W9-AHE-470

entrepreneurship
AND SMALL BUSINESS
3RD ASIA–PACIFIC EDITION

Michael SCHAPER
Thierry VOLERY
Paull WEBER
Kate LEWIS

WILEY

John Wiley & Sons Australia, Ltd

Third edition published 2011 by
John Wiley & Sons Australia, Ltd
42 McDougall Street, Milton, Qld 4064

First edition published 2004

Second edition published 2007

Typeset in 10/12.5 Horley Old Style Regular

© Michael Schaper, Thierry Volery, Paull Weber and Kate Lewis 2011

© Michael Schaper and Thierry Volery, 2004, 2007

The moral rights of the authors have been asserted.

National Library of Australia
Cataloguing-in-publication data

National Library of Australia Cataloguing-in-Publication entry

Title:	Entrepreneurship and small business/Michael Schaper ... [et al.]
Edition:	3rd Asia-Pacific ed.
ISBN:	9781742164625 (pbk.)
Notes:	Includes index.
Target Audience:	For tertiary students.
Subjects:	Small business — Pacific Area — Textbooks.
	Entrepreneurship — Asia — Textbooks.
	Entrepreneurship — Pacific Area — Textbooks.
Other Authors/ Contributors:	Schaper, Michael.
Dewey Number:	658.022

Reproduction and Communication for educational purposes
The Australian *Copyright Act 1968* allows a maximum of one chapter
or 10% of the pages of this work, whichever is the greater, to be
reproduced and/or communicated by any educational institution for
its educational purposes provided that the educational institution
(or the body that administers it) has given a remuneration notice to
Copyright Agency Limited (CAL).

Reproduction and Communication for other purposes
Except as permitted under the Act (for example, a fair dealing for
the purposes of study, research, criticism or review), no part of this
book may be reproduced, stored in a retrieval system, communicated
or transmitted in any form or by any means without prior written
permission. All inquiries should be made to the publisher at the
address above.

Cover and internal design images: © Alfred Krzemien. Used under
licence from Shutterstock (main image); © Mahesh Patil. Used under
licence from Shutterstock (icon in text)

Printed in Singapore by
Craft Print International Ltd

10 9 8 7 6 5 4 3 2 1

About the authors

MICHAEL SCHAPER

Michael Schaper (BA, MComm, PhD) is an adjunct professor at Curtin Business School, Curtin University of Technology, Western Australia, and is also deputy chairman of the Australian Competition and Consumer Commission. Michael was previously dean of Murdoch Business School and head of the School of Business at Bond University, and held the foundation professorial chair in Entrepreneurship and Small Business at the University of Newcastle, Australia. He has extensive experience in the area of small business through his previous roles, which have included appointments as Small Business Commissioner for the Australian Capital Territory, and as President of the Small Enterprise Association of Australia and New Zealand.

Before his academic career, Michael worked for several years as a professional small business adviser in Australia. In addition, he ran his own business and was involved in numerous other start-up projects. He holds a PhD and a Master of Commerce degree from Curtin University of Technology, as well as a Bachelor of Arts from the University of Western Australia. Michael is the author or co-author of eight books, all in the field of business management, numerous journal articles and has been an occasional columnist for *The Australian Financial Review*, *The Australian* and *Business Review Weekly*.

THIERRY VOLERY

Thierry Volery is Professor of Entrepreneurship and Director of the Swiss Institute for Entrepreneurship and Small Business at the University of St Gallen, Switzerland. From September 1999 until 2002, he was Professor of Entrepreneurship and Management at EM Lyon Business School, France. He was previously a senior lecturer in Entrepreneurship and International Business at Curtin University of Technology in Perth, Western Australia.

Thierry has been a visiting professor at the China Europe International Business School (CEIBS) in Shanghai and at the Graduate School of Management, University of Western Australia. He has served on several editorial boards, including the *Journal of Small Business Management*, the *International Small Business Journal*, the *Journal of Enterprising Culture* and the *International Journal of Educational Management*. He holds a doctorate in business economics and social sciences from the University of Fribourg, Switzerland. His research interests include the nature of entrepreneurial work, the health of entrepreneurs and innovation in small firms.

PAULL WEBER

Dr Paull Weber comes from a banking background, where he directly managed over 40 staff and a portfolio of high net-worth business owners. He began his academic 'sea change' in 2001, completing an Honours degree, a research Masters degree and his PhD in six years. He has taught management and marketing courses in small business management, entrepreneurship, marketing communications and marketing principles. His research activities have been concentrated in the areas of mature entrepreneurship, lifestyle entrepreneurship, small business success metrics, organisational commitment and intranet effectiveness.

Paull has contributed several book chapters, journal articles and case studies in the disciplines of entrepreneurship and tourism. He is currently the lead investigator in a long-term initiative to benchmark small business performance across all industry types in Western Australia. He is also the deputy chair of Business Foundations, a business incubator, advisory and training organisation that assists more than five hundred businesses each year.

KATE LEWIS

Dr Kate Lewis is a senior lecturer in the School of Management, and a research associate of the New Zealand Centre for Small and Medium Enterprise Research, at the Wellington campus of Massey University, New Zealand. She is also an associate fellow of the New Zealand Work and Labour Market Institute (Auckland University of Technology) and a vice-president of the Small Enterprise Association of Australia and New Zealand. Her research is primarily focused on entrepreneurship and small firms, and she has a particular interest in youth entrepreneurship. Other areas of work include enterprise policy and business assistance, environmental management and small firms, gender and entrepreneurship, and entrepreneurial identity.

Contents

CHAPTER 6   Market research and strategy formulation   127

CHAPTER 7   Preparing a business plan   155

CHAPTER 7 APPENDIX Sample business plan   175

CHAPTER 8 Legal issues   195

CHAPTER 14 Financial information and management   341

Preface

Although there are many different career options in business, few offer as much potential for personal achievement and independent wealth creation as starting or running your own business. Entrepreneurs are people who conceive of new business opportunities, take the risks and then turn their ideas into successfully functioning enterprises. Small business owner–managers are the people who are responsible for the day-to-day organisation and operation of small firms. Both groups are at the forefront of many of the new ideas, new markets, new jobs and new wealth-generating activities taking place all over the world today.

Like any area of potentially high rewards, there are many risks involved in new projects. Failure rates are often much higher than for established firms; and operating systems, human resources and financing options are often different and much more limited than in larger organisations. For these reasons, intending entrepreneurs and small business owner–managers need to carefully prepare themselves before starting out on their venture.

There are many textbooks available on these subjects, but most continue to focus solely on a particular country. Even today, the majority of English-language books available are British, Australian or American, and often ignore or downplay the important legal, marketing and operational variations that occur across the Asia–Pacific region.

For this reason, we have written *Entrepreneurship and Small Business: 3rd Asia–Pacific Edition*, a comprehensive, multinational textbook that focuses on a number of different jurisdictions and countries in the region: Australia, New Zealand, Singapore, Malaysia, India, Hong Kong and China. New business ventures and established small businesses are key driving elements in each of these economies.

Finally, a word about terminology — as explained in chapter 4, it is recognised that the terms *small business* and *entrepreneurship* are not synonymous. Entrepreneurship is mainly about the creation and growth of a business venture, whereas small business management covers the daily control of a small firm. However, there is often considerable overlap between the two sets of activities. Many entrepreneurs start off by creating a small firm that subsequently grows into a larger enterprise. Both entrepreneurs and small business owner–managers are required to be familiar with many of the same technical skills and business concepts. Therefore, in the parts of this book that apply to both entrepreneurs and small business operators, we have used the terms *entrepreneur* and *small business owner–manager* interchangeably.

Whether you want to build an entrepreneurial success story or just a profitable small local enterprise, or are simply seeking to better understand these types of businesses, this book will provide the information you need. We hope you find it useful.

Michael Schaper, Thierry Volery, Paull Weber and Kate Lewis
June 2010

Acknowledgements

No book is ever solely the work of its authors. Many other people play an important part in preparing a textbook of this magnitude, and without them it is doubtful our project could have been completed in time. In particular, we would like to acknowledge the help of Geoff Baker (Murdoch University) and Ilana Boon (University of the Sunshine Coast) for research work and editing, Darryl Cahill and accounting staff (RMIT) for additional cases, as well as Dan Logovik (John Wiley & Sons Australia), who provided a substantial amount of professional assistance in the development and refinement of this third edition.

We are also indebted to the practitioners who provided access to companies as well as information and suggestions on profile and case drafts. Our special thanks go to Narayana Murthy (Infosys), Chris Anderson and Duane Dalton (Pita Pit), Jack Hughes (Darwin Region Business Enterprise Centre), Justin Miller (Sensear), Andrew Monteiro (Journal IT), Eric Rongley (Bleum), Brenda Bourne (Webwoman), Steven Quayle (3Floorsup), Damian Knowles (Howling Wolves), Charles Bellow (Local Chambers), Carolyn Cresswell (Carman's Fine Foods), Janet Sayers (Sand and Sea), Mohshin Aziz (AirAsia), Phillip Mills and Jill Tattersall (Les Mills International).

The authors and publisher would also like to thank the following copyright holders, organisations and individuals for their assistance and for permission to reproduce copyright material in this book.

Images

• © Pearson Education UK, **6**/from 'Strategic Entrepreneurship Third Edition' by Philip A. Wickham, Prentice Hall Financial Times, © 2004, reprinted with the permission of Pearson Education Limited • © Elsevier, **31**/Reprinted/adapted from 'Journal of Business Venturing' Vol. 16, Chirstian Bruyat & Pierre-André Julien, 'Defining the Field of Research in Entrepreneurship', p. 174, © 2000, with permission from Elsevier • © John Wiley & Sons, Inc, **106**/from The Portable MBA in Entrepreneurship 2nd ed by William D. Bygrave, 1997. Reprinted with the permission of John Wiley & Sons Inc • © Simon & Schuster, Inc., **129**/Adapted with the permission of The Free Press, a Division of Simon & Schuster Adult Publishing Group, from COMPETITIVE ADVANTAGE: Creating & Sustaining Superior Performance by Michael E. Porter. Copyright © 1985, 1998 by Michael E. Porter. All rights re. • © Marc J. Dollinger, **146**/from 'Entrepreneurship 2e' by Marc J. Dollinger, Prentice Hall US, © 1999, p. 31. Reproduced with the permission of Marc J. Dollinger • © John Wiley & Sons Australia, **147**/Adapted from A. Osterwalder, The business model ontology: A proposition in a design science approach, unpublished PhD thesis, University of Lausanne, p. 44; **301**/Sonja Stambulic • © Wiley Blackwell Publishers, **426**/from 'Toward a Reconciliation of the Definitional Issues in the Field of Corporate Entrepreneurship' by Pramodita Sharma & James J. Chrisman, Spring 1999, Entrepreneurship Theory & Practice, Reproduced with the permission of Blackwell Publishing • © Corporate Executive Board, p. **429**/Adapted from 'The New Venture Division: Attributes of an Effective New Business

Incubation Structure', Corporate Executive Board, Washington, 2000, p. 4 • ©
Booz Allen Hamilton, **431**/from e-Business & Beyond: Organizing for Success
in New Ventures by Gary Neilson, Bill Jackson, Jill Albrinck, David Kletter,
Jennifer Hornery, Maurisio Mauro, Paul Hyde & Rob Schuyt. Reprinted with
permission from Booz Allen Hamilton Inc., © 20.

Text

• © Emma Isaacs, **50–1** • © Harvard Bus. School Publishing, **63–4**/Reprinted
by permission of Harvard Business Review. 'The Disruptive Playbook' from
'Mapping Your Innovation Strategy' by Scott D. Anthony & Lib Gibson,
May 2006. Copyright © 2006 by the Harvard Business School Publishing
Corporation; all rights re. • © Narayana Murthy, **66–7** • © Kimberley Hill, **86**
• © Jessica Kiely-Schebesta, **92** • © Michael à Campo, **99–100**/Reproduced
with the permission of Michael à Campo • © Carolyn Cresswell, **112** • © Pita
Pit, **124–5** • © Journalists Copyright, **143**/'Bypass operations', by Kristen Le
Mesurier, BRW, April 24, 2008 • © Daryll Cahill, Dr., **165–6**/Reproduced with
the permission of Dr. Daryll Cahill.; **337–8**/Case study and solution prepared
by the Small Business staff, School of Accounting and Law, RMIT University
• © Damian Knowles, **170–1** • © Commonwealth Copyright Admin, **211**/
IP Australia. www.ipaustralia. Copyright Commonwealth of Australia, repro-
duced by permission • © Infego Communcations, **233–4**/The Maverick, by
Vikki Bland, Unlimited, 27 Jan, 2008 • © BECNT, **249–50** • © Leighton Jay,
251/from Jay, L. & Schaper, M. (2002) The Utilisation of Business Advisory
Services by Home-Based Businesses in Western Australia Paper Presented
to the 15th Annual Small Enterprise Association of Australia & New Zealand
(SEAANZ) conference, 22–24 • © Justin Miller, **274–5** • © Allen and Unwin,
276/Reproduced from How to Organise and Operate a Small Business in
Australia by J. English © 1998. Reproduced with permission of Allen & Unwin
www.allen-unwin.com.au • © Andrew Monteiro, **301–2** • © Michael Schaper,
Professor, **320–1**/from The Australian Small Business Guide to Hiring New
Staff by Michael Schaper, Business Publishing, 2000 • © Aileen Ng, **325** • © John
Wiley & Sons, Singapore, **327–8, 353–4**/Fernandez JA & Underwood L, 2009,
China Entrepreneur: Voices of Experience, ISBN: 0470823216. Reproduced
with permission of John WIley & Sons, Asia • © Brenda Bourne, **389** • © Steven
Quale, **393–5** • © Michiel Leenders, Prof and, **419–20**/Reproduced with the
permission of the authors, Professor Emiritus Michiel R. Leenders and Louise
A. Mauffette-Leenders and Les Mills International (LMI) • © AirAsia, **427–8**/
Reproduced with the permission of Mohshin Aziz.• © Janet Sayers, **462–3**

PART **1**

The nature of small business and entrepreneurship

CHAPTER 1

Entrepreneurship: definition and evolution

Learning objectives

After reading this chapter, you should be able to:

- provide a definition of entrepreneurship
- state the key elements of entrepreneurship
- explain the process of new venture creation
- explain the role of entrepreneurship in economic growth
- discuss the common features of entrepreneurship in the Asia–Pacific region.

Entrepreneurship takes a variety of forms in both small and large firms, in new firms and established ones, in the formal and informal economy, in legal and illegal activities, in innovative and more conventional business ventures, and in all regions and economic sub-sectors. Today it is widely claimed that entrepreneurship is one of the most powerful drivers of growth and prosperity in the modern global economy. Few factors have as great an impact in creating jobs, producing innovation, or generally contributing to a dynamic and competitive economy.

The importance of entrepreneurship is perhaps best illustrated in the Asia–Pacific region. The transformation of this region and the emergence in the 1990s of the newly industrialised economies, or so-called tigers, such as Hong Kong, Singapore, South Korea, Malaysia and Thailand, are largely due to entrepreneurial activities. During the same period, the Australian and New Zealand economies were significantly liberalised, introducing new opportunities for entrepreneurs. These changes contributed to sustained economic growth.

More recently, entrepreneurship has transformed the economy of two 'sleeping giants' in Asia — India and China. India has, over the past couple of decades, broken away from the Licence Raj and has witnessed a profound entrepreneurial transformation. Since 1991, when the government started opening up the economy, the country's mood has changed to one of business friendly rules and can-do optimism. Communist China's conversion to entrepreneurship is even more surprising. Privately owned small and medium-sized enterprises (SMEs) now account for approximately two-thirds of the economy. More than sixty Chinese companies are traded on the NASDAQ. Since 2002, entrepreneurs can officially become members of the Chinese Communist Party; and today, the Central Party school offers special courses for entrepreneurs (who are known as 'red capitalists').[1]

This chapter focuses on defining the notion of entrepreneurship and examines the role of entrepreneurship as a catalyst for economic growth. The nature of entrepreneurship within the Asia–Pacific region is discussed.

Defining entrepreneurship

Industrial Revolution
The term used to describe the changes brought about by the introduction of technology and methods of mass production in the eighteenth and nineteenth centuries.

Entrepreneurship stems from the French word *entreprendre* meaning 'to undertake' or 'to take in one's own hands'. During the **Industrial Revolution** the term *entrepreneur* was used to describe the new phenomenon of the individual who had formulated a venture idea, developed it, assembled resources and created a new business venture.[2] The entrepreneur has thus emerged as a pivotal figure who operates within a market.

Entrepreneurs such as John Rockefeller (who formed Standard Oil), Andrew Carnegie (who advanced the mass production of steel and lowered its cost), James Watt (who improved on existing ideas and made a workable steam engine), Thomas Edison (who brought the benefits of electricity through new appliances), and William Jardine and James Matheson (who founded Jardine Matheson and sent the first private shipments of tea to England) all contributed to the Industrial Revolution. Entrepreneurs are risk-taking people who react to opportunities, bear uncertainty and serve to bring about a balance between supply and demand in specific markets. Since the Industrial Revolution, many economists have directed their attention to entrepreneurship and contributed to the understanding of the concept.

Towards a definition of entrepreneurship

Entrepreneurship remains difficult to define because it is a multi-faceted phenomenon that spans many disciplinary boundaries. Different studies of entrepreneurship have adopted different theoretical perspectives, units of analyses and methodologies. For example, topics in entrepreneurship have been researched by psychologists, sociologists, historians, finance experts and organisation scholars. The focus of research has varied greatly: the entrepreneur, the social network of the entrepreneur, the new organisation, the new product or service offering, and sometimes the framework conditions of a whole country have been examined.

Therefore, it is not surprising that there is no agreed definition of entrepreneurship, and uncertainty exists regarding what constitutes entrepreneurship as a field of study. One of the main obstacles to building a definition of entrepreneurship stems, perhaps, from the fact that until the late 1990s, most researchers defined the field solely in terms of who the entrepreneur was and what he or she did. The problem with this approach is that entrepreneurship involves the linking of two conditions: the presence of lucrative opportunities and the presence of enterprising individuals.[3] By defining the field in terms of the individual alone, early research in entrepreneurship generated incomplete definitions that do not withstand scrutiny.

Consequently, we define **entrepreneurship** as the process, brought about by individuals, of identifying new entrepreneurial opportunities and converting them into marketable products or services. Therefore, as suggested by Shane and Vankataraman,[4] the field of entrepreneurship involves the study of *sources* of opportunities; the *processes* of discovery, evaluation and exploitation of opportunities; and the set of *individuals* who discover, evaluate and exploit those opportunities.

Entrepreneurship
The process, brought about by individuals, of identifying new opportunities and converting them into marketable products or services.

The key elements of entrepreneurship

Much of the argument over the definition of entrepreneurship revolves around the factors considered necessary for entrepreneurship to occur. As depicted in figure 1.1, five factors have been commonly cited for entrepreneurship to take place: an individual (the entrepreneur), a market opportunity, adequate resources, a business organisation and a favourable environment. These five factors are considered contingencies — something that must be present in the phenomenon but that can materialise in many different ways.[5] The entrepreneur is responsible for bringing these contingencies together to create new value.

The entrepreneur

Entrepreneurship requires at least one motivated person. The entrepreneur is the cornerstone of the entrepreneurial process — the chief conductor who perceives an opportunity, marshals the resources to pursue this opportunity and builds an organisation that combines the resources necessary to exploit the opportunity. Researchers have hypothesised a number of factors that influence the way opportunities are recognised and exploited by entrepreneurs. Among these, four have been identified as especially important: active search of opportunities, entrepreneurial alertness, prior knowledge and social networks.

FIGURE 1.1 The key elements of entrepreneurship
Source: Adapted from P.A. Wickham, *Strategic Entrepreneurship*, Prentice Hall, Harlow, 2004, p. 134.

- *Active search of opportunities.* Many of the erstwhile studies in entrepreneurship implicitly assumed that recognition of an opportunity is preceded by a systematic search for available opportunities.[6] Similarly, entrepreneurs are more likely than managers to engage in an active search for opportunities and potentially untapped sources of profit.[7] These findings indicate that actively searching for information is an important factor in the recognition of many opportunities by entrepreneurs, although such searches must be carefully directed in order to succeed.
- *Entrepreneurial alertness.* Kirzner was the first to use this term to explain the recognition of entrepreneurial opportunities.[8] He defined 'alertness' as a propensity to notice and be sensitive to information about objects, incidents and patterns of behaviour. Individuals with high alertness show a special sensitivity to maker and user problems, unmet needs and novel combinations of resources. Therefore, alertness emphasises the fact that opportunities can sometimes be recognised by individuals who are not actively searching for them. But what are the foundations of entrepreneurial alertness? It has been suggested that alertness rests mainly on the creativity and high intelligence capacities of individuals.[9] These capacities help entrepreneurs to identify new solutions for the market and customer needs and, at the same time, to develop creative ways to attract resources.
- *Prior knowledge.* People tend to notice information that is related to information they already know. A wealth of evidence indicates that information gathered through a rich and varied life (especially through varied work experience) can be a major plus for entrepreneurs in terms of recognising opportunities. Each person's prior idiosyncratic knowledge creates a *knowledge corridor* that allows

him or her to recognise certain opportunities[10] but not others. Therefore, any given opportunity is not obvious to all would-be entrepreneurs.

- *Social networks.* The way people are connected through various social relationships, ranging from casual acquaintances to close familial bonds, also plays an important role in opportunity recognition, resource acquisition and the development of an organisation.[11] The shape of the social network helps determine a network's usefulness to its individuals. Small, tight networks can be less useful to their members than networks with lots of loose connections (weak ties) to individuals outside the main network. More 'open' networks, with many weak ties and social connections, are more likely to introduce new ideas and opportunities to their members than closed networks with many redundant ties.[12] In other words, a group of friends who do things only with each other already share the same knowledge and opportunities. A group of individuals with connections to other social networks is likely to have access to a wider range of information and resources. To achieve individual success, it is better to have connections to a variety of networks rather than many connections within a single network.

These four factors characterising entrepreneurs have been studied separately and viewed as largely independent aspects of opportunity recognition and resource acquisition. Recently, however, an integrative framework has been proposed, drawing on the research in cognitive science — the study of human intelligence that embraces various academic disciplines, such as psychology, linguistics, neuroscience and economics. This approach suggests that entrepreneurs use cognitive frameworks they possess to 'connect the dots' between changes in technology, demographics, markets, government policies and other factors. The pattern they then perceive in these events or trends suggests ideas for new products or services — ideas that can potentially serve as the basis for new ventures.[13]

Opportunity

In broad terms, an **opportunity** can be defined as a situation in which a new product, service or process can be introduced and sold at greater than its cost of production.[14] But opportunity describes a range of phenomena that begin unformed and become more developed through time.

In its most elemental form, what may later be called an opportunity may appear as 'imprecisely defined market needs, or unemployed resources or capacities'.[15] Imprecisely defined market needs are the source of *market-pulled opportunities*. Prospective customers may or may not be able to articulate their needs, interests and problems. Even if customers cannot do so, the role of the entrepreneur is to recognise these needs and to develop an offer in which customers will perceive some value.

Under-utilised or unemployed resources, as well as new technologies or capabilities, may also offer possibilities to create new value for customers. In this case, entrepreneurs first identify resources that are not optimally used, and then seek a better use or combination of these in a specific market. This type of opportunity can be called *market-pushed opportunities*. For example, the technology for making a material with the combined properties of metal and glass may be developed before there are any known applications. Similarly, new medical

Opportunity
A situation in which a new product, service or process can be introduced and sold at greater than its cost of production.

compounds may be created without knowledge of their potential applications in the field of medicine.[16]

Resources

Having distilled an opportunity, would-be entrepreneurs must be willing and able to marshal resources in order to pursue the opportunity and transform their idea into an organisation. A resource is any thing or quality that is useful. As detailed in chapter 6, the resource-based theory recognises six types of resources: financial, physical, human, technological, social and organisational.

For the entrepreneur, constructing an initial resource base is an exceptional challenge. The venture's lack of a reputation and a track record creates a heightened perception of risk on the part of potential resource providers. In the majority of new ventures, initial resource endowments are incomplete; entrepreneurs, therefore, act as if they are trustworthy in order to gain access to other resources. They may use time-relevant language or symbols (e.g. polished business plans, stories, or stylish offices) to create an image of success that will encourage providers to commit resources to the venture. In this way, some resources (social, for example) are leveraged to obtain others (financial, for example). If social capital is favourable, it can be converted into tangible and intangible benefits, including increased cooperation and trust from others, finance, or assets and equipment purchased at less expensive prices.[17]

Organisation

Many different types of organisational arrangement exist for the exploitation of entrepreneurial opportunities. Although most media attention and research in entrepreneurship has focused on new independent start-ups, other possible types of organisational structure include corporate ventures, franchises, joint ventures and business acquisitions. This indicates that entrepreneurship can take place in diverse environments, and that there are many ways to become an entrepreneur. The creation of corporate ventures or start-ups inside a corporation, in order to develop, produce and market a new product or service, is an illustration of this point. The new entity can be either a new internal division or a new subsidiary in the established corporation. Joint ventures, licences, franchises and spin-offs (business operations derived as secondary developments of a larger enterprise, which become separate legal entities) are other examples of possible organisational arrangements.

Sometimes it is not necessary to build an organisation from scratch to exploit new opportunities and to combine resources. For example, the acquisition of a business can be an alternative to a start-up if the entrepreneur wants to use an existing vehicle to 'hit the ground running'. In this case, the buyer can introduce substantial innovation along the lines of new products or new processes to give the business a boost. The takeover of a family business by the next generation and the redeployment of its resources according to a new business model comprise another example.

Many believe that for a venture to be deemed entrepreneurial it is not sufficient for the owner to launch an organisation; the venture must also represent innovation. However, everyday evidence shows that starting a business venture does not always demand much originality or power of invention. The fresh, new firm may be a mere clone of another one in a neighbouring town. As will be explained in chapter 3, the extent of innovation can vary greatly, and the extension, duplication or synthesis of existing products, services or processes can also be considered innovation.

Environment

The environment plays a critical role in entrepreneurship. Entrepreneurs operate in an environment that can be more or less rich in opportunities, and where several conditions influence the pursuit of these opportunities. For example, opportunities can emerge because of market inefficiencies that result from information asymmetry across time and place, or as a result of political, regulatory, social or demographic changes.

There are two levels of the environment that exert an influence on the emergence of a business venture: the community level and the broader societal level. At the community level, both the number of organisations in an industry (also called population density) and the strength of the relationship between these organisations are important to entrepreneurs. Individuals trying to create business ventures in a population with high density will find more opportunities for acquiring effective knowledge and creating extensive social networks, but they will also encounter more intensive competition.

At the societal level, at least two aspects shape the environment for organisation: cultural norms and values, and government activities and policies. Changing norms and values alter entrepreneurial intentions and the willingness of resource providers to support new ventures. Government actions and political events create new institutional structure for entrepreneurial action, encouraging some activities and impeding others.[18]

There is abundant evidence that regulatory and administrative burdens can negatively affect entrepreneurial activity. For example, excessively stringent product and labour market regulations have implications for firm entry and exit.

Entrepreneur profile

Graeme Wood, Wotnews

Graeme Wood is a serial entrepreneur. Anyone who thought that he would put his feet up in October 2007 when he stepped down as CEO of the online accommodation group Wotif.com got it wrong. A few months later he took a 50 per cent stake in news aggregation site Plugger, which was later rebranded as Wotnews. 'For me, it's the thrill of a good idea, and that's still what motivates me,' he says. 'When I stumble across an opportunity, I have to do something about it.' Except for an unlikely foray into egg trading in Queensland's new deregulated market in the early 1990s, Graeme Wood has favoured business in software development and information technology services. 'In business, I don't like getting involved in anything I don't understand,' he says.[19]

In 2000, he launched the accommodation website Wotif.com with two other business partners. The easy-to-use website and booking engine advertises vacant rooms at discounted prices available up to 28 days in advance. The idea behind Wotif.com was convincing hotels that instead of leaving unsold rooms empty, they could offer them online at a discount. Wood wanted to apply yield management — a practice that began in the airline industry during the 1970s — to the hospitality industry. Airlines were among the first to maximise efficiency by lowering prices in response to demand — an attempt to ensure all seats were occupied before take-off.

Wood remained unfazed by the dotcom crash. 'The dotcom bubble had burst, but I think a good idea is still a good idea no matter what the market circumstances are,' he says. 'So this struck me as being a good idea that needed to be pursued, because if I didn't do it somebody else would.'[20] In May 2006, Wotif.com listed on the Australian Stock Exchange with its shares being heavily oversubscribed. Today, Wotif.com has expanded to more than 400 staff, selling accommodation in nearly 50 countries. Each month the site attracts over three million visits and handles 200 000 bookings.

Wood's latest business, Wotnews, is still in its infancy. The company's technology platform aggregates business news from 3500 sources — including mainstream media, blogs, industry associations and government bodies — and targets individual and enterprise users in finance, media and professional services. He was introduced to Plugger team (as the company was then known) in late 2007 and he liked what he saw.[21] 'I thought they were clever blokes who had a history of delivering on technology projects, which is pretty rare,' he remarks. But he also identified an opportunity: 'The opportunity exists because the established media players who could have take advantage of it have other priorities, protecting old legacies and attitudes. They are resisting change and suffering accordingly. That's how Wotif snuck into the hospitality industry unnoticed.'[22]

The process of new venture creation

Not everyone has the potential to launch a business venture, and not all those with such a capacity will necessarily attempt to do so. Of those who do attempt it, not all will succeed in creating a new venture. The model of new venture creation proposed in figure 1.2 explains these observations. Yet, we know that each venture is different, and no single complete model exists to explain how a venture gets off the ground. Entrepreneurs have different personalities and backgrounds as well as different goals; all have a different time frame and aspire to launch their ventures in various industries. Thus, the model presented in figure 1.2 allows for this diversity, rather than specifying a particular path.

Central to the process of new venture formation is the founding individual. Whether the entrepreneur is perceived as a hard-headed risk-bearer or a visionary, he or she is perceived to be different in important ways from the non-entrepreneur, such as the manager, and many believe these differences lie in the psychological traits and background of the entrepreneur. There have been many attempts to develop a psychological profile of the entrepreneur. The need for achievement, the level of confidence and a risk-taking propensity are the three psychological traits that have been used in many studies and shown a high degree of validity in differentiating among types of entrepreneur. Another approach has been to study the background, experience and aspirations of entrepreneurs.

Entrepreneurs do not operate in a vacuum; they respond to their environments. At the opportunity recognition stage, the entrepreneur perceives market needs and/or underemployed resources, and recognises a 'fit' between particular market needs and specified resources. A favourable political, economic, social and infrastructure environment facilitates the emergence of new business ventures. Figure 1.2 shows that the initiation of new ventures requires the combination of the right person in the right place. The typical would-be entrepreneur is constantly attuned to environmental changes that may suggest an opportunity.

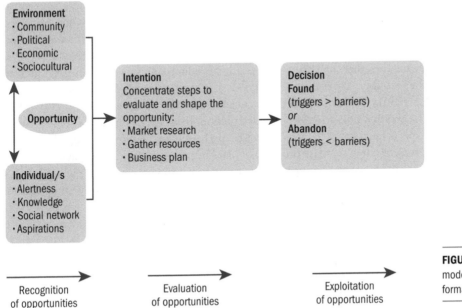

FIGURE 1.2 A model of new venture formation

People may have the propensity to found and develop a business in an environment conducive to entrepreneurship. They may even have identified a promising opportunity, but the actual decision to launch the venture arises from a clear intention, and this implies action. In new venture formation, intention is a conscious state of mind that directs attention towards the goal of establishing the new organisation.[23] With the expression of intent ('I intend trying to start a business'), the hopeful entrepreneur takes some concrete steps towards evaluating the business opportunity and gathering resources for launching the venture. Such steps can include the formulation of strategy, the development of a prototype, market research, the identification of potential partners, and the drafting of a business plan.

Just as the would-be entrepreneur must decide to attempt to establish a business, he or she must finally decide whether to proceed with or abandon the attempt. The decision may be triggered by a specific event or simply by the accumulated weight of confirmatory or contradictory information. Although some precipitating events, such as a dismissal, job frustration, graduation or inheritance, may trigger the launch of the business venture, it is often the passion of the individual, sustained ultimately by motivation, that pushes the entrepreneur to 'take the plunge'. If the venture is launched, the triggers have prevailed over the perceived barriers to start-up. Alternatively, if the person decides to abandon the attempt, then the hurdles are perceived to be greater than the advantages.[24]

The role of entrepreneurship in economic growth and development

Creative destruction
The process of simultaneous emergence and disappearance of technologies, products and firms in the marketplace as a result of innovation.

At a macro level, entrepreneurship is a process of **creative destruction**. By this, Schumpeter[25] referred to the simultaneously destructive and constructive consequences of innovation. The new destroys the old. Entrepreneurs are central to the process of creative destruction; they identify opportunities and bring the new technologies and new concepts into active commercial use. However, a good proportion of creation is non-destructive, and many innovations satisfy new demands rather than displacing existing products and services. Research showed that roughly 70 per cent of the goods and services consumed in the early 1990s bore little relationship to those consumed a century earlier.[26] And even when the creation does involve some destruction, there are nevertheless some positive aspects to consider for society. For example, the innovations developed by entrepreneurs often increase productivity and improve general living standards.

In other words, entrepreneurial capitalism produces a bigger pie, and allows more people to exercise their creative talents. But it is disruptive nonetheless. It increases the rate at which enterprises are born and die, and forces workers to move from one job to another. By studying economic history, we can learn valuable lessons about the conditions that allow entrepreneurs and growth to flourish.

Values, politics and economic institutions

Science and technology, in a given culture, can sometimes progress rapidly and then suddenly stop. Consider China's dazzling supremacy in science and technology at the start of the fifteenth century. Curiosity, the instinct for exploration and the drive to build had created in China all the technologies necessary for launching the Industrial Revolution — something that would not occur for another 400 years. China had the blast furnace and piston bellows for making steel; gunpowder and cannon for military conquest; the compass and the rudder for exploration; paper and moveable type for printing; the iron plough, the horse collar and various natural and artificial fertilisers to generate agricultural surpluses; and in mathematics, the decimal system, negative numbers, and the concept of zero. All of these put the Chinese far ahead of Europeans. Yet the Industrial Revolution took place in Britain and Europe in the eighteenth and nineteenth centuries, and the Chinese rejected and ultimately forgot the technologies that could have given them world dominance. Essentially, this was due to a lack of entrepreneurship in China, caused by three broad, overlapping factors: values, politics and economic institutions.[27]

Values

Entrepreneurship is a process of economic change. So a readiness for change, or at least the willingness to live with it, is essential if a society is to get richer (except by conquest). This helps to account for China's falling behind. Chinese civilisation came under the domination of a bureaucratic elite, the mandarins, who gave continuity and stability to Chinese life, but were also a conservative influence on innovation, resisting the introduction of new techniques unless they provided a clear benefit to the bureaucracy.[28] As a result, the mandarins often blocked change; at the end of the fifteenth century they ended long-standing sea-trade ventures, choking off commerce and shipbuilding alike.

Acquisitiveness is another value that sustains growth. As change agents in a society, entrepreneurs have a regard for the material, and they are willing to exploit nature for human benefit. Yet naked greed is no use. Growth is based on sustainable development; it requires investment, and investment is deferred gratification. The enlightened self-interest praised by economist Adam Smith combines the desire for wealth with prudence and patience.

Politics

Values are a powerful entrepreneurial catalyst at the individual level. At a macro level, politics provides a framework for entrepreneurship. Economic institutions are the tools used by entrepreneurs to capitalise on opportunities and convert those opportunities into marketable products or services.

Once again, China provides a good example of the influence of politics over entrepreneurship. The Ming dynasty (1368–1644) was one of the most stable Chinese dynasties but also one of the most autocratic. The sprawling bureaucracy needed by the highly centralised government was continued by the subsequent Qing dynasty, which lasted until the imperial institution was abolished in 1911. What was chiefly lacking in China for the further development of capitalism was not mechanical skill, scientific aptitude or sufficient accumulation of wealth, but scope for individual enterprise. There was no individual freedom, no security for private enterprise, no legal foundation for rights other than those of the state, and no guarantee against arbitrary extortion by officials or intervention by the state.

If too much order (as in China) impedes entrepreneurship, conversely too much chaos is just as bad. Consider Russia in the 75 years before the Russian Revolution of 1917. Creativity flourished in the chaos of the dying empire. Great authors such as Tolstoy, Dostoevsky, Chekhov, Turgenev and Gogol emerged during this period. Likewise, in the world of music, many Russian artists of that period are still played in concert halls. In science, Russia was a leader and produced several Nobel laureates. However, without some degree of order it was impossible for the Russians to use that creativity to develop a successful economy. Chaos led to more chaos and ultimately to the Russian Revolution. Order was reimposed and creativity died.[29] Successful societies create and manage a tension between order and chaos without letting either of them get out of hand. New ideas are easily frustrated if societies are not receptive to the chaos that comes from change, yet societies have to maintain an appropriate degree of order to take advantage of creative breakthroughs.

Economic institutions

Economic institutions are part of the framework conditions influencing entrepreneurship. In the West, where the state was, and is, a central institution, the economic sphere came to be separated from political control under a variety of pressures. This led to a spawning of other institutions, such as property rights, stock exchanges, banks, courts, laws of contract and so on.[30] With time, these allow a flourishing of many different types of economic enterprise that are different in size, ownership and organisation. Here was yet another form of pluralism that existed in Europe, but not in China or in Japan before the Industrial Revolution — just as governments competed, so did the entrepreneurs and the different forms of organisation.

The relationship between entrepreneurship and economic growth

It is the quality of entrepreneurs' performances that determines whether capital grows rapidly or slowly, and whether this growth involves innovation and change, that is, the development of new products and new production techniques. Differences in growth rates between countries and between different periods in any one country can therefore be traced back largely to the quality of entrepreneurship. Fundamentally, economic growth occurs not because of broad improvements in technology, productivity and available resources, but because entrepreneurs (a) improve their technology, organisation and processes, (b) become more productive and innovative and (c) force other firms out of business. As this ongoing creative destruction occurs, new and better jobs than the lost ones are created, the overall level of productivity rises, and economic well-being increases.

Business dynamics
Also called business churning; the extent to which firms enter an industry, grow, decline and exit an industry.

One indicator of creative destruction is the **business dynamics** taking place within the national economy.[31] This is the extent to which firms enter an industry, grow, decline and exit an industry. Despite the recognition that business dynamics are a necessary feature of economic growth, it is often hard for public opinion and government to accept the destructive dimension of entrepreneurship. It is illusory to think that society can benefit from the growth and progress generated by entrepreneurial activities (new products and services, job and wealth creation) without incurring enterprise restructuring and bankruptcies and their inevitable consequences (removal of products from the marketplace, staff retrenchments, losses by investors).

The level of entrepreneurial activity is a function of the degree to which people recognise the opportunities available and their capacity (motivation and skills) to exploit them. Entrepreneurial activity is, in turn, shaped by a variety of factors (referred to as entrepreneurial framework conditions) that help to foster start-ups. Such factors include the availability of start-up financing, education and training in entrepreneurship, 'incubator' facilities, government policies, and programs targeting the development of entrepreneurship.

At a broader level, there is a relationship between national conditions, such as legal institutions, general infrastructure, labour and financial markets, and the performance of established firms. History shows that the process of innovation and entrepreneurship consists of an accumulation of numerous institutional, resource and proprietary events involving many factors from the public and private sectors.[32] Finally, social values, politics and institutions shape the macro context within which entrepreneurial processes occur. It is important to recognise, however, that although government agencies and educational institutions can create conditions in which entrepreneurship can prosper, it is ultimately up to individuals and firms to take up the challenge of launching new activities.

Measuring entrepreneurial activity

Given the fact that there are many different institutional ways of exploiting opportunities, measuring entrepreneurial activity in the economy is a difficult task. Substantial attention has been given recently to fast-growing new firms in expanding industry sectors, and this has provided anecdotal evidence that some countries are more entrepreneurial than others. The Global Entrepreneurship Monitor (GEM)[33] is an international research consortium that aims to go beyond such impressionistic evidence and to systematically assess two things: (1) the level of start-up activity, or the prevalence of embryonic firms and (2) the prevalence of those that have survived the start-up phase.

First, start-up activity is measured by the proportion of the adult population in each country currently engaged in the process of creating a business. Second, the prevalence of new firms is measured by the proportion of adults in each country involved in operating a business that is less than 42 months old when the survey is completed. For both measures, the research focus is on entrepreneurial activity in which the individuals involved have a direct, but not necessarily full, ownership interest in the business. Combining these measures provides an excellent index of the total level of entrepreneurial activity.

How entrepreneurial are the people of different countries?

The overall level of entrepreneurial activity for a selection of countries participating in the GEM project is presented in figure 1.3. The vertical bars represent the precision of each estimate based on the size of the sample in each country at the 95 per cent confidence interval. The range in prevalence rates shows a tenfold difference, from a low of 3.8 per cent in Hungary to 14.4 per cent in Brazil. When countries are grouped according to a global region, it appears that entrepreneurial efforts are not uniformly distributed around the world. Without question, entrepreneurial activity is quite low and uniform across most developed European countries. Anglo-Saxon countries have a relatively high level of activity compared with European countries. Latin America has among the highest and most uniform levels of activity. The situation in Asia is contrasted: while Japan and Singapore have a low rate of entrepreneurial activity, Hong Kong SAR, China and India are the most entrepreneurial countries in the region.

The GEM study uncovered a dynamic dimension to entrepreneurial activity. Respondents were asked to indicate whether they were starting and growing their business to take advantage of a unique market opportunity (opportunity entrepreneurship) or because it was the best option available (necessity entrepreneurship). In the case of necessity entrepreneurship, people launch a business venture not so much to pursue a unique opportunity but because they have no other way of making a living. Cross-national comparisons indicate that from 3 per cent of adults in Japan to over 16 per cent in New Zealand are engaged as opportunity entrepreneurs. The level of necessity entrepreneurs had an even greater variation, from virtually none in Europe to 5 per cent or more in India and China. The analysis indicated that developing countries generally have a higher prevalence rate for necessity entrepreneurship.

People are finding it easier in this information age to establish a new business; conversely, incumbents are finding it more difficult to defend their territory.

Whereas it took twenty years for a third of Fortune 500 companies' composition to change from 1960 (testament to its stability), now it only takes four years.[34] There are many reasons for this. First, the information revolution has helped to lower transaction costs (the information, negotiation and control costs involved in every economy transaction) and to unbundle existing companies. Second, the economic growth is being driven by industries, such as computing and telecommunications, where innovation is particularly important. Third, advanced economies are characterised by a shift from manufacturing to services. Service firms are usually smaller than manufacturing firms, and there are fewer barriers to entry.

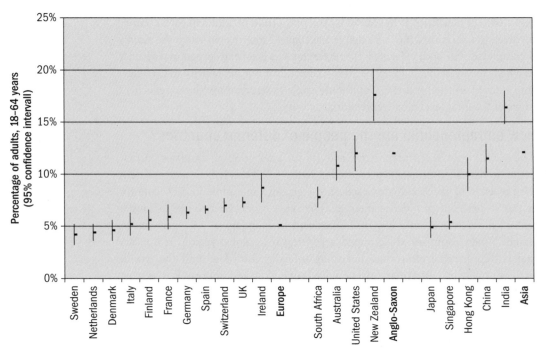

FIGURE 1.3 Total entrepreneurial activity by country and region (mean 2006–09)
Source: GEM Consortium www.gemconsortium.org.

Common features of entrepreneurship in the Asia–Pacific region

Entrepreneurship styles, habits and environments vary significantly across the Asia–Pacific region. At first glance, there appears to be little in common in setting up a business in Australia, Malaysia or Hong Kong. Despite the differences, there are some key features in Asia–Pacific entrepreneurship that distinguish it from European and American entrepreneurship. For example, a common characteristic is the key role played by the state in the development of entrepreneurship. Another common denominator is the presence of ethnic entrepreneurs. For instance, Chinese people living outside the current administration of the People's Republic of China have been at the heart of the region's economic boom.

Most ethnic Chinese who left the mainland (known as *huaqiao*) did so with little wealth and could not rely on the governments of other South-East Asian countries for assistance. Often battling prejudice and discrimination, these families created their own businesses and, in the process, developed much of the modern private sector throughout South-East Asia. Wary of their new local governments, the ethnic Chinese discovered that a common background provided a basis for mutual trust and, therefore, presented an opportunity for business and trade throughout the Asia–Pacific region. Language, culture and ethnicity served as common ground, but family provided the most reliable and secure assurances in an area where formal business agreements were difficult to enforce. Today, companies owned by ethnic Chinese families in Singapore, Malaysia, Thailand, Indonesia and the Philippines make up about 70 per cent of the private business sector in those countries and are rising influences in Vietnam, Australia and New Zealand.[35]

Ethnic Indians constitute another sizeable segment of the immigrants of diverse nationalities in the Asia–Pacific region. In terms of sheer numbers, they are the third largest group, behind the British and the Chinese. Over 15 million people of Indian origin have settled in 70 countries. They are significant minorities in Malaysia, Singapore and Sri Lanka, and have made important contributions to the development of entrepreneurship across the Asia–Pacific region. For example, one of the main reasons behind the emergence of Silicon Valley as the world hub of high-tech industries has been the presence of ethnic Indian entrepreneurs. In addition, the pyramid structures of Asian firms, and the active role of the state are further common features of entrepreneurship in the Asia–Pacific region.

Sociocultural features of ethnic Chinese

Redding[36] suggested that the impact of Chinese culture has worked through the two main determinants of social structures, which in turn affect the workings of organisations. These are (1) the rules that govern the stabilisation and legitimisation of authority, that is, the vertical dimension of order and (2) the rules that govern the stabilisation of cooperation, that is, the horizontal dimension of order.

The norms for vertical relationships are taught via Confucian concepts. The Confucian ethical system regulating social behaviour has three principal ideas: benevolence (*ren*), righteousness or justice (*yi*) and propriety or courtesy (*li*). Regulation is certainly the appropriate term. Confucianism is a secular system developed at a time of chaos to allow harmony to coexist with rigid hierarchy. This worked by providing a set of principles for action, most of which surround the role of the father as the pivot of the social system.

As a result, the style of leadership adopted commonly has a paternalistic flavour, and the adoption of such a style by the business owner sets the tone for other managers to echo it with their subordinates. This style can also bring with it nepotism and autocracy, as social interaction in the Confucian system is very much a tradition. Organisation charts and job descriptions are replaced by social deference. People come into the organisation pre-programmed to understand hierarchy instinctively.

Similar considerations apply to the rules for horizontal order, particularly in the development and handling of relationships. This begins with a clear distinction between in-group members or insiders (*zijiren*) and out-group members or outsiders (*wairen*). Chinese people typically maintain expressive ties with close family members, mixed ties with friends and other kin, and instrumental ties with strangers or out-group members with whom there is no lasting relationship.[37] Social interaction expectations, norms and behaviours differ among these three kinds of ties.

Western and Eastern entrepreneurs and firms have a different approach to relationships. To most Western firms, relationships are secondary — a company tends to decide which business or projects it is interested in and then cultivates the necessary connections. Asian companies believe that relationships come first and that investment opportunities flow from them. This philosophy finds its root in the historic uncertainty and separateness felt by expatriate Chinese. Many local firms in the Asia–Pacific region were established by Chinese migrants and their offspring in not-so-friendly environments, away from their country of origin, in countries with rules-based, yet, weak systems. Consequently, expatriate Chinese tended to rely mainly on relationships with extended families and clans to build up the business and reduce risk. The interlocking relationships soon extended to local officials keen to benefit from Chinese entrepreneurial skills. This web of connections, or *guanxi*, is still paramount with most ethnic Chinese groups in the Asia–Pacific region.

Ethnic Indians

Although expatriate Indians are often described as a fractionalised community from diverse Indian regions, castes and religions, they nevertheless have unity in their diversity. The vast majority adhere to some form of the caste system, and Hindu mythology pervades their culture. India has also instituted an exceptional education system that has trained a ready core of highly skilled and highly educated professionals and entrepreneurs who are familiar with the English language and Western ways. As a result, most of the recent migrants to Australia, New Zealand, Singapore and the United States are capable of quickly stepping into middle- and upper-level jobs.

Like their less educated counterparts, most high-tech Indian immigrants rely on ethnic strategies to enhance entrepreneurial opportunities. Seeing themselves as outsiders to the mainstream technology community, foreign-born engineers and scientists in Silicon Valley have created social and professional networks to mobilise the information, know-how, skill and capital to start technology firms. Combining elements of traditional immigrant culture with distinctly high-tech practices, these organisations simultaneously create ethnic identities within the region and aid professional networking and information exchange.

India has begun to reverse its brain drain, as many Indian-born scientists, professionals and entrepreneurs are returning to their mother country. Between 2003 and 2005, approximately 5000 technologically proficient Indians, each with more than five years of working experience in America, returned to India.[38] Such people have helped to fill some of the skills gap created by the country's recent boom. India's entrepreneurial tradition stretches a long way back; for example, the Marwari baniyas merchant community extended their trade networks to many regions of India and even to neighboring countries, building their wealth by bargaining hard with those outside their circle. However, the new generation of entrepreneurs usually launch a business based on merit and professionalism rather than kinship ties.[39]

The pyramid structures of Asian family firms

Another common feature of entrepreneurship in the Asia–Pacific region relates to the type of ownership and structure of the enterprises. Most of the businesses across the region are family-owned, although the proportion of family businesses is lower in Australia and New Zealand compared with Asia. In India, for example, a third of the firms in the 1990s belonged to wider business groups, controlled by families or corporate 'promoters'. In Hong Kong, 15 families control corporate assets worth 84 per cent of GDP.[40]

Although all countries in the region basically have the same legal structures under which businesses operate, most Asian companies have a distinctive feature. Control of firms is enhanced through 'pyramids' — complex and opaque structures of private holding companies, layer upon layer of subsidiaries, and cross-holdings — where voting rights exceed formal profit rights. Most of these pyramids have been established by overseas Chinese entrepreneurs, and their purpose is to draw outside capital into the family group and retain control over the use of this capital within the family.

The pyramid scheme functions like this: let's say a family holds a 51 per cent controlling stake in a company at the pyramid's apex. Similar stakes are then held in the second and third tiers of companies. Thus, control of the entire pyramid from top to bottom is maintained, even though the family's financial commitment decreases proportionally from tier to tier. In this case, the second tier is only 26 per cent (51 per cent of 51 per cent), whereas the third tier stakes are only about 13 per cent.[41]

This discrepancy between the family's control (voting rights) and ownership (profit rights) creates an opportunity and, indeed, an incentive to expropriate minority shareholders in second and third tier companies. How? One way is for the controlling family to make these companies pay miserly dividends. Better still, the family could make a second tier company sell an asset to third tier company at an artificially low price, or make second tier company buy an asset from a third tier company at an inflated price.

The role of the state

Over the past decades the state has played a ubiquitous role in entrepreneurship in virtually all Asia–Pacific countries. Encouraging entrepreneurship has been increasingly recognised by governments across the region as an effective means of creating jobs, increasing productivity and competitiveness, alleviating poverty and achieving societal goals. It is, therefore, not surprising that the state has been a strong promoter of entrepreneurship to the extent that it has even become an entrepreneur itself — hence the term 'state entrepreneurship'.

Promotion of entrepreneurship and SMEs

Every country in the region has engaged in some sort of promotion of entrepreneurship and of SMEs. Singapore was among the first to promote entrepreneurship, developing a comprehensive policy to deal with related matters, and creating an environment conducive to entrepreneurial activites — thus, earning the country a high ranking in the Work Bank league tables for ease of doing business. Along with its big investments in digital media, bioengineering and clean technology, the government has set up a public venture-capital fund, created huge incubators and used financial incentives to lure foreign scientists.[42]

A comprehensive network of small business agencies has also been set up by the various states in Australia. Likewise, Malaysia has taken a dynamic approach to the promotion of entrepreneurship by creating a ministry totally dedicated to entrepreneurial issues. The Ministry of Entrepreneur Development was set up in 1995 to assume full responsibility for all the functions of the Ministry of Public Enterprise, which was abolished.

State entrepreneurship

Governments have traditionally played an important role in a few 'sensitive' sectors in all Asia–Pacific countries. Those sectors include telecommunications, media, real estate, natural resources and banking. Even in countries labelled 'free market economies', such as Australia and Singapore, the government still owns companies in those sectors, although the telecommunications sector has recently been deregulated and government icons, such as Telstra in Australia and SingTel in Singapore, have been partially privatised.

Singapore is certainly the champion of state entrepreneurship. In the 1960s and 1970s, the government initiated many enterprises in key sectors, including manufacturing, shipping, air transport, international trade and long-term finance. The main vehicle for state entrepreneurship in Singapore is government-linked companies (GLCs). These enterprises are formed under holding companies, which in turn depend on a ministry.[43] Examples of GLCs are Sambawang (infrastructure, marine engineering, information technology and leisure activities), Development Bank of Singapore (banking), Neptune Orient Lines (shipping) and Singapore Airlines (air transport). Consequently, public servants have often played the role of entrepreneurs in Singapore.

Similarly, the Malaysian government controls companies in various industries, including printing (e.g. Percetakan Nasional Malaysia Berhad, or PNMB), banking (e.g. Bumiputra-Commerce Bank, Danamodal Nasional Berhad), oil and gas (e.g. Petronas), air transport (Malaysia Airlines) and conglomerates, such as UDA Holdings Berhad with activities in property development, hospitality and retail. The picture was much the same in Indonesia until 1999, when the Wahid government, under International Monetary Fund pressure, was forced to privatise and dismantle state monopolies.

In China, the state-owned enterprises left over from the state planning era still represent about one third of the economy. Although these enterprises are now under severe scrutiny over their performance, almost all of them benefit from protective barriers in their home market. Such an example would be the world's biggest mobile operator China Mobile as its competition has been limited by ministerial decree to a handful of domestic companies. The government regulates other areas of strategic interest, such as steel, energy and finance, in a similar fashion.[44]

Emerging trends

The new millennium brought profound changes that have affected entrepreneurship in the Asia–Pacific region. The main force behind those changes lies in the rise and supremacy of the free-market economy as a framework for entrepreneurship. This trend has its roots in the collapse of the communist system; trade liberalisation led by the World Trade Organization; and the Asian financial crisis (1997–98).

Deregulation and privatisation

All countries in the Asia–Pacific region embarked on some program of deregulation and privatisation in the 1990s. Some countries moved towards deregulation on their own initiative, such as New Zealand, Australia, Singapore and Vietnam. Others, such as Thailand and Indonesia, were more or less forced to follow after the Asian financial crisis. Many laws restricting entrepreneurial endeavours, particularly for ethnic Chinese and foreign nationals, have been scrapped or watered down. Furthermore, several state-owned companies were totally or partially privatised in the 1990s. This change has created new opportunities for would-be entrepreneurs, and considerably improved the environment for entrepreneurship.

Adoption of Western ideas

Western ideas have spread quickly into South-East Asia through different channels, such as films, television, advertising, internet and education systems. For example, many of the ethnic Chinese entrepreneurs who built huge conglomerates are preparing to hand over those companies to members of the next generation, who have often been educated in American, British or Australian universities where they learned Western ways of doing business. Buzan and Segal[45] suggested that we are moving into a 'Westernistic age' marked by the fusion of Western and other cultures. The power of the West has been, and still is, based on forms of social, economic and political organisation that allow individuals to make more of their human potential than had been previously possible. Some parts of Western ideology still encounter strong resistance in South-East Asia, notably democracy, civil society and human rights. But, as Japan, Korea, Singapore and Taiwan demonstrate, 'Westernisation' does not mean becoming identical to the West or losing one's own culture.

Convergence, in other words, has limits; although it appears to be quite widespread in matters of routines and practices, such as factory layouts, accounting practices, and technical standards, there is a realm of beliefs, attitudes and meanings where convergence is difficult to find. Differences, therefore, remain salient between the countries in the region, at both cultural and institutional levels.

Adoption of rules-based systems

South-East Asian economies have traditionally been based on relationships. Business transactions were made on the strength of personal agreements rather than on contracts. Transactions in the Chinese *guanxi* system are still mainly private. They are neither verifiable nor enforceable in the public sphere. After the 1997–98 financial crisis, Asia's governments made a big effort to clean up their financial and regulatory regimes. Stronger rules-based systems were introduced, with stricter insider-trading and contract laws and more rigorous competition policies. Consequently, the usefulness of *guanxi* in gathering information and providing finance and personal favours has begun to decline. As Asia's markets become more rules-based, its entrepreneurs are increasingly prepared to deal with contracts outside the traditional network.

Other recent changes relate to the corporate governance and human resource practices of medium and large companies in South-East Asia. We can observe an increased disclosure in public accounts, the search for an image of good management, and the employment of 'outsiders' in key positions to deal with Western sources of capital and technology.

Emergence of an entrepreneurial society

The rise of the entrepreneur, which has been gathering speed over the past two decades in the Asia–Pacific region, can be felt both at the economic and broader societal levels. Masses of new entrepreneurs are storming onto the world market, as a result of the opening up of China and India. About 65 per cent of China's economy is now dominated by SMEs serving local markets or engaged in global supply networks of the 'workshop of the world'. With this surge of entrepreneurial capitalism, the ideology of family status by seeking private wealth is reemerging. The masses of Asian entrepreneurs not only adapt Western ideas into their local markets but also transcend these ideas with their own technological advances. These effects are now being experienced by the entire world.

Entrepreneurship in Australia, for many, has become synonymous with decency, fairness and honesty in business. Big companies are, in contrast to the 1990s, seen as the bad guys by consumers who now embrace entrepreneurs and the brands they endorse. The perception of entrepreneurship among consumers has become so positive that consumers now regard an entrepreneurial attitude, personality and inventiveness as three of the foremost qualities they look for in a brand.[46]

The rapid growth of entrepreneurialism in countries such as China and India is felt at the societal level, reflected in attitudinal changes spilling over not only into mainstream business but also politics and civil society. Often outstripping their respective countries' abilities to keep up with their laws to regulate them, entrepreneurs continue to create their own rules and invent new ways of doing things ahead of social norms and customs.[47]

SUMMARY

Entrepreneurship is the process of people identifying new opportunities and converting them into marketable products or services. Therefore, the field of entrepreneurship involves the study of (1) sources of opportunities; (2) the processes of discovery, evaluation and exploitation of opportunities; and (3) the set of individuals who discover, evaluate and exploit those opportunities. Five factors have been commonly cited for entrepreneurship to take place: an individual (the entrepreneur), a market opportunity, adequate resources, a business organisation and a favourable environment. These five factors are considered contingencies — something that must be present in the phenomenon of entrepreneurship but that can materialise in many different ways. The entrepreneur is responsible for bringing these contingencies together to create new value.

At a macro level, entrepreneurship has been referred to as a process of creative destruction and a catalyst for economic growth. Entrepreneurs identify opportunities and bring the new technologies and concepts into active commercial use. In doing so, they create new business ventures, jobs and wealth, but they also force out of the marketplace the enterprises which failed to innovate. However, measuring entrepreneurial activity in the economy is a difficult task because there are many different institutional forms for exploiting opportunities. The Global Entrepreneurship Monitor, an international research consortium, showed that the level of entrepreneurial activity differed significantly between countries. This difference reflects major variations in the degree to which the opportunities are perceived to exist, rather than differences in opportunities themselves.

While studying entrepreneurship styles, habits and environments across the Asia–Pacific region, we can identify three common features: (1) the key role played by the state in the promotion and development of entrepreneurship; (2) the pyramid structures of Asian firms, which are mainly family-owned; and (3) the presence of ethnic Chinese and ethnic Indian entrepreneurs who have been at the heart of the region's economic boom.

Following the 1997 Asian financial crisis and the spread of the free market, the region has undergone major changes. Among these, the movement for privatisation and deregulation, the adoption of Western ideas, the emergence of rules-based systems, and the increased pressure for disclosure are likely to have profound effects on entrepreneurship and small businesses. These trends have led to the rise of the entrepreneurial society, which recognises and celebrates the vital economic and societal roles played by entrepreneurs.

REVIEW QUESTIONS

1. What are the key elements of entrepreneurship?
2. What are the critical stages in the process of new venture formation?
3. What are the central factors necessary for entrepreneurship to thrive in a country?
4. What are the common features of entrepreneurship in the Asia–Pacific region?
5. What are the emerging trends affecting entrepreneurship in the Asia–Pacific region?

DISCUSSION QUESTIONS

1. Why is it often said that entrepreneurship is a complex phenomenon? Identify different dimensions of or approaches to this phenomenon.
2. Why does only a small proportion of the population set up new business ventures and become independent entrepreneurs?
3. What are the main benefits of entrepreneurship?
4. Are state entrepreneurship and the position of some public servants as entrepreneurs likely to diminish in the near future? Why or why not?
5. Can entrepreneurship be taught and learned?

SUGGESTED READING

Baumol, W., Litan, R., & Schramm, C., *Good Capitalism, Bad Capitalism, and the Economics of Growth and Prosperity*, Yale University Press, New Haven, 2008.

Khanna, T., *Billions of Entrepreneurs: How China and India are Reshaping their Futures and Yours*, Harvard Business School Press, Boston, 2007.

Shane, S., *A General Theory of Entrepreneurship: The Individual–Opportunity Nexus*, Edward Elgar, Aldershot, 2003.

Case study

Green Building Material

In January 2010, Rajat Bhattacharya, Raghu Bezawada and Vikas Tuli had just completed their MBA, wherein they wrote a business plan as part of the entrepreneurship course requirement (for which they received commendation). Now they are seriously wondering if they should launch the business upon their return to India. They identified an opportunity to manufacture reasonably priced eco-friendly building materials (primarily bricks) from fly ash. The company would initially manufacture a single type of brick by setting up a manufacturing unit in Hyderabad, the fourth largest city of India. They even had a name for the company: Green Building Material Pvt. Ltd. (GBM).

The booming construction industry in India

The Indian real estate industry has been booming since the beginning of the millennium. The industry is expected to grow at 30 per cent per annum to reach A$90 billion by 2015 from the existing A$12 billion. A variety of factors contribute to this upbeat mood. First, there is a chronic housing shortage, which has been amplified by the demographic pressure. Various sources peg the nationwide housing shortage at 20 million residential units and it is continuously increasing. Second, demand for commercial and office space has been fuelled by the growing economy. The information, communication and technology sector alone would require 50 to 70 million square feet of space over the next three years. The three would-be entrepreneurs also discovered that there are over 200 shopping centres under construction or in the active planning stage in India.

Traditionally, the construction industry in India has been heavily dependent on clay bricks. The current countrywide demand amounts to over 100 billion bricks per annum. This booming industry is facing a constant shortage of this type of building material. Yet, there are many problems associated with the manufacturing and usage of clay bricks. First, the manufacturing of clay bricks is a seasonal business since they cannot be manufactured during the rainy season. Second, clay bricks are not environment friendly since they require fertile top-soil as a raw material, and a lot of fossil fuel is used during the firing. As a result, clay bricks manufacturing is one of the most carbon intensive industries in India, representing about 17 per cent of the country's carbon dioxide emissions.

In terms of customer segments, the company plans to target three main segments: builders (companies building commercial and residential real estate); contractors dealing with government projects; and individuals building their own houses. The team has already spoken to several builders in Hyderabad and two of them, Castle Constructions and Rehman Constructions, have formally expressed their interest in buying fly ash bricks.

Fly ash bricks

GBM plans to produce and commercialise fly ash bricks as an alternative to clay bricks. Fly ash bricks offer a number of advantages over traditional clay bricks. They are of better quality; they can be produced at a lower cost; they are 'eco-friendly' since they use up fly ash (an environmentally unfriendly residue from thermal power plants); they do not require kilns for burning in the production process, thereby reducing harmful carbon emissions; and they do not use up fertile top soil.

Fly ash is a readily available and cheap material. The 80-odd thermal power stations in India use bituminous coal and produce large quantities of fly ash. Altogether, they produce around 150 million tons of fly ash a year, which if not reused could eventually lead to an environmental catastrophe. At present about 73 000 acres of land is occupied by fly ash dumps; and thermal power plants are desperate to get rid of these.

To promote the usage of fly ash, various state governments have started offering incentives to entrepreneurs planning to use the commodity. A number of states like Andhra Pradesh, Orissa, Tamil Nadu, and Rajasthan have announced fiscal and policy incentives for usage of fly ash based products. For example, in Hyderabad, in the state of Andhra Pradesh, all major thermal power plants offer free fly ash, free land (at the site of the power plant) and free electricity to entrepreneurs planning to make products using fly ash.

The main competitors for GBM are the small and micro clay brick manufacturers. GBM's fly ash bricks would be competitively priced at A$0.043 (INR 1.60) per brick compared to the price of clay bricks stated at A$0.056 (INR 2.10) per brick. The market research showed that a large proportion of potential customers treat cost and quality as key considerations in buying bricks. The quality of GBM fly ash bricks is superior to clay bricks in all aspects. GBM has also priced its product in view of the price that potential builders are willing to pay.

Management and finance

All three friends plan to be involved in the management of GBM. Rajat Bhattacharya is an IT professional and he has already gained project management experience in the financial services industry. He will be the head of finance in the new company. Raghu Bezawada is an electronics engineer and he has entrepreneurial experience in real estate in Hyderabad. As such, he has numerous contacts with builders in this region. He will be the head of marketing. As for Vikas Tuli, he is a mechanical engineer with extensive experience in production at Hindustan Machine Tools. He will be the head of operation and procurement.

During the preparation of the business plan, the team approached Mr. Appi Reddy, a retired divisional engineer at Vijayawada & Kothagudam thermal power stations. Mr. Reddy has 30 years of experience in various operation and marketing functions in the energy industry. Most importantly, he has high level contacts in all major power plants in South India. He agreed to become the managing director at GBM and to mentor the three young, dynamic would-be entrepreneurs.

The production process is relatively straight forward. Fly ash, sand, lime, and gypsum are first transformed into a homogenous mix before being fed to the brick-making machine. This machine compresses the raw materials. The shape and size of the bricks can be easily changed depending upon customers' requirements. The price for one of these machines is just under A$20 000. GBM plans to install two machines in the first year in Hyderabad. In the second year, two other factories (one in Chennai and one in Vishakapatnam) will be launched.

As shown in table 1.1 the company will be cash flow positive right from the first year of its operation, even though, according to Rajat, 'it targets very modest sales revenue in the first year of operations'. The three friends want to raise A$50 000 to launch GBM and A$130 000 in the second year to invest into the new factories.

TABLE 1.1 Cash flow previsions for the first three years (in A$)

Cash flow	Year 1	Year 2	Year 3
Opening cash balance	0	32 093	470 986
Cash inflows			
Capital funds	50 000	130 000	
Sales	310 573	2 017 557	2 017 557
Total cash inflows	360 573	2 147 557	2 017 557
Cash outflows			
Cost of machinery	39 730	119 189	0
Cost of raw materials	119 085	725 848	725 848
Land leasing cost	8 108	17 838	17 838
Electricity	9 705	47 286	47 286
Labour cost	21 892	116 757	116 757
Administrative expenses	8 919	45 405	45 405
Transport cost of raw material	96 084	312 091	312 091
Transport cost of finished product	24 957	324 250	324 250
Total cash outflows	328 480	1 708 664	1 589 475
Net cash flow	32 093	438 893	428 082
Closing cash balance	32 093	470 986	899 068

This is a fictional case.

Questions

1. What is your assessment of GBM as a business opportunity? Is it more than just a business idea?
2. At what stage of the new venture creation process are the three would-be entrepreneurs today?
3. If you were in the position of Rajat, Raghu and Vikas would you now proceed with the launch of GBM?
4. What are the next steps they should follow in order to launch GBM?

ENDNOTES

1. 'The more the merrier, Special report on entrepreneurship', *The Economist*, 14 March 2009, p. 11.
2. R. Cantillon, *Essay on the Nature of Commerce* (1755), trans. H. Higgs, Macmillan, London, 1931.

3. S. Vankataraman, 'The distinctive domain of entrepreneurship research', in J. Katz, (ed.), *Advances in Entrepreneurship, Firm Emergence and Growth*, JAI Press, Greenwich, Conn., 1997, pp. 119–38.

4. S. Shane & S. Vankataraman, 'The promise of entrepreneurship as a field of research', *Academy of Management Review*, vol. 25, no. 1, 2000, pp. 217–26.

5. P. Wickham, *Strategic Entrepreneurship*, Prentice Hall, Harlow, 2004.

6. S. Shane, *A General Theory of Entrepreneurship: The Individual-Opportunity Nexus*, Edward Elgar, Aldershot, 2003.

7. B. Gilad, S. Kaish & J. Ronen, 'The entrepreneurial way with information', in S. Maital, (ed.), *Applied Behavioural Economics*, vol. II, Wheatsheaf Books, Brighton, 1989, pp. 480–503.

8. I. Kirzner, *Competition and Entrepreneurship*, University of Chicago Press, Chicago, 1973.

9. S. Shane, *see* note 7.

10. S. Shane, 'Prior knowledge and the discovery of entrepreneurial opportunities', *Organization Science*, vol. 11, no. 4, pp. 448–69.

11. R.P. Singh, G. Hills, R. Hybels & G. Lumpkin, 'Opportunity recognition through social networks of entrepreneurs', *Frontiers of Entrepreneurship Research*, Babson College, Wellesley, 1999, pp. 228–41.

12. M. Granovetter, 'The strength of weak ties', *American Journal of Sociology*, vol. 78, no. 6, 1973, pp. 1360–80.

13. R. Baron, 'Opportunity recognition as pattern recognition: how entrepreneurs "connect the dots" to identify new business opportunities', *Academy of Management Perspectives*, February 2006, pp. 104–19.

14. M. Casson, *The Entrepreneur: An Economic Theory*, Barnes & Noble Books, Totowa, NJ, 1982.

15. I. Kirzner, 'Entrepreneurial discovery and the competitive market process: an Austrian approach', *Journal of Economic Literature*, vol. 35, 1997, pp. 60–85.

16. A. Ardichvili, R. Cardozo & S. Ray, 'A theory of entrepreneurial opportunity identification and development', *Journal of Business Venturing*, vol. 18, no. 1, 2003, pp. 105–23.

17. C. Brush, P. Greene & M. Hart, 'From initial idea to unique advantage: the entrepreneurial challenge of constructing a resource base', *The Academy of Management Executive*, vol. 15, no. 1, February 2001, pp. 64–78.

18. H. Aldrich & M. Martinez, 'Many are called, but few are chosen: an evolutionary perspective for the study of entrepreneurship', *Entrepreneurship Theory & Practice*, vol. 25, no. 4, 2001, pp. 41–56.

19. L. d'Angelo Fisher, 'Money makers', *BRW*, 12 February, 2009, p. 19.

20. J. Mehlman, 'Making money when you sleep', *Nett Magazine*, 30 March, 2009, p. 1.

21. SmartCompany, 'Wotif founder Graeme Wood buys stake in news site Plugger', www.smartcompany.com.au, 25 September 2008.

22. L. d'Angelo Fischer, see note 19.

23. B.J. Bird, *Entrepreneurial Behavior*, Scott, Foresman & Co., Glenview, Ill., 1989.

24. T. Volery, N. Doss, T. Mazzarol & V. Thein, 'Triggers and barriers affecting entrepreneurial intentionality: the case of Western Australian nascent entrepreneurs', *Journal of Enterprising Culture*, vol. 5, no. 3, 1997, pp. 273–91.

25. J.A. Schumpeter, *The Theory of Economic Development*, Harvard University Press, Cambridge, Mass., 1934.

26. 'The entrepreneurial society, Special report on entrepreneurship', *The Economist*, 14 March 2009, p. 18.

27. L.C. Thurow, *Building Wealth: The New Rules for Individuals, Companies and Nations*, HarperCollins, New York, 1999.

28. R. Marsh, *The Mandarins: The Circulation of Elites in China, 1600–1900*, Free Press, Glencoe, Ill., 1961.

29. L. Thurow, *Building Wealth*, Harper Business, New York, 2000.

30. W.E. Williamson, *The Economic Institutions of Capitalism*, Free Press, New York, 1985.

31. Z.J. Acs, B. Carlsson & C. Karlsson (eds), 'The linkages among entrepreneurship, SMEs and the macroeconomy', in *Entrepreneurship, Small and Medium-Sized Enterprises and the Macroeconomy*, Cambridge University Press, Cambridge, Mass., 1999, p. 16.

32. A. Van de Ven, 'The development of an infrastructure for entrepreneurship', *Journal of Business Venturing*, vol. 8, no. 4, 1993, pp. 211–30.

33. More information on the Global Entrepreneurship Monitor is available at www.gemconsortium.org.

34. 'Global heroes – Special report on entrepreneurship', *The Economist*, 14 March 2009, p. 6

35. M. Weidenbaum & S. Hughes, *The Bamboo Network: How Expatriate Chinese Entrepreneurs are Creating a New Economic Superpower in Asia*, Free Press, New York, 1996.

36. G.S. Redding, *The Spirit of Chinese Capitalism*, de Gruyter, New York, 1990.

37. W.K. Gabrenya & K.K. Hwang, 'Chinese social interaction: harmony and hierarchy on the good hearth', in M.H. Bond (eds), *The Handbook of Chinese Psychology*, Oxford University Press, Hong Kong, 1996, pp. 309–21.

38. See note 1

39. 'Entrepreneurship in India', *The Economist*, www.economist.com, 18 December 2008.

40. S. Claessens, S. Djankov & L. Lang, 'The separation of ownership and control in East Asian corporations', *Journal of Financial Economics*, no. 58, 2000, pp. 81–112.

41. 'Pharoah capitalism', *The Economist*, 14 February 2009, p. 81.

42. Finfacts Irland, 'Lands of Opportunity: Israel, Denmark and Singapore — and what about Ireland?', www.finfacts.ie, 16 March, 2009.

43. S. Choo, 'Developing an entrepreneurial culture in Singapore: dream or reality', *Asian Affairs*, vol. 36, no. 3, November 2005, pp. 361–73.

44. 'Time to change the act', *The Economist*, 21 February, 2009.

45. B. Buzans & G. Segal, *Anticipating the Future*, Simon & Schuster, New York, 2000.

46. Grey Group, *Eye on Australia 2005*, Grey Group, Melbourne.

47. Khanna, T., *Billions of Entrepreneurs: How China and India are reshaping their Futures and yours*, Harvard Business School Press, Boston, 2007.

CHAPTER 2

The personality of entrepreneurs

Learning objectives

After reading this chapter, you should be able to:

- explain the relationship between the entrepreneur and new value creation

- explain why and how entrepreneurs discover and exploit opportunities

- list the roles and characteristics of entrepreneurs

- identify the relevant performance measures for an entrepreneur

- define the risks of a career in entrepreneurship

- explain entrepreneurial behaviour in a social context.

The individual entrepreneur plays a central role in new venture formation. This chapter identifies and discusses the personal dimensions that can explain or affect the entrepreneurial process. Firstly, it is essential to understand the relationship between individuals and opportunities. We show that entrepreneurs can be understood only in relation to their project, and that individual differences matter in the discovery and exploitation of opportunities. Secondly, the roles and characteristics of entrepreneurs are examined from an economic and psychological perspective. Thirdly, the chapter identifies the social contexts that affect the situations in which entrepreneurial opportunities emerge and are pursued. Three features of a person's social context are reviewed: the stage of life, the role and importance of social networks, and ethnicity.

Individuals and opportunities

The entrepreneur is the central actor in the creation of a new venture. Economic circumstances, social networks, marketing, planning, finance and even public agency assistance are all important. But none of these alone will create a new venture. For that we need someone who can pull all the possibilities together, who identifies and shapes a business opportunity, and who has the motivation to persist until the job is done. The entrepreneur is responsible for creating new value (an innovation and/or an organisation). This section shows how entrepreneurs are intricately related to their project. We explain why some opportunities are discovered and exploited by certain individuals and not by others. Then we outline how the exploitation of opportunities is organised in the economy.

The relationship between the individual and the opportunity

Initially, an opportunity is generally recognised by a single individual who may decide to pursue it alone or with others. That opportunity becomes an entrepreneurial project, and a process of new value creation is initiated. At this stage, budding entrepreneurs clearly express their entrepreneurial intention. As a project matures, it gradually places constraints on the entrepreneur. Frequently, the project also influences the entrepreneurs, as they define themselves to a large extent by the relative success of the venture. The project occupies a large part of the person's life (activities, goals, means, interest) and usually influences the person's social network.[1] For example, emerging entrepreneurs are always alert to resources (information, finance, contacts) that could help them to evaluate and shape the project they pursue. A business seminar, an alumni meeting or even a holiday can bring forward valuable information and contacts for would-be entrepreneurs. In short, many aspects of life, usually seen as independent of a person's business venture, will be seen by the entrepreneur as another arena in which to foster the new enterprise.

Defining the concept of dialogic

Dialogic *A system with a circular causality process.*

Bruyat and Julien[2] see the relationship between the individual and opportunity as a **dialogic**, or a system with a circular causality process. This means that two or more elements are combined into a single unit without losing their individual aspects. Dialogic relationships must be studied as a whole to be understood. (The symbol ⇔ is used to represent a dialogic relationship.) In terms of entrepreneurship, this dialogic means that the individual can be called an entrepreneur only because he or she is pursuing a project to commercialise a new product or service and, in turn, that this entrepreneurial project exists only because there is an individual who has identified this opportunity and is pursuing it.

Entrepreneurship is concerned mainly with a process of change, emergence and creation, for the individual as well as a business opportunity. Figure 2.1 shows the dialogic relationship between the individual and opportunity. The amount of value creation can vary a great deal. In fact, many entrepreneurs create little value — they set-up business ventures that merely adapt or improve an existing business concept and, as a consequence, commercialise products and services that are largely identical to what is already available in the marketplace. The importance of change in the individual can also vary a great deal. The changes may affect the entrepreneur's knowledge, relationships or social status and require the person to engage in learning new skills.[3] As a consequence, becoming an entrepreneur can trigger some profound changes for both the entrepreneur and the environment or industry in which he or she evolves. Figure 2.1 shows four types of entrepreneurial outcome built on individual ⇔ opportunity dialogics.

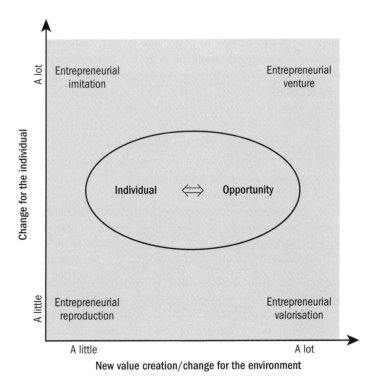

FIGURE 2.1 Typology of entrepreneurial outcomes

Source: Adapted from C. Bruyat & P.A. Julien, 'Defining the field of research in entrepreneurship', *Journal of Business Venturing*, no. 16, 2000, p. 174.

- *Entrepreneurial reproduction*. This entrepreneurial outcome implies little new value creation (innovation) and few changes for the individual. For example, suppose that a chef employed in a restaurant decided to open his own restaurant in a promising location. The competitive advantage of this restaurant might be the location, a specific type of cuisine, or the services offered (high-standard service, live music, home delivery, long opening hours). The entrepreneur chef becomes self-employed by performing an activity that he is already good at. So, in the case of entrepreneurial reproduction, entrepreneurs often concentrate their activities on an aspect of operational efficiency — that is, doing things better or more efficiently and thus adding value to the products or services.

- *Entrepreneurial imitation.* In this outcome, entrepreneurs make great changes in their knowledge, relationships and habits but there is little significant new value creation. In such projects there is usually a great deal of uncertainty, lengthy learning processes and possibly costly mistakes. Urban professionals who set-up or buy a 'lifestyle business' in the countryside, such as a bed-and-breakfast, restaurant or winery, are typical examples of entrepreneurial imitations. These people can have a variety of backgrounds (lawyer, clerk, engineer) and venture into a totally new industry for which they have to learn new skills. However, the level of innovation in the new venture is often marginal.

- *Entrepreneurial valorisation.* In this outcome, the entrepreneur sets up an innovative business in his or her field of expertise, hence capitalising on in-depth knowledge and possibly several years of industry experience. Although entrepreneurial valorisation (assigning a value to the entrepreneur's specific qualities) is most likely to take place in high-technology industries, such as software development, biotechnology and fine mechanics, it can also happen in more traditional industries. Consider the case of Ray Kroc, the founder of McDonald's. At age 52, Ray Kroc was the exclusive distributor for a company that produced 'multi-mixer' milkshake machines. Impressed by a small chain of hamburger restaurants based in California that used the multi-mixers, Kroc bought the restaurants from the owners, the McDonald brothers. His vision was for McDonald's to be the world's best quick-service restaurant experience. Being the best meant providing outstanding quality, quick service, cleanliness and value (low-price strategy). Kroc's key innovation was to standardise products, services and procedures in order to expand as quickly as possible through the franchising system. In doing so, Kroc also created the fast-food industry.

- *Entrepreneurial venture.* Entrepreneurial ventures are less common, but if they are successful they create major changes in the environment and sometimes create new industries; examples are Microsoft, eBay, Google and Creative Technology. Entrepreneurial ventures entail a great deal of uncertainty because they result from significant changes for the entrepreneur coupled with radical innovation. Because the results of the process depend on the entrepreneur's ability to pick up skills quickly and the speed with which the market takes up the innovation, the results of these projects are less predictable.[4]

Figure 2.1 can be used to chart a specific case, which would be shown by a pathway within the matrix. An entrepreneur can, for example, start a business along the lines of entrepreneurial reproduction and later introduce a significant innovation into the market, thereby moving towards entrepreneurial valorisation. In some cases, the entrepreneurial phase may be destroyed by the cessation of new value creation once the business has been established. This often happens with entrepreneurial reproduction and entrepreneurial imitation. In such cases, the entrepreneur may introduce an innovation at the time the business venture is launched. But once the business is successfully established in the market, there is hardly any innovation or growth taking place.

The discovery and evaluation of entrepreneurial opportunities

It was suggested in chapter 1 that the initiation of new ventures requires the combination of the right individual in the right place. In other words, it is necessary to have both an environment rich in opportunities and people who are able and motivated to pursue those opportunities. Drucker[5] identified three different categories of opportunity:

- inefficiencies within existing markets due to either information asymmetries or the limitations in technology in terms of satisfying certain known but unfulfilled market demands
- the emergence of significant changes in social, political, demographic and economic forces
- inventions and discoveries that produce new knowledge.

It is one thing for opportunities to exist, but an entirely different matter for them to be discovered and exploited. Opportunities rarely present themselves in neat packages. They almost always have to be discovered and shaped. Why are these opportunities discovered and exploited by certain people and not by others? Essentially, it is because people are different and these differences matter.[6] There are four main differences to consider: psychological characteristics, information and knowledge availability, creative processing and cognitive **heuristics**.

Psychological characteristics

Among the almost endless list of entrepreneurial traits suggested, the need for achievement, the ability to control events in one's life and a risk-taking propensity have received wide attention in the literature and show a high level of validity. Entrepreneurs are typically those people who relentlessly pursue their project, feel that they can control their life and are able to take risks. These characteristics are discussed later in this chapter.

Information and knowledge availability

Specific knowledge and 'knowledge corridors' play a critical role in motivating the search for opportunities. Opportunities can be identified and exploited by people who have the ability to obtain information not possessed by others. Consequently, they can build knowledge about, for instance, a specific industry or market. Specific knowledge by itself may be sufficient for the launch of a successful enterprise, but networks and social relationships can be a crucial source of information and resources for identifying and shaping ongoing opportunities. Networking allows entrepreneurs to enlarge their knowledge of opportunities, increase their sphere of action, gain access to critical resources (e.g. customers, suppliers, finance, premises) and acquire knowledge that allows them to avoid and deal with business development obstacles.

Heuristics
Simplifying strategies that can be used to make judgements quickly and efficiently. Heuristics result from cognition, i.e. the intellectual processes through which information is obtained, transformed, stored, retrieved and used.

Creative processing

The ability to make the connection between specific knowledge and a commercial opportunity requires skills, aptitudes, insight and circumstances that are neither uniformly nor widely distributed. Creative processing refers to the way people approach problems and solutions — their capacity to put existing things together in new combinations. It has often been suggested that entrepreneurs see how to put resources and information together in different ways; they have the knack of looking at the usual and seeing the unusual. Consequently, they can spot opportunities that turn the commonplace into the unique and unexpected.[7] People have different creative processing abilities because they use different schemas — that is, mental structures used to organise our knowledge of the social world according to theme or subject.

Cognitive heuristics

Heuristics are simplifying strategies that can be used to make judgements quickly and efficiently. In business, this decision process is often referred to as trial and error — a mostly unconscious journey from one event to another, picking up pieces of knowledge and experience both positive and negative. People then filter these data through their own mental set, and establish a pattern of behaviour. Since individuals have different business and social experiences, they will make different judgements about a specific situation. Some will consider this situation to be an opportunity and decide to pursue it.

Entrepreneurs appear to differ from other types of people in the use of cognitive mechanisms. For example, it has been suggested that entrepreneurs are more likely than non-entrepreneurs to experience regret over previously missed opportunities. Previous entrepreneurial experience also provides a framework for processing information and allows informed, experienced entrepreneurs to identify and take advantage of opportunities.[8]

The decision to exploit entrepreneurial opportunities

Although the discovery of an opportunity is a necessary condition for entrepreneurship, there is more to it than that. After having identified and assessed an opportunity, potential entrepreneurs must decide whether they want to *exploit* it. Why, when and how do some people and not others exploit the opportunities they discover? The answer again appears to depend on the joint characteristics of the individual and the nature of the opportunity.[9] Entrepreneurs tend to exploit opportunities that have a high expected value. Such opportunities are likely to generate a profit large enough to compensate for the opportunity cost of other alternatives, the time and money invested in the development of the project, and the risk associated with the project. In particular, exploitation is more common when expected demand is large, industry margins are high, the technology life cycle is young, and the level of competition in the industry is low.

Individual differences matter too. Firstly, individuals have different opportunity costs. The **opportunity cost** principle states the cost of one good in terms of the next best alternative. For example, suppose a public servant decides to launch a business venture. The opportunity cost of the entrepreneurial profit is the alternative income that he or she might receive by remaining a government employee.

Opportunity cost
The cost of passing up one investment in favour of another.

Since people have different incomes and wages, they are likely to make different decisions about whether or not to exploit any given opportunity. Secondly, the decision to exploit entrepreneurial opportunities is also influenced by individual differences in risk perception, optimism, tolerance for ambiguity and need for achievement. The different psychological characteristics of the entrepreneur will be discussed in detail later in this chapter.

Triggers and barriers to start-ups

So far, little research has focused on would-be entrepreneurs and the factors likely to influence their decision to launch a new venture. However, certain triggers and barriers often appear to play a role in the decision to exploit an opportunity.[10] For example, the following triggers have been identified:

- *Material rewards*. Many entrepreneurs launch their own business venture because they want to be rewarded according to their effort, and because of the anticipated financial gains. For example, 40 per cent of the Fast 100 owners — *BRW*'s list of Australia's fastest growing companies — draw a salary in the first year in business and, for the majority of them, this salary is over A$100 000 per year.[11] Launching or buying a business can also represent an interesting investment option for those who have savings.
- *Creativity*. When asked about the variables that motivate the launch of a new venture, many entrepreneurs mention: 'to take advantage of my own talents', 'to create something new' and 'to realise my dreams'. Altogether, these variables translate the desire and the ability to bring something new into existence.
- *Desire for autonomy*. Entrepreneurs want to be independent, and they express the desire to work at a location of their choice, set their own hours of work and be their own boss.

The launch of a new business venture can be a long and difficult process, and entrepreneurs can face all sorts of hurdles while trying to realise their dreams. If these barriers are too high, entrepreneurs may eventually abandon the opportunity. The following barriers appear to play an important role in the start-up process:

- *Lack of resources*. Would-be entrepreneurs often think that they do not possess the necessary marketing and management skills. These personal deficiencies are often worsened by a lack of information on start-ups and the difficulty of finding sufficient finance.
- *Compliance costs*. High taxes and the cost of complying with government legislation are perceived as a major hurdle. Such compliance costs are often referred to as 'red tape'.
- *Hard reality*. Setting up a business venture is often harder and riskier than initially expected. The future is perceived as very uncertain and, as a result, a certain fear of failure emerges while the would-be entrepreneur gathers resources and processes information to launch the venture.

Some precipitating events, such as dismissal, job frustration, graduation or an inheritance, may also trigger the launch of the business venture. However, when the importance of each trigger is examined, it is often the desire to create something new — sustained ultimately by the passion and motivation of the individual — that pushes the entrepreneur to 'take the plunge'.

Modes of exploitation

Another critical question concerns how the exploitation of entrepreneurial opportunities is organised in the economy. Two major institutional arrangements exist — the creation of new firms (hierarchies) and the sale of opportunities to existing firms (markets) — but the common assumption is that most entrepreneurial activity occurs through new independent start-ups. However, people within organisations who discover opportunities sometimes pursue those opportunities on behalf of their current employer. In contrast, independent actors sometimes sell their opportunities to existing enterprises and, sometimes, establish new businesses to pursue the opportunities. Other institutional forms, such as joint ventures or franchises, are also possible.

Understanding the profile of an entrepreneur

It is difficult to identify and find entrepreneurs and to determine what they do. Is the artisan, the small business owner–manager or even the manager of a large corporation an entrepreneur? Are entrepreneurs found in private businesses only, or can they be in government and not-for-profit organisations as well? This section reviews the two basic schools of thought on the profile of the entrepreneur: the economists who consider the entrepreneur as an agent who specialises in certain roles, and the behaviourists who concentrate on the creative and intuitive characteristics of entrepreneurs. Later sections present the different risks associated with a career as an entrepreneur, and discuss the relevant performance measures to be considered in entrepreneurship.

The roles of entrepreneurs: an economic perspective

From an economic point of view, entrepreneurship is considered as a function, so entrepreneurs have been all but banished from the theory of the firm and the market. Microeconomics instead gives pride of place to prices. Guided by the wages and interest rates they must pay, businessmen choose from different techniques of production (labour-intensive when workers are cheap, capital-intensive when they are scarce) but they do not reinvent or revolutionise them. Guided by the price their wares will fetch, they decide to make more goods or fewer. In other words, as Casson noted, 'The entrepreneur is what the entrepreneur does'.[12] The status of the entrepreneur can then be analysed in terms of a division of labour that explains this function based on certain roles, such as risk bearer, arbitrageur, innovator, and coordinator of scarce resources.

Risk bearer

Cantillon[13] described an entrepreneur as a person who pays a certain price for a product to resell it at an uncertain price, thereby making decisions about obtaining and using resources while assuming the risk of enterprise. According to this view, merchants, for example, are specialised bearers of risk. Manufacturers can also be bearers of risk in that they purchase the labour of workers before the product of that labour is sold. Consequently, entrepreneurs should be regarded as calculated risk takers.

Risk exists when uncertain outcomes can be predicted with some degree of probability. An entrepreneur is prepared to accept the remaining risk that cannot be transferred through insurance. It was Knight who first developed the distinction between risk, which is insurable, and uncertainty, which insurers will not touch because they have no way of typing and calibrating it. Knight's thesis is that an entrepreneur's new business venture is in some aspects unique, and the relative frequencies of past events are not sufficient to estimate the probabilities of future returns of the venture. Uncertainty, which cannot be eliminated or insured against, is therefore the source of profit:

> Profit arises out of the inherent, absolute unpredictability of things, out of the sheer brute fact that the results of human activity cannot be anticipated and then only in so far as even a probability calculation in regard to them is impossible and meaningless.[14]

Faced with uncertainty, people must rely on their own judgement, because they have no outside information to refer to. It is on this resource — good judgement — that entrepreneurs earn a profit.

Arbitrageur

For other economists,[15] the entrepreneur is the key figure in the market economy. In a continually changing environment, entrepreneurs move the economy towards equilibrium through speculation and **arbitrage**. The main function of the entrepreneur in this context is one of price discovery. The motivation for price discovery is the prospect of a temporary monopoly gain if the entrepreneur can benefit from being the first to exploit the price differences. Profit is the reward for recognising a market opportunity and providing the intermediary function. Freedom of entry ensures that the entrepreneur receives only a normal profit once the costs of discovery are allowed for.

Arbitrage
The action of taking advantage of a discrepancy in value that exists in the marketplace. Those who ferret out such discrepancies in value and realise profits by acting on them are called arbitrageurs.

Innovator

Schumpeter[16] broke with traditional economics because it sought, and still seeks, to optimise resources within a stable environment. He suggested that dynamic disequilibrium brought on by the innovating entrepreneur, rather than equilibrium and optimisation, is the norm of a healthy economy. According to this perspective, the entrepreneur is an innovator who carries out new combinations: introducing a new technology or product, discovering a new export market or developing new business organisations. Schumpeter added that innovations are, as a rule, embodied in new firms. Thus the agent of change is the entrepreneur who, hitting upon the prospective profitability of some unnoticed commercial application, undertakes a new venture by implementing an innovative idea. Banks — the venture capitalists of Schumpeter's era — selected the investment projects to finance.

Coordinator of scarce resources

Another economist, Say,[17] described the entrepreneur as a coordinator and supervisor of production. The entrepreneur is the plucky up-start who shifts economic resources out of an area of lower productivity and into an area of higher productivity and greater yields. Entrepreneurs, however, may not have all the resources (e.g. money, labour, premises, technology) necessary to launch a business venture. Therefore, a critical role of the entrepreneur involves convincing resource holders to commit some resource to the new venture and coordinating these scarce resources. To achieve this, the entrepreneur must have judgement, perseverance and knowledge of the world of business.

The characteristics of entrepreneurs: a behaviourist approach

The second category of researchers who study entrepreneurs are the behaviourists, including psychologists and sociologists. Early studies in entrepreneurship typically focused on the psychological characteristics and the personality of the individual as determinants of entrepreneurial behaviour. The most common characteristics are shown in figure 2.2.

Self-confidence	Tolerance of ambiguity
Risk-taking propensity	Responsiveness to suggestions
Flexibility	Dynamic leadership qualities
Independence of mind	Initiative
Energy and diligence	Resourcefulness
Hard-work ethic	Good communication skills
Creativity	Perseverance
The need for achievement	Profit-orientation
Internal locus of control	Perception with foresight

FIGURE 2.2
Characteristics of successful entrepreneurs

Among the almost endless list of entrepreneurial traits suggested, only three have received wide attention in the literature and show a high level of validity:[18] the need for achievement, internal locus of control and a risk-taking propensity.

The need for achievement

Of all the psychological measures presumed to be associated with the creation of new ventures, the need for achievement has the longest history. The **need for achievement** — a person's desire either for excellence or to succeed in competitive situations — is a key personal attribute of successful entrepreneurs.[19] Successful entrepreneurs are highly motivated in what they do. They are typically self-starters and appear internally driven to compete against their own self-imposed standards. High achievers take responsibility for attaining their goals, set moderately difficult goals and want immediate feedback on how well they have performed.

Need for achievement
A person's desire either for excellence or to succeed in competitive situations.

Locus of control
The extent to which individuals believe that they can control events that affect them.

Internal locus of control

Locus of control refers to the extent to which people believe they can control events that affect them. People with a high internal locus of control believe that events result mainly from their own behaviour and actions. Those with a high external locus of control believe that powerful others, fate, or chance mainly determine events. Effective entrepreneurs believe in themselves, and have a perception that they can control the events in their lives and can, therefore, guide their own destiny. This attribute is consistent with a high-achievement motivational drive and a need for autonomy.

What seems to underlie the internal locus of control is the concept of 'self as agent'. This means that individuals' thoughts control their actions, and that when they realise this executive function of thinking, they can positively affect their beliefs, motivation and, to a certain extent, their performance. As a result, the degree to which they choose to be self-determining is a function of their realisation of the source of agency and personal control.[20] In other words, we can say to ourselves, 'I choose to direct my thoughts and energies towards accomplishment. I choose not to be daunted by my anxieties or feelings of inadequacy.'

Risk-taking propensity

Although entrepreneurs are not gamblers, they are characterised by a propensity to take calculated risks. In a world of change, risk and ambiguity, successful entrepreneurs are those who learn to manage the risk, in part by transferring a portion of the risk to others (investors, bankers, partners, customers, employees and so on). However, risk-taking propensity is strongly influenced by cognitive heuristics. Entrepreneurs may not think of themselves as being any more likely to take risks than non-entrepreneurs yet, nonetheless, they are predisposed to categorise business situations more positively.[21] Thus, entrepreneurs may view some situations as opportunities, even though others perceive those same situations as having little potential.

The characteristics approach eventually reached a dead end, as it could only partially answer the question: 'What makes people set-up new ventures?' The study of the demographic background of entrepreneurs (age, gender, previous employment) was another attempt to understand these people and uncover a pattern. Demographic studies generally confirmed that entrepreneurs tend to be better educated; to come from families where the parents owned a business; to start ventures related to their previous work; and to locate their ventures where they are already living and working. Overall, these studies provided mixed results.[22] This is not surprising — being innovators and idiosyncratic, entrepreneurs tend to defy stereotyping.

Entrepreneur profile

Jack Ma, Alibaba

Rail-thin and ever-energetic, Jack Ma has been dubbed the 'father of the internet in China'. After discovering the web on a visit to America in the mid-1990s, he returned to Hangzhou, his native city near Shanghai, and founded Alibaba. The company makes it easy for millions of buyers and suppliers around the world to do business online though three marketplaces: a global marketplace (alibaba.com) that connects small and medium-sized importers and exporters in China with counterparts worldwide; a Chinese marketplace for domestic trade in China; and a Japanese marketplace facilitating trade to and from Japan.

Ma recalls that two distinctive events changed his vision of the world and established his pathway to entrepreneurship. He developed an interest in learning English when he was 12, travelling by bike every day to a Hangzou hotel to offer his services as a free guide, which allowed him to improve his English.

'Those years deeply changed me. I started to become more globalised than most Chinese. What I learned from teachers and books was different from what foreign visitors told us.'

His second defining moment was in 1979, when he befriended an Australian family, became pen pals and six years later they invited him to travel and stay with them for a summer holiday.

'I went in July, and these 30 days changed my life. I was educated that China was the richest, happiest country in the world... So when I arrived in Australia, I realised that everything is different from what I was told.'[23]

Ma recognised the potential of internet early on but he seldom mentions technology. Whereas most entrepreneurs are geeks (e.g. Yahoo!'s or Google's founders), Ma came across his first computer in 1995 on a trip to Seattle. 'Someone as dumb as me should be able to use the technology,' he says.[24] So he presented his vision to a few close friends and he raised US$60 000 to launch Alibaba in 1999. He handled early difficulties by being flexible, and he ascribes Alibaba's survival and success to the fact he 'knew nothing about the technology; we didn't have a plan and we didn't have money.'[25] In truth, Ma had powerful backers early on, including Goldman Sachs and Softbank. Alibaba went public in 2007 as the second-biggest internet IPO in history after Google. Today, it is the world's largest business-to-business e-commerce platform.

Ma encourages people to shape their own destinies by starting their businesses to survive the economic downturn, rather than relying on the government or other businesses to relieve their situation. At the Alibaba annual shareholders meeting in 2009, he reminded his audience that it was the people who spotted opportunities others missed who made the great fortunes of the world. He also surprised 80 business school students with a gift of 100 shares, telling them he hoped the gift would be an incentive for them to deepen their interest in entrepreneurship, beyond just following Alibaba's performance.[26]

The risks of a career in entrepreneurship

There are four types of risk to be considered before embracing a career in entrepreneurship: (1) financial risks, (2) career risks, (3) social risks and (4) health risks. All would-be entrepreneurs must ask themselves if they are prepared to live with these risks, and they should prepare strategies to minimise them.

Financial risks

Collateral
Property used as security for a loan. If the debt is not paid, the lender has the right to sell the collateral to recover the value of the loan.

Entrepreneurs usually invest large amounts of their own money to launch a new business venture. They have to commit part or all of their own savings to the venture, and offer some **collateral** to raise finance. After start-up, most of the profits are usually reinvested in the business to expand the activities. Entrepreneurs risk losing all or part of the money invested in their business if, for example, they go bankrupt.

There are different ways for entrepreneurs to reduce financial risks. In order to set-up the business, one strategy is to borrow funds from bankers, venture capitalists or partners. Another strategy is to place personal assets in the spouse's name so that these assets cannot be seized if the firm goes bankrupt. The legal structure of the business can also help to minimise financial risks. For example, entrepreneurs who operate a business as a sole proprietorship or as a partnership face unlimited liability, whereas for a company the liability of the owners is limited to the unpaid value of the shares they hold.

Career risks

A question often asked by would-be entrepreneurs is whether they will be able to find a job or go back to their old job if their venture fails. This is a major concern, especially for well-paid professionals and people close to retirement age. Such people must ask themselves whether they are prepared to accept a lower paid job, not necessarily in their field of expertise, if they have to go back to being an employee. One way to minimise career risk is to launch a business on a part-time basis while still retaining the current job. Should the attempt fail, the person will have a fall-back position and income.

Social risks

Starting a new venture uses much of the entrepreneur's energy and time. Consequently, family and social commitments may suffer. To minimise subsequent reproaches and disappointments, any decision to set-up a new business venture should involve the family. This might help would-be entrepreneurs to identify potential family problems that can arise from long working hours, reduced holidays and stress. Discussing the entrepreneurial project also helps to build commitment within a family. Successful entrepreneurs almost invariably recognise the support of their spouses and/or family in their career.

Another type of social risk is linked to the image of the failed entrepreneur. Some societies have little tolerance for failure. A typical example is the *kia su*, or 'afraid to lose' attitude that is pervasive in Singaporean culture. This typifies a mentality where failure is perceived to be a disgrace and to bring shame on the individual and the family.

Health risks

Entrepreneurship is a rigorous activity, not only physically but also mentally. In many instances, work and its demands dominate the lives of entrepreneurs. A clear separation of work and non-work is generally hard to achieve, and a normal work day can extend to 10 or 12 hours. There is evidence that entrepreneurs experience higher job stress and psychosomatic health problems than people who are not self-employed.[27] Would-be entrepreneurs should make sure that their health can cope with the demands and challenges of starting and running a business.

The source of many health problems is stress, which stems from the discrepancies between a person's expectations and their ability to meet demands. One of the solutions for reducing stress is to create an environment that discourages it — for example, by having a place where everything can be kept organised.

Relevant performance measures

Entrepreneurship is concerned with the discovery and exploitation of profitable opportunities for private wealth and, consequently, for social wealth as well. There may be many motives for starting a business, such as acquiring higher social status or a new lifestyle, but the financial dimension cannot be ignored. After all, a business must generate a profit to stay in the marketplace, and entrepreneurs must be able to use a simple standard measure — a monetary unit — to assess their performance. The relevant benchmarks in entrepreneurship are: (1) the absolute level of economic performance that provides a return for enterprising effort and (2) the social contribution of the individual effort.

Superior performance relative to other enterprises is not a sufficient measure of success in the case of entrepreneurship because profit must exceed some minimum threshold in order to compensate opportunity seekers for their efforts. Just to break even, profits must compensate for bypassed alternatives (opportunity cost) and for the cash, effort and time invested in the venture (liquidity premium), as well as covering a premium for risk and a premium for uncertainty.

- *Opportunity cost.* Economists use this term to refer to what is given up when a certain course of action is chosen. For example, when choosing to set-up a business and become self-employed, entrepreneurs must give up a regular salary and holidays (if they are employees). Opportunity costs are particularly high for well-paid professionals and executives.
- *Liquidity premium.* The entrepreneurial process generally requires substantial investments in order to evaluate and exploit opportunities. Most would-be entrepreneurs invest their own money in pre-start-up activities, such as building a prototype, paying a consultant to conduct professional market research, and registering a patent or trademark. In addition, they spend a considerable amount of their own time and effort in fine-tuning the business concept and convincing various resource holders (such as venture capitalists, suppliers, clients and potential employees) to take part in the enterprise.
- *Risk premium.* In economics, risk denotes the possibility of a loss. Risk is present when future events occur with measurable probability. It is measurable because it relates to situations that have many precedents and where, as a consequence, the odds of success can be calculated. The risk premium depends on the outcome probability of the business venture. For example, if the odds of success are relatively high because the entrepreneur has developed a promising product (good trial tests) that can be protected (by a patent or registered trademark) and for which there is a familiar market, then the risk premium is relatively low.
- *Uncertainty premium.* Uncertainty is not measurable, and so cannot be quantified and handled through insurance or other arrangements. Uncertainty occurs in circumstances that cannot be analysed either on rational grounds, because they are too irregular, or through empirical observation, because they are unique. Uncertainty is therefore present when the likelihood of future events is indefinite or incalculable. The uncertainty premium is particularly high if the entrepreneur has no previous experience of the industry in which

the business venture is to be established, and if the venture is based on radical innovation implying emerging technology.

As depicted in figure 2.3, results that fall below the sum of the above four components represent an economic loss for the entrepreneur, even if the sum is far above the performance of rival firms. Only the surplus above this minimum can be counted as the entrepreneur's reward.

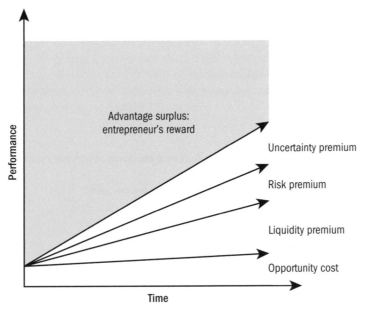

FIGURE 2.3 Relevant performance measures for entrepreneurs

Source: Adapted from S. Venkataraman, 'The distinctive domain of entrepreneurship research', in J. Katz (ed.), *Advances in Entrepreneurship, Firm Emergence and Growth,* vol. 3, Jai Press, Greenwich, Conn., 1997, p. 134.

What would you do?

Should I take the plunge?

A native Singaporean, you have already completed a diploma at a local polytechnic and an apprenticeship as a chef, before performing a three-year stint as a food and beverage (F&B) assistant manager in a local five-star hotel. You are currently finishing your Bachelor of Hospitality Management at renowned Australian university, having believed that a university degree abroad was a natural progression in a promising career in hospitality. Upon completion of your degree, you initially planned to move back to Singapore and to become an F&B manager or a hotel assistant manager.

Now you are having second thoughts, and may want to launch your own business with a classmate who is also your girlfriend and the daughter of a rich Australian entrepreneur. You are in the process of writing a business plan to raise A$150 000 from an investor to set-up 'Noodleman'. The business will provide high quality, fast-served Asian style meals, based on a central theme of noodles. The meals will be delivered fresh, faster than other noodle-based products. Adopting a similar distribution model to mobile coffee companies in Australia (e.g. Cappuccino Xpress, Espresso Mobile Café, Kiss Cafe), Noodleman meals will be provided through mobile vending units. To date, you have already invested over two months of work to ➡

develop recipes, and to write a first draft of the business plan. Together with your girlfriend, you also have invested A$10 000 each to build a mobile vending unit prototype, which has been successfully tested over a couple of weekends, generating sales of A$700 and a net profit of A$200 per day.

Valued at A$8.2 billion in 2009, the Australian market for 'fast' food is large and segmented, with Asian style foods representing two of the top three choices in capital cities. However, your research indicates that the market is approaching saturation, and it is heavily segmented on quality, style, modality and price. Your girlfriend thinks that Noodleman can rapidly expand through a franchise system and become the benchmark in the mobile vending noodle business. However, you know that there are strong competitors in the noodle business, including Wagamama and Noodle Box, and that you have to work on average 10 hours per day during the first months to launch the business. Is it worth it? You are also tempted to move back to Singapore where you could quickly get a stable job through your established network. You would make at least A$60 000 as a F&B manager and have four weeks' annual leave.

Questions
1. **From a personal perspective, what performance measures should you take into account when assessing this opportunity?**
2. **What are the risks involved in launching this business venture?**

Entrepreneurs in a social context

The social context is crucial to understanding the situations in which entrepreneurial opportunities will emerge and be pursued.[28] Three features of a person's social context are important to the perception of entrepreneurial opportunities and the decision to seize them: (1) the stage of life, (2) position in social networks and (3) ethnicity.

Stage of life and entrepreneurial behaviour

Most societies have developed stable and widespread expectations about the appropriate times for major life events. Societal institutions are often organised around these social conventions, such as the age at which schooling should begin, the age at which marriage is appropriate, the age of retirement and so on. One critical life event is starting a job, which usually occurs immediately after completing an educational program. If the decision to become an entrepreneur was a common event for members of society, it would not be surprising to find major regularities in its relation to a stage of life. In reality, however, that is not the case. Entrepreneurial activity involves a minority of the population, and there is no general theory indicating the stage of life that is best for launching a business venture.

Entrepreneurs are more effective at building ventures from scratch once they have attained a certain level of maturity and self-knowledge, but they can achieve this without spending most of their working lives in corporate jobs. Wasserman[29] identified two main points in favour of leaping sooner rather than later. First, long stretches in corporate positions often prevent executives from developing the versatility that new ventures generally require. As an executive they may become used to delegating, leaving the specialists to deal with HR,

IT and financial issues. This is a luxury that start-ups can ill afford. Second, employees who linger until they reach senior positions maybe age themselves out of what could otherwise be a satisfying career in start-ups.

Empirical research has shown that those people most likely to pursue entrepreneurial opportunities are men (women's participation rate being about half that of men across all countries in the Global Entrepreneurship Monitor) with post-secondary education, aged between the ages of 25 and 44, and with an established career record. Although not everyone with these characteristics starts new firms, this set of features is to some extent unique and predictable.

Social networks and entrepreneurial behaviour

Humans are social animals, which means that we relate to others; we all have a **social network**. A person's self-image determines what connections are made, and a person's identity is shaped by his or her network. Every tie is unique. The networks that entrepreneurs build for themselves and their ventures stand out in a number of respects:

- The networks are genuinely personal, intertwining business concerns and social commitments in individual ties. By way of personal networking, entrepreneurs make their planned venturing career into a way of life. Personal resources (e.g. information, money, labour) are mobilised to set-up new ventures that are alien to the market.[30]
- The spatial dimension is relevant. For historical, practical and symbolic reasons, many entrepreneurs and their firms are attached to a place. This means that the local and regional socioeconomic environment is both a major determinant and a major outcome of entrepreneurial activity.

Although networks are important in both Western and Eastern cultures, they are central to many Eastern cultures and particularly to the Chinese. The Chinese navigate complex networks of connections (*guanxi*) that expand throughout their lives. Each person is born into a social network of family members, and as the person grows up, group memberships involving education, occupation and residence provide new opportunities for expanding this network. The *guanxi* philosophy has deep roots. Many South-East Asian firms were established by migrant Chinese or their offspring, who built up networks in which extended families and clans did business with each other in order to reduce risk. The relative permanence of such social networks contributes to the importance and enforceability of the Chinese conception of reciprocity (*bao*).

But how can entrepreneurs build an effective network? In fact, networks have to be carefully constructed through relatively high-stake activities that bring the entrepreneur into contact with a diverse group of people. Most personal networks are highly clustered — that is, your friends are likely to be friends with one another as well. And, if you made those friends by introducing yourself to them, the chances are high that their experiences and perspectives echo your own. However, because ideas generated within this type of network circulate among people with shared views, a potential winner can wither away and die if no-one in the group has what it takes to bring it to fruition. But what if someone within that cluster knows someone else who belongs to a whole different group? That connection, formed by an information broker, can expose the

Social network
The sum of relationships that a person maintains with other people as a result of social activity.

entrepreneur's idea to a new world, filled with fresh perspectives and resources for success. Diversity makes the difference.[31]

Ethnicity and entrepreneurship

Ethnic and religious affiliations have historically played an important role in entrepreneurship, and there is substantial information about the extent to which various ethnic groups or new immigrants engage in entrepreneurial behaviour in the Asia–Pacific region. The main explanation of ethnic entrepreneurship is that it is a response to the lack of opportunities in the dominant culture. In this situation, entrepreneurship is very often a necessity triggered by a variety of push factors, such as ethnic discrimination in the host society; lack of recognition of qualifications; poor use of local language; and limited opportunities. However, entrepreneurship can also be a first choice between different career alternatives, and this might result from different pull factors, such as the presence in the family of entrepreneurs who act as role models; high social status given to the entrepreneur in the culture of the immigrant; perception of good entrepreneurial opportunities in the family and ethnic network; and availability of resources in the ethnic network.

Ethnic Chinese entrepreneurs in South-East Asia

In South-East Asia, there is substantial evidence that entrepreneurship, which is a crucial factor in development, has been steadily supplied by an ethnic minority — the expatriate Chinese. Historical evidence shows how domestic economies in the region faltered when ethnic Chinese entrepreneurs were not allowed to operate.[32] Usually, both push and pull factors have influenced ethnic Chinese entrepreneurship. Ethnic Chinese have often been discriminated against, having, for example, been barred from public service positions and land ownership, and allowed only limited access to tertiary education. As a consequence, they have often had no alternative but to become self-employed. At the same time, guanxi has provided ethnic Chinese privileged access to entrepreneurial opportunities and to resources. Initially, ethnic Chinese entrepreneurs fulfilled an intermediation function, particularly in their role as traders. They filled a gap in the existing market by providing goods and services that were not available. Today, although many are still engaged in trading and entrepreneurship, considerable numbers of ethnic Chinese have moved to banking and finance, transport, real estate, property development and hotel and travel services.

The situation in Australasia

In multicultural Australia and New Zealand, the growth of self-employment among ethnic minorities has been a conspicuous feature of entrepreneurial activities. In Australia, research has shown that ethnic business creation is positively related to pull and push motivations.[33] However, it was found that first-generation ethnic entrepreneurs were more influenced by push motivation, whereas third-generation ethnic entrepreneurs were more influenced by pull motivation. The first-generation ethnic entrepreneurs placed significantly greater importance on economic necessity and unemployment — both push motivators. The second-generation ethnic entrepreneurs gave greater importance to opportunities in Australia for doing business and making links to the country of origin — both pull motivators. The third-generation ethnic entrepreneurs went into business largely due to pull motivators, such as opportunities in Australia; links for doing business in the country of origin; and ethnic networks. Thus, the current trend reveals that ethnic business operators do not enter business activity as a last resort but as a positive choice.

SUMMARY

The entrepreneur and opportunities are the essence of the entrepreneurial process. Entrepreneurs are intricately related to the opportunity they pursue, and together they form a system called a 'dialogic': a system with a circular causality process. It is one thing for opportunities to exist, but an entirely different matter for them to be discovered and exploited. Four types of person-related difference (psychological traits, information availability, creative processing and cognitive heuristics) can explain why some opportunities are discovered and exploited by certain individuals and not by others. Although the discovery of an opportunity is a necessary condition for entrepreneurship, it involves more than that. After having identified and assessed an opportunity, potential entrepreneurs must decide whether they want to *exploit* the opportunity. This decision again appears to be a function of the joint characteristics of the opportunity and of the nature of the individual. There are two schools of thought on the entrepreneurial perspective in individuals: the economic perspective considers that the entrepreneur is an agent who specialises in certain roles, such as risk-bearing, arbitrage, innovation and coordination of scarce resources; the behaviourist approach, on the other hand, has identified three recurrent entrepreneurial traits — the need for achievement, the internal locus of control, and risk-taking propensity.

When considering a career in entrepreneurship, people should also consider the four types of risk (financial risk, career risk, social risk and health risk) and prepare strategies to avoid or minimise them. Similarly, would-be entrepreneurs must be careful to have the correct performance measures in mind. Just to break even, profits must compensate for bypassed alternatives (opportunity cost) and for the cash, effort and time invested in the venture (liquidity premium), and they must cover a premium for risk and for uncertainty.

The social context is crucial to understanding the situations in which entrepreneurial opportunities will emerge and be pursued. Three features of a person's social context appear to play a role in relation to the perception of entrepreneurial opportunities and the decision to seize them: the stage of life, social networks and ethnicity.

REVIEW QUESTIONS

1. Drawing on the individual ⇔ opportunity relationship (or dialogic), what are the four different types of entrepreneurial outcome possible?
2. Why are existing entrepreneurial opportunities discovered and exploited by certain individuals and not by others?
3. Which entrepreneurial traits suggested from the behaviourist approach have received wide attention in the literature and show a high level of validity?
4. What types of risk should be considered before embracing a career in entrepreneurship?
5. To what extent does the social context play a role in entrepreneurship? What are the key features of a person's social context to consider?

DISCUSSION QUESTIONS

1. Identify major changes that create opportunities for entrepreneurs.
2. Why is there a wide variation in entrepreneurial activity among countries worldwide?
3. Are entrepreneurs born or made?
4. If a would-be entrepreneur evaluates all the potential risks before starting a business, does it mean that the business venture will not fail?
5. Social networks are recognised as important elements for ethnic Chinese entrepreneurs. Are these networks equally important for entrepreneurs of other ethnic origins?

SUGGESTED READING

Bjerke B., *Understanding Entrepreneurship*, Edward Elgar, Cheltenham, 2007.

Sarasvathy S., *Effectuation: Elements of Entrepreneurial Expertise*, Edward Elgar, Cheltenham, 2008.

Shane S., *The Illusions of Entrepreneurship*, Yale University Press, New Haven, 2008.

Case study

Emma Isaacs

Emma Isaacs was not predestined to become an entrepreneur: following the advice of her high-school career counsellor, she originally planned to become an HR manager with a large corporation, and she started with a work-experience stint with a local company while she was still at school. She enrolled at university to pursue a business degree with a major in HR while working part-time at Staff it, a recruitment company. However, she quickly realised that university 'wasn't her thing'. After six months, she dropped out and accepted a 50 per cent share in Staff it and became an entrepreneur at age of 18.[34] Twelve years later, the Sydney-based woman now runs four businesses in networking, event management and fitness.

The debut as a serial entrepreneur

Isaacs' first business, Staff it, reflected her interest in HR. She ran the recruitment agency for eight years before selling it. During that time, she won several recruitment industry awards and Westpac's Small Business of the Year award in 2005. However, she needed a new challenge. That same year, Isaacs was asked to attend a networking function called Business Chicks. Curious, she went along to check it out. 'When I attended my first Business Chicks event I was blown away. I knew there was something very different about Business Chicks, and you could tell everyone in the room thought the same,'[35] she says.

In 2000, Business Chicks was set-up as an arm of the charity Kids Helpline. Isaacs soon learned that Business Chicks was for sale. And, never one to miss an opportunity, she started her due diligence, and a few months later she was awarded the right to purchase the business. 'It was an ambitious undertaking for me running a thriving recruitment business and 'inheriting' another project that required my full attention — and I didn't understand the significance of purchasing Business Chicks at the time. I just thought I was doing a nice thing for charity. I didn't know that it would become my 'full time gig' when I eventually sold out the recruitment company,'[36] she smiles.

In just over four years, Business Chicks became one of Australia's largest business groups for women, expanding its membership from 250 to over 25 000 members. The national community seeks to enrich the lives of women in business through the magazine it publishes, *Latte*. It is therefore more than just an enterprise organising networking events. Rather, Isaacs sees it as a community designed to inspire and nurture women in business. Through Business Chicks they can connect with others, and for some, it's like an instant family.

Today, Business Chicks is in every state in Australia, and sometimes up to 900 participants attend a single networking event. The impressive figures have been gained by word of mouth — there is no external promotional budget. 'We put a lot of resources into providing benefits to members — to give them value. We've really expanded the offering,'[37] Isaacs says. Business Chicks is a membership enterprise with an annual fee of A$99. Additional revenue is generated by the workshops and events. Events still help raise money for Kids Helpline, thereby achieving one of the initial goals of the network.

Three other business ventures

In addition to Business Chicks, Isaacs also owns a women's magazine, *Latté*; another business network, the Last Thursday Club; and a fitness centre, Studio Bodyfit. *Latté* is Business Chicks' bi-monthly glossy magazine and it is mailed to all members. More recently, Isaacs expanded further in the industry by purchasing the Last Thursday Club, a networking business that holds networking events for entrepreneurs, innovators and business leaders. It's held on the last Thursday of every month (hence the name) in Sydney. 'It's a different product, we're crystal clear about our mission for Last Thursday Club. All we do is two things — networking and education,' says Isaacs. The Club targets the corporate, SME and entrepreneurial sector.

Isaacs also finds time in her diary to give back to society, and she recently joined the board of the Entrepreneurs Organisation - Sydney. Married to a like-minded entrepreneur (they met through the Entrepreneur Organisation), the topic of business punctuates some of their spare time. When they go on holiday, however, they made a pact not to talk about their business ventures. 'You have to leave the BlackBerry and the laptop at home,' Isaacs says, 'Your working place is so hectic that holidays need to be for relaxing.'[38]

For Isaacs, life is very much in the fast lane, with no concrete career path laid before her:

'If you speak of career path, I'd say I want to spend my life building hundreds of businesses. You have to have the core set of skills to be an entrepreneur, but I don't think it matters if you don't have knowledge of the industry or product. For me, it's about having a really great life, to do whatever I want. I want to have the freedom to be creative. I encourage this. I say, let's try different things, and learn from the mistakes. If you're doing what you love, you would also want to make the world a better place.'[39]

Questions

1. Drawing on the individual ⇔ opportunity dialogic, what type of entrepreneurial outcome represents the various business ventures founded or bought by Emma Isaacs?
2. What are the typical entrepreneurial characteristics displayed by Emma?
3. How can Emma develop synergies between her existing business ventures and improve her offering?

ENDNOTES

1. C. Bruyat & P.A. Julien, 'Defining the field of research in entrepreneurship', *Journal of Business Venturing*, no. 16, 2000, pp. 155–80.
2. ibid.
3. ibid.
4. ibid.
5. P. Drucker, *Innovation and Entrepreneurship*, Harper & Row, New York, 1985.
6. S. Vankataraman, 'The distinctive domain of entrepreneurship research', in J. Katz (ed.), *Advances in Entrepreneurship, Firm Emergence, and Growth*, Jai Press, Greenwich, CT, 1997.
7. D.G. Mitton, 'The complete entrepreneur', *Entrepreneurship Theory and Practice*, vol. 13, no. 3, 1989, pp. 9–20.
8. S. Kaish & B. Gilad, 'Characteristics of opportunities search of entrepreneurs versus executives: Sources, interests, general alertness', *Journal of Business Venturing*, no. 6, 1991, pp. 45–61.
9. S. Shane & S. Vankataraman, 'The promise of entrepreneurship as a field of research', *Academy of Management Review*, vol. 25, no. 1, 2000, pp. 217–26.
10. T. Volery, N. Doss, T. Mazzarol & V. Thein, 'Triggers and barriers affecting entrepreneurial intentionality: The case of Western Australian nascent entrepreneurs', *Journal of Enterprising Culture*, vol. 5, no. 3, 1997, pp. 273–91.
11. R. Skeffington, 'Follow that Ferrari', *Business Review Weekly*, October 13–19, 2005, pp. 111–12.
12. M. Casson, *The Entrepreneur: An Economic Theory*, 2nd edn, Edward Elgar, Cheltenham, 2005.
13. R. Cantillon, *Essai sur la Nature du Commerce en Général* (1755), trans. H. Higgs, Macmillan, London, 1931.
14. F. Knight, *Risk, Uncertainty and Profit*, Houghton Mifflin, Boston, 1921.
15. Mainly the Austrian economists like F.A. Hayek, *Individualism and Economic Order*, Routledge, London, 1959; I.M. Kirzner, *Competition and Entrepreneurship*, Chicago University Press, Chicago, 1973.
16. J.A. Schumpeter, *The Theory of Economic Development*, Harvard University Press, Cambridge, MA., 1934.
17. J.B. Say, *A Treatise on Political Economy* (1803), trans. by C.R. Prinsep, Grigg & Elliot, Philadelphia, 1843.
18. W.B. Gartner, 'A conceptual framework for describing the phenomenon of new venture creation', *Academy of Management Review*, vol. 10, no. 4, 1985, pp. 696–706.
19. D.C. McClelland, *The Achieving Society*, Free Press, New York, 1967.
20. B.L. McCombs, 'Motivation and lifelong learning', *Educational Psychologist*, vol. 26, no. 2, 1991, pp. 117–27.
21. L.E. Palich & D.R. Bagby, 'Using cognitive theory to explain entrepreneurial risk-taking: Challenging conventional wisdom', *Journal of Business Venturing*, no. 10, 1995, pp. 425–38.
22. T. Mazzarol, T. Volery, N. Doss & V. Thein, 'Factors influencing small business start-ups: A comparison with previous research', *International Journal of Entrepreneurial Behaviour and Research*, vol. 5, no. 5, 1999, pp. 48–63.
23. R. Fannin, How I did it — Alibaba, *Inc. Magazine*, January 2008, p. 105.
24. *The Economist*, 'China's pied piper', 21 September 2006.
25. A. Ignatius, 'Jack Ma', *Time*, 30 April, 2009.
26. Alibaba.com, 'Jack Ma gives students 100 reasons to care about Alibaba.com', www.alibaba.com, 7 May 2009.
27. M. Jamal, 'Job stress, satisfaction and mental health: An empirical examination of self-employed and non-self-employed Canadians', *Journal of Small Business Management*, vol. 35, no. 4, 1997, pp. 48–57.
28. P.D. Reynolds, 'Sociology and entrepreneurship: Concepts and contributions', *Entrepreneurship Theory and Practice*, vol. 16, no. 2, 1991, pp. 47–70.

29. N. Wasserman, 'Planning a start-up? Seize the day...', *Harvard Business Review*, January 2009, p. 27.
30. B. Johannisson, 'Paradigms and entrepreneurial networks — some methodological challenges', *Entrepreneurship and Regional Development*, vol. 7, no. 3, 1995, pp. 215–31.
31. B. Uzzi & S. Dunlap, 'How to build your network', *Harvard Business Review*, December 2005, pp. 53–60.
32. A.R. Gambe, *Overseas Chinese Entrepreneurship and Capitalist Development in Southeast Asia*, LIT Verlag, Hamburg, 1999.
33. M.S. Chavan, 'The changing role of ethnic entrepreneurs in Australia', *The International Journal of Entrepreneurship and Innovation*, vol. 3, no. 3, 2002, pp. 175–82.
34. L. D'Angelo Fisher, 'No fear here', *BRW*, February 12–18, 2009, p. 22.
35. N. Card, 'High flyer is running hard', *My Business*, April 2008, p. 27.
36. Growth Business, 'Gen Y rules, ok!', *Growth Business*, October/November 2007, p. 9.
37. M. Kaplan, 'Emma Isaacs is both intimidating and inspiring', *The Australian*, 28 March, 2009.
38. D. Bela, 'Think tank to develop ideas', *mx Career One*, June 2008.
39. M. Kaplan, 'Chicks coming out of their shells', *The Australian*, 28 March, 2009.

CHAPTER 3

Creativity, innovation and entrepreneurship

Learning objectives

After reading this chapter, you should be able to:

- use a series of creativity techniques

- define and explain the sources of innovation

- discuss the different innovation types

- explain the link between creativity, innovation and entrepreneurship

- outline the steps to follow in order to screen opportunities.

Creativity and innovation are an integral part of entrepreneurship. Drucker remarked, 'Innovation is the specific instrument of entrepreneurship.'[1] Just as entrepreneurship is crucial for the economy in general, innovation has become an important tool for managers who want to adopt an entrepreneurial approach. Promoting creativity and innovation is important for small and medium-sized enterprises that want to maintain their competitive advantage. Creativity and innovation are the essence of entrepreneurship and the engine of small business growth. It is the ability to innovate that determines much of what an organisation is able to do. Innovation does make a huge difference to organisations of all shapes and sizes. The logic is simple: if we don't change what we offer the world (products and services) and how we create and deliver them, we risk being overtaken by others who do.[2] This chapter explains the role of creativity and innovation in the entrepreneurial process. It details the three components of creativity, explains different creativity techniques and discusses the factors influencing creativity. The different sources and categories of innovation are then presented. It is shown that creativity, innovation and entrepreneurship can be approached as a flow of knowledge, which is developed and transmitted mainly by social networks.

Creativity

Creativity *The production of new and useful ideas.*

Creativity is the point of origination for innovation and entrepreneurship. In business, it can be defined as the production of new and useful ideas.[3] Creativity is the process through which invention occurs — the enabling process by which something new comes into existence. Reaping the fruits of innovation begins with creative ideas. It is therefore not surprising that successful, innovative companies systematically encourage the development of ideas. Those ideas are then screened to see whether they lead to a potential innovation. Experience shows that entrepreneurial companies need to generate hundreds of ideas to end up with four plausible programs for developing new products, and four development programs are the minimum to obtain just one winner. Therefore, it is crucial to create a corporate culture that allows ideas to blossom. 'You have to kiss a lot of frogs to find a prince,' said Art Fry,[4] the inventor of Post-It notes at 3M. 'But remember, one prince can pay for a lot of frogs.'

The three components of creativity

Creativity is usually associated with the arts and is seen as the expression of highly original ideas. In business, originality is not enough. To be creative, an idea must also be appropriate — that is, useful and actionable. In the end, it must fulfil a need in the marketplace and generate profit. To most people, creativity refers to the way people think — how inventively they approach problems, for instance. Indeed, thinking imaginatively is one part of creativity, but knowledge and motivation are also essential.[5]

Creative thinking skills

Creative thinking refers to how people approach problems and solutions — their capacity to put existing ideas and knowledge together in new combinations. The skill itself depends on personality, as well as on how a person thinks and works. People are more creative if they feel comfortable disagreeing with others, i.e. if they try out solutions that depart from the status quo. As for working style, people are more likely to achieve creative success if they persevere with a difficult problem. Indeed, plodding through long dry spells of tedious experimentation increases the probability of truly creative breakthroughs. So, too, does a work style that uses 'incubation', which is the ability to set aside difficult problems temporarily, work on something else, and then return later with a fresh perspective.

Further, personality is strongly influenced by cognition, the mental activity by which an individual is aware of and knows about his or her environment, including such processes as perceiving, remembering, reasoning, judging and problem solving. Creative thinking is based on the same kinds of cognitive processes that we use in ordinary, everyday thought — retrieving memories, forming mental images, and using concepts.[6]

Knowledge

Expertise or knowledge encompasses everything a person knows and can do. This knowledge can be acquired in different ways: through formal education, practical experience or interaction with other people. Knowledge constitutes what Simon called his 'network of possible wanderings',[7] the intellectual space that he uses to explore and solve problems. The larger this space, the better.

Motivation

Knowledge and creative skills are a person's raw material — the person's natural resources. But a third factor — motivation — determines what people will actually do. Scientists can have outstanding educational credentials and a great ability to generate new perspectives on old problems. But if they lack the motivation to do a particular job, they simply will not do it; their expertise and creative thinking will either go untapped or be applied to something else. However, all forms of motivation do not have the same impact on creativity.[8] In fact, there are two types of motivation — extrinsic and intrinsic.

Extrinsic motivation comes from outside a person, whether the motivation is a 'carrot' or a 'stick'. If the manager promises to reward employees financially if a project succeeds, or threatens to fire them if it fails, employees will certainly be motivated to find a solution. However, this sort of motivation 'makes' employees do their jobs in order to get something desirable and to avoid something painful. The most common extrinsic motivation that managers use is money, which does not necessarily stop people from being creative. But in many situations it does not help either, especially when it makes people feel they are being bribed or controlled. More importantly, money by itself does not make employees passionate about their jobs.

Conversely, passion and interest — a person's internal desire to do something — are what intrinsic motivation is all about. When people are intrinsically motivated, they work for the challenge and enjoyment of it. The work itself is motivating. Consequently, people will be most creative when they feel motivated mainly by the interest, satisfaction and challenge of the task itself and not by external pressure.

Creativity techniques

Several techniques can be used to get the initial 'creative spark', and most can also be used to fine-tune an entrepreneurial opportunity during the innovation stage. Among the most popular creativity techniques are problem reversal, forced analogy, attribute listing, mind maps and brainstorming.

Problem reversal

Problem reversal *The action of viewing a problem from an opposite angle by asking questions such as 'What if we did the opposite?' and 'What is everyone else not doing?'*

The **problem reversal** technique is based on the premise that the world is full of opposites.[9] Any attribute, concept or idea is meaningless without its opposite. The great Chinese thinker Lao Tzu stressed the need for the successful leader to see opposites all around. For example, he noted the importance of action through inaction (*wu wei*), of letting go and not resisting nature's way of achieving balance. As a result, his philosophy maxims were often expressed as opposites: 'Be upright without being punctilious. Be brilliant without being showy.' All behaviour consists of opposites. To stimulate our creativity, we have to learn to see things backwards, inside out and upside down.

- State the problem in reverse. Change a positive statement into a negative one. For example, if you are trying to improve customer service, list all the ways one could make customer service *bad*. People are often pleasantly surprised at some of the ideas they come up with.
- Figure out what everybody else is *not* doing. For example, Apple did what IBM did not — it was the first computer manufacturer to provide a graphical user-interface. Japanese car manufacturers made small, fuel-efficient cars, whereas American car manufacturers focused on large cars.
- Change the direction or location of perspective. For example, examine a particular problem or question from the perspectives of the producer, distributor and client. Similarly, the problem may be different if people are city dwellers or country dwellers or from different nations.
- Turn defeat into victory. If something turns out badly, think about the positive aspects of the situation. One of the most popular products ever developed by 3M, the Post-It note, came about because a 3M engineer took some glue that did not stick properly and put it on small, colourful pieces of paper. This glue was originally considered an innovation failure.

Forced analogy

Forced analogy *Also called forced relationship; the action of making an association between two unlike things in order to obtain new insights.*

Forced analogy is a useful and fun method of generating ideas. This technique takes a fixed element, such as the product or some idea related to the product, and forces it to take on the attributes of another unrelated element. This forms the basis of a free flow of associations from which new ideas may emerge. As before, one should judge the value of the ideas after the process is complete.

Forcing relationships is one of the most powerful ways of developing new insights and new solutions. A useful way of developing the relationships is to have a selection of objects or cards with pictures to help you generate ideas. Choose objects or cards at random and see what relationships you can force. Use mind-mapping or a matrix to record the attributes, and then explore aspects of the problem at hand. For example, Olson[10] described the problem of examining a corporate organisational structure by comparing it with a matchbox. This comparison is summarised in table 3.1.

TABLE 3.1 Forced analogy between a matchbox and a corporation

Attributes of a matchbox	Analogy with the corporation
Striking surface on two sides	The protection an organisation needs against strikes
Six sides	Six essential organisational divisions
Sliding centre section	The heart of the organisation should be 'slidable' or flexible
Made of cardboard	Inexpensive method of structure, disposable

Attribute listing

Attribute listing ensures that all possible aspects of a problem have been examined. List all the major characteristics or attributes of a product, object or idea. Then, for each attribute, list ways each of the attributes could be changed. After all the ideas are listed, evaluate each idea — bringing to light possible improvements that can be made to the design of the product. Consider the following situation: a person in the business of making torches is under pressure from competitors and needs to improve the quality of the product. As table 3.2 shows, by breaking down the torch into its component parts — casing, switch, battery, bulb and weight — and by studying the attributes of each component, it is possible to develop ideas on how to improve each one.

Attribute listing *The identification and listing of all major characteristics of a product, object or idea.*

TABLE 3.2 Attribute listing – improving a torch

Feature	Attribute	Ideas for improvement
Casing	Plastic	Metal
Switch	On/off	On/off low beam
Battery	Power	Rechargeable
Bulb	Glass	Plastic
Weight	Heavy	Light

Attribute listing is a very useful technique for quality improvement of complicated products, procedures or services. It can be used in conjunction with some other creative techniques, especially idea-generating ones such as brainstorming. This allows the entrepreneur to focus on one specific part of a product or process before generating ideas.

Mind maps

The human brain is very different from a computer. Whereas a computer works in a linear fashion, the brain works *associatively* as well as linearly — comparing, integrating and synthesising as it goes. Association plays a dominant role in nearly every mental function, and words themselves are no exception. Every word and idea has numerous links attaching it to other ideas and concepts. **Mind maps** are an effective method of note-taking and useful for the generation of ideas by association.[11] Mind mapping (or concept mapping) involves writing down a central idea, and thinking up new and related ideas that radiate out

Mind maps *A visual method of mapping information to stimulate the generation and analysis of it.*

from the centre. By focusing on key ideas written down in your own words, and then looking for branches out and connections between the ideas, knowledge is mapped in a manner that helps you understand and remember new information.

To make a mind map, start in the centre of a page with the main idea and work outwards in all directions, producing a growing and organised structure composed of key words and key images. Mind maps are a way of representing associated thoughts with symbols rather than with extraneous words — the mind forms associations almost instantaneously, and 'mapping' allows us to record ideas more quickly than if we were expressing them using only words or phrases. Because of the large amount of association involved, mind maps can be very creative, tending to generate new ideas and associations that have not been thought of before. Every item in a map is, in effect, the centre of another map.

The creative potential of a mind map is useful in brainstorming sessions. Start with the basic problem as the centre, and generate associations and ideas from it in order to arrive at a large number of possible approaches. By presenting thoughts and perceptions in a spatial manner and by using colour and pictures, a better overview is gained and new connections can be seen.

Brainstorming

Brainstorming
A conference technique by which a group tries to find a solution for a specific problem by amassing spontaneous ideas from its members.

The term **brainstorming** has become a commonly used generic term for creative thinking. More concisely, brainstorming is the generation of ideas in a group based on the principle of suspending judgement — a principle that has proved to be highly productive in individual effort as well as group effort. The 'generation' phase is separate from the 'judgement' phase of thinking.

Brainstorming works best when a group of people follows four rules:

- *Suspend judgement.* When ideas are suggested, no critical comments are allowed. All ideas are written down. Evaluation is reserved for later — people have usually been trained to be so instantly analytical and practical in their thinking that this is very difficult to do, but it is crucial. To create and criticise at the same time is like watering seedlings while pouring weedkiller onto them at the same time.

- *Think freely.* Every idea is accepted and recorded. Freewheeling, wild thoughts are fine, as are impossible and unthinkable ideas. In fact, in every session, there should be several ideas so bizarre that they make the group laugh. Remember that practical ideas often come from silly, impractical, impossible ones. By allowing people to think outside the boundaries of ordinary, normal thought, brilliant new solutions can arise. Some wild ideas turn out to be practical too.

- *Encourage people to build on the ideas of others.* Improve, modify, build on the ideas of others. What's good about the idea just suggested? How can it be made to work? What changes would make it better or even wilder? This is sometimes called tagging on, piggybacking or hitchhiking.

- *Quantity of ideas is important.* Concentrate on generating a large stock of ideas so that they can be sifted through later on. There are two reasons for wanting a lot of ideas: (1) the obvious, usual, stale, unworkable ideas tend to come to mind first, so the first ten or so ideas probably won't be fresh and creative; (2) the larger your list of possibilities, the more you will have to choose from, adapt or combine. Some brainstormers aim for a fixed number, such as 20 or 30 ideas, before quitting the session.

Factors influencing creativity

The traditional psychological approach, which focuses on the characteristics of creative people, contends that the social environment can influence both the level and the frequency of creative behaviour.[12] The encouragement of creativity, autonomy, resource availability, workload pressures and mental blocks are important factors to consider in this respect. Since creativity, innovation and entrepreneurship can also take place in an established organisation, these factors should be of prime interest to managers who want to promote an entrepreneurial spirit.

Encouragement of creativity

Encouragement of the generation and development of ideas appears to operate at three major levels within organisations:
- Organisational encouragement plays an important role, and several aspects are perceived as operating broadly across the organisation — such as encouragement of risk-taking and of idea generation, valuing innovation from the highest to the lowest level of management, and fair, supportive evaluation of new ideas.
- Encouragement from supervisors indicates that project managers or direct supervisors can promote creativity. Open supervisory interactions and perceived supervisory support operate on creativity largely through the same mechanisms that are associated with fair, supportive evaluation; under these circumstances, people are less likely to experience the fear of negative criticism that can undermine intrinsic motivation.
- Encouragement of creativity can occur within a group itself, through diversity in team members' backgrounds, mutual openness to ideas, constructive challenging of ideas, and shared commitment to the project.

Autonomy

Creativity is fostered when individuals and teams have relatively high autonomy in the day-to-day conduct of work, and a sense of ownership and control over their own work and their own ideas. In addition, people produce more creative work when they perceive themselves as having a choice in how to go about accomplishing the tasks they are given.

Resources

It is generally admitted that resource allocation on a project is directly related to the project's creativity levels. Apart from the obvious practical limitations that extreme resource restrictions place on what can be accomplished, perceptions of the adequacy of resources may affect people psychologically by affecting their beliefs about the intrinsic value of the projects they have undertaken.

Pressures

The evidence that exists about pressures suggests seemingly paradoxical influences. Some research has found that, although extreme workload pressures can undermine creativity, some degree of pressure can have a positive influence if it is perceived as arising from the urgent, intellectual, challenging nature of the problem itself.[13] Similarly, time pressure is generally associated with high creativity in scientists involved in research and development, except when that pressure reaches an undesirably high level. Thus, two distinct forms of pressure can be identified: excessive workload pressure and the pressure of challenge. The former is likely to have a negative influence on creativity, whereas the latter will have a positive influence.

Mental blocks

In addition to organisational constraints, creativity can be impeded at the individual level because of various mental blocks. Prejudice and functional fixation are two examples of mental blocks.

Prejudice stems from the preconceived ideas we have about things. These preconceptions often prevent us from seeing beyond what we already know or believe to be possible, and thus inhibit the acceptance of change and progress. Consider the problem of how to connect sections of aeroplanes with more ease and strength than by using rivets. A modern solution is to glue the sections together. Most people would probably not think of this solution because of the prejudice about the word and idea of glue. But there are many kinds of glue, and the kind used to stick plane parts together makes a bond stronger than the metal of the parts themselves.

Sometimes we see an object only in terms of its name, rather than in terms of what it can do. This type of mental block is a *functional fixation*. Consider the case of shopping centres. Traditionally, these were considered to be places where people went to buy something specific, until it was discovered in the mid-1990s that many people go shopping for entertainment. 'Borders — books and music' recognised this new trend. Its shop on Orchard Road in Singapore offers a huge selection of books and compact discs, a cafe and a bistro. The revolutionary thing about Borders is that, with its cosy armchairs and well-informed staff, it actually encourages shoppers to browse.

There is also a functional fixation when it comes to people's roles. Think how most people would react if they saw their dentist mowing their lawn, or their car mechanic on a television show promoting a book. In Australia, Australia Post uses its dense logistics network throughout the country to deliver products other than mail — it also delivers groceries and organic fruit and vegetables that have been ordered online through various companies, including Only Australian Groceries, Coles Online and Ecofy.

What would you do?

Weight management

You have just come across an Australian health survey with findings that indicate 19 per cent of males and 22 per cent of females aged 25 years or over are obese, and an additional 48 per cent of males and 30 per cent of females are overweight. Further research suggests that obesity has become the number one public health issue in Australia and in many other industrialised countries. According to the World Health Organisation 'obesity has reached epidemic proportions globally, with more than 1 billion adults overweight — at least 300 million of them clinically obese — and is a major contributor to the global burden of chronic disease and disability'.[14]

The conditions of overweight and obesity are defined as the excessive accumulation of body fat, which is often classified using the body mass index (BMI), a weigh-for-height index. Whereas a BMI of 18.5–24.9 is considered to be a healthy weight range, BMIs of 25 and 30 or more are considered overweight and obese respectively. Both of these conditions expose individuals to a greater risk of health problems, including diabetes, cardiovascular disease, musculoskeletal disorders and some forms of cancer.

Various discussions with health experts made you aware that effective weight management for individuals involves a range of long-term strategies. These include prevention, weight maintenance and weight loss, and you sense that each of these areas represent a huge number of entrepreneurial opportunities.

Questions

1. Use two creativity techniques to generate new ideas in the area of weight maintenance. What ideas can you identify?
2. Which of the ideas that you identified has the potential to generate a sustainable profit? Why?
3. To what extent do obesity prevention, weight maintenance and weight loss relate to each other? Use a mind map to show the relationships.

Innovation

Ideas are not enough for innovation, let alone entrepreneurship, to occur. Many people who are full of ideas simply do not understand how an organisation operates in order to get things done, especially new things. Too often there is an assumption that creativity automatically leads to actual innovation, but this is not true. Once a business opportunity or idea has been identified, it needs to be shaped and assessed, and eventually it has to materialise in a prototype, formula, patent or business plan.

Entrepreneurship can occur with little, if any, innovation. Most of the 'new' products and services launched in the marketplace, and the business ventures set-up to produce them, are more or less copycats. Thus, the presence of innovation is viewed as a *sufficient* condition for entrepreneurship but not a *necessary* one. Moreover, newness or uniqueness of innovation is a matter of degree, in terms of the tangible characteristics and the relevant market.

It is therefore important to understand that innovation is a multidimensional concept, and that it is not necessary to reinvent the wheel to become an entrepreneur. For example, it is possible to innovate along several dimensions — product, service and process. In addition, the extent of innovation can vary greatly. For example, technological product innovation can be accompanied by additional managerial and organisational changes. This section discusses the various categories and sources of innovation.

Incremental versus disruptive innovation

When defined as an outcome, innovation is the tangible product, service or process that is adaptable or diffusable, meaning it can be used in various contexts by different individuals. More broadly, however, the change in condition, outcome or relationship that results from the innovation process itself may be either *incremental* or *disruptive*. The characteristics of incremental versus radical innovations are presented in table 3.3.

TABLE 3.3 Characteristics of incremental and disruptive innovation

Incremental innovation	Disruptive innovation
• Steady improvements	• Fundamental rethink
• Based on sustaining technologies	• Based on disruptive technologies
• Obedience to cultural routines and norms	• Experimentation and play/make-believe
• Can be rapidly implemented	• Need to be nurtured for long periods
• Immediate gains	• Worse initial performance, potential big gains
• Develop customer loyalty	• Create new markets

Incremental innovation

Incremental innovations are improvements of existing products that enhance performance in dimensions traditionally valued by mainstream customers. They make existing products and services better. Such innovations include, for example, bigger, more powerful mainframe computers. They usually come from tweaking existing designs and listening to big clients, who usually just want steady improvements that yield higher margins. Incremental innovations use established technologies and can be easily and rapidly implemented. Such innovations are a strong suit for established companies that continuously improve their products. But they almost inevitably hit a point at which they offer more quality or features than customers need, want or can afford. In pursuing higher margin business from demanding customers, established firms sacrifice the low end. This creates openings for disruptive innovations, which usually debut at the bottom of the market, among new customers.

Whatever the type of innovation, it remains fundamentally an application of knowledge. This notion lies at the heart of all types of innovation, be they product-, service- or process-oriented and disruptive or incremental. Table 3.4 lists some examples of incremental innovations with this central characteristic (application of knowledge) in mind.

TABLE 3.4 Types of incremental innovation

Type of innovation	Principle and example
Extension	Improvement or new use of an existing product, service or process, such as the development of desktop, notebook and laptop computers based on the mainframe.
Duplication	Creative replication or adaptation of an existing product, service or concept. Duplication can take place across different markets or industries, e.g. fast-food chicken outlets such as Chicken Treat or Red Rooster in Australia were adapted from the Kentucky Fried Chicken model from the USA; or the franchise may be adapted to suit a variety of sectors such as petrol stations, cleaning and childcare, with the concept having originated in the fast-food industry.
Synthesis	Combination of an existing product, service or process into a new formulation or use, such as the fax (telephone + photocopier) or the multi-purpose smartphone (telephone + camera + organiser + internet + music player + GPS).

Disruptive innovation

Conversely, disruptive innovations change the value proposition. Disruptive innovations, such as personal computers, underperform existing products but they are also simpler, less expensive, more convenient, adequate and easier to use. They cause fundamental changes in the marketplace. Such innovations are based on new technologies, and often present teething troubles that spoil the clients' bottom line. Invariably, breakthrough innovations require a fundamental rethink. Sometimes they come from dusting off ideas that failed to make it in the past, but more often they stem from the sheer stubbornness of would-be entrepreneurs who refuse to abandon their pet ideas.

Coming up with mould-breaking innovations is very different from making incremental improvements. Important as they are, steady improvements to a company's product range do not conquer new markets. Existing corporations, therefore, face the difficulty of choosing between sustaining technologies, which deliver improved product performance, and disruptive ones, which may initially result in a worse performance. This is what Christensen called the 'innovator's dilemma'.[15] Truly important breakthrough innovations built on disruptive technologies are initially rejected by clients who cannot currently use them. This rejection can lead firms with a strong client focus to allow their most important innovations to languish. The fatal flaw in these firms is their failure to create new markets and find new customers for these products of the future. As they unwittingly bypass opportunities, they open the door for more nimble, entrepreneurial companies to catch the next great wave of industry growth. The transistor was a disruptive technology for the vacuum-tube industry in the 1950s, just as the personal computer disrupted the typewriter industry in the 1980s.

As shown in table 3.5, entrepreneurs seeking to create value through disruptive innovations can take one of three basic approaches, each of which is suited to certain circumstances.

TABLE 3.5 Disruptive approaches

1. The back-scratcher: scratch an unscratched itch
What it is: Makes it easier and simpler for people to get an important job done
When it works best: When customers are frustrated by their inability to get a job done, and competitors are either fragmented or have a disability that prevents them from responding
Historical examples: Federal Express, mobile phones
Current examples: Procter & Gamble Swiffer products, instant messaging technology

2. The extreme makeover: make an ugly business attractive
What it is: Find a way to prosper at the low end of established markets by giving people good enough solutions at low prices
When it works best: When target customers don't need and don't value all the performance that can be packed into products, and when existing competitors don't focus on low-end customers
Historical examples: Nucor's mini-mill, backpacker accommodation
Current examples: Budget airlines such as AirAsia, Jetstar Asia, Tiger Airways, Virgin Blue

TABLE 3.5 continued

3. The bottleneck buster: democratise a limited market

What it is: Expand a market by removing a barrier to consumption

When it works best: When some customers are locked out of a market because they lack skills, access or wealth. Competitors ignore initial developments because they take place in seemingly unpromising markets.

Historical examples: Personal computers, Sony Walkman, eBay

Current examples: Blogs, home diagnostics, social networks such as Facebook or Twitter

Source: Adapted from S. D. Anthony & L. Gibson, 'Mapping your innovation strategy', *Harvard Business Review*, May 2006, p. 107. Copyright © 2006 by the Harvard Business School Publishing Corporation; all rights reserved. Reprinted by permission of Harvard Business Review.

Cost innovation

Traditional thinking associates innovation with new product/service development or added functionality, for which customers are expected to pay a premium. Although innovating to provide products of on-par or greater functionality at lower prices seems counterintuitive, some savvy companies in emerging markets have done so, in order to attract value-conscious consumers. This 'value for money' segment, which comprises people who ascribe importance to efficiency (doing the same for less), effectiveness (doing more at the same cost) or economy (doing and spending less), is expected to grow in emerging markets and developed countries alike.[16]

Products or services that in some aspects appear inferior, despite their greater affordability and ease-of-use, are cost innovation strategies, disruptive to current offerings. Emerging giants initially relied on cheaper labour to produce low cost products and services, but now others are using cost innovation to gain a competitive advantage. This capability not only helps those entrepreneurs establish a stronghold in their home countries, but also allows them to crack the value-for-money segments in developed markets.[17]

Cost innovation can be delivered in three ways:

- *Selling high-end products at mass-market prices.* Consider Aravind, the world's largest eye-hospital chain, based in Madurai, India. Aravind's founders used a pricing structure tiered so that wealthier patients were charged more (for example, for better meals or air-conditioned rooms), allowing the firm to cross-subsidise care for the poorest. In addition, the company benefits from economies of scale: its staff screens over 2.7 million patients a year via clinics in remote areas, and refers over 285 000 of them for surgery at its hospitals.[18] Aravind's model does not just depend on providing affordable services on a large scale, but on a clever combination of pricing, scale, technology and process.
- *Offering choice or customisation to value customers.* China's Goodbaby sells customers 1600 kinds of children's strollers, car seats, bassinets, baby walkers, high chairs, and tricycles — four times more than its rivals offer but at comparable prices. The Shanghai-based company offers a wide range of products that meet practically every need, from strollers that can handle uneven surfaces to those that fold away with a few simple movements. As a A$500 million company, Goodbaby can do this, in part, because it invests 4 per cent of its annual revenues in R&D, which is twice the average for the toy industry.[19]

- *Turning niches into mass markets* (see approach 3 in table 3.5). China's Haier captured 60 per cent of the US wine-refrigerator market in less than a decade by lowering prices so much that a small, under-guarded niche became a volume business.

Sources of innovation

Most innovations result from methodically analysing seven areas of opportunity, some of which lie within particular companies or industries, and some of which lie in broader social or demographic trends.

Sources of innovation within companies or industries

Drucker[20] identified four such areas of opportunity within a company or an industry:

- *Unexpected occurrences*. Unexpected successes and failures are productive sources of innovation because most people and businesses dismiss them, disregard them and even resent them. Many innovations are the result of unexpected successes, particularly in the pharmaceutical industry. For example, the antibacterial effect of penicillin was discovered accidentally by Alexander Fleming in 1928. The discovery of the Pfizer blockbuster Viagra was also an accident. In 1991, a group of scientists at Pfizer, led by Andrew Bell, David Brown and Nicholas Terrett, discovered a series of chemical compounds that were useful in treating heart problems such as angina. The compounds were patented as Sildenafil. In 1994, Terrett discovered during the trial studies of Sildenafil as a heart medicine that it also allowed men to reverse erectile dysfunction. The drug acts by enhancing the smooth muscle relaxant effects of nitric oxide, a chemical that is normally released in response to sexual stimulation.
- *Incongruities*. These occur whenever a gap exists between expectations and reality. For example, in 1971, when Fred Smith proposed overnight mail delivery, he was told: 'If it were profitable, the US Postal Office would be doing it.'[21] It turned out Smith was right. An incongruity existed between what Smith felt was needed and the way business was currently conducted — and Federal Express, the world's first overnight delivery network, was born in the United States.
- *Process needs*. These exist whenever a demand arises for the entrepreneur to innovate as a way of answering a particular need. For example, eye surgeons long knew how to perform cataract surgery. An enzyme that made the process easier had been known for decades, but was not usable because it was too hard to preserve. In the 1950s an entrepreneur named William Conner figured out how to preserve the enzyme. He and a colleague set-up the Alcon Prescription Laboratory (now Alcon Laboratories Inc.) to manufacture and market this new product.
- *Industry and market changes*. There are continual shifts in the marketplace, which are caused by changes in consumer attitudes, advances in technology and industry growth. Industries and markets undergo changes in structure, design and definition. Indeed, when market or industry structures change, traditional industry leaders often neglect the fastest growing market segments. New opportunities rarely fit the way the industry has always approached the

market, defined it or organised to serve it. An example is found in the health-care industry in South-East Asia, where private medical centres are imitating five-star hotels to win a share of wealthy sick customers.

Sources of innovation in the social environment

Three additional sources of opportunity exist outside a company in its social and intellectual environment:

- *Demographic changes.* Of the external sources of innovation opportunity, demographics are the most reliable. Census data, for instance, provide a precise picture of the actual demographic structure of a country, and from these data it is relatively easy to extrapolate the future age structure. In Australia and New Zealand, two countries that have integrated a large number of migrants over the past decades, 'ethnic food' is one of the fastest growing market opportunities for entrepreneurs. Another demographic trend in the industrialised countries is the ageing population. This creates many opportunities in the field of assistive technology.
- *Perceptual changes.* Sometimes the members of a community can change their interpretation of facts and concepts, and thereby open up new opportunities. What determines whether people see a glass as half full or half empty is mood rather than fact, and a change in mood often defies quantification. But it is not esoteric. It is concrete and it can be tested and exploited for innovation opportunity. Perceptual changes can particularly affect dimensions, such as acceptability, beauty, time and distance. For example, commuters living in suburbs of big cities often perceive a 50-kilometre or one-hour journey to their workplace as acceptable, whereas residents in small towns would not.
- *New knowledge.* Among history-making innovations, those based on new knowledge — whether scientific, technical or social — rank high. Knowledge-based innovations differ from all others in the time they take, in their casualty rates, and in their predictability, as well as in the challenges they pose to entrepreneurs. They have, for instance, the longest lead time of all innovations. To become effective, innovation of this sort usually demands not one kind of knowledge but many. Innovations in bioscience are a case in point. In recent innovations awards organised by *The Economist*, the category receiving the largest number of nominations was bioscience.[22] Interestingly, many of these could just as easily have been classified under nanotechnology. Clearly, innovations in bioscience are built on the combination of new knowledge from several fields.

Entrepreneur profile

Narayana Murthy, Infosys

In 1981, Narayana Murthy founded Infosys with six colleagues. The Bangalore-based company defines, designs and delivers technology-enabled business solutions. In 1999, Infosys became the first Indian company to be listed in the NASDAQ stock exchange. Today, the company is a global leader in IT services and consulting with revenues of over US$4.8 billion. Murthy retired from the operative management in 2006, at the age of 60, to become non-executive chairman and 'chief mentor'.

In 1974, on a journey through Eastern Europe by train, Murthy was suspected to have criticised the situation in Bulgaria in his talk with a passenger, and was detained by the local police. He suffered from hunger and cold during his 70 hours detention. This experience changed him from 'a confused leftist into a determined, compassionate capitalist'. He concluded that 'entrepreneurship resulting in large-scale job creation was the only viable mechanism for eradicating poverty in societies.' So he began to look for an opportunity to create wealth. He found that the salary of IT employees in India was only about one-tenth of their counterparts in California. He then thought that Indian software engineers can produce quality software on time at an affordable price for the US corporations.

During the first years, the company operated by dispatching its staff to the countries where the clients were located, and directly turning to the next project after one was completed. This mode was called 'body shopping', and it relied on the competitive advantage arising from a cheaper labour force. Later, along with the increase of clients and the enlargement of the project scale, the personnel dispatching cost increased too. This prompted Murthy to develop a new operation mode that he baptised 'business process outsourcing', whereby Infosys would acquire the projects abroad and complete them in India. This not only saved dispatching costs but also improved speed and efficiency, as the operation would be run continuously because of the time difference with India. 'We pioneered the global delivery model, which emerged as a disruptive force in the industry, leading to the rise of offshore outsourcing,' recalls Murthy.

This marked a clear shift in the competitive approach of Infosys, from cost to service to achieve market superiority. In order to develop superior value, Infosys focused on two tasks: first, it developed software service in four fields, including finance, health, telecommunication, and engineering; second, as the company knew little about the countries where the clients were based, it trained the local staff to create an image of a local company, with their help. The business concept of Infosys is based on globalisation: 'sourcing capital from where it is the cheapest, producing where it is most cost-effective and selling where it is most profitable, all without being constrained by national boundaries,' says Murthy.

Today, Murthy thinks that the largest challenge faced by Infosys is how to recruit the best employees and retain them. 'From my viewpoint, the excellent persons are the soul of the company,' he says. 'Infosys longevity will depend on how well we build on our people resources.' He is determined that the first mission of the company is 'to respect the personality". Employees are encouraged to debate ideas and to challenge each other but to be polite, as he says 'You may criticise, but not be impolite.' Murthy and his co-founders think that 'being modest is a key value', and they required the employees to promote this moral character of respect to other persons or enterprises, including the competitors.

Source: Based on author's interview with Narayana Murthy

Linking creativity, innovation and entrepreneurship

While still oversimplified, figure 3.1 is a representation of the links between creativity, innovation and entrepreneurship as a process model. It can be regarded as a logically sequential (though not necessarily continuous) process that can be divided into a series of interdependent stages. The overall process can be thought of as a complex set of communication paths over which knowledge is transferred. These paths include internal and external linkages. At the centre of the model, innovation represents the firm's capabilities and its linkages with both the marketplace and the science base. As shown in figure 3.1, the entrepreneurial process is influenced by two main factors. On the one hand, the unsatisfied needs in the marketplace are one source of opportunity for developing and commercialising new products or new services (pull factors). On the other hand, technological progress, such as powerful computers, microscopes, digital networks and scanners, combined with the advance of science produce knowledge at an exponential rate (push factors). New knowledge can be a formidable source of opportunity for people who are able to use this knowledge to answer needs that are often unformulated.

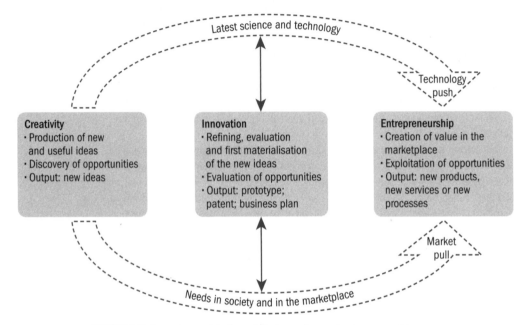

FIGURE 3.1 A process model of creativity, innovation and entrepreneurship

Many people see the successive stages of ideas generation (creativity), ideas evaluation (innovation) and ideas implementation (entrepreneurship) as being distinct and separate. In fact, these stages can overlap, and entrepreneurship is not necessarily a linear process. Two important concepts are developed in this section:

• It is shown that these three stages essentially consist of creating new knowledge.
• It is suggested that this knowledge is developed and formulated through different types of social network.

Knowledge development during the entrepreneurial process

What creativity, innovation and entrepreneurship all have in common is that they are concerned with knowledge development. In other words, the creativity–innovation–entrepreneurship process is like an assembly line of knowledge and ideas. Knowledge is an intangible commodity, but it lies at the core of the three stages.

During the creativity stage, knowledge is present in an exceptionally raw form. It might just consist of ideas and sketches drawn on a piece of paper. During the innovation stage, knowledge is further refined, and the initial idea should pass the 'feasibility test'. At this stage, knowledge is often codified, for instance in the form of a formula or patent. However, the best patent does not constitute a finished product. For this we need an entrepreneur who is able to organise and coordinate resources to manufacture and market the product that integrates the patented technology. During the entrepreneurship stage, knowledge is embedded in the product or service marketed. It is the extent to which the entrepreneur can generate, explain and protect this knowledge that will ensure the firm has a competitive advantage.

Therefore, the development and deployment of unique resources and distinctive skills are necessary for achieving organisational survival, profitability and growth. Such resources and skills are also referred to as competencies, which must be sustained by continuous learning. Knowledge constitutes the essence of competencies, and the way organisations create new knowledge is intrinsically related to the creativity–innovation–entrepreneurship process.

In the case of established organisations, the crucial role that corporate entrepreneurship activities play in the creation of knowledge has been recognised.[23] Formal and informal corporate entrepreneurship activities can enrich a company's performance by creating new knowledge that becomes the basis for building new capabilities or revitalising existing ones. Indeed, some of the most important contributions of corporate entrepreneurship may lie in the development of critical capabilities that are much needed for the creation and commercialisation of new knowledge-intensive products, processes or services.

Developing and disseminating knowledge through social networks

Social networks are the catalyst for the development and dissemination of knowledge, both for emerging and established organisations. Would-be entrepreneurs' personal networks — the set of people to whom they are directly linked — affect their access to social, emotional and material support. Network relationships and contacts are basic to (1) identifying opportunities and (2) obtaining the knowledge and resources required to exploit opportunities. Regardless of their abilities, would-be entrepreneurs who are low on the socioeconomic scale and who possess poor networking skills may find themselves cut off from emerging opportunities and critical resources.

Social networks can be characterised by three main features: their diversity, their affective or emotional strength, and their structural equivalence — that is, the degree to which actors in the network have similar/dissimilar social relationships. Diversity arises from the various characteristics (in terms of age, gender, ethnicity, education and occupation) of the people forming the network. Diversity in network ties, for example, is essential for would-be entrepreneurs, as it widens the scope of information about potential innovations, business locations, assistance schemes and sources of capital. Therefore, a network of uniform or similar ties will be of limited value to an entrepreneur.[24]

The relationships between the people in the network can be strong, weak or indeterminate/fluctuating.[25] The most durable and reliable relationships in personal networks are strong ties, which are usually of long duration. Strong ties are built on mutual trust and are not governed by short-term calculations of self-interest. Weak ties, on the other hand, are superficial or casual and normally involve little emotional investment. Weak relationships are typically of shorter duration and contact is less frequent. The loosest ties — fluctuating ties — can best be described as contacts. This type of network relationship is created for pragmatic purposes with strangers with whom the individual has generally had no previous contact.

From creativity to entrepreneurship: screening opportunities

The creativity–innovation–entrepreneurship process essentially entails identifying and evaluating opportunities. During this process, business ideas will be assessed to determine if they represent an entrepreneurial opportunity — a situation where sustainable value and wealth can be created. There are many different tools available for evaluating entrepreneurial opportunities, most of which have been developed by venture capitalists and business consultants. One such tool is depicted in figure 3.2. The process consists of a series of strict filters that are first used to screen for opportunities in order to identify those that offer a significant, commercial viable potential to be exploited. Versions of the screen, sometimes known as the Schrello screen or the R-W-W ('real, win, worth it') screen have been circulating since the 1980s, and have been used by large corporations to assess business potential and risk exposure in their innovation portfolio.[26] Any tool that aims to assess an opportunity should address three critical issues:

- *Product feasibility* — Is it real? Can the product be made or service delivered using currently available, or at least feasible, technology?
- *Market feasibility* — Is it viable? Does anyone want it? Has the product any features that someone values and would be ready to pay for?
- *Economic feasibility* — Is it worth it? Can the product be developed, manufactured and distributed while generating a profit?

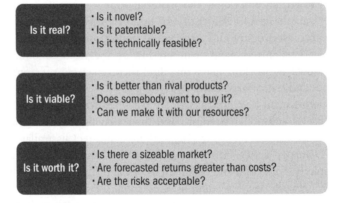

FIGURE 3.2 Feasibility analysis: structured process to screen opportunities

Is it real? Establishing the novelty, patentability and technical feasibility

The first step of the process consists of determining the novelty, the patentability and the technical feasibility of the product or service delivery. Typically, about

50 per cent of opportunities would not pass this filter because the innovation is not genuinely novel, it cannot be patented or the entrepreneur does not own the technology; someone else, somewhere else, has already disclosed and/or patented it.

Is it novel?

Quite a few 'inventions' are not novel — findings in one field turn out to be well known in another, a situation not helped by specialist scientific jargon and acronyms. Many would-be entrepreneurs are in fact reinventing the wheel. An initial search on the internet might quickly reveal that an invention is not novel, since most leading scientific groups these days use the internet extensively to post details about themselves and their work. It is also easy to conduct a patent search via the websites of the main patent registration authorities in the world, such as the US Patent and Trade Mark Office (www.uspto.gov) and the European Patent Office (www.european-patent-office.org).

Is it patentable?

As explained in detail in chapter 8, a patent is a right granted for any device, substance, method or process that is new, inventive and useful. Double-checking that the 'innovation' meets these basic requirements can potentially save a lot of work. Although commissioning a patent search costs money, it is not prohibitively expensive, although the use of a professional patent lawyer is recommended.

Other new and useful innovations such as artistic creations, mathematical models, plans and schemes are not patentable, but can be protected by other intellectual property rights. Trademarks, copyrights and design rights may, therefore, have a valuable role, and should be included in the search at this stage. In any case, if the innovation is not patentable, a clear concept of the product or the service must be laid out.

Is it technically feasible?

How do you find out whether a product idea is feasible? One way is to conduct a peer review. Under suitable non-disclosure agreements, opinions should be sought from other leading professional scientists in the relevant technical field. They should also be able to inform you of any rival technologies. In addition, the development of a product prototype is recommended at this stage. Prototyping can help identify technical challenges and provide useful insight into possible manufacturing challenges for subsequent mass production.

Is it viable? Showing the superiority of the product and market interest

The question of product viability is the point at which 30 per cent of 'innovations' fail. Cases of scientific fraud are few but do occur. More frequently there are misinterpreted results or, quite simply, a better product already exists.

Is it better than rival products?

An internet search should now be conducted using a search engine such as Google. Again, a skilled search will swiftly lead to the discovery of existing products if they are available. Separate searches should be conducted for each application of the technology, and they should be carried out in two ways: first, for the exact product, and second, for products that perform the same function. Which offers commercial benefit? Which is faster, cheaper and easier? Note that there are three types of commercial advantage: (1) the saving of time in comparison to existing products (time to market or to money); (2) the saving of money in comparison to existing products; or (3) the enabling of future, valuable products of a type not currently available. Potential applications can be dismissed because the technical advantages do not translate into commercial advantages. 'Smaller is only better if smaller is needed.'

Remember that the market is indifferent to how the technology works, instead buying the benefits that technology can provide. Through close examination of rival technologies, it is possible to determine which technical attributes are advantages. A good rule of thumb is that the new technology should have at least one feature that promises to be ten times better than its rivals, and this should be quantifiable in a definite measure, such as dimension, speed, time, range or availability.

Does somebody want to buy it?

The next filter aims to check that there are indeed potential buyers — whether individuals or companies — willing to adopt and pay for the commercial advantages. These buyers should then be contacted to verify that they would value the offered advantages if the development proved successful, and to determine what they would require in order to make such a decision. There is no greater reassurance of the viability of a novel technology than potential customers who clearly state that they would like to obtain, and are willing to pay for, the commercial advantages that the technology could offer.

It is not necessary to consider every potential customer at this stage; only a few 'lead buyers' should be contacted. Note that any 'not interested' answer from a potential buyer is only on behalf of that buyer alone — this individual does not speak for the industry as a whole or all existing rivals. Again, it is worth checking why an offer has been rejected, as this allows any perceived or actual inadequacies to be addressed. Therefore, it is more effective at this stage to take a qualitative approach that involves contacting key potential customers to seek their opinions and discuss the product offering in detail.

Do we have superior resources?

After establishing that the offering can win, the entrepreneur must determine whether or not the company's resources, management and market insight are better than those of the competition. If not, it may not be possible to sustain advantage, no matter how good the product. Further details on the attribute of strategic resources are provided in chapter 6.

Is it worth it? Showing a positive return

Will the product be profitable at an acceptable risk? Few products launch unless the entrepreneur — or the top management in the case of a large company — is confident that the forecasted return is greater than costs. A successful launch requires projecting the timing and amount of capital outlays, marketing expenses, costs, and margins; and applying time to breakeven, cash flow and other financial performance measures. The business plan is the document that provides an overview on the economic feasibility of the project. It involves planning resources and developing a budget, which is then compared with the end-point value (the sales projections derived from a market survey) to ascertain the true market size that can realistically be captured.

What is the market size and attributes?

Would the market size and attributes lead to the advantages actually being paid for? In other words, are the applications viable or would the market either ignore their benefits (as nice but not needed) or wish to absorb the benefits (taking them if offered but not paying for them)? To find this out, questions must be asked about the size of the markets, the openness of the markets to new products or attributes, and the rate and direction of change in the markets. The result of this inquiry helps to identify potential market segments, determine paths to the market and ultimately generate sales projections.

Drafting a business plan

The information gathered can be used to determine the commercial viability of a new start-up, product offering or purchase of a business. Usually, the feasibility analysis will be summarised in a business plan — the comprehensive document that serves as a 'roadmap' for new business ventures.

In chapter 7, the specific contents of a business plan are examined in detail. An examination of the plan will show that it essentially involves answering a great many questions, which can only be done effectively if accurate research is conducted beforehand.

SUMMARY

This chapter has explained the role of creativity and innovation in the entrepreneurial process. Creativity is the point of origination for innovation and entrepreneurship. It can be defined as the production of new and useful ideas in any domain. Within every individual, creativity is a function of three components: creative thinking skills, knowledge and motivation. Several techniques can be used to obtain the initial 'creative spark'. Among the most popular creativity techniques are problem reversal, forced analogy, attribute listing, metaphorical thinking, mind maps and brainstorming. At the same time, several factors can influence creativity. Encouragement, autonomy, resource availability and workload pressures are important factors in this respect.

Innovation is the successful implementation of creative ideas within an organisation. Most innovative business ideas come from methodically analysing several areas of opportunity, some of which lie within particular companies or industries, and some of which lie in broader social or demographic trends. Innovation is a multidimensional concept. When considering the extent of innovation, it is possible to distinguish between disruptive and incremental innovation. Innovation can also concern different elements, such as a product, a service, a process or a combination of these.

The successive stages of ideas generation (creativity), ideas evaluation (innovation) and ideas implementation (entrepreneurship) can overlap and are not necessarily a linear process. These three stages essentially consist of creating new knowledge, which is developed and formulated through different types of social network. However, a good idea is not enough to start-up a business venture. The idea must be screened in order to identify significant, commercial opportunities, which will create value for the entrepreneur and the customer. The screening process to establish the feasibility of the opportunity must address the product feasibility (is it real?), the market feasibility (is it viable?) and the economic feasibility (is it worth it?).

REVIEW QUESTIONS

1. What are the different components of creativity?
2. What are the factors that can affect creativity?
3. What are the different sources of innovation?
4. What do creativity, innovation and entrepreneurship have in common?
5. What are the key steps to screening an opportunity?

DISCUSSION QUESTIONS

1. Can everyone learn to be creative?
2. How is it that one often meets a lot of creative people with business ideas, but that only a very small proportion of them will actually become entrepreneurs?
3. Why do seasoned entrepreneurs often say: 'You don't need to reinvent the wheel to become an entrepreneur'?
4. Why do consumers fail to buy innovative products even when they offer distinct improvements over existing ones?

SUGGESTED READING

Bhidé, A., *The Venturesome Economy: How Innovation Sustains Prosperity in a More Connected World*, Princeton University Press, Princeton, 2008.

English, J. & Moate, B., *Discovering New Business Opportunities*, Allen & Unwin, Crows Nest, 2009.

Fannin, R., *Silicon Dragon: How China is Winning the Tech Race*, McGraw Hill, New York, 2008.

Inventors, http://inventors.about.com (website about famous inventions with A-to-Z lists, timelines and history essays).

Case study

NoWaterWash

Nina Lim is never short of ideas. As a teenager, she set-up her own part-time business designing websites for entrepreneurs and student associations, while pursuing her studies at National Junior College in Singapore. Nina has always been interested in entrepreneurship, and she regularly attends the Action for Community for Entrepreneurship (ACE) — a network promoting entrepreneurship. Now, she is two months away from completing her Masters in Material Sciences at Nanyang Technological University (NTU), and she has just launched NoWaterWash with Tim, a fellow NTU business student. The pair is contemplating entering 'The BIG Idea' — a business plan competition held at their university — but they are still unsure about the range of products they should provide, and the markets they could target. In addition, a concrete business model has yet to be developed.

The technology

NoWaterWash is an innovative car wash process that does not require water. 'We use a unique 2-in-1 wash and polish product, which uses a polymer compound to lift dirt from the surface of the paint and encapsulate it in a lubricating film. The dirt is then removed with a soft cloth treated with nanoparticles, says Nina. This washing process reveals a shiny surface that is protected by a thin polymer coating. Whereas traditional car wash products are wax-based, tend to deteriorate rapidly in the sun and dull the paint's appearance over time, the polymer coating lasts for up to six weeks and keeps the car looking shinier for longer.

The real innovation in the washing process consist less in the use of polymer compound, which can be readily bought from selected chemical suppliers, than in the nanotechnology treatment of the cloth used to remove the dirt. The technology has been developed by Nina, together with her supervisor, as part of her masters thesis. The university has successfully lodged a patent to protect the technology, which is licensed exclusively to NoWaterWash.

The technology is proven. Nina and Tim washed a sample car panel over a hundred times to show the efficiency of the process, and demonstrate that it does not damage the paintwork. They have also started to wash about ten friends' cars per week since they registered the company three months ago. The pair has invested just a few hundred dollars in equipment so far, and since the entire washing process is waterless, it can be done anywhere — in a car park or on the street. Now, word of mouth is kicking in, and a journalist from the *Straits Times* even wants to write an article about the young entrepreneurs.

The market potential

Nina came across the NoWaterWash idea during an exchange semester in Brisbane. Drought is part-and-parcel of life is Australia, and most of the states are affected by water restrictions. As a result, it is forbidden to wash cars during periods of high water restriction in Brisbane. Water resources are also precious in Singapore, given the small amount of land and its large urban population. In 2001, the city-state even launched NEWater — the branded name given to reclaimed water from wastewater that has been purified.

At the beginning, Nina and Tim plan to offer two types of 'packages': the basic and the premium NoWaterWash. The basic package will comprise the cleaning and polishing of all exterior surfaces of the car, including glass treatment, tyres and wheel protections. 'This is perfect when your car is ok on the inside, but showing the effect of being out and about on the outside. We plan to charge S$45 for this service' says Nina. The premium NoWaterWash is a full makeover, inside and out, and it will cost S$65. This package includes windows cleaning inside and out, cleaning and conditioning of the dash and trims, and vacuuming carpets and seats.

While the ecological dimension of the service certainly remains a big selling argument for green customers, Nina says that 'The main benefit of a waterless product is that it gives us great flexibility. We go wherever the client is and we don't depend on a specific location. This allows us to save on infrastructure cost and to offer a competitive price for our service.' Car owners do not need to drive to a washing station. Therefore, NoWaterWash offers a service that saves time and gives greater convenience.

Tim conducted some preliminary market research and found from the Land Transport Authority website that there are currently just over half a million cars registered in Singapore. This is more than enough to start the business. However, Nina thinks that they could expand the service range, and that they could target some specific segments in the local market. In addition, she realised from her journey in Australia that there is a huge potential market overseas.

Questions

1. Use one or several creativity techniques to identify new types of services and additional customers for NoWaterWash.
2. Is the feasibility of NoWaterWash established? Outline what has already been done, and the next steps that Nina and Tim might have to take.
3. What business model would you recommend that NoWaterWash adopt to enter the market and rapidly expand in Singapore and abroad?

ENDNOTES

1. P.F. Drucker, *Innovation and Entrepreneurship*, Harper & Row, New York, 1985, p. 30.
2. Bessant, J. & Tidd, J., *Innovation and Entrepreneurship*, John Wiley, Chichester, 2007.
3. R.W. Woodman, J.E. Sawyer & R.W. Griffin, 'Toward a theory of organizational creativity', *Academy of Management Review*, vol. 18, no. 2, 1993, pp. 293–321.
4. 'Leaps of faith: A survey of innovation in industry', *The Economist*, 20 February 1999, pp. 12–16.
5. T. Amabile, 'How to kill creativity', *Harvard Business Review*, September–October 1998, pp. 77–87.
6. T. Ward, R. Finke & S. Smith, *Creativity and the Mind*, Plenum Press, New York, 1995.
7. H. Simon, *Administrative Behavior*, Free Press, New York, 1997.
8. T. Amabile, *Creativity in Context: Update to the Social Psychology of Creativity*, Westview, Boulder, CO, 1996.
9. C. Thompson, *What a Great Idea!*, Harper Perennial, New York, 1992.
10. R. Olson, *The Art of Creative Thinking*, Harper Collins, New York, 1986.
11. T. Buzan, *Mind Maps at Work*, Penguin Book, New York, 2005.
12. T. Amabile, R. Conti, H. Coon, J. Lazenby & M. Herron, 'Assessing the work environment for creativity', *Academy of Management Journal*, vol. 39, no. 5, 1996, pp. 1154–84.
13. T. Amabile, C.N. Hadley & S.J. Kramer, 'Creativity under the gun', *Harvard Business Review*, Special Issue, August 2002, pp. 52–63.
14. World Health Organisation, 'Obesity and overweight', WHO, www.who.int.
15. C.M. Christensen, *The Innovator's Dilemma*, Harvard Business Press, Boston, 1997.
16. P.J. Williamson & M. Zeng, 'Value-for-money strategies for recessionary times', *Harvard Business Review*, March 2009, pp. 66–74.
17. ibid.
18. The Economist, 'Lessons from a frugal innovator', *The Economist*, 18 April 2009, p. 63.
19. P.J. Williamson & M. Zeng, see note 16.
20. Drucker, see note 1.
21. D.F. Kuratko & R.M. Hodgetts, *Entrepreneurship: A Contemporary Approach*, Dryden Press, Fort Worth, 1998.
22. 'Comeback kid?', *The Economist Science Technology Quarterly*, 21 September 2002, p. 3.
23. S. Zahra, A. Nielsen & W.C. Bogner, 'Corporate entrepreneurship, knowledge and competence development', *Entrepreneurship Theory and Practice*, vol. 23, no. 3, 1999, pp. 169–89.
24. M. Granovetter, *Getting a Job: A Study of Contacts and Careers*, University Press, Cambridge, MA, 1974.
25. H.E. Aldrich, *Organizations Evolving*, Sage Publications, London, 1999.
26. G. Day, 'Is it real? Can we win? Is it worth it? Managing risk and reward in an innovation portfolio', *Harvard Business Review*, December 2007, pp. 110–20.

CHAPTER 4

Small business: definitions and characteristics

Learning objectives

After reading this chapter, you should be able to:

- define what constitutes a small business
- identify the key characteristics that make small businesses different from other types of business organisation
- list the advantages and disadvantages of starting and operating a small business
- outline the importance of small business in the economy
- explain the difference between small business management and entrepreneurship.

What is a 'small business'? Small firms are now recognised as a vital and significant part of the economy in the Asia–Pacific region and as one of the keys to national goals, such as wealth creation and employment growth. In this respect, it is often claimed that 'small business is big business'. But what constitutes a small enterprise? How does it differ from a large one? Are there any characteristics of a small business that are unique?

This chapter examines and explains the essence of small business. It is necessary to understand how the concept of a small business can be defined, and to explain the intrinsic characteristics of such firms: how they operate, the way they differ from larger enterprises, the advantages and drawbacks of owning and managing a small business and the factors that contribute to their success and failure. We examine the importance of the small business sector in different Asia–Pacific economies, and conclude by looking at the differences between entrepreneurs and small business owner–managers.

Defining small business

Small businesses are the most common form of business worldwide, but researchers have always had difficulty in satisfactorily defining them and separating them from larger firms. As most small business researchers would argue, a small firm is not just one that is smaller than a larger organisation; it is also a business that is often managed in ways fundamentally different from a large corporation.[1] In this section, we examine the different ways that business organisations can be classified.

Generic definitions

There are essentially two broad ways in which to define a business. The first approach is to focus on the *qualitative* or *intangible characteristics of the firm* — in other words, the way in which it does things and is managed.[2] This is a useful mechanism for understanding how a small firm is organised, how it operates and who runs (or manages) it on a day-to-day basis.

During the last 30 years, a number of qualitative criteria have been suggested as key defining features of a small firm. In a general sense, a business has been regarded as small if it has the following characteristics:

- *It is independently owned and operated.* The business is not part of a larger corporation nor effectively controlled by another firm. In other words, the owners of the business are not answerable to anyone else for the decisions they make.
- *The owners contribute most, if not all, of the operating capital.* They take on the responsibility of funding the business idea and bearing the risk, such as potential bankruptcy, if the project fails; and they are entitled to most of the profits if it succeeds.[3]
- *The main decision-making functions rest with the owners.* The owners usually also work full time in the firm; thus, they are often referred to as owner–managers. Most of the critical decisions are made by one or two people, since the firm is rarely big enough to support a group of professional specialists in areas such as marketing, administration, finance or logistics.[4]

- *The business has a small market share.* Typically the firm does not dominate its industry; rather, it is just one of many businesses competing for a limited pool of customers.[5]

Qualitative definitions are particularly useful in helping to understand the nature of the business, the role of the owner and the way the business is run, since such explanations focus on the people who work within the firm and control the firm, and the way they behave. However, it can be extremely difficult to measure and analyse these characteristics, since such qualitative definitions are often based on subjective concepts.

The alternative is to look at some *quantitative aspects of the business.* These are empirical measures that are relatively easy to define and measure. Some common quantitative variables used to categorise and sort businesses include:[6]
- the number of staff (if any) that work in the firm
- annual wages and salaries expenditure
- legal structure of the firm
- the total annual turnover (sales revenue) that the business generates
- the dollar value of the assets (such as office equipment, factory machinery and/or property) that the business owns
- the share of ownership that is held by the owner–manager/s.

As simple as these indicators might appear, they are still not perfect. All statistical measures are subject to interpretation and can have their own problems of definition. For example, if the number of employees is to be used as the yardstick, then what constitutes an 'employee'? Does it mean only permanent employees, or should part-time and casual staff be included as well? If assets are the indicator of size, how is it possible to compare two businesses that have similar asset bases if one leases all its equipment and the other purchases its equipment?

With so many issues to consider, it is clear that striking a balance between all these different qualitative and quantitative criteria can sometimes prove difficult. The task is made even more complicated by the fact that small businesses are found in every country in the world and in every industry, and they take many different organisational, legal and operating forms. Collectively, they represent a heterogenous (exceptionally diverse) sector.[7] However, as a general definition, a **small business** can be defined as an independent firm that is usually managed, funded and operated by its owners, and whose staff size, financial resources and assets are comparatively small in scale.

As at least one researcher has pointed out, no classification system will ever be complete enough to cover all types of small business; every firm is unique in one way or another.[8] Indeed, it is not surprising that there is no universally agreed-upon definition of what exactly a small business is. However, the above typologies do provide a method of understanding the basic ways in which small firms operate: independently, with limited resources, and with one or two key individuals taking most of the responsibility, risk and rewards in the project. It is these characteristics which set small enterprises apart from all other types of business organisation.

Small business *A small-scale, independent firm usually managed, funded and operated by its owners, and whose staff size, financial resources and assets are comparatively limited in scale.*

National definitions of small business

Given the lack of a common set of definitions, it is not unusual to find that throughout the Asia–Pacific region widely varying terms are used to define and categorise a small business (see table 4.1). They range from relatively simple frameworks, such as that used in New Zealand, to quite complex criteria, such as is found in Malaysia.

In Australia, the most commonly cited definition is that provided by the Australian Bureau of Statistics (ABS), which uses a combination of both qualitative and quantitative measures. The ABS describes a small firm as, first, having a number of qualitative characteristics: it must be independently owned (not part of a larger organisation) and managed by an individual or a small number of persons. Once these criteria are met, then a quantitative value, the number of staff, is used as an additional measuring tool.[9]

According to the ABS, there are four main categories of business:[10]

- *micro-enterprises*, which employ fewer than five staff — this includes self-employed people who work on their own
- *small businesses*, which have between five and 19 staff
- *medium-sized businesses*, consisting of firms employing 20–199 people
- *large firms*, consisting of businesses with more than 200 staff.

TABLE 4.1 Summary of the various definitions of small businesses

Country	Criteria
Australia	Micro-enterprise: <5 employees Small business: 5–19 employees Medium-sized enterprise: 20–199 employees Large firm: 200+ employees
New Zealand	Small or medium-sized firm: <20 full-time employees Large firm: 20 or more full-time employees
Hong Kong	A small or medium-sized firm is one that has: <100 employees if it is in the manufacturing sector, or else <50 employees if it is in any other sector
Malaysia	Can be based on either annual sales revenue or number of staff employed. Turnover-based definition: Micro: <RM250 000 (Malaysian ringgit) (manufacturing sector); <RM200 000 (other sectors) Small: RM250 000–RM10 million (manufacturing); RM250 000–RM1 million (other sectors) Medium: RM10–25 million (manufacturing); RM1–5 million (other sectors) Large: >RM25 million (manufacturing), RM5 million (other sectors) Staff-based definition: Micro: <5 full-time employees Small: 5–50 staff (manufacturing sector); 5–19 (other sectors) Medium: 51–150 staff (manufacturing sector); 20–50 (other sectors) Large: >150 (manufacturing); >50 (other sectors)
Singapore	Manufacturing firms with net fixed assets investment not exceeding S$15 million Non-manufacturing enterprises with <200 employees
China	The definition varies from industry to industry, but is typically: Micro enterprise: <7 staff Small business: <500 staff, or annual sales of <30 million yuan Medium business: <2000 staff, or annual sales of <300 million yuan

Country	Criteria
India	Micro business: a firm where the investment in plant and machinery does not exceed 2.5 million rupees (manufacturing and agro-businesses) or 1 million rupees (services, primary agriculture and information & communication technology (ICT)) Small business: investment in plant and machinery is between 2.5 million and 50 million rupees (manufacturing and agro-businesses) or 1 million to 20 million rupees (services, primary agriculture and information & communication technology (ICT)) Medium business: investment in plant and machinery is 50–100 million rupees (manufacturing and agro-businesses) or 20–50 million rupees (services, primary agriculture and information & communication technology (ICT)) Large firm: investment over 100 million rupees (manufacturing and agro-businesses) or 50 million rupees (services, primary agriculture and information & communication technology (ICT))

Sources: OECD 1997, *Globalisation and SMEs*, vol.2; ABS, Small Business in Australia 2001, 2002; NZ Ministry of Economic Development, *SMEs in NZ: Structure and Dynamics 2008*; SPRING Singapore 2009; SME Corp. 2009, Definition of SMEs; Financial Secretary's Office 2009, *2008 Economic Background and 2009 Prospects*, SAR Hong Kong; NBS of China n.d., Statistical grouping sizes enterprises (Provisional); *Ministry of Small-Scale Industries 2006–07 Annual Report*. For full source details see endnotes.[11]

Collectively, micro-enterprises, small businesses and medium-sized firms are referred to as SMEs (small and medium-sized enterprises). The terms *small business* and *SME* are sometimes used interchangeably by academic researchers, since medium-sized firms share many of the characteristics of their smaller counterparts. As a result, some of the data about small firms are usually embedded among results covering the whole SME sector. Likewise, the term *small business* usually includes micro-enterprises as well, unless the two have been specifically separated. (In this book, when referring to Australian firms, the term *small business* includes both micro-enterprises and small businesses as defined by the ABS.)

A somewhat similar definition is used in New Zealand, where the Ministry of Economic Development labels an SME as a firm that employees less than 20 staff. Using this measure, it is estimated that SMEs account for 97 per cent of all business enterprises trading in that country.[12]

Definitions for Hong Kong, Singapore, Malaysia, China and India are based on a number of categories, which usually include both the number of employees and/or another quantitative variable, such as the industry sector within which the firm is based. In these countries, the term *SME* is frequently employed instead of *small business*.

In recent years there have been some attempts to introduce common international definitions, so that SME distributions can be studied and compared from one country to another. However, there are numerous problems involved in developing such a data set. For example, some countries collect information based only on surveys, while others rely on taxation information; likewise, some nations exclude the self-employed but others do not. Thus, international comparative data remains very limited at present.[13]

Characteristic features of a small business

Apart from formal definitions, there are several other characteristics that separate small firms from other types of business. Many of these indicate that the art of establishing and managing a successful small firm is often quite different from the skills required in managing larger firms, government agencies or not-for-profit organisations. In this section, we examine the general or typical characteristics of small businesses, before comparing small businesses with larger corporations. The advantages and disadvantages of operating a small firm are examined and spelt out, and we look at the factors that contribute to success and failure among small business owner–managers.

General aspects

As the qualitative definitions at the start of this chapter have shown, a number of features are typical of most small enterprises:

- *Owned by just one or two individuals*. These key people are usually responsible for almost all of the critical events in the life of the business: they conceived the original idea, establish the venture, oversee its daily activities, employ other staff, decide what will be sold, and ultimately are often responsible for ceasing activities.[14]
- *Financing provided by the owner*. Capital from external investors is often hard to come by, so most start-up funding and working capital is provided by the owner and from retained profits within the enterprise.[15]
- *Limited market share*. Most small enterprises can cater to only a relatively limited number of customers; their size and resources preclude them from being the dominant player in their industry.[16]
- *Limited life span*. Few small firms remain in existence for more than 10–15 years.[17] Although there are clearly exceptions to this rule, the life of a small enterprise is often marked by a relatively high business-closure rate, the cumulative effect of which is that most go out of operation after a decade.
- *Sometimes run on a part-time basis*. Many firms, especially ones run from home, are in fact part-time ventures. They may be run by someone as a form of casual income supplement, or constructed as part of a 'portfolio career' that combines self-employment with part-time work for another organisation.
- *A low level of net profit*. Although the opportunity to make a windfall always exists, the reality is that many firms report a low level of net profit. This relatively poor financial return often results in owner–managers earning an income well below average annual salaries for wage-earners.[18]
- *Limited product or service offering*. Rather than trying to be a comprehensive provider, most small firms tend to specialise in one or two things that they do best. By concentrating on their core areas of strength, they can maintain a competitive advantage that helps them survive against larger rivals.
- *Often home-based*. As is discussed in chapter 18, in some countries such as Australia the majority of small firms are located in the owner's personal residence. Home-based enterprises are also common throughout much of the Asia–Pacific region, and have grown rapidly in recent years in countries such as Singapore.[19]
- *Geographically limited to one or two locations*. Even when a small firm is located in commercial premises, it usually has only one or possibly two outlets; the existence of a multi-branch operation is usually restricted to a limited number of aggressively growing firms.

- *Often a family-based business.* Often, ownership and managerial control is vested in the members of the founder's family. Although outsiders may work in the enterprise, they rarely reach the position of chief executive officer. (Note, however, that not all small businesses are family businesses, or vice versa: several notable large firms, such as the Lowy or Murdoch family empires, are also effectively controlled by just one family.)
- *Located only in the private sector.* All economies consist of three essential sectors: the public sector (which represents government agencies, trading entities and departments); the private sector (business organisations principally owned by private individuals and groups); and the not-for-profit sector (non-government organisations that deliver services in the welfare, conservation, education, health and related areas). Although enterprises in all three sectors carry out commercial activities, genuine small firms are found only in the private sector.

A PROFILE OF A 'TYPICAL' SMALL BUSINESS OWNER

Is it possible to construct a picture of what might be termed a 'typical' owner-manager? As any statistician will point out, the concept of 'average' is rarely a valid way of constructing an image of a group of people. A more accurate way is to look at the mode: the most frequently occurring event within a given set of descriptors. Over the last fifteen years, data collected by the Australian Bureau of Statistics[20] has allowed researchers to identify the most common modal features of small business owners in Australia. The typical business owner-manager in Australia:

- is male (most small businesses are owned by men)
- was born in Australia
- works as a tradesperson or professional (these are the two largest occupational groups that owners come from)
- is aged between 25 and 55 years
- has completed a secondary school education or trade qualification
- has been trading for between one and five years
- used personal financial resources to start and fund the enterprise
- has not undertaken any formal management training
- does not use a business plan.

Differences between small and large businesses

Small organisations are not just 'shrunken' large enterprises. As the previous section of this chapter implies, there are often substantial differences between large and small firms. These variations are not just about the size of the firm. They also relate to many aspects of the organisation's activities, operations and management methods. Some of the major differences have been statistically measured,[21] and the following are features of small business:

- *More female owner–managers.* There are more women who are the owner–managers of small businesses than there are women who are chief executives or owners of large corporations.
- *Managers have fewer qualifications.* In general, fewer small business owner–managers hold formal tertiary or technical degrees and diplomas, either in business or in their particular area of expertise, than do executives in large corporations.

- *Fewer union employees.* Due to the informal nature of the workplace, employment relationships and job contracts tend to be negotiated directly between the manager and the staff member rather than through the agency of a trade union.
- *Fewer hours of operation each week.* Although one might expect small firms to operate for longer hours than large ones, in some countries (such as Australia) the large number of part-time, home-based operations skews the results towards a low average number of operating hours.
- *Less likely to use formal management improvement and planning techniques.* Whereas large organisations have adopted many systems and procedures to enhance performance, such as quality assurance, total quality management, or just-in-time delivery systems, smaller firms are much less likely to do so. Many more large corporations have a business plan than do small firms.
- *Less likely to access government assistance.* Although governments often provide services specifically designed to help small businesses in areas such as planning, marketing and human resources, uptake of such programs tends to be limited.
- *Less likely to export.* Trading overseas is an important means of expanding a business, and is especially important for nations with small domestic markets, such as New Zealand and Singapore. Despite this, most small and medium-sized enterprises tend to focus on their local market, and do not export.
- *Less external financing.* Most funding to start the venture comes from the owner; finance for subsequent growth is usually met by reinvesting profits and/or additional capital contributions from the owners.
- *Less likely to want to grow bigger.* For many small business owners, the goal is to have a successful business, not to constantly grow larger. This is a key difference in separating genuine growth-oriented entrepreneurs from conventional small-firm owner–managers.
- *More likely to fail.* As Storey[22] has noted, one of the fundamental characteristics of small businesses is their higher failure rate. Although the overall level of business exits is quite low, there is nevertheless a clear link between firm size and business exit rates. This issue is discussed in more detail later in this chapter.
- *Differences in managerial perspectives.* This issue is harder to quantify and measure, but just as important. Small businesses rely heavily on their owner–managers, but have extremely limited physical and financial resources. Their managers often think, plan and implement decisions with a very different perspective from that of their counterparts in large corporations. The way in which small-firm owner–managers operate their businesses, the way they market their firm, the level of personal risk they face and their degree of sophistication differs significantly from the approach of professional corporate managers. Compared with their counterparts in large firms, small-firm owner–managers plan for shorter time frames, use less formal communication forms and are more personally involved in more areas of the firm.[23] Table 4.2 below summarises some of these key differences.

TABLE 4.2 Some typical differences between SMEs and large firms

	SMEs	Large firms
Planning timeframe	Short-term timeframe; intuitive	Long-term; formalised
Number of owners	1–2	Multiple shareholders
Organisational structure	Adhocracy	Bureaucracy
Management	By owner	By professional executives
Number of business establishments	Single	Multiple
Product/service range	Limited	Limited or wide
Knowledge base	Limited; ad hoc	Sophisticated; extensive; widely dispersed
Internal communication systems	Informal; personalised	Systematic; structured
Management skills	Wide range; little formal training	Specialist; technical skills focus
Personal income of managers	Contingent on firm performance; highly variable	Usually fixed
Personal interests	Directly affect firm performance	Minimal role
Quality control	Informal; personal benchmarks	Standardised
Firm objectives	Personalised	Set by corporation and shareholders

Sources: Carter, S. 1996, 'Small Business Marketing' in Warner, M. (ed.) *International Encyclopedia of Business and Management,* London: Routledge, pp. 140–56; Gibb, A.A. 2000, 'SME Policy, Academic Research and the Growth of Ignorance, Mythical Concepts, Myths, Assumptions, Rituals and Confusions', *International Small Business Journal,* vol. 18, no. 3 (May), pp. 13–35.

The advantages and disadvantages of operating a small business

Another critical issue to examine in any analysis of small business is the reason people choose to work in a small business. Small business owners must face a number of challenges, and success is rarely guaranteed. Why, then, do people choose either to start a new small-scale business venture or to buy an existing firm?

The key factor that often drives people to start their own business enterprise is a desire to be independent. The dream of 'being your own boss' is very attractive to people who want to have more direct control over their own working life, their personal income and their capacity to make decisions (see the Entrepreneur Profile of Kimberley Hill, the solo operator of Lovie's Test and Tag).

A second factor is the ability to fulfil personal goals and interests. Running a business can allow people to follow a dream or an opportunity that they have long been interested in. It can also let them apply their energies and enthusiasm to a field in which they already have a personal interest and talent. It is not unusual, for example, for owner–managers to turn their hobby interests into a full-time business.

Entrepreneur profile

Lovie's Test and Tag

Sometimes the most successful small businesses have nothing to do with the owners' original career goals, as Kimberley Hill's story demonstrates. After working in hospitality as an employee for seventeen years, Kimberley looked at moving into business. She first considered buying a small café, but the hours and risk turned her off. Instead, in 2007, she started her own electrical safety testing and tagging business in the Hawkesbury region of New South Wales, Australia.

'I knew nearly nothing about electrical safety when I started. But I knew that New South Wales had the highest safety standards in the country, and electricians didn't enjoy their new responsibility. So I did an electrical safety course, followed by a small business development course. Out of these came a business plan, and I've stuck to that pretty closely since.'

Under New South Wales regulations, mobile electrical devices, such as power tools, need to be certified every few months. So the enterprise is all about repeat business. Getting the customers was the biggest challenge. However, her unique personal branding gave her a big advantage. Her work truck was already painted pink, so she decided to make site visits in pink overalls, cutting a unique figure in a field that has historically been a male-dominated industry. And her website, www.loviestestandtag.com.au, also features a pink colour scheme.

With a moderate investment in equipment, she quickly surpassed the service of ordinary electricians, and now her professionalism is instantly recognised in her area.

Kimberley works from home, spending about half of her time on the road. Her expenses are her car, mobile phone, laptop and some safety testing equipment. She works about 30 hours per week, which gives her enough free time for her other interests, craftwork and care of animals.

At the moment Kimberley is content to build her business in the Hawkesbury, but she is beginning to investigate franchising. Electrical safety standards vary from state to state in Australia, and so the viability of the core business may need to be carefully considered. However, it's an opportunity that she is keen to consider in due course.

Profile prepared by Geoff Baker, Murdoch University Business School.

If properly managed, there are also potential financial opportunities. A well-run business can be a highly profitable one, producing a better income for the owner than would be earned as an employee for someone else. A business can also become an asset that produces ongoing (residual) income or that can be sold at a later stage for a substantial capital gain.

Finally, there may be family benefits from establishing a firm, especially if it is managed with a long-term vision. A successful business can provide opportunities for children to inherit wealth and income that their parents could not otherwise hope to provide.

On the other hand, the disadvantages of going into small business for oneself are relatively clear. A main consideration is uncertainty. There are few, if any, guaranteed outcomes in being a business owner–manager. For many firms, ambiguity and constant change are almost a given. There can be major fluctuations in sales income, profitability, government regulations, competitors and market dynamics from one year to another.

A second variable is the potential for financial loss. If the business fails to make a profit, then the owner will usually be out of pocket. Even if a profit is made, it may be lower than expected, which will in turn produce a lower return on investment. Finally, if the business collapses, then the owner may lose all the original investment, and possibly even personal assets (such as the family home) if these have been used to help guarantee a bank loan.

There are increased responsibilities that come with being an owner–manager. As 'the boss', the small business owner must make decisions about hiring and firing staff, dealing with customer complaints, day-to-day problems, financial control of the enterprise, and legal responsibility for compliance with government rules. This often substantially increases the pressure on the owner, which may be hard to avoid or overcome. Personal stress is common for business owner–managers.

Factors leading to success and failure

The process of small business formation and development is a hazardous one, and it seems logical to conclude that the risk of failure will be high, especially in the early years of a business's existence. At the macro (economy-wide) level, the turnover of firms is a natural and inevitable phenomenon in any market-based economy, which has a number of beneficial effects. The emergence of new enterprises often indicates the creation of new, innovative products and services, and it also provides new job opportunities within the community. The demise of a business can also be positive, in that it frees up finance, managers and personnel for new businesses.[24] At the individual level, however, there can be a high cost from business turnovers, including unemployment and the loss of personal financial assets and self-esteem. It is important, therefore, to understand the factors that lead to business success and failure.

The causes of failure have been more extensively discussed and researched than the reasons for success. Theoretically, almost every aspect of business can potentially cause a business to fail if not dealt with properly. However, there are a number of general trends that appear to indicate the most common areas of likely failure (see figure 4.1). Researchers in Singapore, Malaysia and Australia have found that problems could be grouped into four functional areas: finance, marketing, production and personnel.[25] In addition to these specific organisational problems, a fifth critical area was identified: personal factors, such as a lack of time, having to perform too many different duties, being unable to sell oneself, being too conservative and having difficulty in generating ideas.

Abdul Rashid's Malaysian research found that the problems of the business owner vary depending on the stage of business development. At the initial level, finance and marketing issues were a key concern, whereas in slightly older firms, personal and family matters seem to be more important, especially for women.[26]

In Singapore, Soh-Wee studied start-up and early development problems confronting young small business owner–managers. Her findings show that the rising costs of doing business and the difficulty of obtaining finance are the most pressing problems facing young business owner–managers. The loss of control over one's workforce is the next most important problem. Inadequate technical and managerial knowledge, as well as strong competition, however, were perceived to be less important.[27]

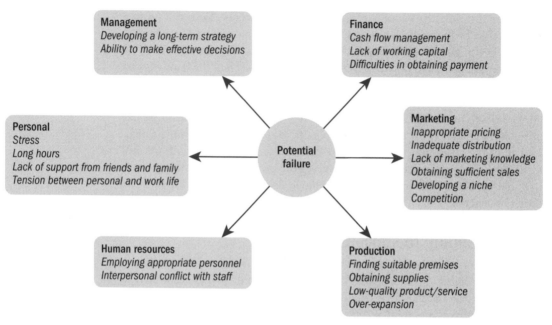

Management
Developing a long-term strategy
Ability to make effective decisions

Finance
Cash flow management
Lack of working capital
Difficulties in obtaining payment

Personal
Stress
Long hours
Lack of support from friends and family
Tension between personal and work life

Potential failure

Marketing
Inappropriate pricing
Inadequate distribution
Lack of marketing knowledge
Obtaining sufficient sales
Developing a niche
Competition

Human resources
Employing appropriate personnel
Interpersonal conflict with staff

Production
Finding suitable premises
Obtaining supplies
Low-quality product/service
Over-expansion

FIGURE 4.1 Some potential factors leading to failure facing small business managers

Another way of analysing the causes of failure is to break possible contributing factors down into two groups: problems within the organisation itself and external variables. The former group includes bad management practices, poor product/service quality, employing the wrong staff, a lack of sufficient capital and cash flow (liquidity) and personal shortcomings of the owner, such as a tendency to autocratic decision making or poor time management.[28] External causes of business failure can include the activities of competitors, change in market demand, economic recession, change to government policies and laws and the introduction of new technologies or processes. Research studies in Singapore showed that internal factors are the predominant cause of business failures in that country.[29]

Just how high is the rate of small business failure? This is a difficult issue to measure. So-called failures can occur when a business goes into bankruptcy, is sold to another owner, is merged with another firm or is liquidated by the owners,[30] although even in these cases it is not always possible to determine the causes of such events. In fact, there is no single definition of business failure. For example, financial failure can mean anything from making a trading loss each year to simply not making a satisfactory level of profit or sufficient return on capital invested. In terms of the firm's marketing performance, a business could be considered a failure if its product recognition is low, its market share declines or its original market ceases to exist, even if it still trades at a profit. In addition, a firm may have gone out of existence for other reasons, such as the owner's wish to retire, ill health of the owner, or even a merger with another firm to create a bigger enterprise. For these reasons, the use of the word *failure* is often inappropriate.

The concept of **business exits** may be more appropriate. An exit refers to any situation in which a business ceases to exist, and can include closure, liquidation, bankruptcy, sale or transfer to another owner, or merger. A number of different studies have indicated that exit rates can be difficult to measure accurately, and can change over time. For example, one study of exits in Australia during the late 1990s indicated that approximately 7.5 per cent of all businesses cease trading each year;[31] another conducted during the early 2000s indicated an exit rate closer to 8 per cent;[32] and the most recent one, covering businesses between 2003 and 2007, suggested the annual rate was just over 10 per cent.[33] Despite the variation in these figures, some trends are clear: micro-businesses have the highest exit rate of all types of business, while large firms are least likely to cease trading; sole proprietors are more likely to exit than other types of business structure; and firms with very low turnover have the highest probability of early exit.[34]

In New Zealand, survival rates are somewhat similar to those in Australia. For example, about 80 per cent survive their first year of trading, two-thirds survive to the end of their second year, just under half survive their fifth year and just over a third survive for seven years. Long term, these suggest an exit rate of about 10 per cent per annum. As is also the case in Australia, non-employing firms in NZ are less likely to survive than employing firms.[35]

Survival rates have not been studied in as much detail in other Asia–Pacific countries, but analysis of existing data by the government agency Statistics Singapore indicates that about half of all business enterprises are still in existence after five years of trading.[36]

The important point to note is that few firms 'fail' as such. Most businesses will still be in existence after several years. Even those that do cease operating usually do so for reasons other than actual failure.[37]

Just like the measurement of failure, evaluating success rates and the factors that contribute to them can be difficult. There have been various suggestions about how 'success' in small business can be measured. Kelmar,[38] in his review of several studies published in this field, noted that most authors indicated that marketing characteristics are particularly important. For example, success is often deemed to occur when a business shows that it can profitably sell its goods or services in the marketplace. This is followed by financial considerations, such as a growing level of profit, whereas measures of management rank third. If one looks more closely at the characteristics indicated under these generic headings, it appears that growth constitutes the predominant indicator of success. This classification is rather broad in its interpretation, and includes business growth, employment growth, productivity growth, profit growth and sales growth. Other important indicators of success may be more subjective: the amount of income the owner earns, the amount of free time he or she has, or the level of personal satisfaction regarding business achievements. Interestingly, a small business can be both a success and a failure simultaneously. It is possible, for example, for a firm to have a very poor financial return and, yet, at the same time, provide the owner with a feeling of satisfaction because some personal psychological needs, such as feelings of independence, are being met by the firm.

Given the wide range of possible ways of measuring success and the difficulties of doing so, it is not surprising that the number of studies in this area is relatively limited. Interestingly, most small business operators tend to regard

Business exit
Any situation in which a business ceases to exist, through closure, liquidation, bankruptcy, sale or transfer to another owner, or merger.

themselves as a success, despite what others might think of their performance. The Australian Bureau of Statistics, for example, found that 90 per cent of small-firm owners regarded themselves as successful.[39]

The economic significance of the small business sector

Small firms are more than just an interesting phenomenon; they are also a critical component in the structure of any economy. Although the economic basis of countries in the Asia–Pacific region varies substantially, ranging from agricultural-based production in Indonesia and mass-scale manufacturing in China through to high-tech service industries in Singapore and Hong Kong, all of them possess one common factor: a sizeable small business sector.

General importance

More specifically, small firms are important to all national economies because they provide:

- *Employment opportunities for people.* This includes the self-employment of the business owner–manager and the conventional jobs provided to the staff who work for the owner. Although there are no hard and fast rules, generally speaking small businesses account for about half of all the jobs in the private sector of most countries.
- *The next generation of large firms.* Large organisations are not permanent; they too are born, exist and eventually exit the marketplace. Many of the large corporations that dominated the stock exchanges of Australia and New Zealand at the start of the 1960s, for example, are no longer in existence. They have been replaced by other firms that started out as small-scale ventures and have since grown in size to join the ranks of large enterprises. Although it is difficult to predict which small businesses will succeed and become the leviathans of the future, one thing is clear: without an ample supply of small firms, there can be no 'next generation' of large ones.
- *Competition.* When a market is dominated by only one or two firms, then customers can often suffer from high prices, low-quality products and poor service. In contrast, the existence of a number of competitors serves to keep businesses responsive to the needs of their clients, and ensures that customers have a choice in what they buy, where they buy it and for how much. If such competition were removed from the marketplace, the range of offerings available would be much smaller.
- *Innovation.* The existence of small firms not only acts as a catalyst for competition but also serves as a spur for innovation. Competition encourages firms to constantly seek new and better ways of providing improved goods and services; to find more efficient and effective ways of managing the business; and to adopt new production methods. In addition, small firms can also be used as a vehicle for launching an innovation if no large firm or government agency is willing to take the risk.
- *An outlet for entrepreneurial activity.* As mentioned in chapter 1, entrepreneurs often use a small business as their vehicle for launching a new business idea or

for experimenting with an innovative product or service. If small firms did not exist, or could not be started easily by enthusiastic entrepreneurs, there would be few opportunities in which to test ideas and offer them in the marketplace.

- *Exports.* To survive, some small firms also have to seek markets beyond their own national boundaries. In Singapore, for example, a small national market imposes substantial limits on the opportunities for future growth. Many Singaporean firms have chosen to expand by offering their products to the neighbouring nations of Malaysia and Indonesia. A similar situation applies to small firms in New Zealand, many of which have found new markets in Australia and the Pacific islands.
- *Specialised products and services.* Because of their limited size and resources, small businesses are often better able to survive by focusing on a specific range of activities. An example of this is Jessica Kiely-Schebesta's career-development business, which is profiled in this chapter. Many of these products or services appeal to a small niche market, but not to a large group of customers. For example, stamp-collecting shops or horse-drawn caravan holidays will appeal to small groups of people interested in buying such goods or services, and this demand will be enough to support one or two people in a full-time occupation at a modest level of profitability. However, the scope is so limited that no large corporation would be interested in such offerings.
- *Support to big business.* Many large corporations actually rely on small businesses for their own survival. They use such firms to provide them with materials, support and ideas. Big businesses, such as manufacturers, often source many of their component parts, casual labour and consultancy services from smaller firms, as well as relying on small retail shops to sell their products to the public. Although it tends to be overlooked, large and small firms often have a symbiotic (mutually beneficial) relationship rather than a competitive one.
- *Decentralisation.* Most economic activity takes place in large cities, where the population is highly concentrated, infrastructure is reliable, transport costs are lower, there is ready access to skilled labour and most resources, and marketing to a concentrated cluster of consumers is more cost-effective. However, many people live outside major cities, often in small towns, villages and isolated communities. It can be difficult for them to attract large corporations to their region, mainly because the consumer base is so small. For these people, small firms are the main means of purchasing goods and finding employment.
- *Distribution of economic resources, wealth and opportunities.* When an economy is dominated by a relatively limited number of large enterprises, the imbalance can restrict wealth, financial assets and opportunities to a small clique of highly influential business owners and senior managers. In contrast, a nation with a flourishing small business sector is one that provides numerous opportunities for many people to build wealth and create their own economic future.
- *Flexibility in the overall economy.* Finally, a society with a large number of small firms is one with a higher capacity to withstand economic upheaval and change. A diverse range of firms, in many sizes and industries, can act as a buffer and increase flexibility in responding to adverse change.

Jessica Kiely-Schebesta, The Frank Team

Jessica's first business was more of a pastime than a planned commercial venture. At the age of 19, she began an in-home tutoring service, New Horizon Tutoring, for high-school students while she completed her degree in Economics and Social Science at Sydney University. Jessica had other university students working for her as tutors and, like many other small ventures, the business was managed on a fairly informal basis: there was no business plan, and she ran the business from her bedroom. After finishing her degree she then ran the business full time for a year, and expanded its operations through different parts of Sydney. It was while she was running this firm that she started her second one.

In 2001 she started The Frank Team, with a partner. Like her first business, it grew organically out of her passions. However, unlike the first, she developed a business plan, conducted market research and started with a small amount of capital to formally create the business entity.

'We were involved in a local council youth committee, and we wanted some training in events management, strategic planning, PR skills and related areas,' Jessica explains. But we couldn't find anything that fitted our niche. So we trained ourselves, and then started to provide the same services to others.'

'The Frank Team started with providing help to local youth committees, and then got into careers programs in schools and tertiary organisations. We now also provide young entrepreneur training, backed up by a networking website, www.youngentrepreneurs.net.au.'

The Frank Team today employs three full-time staff, and has 15 contract presenters working around Australia.

'Our next challenge is to consolidate our careers service across Australian schools in all of the states, which means systematically pursuing Australian schools and tertiary organisations through our marketing plan. We have also just launched a short course program for young people getting into business. Currently, we have six-week and one-day versions running in New South Wales, but with our multistate presence we could grow this around the country.'

You can learn more about The Frank Team by visiting the website, www.frankteam.com.au.

Profile prepared by Geoff Baker, Murdoch University Business School.

Global significance

Across the world, small businesses represent the majority of all trading enterprises. While large firms still account for much employment (about 30–40 per cent in most countries), the majority of exports and about 50 per cent of economic value added, they are more than matched by SMEs in terms of overall economic significance. Recent counts of small business indicate that they typically constitute over 90 per cent of all firms in a country, and that the very smallest of firms (micro-enterprises) usually account for at least 75 per cent of all businesses.[40]

Table 4.3 provides a summary of the distribution of private sectors by size, across a number of key developed economies. As has previously been noted[41], the distribution of firms in most stable open-market economies is such that SMEs appear to account for no less than 95 per cent, or nineteen out of every twenty firms in existence. Conversely, large firms rarely exceed a '1 in 20' distribution rule. Micro-firms predominate over all other firms, giving rise to a pyramid-type structure in each economy, whereas large businesses are the numerically smallest cohort. Although it is not shown here, recent research also appears to confirm that these proportions and distributions have not changed much over the last 20 years. In other words, the pattern of firm distribution appears to be relatively fixed and enduring.[42]

TABLE 4.3 Counts of firms by size in selected nations and geographic regions

	European Union 2005	UK 2007	USA 2005
Micro-businesses	18 040 000 (91.8%)	4 480 000 (95.7%)	20 390 000 (77.3%)
Small business	1 350 000 (6.9%)	167 000 (3.6%)	5 360 000 (20.3%)
Medium enterprises	210 000 (1.1%)	27 000 (0.6%)	610 000 (2.3%)
Large firms	40 000 (0.2%)	6000 (0.1%)	17 000 (0.06%)
Total	19 640 000 (100%)	4 680 000 (100%)	26 380 000 (100%)

Sources: Schiemann, M. (2008) *'Enterprises By Size Class – Overview of SMEs in the EU'* Eurostat publication 31/2008, 2008, http://epp.eurostat.ec.europa.eu; UK Department for Business Enterprise & Regulatory Reform (2008), *Statistical Press Release, 30 July*, http://stats.berr.gov.uk; US Small Business Administration, *The Small Business Economy 2008: A Report to the President*, Small Business Administration, Washington, 2009, p. 278. Figures are rounded.

Australia

The number of small private sector firms in Australia has grown substantially over the last twenty years. At the last published count of firms (in 2007), the Australian Bureau of Statistics reported that there were just over 2 million firms registered with the Australian Taxation Office that were considered to be actively trading. The biggest group of firms were micro-enterprises, followed by small businesses. As table 4.4 indicates, some 95.8 per cent of all private sector firms were found in these two categories; the number of medium and large firms constituted only 3.2 per cent of all firms. Although the method of counting of businesses has changed somewhat over the years,[43] the ABS data has consistently shown a continued growth in the number of SMEs. Some sectors of the economy have particularly large numbers of small businesses, such as the property and business services sector, construction, primary industries and retail trade.[44] The majority of firms are also home-based (a phenomenon which is discussed in more detail in chapter 18).

TABLE 4.4 Actively-trading private sector firms in Australia in 2007

Micro-businesses (0–4 employees; includes self-employed persons)	1 699 277 (84.5%)
Small business (5–19 employees)	228 313 (11.3%)
Medium-sized (20–199 employees)	78 304 (3.9%)
Large (200+ staff)	5876 (0.3%)
Total	2 011 770 (100%)

Figures include agricultural enterprises; totals are rounded.

Source: Australian Bureau of Statistics, *Counts of Australian Businesses, including Entries and Exits*, cat. no. 8165.0, ABS, Canberra, p. 18, 2007.

New Zealand

In New Zealand in 2007 there were 448 000 small and medium-sized businesses, representing 97 per cent of all firms in the country. Together, these enterprises employed 595 000 people (about 31 per cent of all employment in the country), and generated approximately 39 per cent of national economic output, even though the typical small firm in New Zealand employs only five people. Similar to the Australian experience, the majority of small firms are found in the services and related areas, including such fields as personal services, finance and insurance, construction, property and business services, the cultural and recreational industries, and communications services.[45]

Hong Kong

Statistics gathered in the Hong Kong Special Administrative Region cover both small and medium-sized firms. In December 2008, there were over 266 000 SMEs in the Hong Kong Special Administrative Region, representing 98 per cent of all business enterprises. In aggregate, they employed about 1.2 million people — almost half of the private sector workforce.[46] In Hong Kong's SME sector, the majority of employees are usually family members, and most firms employ fewer than 10 people.[47] There is a strong focus on trade and hospitality: the greatest number of SMEs are found in the import/export field, in restaurants and hotels, and in the wholesale and retail trade sectors.[48]

Singapore

In 2009 there were an estimated 161 000 small and medium-sized enterprises in Singapore. These made up 99 per cent of all firms in the republic, and they employed about 60 per cent of the workforce. Although many multinational corporations in the Asia-Pacific region are based in Singapore, it is clear that much of the country's economic activity is still generated by SMEs: small and medium-sized firms account for almost half of the total national economic output.[49]

Malaysia

Sometimes SMEs are also referred to as small and medium industries (SMIs) in Malaysia. In 2005, using a revised business census methodology, there were approximately 510 000 SMEs in the country, representing 99.2 per cent of all business establishments. Micro-enterprises accounted for 78 per cent of all firms; small firms represented 18 per cent and medium-sized businesses constituted 2 per cent of the business population.[50] SMEs account for almost a third of national economic output in the country, employ over 55 per cent of the private sector workforce and account for about one-fifth of national exports.[51]

China

Official business statistics about the SME sector are somewhat limited at present. However, the China Association of Small and Medium Enterprises estimated that in 2006 there were approximately 42 million small and medium-sized businesses, accounting for over 99 per cent of all businesses — although many of these were state or collectively owned, making it difficult to accurately determine the private-sector component. Privately-owned firms registered with the Industry and Commerce Department accounted for 4.3 million firms.[52] It is estimated that SMEs account for approximately 75 per cent of the workforce in urban areas (rural data is more difficult to come by) and generate approximately 60 per cent of China's industrial output.[53]

India

Many businesses in India are not formally registered, making it, like China, difficult to accurately assess the true size of the small business sector. The federal Ministry of Micro, Small and Medium Enterprises states that, in 2009, there were almost 13 million such businesses formally registered and trading, employing 31 million people, although this figure is probably an underestimate of the true size of the SME sector. These firms accounted for 33 per cent of all exports, and almost 40 per cent of the nation's industrial outputs.[54]

Entrepreneur or small business owner–manager?

A final but extremely important issue when examining the nature of small firms is the difference between small business management and entrepreneurship. Among the general community and even in parts of the business world, the small business owner–manager is often regarded as an entrepreneur and vice versa. This is not surprising, since the two roles are closely related and even overlap in many respects. However, the two concepts, although similar, are not synonymous.

How do small business owner–managers differ from entrepreneurs? Entrepreneurs discover, evaluate and exploit new business opportunities. Although they may start-up new small businesses as their vehicles for doing this, they may equally operate through the forum of an existing large firm, a government agency or a not-for-profit organisation. In contrast, a *small business owner–manager* is a person who runs an existing small business; there may be little innovation, idea-generation or risk involved in such a project.

The term *entrepreneur*, as mentioned in chapter 1, best describes a person who develops new ideas, starts an enterprise based on these ideas and provides added value to society based on independent initiative. Not all small business owners fit this category, since many small firms do not actively seek out new ideas or business opportunities. For example, people who leave a job with a large corporation or government agency and simply recreate the same job on an outsourced basis with a separate legal business entity are really just small business operators, rather than true entrepreneurs. They are not developing any innovative ideas or taking substantial risks, but recreating their old job under a different format.

The distinction between the two terms is often subtle, but still important. The person who establishes a fast-food franchise chain is called an entrepreneur, but the local owner–manager of a solitary, long-established restaurant is best called a small business operator. Distinguishing factors are that entrepreneurs have a vision for growth, a commitment to innovation, persistence in gathering the necessary resources and an overriding need to achieve. The small business operator does not always exhibit these characteristics, and they are not always necessary for the successful management of a small-scale firm[55] (see table 4.5).

TABLE 4.5 Differences between entrepreneurship and small business management

	Entrepreneurship	Small business management
Definition of the field	The process whereby an individual discovers, evaluates and exploits an opportunity independently	The administration of a small, independent business venture
Firm size	Large, medium or small	Small
Degree of risk involved	Very variable	Generally lower risk
Number of people involved in the business	Can range from very small to very large	Small
Economic sector	Found in private, government and not-for-profit sectors	Found only in private sector
Growth focus	High	Variable
Key individual	Entrepreneur	Owner–manager
Key attributes of the individual	High need for achievement (set-up a business to realise a dream); high internal locus of control; high risk-taking propensity; creative and innovative; growth-oriented	Moderate need for achievement (run a business to make a living); good organisational skills to manage efficiently; no/ little innovation; moderate growth

People can also hold these different titles at different points in their working lives. For example, some people start out as entrepreneurs (creators of a new, innovative business), but can then be called a small business owner–manager once the business venture has been established and they no longer have any ambition for innovation and growth. Conversely, a small business manager can also become an entrepreneur — for example, a person may buy an existing business with the initial purpose of running a 'lifestyle business', but may subsequently take up various opportunities to expand the business, such as introducing new product lines, developing new markets, or providing additional services to clients.

The shirt on his back

Sometimes the simplest choices are the hardest ones. For many years, your father has operated a small kiosk in the local weekend street markets. A long time ago he had a clever idea that has since blossomed: directly importing cheap sarongs and shirts from Indonesia, and selling them to the many tourists, students and low-income earners who visit the markets. As the only clothing vendor in the night street markets, business has been good for your father. Income from the business is not huge, but it's worthwhile — averaging a net profit of about A$300 per day, once the cost of the shirts, stall fees and business operating costs are taken into account. The street markets operate every Thursday, Friday, Saturday and Sunday, leaving three days per week free to either spend on other pursuits or leisure.

You already know the business well, since you have frequently helped your family staff the stall on weekends. Your father has now indicated that he wants to retire, and is prepared to sell you the business. If you're prepared to give him A$200 a week for the next three years, the enterprise can all be yours. It's a very reasonable price, and much less than you would pay on the open market.

However, just after you have finalised the verbal agreement with your father, you receive a phone call from a much larger stall trader in another city. She tells you that she plans to move into your markets within the next six months, as part of a national expansion plan. She is prepared to pay you A$35 000 for the business, and give you the chance to work for her. Otherwise, she warns, be prepared to face stiff competition in the immediate future.

Questions

1. **List the different options that you have for the next 12 months, and the advantages and disadvantages of each course of action.**
2. **Would a typical small business owner react differently to this situation than an entrepreneur? Explain your reasoning.**

SUMMARY

There is no single definition of what constitutes a small business, and a variety of both qualitative and quantitative factors can be used to separate small firms from other businesses. From a qualitative perspective, the business has to be independently owned and operated, closely controlled and funded by the owner, and the principal decision-making functions must rest with the owner–manager. In addition, the small business can be defined using a variety of quantitative indicators, such as number of employees, value of assets, turnover, and share of ownership retained by the owner–manager. Small businesses form a vital part of the economy throughout Australia, New Zealand and the rest of the Asia–Pacific region.

Small firms share a number of typical characteristics that separate them from other types of business organisation. Some of these differences include a smaller market share, a small ownership base, a limited life span and limited net profit. Compared with larger firms, small businesses are more likely to be operated from home, to be run by a family and to have female managers. There are few formal planning procedures, less access to outside capital, less government support and a greater likelihood of 'failure' or exit.

The advantage of owning a small business includes flexibility, personal achievement and the freedom to pursue one's own goals. The disadvantages include an increased exposure to uncertainty and risk, financial loss and personal stress.

Most small businesses face a series of generic problems in the first years of operation. These difficulties fall into four main functional areas — finance, marketing, production and personnel — plus personal difficulties that are caused by running the business. These problems may eventually lead to the failure of the business. Some studies show that internal problems, such as poor management within the firm, are usually the underlying causes of failure; other research points to external circumstances (such as recession or the lack of available capital) as a key determinant of small business failure. Measuring success in a small firm is also difficult.

Small businesses are a major economic force throughout the Asia–Pacific region. They provide many of the jobs and a good proportion of GDP in each country, as well as support to large firms, flexibility in the overall economy, and the more equitable distribution of economic resources, wealth and opportunities.

The concept of small business management differs from the concept of entrepreneurship. Whereas small business management is concerned mainly with the art of managing a small-scale commercial firm, entrepreneurship can be viewed as the process of identifying new market opportunities and converting them into a marketable product or service.

REVIEW QUESTIONS

1. List the main qualitative and quantitative criteria used to define a small business.
2. Outline the economic significance of SMEs in the Asia–Pacific region.
3. How does a small business differ from a large one?
4. What is a business exit and how does it differ from the concept of business failure?
5. List the general characteristics of a small business.

DISCUSSION QUESTIONS

1. Why do so many different countries seem to have similar proportions of SMEs in their business populations?
2. Is there any meaningful difference in the definitions of small business and entrepreneurship?
3. Why do countries use different definitions of a 'small business'?

SUGGESTED READING

Australian Bureau of Statistics, *Counts of Australian Businesses, including Entries and Exits*, Cat. no. 8165.0, ABS, Canberra, 2007.

Ministry of Economic Development (MED), New Zealand, *SMEs in New Zealand: Structure and Dynamics 2008*, MED, Wellington, 2008.

Organisation for Economic Co-operation and Development (OECD) *Measuring Entrepreneurship: A Digest of Indicators*, Paris: OECD Statistics Directorate, 2008.

Ronir — a tale of two perspectives

Four years ago, Dan and Alice purchased the Ronir Restaurant in Melbourne. Although the site had previously been a restaurant for a number of years, lately it had been closed for some months. Both Alice and Dan were in their early 30s, and each of them had previously operated their own restaurant, where they enjoyed the sense of freedom and control that comes with being the decision maker, so they were keen to become business owners again.

There was no goodwill included in the purchase price, and the acquisition cost was relatively low. By using their own funds, getting some help from their families, and utilising finance leasing for kitchen equipment, restaurant tables and chairs, they were able to self-finance the full amount of capital needed to establish the business. Neither owner had wanted to be indebted to the banks. Although a small overdraft had been set-up with the purchase of the business, trade credit was used in preference to the overdraft for any short-term cash flow issues. This was easily obtained because of the good relationship fostered by Dan and Alice with their suppliers.

The new owners refurbished the premises so that it could seat approximately 40 customers at a time, and they opened for breakfast, lunch and dinner, seven days a week. After a short while, and contrary to their business plan, they decided that breakfast and lunch were not going to be profitable so they stopped providing these. However, evening meals were quickly becoming popular. The restaurant was soon taking an average of 90 diners per night.

Ronir served traditional Italian food, made with local ingredients at a very affordable price. Patrons came largely from the local area and neighbouring suburbs, and many guests were dining there more than once a week.

In the early years of Ronir, Dan and Alice wanted to create a restaurant with an atmosphere, service and cuisine that would communicate their personality, but also provide them with a comfortable income. Ronir soon gained a reputation for providing great food at reasonable prices. Since many restaurants often lose sales when patrons cancel, the owners made the decision not to take bookings, and a customer waiting list formed each night. On busy nights customers sometimes waited for over an hour before being seated. They would either wait at the small bar inside the premises, or go to a nearby hotel for a pre-dinner drink and wait to be called by the restaurant when a table became free.

Three floor staff, including Alice, were needed to wait on tables. Alice had completed one year of a Commerce degree at university, so initially she looked after the bookkeeping side of the restaurant as well. Alice also compiled the wine list and ordered wine, managed staff rosters and dealt with hiring, firing and paying staff. Dan worked principally as the head chef, in charge of a small team that consisted of a second chef, an apprentice chef and a kitchen hand. Both Alice and Dan were now working quite long hours — about fifty a week — but were taking home an income slightly above the average wage.

Two years ago, the two partners brought in a third business owner. The workload was becoming too great for them to manage, so they decided to invite a 'friend of a friend' to buy into the partnership. Jennifer had strong management and financial experience, and took on the financial responsibilities of the business, as well as staffing and marketing. She also computerised what had previously been a manual accounting system.

Jennifer noticed that some enquiring customers would not wait for a table, often moving to other nearby restaurants where they could get a table straight away. With Ronir at capacity, and prices very low, net profit had stabilised at approximately 5 per cent. Jennifer believed that by increasing prices and renegotiating trade terms, she could more than double the net profit margin without reducing the number of diners seated each night. However, Dan and Alice felt uncomfortable with this change in direction. They took great pride in the fact that it was difficult to get a seat at their restaurant, and were unwilling to tamper with a 'successful' formula.

In addition to increasing profitability, Jennifer wanted to grow the business by increasing the seating capacity, and possibly even opening further restaurants. Although in principle each of the owners agreed with this new strategy, tensions soon developed. Alice and Dan liked the way things had traditionally been done and the stability associated with the past. They were becomingly increasingly uncomfortable with Jennifer's new systems, and the more formal procedures needed for her proposed growth strategy.

Case study prepared by Michael A'Campo, The University of Newcastle, Australia.

Questions

1. **What are the qualitative and quantitative points that may define Ronir as a small business?**
2. **Are all three owners entrepreneurs? Justify your answer.**
3. **Compared to a large business, why are the management perspectives different for a small business?**

ENDNOTES

1. J.A. Welsh & J.F. White, 'A small business is not a big business', *Harvard Business Review*, vol. 59, no. 4, 1981, pp. 18–32.
2. G.G. Meredith, *Small Business Management in Australia*, 4th edn, McGraw-Hill, Sydney, 1993.
3. Government of the United Kingdom, *Committee of Inquiry on Small Firms* (Bolton Report), HMSO, London, 1971.
4. Department of Trade and Industry, *Report of the Committee on Small Business* (Wiltshire Report), AGPS, Canberra, 1971.
5. G. Meredith, *A National Policy for Small Enterprise Development*, University of New England, Armidale, 1975.
6. Australian Bureau of Statistics, 'Defining businesses by size', *Small Business in Australia 1999*, ABS, Canberra, 2000, pp. 135–50.
7. P.A. Julien, *The State of the Art in Small Business and Entrepreneurship*, Ashgate, Aldershot, 1998, p. 3.
8. ibid, p. 133.
9. ABS, *see* note 6, p. 149.
10. Australian Bureau of Statistics, *A Statistical View of Counts of Businesses in Australia*, ABS, Canberra, 2005, p. 7.
11. OECD, *Globalisation and SMEs*, vol. 2, OECD, Paris, 1997, pp. 119–21; Australian Bureau of Statistics, *Small Business in Australia 2001*, ABS, Canberra, 2002; NZ Ministry of Economic Development (MED), *SMEs in New Zealand: Structure and Dynamics 2008*, MED, Wellington, 2008; Singapore Standards, Productivity and Innovation Board (SPRING), 'SPRING's Performance Indicators', 2009 www.spring.gov.sg; Small and Medium Industries Development Corporation, Malaysia, *Definition of SMEs*, 2003, www.smidec.gov.my; SME Corp. 2009, *Definition of SMEs*, www.smecorp.gov.au; Financial Secretary's Office, February 2009, *2008 Economic Background and 2009 Prospects*, Government of the HK Special Administrative Region, Hong Kong; National Bureau of Statistics of China n.d., Statistical grouping sizes enterprises (Provisional), China Statistical Information Network; Indian Ministry of Small Scale Industries 2007, *Ministry of Small-Scale Industries 2006–07 Annual Report*, http://msme.gov.in, p. 9.

12. Ministry of Economic Development (MED), New Zealand, *SMEs in New Zealand: Structure and Dynamics 2008*, MED, Wellington, 2008, pp. 4–5.
13. P.E. Atkinson, 'Strengths and Weaknesses of SME Statistics Systems: The Users' Perspective' OECD presentation of identified key issues, Special Workshop on 'SME Statistics: Towards a More Systematic Statistical Measurement of SME Behaviour', 2nd OECD Conference of Ministers responsible for SMEs, Istanbul, 3–5 June 2004, www.oecd.org; Ministry of Economic Development, New Zealand, *SMEs in New Zealand: Structure and Dynamics*, MED, Wellington, 2005, p. 4.
14. Department of Trade and Industry, *see* note 4.
15. Government of the United Kingdom, *see* note 3.
16. G. Meredith, *see* note 5.
17. I. Bickerdyke, R. Lattimore & A. Madge, *Business Failure and Change: An Australian Perspective*, Productivity Commission, Canberra, 2000.
18. Department of Employment, Workplace Relations and Small Business, *A Portrait of Australian Business: Results of the 1996 Business Longitudinal Survey*, AGPS, Canberra, 1998, p. 38.
19. K. Goh & T.W. Chian, Profile of home offices in Singapore, Statistics Singapore Newsletter, March 2004 http://www.singstat.gov.sg.
20. Australian Bureau of Statistics, Counts of *Australian Business Operators*, Cat. no. 8175.0, ABS, Canberra, 2008; Department of Industry, Science and Tourism, *The 1995 Business Longitudinal Survey*, AGPS, Canberra, 1997.
21. ibid.
22. D.J. Storey, *Understanding the Small Business Sector*, Routledge, London, 1994.
23. S. Carter, 'Small business marketing', in M. Warner (ed.), *International Encyclopedia of Business and Management*, Routledge, London, 1996, pp. 140–56.
24. I. Bickerdyke, R. Lattimore & A. Madge, *see* note 18.
25. H. Ahmad & P.S. Seet 'Dissecting behaviours associated with business failure: A qualitative study of SME owners in Malaysia and Australia', *Asian Social Science*, vol. 5, no. 9, September 2009, pp. 98–104; S. Cromie, 'The problems experienced by young firms', *International Small Business Journal*, vol. 9, no. 3, 1991, pp. 43–61; A. Rashid & M. Zabid, pp. 290–8, and C.W.L. Soh-Wee, pp. 345–66, in Low Aik Meng and Tan Wee Liang (eds), *Entrepreneurs, Entrepreneurship and Enterprising Culture*, Addison-Wesley, Singapore, 1996; S.T. Fock & D.G. G, 'Enterprise 50: Successful growing enterprises of Singapore: an exploratory study of success factors', *International Journal of Entrepreneurship and Innovation Management*, vol. 1, no. 3–4, 2001, pp. 299–316; B.C. Ghosh, T.W. Liang, T.T. Meng & B. Chan 'The key success factors, distinctive capabilities, and strategic thrusts of top SMEs in Singapore', *Journal of Business Research* vol. 51, no. 3, March 2001, pp. 209–21.
26. A. Rashid & M. Zabid, 'Management practices, motivations and problems of successful women entrepreneurs in Malaysia', in Low Aik Meng & Tan Wee Liang (eds), *Entrepreneurs, Entrepreneurship and Enterprising Culture*, Addison-Wesley Publishing, Singapore, 1996, pp. 290–8.
27. C.W.L. Soh-Wee, 'Start-up and early business development challenges confronting young entrepreneurs in Singapore', in Low Aik Meng and Tan Wee Liang (eds), *Entrepreneurs, Entrepreneurship and Enterprising Culture*, Addison-Wesley Publishing, Singapore, 1996, pp. 345–66.
28. J.C. Collins & C.I. William, *Managing the Small to Mid-Sized Company — Concepts and Costs*, Irwin, Chicago, 1995.
29. L.G. Theng & J.L.W. Boon, 'An exploratory study of factors affecting the failure of local small and medium enterprises', *Asia Pacific Journal of Management*, vol. 13, no. 2, October, 1996, pp. 47–61.
30. J. Watson & J. Everett, 'Defining small business failure', *International Small Business Journal*, vol. 11, no. 3, 1993, pp. 35–48.
31. Australian Bureau of Statistics, *Business Exits in Australia*, cat. no. 8144.0, ABS, Canberra, 1997.

32. Australian Bureau of Statistics, *Experimental Estimates, Entries and Exits of Business Entities, Australia*, Cat. no. 8160.0.55.001, ABS, Canberra, 2005, p. 5.

33. Australian Bureau of Statistics, *Counts of Australian Businesses, including Entries and Exits*, Cat. no.8165.0, ABS, Canberra, 2007, pp. 67.

34. Australian Bureau of Statistics, *Counts of Australian Businesses, Including Entries And Exits*, Cat. no. 8165.0, ABS, Canberra, 2007, pp. 67.

35. Statistics New Zealand, NZ Business Demography Statistics: February 2008, www.stats.govt.nz, 2008, p. 10.

36. Statistics Singapore, 'Survival rates of enterprises', *Statistics Singapore Newsletter*, September 2003, p. 17.

37. B. Headd, 'Redefining business success: Distinguishing between closure and failure', *Small Business Economics*, vol. 21, No. 1, August, 2003, pp. 51–61.

38. J.H. Kelmar, 'Measurement of success and failure in small business: A two-factor approach', *Journal of Enterprising Culture*, vol. 1, no. 3, 1994, pp. 421–36.

39. Australian Bureau of Statistics, *Characteristics of Small Business, Australia*, ABS, Canberra, 2002.

40. Organisation for Economic Co-operation and Development (OECD) *Measuring Entrepreneurship: A Digest of Indicators* Paris: OECD Statistics Directorate, 2008.

41. M. Schaper, L.P. Dana, R.B. Anderson & P. Moroz 'Distribution of firms by size: Observations and evidence from selected countries', *International Journal of Entrepreneurship and Innovation Management* (in press), 2009.

42. M. Schaper, 'Distribution patterns of small firms in developed economies: Is there an emergent global pattern?', *International Journal of Entrepreneurship and Small Business*, vol. 3, no. 2, 2006, pp. 183–9.

43. Only firms considered to be actively trading, collecting the Australian Goods and Services Tax (GST) and with an Australian Business Number (ABN) are reported in this count, whereas the previous ABS publication cited in the second edition of this book (*ABS Business Register: Counts of Businesses*, Cat. no. 8161.0.55.001, ABS, Canberra, 2005, p. 17) did not have such restrictions and significantly overstated the number of active businesses in existence.

44. Australian Bureau of Statistics, *Counts of Australian Businesses, including Entries and Exits*, Cat. no. 8165.0, ABS, Canberra, 2007, p. 10.

45. Ministry of Economic Development, New Zealand, *SMEs in New Zealand: Structure and Dynamics 2008*, MED, Wellington, 2008, pp. 7–10.

46. Trade and Industry Department, Hong Kong Special Administrative Region, *SMEs in HK*, 2009, www.success.tid.gov.hk.

47. T. Fu-Lai Yu, *Entrepreneurship and Economic Development in Hong Kong*, Routledge, London, 1997.

48. Trade and Industry Department, Hong Kong Special Administrative Region, loc. cit.

49. Singapore Department of Statistics (Statistics Singapore), *Profile of Enterprirses in Singapore*, 2009 http://www.singstat.gov.sg, (accessed 24 September 2009); Singapore Standards, Productivity and Innovation Board (SPRING), 'SPRING's Performance Indicators', 2009, www.spring.gov.sg.

50. Bank Negara Malaysia, *Small and Medium Enterprises (SME) Annual Report 2005*, Kuala Lumpur, Bank Negara Malaysia, 2006, p. 21.

51. Bank Negara Malaysia *Small and Medium Enterprise (SME) Annual Report 2007*, Kuala Lumpur, Bank Negara Malaysia, 2008, p. 34.

52. China Association of Small and Medium Enterprises, www.ca-sme.org; China Daily, *China Launches Association For SMEs*, 12 December 2006, www.chinadaily.com.cn.

53. Embassy of the United States in China, *China's Small And Medium Enterprises: Room To Grow With WTO*, 2002, www.usembassy-china.org.cn.

54. Ministry of Micro, Small and Medium Enterprises, Government of India (2009), About Us, http://msme.gov.in.

55. D.H. Holt (1992), *Entrepreneurship: New Venture Creation*, Prentice Hall, Englewood Cliffs, NJ, p. 11.

PART 2

Getting into business

CHAPTER 5

Options for going into business

Learning objectives

After reading this chapter, you should be able to:

- explain the three major issues that all prospective entrepreneurs and small business owners must consider before going into business
- compare and contrast the advantages and disadvantages of starting a new business
- outline the factors to take into account when purchasing a business
- explain the different ways of calculating a business purchase price
- describe how a franchise operates
- use the '6 step' process to organise your strategy for going into business.

Entering into the business world as the owner–manager of a firm is a complicated, time-consuming activity. It is a decision that should not be taken lightly, and involves a careful weighing up of both the advantages and disadvantages of going into business.

Several different options are available to people intending to go into business. Although starting a new firm is often the most popular choice, it is not always the most appropriate one. Sometimes it may be more beneficial to purchase an existing enterprise, with its own established production processes and customer base. Another avenue to consider is that of franchising, where a person buys the right to use a pre-existing operating and selling system. In this chapter, each of these options is considered in detail, and different methods of calculating purchase prices and costs are examined. Also, the steps involved in deciding on a business start-up, a purchase or a franchise are explained. This knowledge can help prospective entrepreneurs and small business owners to make a more informed and accurate decision about the most appropriate way for them to go into business.

Issues to consider before going into business

Before examining each of the various business options available, it is best to understand the framework in which new, small entrepreneurial ventures begin. As discussed in the previous chapters, any business venture is driven by three forces: the entrepreneur or small business owner; the resources that he or she has; and the nature of the business opportunity itself (see figure 5.1). Each of these has a major bearing on the methods and strategy used when going into business.[1]

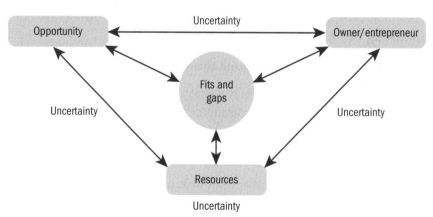

FIGURE 5.1 Three issues to consider before going into business

Source: W.D. Bygrave, 'The entrepreneurial process', in *The Portable MBA in Entrepreneurship*, 2nd edn, John Wiley & Sons, New York, 1997, p. 11.

The entrepreneur/small business owner: personal goals and abilities

Personal self-awareness is important for a successful business venture. Effective owners or entrepreneurs have a thorough and honest understanding of their own personal strengths and weaknesses and a clear idea of their own (as opposed to their prospective business's) goals before they commit themselves to the business.

The amount of prior knowledge and enthusiasm they have for the industry sector they wish to work in is important. Most business owners find that their chances of success are greater if they are involved in an industry in which they already have some experience and in which they enjoy working.

Business owners should also have a clear idea about why they are going into business and what they hope to achieve. Such personal goals may include:

- a certain level of personal income each year ('to make $X per year')
- a specified (percentage) return on investment for funds invested in the project
- personal freedom ('being my own boss')
- providing job opportunities for other family members
- growing the business into a larger enterprise within a certain time period.

The prospective business owner's personal risk profile also needs to be considered. No business is ever guaranteed. There will always be uncertainty about whether a firm will succeed. Going into business inevitably involves risking a certain amount of one's own money, credibility, time, enthusiasm and, sometimes, health and wellbeing. Just how much risk a person is willing to take on is an important determinant in assessing business options.

Individual business owners, like other members of the community, can usually be classified into one of at least three different categories of risk-related behaviour. *Risk-averse people* are usually unwilling to bet much, if anything, on their new venture. For these people, business operations with a proven track record (such as a franchise or well-established existing business) are a preferred option. *Moderate risk takers* will usually be willing to invest up to, but not beyond, a predetermined amount of resources. They will usually choose to buy an established firm or a new business that has been soundly researched and whose viability is reasonably self-evident. *High risk takers*, who often put up most of their own personal resources, are usually people who start up new businesses, especially in 'cutting-edge' and capital-intensive markets, where the chances of failure are much higher, although the potential return on investment is also more lucrative.

Resource availability

Access to resources can be a key determinant of the business option chosen. Business ventures require the owner/entrepreneur to have or obtain numerous resources.

The most obvious of these resources is finance. Prospective small business owners or entrepreneurs who do not have a great deal of money will be limited in their choices, and they will usually opt for a new business in a field where both **entry costs** (the price involved in starting the firm) and **exit costs** (the price involved in liquidating the enterprise if it does not prove to be viable) are low. For example, service-sector businesses generally have low entry and exit costs, whereas the reverse is true for manufacturing and retail firms.

Almost as important is a supply of personnel for the venture. A committed team of employees can allow a business project to be much larger in scale and

Entry costs *The price of starting up or buying a business enterprise.*

Exit costs *The price involved in liquidating or closing a business enterprise.*

ambition than a solo venture; on the other hand, difficulties in employing appropriately trained staff can cripple otherwise viable projects.

Another important resource is time. Some business ideas can take a long time to reach fruition, and this may not always coincide with the desires of the entrepreneur. Some people are prepared to spend a lengthy period of time getting their idea right, whereas others may have a more pressing need or desire to realise an immediate financial return on their investments. Starting a new business may prove to be a useful option in the former case, but not in the latter.

The opportunity

Different business opportunities also impose implicit constraints on the type of business chosen. If a person wants to run a McDonald's store, for example, then there is only one option: enter into a franchise arrangement with the parent company. Alternatively, if an entrepreneur has a unique product idea that has not been previously tested in the market, then a start-up operation is probably most appropriate, since it will allow the owner–manager to structure the venture in a way that best suits the unique circumstances.

Starting a new business

Once personal goals have been set, available resources determined and the business opportunities examined, the choice of business option can be made. The first option that usually springs to mind for most budding small business owners or entrepreneurs is starting their own business operation as a totally new venture.

The advantages of starting a new business

Sometimes intending business operators find that they have to start their own enterprise simply because there is no existing business available for purchase. Alternatively, they may find that the only firms available for sale on the open market are too expensive, or the asking price is, in some other way, considered unreasonable. However, starting a new business venture does provide a number of opportunities that other forms of business management do not offer; these are outlined as follows.

Ability to determine business direction

Ideally, a new business start-up allows the owner of the venture to exert near-total control over the enterprise — depending on the ownership structure. The products to be sold, the target customer base, the organisational culture and management structures of the enterprise, and the financial strategy of the business can all be determined by the entrepreneur, since he or she will be personally responsible for building each of these elements. In contrast, the purchase of an existing business usually means that the new owner has to assume responsibility for many unfamiliar operating procedures that may take some time to change, if they can be altered at all.

Flexibility

Because a new business is a 'blank slate' at its inception, it can be moulded and shaped to fit the needs of both the owner and the market. In contrast, an existing business has established systems and procedures, a strong organisational culture driven by the current staff, and defined ways of operating, all of which preclude rapid change. From this perspective, a new business is seen to be more flexible and to have a greater capacity to innovate than its established counterpart. In addition, the start-up business owner is able to build up the project slowly over time, and get it right as it progresses.

Cost minimisation

Properly handled, many new small businesses (especially micro-enterprises) can start trading with a lower cost base than established businesses, since they do not have the ongoing costs of their established competitors or any of the inefficiencies that may have built up over time. While a new business can sometimes be successfully commenced with lower fixed costs, purchasing an existing business may result in the new owner paying for several additional unwanted items, such as the purchase of goodwill, existing assets or stock on hand, regardless of whether the new owner wishes to use them or not.

Lifestyle goals

A new business allows the owner to develop a particular desired lifestyle. For example, many people seek self-employment because they no longer wish to have a 'boss' to whom they are answerable. For others, a new business may bring with it the opportunity to work more convenient hours, to spend more time with friends and members of their family, to work from home, to build an asset they can pass on to their children, or to avoid a stressful environment in their current workplace.

What would you do?

Start-up team or solo franchisee?

Jacob is 28 years old and is currently at university in his final year of a business degree, majoring in marketing and IT. He has worked in a variety of jobs, including working for a large firm and in a franchised operation, and has spent time overseas. He is engaged and his fiancé is pregnant with their first child. They have recently purchased their first house. You are a business start-up consultant and Jacob has come to you for guidance, as he is contemplating working for himself after he completes his degree.

Jacob tells you that he is interested in two prospective business opportunities. The first involves purchasing the franchise license for a home maintenance business that has been operating in his local area for the past five years. Jacob knows the current owner (48-year-old Tom), as Jacob has worked for him as a summer job. Jacob is interested in this opportunity because Tom has told him that he never invested as much time and money in the franchise as he might have.

The second opportunity Jacob tells you about involves him starting up a new business with two fellow university students. Matt and Lisa have invited Jacob to be part of their start-up team for a street clothing business. They have already attracted an angel investor, and want to launch both a retail and online store.

Jacob has come to you for advice prior to assessing the financial dimensions of each opportunity. He wants to primarily be guided by your assessment of which opportunity best fits his skills and background, as well as his current personal circumstances.

Questions

1. **What advice will you give Jacob? Explain your reasons.**
2. **Do a SWOT (strengths, weaknesses, opportunities and threats) analysis of the option you have advised Jacob to take.**

The disadvantages of starting a new business

Despite the benefits outlined above, starting a new business can be very risky. There are several limitations and drawbacks that can potentially destroy or weaken the viability of a new business venture.

Raising capital

Because a new business does not have any established financial history or resources to draw on, financing the business venture can be difficult. Many financial institutions are reluctant to extend credit to unknown and unproven enterprises, and the business owners may find that they have to provide much, if not all, of the initial capital themselves. If the intending business owner does not have the necessary access to finance, the business may quickly fail from a lack of sufficient start-up funds or working capital.

Lack of an established customer base

By definition, the formation of a new business means that the entity does not yet have any customers of its own. Although the owner may be in a position to attract customers through personal networks and previous industry experience, there are rarely enough to immediately create a viable business. Instead, the business owner will need to invest a considerable amount of time, energy and money in researching and marketing to a defined target market base.

Cash flow shortages

Lack of capital and a shortage of customers may mean that the business's cash flow will be under severe stress during the early days of its existence. This cash flow shortage is common in new businesses, and may exist for a few months or even several years. When cash flow is tight, a sudden unexpected change in the business environment (such as an interest rate increase, a currency devaluation or additional unplanned expenses) may mean that the business can no longer pay its bills on time.

Learning curve expenses

Because a new enterprise is one in which nobody has previously done the work required, there will be a considerable number of one-off events where the owner will have to invest time, effort and money to get the business working effectively (frequently referred to as a *learning curve*). For example, the operator of a new business must develop a name and brand, decide on suitable premises, recruit and train staff, devise an initial marketing campaign and make the firm known in the marketplace. Much of this will not result in the direct generation of customer sales, but it is still necessary. However, because this is a new activity, it is likely to take far longer than it would in an established business.

Costs of a start-up venture

Regardless of the type of business venture being explored, some costs are common to all new enterprises. Any starting business will need to meet the following costs:

- licences and permits required to operate the business
- working capital
- telecommunications and information technology equipment
- operating plant and equipment
- staff recruitment expenses
- insurance
- raw materials (or trading stock)
- rental of premises (unless working from the owner's home)
- office supplies and equipment.

These are just the most basic of all expenses, but they will still typically add up to a significant amount of money for even the simplest and most budget-conscious enterprise.

Purchasing an existing business

Sometimes commercial goals and ambitions are best fulfilled by the acquisition of a firm that is already operating — sometimes also referred to as a *going concern*.

The main advantage of purchasing an existing business is that it allows a proprietor to begin trading immediately, since an established business operation, cash flow, staff, product range and customer base already exist. It is also easier to arrange finance for the venture, and the established track record of the firm allows the prospective owner to make a more objective evaluation of likely future performance than would be the case if starting a new enterprise. In many respects, the advantages of buying an existing firm are the mirror opposite of the disadvantages of starting a new firm, as mentioned above.

Potential businesses can be found in a variety of ways. They may be advertised for sale by a business broker (an agent who specialises in listing and selling businesses, and who may often focus on one or two particular industries); listed by the current owner in a newspaper, trade publication, magazine or online advertisement; sold through accountancy firms; or, in the case of extremely troubled businesses, disposed of via insolvency or bankruptcy trustees. Another option is to approach existing owners to see if they are willing to sell. This was the case with Carolyn Cresswell, whose story appears in the following Entrepreneur profile.

Although accurate market research and an honest appraisal of business opportunities are critical to the launch of a brand-new firm, the issues involved in the purchase of a going trading concern are more complex. In addition to such market analysis, the prospective purchaser must also be able to correctly calculate a purchase price, and know the appropriate issues to investigate before making an offer.

Carolyn Creswell, Carman's Fine Foods

In 1992, at the age of eighteen, Carolyn Creswell was studying for her Bachelor of Arts degree while also working one day a week in a bakery making muesli. Nine months after starting work, she was told that the business was to be put up for sale and she would lose her job. So, using her savings, she bought it herself.

'It was a very small, very basic business at the time. There was no registered business, no bank account, about 80 clients, and just a few people working to a recipe, in space sub-let from a Melbourne baker.'

Rather than lose her job, Carolyn decided to confront the challenge head on. Together with a workmate, they bought the tiny business for A$1000 each.

Carman's (a synthesis of the two purchasers' names) was born. In 1994, Carolyn bought out her partner, and today still directly manages the firm herself. The product range now includes muesli, muesli bars, porridge, biscuits and organic honey, which are distributed to thousands of outlets Australia-wide. These outlets include major Australian supermarket chains Coles and Woolworths, as well as Myer, David Jones and numerous health stores. Her products are now exported to 26 countries. For example, they are on the shelves of Sainsburys in the United Kingdom and Wholefoods Market in the US. In 2009 Carolyn was one of the first small businesses to secure its products in the Melbourne outlet of American wholesale warehouse Costco.

Turnover in the first year was A$80 000, but has now grown a hundredfold. In 2005 Carolyn's work was recognised when her firm was listed on the prestigious *BRW* Fast 100 — a list of the nation's 100 fastest growing firms — and in 2007 she won the Ernst and Young Entrepreneur of the Year award.

'Lots of people think about starting up a business but get scared. Don't. Just give it a go. You don't need a huge amount of money or a fancy setup. You can work from your bedroom. It doesn't have to be a big deal. But if you want it, then you've got to commit and start somewhere.'

The initial investment of A$1000, along with the bare basics provided by the existing business concept, have enabled Carolyn to create a highly successful business.

For more information, see www.carmansfinefoods.com.au.

Source: Based on an interview with Carolyn Cresswell.

Establishing a purchase price

How much is a business worth? As more than one economist has noted, an item is worth whatever someone is prepared to pay for it. Such a refrain may be of little consolation to a buyer who is trying to negotiate a complex deal, and who needs to have some realistic understanding of what constitutes a 'fair' price.[2]

The methods for establishing a reasonable purchase price tend to fluctuate, and can be prone to trends and fads among advisers as to what is the 'best' method. The definition of what constitutes a best price also depends on whether one is a purchaser (to whom a lower price is preferable) or a vendor (to whom the highest possible selling price is critical). Finally, different industries also tend to favour different valuation methods, which can make the task even more complicated.

Generally speaking, there are several different ways in which the price of an existing business can be set. Purchase prices can be broken down into three broad categories — market-based valuations, asset-based valuations and earnings-based valuations.[3]

Market-based valuations

In an efficient and open marketplace, the price of a business should be easily determined by reference to previous sales. If a similar business has been sold in the past, then that price can be seen as an accurate reflection of what the current business is worth. According to this school of thought, the open marketplace is the best judge of a firm's worth.

There are two main types of market-based valuation:

- *The going market rate method.* As its name suggests, this is simply the 'current market' price for a particular type of firm. It is usually established by reference to recent selling prices for other firms of a similar size and industry type. For example, if a small IT firm in a particular city was recently sold for A$350 000, then the next such firm put up for sale will be priced at about the same amount.

Selling price = Selling price of similar firms

Although such a technique may not fully reflect a firm's own particular strengths or weaknesses, it is a useful starting point in working out a final price. Current market rates can often be determined by studying similar businesses advertised for sale online, in newspapers or via a business broker.

- *Revenue multiplier method.* A slightly more sophisticated approach is to adopt one of a number of 'rules of thumb' (informal guidelines) on pricing. The most common of these is the use of a revenue multiplier. This technique is often used in the purchase of professional practices, such as businesses run by doctors, dentists and accountants. In most such industries there is a common 'industry multiplier' that is used to estimate the most likely purchase price of the practice. The selling price is established by multiplying the annual turnover of the business by this multiplier.

Selling price = Turnover × Standard industry multiplier

For example, an accountancy practice may use an established industry multiplier of 0.7 or 1.0. If the annual turnover of the firm is A$225 000 and the multiplier applied is 0.7, then the asking price would be A$157 500. Whether one uses the going market rate or the revenue multiplier method, such approaches avoid the need to undertake detailed calculations or complex financial analysis. The techniques are simple and easy to understand, especially for entrepreneurs and small business owners who are not familiar with valuation methodologies. However, such methods have a number of serious weaknesses. The price reached is largely dependent on broader sales trends, and may not fully recognise the special circumstances of the individual business being considered. If prices in the market as a whole become overinflated, then the purchaser will pay more for the business than it would otherwise be worth. Moreover, these methods do not take into account the future earnings potential of the business or the value of the assets in hand. Finally, it can often be difficult to collect accurate information about market prices, since few small businesses are sold by public tender or share floats, or in other public forums.

Asset-based valuations

An alternative to relying on market forces is to set a price after examining the assets and liabilities of the business. This involves examining present and historical data about the business, which is usually found among the financial records ('books') in the balance sheet.

- *Book value.* In this process, the asking price is set by first calculating the worth of all the firm's assets. These may be tangible items, such as stock on hand, equipment, property, vehicles, furniture and fittings and intangible commodities, such as intellectual property rights and goodwill. The liabilities of the business are then subtracted to produce a final value.

Selling price = Tangible assets + Intangible assets − Liabilities

- *Adjusted book (net asset) value.* In practice, the simple book value method is really only the starting point in price calculations. Relying on the books of accounts means that only historical information is referred to, rather than contemporary information. For example, a building may be shown on the balance sheet at the price paid for it several years ago (less depreciation), but it may actually be worth much more today because of a general increase in property asset prices. To overcome this, valuers often adjust the initial book value in a number of ways. The assets may be revalued to reflect their current worth, as may the liabilities. This is a somewhat subjective measure, which can vary from one valuer to another.

Goodwill *An intangible commodity; the extra value ascribed to a business, piece of intellectual property, brand name, or other business-related activity.*

Similarly, the question of determining exactly what constitutes **goodwill** is extremely problematic. At its simplest, goodwill is simply the extra value a purchaser is prepared to pay because of the firm's unique position. This may be something as simple as a track record of consistent net profits, or it may be something less easily measured but just as important to its success, such as a highly favourable location, a well-known brand name, a good reputation in the local community or a loyal customer base. In many cases, one or two years' net profits may be used as a proxy measure for the sum of a firm's goodwill.

- *Liquidation value.* Sometimes a prospective purchaser of a business may plan to break up and sell the various assets of the firm rather than continue to operate it as a going concern. During the 2000s, for example, a number of entrepreneurs made considerable profits by purchasing large corporations and then selling off their assets. When this is a possibility, the book value may have to be adjusted to see what the business is worth when it is liquidated. To do so, the individual assets of the business are valued at the price they are likely to receive if sold quickly. In many respects, a liquidation price represents a floor or bottom price below which the vendor will not go, since he or she could sell the assets as stand-alone items for the same amount.[4]

- *Replacement value.* If a liquidation price represents the lowest price a vendor will accept, then the replacement book value often equals the highest price purchasers will usually want to offer. In this exercise, the cost of replacing all the firm's tangible assets (at current market costs) is calculated. This is the price an entrepreneur or small business owner would have to pay if starting up a similar business rather than buying the current one. Unless there are substantial intangible assets, such as goodwill, this is the maximum price worth paying for the business.

Earnings-based (cash flow) valuations

In contrast to the historical or present-day focus of book valuations, some purchasers are more concerned about the potential of the business they want to buy. From this perspective, future earning power and the ability to produce cash income (which can, in turn, be used to provide working capital, grow the business, reduce debt and reward the owner) are most important.

- *Return on investment.* The capitalised value method — commonly referred to as the return on investment (ROI) technique — is one of the most widely accepted and used valuation tools.[5] It is based on the assumption that the risk and return of a business should be reflected in its selling price. It works on a formula that includes the estimated future profit:

$$\text{Selling Price} = \frac{\text{Net annual profit}}{\text{ROI}}$$

Different industries have different levels of risk, and therefore differing ROI. As in all investment decisions, a higher level of risk is often associated with a higher level of return. In other words, if investors in a business are prepared to be exposed to a high chance that the business will fail and their money will be lost, then they are entitled to a higher ROI. However, because they are riskier enterprises, the selling price of such firms is likely to be low. Future income cannot be guaranteed to the purchaser.

- *Discounted cash flows.* A common but more complex analytical tool is the use of discounted cash flow (DCF) models. Originally devised for use in the assessment of capital budgets, this model discounts the future cash income generated by the business to its current value. The fundamental principle governing this procedure is the assumption that the valuation of the business is equal to the present value of the sum of its estimated future cash flows. In other words, if a business is expected to generate a healthy cash flow for the next 10 years, how much is that prospective cash flow worth in today's dollars?

This future cash stream usually includes both annual cash flows and the terminal value expected when the business is sold. Such a valuation approach gives a dynamic rather than a static perspective of the firm, since the selling price is based on future cash-creating activities.

The estimated value of the firm today, employing the discounted cash flow technique, can be estimated using the following formula:

$$\text{Value} = \sum_{t=1}^{n} \frac{\text{CF}_t}{(1+r)^t} + \frac{\text{Terminal value}}{(1+r)^n}$$

CF_t = expected cash flow in period t
r = required rate of return, or discount rate, or opportunity rate
n = number of periods considered in the analysis

Terminal value = value of the business after the forecast period (at the end of time period *n*). The terminal value is calculated using the expected liquidation value of the business at the end of the time frame under consideration.

This is a more complex analytical tool, and its effectiveness depends on whether realistic assumptions, such as the required rate of return, are used.

Choosing between valuation methods

In reality, the above valuation methods rarely provide a complete guide to a final purchase price. Indeed, the techniques discussed above are only some of the more common ones used. There is a wide variety of methods that can be used, and many different ways they are calculated and names they are known by.

For these reasons, the approaches described are perhaps best treated as guidelines that can be used to establish a negotiating stance. In theory, if used effectively, the various methods should all produce broadly similar valuations.[6] However, this is rarely the case in practice.

Most entrepreneurs and small business owners tend to place greater reliance on some methods than on others. The arguments that 'cash is king' and that a solid predictable stream of income is central to future success lead some people to favour cash flow (earnings) valuations. However, due to the relative complexity of such calculations and the difficulty of predicting future earnings, some purchasers prefer to use an asset-based method. This has the advantage of being easier to calculate and understand. Market-based prices are the easiest of all for small business owners to use but, since few small firms are publicly traded, information on the purchase price of other similar businesses is usually difficult to obtain.[7]

Questions to ask

Ill-will *Negative perceptions or attitudes towards a firm; an intangible commodity that detracts from the overall value of a business.*

Researching information about an existing business for sale usually requires at least as much, if not more, effort than starting up a firm. For example, the purchase will often entail assuming responsibility for debts or liabilities incurred by the previous managers. These may include unpaid tax bills, accrued staff leave entitlements, legal actions outstanding against the firm, or creditors whose accounts are due. It is important to note that in many jurisdictions, such liabilities continue to rest with the business itself, regardless of the change of ownership. These liabilities may not be apparent unless a thorough examination of the business's accounts and records is made before purchase. Less obvious, but still significant, are other potential liabilities, such as undesirable or poorly trained staff, products with a poor reputation in the marketplace, or a large base of unsatisfied previous customers — all this comprises **ill-will**. In addition to current or potential liabilities, there is always the risk that a dishonest or negligent vendor has misled the purchaser.

Due diligence *A process of detailed scrutiny aimed at obtaining all the information needed to comprehensively evaluate a business for purchase, and to establish whether the projected business is a worthwhile investment.*

Overcoming this requires the purchaser and advisers to conduct a **due diligence** study. Due diligence is the detailed scrutiny of a business in order to obtain all the information needed to comprehensively evaluate it, and determine whether it is a worthwhile investment. Such an investigation is best performed by a team assembled by the prospective purchaser, and should include accountants, legal advisers, a business broker and specialist consultants. Common questions that should be asked include:

- Why is the vendor selling?
- Will existing staff remain if the business is sold?
- What current liabilities does the business have?
- Are there any outstanding taxation debts?
- Is there any outstanding litigation against the firm?
- Can all licences and permits to operate be transferred to the new owner?
- How accurate and honest are the financial accounts that have been provided?
- What is the level of accrued staff leave that will have to be paid?
- What is the likely future state of the industry — is demand increasing or decreasing?
- Is the lease on the premises secure? Is it transferable to a new business purchaser? How long does the existing lease run?
- Will suppliers continue to provide stock, and at the same price as they have previously?
- What is the condition of the physical assets? Will any need to be replaced in the near future?
- Will customers remain loyal to this business once the current proprietor has departed?

Other issues

When negotiating the purchase of a business, it makes good sense to include a **restraint of trade clause** in the final contract of sale. This prohibits the vendor from establishing a rival business within a reasonable distance of the premises. Although such clauses are often limited by the courts, they do prevent the vendor from selling a firm and then using the proceeds to become a competitor.

In addition to the purchase price, buyers should also be aware that they will face ancillary costs. These can include the accountant's fees, for reviewing the books of the business; legal fees, for the contract of sale; valuation costs; government taxes, such as stamp duty, on the sale transfer and contract registration; and bank fees, when loans are established to pay for the business.

Entering a franchise system

Franchising has become an increasingly popular form of business system over the last 30 years.[8] Although franchising has been in existence for well over a century, it is still relatively new in many industries. It provides another avenue through which people can begin their own business, and many franchises now exist in such diverse fields as petrol retailing, motor vehicle distribution, real estate sales, personal services, professional practices, fast food and retail sales.

At its simplest, a **franchise** is an arrangement whereby the originator of a business product or operating system (commonly referred to as the **franchisor**) gives a prospective small business owner (the **franchisee**) the right to sell these goods and/or to use the business operations system on the franchisor's behalf. A 2008 survey of franchising in Australia reported that there were in excess of

Restraint of trade clause *A contractual restriction on the right of a business vendor to operate a similar business in rivalry with the new purchaser of the firm.*

Franchise *An arrangement whereby the originator of a business product or operating system permits another business owner to sell the goods and/ or to use the business operating system on the originator's behalf.*

Franchisor *A business or individual who owns the rights to a particular business franchise system or product.*

Franchisee *The business/person given contractual permission by the original owner of a system or product to operate a business franchise system or sell a product.*

1100 franchise systems operating, and that there had been much growth in the number of franchise systems between 2006 and mid 2008. The sector generated sales turnover of A\$130 billion and employed 413 000 people. Franchises represented 3.7% of all small and medium-sized enterprises.[9] Data collected in 2006 from national franchise associations around the world found that New Zealand had 350 franchise systems; China had 2100; Hong Kong had 74; India had 850; and Singapore had 380.[10]

Product franchise *A franchise to sell a particular product or service.*

There are two basic types of franchise. A **product franchise** gives a small business operator the right to sell a particular commodity or set of goods. In this arrangement, the franchisee is used as a distribution mechanism for a good or service, and has a large measure of independence as to how the business will be set up and operated. The franchisor's role is limited to ensuring that sufficient stock is made available, and that the franchisee is selling the product at a satisfactory price and providing customers with suitable after-sales service and support. One of the first such franchises was created to distribute and sell sewing machines; today, many other individual products (including clothing, vehicles and household goods) are sold via this system.

Business system franchise *An arrangement whereby the franchisor supplies the product, and gives comprehensive guidelines on how the business is to be run.*

In contrast, a **business system franchise** is a more detailed agreement between the two parties. In this arrangement, the franchisor not only supplies the product but also gives comprehensive guidelines on how the business is to be run. The franchisee is expected to follow a predetermined set of rules about all aspects of managing and operating the business. This will usually include pricing; production processes; marketing; staff recruitment, remuneration, training and evaluation; product offerings and promotional methods; recordkeeping; operating hours; use of different suppliers; store layout and fittings and so on. A well-known example of a business system franchise is that operated by fast-food giant McDonald's. The store proprietors (franchisees) are usually expected to follow a comprehensive set of instruction manuals and operating systems written by the franchisor, and they are usually given detailed training in these before starting their own restaurant.

The main benefit of the system franchise is that all aspects of organising and operating the business have already been investigated, pre-tested and successfully implemented by the franchisor, and the viability of the franchise has also usually been assessed in advance. There is little, if any, extra management work or market research that the franchisee has to do, apart from going through the actual process of setting up and then overseeing the particular store. In many ways this type of franchise represents a compromise between the previous two business options: although franchisees are still technically starting a new firm, they are also buying in a large body of existing knowledge.

Advantages and disadvantages of franchising

There are many benefits to be gained from entering a franchise arrangement, particularly if it is a business system format. The new business owner is spared the task of developing an operating system, which usually represents a large amount of time and energy in most new small firms. There is less 'learning by mistakes', which can often cause many businesses to falter and fail. As a result, most franchises have a lower failure rate than new independent small businesses.

Customers are usually attracted by the presence of an established product or brand name, which is backed up by the franchisor's ongoing marketing efforts. Most franchisors provide continuing training for franchisees, as well as market research into emerging trends and purchasing behaviour. The cost of raw materials and supplies is often lower, as the franchisor can use the combined power of many franchisees to negotiate discounts. All these advantages mean that raising capital can also be easier, since financial institutions are often more willing to lend money to buy a franchise than they are to start a new, unknown enterprise.

However, access to these systems does not come cheaply. The purchase price for entering into a business system franchise is often quite high, and may be beyond the reach of many small-scale entrepreneurs. In addition to this initial outlay, franchisees are usually expected to pay a proportion of their profits to the franchisor, and may also be required to pay a separate marketing levy.

There are other limitations and drawbacks. Many franchises are sold on a geographical basis. Franchisees are often restricted to serving a set market, and may not expand beyond a predetermined boundary. The opportunities for individual store owners to innovate and change the pre-set rules are limited, since the core appeal of many franchises is their uniformity. If the parent company (franchisor) fails or is poorly run, then the dependent franchisees may also be at risk of collapsing.

It is also important to bear in mind that a franchise is essentially a contractual arrangement, and therefore has a limited lifespan. At the end of a set period, typically from five to seven years, the franchisee will have to negotiate a new contract with the parent franchisor; renewal of the contract is not always guaranteed.

Franchises can be an attractive option to many intending small business owners, especially those who are risk-averse or who have only limited experience in managing their own enterprise. However, franchises are often not suitable for entrepreneurial personalities who have their own ideas about what products to offer and how to manage a firm, and who wish to aggressively increase their market share. More information about franchises can be obtained from the sources listed in table 5.1.

TABLE 5.1 Franchise organisations

Country	Entity
Australia	Franchise Council of Australia, www.franchise.org.au
New Zealand	Franchise Association of New Zealand, www.franchiseassociation.org.nz
Hong Kong	Hong Kong Franchise Association, www.franchise.org.hk
Malaysia	Malaysian Franchise Association, www.mfa.org.my
Singapore	Franchising and Licensing Association (Singapore), www.flasingapore.org
China	China Chain Store & Franchise Association, www.chinaretail.org
India	The Franchising Association of India, www.fai.co.in

Comparison of options

As the preceding discussion and table 5.2 show, there is rarely a clear best choice among the three different types of business avenue. Each of the three forms of market entry (start-up, purchase or franchise) has its own respective advantages and disadvantages.

TABLE 5.2 Differences between businesses

Factor	Start-up	Purchase	Franchise
Market/customer base	Unknown	Defined	Predetermined
Advertising and pricing strategy	Unknown	Defined	Predetermined
Future growth possibilities	Unlimited	Unlimited	Restricted
Staffing flexibility	High	Low	Moderate
Flexibility in managerial decision making	High	Moderate	Low
Risk of failure	High	Moderate	Low
Level of initial financial outlay	At owner's discretion	Substantial	Substantial
Subsequent financial commitments	Nil	Nil	Yes (ongoing levies and royalties)
Goodwill costs	No	Yes	Yes
Ability to raise external funds	Poor	Moderate	Moderate

There is rarely, if ever, a best option that will suit the needs of all entrepreneurs or small business owners. Determining the most suitable mechanism for an entrepreneur or small business owner will usually involve careful consideration of personal goals and financial and other resources, and a clear understanding of the nature of the business opportunity that the prospective owner or entrepreneur wishes to exploit.

Procedural steps when starting a business venture

Once the decision to start a new business has been made, there are a number of steps that, if followed in a logical manner, provide a useful framework for evaluating and then acting on the intended project (see figure 5.2). They are designed to be conducted in a sequential 'lock-step' manner; i.e. each stage must be largely completed before moving on to the next. In this way, if the idea appears unviable at any stage, it can be aborted before too many resources have been committed to the project.

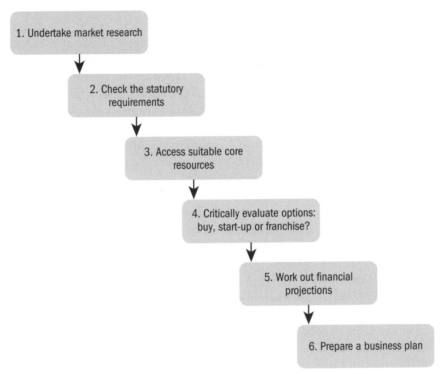

FIGURE 5.2 The process of going into business

1. Undertake market research

Before beginning it is necessary to know whether there really is a demand for the proposed service or product, and whether there is room for another business in the market. This stage involves the collection of critical strategic information, such as data on competitors, general industry trends, the intended target customer base, products, pricing, and production/delivery processes. Such information must be collected in an impartial and accurate manner; this is explained in more detail in chapter 6.

2. Check the statutory requirements

There are many laws that cover small business, and it is the responsibility of all owner–managers to comply with the relevant legislation. This can include rules regarding business names, permission to operate in a particular location, health and safety laws, taxation rules and export permits. In many nations there are several different jurisdictions that apply the laws, from national governments to state or provincial governments and local councils. Failure to obtain the necessary approvals will mean that the business cannot trade, so securing such permits is an important early step in the process.

It is also necessary at this stage to obtain an indication of the likely legal structure of the business. This can be as a sole trader, where the owner retains all rights and liabilities; a partnership, where profits and responsibilities are shared; or a company, which is a more complex legal structure that owns the business and takes responsibility for it. These structures are explained in more detail in chapter 8.

3. Access suitable core resources

Any business venture requires a suitable business address and facilities before it begins operating. For a home-based business, this may be a relatively simple issue; it may involve, for example, ensuring that there are enough desks and chairs and adequate space, or that the local authority will allow the business to operate from a residential location. In contrast, if commercial facilities are required, more attention to detail is needed. The intending owner must ensure that the premises are in a good location, suited to the needs of the business, and that a satisfactory lease contract has been negotiated.

The decision to proceed with a new venture also rests on access to suitable equipment and tools. For example, a mobile carpentry service that cannot obtain work tools and an appropriate vehicle is unlikely to succeed, as is a restaurant that does not have sufficient refrigeration or cooking facilities.

An important but often overlooked aspect of any proposed business start-up is the availability of suitable insurance. Although some insurance policies, such as workers compensation and third-party motor vehicle insurance, are compulsory in many countries and easily obtainable, other policies may be discretionary but very important. For example, an abseiling business that cannot obtain sufficient insurance to cover possible injury claims by clients may need to reconsider its plans, since failure to obtain such coverage could cause the business to fail if faced with a large negligence claim.

These operational issues are examined in more detail in chapter 12.

4. Critically evaluate options: buy, start-up or franchise?

The collection of the preliminary information outlined above should now allow the intending business operator to make a more knowledgeable and honest assessment of the chances of success. At this point, it is also preferable to compare the benefits and disadvantages of the start-up venture model with those of buying an existing business or entering into a franchise. Ideally, this analysis should be done in conjunction with an accountant or other qualified business adviser.

5. Work out financial projections

The intending business owner will need to know each of the following financial considerations before going into business:
- the amount of money required to start (for equipment purchases, advertising, wages, insurance, leases, vehicles, and/or other items)
- the amount of money that will need to be borrowed, and whether the money can be obtained (either from funds the owner already has, or through a financial institution); if funding is not available, then the project may not be viable
- the projected cash flow for the next year
- the projected profit and loss for the whole year (which will show whether the business is viable in the long-term).

If purchasing an existing firm, the prospective owner will also need to see a balance sheet. These documents are discussed in chapter 14.

6. Prepare a business plan

If the decision is made to proceed, the prospective business owner should now develop a more detailed plan for the business, covering as many different aspects of operations, marketing and finance as possible. This provides a blueprint for action and a timeline for implementation, and also helps in the raising of any necessary capital. The contents of a business plan are shown in detail in chapter 7.

SUMMARY

Going into business requires budding small business owners and entrepreneurs to understand the three factors that influence all business ventures: (1) the personal goals, desires, experience and abilities of the owner or entrepreneur; (2) the financial, human and other resources that can be used in the enterprise; and (3) the nature of the business opportunity itself.

There are three very different ways of getting into business: starting a new business, buying an existing operation or entering into a franchise arrangement. Starting a new business involves the wholesale development of a complete business idea, which must cover not only all the issues involved in starting up, but also the task of managing the business on a day-to-day basis once it begins trading. A new business provides maximum flexibility, but also heightens the risk of business failure.

Buying an established enterprise can lower the risk of business failure. It will also provide the owner with an immediate source of cash flow and customers. But this is a more expensive option, and great care must be taken when determining what constitutes a reasonable purchase price. There are three main ways of setting a price: market-based valuations, asset-based valuations, and earnings-based (cash flow) valuations.

Franchises may take the form of either product or business system arrangements. The latter is more comprehensive, and usually has a lower failure rate, but it severely limits the freedom and flexibility of the business owner and can be expensive to enter into.

There are six steps involved in the process of evaluating business options. These start with undertaking market research; understanding the legal requirements pertaining to the proposed business venture; and obtaining all necessary resources required for the business venture. After these first three steps, the intending business owner must critically evaluate which business avenue is the best option. Once this decision has been made, some preliminary financial projections can be made, and then a business plan prepared.

REVIEW QUESTIONS

1. Explain the respective advantages and disadvantages of starting and buying your own business.
2. What are the different formulas used to calculate the selling price of a business?
3. Explain the difference between a product franchise and a business system franchise.
4. What are the six steps to follow when starting a business venture?

5. What are the main differences between the three types of business start-up options?

DISCUSSION QUESTIONS

1. Why is it important to reflect on your personal business goals before choosing a business venture option?
2. If you were preparing to sell your own business, what specific management actions could you take to maximise its selling price?
3. What personality types are best suited to the start-up, purchasing and franchising options, respectively?

EXERCISES

1. A business has an annual profit of A$120 000 and a return on investment of 10 per cent. Calculate the expected purchase price of this business. What would be the impact on the purchase price of the business if instead of 10 per cent, the return on investment was 8 per cent?
2. A firm is expected to continue to generate annual cash flows of A$28 000 per annum for the next five years. In addition, the liquidation value of the firm is estimated to be A$425 000. Using a discount rate of 12 per cent, calculate the expected price of the firm, based on these future cash flows. What would be the impact on the purchase price of an increase in the discount rate to 15 per cent?
3. A business with tangible assets of A$660 000 and liabilities of A$40 000 produces a net profit of A$45 000 per annum, based on an annual turnover of A$490 000. The business has an ROI of 7 per cent and the multiplier used is 1.4. Intangible assets are valued at A$30 000. Calculate the purchase price for this business using each of these methods — book (asset) value, market value (revenue multiplier) and return on investment.

SUGGESTED READING

Australian & New Zealand Business Franchise Guide, CGB Publishing, Victoria, 2009.

Feldman, S., Sullivan, T. & Winsby, R., *What Every Business Owner Should Know About Valuing Their Business*, McGraw-Hill, New York, 2003.

Holmes, S., Hutchinson, P., Forsaith, D., Gibson, B. & McMahon, R., *Small Enterprise Finance*, John Wiley & Sons, Brisbane, 2003.

Case study

Potential in pitas

Entrepreneurs Chris Henderson and Duane Dalton are the managing directors of The Pita Pit franchise group in New Zealand. They are part of the master franchise team (including Duane's wife Tania Dalton and investor Ross Tweedie) that launched the system in New Zealand in 2007. The franchise began originally in Canada in 1995 (founded by John Sotiriadis and Nelson Lang), and has since spread globally to include over 300 restaurants. Chris Henderson was exposed to the franchise system when he was working in California, and this was the start of his journey to bring The Pita Pit home with him.

One of the success factors of The Pita Pit is its commitment to providing food options that have been developed with a view to healthy eating – as well as placing an emphasis on taste and quality. In addition to being a core value of the franchise, this approach has facilitated the creation of a brand that can capitalise on current mega-trends that centre on healthy eating choices, food quality and the origins of what we eat (i.e. sustainability issues). The fresh pita shells are filled (as you wait) with your selection of fresh vegetables and grilled (not microwaved) low-fat protein.

Currently with three stores in New Zealand (Takapuna, North Shore City; Vulcan Lane and SkyCity Metro in Auckland's central business district), Chris and Duane are committed to expanding the system. There are at least six stores scheduled to open soon, and they have recently signed the Master Franchise Rights for Australia. The first Australian store is also scheduled to open soon. The Takapuna Pita Pit has embedded itself within its local environs, and used varying types of engagement to both promote the brand and the links it has with its local community. The Pita Pit already delivers lunches to local schools, sports teams and community groups; and caters for corporate lunches.

The market for Pita Pit stores varies from location to location, but one of the brand's apparent strengths appears to be its appeal to a variety of target groups. The brand, overall, appeals to healthy eaters and sports people; and the locations and appearance of the stores also attract younger customers. The Takapuna store is located amongst offices, retail shops and bars to attract office workers and shoppers for lunch. The store makes hundreds of pitas each and every day. Its close proximity to bars has inspired the store's long opening hours, and means it can capitalise on the custom of patrons after an evening out. The Pita Pit concept is such that its success is not dependent on having a large shop footprint. It can therefore work in other locations such as a more kiosk-like approach or as part of a food court scenario within a shopping complex.

The Pita Pit's website clearly sets out details to inform potential franchisees. The franchise fee is currently set at NZ$30 000 (plus GST of 12.5%) and franchisees receive: support with site selection and documentation, construction guidelines, equipment and operations manuals, marketing assistance, access to authorised suppliers, and an exclusive territory. The ongoing royalties are currently 6% of gross sales and the franchise license is 10 years, with a 10 year right of renewal. Set up fees for a restaurant (recommended to be 80–120 square metres) are listed as being between NZ$175 000 and NZ$275 000 plus GST.

For more information on The Pita Pit, see www.pitapit.co.nz.

Questions

1. You are interested in buying a Pita Pit franchise. What three questions would you ask the master franchise team before you made your decision?
2. What are the advantages of purchasing a franchise instead of starting up your own food store?
3. What are the benefits of franchising a business idea, rather than the start-up entrepreneur expanding the concept through multiple sites?

ENDNOTES

1. J.A. Timmons & S. Spinelli, *New Venture Creation: Entrepreneurship for the 21st Century*, Mc-Graw-Hill, Boston, MA, 2004.
2. Small Business Development Corporation, Western Australia, *A Guide to Buying a Small Business*, SBDC, Perth, 1998.
3. S. Holmes, P. Hutchinson, D. Forsaith, B. Gibson & R. McMahon, *Small Enterprise Finance*, John Wiley & Sons, Brisbane, 2003, p. 315.

4. H.H. Stevenson, M.J. Roberts & H.I. Grousbeck, *New Business Ventures and the Entrepreneur*, 3rd edn, Richard D. Irwin, Homewood, IL, 1989.
5. Small Business Development Corporation, see note 2.
6. D. Waldron & G.M. Hubbard, 'Valuation methods and estimates in relation to investing versus consulting', *Entrepreneurship Theory and Practice*, no. 16 (Fall), 1991, pp. 43–52.
7. R. McMahon, S. Holmes, P.J. Hutchinson & D.M. Forsaith, *Small Enterprise Financial Management: Theory and Practice*, Harcourt Brace, Sydney, 1993.
8. S. Weaven & L. Frazer, 'Current status of franchising in Australia', *Small Enterprise Research*, vol. 13 no. 2, 2005, pp. 31–45.
9. L. Frazer, S. Weaven & O. Wright, *Franchising Australia 2008 Survey, Asia-Pacific Centre for Franchising Excellence*, Griffith University, Brisbane, 2008.
10. La Fédération française de la franchise, *Franchise statistics in the world by region — 2006 update*, 2006, www.franchise-fff.com.

CHAPTER 6

Market research and strategy formulation

Learning objectives

After reading this chapter, you should be able to:

- list the types of secondary information sources commonly available

- list some common forms of primary market research

- explain the different perspectives on strategy

- list the key steps of strategy formulation for new business ventures.

You have your business idea and you have thought carefully about your own motivations and characteristics. Now you need to demonstrate that your idea represents an opportunity to build a business. Put simply, you need to show that there are people who will buy what you are hoping to produce and sell. This requires that you quantify the opportunity and develop an understanding of how much new value might be created. Obtaining information on the opportunity is viewed as an investment in the business, and must be considered as such. Information collected about the industry and the market, together with the firm-specific variables, will assist the entrepreneur in developing a strategy for the business.

In this chapter, we present various methods of market research, drawing from both secondary and primary sources of data, and we examine how strategy is formulated in new business ventures. The value of a well-considered and well-defined strategy is advocated.

The role of market research

One of the most common problems faced by entrepreneurs is a lack of information that relates to their business idea. There is now much evidence to show that a lack of research is a key inhibitor to new venture creation.[1] A lack of effective research can also create less obvious barriers to business survival and growth: for example, many venture capitalists report that the business plans presented to them by entrepreneurs often do not contain in-depth market information and analysis, thus reducing their prospect of obtaining investment capital.[2]

Market research *The use of information to identify and define marketing opportunities and problems.*

Market research refers to the use of information to identify and define market opportunities and problems. It is used to generate, refine and evaluate marketing-related activities within a small firm or to help determine future marketing strategies and sales forecasts for a new business venture.[3] Typical market research activities include identifying target markets for a new product; surveying members of these markets to understand their purchasing behaviour relevant to such products; and estimating the cost of producing an item and supplying it to the marketplace.

What to research?

One of the first issues to be considered is exactly what information should be investigated. As is frequently the case in marketing, a number of alternative frameworks for studying the wider environment are available, the most conventional of which describes it in terms of an 'onion'. This is a useful approach, since it distinguishes between three different degrees of interaction: the market, the industry and the macro-environment.

The market

The market is the primary concern for the entrepreneur. The market consists of the people or firms who could benefit from the use of the new product, who have the means to buy it and who will be offered the opportunity to do so.[4] Some specific information requirements about the market are:
- *The customer profile/s and segment/s.* What is the typical customer profile in terms of socioeconomic or other relevant dimensions? Are there different needs, requirements and buying behaviours among the customers?

- *The product or service.* How should it be tailored to meet customer needs?
- *Price.* What are competitors charging, and what are customers' pricing expectations?
- *Sales and distribution channels.* What is the most appropriate distribution channel to reach the customers?

The industry

The industry is the next category to consider. Porter identifies five forces that determine the attractiveness of an industry, and he regards these as forming the micro-environment, as opposed to the macro-environment. These forces consist of those influences close to a company that affect its ability to serve customers and make a profit. As shown in figure 6.1, the five forces are: the risk of new competitors entering the industry, the threat of potential substitutes, the bargaining power of buyers, the bargaining power of suppliers and the degree of rivalry between existing competitors. A change in any of the forces normally requires a company to reassess its position in the industry.

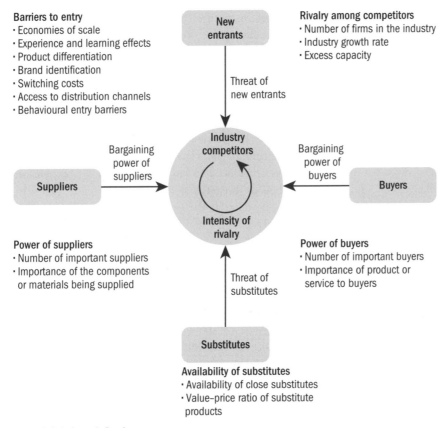

FIGURE 6.1 Porter's five forces

Source: Adapted with the permission of The Free Press, a Division of Simon & Schuster Adult Publishing Group, from M. Porter, *Competitive Advantage: Creating and Sustaining Superior Performance*, Free Press, New York, 1985, p. 6. Copyright © 1985, 1998 by Michael E. Porter. All rights reserved.

The macro-environment

The macro-environment is often not recognised as a force impinging on organisations, and yet it may well contain the major factors that determine the performance of a new business venture. These external factors are most often grouped as the STEP factors (social, technological, economic and political), and they can have dramatic effects on organisations. A political factor such as legislation, for example, determines the boundaries of the actions of most organisations and, yet, it is often 'taken as read', going relatively unnoticed in regard to its effect on organisational performance.

Environmental scanning *Analysing and understanding the internal and external forces that may affect a company's products, markets or operating systems.*

Environmental scanning enables entrepreneurs to understand both the external environment and the interconnections between its various elements. In other words, environmental scanning is 'a kind of radar to scan the world systematically and signal the new, the unexpected, the major and the minor'.[5] Scanning provides intelligence that is useful in determining organisational strategies, and it helps in fostering understanding of the effects of change on an organisation; forecasting; and bringing expectations of change to bear on decision making.

Constraints on research

The ability to conduct effective research is constrained by several limiting factors. Each of these affects the final results that are available to the firm and the entrepreneur.

Cost

All research has a cost. It consumes not only money, but also personal effort by owners or employees. 'Perfect' information, in the sense of data that is easily available, cost free, and fully relevant, is rare. Information is an expense, and costs arise both when the information is originally collected, and when it is stored for future use. Entrepreneurs need to know how much this expense is likely to be, and how much they are prepared to pay. Can the cost be justified? What is the cost of not collecting data? Is there another source of information that is cheaper or easier to use? Does the cost of collection outweigh the benefit of any information derived from it?[6]

Research experience

Firms and individuals familiar with the conduct and analysis of information tend to be better researchers, and to produce more meaningful results than novices in the area. On the whole, the generalist nature of small business management (the fact that the owner has to be competent in many different areas of business) and the lack of research experience by many entrepreneurs mean that few of them have well-developed skills in this area. As a result, the data they collect is often limited in scope and, consequently, value.

Reliability of data

What level of confidence can the entrepreneur have in the information collected? Is the data worth relying on or is further investigation needed to verify the claims made? Over-reliance on one or two key information sources can compromise the results of a study and any conclusions drawn. Wherever possible, it is best to use a variety of sources and research methods, so as to overcome possible bias arising from the use of a single data source.

Personal prejudices

One common problem in research is the tendency to seek out self-verifying information, that is, seeking information that proves one's own biases or claims without adequately considering other contradictory material. Some entrepreneurs and business owners collect only the evidence that supports their initial biases and perspectives, rather than information which provides a fully balanced and objective assessment.[7]

Uniqueness

Some entrepreneurial business ideas are so unusual and so different that there is very little existing research to help assess its viability. This is typically the case with a radical innovation that fundamentally changes the existing way of doing business, or that offers a completely new product with which no-one is familiar. When this occurs, it may be extremely difficult to collect any information that is relevant to the venture idea. However, such occurrences are rare. Most products, services and processes have been trialled previously, and most innovation is, in fact, built on existing ideas and research.[8]

Time

The amount of time available to properly investigate an issue can vary enormously. Some intending business owners believe that a measured, detailed study over a substantial period of time is necessary to gain all of the required information for their business idea; others want to launch their venture as quickly as possible, even if this means compromising the amount of time spent conducting research.

The above limitations mean that most entrepreneurs and owner–managers operate in a situation of what has been termed 'bounded rationality'[9] — that is, their ability to make well-informed and logical decisions is often distorted by real-world constraints and restrictions on the actual information collected. Most of the existing studies of research-gathering among small business owners and entrepreneurs indicate that data collection and analysis tends to be disorganised, limited in scope and heavily skewed towards one or two sources. When market research is undertaken, informal information sources, such as friends and family members, are favoured over more conventional data sources.[10]

Conducting research

The business researcher has two main avenues when seeking and collecting information. One is to consult existing sources of data (secondary information) that will provide a general picture of the current state of knowledge about a particular problem or factor under investigation. Once this step has been completed, it often becomes necessary to investigate some issues in more detail by undertaking original research from primary data sources. Both are important to the information collecting process, although they have different roles to play.

Although it may be tempting and seemingly convenient to rely solely on just one of these research sources, effective research results can really only be obtained by consulting both types. Used together as twin arms of an integrated research strategy, primary and secondary data can allow the entrepreneur to develop a solid understanding of the business venture and the environment in which it operates.

Secondary information

Secondary data

Information from business research that has been done previously.

Data that has already been collected, analysed and published by other parties is broadly defined as **secondary data** (sometimes called 'desk research'); that is, the reader receives the information secondhand.[11] Secondary data sources can take many forms, some of which are discussed below.

Publications

There are numerous books, magazines and industry journals relevant to the modern business environment. General magazines can provide an overview of economic conditions, and feature stories can provide knowledge of competitors and the industry as a whole. Newspapers are also a source of information, both direct and indirect; they contain feature articles, and their advertisements may give a further clue about the marketing activities of competitors.

Although sometimes overlooked, trade magazines are particularly valuable, as they provide direct information about particular industries, product offerings, policy issues and likely future developments. Trade journals rate as one of the most frequently used sources of secondary data for established small businesses.[12]

Business directories

Much information is collated and presented on a commercial basis by a number of private sector organisations, such as Dun & Bradstreet and Kompass. These directories can offer data on company backgrounds, credit risk, trading activities, business locations, office holders, staff size and history (see table 6.1).

TABLE 6.1 Directories and general publications

Country	Publications
Australia	Dun & Bradstreet Australia, www.dnb.com.au Yellow Pages, www.yellowpages.com.au
New Zealand	New Zealand Trade Directory, http://nztrades.com UBD New Zealand Business Directory, www.ubd.co.nz
Hong Kong	Business Directory of Hong Kong, www.business-directory.com.hk Hong Kong Enterprise Directory, www.hked.com
Malaysia	Business Directory of Malaysia, www.eguideglobal.com/my Malaysia Company Directory Index, www.malaysia-index.com
Singapore	Times Business Directory, www.timesbusinessdirectory.com.sg Singapore Business.com, www.singapore-business.com
China (PRC)	Alibaba, www.alibaba.com Business-China.com, www.business-china.com
India	Indian Yellow Pages business directory, www.indianyellowpages.com IndiaMART.com, www.indiamart.com

The Yellow Pages and other similar telephone directories provide an often overlooked source of basic and useful information, such as the number of firms working in a particular industry category, their location and their product offerings. This often constitutes one of the first reference points when attempting to compile a list of competitors.

Private market researchers and competitive intelligence providers

A variety of commercial researchers compile their own databases of company and industry information, which can be purchased by prospective users. However, such companies sell more than just streams of raw facts and figures (data). Instead, they sell processed and meaningful data (information). Performance benchmarks, industry and sectoral analyses, and company financial critiques are just some of the many different items that such researchers can provide information on.

While there are many small businesses and regional players providing these services, there are also several global companies in this field, such as Kroll, Euromonitor International, the Economist Intelligence Unit and Factiva. Kroll, for example, provides a range of services, including business intelligence, investigation services, and background and screening services. Factiva provides business news and information by sifting and analysing information from many mediums. It gathers information from print sources, newswires, websites and company reports, and it provides powerful filtering and results visualisation. Most university libraries subscribe to Factiva.com.

Government bodies

Government departments and agencies are another good source of information and research, although it may take some time to uncover the government agency with the most relevant data for a particular business project. Useful bodies can include statistical authorities and departments of commerce or trade. In countries with a federal or provincial structure, such as Australia and Malaysia, it may be necessary to contact national agencies and the corresponding state department as well. Table 6.2 lists some important national government and statistical websites.

TABLE 6.2 National government and statistics websites

Country	Website
Australia	Business Entry Point, www.business.gov.au
	Australian Bureau of Statistics, www.abs.gov.au
New Zealand	New Zealand Government Online, www.govt.nz
	Statistics New Zealand, www.stats.govt.nz
Hong Kong	HK Special Administrative Region Census and Statistics Department, www.info.gov.hk

TABLE 6.2 continued

Country	Website
Malaysia	Government of Malaysia website, www.gov.my Department of Statistics, www.statistics.gov.my
Singapore	Government of Singapore website, www.gov.sg Department of Statistics, www.singstat.gov.sg
China (PRC)	Chinese Central Government official website, english.gov.cn National Bureau of Statistics of China, www.stats.gov.cn/english
India	National Portal of India, india.gov.in Ministry of Statistics, mospi.nic.in

The internet

The internet is a rich source of information in many different ways. In addition to global search engines, such as Google or Yahoo!, there are some specific national search directories, e.g. Sensis in Australia, that can help find relevant websites quickly. It is important to remember that search terms and concepts need to be relatively detailed to prevent too many irrelevant sites being uncovered, and that the spelling used in many Pacific Rim countries is subtly different from that used by US websites and search engines.

Other electronic sources that are often overlooked are the many virtual communities and blogs that exist online. These are forums in which people with a common interest in a particular topic interact electronically to discuss issues, share ideas and pass on information. It may be possible, for example, to access a chat room dedicated to alternative medicines, and to brainstorm your ideas for a new herbal remedy you wish to develop. Such feedback is free and can usually be obtained very quickly.

Trade shows

Meetings and conventions that bring together manufacturers, distributors, competitors and regulators are an invaluable means of keeping up-to-date with developments in many industries. Trade shows are now common in many industries, including the mining sector, healthcare, tourism, sports retailing and manufacturing.[13]

Industry associations

Many industrial and professional activities are represented by a trade association, chamber of commerce or related body. These are organisations established by business operators in a particular industry or region to promote the interests of members. To this end, such bodies undertake research, survey their members, publish data and promote a greater public knowledge about their industry and its economic significance. Associations are also helpful sources to consult when trying to gauge likely legislative, social and economic changes in an industry sector.

Aussie Play Panels

Your friend Anna Lee is a bright, enthusiastic postgraduate law student at a Sydney university. She recently approached you to get some feedback on her business idea. Anna is a mother of two young children, and she spent most of her childhood between Hong Kong, where she was born, and New York, where her father worked as an investment banker. As a result, she has developed rather sophisticated shopping habits. Anna was surprised to see that many Australian shopping centres do not offer child-friendly recreation areas. An observation of other parents during her shopping indicates that their antics often stop them making a purchase.

However, it was the recent experience of her nine-month-old daughter choking on a piece of Lego at a hairdresser that ultimately triggered her business idea. 'I want to offer retailers something safe for parents and kids, but that doesn't take a huge footprint in the store,' she told you. She came up with the idea of plastic play panels specifically designed for children. The play panels could be configured as a small three-sided column with different playthings and games (e.g. telephone and dial, steering wheel, pole with spinning ball and flaps) mounted on each side. Should the shop lack sufficient space, a play panel with a limited number of games could be affixed to the wall. In addition, Anna plans to offer other items such as soft ride-on animals, soft number blocks that can be used as seats, and small, coloured cubby houses.

Anna has already discussed her idea with her friend Rachel, the owner of her favourite fashion store located in a nearby shopping centre. Rachel confirmed that there was a problem in her shopping centre, particularly with the phenomenon of 'drop and go', where parents drop their children in the toy section of the store or a pet shop, and go off to shop for themselves. 'But the key challenge,' said Rachel 'is to convince the shopping centre management that this is a problem and that your product creates some value.'

Questions

1. What benefits can Anna's product provide to the parents and to the stores?
2. Based on Anna's observations, what market research would you recommend be conducted to show that there is a need for her product?

Primary information

Not all information takes the form of previously collected data. Once the process of secondary information collection has been completed, it will usually become apparent that additional input is needed. At this point, new information must be unearthed. **Primary data** refers to information that is collected first-hand for a specific research problem, and this is generally done once the secondary data process is complete. Primary information (which is sometimes also known as field research) is usually meant to 'fill in the gaps' that secondary research cannot answer.[14] As shown in table 6.3, there are four basic primary data collection techniques: observation, experimentation, surveys and interviews.[15]

Primary data
Information that is collected first-hand for a specific research problem.

TABLE 6.3 Types of primary research

Type of research	Advantage	Disadvantage
Observation	Cheap, convenient	No personal feedback
Experiment	Helps identify causal relationships Key variables can be influenced	Difficult to administer May not replicate actual business situation
Survey: telephone	Quick Can cover wide area	Misses personal cues Not everyone has a phone
Survey: personal	Very rich source of data Can elaborate on issues	Time-consuming, expensive
Survey: mail	Quick Can cover a wide area	Misses personal cues Data usually needs to be manually entered
Survey: email	Quick and cheap Can cover wide area	Misses personal cues Not everyone is online
Focus group	Cost-effective Deep insight into customer views	Time-consuming Difficult to generalise results
In-depth interview	Detailed explanation of an issue Flexible	Time-consuming Difficult to generalise results

Observation

Direct visual evidence of business activities is one of the oldest and most commonly used tools in research. Simply watching consumers in action is an economical yet powerful way of understanding their behaviour. Observation can help solve many different research questions: What products do customers select from a supermarket shelf? How many people actually pass by the proposed business premises during the course of a working day? What retail floor outlet works best in attracting customers to a particular product display? Relatively simple measurements and recordings can be made while observing people in action.[16]

Experimentation

Experiments involve the comparison of groups or individuals who have been differentially exposed to changes in their environment.[17] At its most basic, the experimental method subjects groups of people to a change and then measures the outcome (dependent variable). At the same time, a second group (the control group) is also monitored to see if their outcomes change. An example of experimentation in action is to select a group of shoppers to see if they buy more products when the price is lowered. A second group of shoppers (the control group) would not be offered a lower price, but the number of items purchased (dependent variable) would still be measured. This approach is designed to determine whether a causal relationship exists between variables.

Surveys

Often the most effective way to collect information is by simply asking someone (a respondent) directly. This process requires a **survey** to be conducted, using the collection instrument known as a questionnaire — a series of predetermined questions for individual respondents to answer. This is a powerful research tool, since it allows investigators to collect much more information, in a potentially richer form, than either observation or experimentation permits.

There are many ways to administer a questionnaire. If there is a need to interact with the respondent, then an interview can prove the most adequate collection method. It is not always necessary to organise a face-to-face meeting in order to administer a questionnaire, as interviews can also be conducted over the phone or via a videoconference. The main advantage of the interview lies precisely in the interaction with the respondent. This can prove useful in rephrasing questions, making interjections and observing the non-verbal behaviour of the respondent. If there is no need to interact with the respondent, the questionnaire can then be administered via mail or email.

Survey *A system for collecting information using a questionnaire.*

Interviews

Sometimes it may be more useful to talk to a small group of potential (or actual) consumers together, rather than individually. A **focus group** gathers data relating to the feelings and opinions of people involved in a common situation.[18] It involves a number of people (the best number is between five and 12) having a discussion with a trained interviewer, who solicits their views on a product, service or issue. This allows researchers to more cost-effectively collect data, and it provides a much deeper insight into the nature of consumer preferences and feelings.[19]

In-depth personal interview encourage respondents to talk and explain their views. They probe ambiguous or interesting responses, and generally explore an issue in more detail.[20] Such a personal discussion and question-and-answer session with people can often be a helpful source of knowledge. Conducting an interview can take a lot of time, but may reveal information that would otherwise remain concealed. Detailed discussions with people already working in the industry, retired businesspeople, trade and industry association representatives and academic researchers can help entrepreneurs compile background data for the overall industry analysis.

Focus group *A small group of people with an interviewer trained to solicit their views about a particular issue or product.*

In-depth personal interview *An interview that encourages respondents to explain their views, and which probes responses to explore an issue in greater detail.*

General issues to consider in primary research

Good primary research is often very hard to conduct. Although it may seem straightforward, there are many factors that can distort the results or give rise to erroneous conclusions:

- Is the *sample* — the group of people studied — representative of the general population or target market about which information is being sought?
- How high is the *response rate*? Are the results of the study based on a large number of respondents or on only a few limited replies?
- Has the test been conducted in a *reliable* manner (that is, could another researcher using the same methods and sample collect the same results)?

- Is the information that is collected truly *valid* (that is, does it measure what the researchers claim it measures)?
- How *generalisable* are the results? Can they really be applied to people other than those in the sample group?

Developing a strategy

The immediate objective of gathering information through market research is to determine the feasibility (commercial viability) of a new start-up business, product offering or purchase of a business. However, this information will also help to forecast likely future events, and it will provide the foundation for developing a strategy for the business venture. Strategy is important because of its role in the direction taken by the firm. Without a strategy, firms' short-term decisions will conflict with their long-term goals, so success is likely to be brought about by chance and, thus, cannot be reliably sustained or repeated.

Two perspectives on strategy

The strategy concept can be approached and interpreted from several points of view. It can be seen as a plan, a ploy, a pattern, a position or a perspective. A strategy defines the business's direction and scope, and it will seek competitive advantage. Mintzberg[21] suggested that strategy development process should be about 'capturing what the manager learns from all sources (both the soft insights from his or her personal experiences and the experiences of others throughout the organisation, and the hard data from market research and the like) and then synthesising that learning into a vision of the direction that the business should pursue'. The strategic fit between the internal aspects of an organisation and the external environment determines competitive advantage.

There are two dominating perspectives that explain how to achieve a strategic fit: the market-led view and the resource-based view. The market-led view proposes that firms gain competitive advantage through identifying external opportunities in new and existing markets, and then aligning the firm with these opportunities. This approach is founded in the so-called 'strategy-conduct-performance paradigm'. The basic tenet of this paradigm is that the economic performance of an industry is a function of the conduct (or strategy) of buyers and sellers, which in turn is a function of the industry's structure.[22] In this approach, competitive changes within an industry determine which markets the business venture should enter, stay in or exit. Firms that can successfully adapt to those industry/market requirements will survive and grow, whereas those that fail to adapt are doomed to failure, and exit from the industry/market.

Alternatively, the resource-based view of competitive advantage suggests that, to maximise returns, the business venture should assemble and deploy appropriate resources that provide opportunities for sustainable competitive advantage in the business's chosen market. Competitive advantage is thus created by distinctive, valuable firm-specific resources that competitors are unable to reproduce.

Figure 6.2 combines the market-led and resource-led perspectives to outline a process of strategy development. The model presented recognises that strategy formulation is intimately related to the personality of the entrepreneur.

Typically, the entrepreneur will consider both internal and external factors when developing the desired strategy — a subjective representation of the thinking of key persons in the business venture. This emergent strategy forms a sort of information filter that screens relevant data. There are a number of ways in which the entrepreneur can become aware of the desired strategy content:[23]

- *The entrepreneur's communication of his or her vision.* A vision may lack detail but it should highlight the desirability of achieving certain strategy contents in preference to others.
- *The definition of a mission.* The organisation's mission will specify the key elements of the strategy content. The mission will, at a minimum, be able to provide a test as to what strategy contents are desirable and acceptable.
- *The setting of objectives.* The desired objectives may be defined explicitly by the setting of specific objectives. These may be financial or strategic in nature. Quantified objectives provide means of benchmarking the achievement of a desired strategy content.
- *Informal discussion.* The identification a desired strategy often occurs through an informal process. It may become evident though ongoing discussions about the business and the opportunities offered by the market. These discussions may involve a variety of people both within and from outside the organisation, and they may take place over a period of time.

The realised strategy (products sold, markets targeted, approach to competing) is the outcome of the strategy formulation and the dominant orientation of the firm. This will in turn influence the performance of the firm.

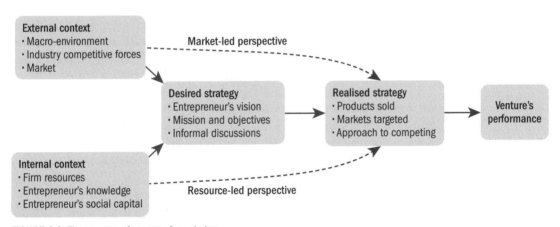

FIGURE 6.2 The process of strategy formulation

Market-led perspective on strategy

Chandler, one of the early thinkers in strategic management, considered strategy as 'the determination of basic long-term objectives of an enterprise, the adaptation of course of action and the allocation of resources necessary for carrying out these objectives.'[24] Therefore, strategy is intricately related to the development of a plan, specifying the enterprise's objectives, developing policies and plans for achieving these objectives, and allocating resources in order to implement the plans. Strategic planning is the highest level of managerial activity, usually performed by the entrepreneur and other key associates. It provides overall direction to the whole enterprise. Strategy formulation involves the following steps:

- *Setting objectives* by crafting a vision statement (a long-term view of a possible future), a mission statement (the role that the organisation gives itself in society), objectives (both financial and strategic) and goals.
- *Conducting a situation analysis*, considering both the internal (organisation-specific) and external (micro-environmental and macro-environmental) factors. Such analysis is usually conducted by examining the strengths, weaknesses, opportunities and threats (SWOT analysis) of the business venture.
- *Selecting a strategy* that will provide the enterprise with a competitive advantage.

This three-step strategy formulation process is sometimes referred to as determining where you are now, where you want to go and how you plan to get there. These three questions are the essence of strategic planning. A strategic plan should not be confused with a business plan. The former is likely to be a short document, whereas a business plan is usually a much more substantial and detailed document. A strategic plan can provide the foundation and framework for a business plan. For more information about business plans, refer to chapter 7.

Formulating a vision, a mission, objectives and goals

The preparation of a strategic plan is a multi-step process covering vision, mission, objectives and goals.

The first step is to develop a realistic vision for the business. This should be presented as a picture of the business's likely physical appearance, size and activities in three or more years' time. In order to formulate a vision, consideration must be given to the future products, markets, customers, processes, location and staffing of the business. For example, Kuala Lumpur-based Macrokiosk has the following vision: 'Macrokiosk's vision is to become the leading mobile messaging technology enabler in Asia.'[25]

In the second step, the business attempts to indicate its purpose and nature by means of its mission. In Macrokiosk's case, the mission is 'to provide scaleable mobile messaging solutions to conveniently disseminate services over borderless markets, and constantly satisfy customers beyond expectations'. A statement such as this indicates what the business is about and is more specific than saying, for example, 'We're in electronics' or, worse still, 'We are in business to make money'.

The third key step is to explicitly state the objective of the business — what it wants to achieve in the medium- to long-term. Aside from the need to achieve regular profits (expressed as return on shareholders' funds), objectives should relate to the expectations and requirements of all the major stakeholders, including employees, and should reflect the underlying reasons for running the business. These objectives could cover growth, profitability, technology, offerings and markets.

Next come the goals. These are specific interim or ultimate time-based measurements, and they are achieved by implementing strategies that pursue the company's objectives. For example, a business might aim to achieve sales of $3 million in three years' time. Goals should be SMART: specific, measurable, achievable, realistic and time-bound. They can relate to factors such as market (sizes and shares), products, finances, profitability, utilisation and efficiency.

SWOT analysis

Once objectives have been identified, the existing and perceived strengths, weaknesses, threats and opportunities are discovered and listed. The aim of any SWOT analysis should be to isolate the key issues that will be important to the future of the organisation, and that will be addressed by subsequent marketing plans. Typically seen by managers as the most useful planning tool of all, SWOT puts some of the key pieces of information into two main categories of factors, internal and external, which can either help or impede the attainment of objectives. The essence of a SWOT analysis is that it precisely identifies:

- *strengths* — attributes of the organisation that are helpful to the achievement of the objective
- *weaknesses* — attributes of the organisation that are harmful to the achievement of the objective
- *opportunities* — external conditions that are helpful to the achievement of the objective
- *threats* — external conditions that are harmful to the achievement of the objective.

As shown in table 6.4, the results of SWOT analysis are often presented in the form of a matrix. Note, however, that SWOT is just one aid to categorisation. It also has its own weaknesses. It tends to persuade entrepreneurs and owner–managers to compile lists, rather than think about what is really important to their business. It also presents the resulting lists uncritically, without clear prioritisation, so that, for example, weak opportunities appear to balance strong threats.

TABLE 6.4 SWOT analysis matrix

Attributes	Helpful to achieving objectives	Harmful to achieving objectives
Internal (attributes of the organisation)	Strengths	Weaknesses
External (attributes of the environment)	Opportunities	Threats

Selecting a generic strategy

A new business venture positions itself by leveraging its strengths. Porter[26] has argued that a firm's strengths can ultimately be divided into the two categories of cost advantage and differentiation. By applying these strengths in either a broad or narrow scope, three generic strategies result: cost leadership, differentiation and focus. They are called generic strategies because they are not firm- or industry-dependent. The development of generic business strategies is often a function of specific industry structure characteristics. That is, the success of any given strategy relates to the firm's ability to engage in activities that lead to increased concentration and to barriers that hinder the entry of other firms. The height of the barriers determines the extent to which superior profits can be gained.

- *Cost leadership*. This strategy emphasises efficiency. By producing high volumes of standardised products or services, the firm can take advantage of economies of scale and learning-curve effects. The product is often a basic no-frills item that is produced at a relatively low cost and made available to a very large customer base. Maintaining this strategy requires a continuous search for cost reductions in all aspects of the business. The associated distribution strategy is to obtain the most extensive distribution possible. Promotional strategy often involves trying to make a virtue out of low-cost product features.[27]

- *Differentiation.* This strategy involves creating a product that is perceived as unique. If this strategy is to be successful, the unique features or benefits must provide superior value for the customer. When customers see the product as unrivalled and unequalled, the price elasticity of demand tends to be reduced, and customers tend to be more loyal. This can provide considerable insulation from competition. However, there are usually additional costs associated with the differentiating product features, and this could require a premium pricing strategy.[28]

- *Focus.* This strategy concentrates on a narrow segment and within that segment it attempts to achieve either a cost advantage or differentiation. The premise is that the need of the targeted segment can be better serviced by focusing entirely on it. A firm pursuing a focus strategy often enjoys a high degree of customer loyalty, and this entrenched loyalty discourages other businesses from competing directly. Firms that succeed in a focus strategy are able to tailor a broad range of product development strengths to a relatively narrow segment of the market that they know very well. The vast majority of start-ups and small businesses pursue a focus strategy.[29]

Blue ocean strategies

Traditional business strategies originate from military models. As companies shape their strategies and plot their objectives, warlike metaphors abound: the business must confront its opponents, render them harmless and gain the advantage. Translated into strategy, this language generates a model for competing in a fixed market and gaining advantage over other entrants in the same field.

Kim and Mauborgne[30] recently suggested an alternative approach based on their conviction that effective strategies must be differentiated from convention. They argue that the only way to beat the competition is to stop trying to beat the competition. They called this approach **blue ocean strategy**. Blue oceans are 'untapped market space, demand creation, and the opportunity for highly profitable growth. Although some blue oceans are created well beyond existing industry boundaries, most are created by expanding existing industry boundaries... In blue oceans, competition is irrelevant because the rules of the game are waiting to be set.'[31]

Blue ocean strategy
A strategy aiming to develop compelling value innovations that create uncontested market space.

The key element of a blue ocean strategy is value innovation: a combination of differentiation and low cost that sets a product line or service apart from its competitors. Examples of value innovation include Starbucks, which made coffee a neighbourhood treat, or The Body Shop, whose natural and affordable cosmetics established a blue ocean in a high-end industry full of pricey competitors. To succeed, a value innovation must demonstrate actual savings and an appreciable benefit that a customer can use immediately.

Yellow Tail is a typical example of value innovation. A wine created explicitly for the US market, Yellow Tail was launched in 2000 by Casella Wines, a small family-owned Australian winery. Casella altered the taste of its wine, making it fruitier and sweeter, and targeted beer and cocktail drinkers by promoting its wine as fun.[32] Breaking with traditional marketing techniques, Casella rejected the idea of relying on wine's elitist tag, with its emphasis on complex taste, ageing and vineyard location. It replaced the wine buff's jargon on the label with a distinctive kangaroo logo (the yellow-footed rock wallaby known to roam the Casella vineyards). As a result of this strategy, Yellow Tail became the top-selling 750-ml-bottle red wine in the USA by August 2003. Casella also grew to be one of the largest wineries in Australia.

Entrepreneur profile

Paul Greenberg and Michael Rosenbaum, DealsDirect

Almost four year ago, the founders of online retailing business DealsDirect.com.au considered leading online retailers such as dStore and David Jones Online as their competitors. But they say they are now neck and neck with the big discount retailers — Kmart, Big W and JB Hi-Fi. It is a sign of how far DealsDirect has come. 'We always had big-picture aspirations, but it's only now that the flag's fallen and the game's on,' co-founder Paul Greenberg says. 'In hindsight, I'd say we've spent the past three years testing the model and conducting research and development.' There is plenty of evidence to suggest that DealsDirect is gaining momentum. In 2008, 58 per cent of households surveyed by AC Nielsen, a market research company, had heard of DealsDirect, and by the end of the year it had outgrown its 5000-square-metre warehouse and distribution centre in Sydney, and moved to a location five times bigger.

Founders Paul Greenberg, 49, and Michal Rosenbaum, 28, started DealsDirect in 2004, well after the tech-wreck when internet use and online transactions were increasing rapidly. Unlike most start-ups, the pair had a head start. Having run a business (Auctionbrokers Australia) on eBay meant they had a ready customer base and plenty of experience. 'It became obvious to us that customers were tiring of the auction format,' says Rosenbaum. 'That was a big opportunity.'

In trying to bypass the middlemen and buy direct from factories in China, they developed relationships with Chinese manufacturers that enabled them to buy in bulk excess stock that the factories wanted to sell quickly and cheaply. The stock is warehoused in Sydney until it is sold. 'That's the difference between us and the competitors we started out with,' Rosenbaum says. 'we're not interested in simply being an online portal. We want to get our hands dirty by controlling the supply chain.'

Initially, one of the biggest challenges for DealsDirect was resistance from distributors in Australia. Put out by an online entrant whose business model was to cut out the middleman and buy direct, and afraid of upsetting the large brands, few established distributors in Australia were willing to supply the site. Greenberg says this attitude is just starting to change. 'We were recently at the toy fair in Melbourne and for the first time the major brands said, "We want to deal with you guys."' he explains. Book distributors are also expressing interest. 'The fact is the big book distributors are losing business to the US because of Amazon.com,' Greenberg says. 'When you think about shipping and time until delivery, we should be competitive. Books will be our next category.'

Source: Kristen Le Mesurier, 'Bypass operations', *BRW*, April 24–June 4, 2008, p. 48.

A resource-based theory of entrepreneurship

The market-led (or industrial organisation) perspective is rather deterministic: competitive advantage is ascribed to external characteristics rather than to the entrepreneur's or venture's competencies and resource-based deployments. In the resource-based perspective, competitive advantage is viewed from the perspective of distinctive resources and competencies that give a firm an edge over its rivals. This perspective considers that firms have different starting points for resources (called resource heterogeneity), and that other firms cannot get them (called resource immobility). New firms emerge to pursue an attractive opportunity as the result of a combination of resources under the leadership of an entrepreneur. Firms usually begin with a relatively small amount of strategically relevant resources and skills, and each company's uniqueness shows how these resources are expected to perform in the marketplace.

According to the resource-based theory,[33] in order to be successful, entrepreneurs must exploit market imperfections based on imperfect information or variations in expectations about prices while adhering to the following simple formula:

1. Buy (or acquire) resources and skills cheaply.
2. Transform the resources into a product or service (production).
3. Deploy and implement (strategy).
4. Sell dearly (for more than you paid — value creation).

Resource types

Resource *Any thing or quality that is useful.*

A **resource** is any thing or quality that is useful. The resource-based theory recognises six types of resource: financial, physical, human, technological, reputation and organisational. These six types are broadly drawn and include all assets, capabilities, organisational processes, firm attributes, information and knowledge.

- *Financial resources.* Financial resources represent money, shares and other assets. Financial resources are generally the firm's borrowing capacity, the ability to raise new equity, and the amount of internal fund generation. Financial resources are seldom the source of sustainable competitive advantage. These resources are valuable, but they are seldom rare; fairly easy to copy; and substitutes do exist.
- *Physical resources.* These resources are the tangible property the firm uses in production and administration (e.g. location, equipment, office space). Complex physical technology cannot provide a basis for a sustainable competitive advantage, as it can be duplicated and reproduced. However, if the method for exploiting the technology is not easy to copy (assuming it is rare and difficult to substitute), the other resources can augment technology to provide a sustainable competitive advantage.
- *Human resources.* The entrepreneur and his or her founding team have two precious types of human resources: human capital (the collective knowledge, skills and abilities of the founding team) and social capital (the ties founding members have with others). Social capital is important because it allows individuals to obtain resources that are otherwise unavailable to them, such as information, capital and access to clients and suppliers. In other words, the founding team is the source of *what* the new venture knows, and also, *who* it knows.

- *Technological resources.* These resources are embodied in a process, system or physical transformation. They constitute physical or legal entities that are owned by a corporation, for example, patents, unique software products and tailored information-system architecture. Technological capital is different from intellectual capital, in that, intellectual capital is embodied in people and is mobile.
- *Reputation.* Reputation encompasses the perceptions that people in the firm's environment have of the firm. Reputational capital can exist at the product or corporate level, and it may be relatively long-lived. The most important aspects of reputation are product quality, management integrity and financial soundness. Even a start-up business can quickly acquire a reputation, for example, by cooperating with a well-established business.
- *Organisational resources.* These resources include the firm's structure, routines and systems. The organisation's structure is an intangible resource that can differentiate it from its competitors. A structure that promotes speed can be the entrepreneur's most valuable resource. Collective remembered history (myth) and recorded history (files and archives) may also be considered organisational resources. The capabilities of a firm — what it can do as a result of team members working together — are also part of organisational resources.

Attributes of strategic resources

Not all resources are strategically relevant for the entrepreneur. **Strategic resources** create competitive advantage, whereas common resources are necessary for carrying out the firm's usual activities but provide no specific advantage. Strategic resources matter because they are the basis of the firm's competitive advantage, which in turn determines its ability to earn a profit. Competitive advantage occurs when the entrepreneur implements a value-creating (above normal profit) strategy that is not simultaneously being implemented by any current or potential competitors.[34] Sustained competitive advantage is competitive advantage with an important addition: current and potential firms are unable to duplicate the benefits of the strategy.

Strategic resources
Resources which provide a sustained competitive advantage to a firm.

The resource-based view of entrepreneurship holds that sustainable competitive advantage is created when firms possess and use resources that are:
- *Valuable* — resources are valuable when they help the organisation implement its strategy effectively and efficiently by exploiting opportunities or minimising threats in the firm's environment.
- *Rare* — these are resources that are not widely available to all competitors.
- *Non-substitutable* — when common resources are not equivalent to the rare and valuable resources of another firm, the rare and valuable resources are said to be non-substitutable; for example, top-management teams cannot be a source of sustained competitive advantage because, even though these teams are valuable, rare and hard to copy, a substitute exists and can be used.
- *Hard to copy* — if a resource cannot be duplicated at a price sufficiently low to leave profits, the resource is said to be imperfectly imitable (hard to copy). Imperfect imitability can stem from:
  - *Historical conditions* — the initial assets and resources used in the firm's start-up are unique for that place and time; firms founded at a different time in another place cannot obtain these resources, so the resources cannot be duplicated.

- *Ambiguous causes and effects* — the relationship between the organisation's resources and its success is not well understood or it is ambiguous, sometimes even to the firm using the high-performing resource.
- *Complex social relationships* — as long as a firm uses human and organisational resources, social complexity may serve as a barrier to imitation. The most complex social phenomenon is organisational culture, which is a complex combination of the founder's values, habits and beliefs, and the interaction of these elements with the newly created organisation and the market.

As figure 6.3 shows, when a firm possesses and controls resources that are valuable, rare, non-substitutable and hard to copy, and it can protect these resources and maintain these four qualities, it will have a competitive advantage in the long term. If a firm has all these qualities but not in full measure and without protection, competitive advantage will be short-lived because competitors will copy and imitate them.

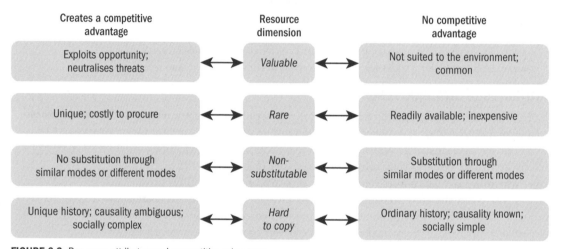

FIGURE 6.3 Resource attributes and competitive advantage

Source: Adapted from M. Dollinger, *Entrepreneurship: Strategies and Resources*, 2nd edn, Prentice Hall, Upper Saddle River, NJ, 1999, p. 31.

Developing a business model

Business model
A conceptual tool describing the elements and relationships that outline how a company creates and markets value.

The terms 'strategy' and '**business model**' have often been used interchangeably. While both concepts are the cornerstone of a firm's competitive advantage, a review of the literature indicates that business models and strategy are linked but yet distinct concepts. A practical distinction describes business model as a system that shows how the pieces of a business fit together, while strategy also includes competition. Therefore, a business model is the conceptual and architectural implementation of a business strategy, and the foundation for the implementation of business processes. In other words, it describes the logic of a 'business system' for creating value.[35]

Components of the business model

An underlying aspiration of companies when formulating a business strategy and business model is the attainment of competitive advantage.

Generally, competitive advantage is manifested in a source (cause) of superior performance. The potential sources are many, but the dominant marker, or anchor, for developing and sustaining a competitive advantage is value creation. Figure 6.4 depicts the different components of the business model. We show that there are two fundamental sources of value creation: customers and the firm.

First, and most important, is the concept of customer value. Customer value is largely concerned with what constitutes value from the customer's perspective. Note the important distinction between 'value' and 'price'. Value is something that customers assign to a product. It is a function of the attributes of the product, such as its performance, design, quality and point-of-sale, and after sales service. Many companies begin with a product idea and a business model and then go in search of a market. Success comes figuring out how to satisfy a real customer who needs to get a real job done. As depicted in 6.4, the building blocks of the customer interface include:

- *The target customer* — Describes the segments of customers a company wants to offer value.
- *The distribution channel* — Describes the various means of the company to get in touch with its customers.
- *The customer relationship* — Explains the kind of links a company establishes between itself and its different customer segments.

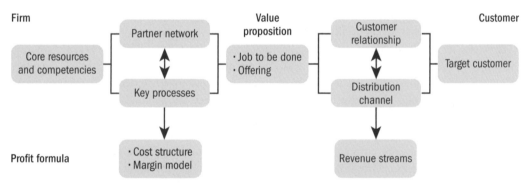

FIGURE 6.4 Business model components

Source: Adapted from A. Osterwalder, *The business model ontology: A proposition in a design science approach*, unpublished PhD thesis, University of Lausanne, 2004, p. 44.

The second battleground in the value creation process is the company's creation and delivery of the things that customers value. This effort entails the acquisition and combination of resources through a series of key processes that allow the firm to deliver value in a way it can successfully repeat and increase in scale. The elements of the firm infrastructure include:

- *Core resources and competencies* — Outline the resources and competencies necessary to execute the company's business model.
- *Key processes* — Describe the arrangement of activities and resources. Key processes include such recurrent tasks as budgeting, manufacturing, sales, and service.
- *The partner network* — Portrays the network of cooperative agreements with other companies necessary to efficiently offer and commercialise value.

The value proposition bridges the gap between the firm and the customer. A successful company is one that has found a way to create value for customers — that is, a way to help customers get an important job done. By 'job' we mean a situation wherein the company solves an important problem or fulfils a need for the target customer. Once the company has recognised the job to be done, it will develop an offering — a product and/or a service — which satisfies the problem or fulfils the need.[36]

The fourth component of the business model is the profit formula. The profit formula is the blueprint that defines how the company creates value for itself while providing value to the customer. A value proposition without a profit formula is unlikely to generate a sustainable business, as many a dot-com start-up found out. The profit formula consists of the following:

- *Revenue streams* — Price × volume.
- *Cost structure* — Direct costs, indirect costs, economies of scale — Cost structure will be predominantly driven by the cost of key resources required by the business model.
- *Margin model* — Given the expected volume and cost structure, the contribution needed from each transaction to achieve desired profits.[37]

Use of business models

Business models can play important roles in business management and, particularly, in regard to emerging ventures. Accordingly to Osterwalder et al.[38] business models fulfill four main roles:

- *Understand and share.* The first area in which business models can contribute is in understanding and sharing the business logic of a firm. Concretely, business models help to capture, visualise, understand, communicate and share the business logic. Experience shows that in many cases entrepreneurs are not always capable of communicating their business model in a clear way. Furthermore, because people use different mental models, they do not automatically understand a business model in the same way. Using a conceptualisation to capture the business model, means that with little additional effort it can be understood, presented graphically and shared with stakeholders.
- *Analyse.* The business model concept can contribute in analysing the business logic of a company. The business model becomes a new unit of analysis. Business models can improve measuring, observing and comparing the business logic of a company.
- *Manage.* Business models improve the management of the business logic of the firm once it is established. The business model concept helps ameliorate the design, planning, changing and implementation of the model. In addition, with a business model approach companies can react faster to changes in the business environment. Finally, the business model concept improves the alignment of strategy, business organisation and technology.
- *Prospect.* A fourth area of contribution refers to the possible future of a company. The business model can help foster innovation and increase readiness for the future through business model portfolios and simulation.

SUMMARY

Comprehensive market research has to be conducted to determine the size of the market and potential segments. When conducting the research, it is useful to consider the industry and the macro-environment, as well as the market. Both secondary and primary information have a role to play in the collection of credible research data. Secondary information sources include print publications, private market researchers, business directories, database vendors, government statistics and official reports, the internet and industry associations. Primary market research can take the form of direct observation, experimentation and surveys. Careful consideration has to be made as to the sample, the type of measuring instrument used, the type of question asked, the response rate, the reliability, validity and potential for the results to be generalised.

The information gathered during the research process will provide the foundation on which to develop a strategy for the business venture. Strategy is important because of its role in the direction taken by the firm. There are two dominating perspectives on the process of making strategy: the market-led view and the resource-based view. However, a new approach on strategy — blue ocean strategy — has recently emerged. Contrary to most corporate strategies based on military models and direct confrontations, blue ocean strategies build new business where none existed, giving innovative entries clear sailing.

Once the strategy has been formulated, the business model outlining the conceptual and architectural implementation of the strategy can be developed. The business model describes the logic of a 'business system' for creating value. It comprises of four key components: the customer interface, the firm infrastructure to deliver value, the value proposition and the profit formula.

REVIEW QUESTIONS

1. What are the factors that act as constraints to effective market research?
2. List and briefly explain the different types of secondary research sources available.
3. Explain the process of strategy formulation.
4. What is the difference between the market-based and resource-based perspective on strategy?
5. What is a business model?

DISCUSSION QUESTIONS

1. What are the limitations of desk research using secondary data?
2. Identify five simple rules for designing an effective questionnaire.
3. Why can a well-defined strategy help the venture?
4. Can an organisation's culture be a source of sustainable competitive advantage?
5. What are the main criticisms of strategic planning?

SUGGESTED READING

Collis, D.J. & Montgomery, C.A., 'Competing on resources', *Harvard Business Review*, July–August 2008, pp. 140–50.

Hair, J.F., Lukas, B. & Miller, K., *Marketing Research*, 2nd edn, McGraw-Hill, Sydney, 2008.

Kim, W.C. & Mauborgne, R., *Blue Ocean Strategy*, Harvard Business School Press, Boston, 2005.

GetTV

In November 2009 Mark Sinclair, co-founder of GetTV was reflecting on the recent discussions he had with the other executives at the company's main office in Hong Kong. GetTV has been one of the first peer-to-peer (P2P) internet protocol television (IPTV) services to launch offerings throughout South-East Asia. Until now, it had followed a B2C strategy, acquiring, transporting and presenting streaming video in one browser for users. Recently, a few broadcasters had asked GetTV if it could provide them with the technology to develop their own IPTV. This would entail a considerable shift in the strategy, in effect, transforming GetTV into a B2B company. Sinclair had to make a decision before the end of the year whether he wanted to pursue this new opportunity.

The company and its partners

GetTV is a new TV distribution service transmitting popular channels in unprecedented quality to users' computers. GetTV is free and works without the need for specialised hardware. Users download the software, the GetTV player, from the company website, and can watch free TV on their computers within minutes. Via their proprietary browser, the company provides users with diverse content of good video quality, while dramatically reducing cost and increasing reach for broadcasters, and enabling advertisers to leverage the best aspects of both web-based and traditional television advertising methods. GetTV's business model is ad-supported. When a user first selects or switches channel, they are served up a 5-second advertisement (the time it usually takes for the stream to buffer). The ads are also hyperlinked so that viewers can access more information.

For users, GetTV is superior to today's IPTVs in three major ways: viewing quality, channel choice, and portability. The company's proprietary P2P streaming technology ensures a video delivery and smoothness that has until now been impossible to achieve.

'In terms of picture quality, this isn't quite on-par with regular digital television, but isn't far off either,' says a GetTV subscriber. Channel choice is a second advantage: consumers are able to watch an array of major television channels in one browser, and they find specialty content often not available elsewhere. Portability is the third advantage: 'You can watch GetTV wherever you can connect your laptop to the internet,' explains Sinclair.

Local broadcasters transmit television programs for general use. There are either public (e.g. Radio Television Hong Kong) or private broadcasters. Broadcasters are important partners in GetTV's business model, since they give the right for their channels to be distributed on the GetTV platform in agreements similar to those with cable or satellite providers. GetTV provides several benefits to broadcasters. First, it increases the 'stickinesss' as it takes broadcasters' brands beyond the living room, in front of viewers on a device (the computer) that is becoming as pervasive as TV. Second, it increases the value of the advertising windows of broadcasters by adding compelling multimedia and interactive elements. GetTV pays either a fee per subscriber or a share of the advertising revenue to major broadcasters, such as MTV in Hong Kong.

Content owners, such as the big studios like Sony Pictures, Paramount and Disney, are a second category of potential partner in the IPTV industry. They are the producer of content (movies, TV series, sport events) and they sell this content to a broadcaster, who packages it and makes it available on a specific channel. Content owners are assured against piracy because no part of the encrypted video stream is stored on the network, and because GetTV's P2P technology allows for geographic targeting of users.

Advertisers benefit from GetTV's model because it combines the best attributes of web-based (banner and targeted-text) advertising methods with the proven effectiveness of TV-style video spots. Most importantly, advertisers will be able to geographically target their spots much more accurately via the viewer's computer IP address, which indicates their physical location. The ability to, for example, target all 'Desperate Housewives' fans in a particular city is of particular utility and is, therefore, worth a premium. The advertisers pay on a cost per mille (CPM) basis, a commonly used measurement in advertising. GetTV currently charges a CPM of HK$1000 (meaning the advertiser pays HK$1000 to display the ad 1000 times).

GetTV's development and current challenges

GetTV was founded in 2006 by Alex Kwok, a professor of Computer Science at the Hong Kong Technological University, and Mark Sinclair, a software product marketing professional. The company raised US$1 million in 2006 and another US$7 million in 2008. It currently employs 30 staff (20 IT specialists, and 10 people in management and office support). Like any peer-to-peer (P2P) application, GetTV relies primarily on the computing power and bandwidth of the participants in the network, rather than concentrating it in a relatively low number of servers.

GetTV has around 1.5 million subscribers across Hong Kong, Singapore and South Korea and will soon become available across the Asian continent. It broadcasts many service channels in real time, including TVB Pearl (one of the two free television services offered in English Language in Hong Kong), BBC World, CNN and Bloomberg.

One of the major challenges GetTV has faced over the past few months is to obtain approval from broadcasters in various countries to provide their channels on its platform. 'When I joined GetTV in mid-2006, I had planned to acquire all the top Asian TV channels by the end of 2006. We are now at the end of 2009 and we are not done yet,' laments Sinclair. There are two types of hurdles that GetTV faces. The first one is related to technology. Broadcasters worry that the internet is open to everyone, and they are concerned about the protection of their content. 'So we have to demonstrate that we can protect their rights, for example, by making sure that channels are viewed only in a specified country,' says Sinclair. The second hurdle is a legal one, because of the way content owners sell their distribution rights. They usually sell the rights separately for theatre, DVD, cable and satellite distribution. 'Because IPTV is a new medium, the broadcasters may not have the right for distribution over the internet, and therefore they cannot grant us this right,' he says.

At the same time, GetTV increasingly receives requests from internet service providers (ISPs) and broadcasters to licence the technology to them. The ISPs are interested in expanding their service range, in addition to providing internet access. One of the possible partners in their view could be GetTV, providing them with the channels for sale to the end user, as the 'Pacific Internet TV' for example.

The broadcasters perceive the internet as a platform to extend their reach and to develop a closer relationship with their viewers, thereby making their brand stronger. 'These players would like to have their brand in front of the viewers, and they would like to position themselves on the internet, rather than through GetTV,' says Mark Sinclair. 'The broadcasters are interested in our technology, and see the internet as another channel to broadcast their channels, along cable and satellite.'

This is a fictional case.

Questions

1. Outline GetTV's business model. Is it likely to disrupt the television industry?
2. Drawing from the market-based and resource-based perspectives, what are the foundations of GetTV's strategy?
3. If you were Mark Sinclair, would you recommend that GetTV follow a B2B strategy? What are the advantages and drawbacks of such a strategy?

ENDNOTES

1. C.G. Brush, 'Marketplace information scanning activities of new manufacturing ventures', *Journal of Small Business Management*, vol. 30, no. 30, October 1992, pp. 41–54.
2. G.E. Hills, 'Market analysis of the business plan: venture capitalists' perceptions', *Journal of Small Business Management*, vol. 23, no. 23, January 1985, pp. 38–47.
3. P. Kotler, S. Adam, L. Brown & G. Armstrong, *Principles of Marketing*, Prentice Hall, Sydney, 2001, p. 93.
4. J. Legge & K. Hindle, *see* note 2, p. 104.
5. J. Pfeffer & G.R. Salancik, *The External Control of Organizations*, Harper & Row, New York, 1978.
6. M. Evans, 'Market information and research', in K. Blois (ed.), *The Oxford Textbook of Marketing*, Oxford University Press, Oxford, 2000, pp. 150–74.
7. W.L. Neuman, *Social Research Methods*, 3rd edn, Allyn & Bacon, Boston, 1997.
8. J.G. Longenecker, C.W. Moore & J.W. Petty, *Small Business Management: An Entrepreneurial Emphasis*, 11th edn, South-Western, Cincinnatti, OH, 2000, p. 154.
9. H.A. Simon, 'Rational choice and the structure of the environment', *Psychological Review*, vol. 63, 1956, pp. 129–38.
10. T.J. Calahan & M.D. Cassar, 'Small business owners' assessments of their abilities to perform and interpret formal market studies', *Journal of Small Business Management*, vol. 33, no. 33, October 1995, pp. 1–10.
11. P. Kotler, G. Armstrong, L. Brown & S. Adam, *Marketing*, 4th edn, Pearson, Sydney, 1998, p. 159.
12. C.G. Brush, *see* note 6.
13. J.R. McColl-Kennedy & G.C. Kiel, *Marketing: A Strategic Approach*, Nelson Thomson, Melbourne, 2000, pp. 617–18.
14. P. Burns, *Entrepreneurship and Small Business*, Palgrave, London, 2001, p. 119.
15. P. Kotler, S. Adam, L. Brown & G. Armstrong, *see* note 8, p. 101.
16. D. Bangs & M. Halliday, *The Australian Market Planning Guide*, 2nd edn, Business & Professional Publishing, Sydney, 1997.
17. W.L. Neuman, *see* note 12, p. 176.
18. J. Hussey & R. Hussey, *Business Research*, Macmillan, London, 1997, p. 155.
19. P. Kotler, G. Armstrong, L. Brown & S. Adam, *see* note 8, p. 166.
20. G.W. Ticehurst & A.J. Veal, *Business Research Methods*, Longman, Sydney, 2000, p. 97.
21. H. Mintzberg, 'The fall and rise of strategic planning', *Harvard Business Review*, January–February 1994, p. 107.
22. J.S Bain, *Barriers to New Competition*, Harvard University Press, Cambridge, MA, 1956.
23. P. Wickham, *Strategic Entrepreneurship*, 3rd edition, Prentice Hall, Harlow, 2004.
24. A. Chandler, *Strategy and Structure*, MIT Press, Cambridge, MA, 1962.
25. Macrokiosk, *Vision*, www.macrokiosk.com.
26. M.E. Porter, *Competitive Strategy*, Free Press, New York, 1980.
27. Ibid.
28. ibid.
29. ibid.
30. W.C. Kim & R. Mauborgne, *Blue Ocean Strategy*, Harvard Business School Press, Boston, 2005.
31. ibid.
32. ibid., pp. 31–35.
33. B. Wernerfelt, 'A Resource-based view of the firm', *Strategic Management Journal*, vol. 5, 1984, pp. 171–80
34. J. Barney, 'Firm resources and sustained competitive advantage', *Journal of Management*, no. 17, 1991, pp. 99–120.

35. A. Osterwalder, Y. Pigneur & C. Tucci, 'Clarifying business models: Origins, present, and future of the concept', *Communication of the AIS*, vol. 15, May 2005, pp. 1–40
36. M.W. Johnson, C.M. Christensen & H. Kagermann, 'Reinventing your business model', Harvard *Business Review*, December 2008, pp. 51–9.
37. ibid.
38. A. Osterwalder, Y. Pigneur & C. Tucci, see note 35.

CHAPTER 7

Preparing a business plan

Learning objectives

After reading this chapter, you should be able to:

- explain what a business plan is

- list the advantages and disadvantages of using a business plan

- state the major elements of a business plan

- explain how plans may differ in a number of variables

- explain the business planning process.

Starting and organising a business venture is a demanding task. Whether one is buying an existing business or beginning a brand-new enterprise, there are always many tasks to do and issues to deal with. One way is simply to deal with each question or problem as it arises. The other strategy, long favoured by business advisers and commentators, is to carefully plan the business venture at the start.

In this chapter the notion of business planning is defined and explained. We also compare the benefits and disadvantages of planning. The major elements of a plan are discussed, as is the process by which an effective plan is prepared and implemented.

The concept of a business plan

Business plan
A written document that outlines the future activity for an existing or proposed business venture.

A **business plan** is a written document that explains and analyses an existing or proposed business venture. It spells out in some detail the business owner's intentions for the future of the firm. As such, it is a forecast or forward projection of a business idea. It explains the goals of the firm, how it will operate and the likely outcomes of the business venture.

In some respects, a business plan can be likened to a 'blueprint' that an architect prepares for a new building, or that an engineer drafts for a new piece of machinery. In each case a document is prepared that gives the reader an overview of what the intended project will look like, how it will work and what activities must take place to reach the final goals.

Business plans can be applied to any type of enterprise, small or large, and can be equally useful to existing firms as well as new businesses. A business plan has three main functions: to communicate the future of the business, to convey the credibility of the business to the reader and, finally, to act as an organising tool that can help to sell the owner's idea and convert it into reality.[1]

Although some research has shown that successful businesses are more likely to use plans than their unsuccessful competitors, the level of business planning undertaken by firms remains stubbornly low[2] — even in recent studies of developed economies such as the UK, typically less than half of businesses have a formal written business plan.[3] In Australia, a comprehensive survey of several thousand enterprises revealed that only 16 per cent of businesses had a formal plan, and that most of these tended to be large, well-established businesses.[4] A detailed analysis of this study, along with similar research conducted in subsequent years, revealed that large firms tended to plan more than their smaller counterparts.[5] A more recent study of Australian small business reveals that only about 40 per cent possess a current business plan document.[6] A large-scale study of New Zealand business practices and performance found that: although most firms in that country did indeed undertake some sort of planning, most of it was relatively short-term in focus, with the most successful firms tending to be the ones more likely to adopt a formal plan.[7] The need for local SMEs to adopt a business plan has also been recognised by a variety of other organisations across the Asia–Pacific region, including the Malaysian Institute of Accountants (MIA) and the World Bank. MIA recognises that more Malaysian SMEs need to possess and use a business plan, so it has developed an extensive business planning guide to facilitate this.[8]

The advantages and disadvantages of planning

A number of benefits can accrue from the development of a business plan.[9] A well-prepared business plan provides a clear statement of direction and purpose for a firm. It allows management and employees of the firm to work towards a set of clearly defined goals, thus enhancing the likelihood of the goals being reached. This allows the organisation to take the initiative in determining its fate, rather than just reacting to events that occur in the outside environment.

Planning also provides a suitable means of periodically evaluating the performance of the firm. Different quantifiable targets, such as sales revenue, the number of items sold, market share and profitability, can be compared with the actual results at the end of the plan period.[10] Entrepreneurs need to assess the reasons for substantial discrepancies between the forecast and the actual results, and initiate action to overcome the gaps.

Because it is a comprehensive document, a business plan encourages managers and entrepreneurs to effectively review all aspects of their operations.[11] The review and decision-making processes involved in business plan construction foster the more effective use of scarce resources, such as staff, time and money; and improve coordination and internal communication. An effective plan demarcates responsibilities — spelling out the roles of key personnel; it helps clarify job expectations and improves the accountability of staff to the owner–manager.

In addition, the very process of collecting information, analysing it and integrating it into a written document can help ensure that the entrepreneur or small business owner has adequately researched the business idea. If properly done, preparation of a business plan will foster skill development in the process of balanced and objective data collection, systematic analysis of the positive and negative results revealed by the research and the development of a comprehensive business response strategy that integrates all activities of the proposed venture with its internal and external environment.

Other people, including professional advisers, accountants, other owners and the firm's staff, can provide feedback on the accuracy of the completed business plan before it is implemented. This can avoid costly mistakes by identifying and eliminating any errors at the start.

However, it is also important to bear in mind that business plans, in themselves, are not a guarantee of success. Although some research indicates that failed firms are less likely to have a business plan than other businesses, the mere possession of a plan does not ensure survival.[12] No plan can promise success, although preparation of such a document does tend to enhance many of the critical and analytical skills that are strived for by successful entrepreneurs.

Plans on their own cannot eliminate uncertainty, because no organisation exists in a completely predictable environment. No forecasts will be completely accurate and no written plan in itself is a guarantee of success, since this will ultimately rely on a combination of both internal and external environmental factors.[13] In addition, many entrepreneurs have often expressed their fear that a high level of planning will reduce their flexibility and room to move, rather than enhance it.[14] In some cases an inflexible over-reliance on a predetermined plan, even in the face of overwhelming evidence of significant changes taking place in the business environment, can do more damage to the business than might otherwise be the case. There is also evidence emerging that the process and focus of plans (on marketing, operations or finance) should change in response to the prevailing environmental circumstances.[15]

There are several other errors that may reduce the effectiveness of a plan. Common failings can include a lack of sufficient detail in explaining the intentions of the entrepreneur or small business owner; relying on outdated, limited or biased information; failure to undertake detailed market research to validate the sales forecasts, expense estimates and marketing plans of the enterprise; and preparing a document that appears self-evident to the writer, but cannot be understood by other readers.[16]

How effective are plans to the overall success of a business? This is a debatable point. For many years, researchers have tried to quantifiably measure the impact of a business plan on a firm's performance. Intriguingly, studies into this question have failed to conclusively show that planning is beneficial.[17] Although many reports show a link between business planning and firm survival or growth, other studies have produced contradictory results.[18] In the absence of clear-cut data to support one side of the argument or the other, it is up to individual business owners to make their own decisions on whether to use a plan, and the extent to which formal planning processes should be incorporated into the management of their business ventures.

Elements of a business plan

There is no universal format for a business plan; the structure of individual documents can vary from one writer to another. Despite this, most documents include a common mix of items, since there are universal issues that are dealt with by all business enterprises.[19] The main issues dealt with in all business plans can be broadly grouped into those relating to marketing, operations and finance (see figure 7.1).

FIGURE 7.1 Central components of a business plan

These three elements — marketing, operations and finance — are universal. All business owners and entrepreneurs need to research their market, know their customers, understand the state of the industry they operate in and have a comprehensive knowledge of the products or services they sell. They must also be able to structure, manage and operate the business in a logical manner, so that it can work effectively on a day-to-day basis. Finally, they must know how much money is required to start the business, its prospective sales turnover and what returns they are likely to receive from it. One possible format of a plan is discussed below. It covers the three core elements of marketing, operations and finances, and considers additional issues that help round out the business idea and explain it comprehensively. At the end of this chapter, there is an example business plan for a small personal consulting business based in Sydney that follows the same plan structure that guides the rest of this book.

Title page

The title page normally shows the name of the business and that of the owner or owners, and provides contact details (addresses, phone and fax numbers, website URL and email addresses).

Executive summary

An executive summary is an introductory segment, briefly summarising the key features that are explained in more detail later in the plan. It is a quick 'snapshot' of the idea, and is often critical in influencing a reader's judgement of the whole document. Typically, it discusses the following items.
- *Business ideas and goals.* This section provides an overview of the business project, what product or service is being sold and what the entrepreneur's goals are. It also indicates where the business expects to be in a year's time and later.
- *Marketing.* How will the products or services of the business be sold? Who will be the main target markets (customer groups), and what are the main elements of the proposed advertising and promotional strategy for the firm?
- *Operations.* Where will the business be located? How many staff will there be, and how will they be organised? What is the legal structure of the business? How will it be managed?
- *Finances.* What profit is the firm expected to make by the end of the business plan time period? What finance is required, and what will it be used for? Where will such capital be obtained from, and what will the repayments be?

Background

In this section, the business owner or entrepreneur sets down the issues driving the business project. These include:
- *Mission statement.* What is the philosophy and overall vision that the owners have for the business? Why do they want to start and run such a venture?
- *Company history.* Many existing businesses already have well-established systems, products and operating processes and a customer base. It is important to briefly outline these before discussing the changes planned for the future. This segment typically explains how long the enterprise has been

in existence, what products or services it sells and its achievements (and problems) to date.

• *Business goals.* What are the goals of this business? It is useful to provide both short-term goals (those for the next 12 months) and long-term ones (those covering the next 2 or 3 years, or perhaps even longer). It is always desirable to provide some specific, measurable targets (such as net profit sought, anticipated sales revenue, number of staff employed, product range offered and market share to be held), rather than vague or ambiguous statements (such as 'to be the best business in our field') that cannot be evaluated or used as a yardstick for subsequent performance appraisal.

An important but often overlooked aspect of goal setting is the development of an exit strategy — what the entrepreneur needs to do to get out of the business. Many entrepreneurs hope to build their wealth by eventually selling their business. A proposed exit strategy is also important for venture capitalists and other investors who usually want to know how their investment will be returned to them.[20] This segment should cover the method of exiting, the timeline for such events and the steps needed to bring the business to this point.

Marketing

The marketing segment provides the rationale for the existence of the business. Among other things, it gives the entrepreneur the opportunity to show what market research has been done, the likely level of demand for the firm's products, what exactly will be sold by the firm and the intended customer base.

• *Market research.* What research has been done to prepare the plan? It is a good idea to list the primary and secondary sources consulted, including any personal communication with experts and their credentials to speak as experts.[21] If appropriate, attach the results of any surveys, or other particularly relevant data, as an appendix.

• *Market analysis.* What is the result of the research? It is especially important to cover the following issues:

  – *Industry*: What are the characteristics of the industry in which the firm will operate? This section is especially concerned with providing an overview of the industry as a whole, rather than the individual business. What is the current state of that industry, and what are the likely prospects for future growth? A common tool used in such analyses is Porter's five forces model, or its less common extension, the six forces model. The six forces model also considers the impact of customers, government, shareholders, the general public and employees collectively as 'other' stakeholders.[22] If deemed appropriate, either of these or other models can be used at this point.

  – *Seasonality*: Are sales in this industry likely to be affected by changes at different times of the year, or is the business cyclical in some other way — perhaps peaking at different times of the day or week?

  – *Competitors*: How many competitors are there, both direct and indirect? Who are the main players and what is known about them, such as where they are located, what they sell, what prices they charge, how long they have been in the industry, their after-sales service, staffing and customers' views of them?

- *Potential strategic allies*: Are there other firms that the business can work with on joint projects, such as cross-referral of work or other ways that provide mutual benefits?
- *SWOT analysis*: Using the above data, as well as one's own understanding of the business idea, it should be possible to construct a table or list that identifies the various *strengths* and *weaknesses* of the business, as well as the *opportunities* and *threats* that it faces.
- *Marketing plan*. In this section, the marketing mix is dealt with.
  - *Products/services and target market*: Describe or list the main product(s) and/or service(s) to be sold by the business. If making a product, how will it be packaged? What is the target market (who are the main groups of customers for the product/service mix)? Describe the main characteristics of each customer group, such as their age, sex, income level, locality and family structure, their motives for buying this product and the likely number of purchasers in each group. Does one target market have priority over others?
  - *Placement (distribution channel)*: How will goods be distributed to customers? What costs and legal issues may be involved?
  - *Promotions and advertising*: How will the venture's goods and services be advertised and promoted to consumers? What media will be used? Who is responsible for promotions, and what is the cost of each method? It is advisable in this section to map out the advertising and promotions schedule for the course of the whole year.
  - *Pricing policy*: What prices will be set? What sort of pricing strategy will be used? Will there be any discounts for bulk purchases or special customer groups? Will credit terms be offered to any clients?
- *Evaluation of marketing*. How will the effectiveness of the marketing program be assessed? What performance indicators will be used to measure success, and how often will this be done?

Some marketers employ the seven Ps of the extended marketing mix to take particular account of service based businesses.[23] In this business plan format, the additional three P's of people, process and physical evidence are dealt with as functions of operations and production management. However, for clarity, the additional three P's are briefly explained below:

- *People*. The staff, family members and contractors that are required to deliver the service must be considered in terms of skills required, the total price that will be paid for their labour, the availability of this labour and the manner in which workers will be motivated to perform and behave.
- *Process*. The delivery of a service requires careful planning of the timing and staging of the service encounter. This includes planning the support activities and technologies required to ensure that service failures are avoided and wait periods are acceptable. The processes must also be designed in such a way as to ensure the safety and wellbeing of the human actors involved.
- *Physical evidence*. Layout and design of the physical infrastructure, artwork and logos; website design; certificates of competency; accreditations for quality; awards for excellence and the demeanour of other customers are all elements that help define customer expectations and satisfaction levels when they are consuming an intangible service.

Operations and production

Organisational details, day-to-day operating processes and other issues that do not have a clear marketing or financial role are usually discussed here.

- *Legal and licensing requirements.* Include the business name, the legal structure of the business and the laws and licences that the business operates under or must obtain.
- *Management details.* Provide background details about the owners and/or managers, including full name, residential address, phone number, email address, date of birth, qualifications, special skills and job history. Is there any other information about the proprietors that could be important? Do the proprietors have any outstanding loans, guarantees or other financial exposure? Have they ever been bankrupt or charged with an offence that could affect their ability to operate the business? What previous business experience do they have?
- *Organisational structure and staffing.* Who will do which jobs in the business? If there will be more staff than just the owner–operator, who else will be employed? What skills and qualifications do they need? How will the firm recruit staff and at what rate of pay? What further training will staff need? If possible, include an organisational chart for the firm.
- *Professional advisers.* Provide the names and contact details of all the outside business and technical advisers the business expects to use. This may include an accountant, a bank manager, an insurance broker and management consultants.
- *Insurance and security needs.* What insurance will be required for the business and how much will it cost? Are there any special security precautions that need to be considered for the business's property and equipment?
- *Business premises.* Discuss and explain all the issues related to location. Where will the business be based? How accessible is this to customers? Is it convenient to local roads and transport services? If the proposed site is to be leased, what rent, lease period, payments and conditions apply? Are any special facilities required (that is, does the business need a certain building size, specialised customer access, special lighting, airconditioning or rest rooms)?
- *Plant and equipment required.* What equipment does the business need? Provide a list of likely needs, along with the type and make, cost, life expectancy, running costs and service and maintenance requirements.
- *Production processes.* Briefly explain how the product is made, including the supply of any raw materials or trading stock, production processes in the premises and any related issues.
- *Critical risks and contingency plans.* All businesses face potential problems and threats that can derail the goals outlined in the business plan, or possibly even destroy the organisation. Although not all of these can be identified in advance, major ones should be discussed here, along with strategies for dealing with such issues if they arise.

Financial projections

In this section, the financial documents are presented, along with background notes and information that help a reader make sense of the financial forecasts.

- *Basic assumptions and information*
  - Explain the assumptions made in estimating income and expenses, and in calculating the various documents. Justify any unusual items, significant omissions or unusual variations in the figures. What estimates have been made about inflation or increases in costs, wages and interest rates?
  - It may be useful to provide details about the bank accounts that the business operates. What financial institution are these with, what type of account is it (savings, cheque or cash management), and what fees are charged? Does the financial institution have the facilities that the business might need e.g. credit card access, mobile credit card scanners and online banking?
  - Does the business currently have any loans or overdrafts outstanding? Provide details about the lender, the amount borrowed, the current balance still outstanding and the terms of the loan.
  - If additional funds are needed by the business, how much and how are they to be raised? If this money is to be borrowed, provide information about the proposed lender, total amount sought, date required, monthly repayments due, interest rate, loan conditions and term (duration) of the loan.
- *Financial forecasts*
  - *Sales mix forecast:* Use market research and/or past performance to determine likely sales revenue for the first 12 months. Estimate the number of items sold each month, sales income from these and cost of goods sold. Because the estimates in the marketing analysis are linked to and supported by the sales mix forecast, these integral parts of the plan are sometimes referred to as the 'backbone' of the plan.[24]
  - *Cash flow forecast:* A cash flow statement summarises the monthly amount of cash movements (cash inflows and cash outflows) and the resulting cash balance for a year.
  - *Projected profit and loss statement:* Also known as a 'statement of financial performance', this shows business revenues, expenses and net profit for the forthcoming year.
  - *Balance sheet:* Also known as a 'statement of financial position', the balance sheet reports a business's financial position at a specific time. It provides details about the assets (financial resources owned by the firm), liabilities (claims against these resources) and net worth of the business. A balance sheet is usually not provided for a new business. (There is no balance sheet in the sample plan in the appendix to this chapter because Blueprints Business Planning Pty Ltd is a new business. However, a sample balance sheet can be found in figure 14.2.)
  - *Personal expenses, assets and liabilities:* Since much of the capital funding for a new or small business venture is provided by the owner, it is often recommended that the business plan contain details about the owner–manager's personal assets and liabilities. In addition, since the owner usually draws income from the business, it is a good idea to include an estimate of likely personal expenses that will need to be drawn from the business. It is important to build in some degree of variation in these estimates since, just like the business, individuals owners will have high expense and low expense months.

- *Analysis of financial forecasts*
  - From the data provided, it may be desirable to conduct ratio analysis or other pertinent calculations. These could include (but are not necessarily limited to) an estimation of break-even point, fixed and variable costs, contribution margins, mark-ups and margins.

Implementation timetable

This section provides a schedule of the activities needed to set up and run the business. It is usually organised on a monthly basis, providing a set of milestones for the owner–manager to work by.

Appendixes

This section includes any extra useful information such as résumés of the entrepreneur and key management personnel, credit information, quotes for major capital purchases, leases or buy/sell agreements, other legal documents, competitors' promotional material, maps of the business site, floor plans of the business premises, service blueprints, process flowcharts and reference sources and key statistics collected during the market research process.

Different types of plans

Not all plans follow a common template. There are many different structures and sometimes also a difference in the emphasis that entrepreneurs/owner–managers put on particular issues.[25] One of the key features of a business plan must be its flexibility — that is, its ability to accommodate the changing needs of the business and its owner, and to be adjusted as circumstances dictate. In this section, we briefly examine some of the major causes of variations among different plans.

Specificity

In some enterprises, business plans are highly specific and detailed. This is often the case, for example, in a very small micro-enterprise, where there may be only an owner–operator involved in the firm. When a firm is new, small and focused on a limited target market with a constricted product range, it is relatively easy to prepare a business plan that covers all details. In contrast, larger firms may find that their plans are more generalised, owing to the diverse range of their business operations and product range, and the high staff numbers they must take into consideration. There are also local political and cultural contexts to be considered. For example, suggesting that all businesses need particular banking facilities overlooks the reality that many business operations may be based in developing countries and regions that have a predominantly cash economy.[26]

Length

There is no one 'ideal' length for a business plan. Some are simple documents with no more than 10 pages, and others can be several hundred pages long. For some organisations (especially smaller ones), a short plan is a good plan.

A document that is too long is unlikely to be regularly consulted and may be left in a desk drawer where it is soon forgotten. Other business ideas, however, may require much more elaborate explanation and detail. This is especially likely where very large sums of money are being committed, there are numerous parties involved in the business venture, the product or service offering is complex or the organisational requirements are substantial.

Audience

To whom is the business plan addressed? Is it written mainly for the benefit of the organisation's owners and employees, or is it geared towards convincing outsiders (such as financiers) that the firm is a worthwhile venture to invest in? This will affect the level of detail and tone of the finished document, as well as the amount of confidential or commercially sensitive material disclosed.

In some cases, external factors will be the driving force behind the decision to prepare such a blueprint. This can occur, for example, when finance is being sought for a business project. Banks, venture capitalists, other financial institutions and private investors will want to know a great deal of detailed information before committing themselves to a new business venture or to the expansion of an existing one.[27] Government assistance to small business also often depends on the presentation of a suitable business plan. In such cases, it is important to ensure that the completed document is well written, logically argued and puts forward a clear case for support from external parties. However, it is often very difficult for entrepreneurs and business owners to determine how much confidential or commercially sensitive information should be released to outsiders.

In other cases, internal factors will be the main reason for developing a plan. For example, an entrepreneur may wish to draw together all his or her thoughts into a cohesive whole and ensure that no important details have been omitted in the development of the business project. Another reason may be to improve coordination of existing activities within the firm or to clarify the production targets the business is expected to reach.[28] When the document is being prepared largely for use 'in house,' it may be easier to commit confidential information to paper. In some cases, the business plan can also identify future staffing needs of the business and help to 'map out' how current or future staffing arrangements will operate. It may also be possible to omit some details that are well known to everyone, since all likely readers of the plan are already involved in the project.

What would you do?

Tangled up at yoga?

Recently, a friend of yours, Kevin, has been considering buying a yoga studio. For the last five years, he has been taking basic yoga lessons every Wednesday evening. Recently the owner, Mr Smythe, has been talking about selling the business.

Kevin is excited about the prospect and has asked Mr Smythe a lot of questions about the operation. Approximately 130 people take lessons each week. Some of these individuals are signed to 10- and 20-lesson contracts, while others come on a casual basis. The current owner could not give any details on the weekly running expenses of the studio, although he did say that he felt the business was very profitable.

Some people pay by credit card and others with cash, but not all of these amounts have been entered in the books. Unfortunately, it isn't possible to pinpoint how many people actually come in for lessons because the instructors sometimes collect the money and pocket their share before giving Mr Smythe the remainder.

Kevin has mentioned that the facilities are 'becoming slightly run down'. Mr Smythe said that he had some major renovations planned but was vague on what these would be, their cost and when they might start.

Mr Smythe runs an advertisement every week in the Sunday edition of the local paper, and believes that his own presence has been important to customers because he arrives at the studio every day at mid-morning, and does not go home until after the last lesson. As a result, Mr Smythe knows all of these people personally, and encourages them to keep up their lessons and bring their friends along.

Mr Smythe says he has a business plan but won't let Kevin see it until an agreement to buy the firm has been signed. 'I can't let any competitors see my goals and strategies in advance,' he says.

Questions

1. Evaluate and discuss Mr Smythe's yoga business. What are the major strengths and flaws of this small business?
2. Do you think Kevin should agree to Mr Smythe's request, and sign the agreement before examining the business plan? Is there any other way to deal with Smythe's concerns about confidentiality?

Case study prepared by the small business staff, School of Accounting and Law, RMIT University

Time frame

A business plan can be geared for a short time period (anything up to a year) or it may have a longer perspective. Short-term plans can afford to be more detailed, whereas a long-term orientation means that the plan must be more generalised in its contents. Many researchers argue that business planning in small firms tends to be overwhelmingly short-term in orientation, and that it is unusual to find a small business with plans that extend beyond a two-year time horizon.[29] Of course, there are always some exceptions to this rule — some firms have been able to successfully use a very long-term time scale to help turn their business around. In general, however, a shorter term focus is used by most small organisations.

Strategic or operational orientation

Strategic plan
A plan that sets out the long-term focus of the business, its mission and its vision, and attempts to understand the environment in which the business operates.

Business plans should not be mistaken for another common business tool, the strategic plan. A **strategic plan** sets out the long-term focus of the business, its mission and vision, and attempts to understand the environment in which the business operates.[30] In contrast, business plans tend to be more focused on operational issues. As the contents of a typical business plan reveal, such documents focus on putting an idea into action, and cover most of the practical day-to-day issues involved in business creation, growth and management. In reality, there is often some overlap between the two. There is also evidence suggesting that the size of an organisation affects the degree of strategic planning. Typically, smaller firms (often recently established) think no more than one or two years ahead. Only when firms grow in size do they start to have a long term focus.[31]

Preparing the document: the business-planning process

Few business plans are written at one sitting. More typically, a plan is the result of a series of logical steps that most entrepreneurs work through, regardless of whether or not they are conscious of the process involved (see figure 7.2). These steps are often iterative; a person may go through some of them several times before finally developing a plan that all parties feel comfortable with. The following sections briefly describe the critical steps in the **business-planning process**.

Business-planning process *A series of logical steps governing the creation, implementation and revision of a business plan.*

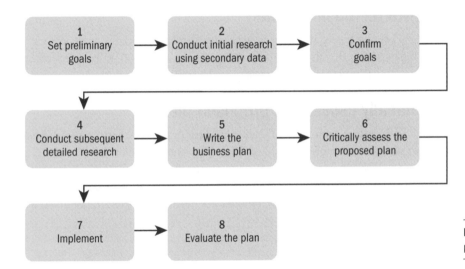

FIGURE 7.2 The planning process

1. Set preliminary goals

All prospective business operators have a vision of what they want to achieve, what business they want to be in and what they want to sell. A useful first point in planning, therefore, is to commit these initial (often vague) goals to paper.[32]

2. Conduct initial research using secondary data

Using the preliminary goals spelled out above, the entrepreneur/small business owner must now collect information from existing data sources that can provide more details on the current state of the industry, and the prospective viability of another entry into the field. At this point, rather than undertaking potentially expensive and time-consuming primary data collection, the entrepreneur may find that secondary data are more useful and easier to gather.

3. Confirm goals

Initial, general research should allow an entrepreneur/small business owner to either confirm or cancel the original goals. Does the business idea now seem viable? If the preliminary research does not clearly indicate that there is room for another market entrant, it may be advisable to abort the business idea at this stage, unless, of course, the intention is to create an entirely new product or service. If the initial idea does seem viable, attention should be turned to developing specific goals and action plans. Where the product or service is entirely new to the market, more emphasis will be necessary on goals related to increasing awareness in the marketplace.

4. Conduct subsequent detailed research

Now is the time to collect detailed information from as many different and specific sources as possible. This is the stage at which all the detailed elements of the business plan (such as marketing, operations and finance) must be investigated.

5. Write the business plan

Once market research results have been obtained and analysed, the entrepreneur/ small business owner must prepare a first version of the proposed business plan, covering all the subject matter suggested in the business plan outline.

6. Critically assess the proposed plan

Once a first draft is completed, the entrepreneur/small business owner should set the plan aside for a brief period of time. They should then return to it with a critical and editorial perspective. Does the document read well? Are all elements integrated? Are there any weaknesses in the argument that must be revised? At this stage, it is often useful to have an outsider evaluate the plan to obtain some unbiased feedback.

7. Implement

Once devised, the business plan must, of course, be put into action. As time unfolds, the entrepreneur/small business owner must adhere to the processes and goals outlined in the original business plan, unless there are strong reasons to do otherwise. If a plan is not implemented, the value of preparing the document in the first place is highly questionable.

8. Evaluate the plan

At the end of a year, or another given time frame, it is necessary to review and evaluate the plan and draw up a new set of forecasts for the future. This is also a useful opportunity to reassess the venture's stated goals to see if they are still realistic or whether some modification is warranted.

When business planning is seen by an entrepreneur or small business owner as an event that occurs only once a year, it can produce an inflexible perspective. On the other hand, those owner–managers and entrepreneurs who treat business planning as an ongoing process are more likely to build firms that are highly responsive to their environment. This latter group regard the business plan as a tool that is constantly reviewed; this allows them to respond quickly to any dramatic or rapid changes in their operating environment. Such responsiveness is especially important for new and small firms that operate in highly dynamic conditions.

SUMMARY

A business plan is a written outline of a business. It may be devised for an existing firm or for a new venture that has not yet been launched. The main advantages of business planning include more complete information gathering, balanced decision making and assistance in raising finance. Disadvantages of a plan can include skewed information seeking, incorrect assumptions, inflexibility and unrealistic expectations.

All business plans, whatever their structure, should cover the key issues of marketing, operations and financing. The major elements of a typical plan can include an executive summary, background on the firm (if an existing enterprise), marketing details, operational arrangements, financial projections, a timetable for implementation and other relevant details.

Plans vary from one business to another. Formats and sequence are often quite different, although all of them should cover the basic issues. In addition, written business plans may have different levels of specificity, be written for different audiences, and cover short-term or long-term time frames.

The business-planning process is an ongoing process by which plans are constructed, implemented and evaluated. It includes the steps of preliminary goal setting, initial information gathering, formulation of set goals, detailed research, plan preparation, critical analysis of the proposed plan, implementation and subsequent evaluation and revision.

REVIEW QUESTIONS

1. List and describe the different types of potential audience for a firm's business plan.
2. Define (in the correct order that they appear) the seven major elements of a business plan.
3. What are the main differences between a strategic plan and a business plan?
4. 'The disadvantages of preparing a business plan outweigh the advantages.' Do you agree with this statement? Explain your reasons.
5. Outline and briefly describe (in the correct sequence) the eight steps involved in the business-planning process.

DISCUSSION QUESTIONS

1. Read section 3 (Marketing) of the business plan for Blueprints Business Planning Pty Ltd in the appendix to this chapter. In your opinion, has sufficient market research been done to prove that the business is potentially viable?
2. If you were the owner of a business but employed a full-time manager to run your firm, who would be best placed to write up the plan?
3. What do you think are the major pieces of information that an investor would look for first in a business plan, and why would an investor look for these items?

SUGGESTED READING

Bangs, D. & Schaper, M., *The Australian Business Planning Guide*, 2nd edn, Allen & Unwin, Sydney, 2003.

Barringer, B., *Preparing Effective Business Plans*, Pearson Education, New Jersey, 2009.

Humphrey, N., *The Penguin Small Business Guide*, Penguin Australia, Camberwell, 2007.

Oliver, L. & English, J. *The Small Business Book: a New Zealand guide for the 21st century*, 5th edn, Allen & Unwin, Crows Nest, 2007.

Case study

From Howling Wolves to howling success

The Howling Wolves Wine Group is a story of innovation, marketing prowess and good strategic and tactical business planning. Allan Waters is the original owner of Harmans Ridge Estate, a 17 hectare property located in the world-famous, premium wine region of Margaret River, Western Australia. Commencing in 1998, he established a hi-tech winery to produce a range of quality wines, using a contract wine-making business model. In 2002, after establishing and refining this business model, Waters joined forces with friends, Vaughan Sutherland, a successful and innovative advertising professional and Damian Knowles, an experienced fine wine retailer, to create the Howling Wolves Wine Group (HWWG). This powerful combination of production, marketing, distribution, wholesale and retail sales expertise is a key factor in the rapid, yet planned, growth of HWWG into some of the most promising markets for premium wines worldwide. The new group was financed internally by loans from the directors in order to maintain tight ownership and control.

The company has a clear strategy to focus on innovation in branding and wine-making technologies to project their premium products and wine-making skills into diverse international markets. The winery crushes over 1600 tonnes of grapes to produce in excess of 1.2 million litres of premium wine each year. Looking beyond this impressive volume of wine production, at the core of any good business model is a quality product that will satisfy customer needs. To ensure the quality of the wines is maintained at these high production volumes, HWWG has employed the skills of one of Australia's most respected wine-makers, Mark Warren. Mark has been recognised by Australia's premier wine critics as the creator of Shiraz and Merlot wines that are among the best to ever come out of the Margaret River region. As well as producing mid-price wines, Warren also oversees the selection of fruit for their super-premium *Small Batch*™ range.

The business plan for HWWG has a geographically segmented strategy operating at multiple price points, with products, brands and entry strategies to suit local markets in Australia, Switzerland, Singapore, Indonesia, the US, India and China. The wines produced range from quality entry-level wines of the *Eight Vineyards* brand, and several styles of white, red and sparkling wines sold under the Howling Wolves *Claw* banner, to the super-premium quality *Small Batch*™ range. Each wine aims to represent exceptional value within their price range, and is designed with global wine markets and trends in mind.

Managing Director of HWWG, Damian Knowles, has some salient stories to tell about when a plan needs to be changed for strategic, tactical or practical reasons. For example, in 2003 the original brand *Howling 'Wolf'* was identified by the Australian Wine & Brandy Corporation (export regulator) as contravening the International Geographic Index because there was already a commune in Germany named *'Wolfe'*, hence the name-change to the plural *Howling Wolves*. This change of branding was slight but still entailed a great deal of unplanned expense in changing signage, bottle labels, packaging, marketing material, websites and all manner of corporate livery.

Because the development of brand names linked with innovation and quality is a key strategic direction for HWWG, clear ownership of trademarks was considered a critical success factor. Registered trademarks have been filed, and the business rigourously defends any identified breaches of their intellectual property. In 2007, the group successfully brought legal action against a new start-up California-based business calling itself *Howling Wolf Wines*, which was forced to cease trading under that name in US markets.

Another strategic marketing and distribution plan was to create the brand *8 Vineyards* for the Asian market. The strategy here was to back up a good entry-level product with a brand name that resonates in Asian cultures. The number 8 is considered a particularly lucky number by the Chinese community. To capitalise on this, the product was placed in the mainland Chinese market prior to the 2008 Olympic Games.

Another change of operational and financial plans was required to enter the Indian market. Because India imposes up to 250% tax on imported wines, a strategic decision was taken to produce the wine in India, to avoid this tax impost. A hi-tech winery modelled around what had been learned at the Australian winery is planned in a 50/50 joint venture with Birhans PL, a well-known Indian distiller and distributor. Premium Margaret River cuttings were grafted to root stock planted on a 100 acre property in Shreepur, a region with a suitable climate and soil profile located about 300 km south of Mumbai. HWWG have enlisted experienced Margaret River region viticulture consultant, Tim Quinlan, to oversee the transport, planting and cultivation in Shreepur. According to the director of the JV company Harshawardhan Apte, the long term plan is to transfer the entire production and distribution of the *8 Vineyards* range to the Indian joint venture.

The nine staff who are directly employed by the group would appear to have an exciting and rewarding future laid out ahead of them. Like any good business planner, HWWG will continue to revise and evolve their strategies and tactics to suit the external environment and respond to opportunities; but it is clear that the central tenet of a strong focus on innovation and branding will form the unique selling proposition of this rapidly globalising SME. When asked about future exit strategies for the directors, Damian muses that this has never been discussed — not one of them wants to leave right now, and why would they!

Questions

1. What do you think are the potential problems for HWWG arising from not having any exit strategy for the directors?
2. What financial and operational risks may the business face in a global market that do not exist in the Australian domestic market?
3. Should HWWG create a separate but jointly prepared business plan with Birhans for the Indian operation? Explain your reasoning.
4. What other geographic markets do you think HWWG should be considering, and why?

Business plan scenario — a blueprint for success?

This scenario should be read in concert with the sample business plan that follows.
For several months, three friends had been thinking about starting their own business. Stephen Molloy, Jessie Jones and Andrew St John had talked about running their own business for a long time, but nothing had gone much further than a talk over coffee now and then.

Finally, in May 2011, Jessie Jones rang her two friends and decided to take action.

'I have an idea for a business,' she told them. 'We'll call it Blueprints Business Planning. Since I have a lot of business experience, I will run it and I will be the starting point for the venture. If you are prepared to put in some money and a little bit of time serving as directors, I think we can eventually grow this into something bigger.'

Andrew and Stephen were intrigued. 'What do we have to do?,' they asked.

'Not much at present,' Jessie said. 'Let me do a draft proposal and then we can meet to discuss it.'

Two weeks later, they met to discuss the results so far. Jessie had exhausted herself preparing an initial business plan for the other two to read, and was quite proud of what she had done in such a short time.

Andrew said, 'I have a few problems with your business plan.' Stephen nodded in agreement.

Jessie was quite hurt. She had put a lot of work into the idea. What should she do now?

Questions

1. Review the sample business plan prepared by Jessie in the appendix to this chapter. What are the strengths and weaknesses of the plan as it currently stands?
2. Should the directors proceed with the project as outlined in the business plan? Why or why not?
3. Why do you think Andrew and Stephen have reservations about the plan? What alternative strategies could Jessie adopt for going into business?

ENDNOTES

1. B. Mainprize & K. Hindle, 'The benefit: a well written entrepreneurial business plan is to an entrepreneur what a midwife is to an expecting mother' *The Journal of Private Equity*, vol. 11, no. 1, 2007, pp. 40–52.
2. S. Kraus, R. Harms & E.J. Schwarz, 'Strategic planning in smaller enterprises — new empirical findings', *Management Research News* vol. 29, no. 6, 2006, pp. 334–44; J.A. Pearce, D.K. Robbins & R.B. Robinson, 'The impact of grand strategy and planning formality on financial performance', *Strategic Management Journal*, vol. 8, no. 2, 1987, pp. 125–34.
3. S.M. Richbell, H.D. Watts & P. Wardle, 'Owner-managers and business planning in the small firm', International Small Business Journal, vol. 24, no. 5, 2006, pp. 496–514.
4. Department of Industry, Science and Tourism, *The 1995 Business Longitudinal Survey*, AGPS, Canberra, 1997.
5. B. Gibson & G. Cassar, 'Planning behavior variables in small firms', *Journal of Small Business Management*, vol. 40, no. 3, 2002, pp. 171–86.

6. P. Weber, L. Geneste, M. Schaper & W. Soontiens, 2009, *Western Australian Small Business Benchmarks 2008 [main report]*, Perth, Curtin University of Technology.

7. S. Knuckey, H. Johnston, C. Campbell-Hunt, K. Carlew, L. Corbett & C. Massey, *Firm Foundations: A Study of New Zealand Business Practices and Performance*, Ministry of Economic Development, Wellington, 2002, p. 45.

8. Professional Accountants in Business (PAIB) & The Malaysian Institute of Accountants (MIA), *Business planning guide: practice application for SMEs*, 2006, mia.org.my.

9. M. Schaper, 'Writing the perfect business plan', *My Business*, October, 1996, pp. 26–7.

10. T.W. Zimmerer, N.M. Scarborough & D. Wilson, *Essentials of Entrepreneurship and Small Business Management*, 5th edn, 2008, Pearson Education Inc, Upper Saddle, New Jersey, pp. 1346.

11. A.M. Hormozi, G.S. Sutton, R.D. McMinn & W Lucio, 'Business plans for new or small businesses: Paving the path to success', *Management Decision*, vol. 40, no. 7–8, 2002, pp. 755–64.

12. S.C. Perry, 'The relationship between written business plans and the failure of small businesses in the US', *Journal of Small Business Management*, vol. 39, no. 3, 2001, pp. 301–9.

13. J.M. Bryson, *Strategic Planning for Public and Nonprofit Organisations: A Guide to Strengthening and Sustaining Organisational Achievement*, Jossey-Bass, San Francisco, 1995.

14. A. Gibb & L. Davies, 'In support of frameworks for the development of growth models of the small business', *International Small Business Journal*, vol. 9, no. 1, 1990, pp. 15–31.

15. M. Gruber, 'Uncovering the value of planning in new venture creation: a process and contingency perspective', *Journal of Business Venturing*, vol. 22, no. 6, 2007, pp. 782–807.

16. 'New study shows six critical business plan mistakes,' *Business Horizons*, vol. 46, no. 4, 2003, p. 83.

17. T. Mazzarol, 'Do formal business plans really matter? An exploratory study of small business owners in Australia', *Small Enterprise Research*, vol. 9, no. 1, 2001, pp. 32–45; B. Honig & T. Karlsson, 'Institutional forces and the written business plan', *Journal of Management*, vol. 30, no. 1, 2004, p. 29.

18. C.R. Schwenk & C.B. Schrader, 'Effects of formal strategic planning on financial performance in small firms: A meta-analysis', *Entrepreneurship Theory and Practice*, vol. 17, no. 3 (Spring), 1993, pp. 53–63.

19. S.R. Rich & D.E. Gumpert, 'How to write a winning business plan', *Harvard Business Review*, vol. 63, no. 3, May–June, 1985, pp. 156–66; W.A. Sahlman, 'How to write a great business plan', *Harvard Business Review*, vol. 75, no. 4, July–August, 1997, pp. 98–108.

20. T. McKaskill, *Finding The Money: How To Raise Venture Capital*, Wilkinson Publishing, Melbourne, 2006, p. 71.

21. B. Barringer, *Preparing Effective Business Plans*, Pearson Education, New Jersey, 2009, p. 108.

22. M.E. Porter, *The Competitive Advantage of Nations*, 2nd edn, Free Press, New York, 1998.

23. A. Kotler & D. Armstrong, *Principles of Marketing* 4th edn, Pearson Education, French's Forrest, NSW, 2009, p. 21

24. Cornwall, J.R. Vang, D.O. & Hartman, J.M, *Entrepreneurial Financial Management: An Applied Approach*, Pearson Prentice Hall, New Jersey, 2004.

25. P.D. O'Hara, *The Total Business Plan*, 2nd edn, John Wiley, New York, 1995.

26. A Kambil, V. Wei-teh Long & C. Kwan, 'The seven disciplines for venturing in China', *MIT Sloan Management Review*, Winter 2006, vol. 47, no. 2, pp. 85–9

27. C. Mason & M. Stark, 'What do investors look for in a business plan? A comparison of the investment criteria of bankers, venture capitalists and business angels', *International Small Business Journal*, vol. 22, no. 3, 2004, p. 227.

28. *How to Prepare, Present and Negotiate a Business Plan*, EPB Publishers, Singapore, 1994.

29. W. Glen & J. Weerawardena, 'Strategic planning practices in small enterprises in Queensland', *Small Enterprise Research*, vol. 4, no. 3, 1996, pp. 5–16.

30. C. Sutton, *Strategic Concepts*, Macmillan, London, 1998, p. 16.

31. S. Maguire, S.C.L. Koh & A. Magrys, 'The adoption of e-business and knowledge management in SMEs', *Benchmarking: An International Journal*, vol. 14, no. 1, 2007.

32. A.M. Hormozi, G.S. Sutton, R.D. McMinn, & W. Lucio, *see* note 11.

Sample business plan

Note: The business plan in this appendix is hypothetical, and is provided solely for the purposes of illustrating the nature and content of a completed plan. The business name, personal details, statistical data and references are fictional; no link with any actual person or organisation is intended.

Blueprints Business Planning Pty Ltd

Business plan for the period July 2011 to June 2012

Blueprints Business Planning Pty Ltd
Australian Business Number (ABN) 99 999 999 999

135 Central Boulevard
Sydney New South Wales, 2000 Australia

Telephone: +61 2 9999 9999
Facsimile: +61 2 9999 9998
Email: jessie@blueprintsbusinessplanning.com.au
Internet: www.blueprintsbusinessplanning.com.au

Prepared June 2011

Contents

Section 1: Executive summary

1.1 Business idea and goals

The main goal is to establish a small, private (proprietary limited) company that specialises in management consulting services for the small and medium-sized enterprise (SME) sector in Sydney and other cities within the state of New South Wales, Australia. The services to be provided will include preparation of business plans, training in small business management skills, and book sales.

The owners plan to begin by employing one person full time (Jessie Jones, a major shareholder) and gradually grow to the point where the business employs three or four people within two to three years of inception. The business intends to generate sales revenue of about A$100 000 and to make a A$2000 profit by the end of its first year of trading.

1.2 Marketing

Blueprints Business Planning Pty Ltd will have two key target markets: small business managers (for whom it will prepare business plans, feasibility studies and associated services) and SME support agencies (for whom it will provide contract services, principally training in small business management skills). There are approximately 200 000 SMEs in the Sydney metropolitan area. Market research indicates that there is currently unmet demand for the products we plan to offer. We will promote the business using a variety of methods, including direct mail, telephone canvassing, a Yellow Pages listing, networking, a website and testimonials.

1.3 Operations

The business will operate with one employee (Jessie Jones, managing director) at start-up and be based from an office at her home. A minimal outlay of equipment and expenses is envisaged at this stage, as most necessary equipment has already been obtained.

1.4 Finance

The business will be self-funding. The directors will provide an initial capital injection of A$10 000, and it is envisaged that the company will generate enough funds from subsequent operations to allow it to operate on a 'no borrowing' policy unless there is a major change in focus.

Section 2: Background

2.1 Mission statement

Blueprints Business Planning Pty Ltd exists to provide business planning services, business education (training) programs and management advice to small and medium-sized organisations.

The company intends to become known as one of the best business planners and advisers in the Sydney marketplace. We want to be known as an organisation that emphasises honesty, accuracy and objectivity in the information we provide to clients; that values confidentiality and sensitivity in all its relations with other parties; and that gives tailor-made responses to individual client needs.

In this way, Blueprints Business Planning Pty Ltd seeks to promote the interests of the following.

- *Clients*. By providing the above services, we can help our clients achieve success in the marketplace and realise their own business goals.
- *The wider community*. Helping businesses become more successful ultimately stimulates local economic development, job creation and wealth distribution.
- *Our employees*. A well-paid, motivated and well-educated staff is essential to ongoing success. In return, employees should expect to receive secure employment, to continually expand and improve their business skills, to be encouraged to try new ideas and approaches and to work in a comfortable, encouraging environment.
- *The owners of the company*. Successful achievement of the company mission should allow the company to operate profitably and to provide a fair return on effort and investment by the owners on a long-term basis.

2.2 Company history

This is a new business that springs from the existing work of Jessie Jones as a management consultant (operating as a sole trader) from August 2001 to June 2011. During this time, Jessie provided training programs, mentoring services and a limited amount of business planning to a range of clients.

2.3 Business goals

The business's goals for the short term (next 12 months) are to employ at least one person full-time on a salary of approximately A$42 000 p.a. (gross), to meet all operating expenses and to generate a net profit of at least A$2000 for future investment. The long-term (next two or three years) goals are to establish a viable consultancy service employing up to five people based in Sydney, delivering services in business planning with its own purchased building.

A future exit strategy has been agreed to by the three foundation shareholders/directors, should any of them wish to liquidate their interest in the business at a later stage. The directors have agreed that, after the end of the third year of trading, any shareholder will have the right to ask for the business to be independently valued; the remaining directors will then have first option to buy out that person's interest. If they do not wish to exercise this right, the shareholder may sell to an outside party.

Section 3: Marketing

3.1 Market research

The following sources were used to prepare this business plan:
- Australian Bureau of Statistics
- NSW Small Business Advisory Network
- personal interviews with several business enterprise centres in and around Sydney
- Institute of Management Consultants, Australia

- a brief survey of SMEs that already use outside consultants
- other existing management consultancies
- a search of the relevant management literature.

3.2 Market analysis

After a review of the industry, the following conclusions were drawn.

(a) *Industry analysis*

There is a definite demand for generic management consulting services, although the industry is still unregulated and ill-defined (Brown 2008, p. 48). Most services provided are aimed at larger corporations since, at the 'bottom end', micro-enterprises are too small to afford business planning services. Accordingly, niche opportunities to provide these services best exist among small to medium-sized (mid-range) businesses (Ziericki 2007). A study of Australian SMEs recently showed that most need more training but are unsure where to find this (Australian Bureau of Statistics 2009, pp. 23–4). This need is especially evident among the 200 000 known SMEs in the Sydney metropolitan region (Sydney Chamber of Commerce 2009).

(b) *Seasonality*

It is estimated that business declines in December and January, which represents the Christmas break and summer holiday period in Australia.

(c) *Competitors*

The business's competitors are very similar to its potential strategic allies. They include:

- other management consultants (especially those who focus on SME training)
- accountancy practices (which also act as advisers to many small firms)
- publicly funded business support agencies (such as business enterprise centres)
- commercial training providers.

The Sydney Yellow Pages lists 123 management consultancies, 3000 accountancy practices, 20 public agencies and 34 commercial training providers in the city. This does not include non-Sydney advisers who are contracted on an 'as needed' basis by firms who wish to use their services.

(d) *Potential strategic alliances*

Potential exists to subcontract work from:

- accountants (that is, those who don't want to do business plans themselves but who do want to offer it as a service to their clients)
- business enterprise centres (such as those who want training courses provided or business plans assessed)
- other management consultants (who may need someone to help if their workload becomes too great).

We intend to focus our efforts on finding a small number of strategic allies (about six) with whom we can form long-term relationships.

(e) *SWOT analysis*

The information on the previous page was used to develop a list of potential strengths, weaknesses, opportunities and threats.

Potential strengths	Jessie's substantial SMEs advisory experience Links to NSW Small Business Advisory Network
Potential weaknesses	One-person operation at present Minimal track record in external consultancies Little skill in preparing tenders
Potential opportunities	Growth in external training programs Growth of ongoing mentoring services Good placement to qualify if sector becomes regulated
Potential threats	Competitors Sensitivity of SMEs to economic downturns

3.3 Marketing plan

3.3.1 Products/services and target market

(a) *Business planning*

Preparation of detailed business plans, covering all parts of a firm's activities

Target markets:
- Small to medium-sized firms (10 to 100 employees).
- Sydney metropolitan area.
- Established companies (preferably two years or older).
- Approximately 200 000 such firms.

Customer buying motives:
- SMEs often need specialist expertise to help in running their firms.
- It is often too difficult to do themselves.
- Such advice is often needed for organisational survival or repositioning.

(b) *Training*

Short, intensive (one- or two-day) courses on marketing, human resources, business planning, basic financial management and record-keeping for SMEs

Target markets:
- New small business owners and existing owners keen to increase their knowledge.
- Central Sydney metropolitan area.
- Sufficient business income (A$200 000+) to be willing to pay for services.
- An estimated 5000 new businesses that start trading each year.

Customer buying motives:
- Owner–managers of SMEs want short, focused courses that develop their own knowledge base and competencies.
- Such courses allow them to acquire useful skills in different aspects of management.
- The increased knowledge helps them to grow their own business.

(c) *Small business development books*

Sales of various book titles, best done in conjunction with training courses (that is, sell books at the end of a particular course).

Target markets:
- Participants in training courses, as discussed above.
- Central Sydney metropolitan areas.
- Sufficient business income (A$200 000+) to be willing to pay for services.

Customer buying motives:
- These books provide more information about materials initially covered in our training courses.

3.3.2 Placement

Since this is a home-based business dealing directly with clients at their premises, no particular distribution arrangements are envisaged as necessary.

3.3.3 Promotions and advertising

To start trading, the business already has a number of secure contracts in place. As such, it is not necessary to actively promote the enterprise to the general community. However, it would be useful to alert other potential clients to its existence, with a view to seeking work from them at a later stage. To this end, the following promotional tools will be used by the business:
- business cards and letterheads
- direct mail followed up by telephone contacts
- listing in the next edition of the Sydney Yellow Pages under 'Management Consultants'
- promotional literature — a series of A4 sheets about the company covering staff of the organisation, services provided, the benefits of using the company and a listing of previous clients
- networking — links to other practising professionals through membership of the Institute of Management Consultants and other local business bodies
- testimonials — a file of positive testimonials from clients that can be used as references for future marketing
- internet — a website and more links to this to be built in over time.

3.3.4 Pricing policy

Charge-out rates for tendered or casual consulting and training services will be A$120 per hour, which is the current market rate (Jones 2010 p. 1). The standard price of preparing a basic 10-page business plan will be A$2000; this figure is comparable to prices charged by other private sector business planners (both fees exclude GST). Any specific costs (such as travel and accommodation) will be additional. These prices are set towards the higher end of those charged within the commercial training sector, but well within the acceptable price range for management consulting services. Terms of payment will be 10 working days (two calendar weeks) and accounts will be tendered on the day that the services are provided.

3.4 Evaluation of marketing

The effectiveness of our marketing strategy will be assessed on a six-monthly basis by analysing sales data to see what draws the company's work. For example, if most work is coming from the distribution of promotional brochures, then this source of promotion will be seen to be effective.

Section 4: Operations

4.1 Legal and licensing requirements

(a) *Business name and legal structure*

Blueprints Business Planning Pty Ltd (Australian Business Number 99 999 999 999) is a proprietary limited company. The company structure has already been registered and established with three shareholders:

Stephen Molloy   (40% shareholding)
Jessie Jones   (40% shareholding)
Andrew St John   (20% shareholding)

who also serve as the directors of the entity.

(b) *Operating laws and licences*

After checking with the Small Business Development Corporation's Business Licence Centre, it appears that no specific licences are needed to operate this business, except for a home-based business permit from the City of Sydney.

4.2 Management details

The managing director of the company will be:

	Jessie Jones
Home address:	135 Central Blvd, Sydney NSW 2000
	Ph: (02) 9999 9999 Fax: (02) 9999 9998
Date of birth:	14 August 1970
Qualifications:	Bachelor of Business (distinction)
Experience:	Owner of café, 1992–2001
	Management consultant and owner of Jones
	Consultancies, 2001–11

4.3 Organisational structure and staffing

Initially, the following tasks of the business will be done by the managing director:

- consulting
- training
- servicing board of directors
- marketing and public enquiries
- bookkeeping and administration of the enterprise.

Two casual trainers will be employed to help deliver the training programs, and to help conduct research and write business plans for clients. Both will report directly to the managing director.

The following is an intended final staffing structure as part of the business's long-term (two to three years) goals:

- *Managing director — business consultancy*
  Duties: Provide business planning, mentoring and occasional training to clients; undertake marketing of the business; provide administrative services and strategic development of the firm
  Salary: Set at approximately A$42 000 per annum in Year 1, rising to A$50 000 by the end of Year 2
  This role will be filled by Jessie Jones.

- *Consultant — general business planning*
  Duties: Conduct business planning and general management consultancy work for clients; undertake office management
  Salary: A$45 000 per annum
  Qualifications required: Aptitude for dealing with the public; small business background; experience in preparing and evaluating business plans; business degree useful, but not essential.
- *Consultant — training activities*
  Duties: Prepare and deliver training courses
  Salary: A$45 000 per annum
  Qualifications required: Aptitude for dealing with the public; small business background; training qualifications (or willingness to obtain); proven ability to deliver effective training sessions; formal educational qualifications preferred.

More detailed job descriptions, employment contracts and ongoing performance appraisal mechanisms will be needed during the second year of operations, or when the employment of full-time staff other than Jessie is necessary (Anderson & James 2008, p. 2). This information must be compiled and entered into that year's business plan. When the business does reach the stage of employing more than one full-time person, it will also use a team-based approach in dealing with specific projects, with different staff members leading the rest of the team on particular assignments.

Training
A minimum of 20 hours professional development must be undertaken by each employee each year, as such training is needed to keep abreast of general developments in the field. One area where specific knowledge is needed is in the preparation of tender submissions.

Professional associations
The managing director will seek to join the Institute of Management Consultants of Australia (IMCA).

4.4 Professional advisers

Accountant
Sunshine Street Accountants
4 Sunshine Street, Midland NSW 2050
Ph: (02) 7999 9999 Fax: (02) 2222 9999 Email: info@sunshinestreet.com.au
Lawyer
Moot & Moot Partners
Suite 1, 1 Main St, Sydney NSW 2002
(Postal address: PO Box 1, Sydney NSW 2045)
Ph: (02) 8999 9999 Fax: (02) 3999 9999 Email: reception@moot.net.au
Insurance broker
To be determined
Bank account
MegaBank Australia
5 St Gregory Tce, Sydney NSW 2000
Manager: Janine Gregory
Ph: (02) 2222 3333 Fax: (02) 2222 3334
Email: Janine.Gregory@megabank.com.au

Bookkeeper
To be determined. This will not be sought unless the managing director can no longer provide this service.

4.5 Insurance and security issues

The following insurance will be required for the business:
- professional indemnity
- public liability
- workers compensation
- director's liability (possibly).

It is estimated that the combined cost for these insurances will be approximately A\$2500 in Year 1 of trading.

Necessary security precautions for the business property and equipment include the provision of a locked filing cabinet for client records. Online security for the website will be needed, and electronic data will be backed up regularly and stored off-site.

4.6 Business premises

(a) *Location*

The business will be based at Jessie's home at 135 Central Boulevard, Sydney NSW 2000. A separate room that can be used as a dedicated office is available, with all required furniture and equipment. The property concerned is owned by Jessie and her husband, so it has security of tenure indefinitely. No rent is payable and no special equipment or fixtures are required.

Training courses will be conducted at specialised venues that can be hired on a daily basis.

(b) *Council and government rules*

A home-based business licence will have to be obtained from the City of Sydney. No other licences apply to the project. Trainers and business planners do not need to be licensed.

(c) *Ability to access target market*

Since most services will be provided on-site at the customer's premises, the office will easily allow the business to access its target markets. The office is located close to most major roads and freeways. Clients will be scattered throughout the metropolitan area, therefore, the firm will need to travel to the client's preferred locations.

4.7 Equipment required

The equipment required for the business will be:
- answering machine
- telephone line
- mobile phone
- computer, printer and scanner
- high-speed internet access
- filing cabinet
- table
- ergonomic office chair.

Quotes from suppliers indicate that the total cost of these items will be approximately A$11 500. All materials required for the proposed training programs (such as TV, video and whiteboard) are provided by commercial training venues.

Likely future needs

If future growth necessitates the use of a fax/modem, the existing home phone line will need to be replaced with a business phone line. Future computing needs will probably include an upgraded system with wireless internet.

4.8 Production processes

An operations manual, updated every six months, will explain procedures and processes within the office. It will also allow the company to apply for quality assurance certification at a later stage, if it wishes to do so.

4.9 Critical risks/contingency plans

The critical risks facing this business and contingencies to deal with them are:
- liability — to be covered by professional indemnity insurance
- injury to the managing director — to be covered by workers compensation
- excessive workload — other directors may take on work, or it may be redirected to other consultancies with whom a strategic alliance has been developed.

Section 5: Financial projections

5.1 Basic assumptions and information

(a) *Calculation of income and expenses*

Expenses have been calculated based on market research and the manager's own knowledge of costs. It is assumed that all accounts revenue will be paid within the month issued (so there is no delayed income on a monthly basis). No provision has been made for the impact of inflation or increases in costs. Pricing and costs for the second year of operations will be reviewed in next year's business plan to take these factors into account.

Depreciation of equipment items purchased in July 2011 is calculated using the straight-line method at 10% per annum of total initial outlay. Book sales assume a gross cost of goods of 60% (that is, a A$20 gross profit on sales price of A$50). Only one year's forecasts have been provided due to the difficulty of forecasting over a longer time period.

(b) *Financing of the business*

The directors will provide an initial capital contribution to the business according to their shareholdings — Stephen Molloy A$4000, Jessie Jones A$4000, Andrew St John A$2000. Sales income for July 2011 is based on commitments or early orders from prospective clients, thus providing initial cash flow and removing the need for short-term debt financing. The overall financing strategy is to operate, wherever possible, with a cash surplus in the bank account at all times. Bank loans will not be required. If necessary, the directors will reduce the wages paid to them during times of cash flow difficulty.

The bank account required for the business is one that:
- has mobile phone/internet banking access
- pays interest on sums below A$5000
- provides monthly bank statements (for reconciliation with accounts)
- has credit card and electronic funds transfer facilities.

For security reasons, a minimum of two directors will be required to verify all accounts.

(c) *Distribution of profits*

Profits in Year 1 will be retained in the business. In future years, annual net profit after tax will be divided in the following manner: three-quarters will be paid to the shareholders at the end of the financial year in accordance with their shareholdings, and the remaining quarter will be kept as retained earnings. The retained capital will be used for reinvestment in the business, mainly to upgrade equipment and to meet unforeseen contingencies. If the business is highly profitable, some of the retained capital may eventually (in two to three years' time) be used to help fund the purchase of permanent business premises.

(d) *Goods and services tax*

No GST figures are shown in any of the financial documents; in other words, all forecasts are net of tax.

(e) *Loans*

The firm has no current loans or debts.

5.2 Analysis of financial forecasts

(a) The owners have decided to use net profit margin as the main indicator of the firm's performance. Based on the projections made in this document, it is estimated for Year 1 that this will be:

$$\text{Net profit margin \%} = \frac{\text{Net profit before tax}}{\text{Sales turnover}} = \frac{\$2320}{\$103\,750} = 2.24\%$$

This figure is relatively low and below industry norms, according to a recent study by Jones (2010), but is not unusual for a business in its first year of trading. We expect margins to increase substantially in Year 2 and Year 3.

In future years, as more data are gathered, it will also be possible to use other ratios to help analyse the financial performance of the firm.

(b) *Break-even point*

Assuming that cost of goods sold is the only variable cost, the contribution margin is equal to the projected gross profit margin (94%).

$$\text{Projected fixed costs} = \$95\,280$$

$$\begin{aligned}\text{Break-even point in dollars} &= \frac{\text{Fixed costs}}{\text{Contribution margin}} \\ &= \frac{\$95\,280}{0.94} \\ &= \$101\,362\end{aligned}$$

5.2.1 Sales mix forecast (All figures are in Australian dollars, A$)

Blueprints Business Planning Pty Ltd
SALES MIX FORECAST
for the period July 2011 to June 2012

	Jul.	Aug.	Sep.	Oct.	Nov.	Dec.	Jan.	Feb.	Mar.	Apr.	May	Jun.	TOTAL
Item: Business planning													
Number sold	2	2	3	3	4	0	1	3	4	5	5	5	37
Selling price	$2 000	$2 000	$2 000	$2 000	$2 000	$2 000	$2 000	$2 000	$2 000	$2 000	$2 000	$2 000	
Total sales income	4 000	4 000	6 000	6 000	8 000	0	2 000	6 000	8 000	10 000	10 000	10 000	$74 000
Cost of goods sold per item	0	0	0	0	0	0	0	0	0	0	0	0	
Total cost of goods sold	0	0	0	0	0	0	0	0	0	0	0	0	0
Item: Training courses													
Numbers sold (hours delivered)	15	15	15	20	20	10	15	20	25	25	25	20	225
Selling price	$120	$120	$120	$120	$120	$120	$120	$120	$120	$120	$120	$120	
Total sales income	1 800	1 800	1 800	2 400	2 400	1 200	1 800	2 400	3 000	3 000	3 000	2 400	$27 000
Cost of goods sold per item	20	20	20	20	20	20	20	20	20	20	20	20	
Total cost of goods sold	300	300	300	400	400	200	300	400	500	500	500	400	4 500
Item: Supplementary books													
Number sold	3	3	3	5	5	2	5	5	6	6	6	6	55
Selling price	$50	$50	$50	$50	$50	$50	$0	$50	$50	$50	$50	$50	
Total sales income	150	150	150	250	250	100	250	250	300	300	300	300	$2 750
Cost of goods sold per item	30	30	30	30	30	30	30	30	30	30	30	30	
Total cost of goods sold	90	90	90	150	150	60	150	150	180	180	180	180	1650
Total sales revenue	$5 950	$5 950	$7 950	$8 650	$10 650	$1 300	$4 050	$8 650	$11 300	$13 300	$13 300	$12 700	$103 750
Total cost of goods sold	$390	$390	$390	$550	$550	$260	$450	$550	$680	$680	$680	$580	$6 150

5.2.2 Cash flow forecast (All figures are in Australian dollars, A$)

Blueprints Business Planning Pty Ltd
CASH FLOW FORECAST
for the period July 2011 to June 2012

	Jul.	Aug.	Sep.	Oct.	Nov.	Dec.	Jan.	Feb.	Mar.	Apr.	May	Jun.	TOTAL
Income													
Sales revenue	$5 950	$5 950	$7 950	$8 650	$10 650	$1 300	$4 050	$8 650	$11 300	$13 300	$13 300	$12 700	$103 750
Capital	10 000												10 000
Sundry													
Total Income	15 950	5 950	7 950	8 650	10 650	1 300	4 050	8 650	11 300	13 300	13 300	12 700	113 750
Expenses													
Cost of goods sold	390	390	390	550	550	260	450	550	680	680	680	580	6 150
Accounting/legal services	1 500		800					200					2 500
Advertising	2 000	100	100	100	180	100	100	100	100	100	100	100	3 180
Bank fees	15	15	15	15	15	15	15	15	15	15	15	15	180
Equipment purchases		11 500											11 500
Equipment leases													0
Insurance	2 500												2 500
Light & power													0
Loan repayments													0
Motor vehicle – fuel	50	50	50	50	50	50	50	50	50	50	50	50	600
Motor vehicle – other costs													0
Petty cash	25	25	25	25	25	25	25	25	25	25	25	25	300

Blueprints Business Planning Pty Ltd
CASH FLOW FORECAST
for the period July 2011 to June 2012

	Jul.	Aug.	Sep.	Oct.	Nov.	Dec.	Jan.	Feb.	Mar.	Apr.	May	Jun.	TOTAL
Postage, printing & stationery	400												400
Rent													0
Repairs & maintenance	100			100			100			100			400
Staff casual wages	2 000	2 000	2 000	2 000	2 000	2 000	2 000	2 000	2 000	2 000	2 000	2 000	24 000
Staff superannuation												6 000	6 000
Staff director's wages	3 400	3 340	4 700	3 220	3 340	3 400	3 220	3 340	3 400	3 220	3 340	3 400	41 320
Telephone	50	50	50	50	50	50	50	50	50	50	50	50	600
Other	100	50	50	50	50	50	50	50	50	50	50	50	650
Total expenses	24 030	6 020	8 180	6 160	6 260	5 950	6 060	6 380	6 370	6 290	6 310	12 270	100 280
Cash surplus/(deficit)	$(8 080)	$(70)	$(230)	$2 490	$4 390	$(4 650)	$(2 010)	$2 270	$4 930	$7 010	$6 990	$430	$13 470
Bank balance													
Start of month	0	(8 080)	(8 150)	(8 380)	(5 890)	(1 500)	(6 150)	(8 160)	(5 890)	(960)	6 050	13 040	
End of month	(8 080)	(8 150)	(8 380)	(5 890)	(1 500)	(6 150)	(8 160)	(5 890)	(960)	6 050	13 040	13 470	

5.2.3 Projected profit and loss statement (All figures are in Australian dollars, A$)

Blueprints Business Planning Pty Ltd
PROJECTED PROFIT AND LOSS STATEMENT
for the period July 2011 to June 2012

Revenues	
Sales revenue	103 750
Less: Cost of goods sold	6 150
Gross profit	97 600
Expenses	
Accounting/legal services	2 500
Advertising	3 180
Bank fees	180
Equipment purchases	11 500
Equipment leases	0
Insurance	2 500
Light & power	0
Loan repayments	0
Motor vehicle – fuel	600
Motor vehicle – other costs	0
Petty cash	300
Postage, printing & stationery	400
Rent	0
Repairs & maintenance	400
Staff wages	24 000
Staff superannuation	6 000
Staff director's wages	41 320
Telephone	600
Other	650
Depreciation	1 150
Total expenses	95 280
Net profit	$2 320

5.2.4 Owner's personal expenses (All figures are in Australian dollars, A$)

Blueprints Business Planning Pty Ltd
OWNER'S PERSONAL EXPENSES: JESSIE JONES
for the period July 2011 to June 2012

	Jul.	Aug.	Sep.	Oct.	Nov.	Dec.	Jan.	Feb.	Mar.	Apr.	May	Jun.	TOTAL
Monthly commitments													
Food	$400	$400	$400	$400	$400	$400	$400	$400	$400	$400	$400	$400	$4 800
Health	100	100	100	100	100	100	100	100	100	100	100	100	1 200
Clothes	80		80			80			80			80	400
Entertainment	200	200	200	200	200	200	200	200	200	200	200	200	2 400
Transport	120	120	120	120	120	120	120	120	120	120	120	120	1 440
Education													0
House payments	1 400	1 400	1 400	1 400	1 400	1 400	1 400	1 400	1 400	1 400	1 400	1 400	16 800
Car payments													0
Other loan repayments													0
Telephone			100			100			100			100	400
Electricity & gas		120			120			120			120		480
Rates			1300										1 300
Personal income tax	900	900	900	900	900	900	900	900	900	900	900	900	10 800
Credit cards	100												100
Other	100	100	100	100	100	100	100	100	100	100	100	100	1 200
Monthly drawings needed*	$3 400	$3 340	$4 700	$3 220	$3 340	$3 400	$3 220	$3 340	$3 400	$3 220	$3 340	$3 400	$41 320

*Shown as 'Staff – director's wages' in cash flow forecast

5.2.5 Owner's personal assets and liabilities (All figures are in Australian dollars, A$)

Blueprints Business Planning Pty Ltd
OWNER'S PERSONAL ASSETS AND LIABILITIES: JESSIE JONES
as at 1 July 2011

Assets

Own house (market value)	$700 000
Other real estate (market value)	0
Motor vehicle (insured value)	25 000
Cash (on hand or in bank)	6 000
Superannuation	84 000
Furniture & personal effects (insured value)	25 000
Other (list if appropriate)	0
Total assets	840 000

Liabilities

Outstanding mortgage (on home)	201 500
Outstanding mortgage (on other real estate)	0
Personal loans	0
Credit cards	100
Current bills	0
Other debts	600
Total liabilities	202 200
Personal worth (total assets minus total liabilities)	$637 800

Section 6: Implementation timetable, 2011–12

2011

July	Apply for home-based business licence
	Open business bank account
	Prepare letterheads, business cards
	Send copy of business plan to accountant and lawyer (for their information)
	Obtain all relevant insurance policies
August	Start direct mail campaign
	Review contents of website
September	Start compiling operations manual
	Visit accountant re: progress to date, recordkeeping
	Enquire re: computing equipment required
October	Enquire with Institute of Management Consultants (Australia) re: membership
November	Prepare promotional brochure
December	Print promotional brochure

2012

January	Staff/directors' retreat to review progress to date
	Review business plan
	Review effectiveness of marketing plan and analyse source of sales to date
	Review operations manual
February	Attend Small Business Development Corporation course on managing business growth
March	Implement benchmarking of advertising by outside adviser
April	Update website
May	Visit accountant re: end-of-financial-year returns
June	Write business plan for 2012–13
	Review and write new marketing plan

Section 7: Appendix — Research reference sources

Anderson, Z. & James, R., *Small Business Employment Guide*, Smiley & Sons, Sydney, 2008.

Australian Bureau of Statistics, *Training Needs in Australian SMEs*, Cat. No. 2222.8, ABS, Canberra, 2009.

Brown, B., 'Revisiting new enterprise opportunities', *Micro-Enterprise Australia*, vol. 6, no. 3, September, 2008, pp. 42–9.

Jones, J., 'Consultancy rates — an overview', *Management Techniques and Issues*, no. 5, January, 2010, pp. 1–5.

Small Business Development Corporation, *Opportunities for New Beginnings*, SBDC, Sydney, 2009.

Sydney Chamber of Commerce, *Survey of Small Organisation Professional Development Needs*, Sydney Chamber of Commerce, Sydney, 2009.

Ziericki, B.B., *Consulting: An Overview of the Personal Services Sector*, available online at Management Myopia website www.managementmyopia.com, 2007.

Legal issues

Learning objectives

After reading this chapter, you should be able to:

- explain the main types of legal structure under which a business may operate

- discuss the pros and cons of each type of legal structure

- describe the various forms of intellectual property

- explain the registration, competition and taxation issues a business must be aware of.

CHAPTER 8

All business activities are, to some extent, regulated by government. Entrepreneurs and new business owners must comply with a variety of regulations and laws that, at first, can appear somewhat confusing and arbitrary. One way of understanding these requirements is to break them down into four components that take place in the following order: (1) choose a legal structure to operate under; (2) protect any intellectual property the business has; (3) determine which operating permits and licences the industry must comply with; and (4) examine any ancillary issues, such as competition and taxation law. Each of these is discussed in detail below.

Legal structures

All businesses must assume a legal form during their existence. Although there are many variations on these in different jurisdictions, in essence there are three main legal structures that a business can operate under: a sole proprietorship, a partnership and a company. Another significant structuring option is to use a trust. In Australia, most businesses are sole proprietorships (38 per cent), although proprietary limited companies are also popular (26 per cent). Trusts and partnerships represent respectively 18 per cent and 15 per cent of the business registered, while other structures constitute 3 per cent.[1]

Sole proprietorship

Sole proprietor *or* **sole trader** *A person who wholly owns and operates a business.*

A **sole proprietor**, sometimes also known as a **sole trader**, is a business in which the owner is synonymous with the firm. There is no distinction in law between the business and the individual owner. All profits and assets of the firm are the owner's, just as any liabilities or debts are also the responsibility of the owner. In Australia, for example, the most common form of legal structure for new start-ups is the sole proprietorship. Note that the term *sole trader* does not mean 'sole employee'. A sole trader, just like a partnership or company, can employ other people.

Advantages and drawbacks of sole proprietorships

The advantages of the sole proprietorship are as follows:
- *Ease of formation.* There are fewer formalities and restrictions compared with other legal forms. The sole proprietorship may also, at a later stage, be converted into a partnership or a company.
- *Total control over the business.* The owner–manager is able to exercise full control over the operations of the enterprise, and retains all the profits generated by the business.
- *Relatively cheap to setup and maintain.* The laws governing the operations of sole proprietorships are usually less onerous than other legal structures, so administrative costs may be quite low.
- *Few regulations.* There are few formalities involved in running a sole proprietorship, as this form is the least regulated of all the business structures. Those formalities that do exist apply equally to other legal structures.

It is these features that many new business operators find attractive, and many small businesses begin life under this structure. However, the sole proprietorship has several drawbacks:
- *Unlimited liability.* Since all assets and liabilities belong to the owner, the individual may be faced with a potentially ruinous set of claims if the firm is

forced into bankruptcy or is the subject of legal action. In these situations, the personal assets of the owner may be seized to satisfy outstanding claims, since legally they are indistinguishable from other assets of the owner/firm.

- *Limited resources.* Sole proprietorships rely heavily on the owner–manager to finance the business start-up and expansion and, therefore, may face funding problems. Similarly, this type of business has limited human resources, as the owner–manager largely relies on personal skills to manage the business.
- *Lack of continuity.* A sole proprietorship has no independent existence and is tied to the owner–manager who runs it. Therefore, the business usually ceases to exist if the business owner dies or is otherwise rendered incapable of operating the business.
- *Tax.* In nations with a high personal tax rate, the inability to separate business income from other personal sources of income may lead to potentially higher rates of personal income tax being paid.

Establishing a sole proprietorship

In Australia, a sole proprietorship may be established by the simple fact of a person trading under his or her own name. Therefore, it can be difficult sometimes to work out if a person is in business or just pursuing a hobby. The Australian Taxation Office[2] considers the following factors to determine if a business exists:

- *Does the activity have a significant commercial character?* It is important to consider whether your activity is carried on for commercial reasons, and in a commercially viable manner.
- *Is there more than just an intention to engage in business?* You need to have made a decision to commence a business, and have done something about it.
- *Does the activity have the purpose of profit as well as the prospect of profit?* Do you intend to make a profit or genuinely believe that you will make a profit, even if you unlikely to do so in the short term?
- *Is there repetition and regularity to the activity?* Businesses usually repeat similar types of activities, although one-off transactions can constitute a business in some cases.

If the person operates the business under another name, the business name must be registered with the appropriate state agency. Renewal of registration varies from state to state. Most firms will also require an Australian Business Number (ABN), which can be obtained online free of charge from the Australian Taxation Office (ATO). Table 8.1 shows the different authorities for registering a sole proprietorship in some countries in the Asia–Pacific region.

TABLE 8.1 Authority and formation for sole traders

Country	Authority
Australia	Individual state agencies and Australian Taxation Office, www.ato.gov.au
New Zealand	Ministry of Economic Development, Companies Office, www.companies.govt.nz
Hong Kong	Business Registration Office, Inland Revenue Department, www.ird.gov.hk

TABLE 8.1 continued

Country	Authority
Malaysia	Companies Commission of Malaysia, www.ssm.com.my
Singapore	Accounting and Corporate Regulatory Authority, www.acra.gov.sg
India	Registration usually at the local value-added tax (VAT) office, but not always necessary depending on state

Partnership

Partnership *A relationship that exists between people carrying on a business in common with a view to making a profit.*

When several people are in business together, this business relationship is called a **partnership**. These people pool their resources, such as capital, time and knowledge, and agree to share the profits as well as the liabilities of the venture.[3] Partnerships are common in husband-and-wife teams. This is an arrangement in which mutual cooperation and trust is very important.

Advantages and drawbacks of partnerships

The main advantages of partnerships are as follows:

- *Ease of formation.* Legal formalities and expenses are few compared with companies.
- *Ease of operation.* A partnership is usually easier to operate, more flexible for tax purposes and cheaper to run than either the smallest company or trust (in Australia).
- *Distinct existence.* Unlike a sole proprietorship, a partnership can be clearly demarcated as a separate entity for marketing and accounting purposes.
- *Combined resources.* A partnership is often an effective vehicle for pooling members' funds, so it is often more effective than a sole proprietorship when it comes to raising finance. It is also a useful mechanism for bringing together people who have different resources to contribute to a business venture.
- *Direct rewards.* Partners directly share the profits, thus providing a direct link between contribution and remuneration.

However, partnerships suffer from several drawbacks, which include:

- *Unlimited joint liability.* Each partner is responsible for the debts and activities of all others. In some countries, the liability of particular classes of partnership may be limited by legislation; similarly, in some professions in some regions, such as dentists and pharmacists, there are various laws that require operators to act either as sole proprietors or as partners (so assuming direct responsibility for their own work).
- *Potential conflicts.* The decision-making process is split among all the partners. Hence, people with a high need for personal control and autonomy may find this arrangement unsatisfactory. Few people anticipate problems when they first join with others in a business venture. However, this informal relationship can easily break down under stress and, as a result, the business may ultimately fail, creating a potential loss for each partner.
- *Lack of continuity.* Most partnership laws stipulate that the partnership ceases to exist if one of the partners dies, becomes incapacitated or simply withdraws

from business. To continue with the business, the remaining partners must usually start a new partnership.

Establishing a partnership

A **partnership agreement** is usually strongly recommended, although it is rarely compulsory. This is a written document spelling out details of the partners in the business, the share of profits they are entitled to, the liabilities they are account-able for, and the roles and responsibilities of the different partners. It also puts in place a mechanism for winding up the partnership or for selling or transfer-ring partners' interests if they no longer wish to be involved in the enterprise. Partners should determine their own positions with regard to these points, and be fully supportive of all the provisions of the proposed agreement.

Partnership agreement *A written document that covers all matters relating to the partnership.*

Although there are many advantages to choosing the partnership form of business, many personal issues need to be considered before entering a partner-ship with another person. Entrepreneurs must ask themselves:

- Do I like and respect the prospective partner/s?
- Do our skills complement each other?
- Do our visions and goals run parallel?

The regulatory requirements governing partnerships are minimal. In Australia, Malaysia and Singapore, a partnership can be established by a minimum of two people and a maximum of twenty. Partnerships do not pay income tax. The share of profit or loss distributed must be declared by the partners in their individual tax returns, and all income is taxed at the personal income rate. The relevant authorities for registering a partnership structure in the Asia–Pacific region are usually the same as for sole proprietorships.

Company

Neither sole proprietorships nor partnerships are particularly effective enti-ties for entrepreneurs who plan to undertake ventures that may expose them to high levels of liability, who need to raise large amounts of capital, or who have a project that will be funded and owned by a large number of people. When this is the situation, a **company** is a more appropriate legal structure.

Company *A separate legal entity that has an existence independent of its owners and managers.*

In a company, ownership is held by a number of shareholders, who may transfer shares to other people and who elect a number of their own members to serve as the directors of the company. The directors are responsible for setting the broad policies of the firm, selecting and overseeing a chief executive officer or managing director, and ensuring solvency and legal compliance. A written constitution (in some jurisdictions known as the memorandum and the articles of association) spells out the basic rules under which the firm is governed and administered. In Australia, the Corporations Act contains replaceable rules gov-erning the internal affairs of a company, but a company can set-up its own con-stitution if it wishes to adopt different rules.

In the specific case of China, foreign companies can choose between three main business structures in order to establish a permanent presence:

1. representative offices
2. joint ventures — the majority of which are 'equity joint ventures' operating as a limited liability company
3. wholly foreign owned enterprises.

Representative offices are the preferred form of establishment but they are hindered by their limited activities. Direct business activities are not possible since representative offices are confined to market research and liaison. A foreign investor may choose a path contingent on many factors: the extent of activity one wants in China; the industry one is investing in; and whether a Chinese partner is necessary to appease the law or to gain from the partner's experience in the Chinese market.

Advantages and drawbacks of companies

Key advantages of a company include the following:[4]

- *Perpetual existence.* A company will continue to exist even if the founder or one of the shareholders dies; rights to their shares are simply transferred to their legal beneficiary.
- *Limited liability.* The liability of the owners of the company (the shareholders) is usually limited to the unpaid value of the shares they hold.
- *Rights of a natural person.* Like an individual, a company may buy, hold and dispose of assets in its own right. It can sue and be sued; can enter into contracts and transactions in its own name; and has a separate legal identity from the individual shareholders. It has its own registered name, corporate office and address.

On the other hand, a company typically faces the following drawbacks:

- *High set-up and maintenance costs.* The laws regulating the operations of corporations are usually tighter than those which apply to partnerships or sole traders.
- *Spread ownership.* Ownership is spread among several people. This can make decision making more difficult, although in Australia it is possible to have one-person firms with only one shareholder, who is also the sole director and managing director of the organisation.

When owner–managers run a company, it seems almost automatic that they take on the role of director. Yet many owner–managers in Australia do so with little understanding of their financial and legal liabilities. Many of them are under the misapprehension that if they set-up a company they will be exempt from personal liability, thinking 'my only risk is the capital that I put into the business'. However, company directors can have a personal exposure to the ATO with regard to preference of action. That arises when the company goes into liquidation within six months of having paid its tax. The liquidator may bring a preference action against the ATO, saying that the money was paid at a time when the company was insolvent, and that there were reasonable grounds for the ATO to suspect that the company was insolvent when it received the payment of the tax. If the liquidator succeeds against the ATO then it is required to pay the money back to the liquidator. In those circumstances, the ATO can pursue the directors personally for the money.[5]

Establishing a company

Although there are several variations on the types of company allowed in various countries, the main distinction is between *private* companies, in which the number of shareholders is limited (usually to 50), and *public* companies, in which shares can be bought and sold on a stock exchange by anyone. Private companies are often designated by the terms Proprietary Limited (Pty Ltd) in Australia, Private Limited (Pte Ltd) in Singapore, or Sendirian Berhad (Sdn Bhd) in Malaysia.

Table 8.2 provides a list of the authorities with which a private limited company must be registered. In all cases, the following formalities must be completed for the company to come into existence:

- A memorandum and articles of association or a constitution must be drawn up for the purposes of registration.
- An application must be made for approval of the name of the company; an existing firm's name cannot be used.
- The requisite fee must be paid.
- The company is incorporated when, on registration, a certificate of registration is issued.

In Australia, most small businesses do not have formal company boards, nor do they tend to include independent directors in their decision making. However, small private companies are increasingly setting up advisory boards that can provide them with the benefits of a directorial board without the expensive salaries. A business venture seeking to establish an advisory board would usually seek out three to five executives and a number of experts who have industry knowledge, access to networks and strategic vision. Unlike the members of a formal board, members of an advisory board just make recommendations rather than decisions.

TABLE 8.2 Authority for registering private limited companies

Country	Authority
Australia	Australian Securities and Investments Commission, www.asic.gov.au
New Zealand	New Zealand Companies Office, www.companies.govt.nz
Hong Kong	Companies Registry, www.cr.gov.hk
Malaysia	Companies Commission of Malaysia, www.ssm.com.my
Singapore	Accounting and Corporate Regulatory Authority, www.acra.gov.sg
China (PRC)	Various authorities must be contacted (including the Ministry of Commerce, and the local Industry and Commerce Administration Bureau)
India	Registrar of Companies (ROC) of the state in which the company's main office is to be located

Trusts

A **trust** exists when a person (the trustee) holds property for others (beneficiaries) who are intended to benefit from that property or from the income of that property. The **trust deed** sets out the terms and conditions under which the trust assets are held and outlines the rights of the beneficiaries. In general, a trust is not

Trust *An obligation imposed on trustees to deal with the trust property (over which they have control) for the benefit of the beneficiaries.*

Trust deed *A written document that evidences the creation of the trust. It sets out the terms and conditions on which the trust assets are held by the trustees, and outlines the rights of the beneficiaries.*

established until it is 'constituted', meaning both that the trust deed is signed and that money, or something of value, is transferred to the trustee. Trusts are a very popular form of ownership structure, particularly in Australia and New Zealand. One of the main reasons is that trusts offer attractions — tax minimisation and other benefits — for families intent on creating wealth for present and future generations by acquiring and holding onto assets. There is also some appeal in running a family business via a flexible trust structure or developing a family estate to survive intergenerational transfers.

Trust structure

In any trust, there is dual ownership of the trust property. As shown in figure 8.1, the trustee is the legal owner of the trust property, and beneficiaries are the equitable owners. The trustee can be one or more persons or a company. The trustee controls and manages the trust property for and on behalf of the beneficiaries. The duties and powers of the trustee are set out in the trust deed. Any kind of property — real estate, shares or business assets — can be the subject of the trust.

Beneficiaries are the equitable or beneficial owners of the trust property. They are the ultimate owners of the property. If there is a conflict between the trustee and the beneficiary, the interests of the beneficiary always prevail. Figure 8.1 shows a simple trust structure in which a company (X Pty Ltd) is the trustee. (Note that other people can act as joint trustees.) In this case, the business is owned by the trustee company.

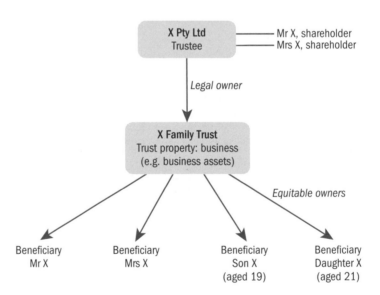

FIGURE 8.1 Trust structure

In Australia, there are four main types of trust that a family or small business might consider:[6]

- *discretionary*, in which the annual distributions of income and capital profits to beneficiaries are at the discretion of the trustee
- *fixed*, in which the income and profit entitlements of the trust beneficiaries are fixed

- *hybrid*, which is a blend of fixed and discretionary; a common structure gives beneficiaries a fixed entitlement to capital and a discretionary entitlement to income
- *unit*, in which a beneficiary has a fixed entitlement to a trust's assets, as well as to a share of trust income in proportion to units held.

Many issues need to be considered before setting up a trust. For example, the current and projected level of income of the entrepreneur is one factor. In essence, the tax treatment of the trust income depends on who is and is not entitled to the income as of 30 June each year. A family with at least one taxpayer who is within the top personal tax rate may have good reason to set up a family trust. The sophistication of the entrepreneur's financial affairs is another factor to consider. It is essential, therefore, to do your homework and get good advice.

Once people have established that they need a trust, the next step is working out what is involved in setting up and running it. Establishment costs depend on how complicated a person's financial affairs are and the professional help employed to set-up the trust. It is possible to buy an off-the-shelf trust deed for A$1500, but it should cover all circumstances. For example, a person may want to place restrictions on who will be the beneficiaries. Expenses could therefore range from A$1500 for something small and simple to several thousand dollars for a more complex trust.

Advantages and drawbacks of a trust

In addition to tax minimisation potential, trusts offer a number of other advantages:
- *Income splitting*. A family trust can boost family income if the investments held in the family trust are allocated to a spouse and children. Since the income is spread over several family members, each family member's income falls into a lower tax bracket. However, children under 18 are not efficient beneficiaries because of the penalty tax regime that exists for this group.
- *Capital gains tax*. Discretionary trusts are able to pass on the 50 per cent capital gains tax discount to beneficiaries tax-free; companies are not able to do this for their shareholders.
- *Control*. Although the assets are owned by the trust, control remains firmly with the family via the trustees, which could be individuals or a private company with family members as directors.
- *Asset protection*. Trusts can allow private family assets to be isolated from business assets and protected if a business collapses. In a matrimonial conflict, a trust enables assets to be protected from an estranged spouse, although changes have been made in this area via family law amendments.
- *Stability*. Trusts can be very stable structures and last beyond the death of the original trustees. If the shares in the company are transferred to trustees before death, a trust can be used to prevent the unnecessary liquidation of a family company. The terms of the trust will ensure that the individual's wishes are observed. This may be particularly advantageous if the family members have little business experience, or if they are unlikely to agree on the correct way to manage the business.

Nevertheless, there are a number of limitations and drawbacks to trusts:

- *Small business capital gains tax (CGT)*. Entrepreneurs establishing a trust need to be aware of the pitfalls concerning the various small business CGT concessions — it may be difficult to qualify for some, and entrepreneurs need to know the rules.
- *Divorce and death*. Potential conflicts can arise involving divorce or partners of beneficiaries who have remarried after a beneficiary's death.
- *Hiding assets*. Entrepreneurs should not expect to be able to hide assets from creditors by setting up a family trust for their personal assets just before their business collapses. Courts can order the repayment of personal or business money directed into a trust within five and a half years of a collapse, especially if legal action has already been taken against the business.
- *Legislative risk*. The tax advantages trusts can offer continue to make them targets for government and regulators. In 2002 the Australian government decided to shelve draft legislation for a new family trust regime, but there is no guarantee regulators will not attempt to make changes in the future.

Comparing legal structures

The choice of legal structure should take into consideration the type and profitability of the business venture and the relationship, family, financial and tax positions of the people going into business. The set-up and running costs of the structure should be considered in relation to perceived benefits. Table 8.3 details some of the differences between the four main legal forms of ownership discussed above. Ideally, the structure chosen should:

- comply with legal requirements
- be simple and cost effective
- maximise protection of assets
- minimise personal liability
- minimise both income and capital gains tax
- allow for admission of new partners or investors
- be flexible.

TABLE 8.3 Differences between legal structures

Feature	Sole proprietor	Partnership	Company	Trust
Formation cost	Low	Moderate	High	Moderate/high
Personal liability of owner/s	Unlimited	Unlimited	Limited	Limited
Ability to raise external capital	Low	Moderate	Moderate/good	Moderate
Permanence	Limited to owner's lifetime	Usually limited; may be overcome by agreement	Enduring	Enduring
Ongoing cost of compliance	Low	Low	High	Moderate/high
Privacy	High	Moderate	Low	High

There is no single business structure that is right for every business. Every decision involves some trade-offs. At the start-up stage, the focus tends to be on cost and simplicity. Entrepreneurs are looking for a structure that has low set-up and running costs. In many cases, the simpler the structure the better, as this requires less management time, less formalisation and fewer operations. The problem comes, however, when businesses mature beyond start-up stage. Often they have earned their goodwill and developed assets, so the cost of restructuring runs high.

Evolving a business from 'start-up' to 'grown-up' means making structural adjustments. In most cases, high-growth business ventures will choose between companies and trusts, or a mix within the structure. Companies and trusts will normally provide a higher level of asset protection and risk management. The objective should be to protect the assets of the owners and shareholders from risks associated with the business. These two structures also separate the operations of the business's assets, so they can be dealt with separately and different risk exposures within the business can be quarantined. It is not uncommon to see the intellectual property of brand goodwill held within a passive entity, and then licensed to the operating entities for their use.[7]

What would you do?

Choosing a legal structure for Zomp Apparel

Patricia Budiyanto and Suzy Elenawati met in Subang Jaya, Malaysia, during their first year at a private college that offers international study programs. Shortly after their arrival at college, both girls joined the Indonesian Students Association and were elected to the board of the association, with Patricia as treasurer and Suzy as events organiser. This meant they often had to collaborate on preparing budgets for various events. They got on so well that they decided to share a flat during their second year of study. During this time, they discovered that they had a shared passion for trendy, designed underwear.

Over the past six months, Patricia and Suzy have organised several 'parties' where they presented and sold their products to female friends. The parties are modeled on Tupperware parties – a pioneer in direct marketing – where a host invites friends and neighbours into their home to see the product line. Patricia and Suzy use a software application to design unique underwear, which are manufactured by a local subcontractor. They even found a brand, 'Zomp Apparel', for their product. Their parties were an immediate success because their friends valued the innovative product design (each piece is unique), and because they could see the product during a private fashion parade. A majority of Malaysians are Muslim, and the two girls discovered that many of their girlfriends preferred to shop with others girls, particularly when it came to underwear. Zomp Apparel parties provides this intimacy in an atmosphere of fun. The two friends are now in the middle of their third and last year of study, and Patricia has suggested that they start a business together in Kuala Lumpur. The main hurdle at this stage is funding. They both have about RM20 000 in savings, just enough to finance the first large production batch.

Questions

1. Are Patricia and Suzy already in business at this stage? Explain your reasoning.
2. What legal structure would you recommend Patricia and Suzy adopt for their business after their graduation?
3. What steps should they take to establish this structure?

Intellectual property

Intellectual property (IP), in business terms, means proprietary knowledge. This can result from an invention, original design or the practical application of a good idea, and it is a key component of success for many entrepreneurs. It is often the competitive edge that sets successful small businesses apart and, as world markets become increasingly crowded and competitive, protecting a firm's intellectual property is essential.

Intellectual property is often a valuable asset, and it is important to clearly identify and safeguard it. It may be the business's name, a brand logo, a graphic design or an invention. Failure to protect such property can put a key asset of the business at risk.

As shown in table 8.4, specific government bodies deal with intellectual property issues in several countries. These agencies provide information about the latest legislation, costs and procedures in relation to the five main types of intellectual property rights — patents, trademarks, industrial designs, copyrights and trade secrets.

TABLE 8.4 Intellectual property agencies

Country	Authority
Australia	IP Australia, www.ipaustralia.gov.au
New Zealand	Intellectual Property Office of New Zealand, www.iponz.govt.nz
Hong Kong	Intellectual Property Department, www.ipd.gov.hk
Malaysia	Intellectual Property Division, Ministry of Domestic Trade and Consumer Affairs, www.mipc.gov.my
Singapore	Intellectual Property Office of Singapore, www.ipos.gov.sg
China (PRC)	State Intellectual Property Office of the PRC, www.sipo.gov.cn
India	Controller General of Patents, Designs & Trade Marks, www.ipindia.nic.in

Patents

Patent *A legal document giving inventors the exclusive rights to their invention for a number of years.*

A **patent** is an exclusive right to exploit (produce and sell) a particular product or use a specific process for a certain period of time. Patent laws are intended to encourage inventions and new technology, and to protect these for a limited period. In most countries, the standard length of protection is 20 years, and the patent can be renewed after this initial period.

A patent can be granted to someone who has created something that is inventive, new and useful. Essentially, the invention must be new and not obvious to people who understand the technology. This means that if an inventor demonstrates, sells or publicly discusses the invention before applying for a patent, the right to protection will be lost. It is also a good idea to do a search of existing inventions before applying for a patent, in case the invention is already known. Table 8.5 lists the relevant patent legislation and length of protection.

TABLE 8.5 Patent legislation and length of protection

Country	Legislation	Length of protection
Australia	*Patents Act 1990*	20 years (standard); 8 years (innovation)
New Zealand	*Patents Act 1953*	20 years
Hong Kong	*Patents Ordinance 1997*	20 years (standard); 8 years (short term)
Malaysia	*Patents (Amendment) Act 2000*	20 years
Singapore	*Patents (Amendment) Act 2004*	20 years
China (PRC)	*Patent (Amendment) Law 2000*	20 years ('invention' patent); 10 years (petty)
India	*Patents (Amendment) Act 2005*	20 years

In Australia, there are two types of patent:
- the *standard patent* gives long-term protection and control over an invention for up to 20 years
- the *innovation patent* is a relatively fast, inexpensive protection option that lasts for a maximum of eight years. It provides local industry with a relatively cheap patent right, and it is quick and easy to obtain. This patent system is designed to protect inventions that are not sufficiently inventive to meet the inventive threshold required for standard patents. It is an attractive option for SMEs.

A patent is often referred to as a monopoly granted by the government to an inventor for a limited period in return for the disclosure of the invention so that others may gain the benefit. Hence, the patent may also be viewed as a reward for creative innovation and intellectual advancement, and the exclusive rights give the inventor the incentive to innovate.[8] The patent owner has the right to sue for any infringement, regardless of whether the owner uses, sells or makes any product using the patent. It is up to the owner of a patent to bring an action, usually under the civil law, for any infringement of patent rights.

The process of registering a patent varies slightly from one country to another, but always starts with the completion of an application form stating the applicant's request for the grant of the patent and the names of the inventor/s, plus any other descriptions, claims and drawings. The authority then determines whether the patent lodged supports a genuine invention and conducts a thorough search process. If there are no adverse findings or opposition, the authority publishes the application and makes known its details to the public. The cost involved in filing an application is minimal. However, the process of registration (search, opposition, publication) takes several months and can amount to between S$4500 and S$6000 in Singapore and between A$5000 and A$7000 in Australia. These figures can be substantially higher if the specialist services of a patent attorney are used, and if inventors want protection overseas.

Most inventors wanting protection overseas lodge a patent cooperation treaty (PCT) application, which lasts for 18 months and covers 124 countries. Then comes the cumbersome and expensive step: to extend the protection beyond this initial period, inventors must then file individual applications in each country where they want protection. The complexity and cost of filing international patents provides a business opportunity for entrepreneurs. For example, inovia, www.inoviaip.com, is a start-up providing a software system that allows the user to apply for international patent protection at a substantially lower cost than by using the conventional legal channels.

The most significant changes in the patent landscape have taken place in China, where the intellectual property regime has been tightened in recent years, and where Chinese companies have become increasingly eager to file and defend patents. No longer content to be just the workshop of the world, China is now the world leader in patent applications, with 800 000 patents filed in 2008. The majority of these are 'petty' patents of moderate technology that require minimal review and last only 10 years. Increasingly though, firms are filing 'invention' patents that are thoroughly scrutinised and, like most other countries, receive 20 years of protection.[9]

Trademarks

Trademark *A word, phrase, logo, symbol, colour, sound or smell used by a business to identify a product and distinguish it from those of its competitors.*

A trademark is a 'sign' used to distinguish the products or services of the trademark owner from those of competitors. A **trademark** can be a letter, number, word, phrase, shape, logo, picture, aspect of packaging or combination of these. One trademark that is known all over the world is the 'golden arches' of McDonald's. The right to use a trademark can be assigned or licensed to someone else for the specified product or service. Registered trademarks are identified with an ®.

A trademark may be a valuable marketing tool, as consumers often associate products or services bearing a particular trademark with a certain quality or image. Whereas a patent protects the function, the trademark protects the look of a business.[10] For this reason, it is recommended that for each new product or service developed and introduced, trademarks should be given an equal amount of consideration. In the People's Republic of China, trademark law was modified in 2001 to offer significant protections to foreign trademark owners. However, trademark piracy remains a rampant problem, despite the effective and speedy administrative procedures available to trademark owners under the State Administration for Industries and Commerce. Table 8.6 shows trademark legislation and length of protection.

A combination of good business operations and imaginative intellectual property protection can be used by new businesses to gain a competitive advantage and earn valuable market share. Some people still think of trademarks as the brand name of a product and its logo. However, in 1995 the Australian Trade Marks Act expanded the range of items that could be registered. These items, dubbed 'non-traditional trademarks', include shapes, colours, sounds and smells. One company that capitalised on a non-traditional trademark is Eagle Boys Dial-A-Pizza. The company, through trademark registration of their fuchsia lighting and innovative two-tiered pizza boxes, developed valuable assets that have been incorporated into its franchising, and have earned it exceptionally high product recognition. Within months of opening its first outlet in 1986, Eagle Boys had registered a trademark; the company then gained the exclusive right to use the fuchsia glow in its shopfronts, a landmark move in the trademark registration system.[11]

A common error that many entrepreneurs make when seeking trademark protection is to assume that it also protects the business name of the firm. A recent survey by IP Australia showed that an alarming 85 per cent of small businesses believed that business name registration would stop other businesses using the same name. Moreover, 80 per cent of small businesses assumed that registering their business name automatically gave trademark protection.[12] Therefore, registering a trademark is essential in protecting the business brand and intellectual property. One solution for small businesses is to register their business name as a trademark.

TABLE 8.6 Trademark legislation and length of protection

	Legislation	Length of protection
Australia	*Trade Marks Act 1995*	10 years, renewable every 10 years thereafter
New Zealand	*Trade Marks Act 2002*	10 years, renewable every 10 years thereafter
Hong Kong	*Trade Marks Ordinance*	10 years, renewable every 10 years thereafter
Malaysia	*Trade Marks (Amendment) Act 2000*	10 years, renewable every 10 years thereafter
Singapore	*Trade Marks (Amendment) Act 2004*	10 years, renewable every 10 years thereafter
China (PRC)	*Trade Mark Law (Amendment) 2001*	10 years, renewable every 10 years thereafter

Industrial designs

A design refers to any aspect of the shape or configuration of the whole or part of an item.[13] The right provided by a design registration is in many ways similar to that provided by a patent, but the protection is limited to the appearance of the product, such as its shape or pattern. Whereas a patent aims to provide protection for the underlying invention, a registered design protects the visual appearance of a product. For example, the *Australian Designs Act 2003* protects the visual feature in relation to a product, which includes the shape, configuration, pattern and ornamentation of the product.

Despite this narrow form of protection, good industrial design of a product is becoming increasingly important for gaining a marketing edge, and registration does provide a means of protecting the subtleties of a design that might have taken a designer many hours of work and thousands of dollars to achieve.

Designs are protected in Australia, New Zealand, Malaysia, Singapore and the Hong Kong Special Administrative Region (SAR). In a major move to increase the protection of intellectual property, the Hong Kong SAR established its own independent design registry in June 1997. The designs registration system is similar to the patent system, but separate from the system operating in other parts of China.

Copyright

Copyright covers literary, dramatic, musical or artistic works. It is the exclusive right to produce or reproduce a work by making copies of it or performing it, or to license others to do so.[14] Many copyright laws also contain provisions for the

Copyright *The exclusive right granted by law to a copyright holder to make and distribute copies of, or otherwise control, their literary, musical, dramatic or artistic work.*

protection of 'works of applied art', such as artistic jewellery, furniture, greetings cards and wallpaper. Originators of copyright material have a number of rights, the most explicit being 'economic rights'. The most important right of the originator is the exclusive right to reproduce. The originator's other rights include performing the work in public, broadcasting it, publishing it and making any adaptation of the copyright work.[15]

Copyright protection is an automatic right that arises when a work is created — the material is protected from the time it is first written down, painted, drawn, filmed or taped. In Australia, for example, copyright protection is provided under the *Copyright Act 1968*. Australian law regards an employer as the owner of copyright if the author was, when the work was created, an employee and was employed for the very purpose of creating the work.

Singapore and Hong Kong have taken important measures to investigate and curb intellectual property piracy problems that are particularly acute in the computer software and entertainment industry (CDs and books being a prime example). Singapore set-up a dedicated Intellectual Property Warrant Rights Unit (IPRWU) in 1995. Similarly, the Hong Kong SAR Copyright Ordinance 1997 provides stiff penalties; those who indulge in copyright piracy are liable to a maximum fine of HK$50 000 per infringing article and a term of imprisonment of up to four years.[16] Importing or exporting pirated articles is also a criminal offence.

Trade secrets

Most companies (including start-ups) have a wealth of information that is critical to their success, but does not qualify for patent, trademark or copyright protection. Some of this information is confidential and therefore needs to be kept secret in order to help the business maintain its competitive advantage. Sometimes entrepreneurs also find it too expensive to patent their invention or they do not want to attract the attention of potential competitors. Therefore, before filing for protection, entrepreneurs should consider the market for their product. The Chairman of the Inventors Association of Australia, Stuart Fox, commented: 'If you are short of funds, don't mortgage the house and spend heaps on patents. Look at whether you can get the idea into production and sell it to customers.'[17]

Trade secret *Any idea, formula, pattern, device, process or information that provides a business with a competitive advantage.*

A **trade secret** is any idea, formula, pattern, device, process or information that provides the owner with a competitive advantage in the marketplace. Trade secrets include marketing plans, product formulas, financial forecasts, employees' rosters and laboratory notebooks. The medium in which information is stored has no impact on whether it can be protected as a trade secret. As a result, written documents, computer files, videotapes and even the employees' memory of various items can be protected from unauthorised disclosure.[18]

Unlike patents, trademarks and copyright, there is no single government agency or legislation that regulates trade secrets. Therefore, it is the firm's responsibility to protect itself by exercising caution in storing and communicating information. Companies often use confidentiality agreements to prevent employees from revealing their secret or proprietary knowledge during and after employment. If an agreement is breached, the employer will have evidence of the agreed terms and subsequent protection by law.

Katherine Drayton, The Sand Wedge

The Sand Wedge is a beach chair with a difference. Unlike a traditional folding beach chair that is heavy and can only be used as a seat, the compact and lightweight Sand Wedge is a back-pack, a beach bag, beach seat and sun lounge all in one. Hitting the surf was a fun family activity for Katherine Drayton, but in getting from the car to the beach she often found herself being loaded up with beach chairs, umbrella and a beach bag overflowing with towels. 'This was when I started wondering how I could make this whole experience better. I thought, what could I design that would hold most of the things I need for the beach, that could be carried as a back-pack and leave those much needed hands free for the other larger necessities,' says Katherine.

'When I made my first Sand Wedge it was really just for me. I showed my idea to family members; they thought it was great and joked about me going on [ABC television's] *The New Inventors.*' As Katherine further developed the concept, she began to think they may be right, and looked into getting a patent or at least researching if it was possible. 'I thought the new buzz word was IP, and making sure you own the rights to your invention' says Katherine.

Katherine went on a search mission to see if anyone had invented something that was similar to her concept. She says, "Do as much research as you can yourself to begin with because patent attorneys can cost a lot of money, and there is no guarantee that your invention will be accepted for registration.' Finding there was nothing like the Sand Wedge protected in Australia or the US, Katherine decided to go ahead with getting IP protection. To start with, she saw a patent attorney to learn more on what a patent was and what it actually protected. She then decided to use the patent attorney to file a provisional patent application, which gave her 12 months to research the product's viability on the market.

Katherine also decided to get a design registration within that 12 months, as a patent protects the way something functions, and a design registration protects the way something looks. 'I currently have IP protection in the form of an innovation patent, a design registration and have my logo trademarked, so I own all the IP related to my business,' says Katherine. Getting IP protection was important for Katherine, firstly to ensure ownership of the rights to her invention, and then to be able to commercially exploit those rights. 'My plan was initially to get proof of marketability, and then see if I could sell the rights to my idea. Now as my business grows, which still was in my initial plan, I am getting more attached to my business, and to where this whole idea is taking me.'

Source: IP Australia, 'Life's a beach', Smart Start Case Studies, Commonwealth of Australia, www.ipaustralia.gov.au.

Other legal issues

Once the legal structure of the business has been established and any intellectual property has been protected, the entrepreneur/business owner needs to examine other, more generalised legal matters that may be relevant to the enterprise. Because there are so many, and they depend on the nature of business activity being undertaken, it can be difficult to cover all these in advance. Some of the more common legal matters concern licences and permits; registering for a business number and for the goods and services tax (GST); competition law; and taxation.

Licences and permits

Regardless of the business structure chosen, each industry has its own set of regulations that participants must comply with. Therefore, in addition to formally registering a business entity, a business owner must ensure that the firm can comply with all necessary permits and licences imposed by government. For example, hairdressers often need to be registered by a board before they can operate. Doctors and dentists need an appropriate degree and professional registration before they can open a practice. Restaurant premises must be approved by health authorities to ensure food is hygienically prepared. In most countries, local government authorities have strict zoning rules about what business activities can take place in particular localities, and whether a business can be operated from home.

Licences take a variety of forms and are administered by a number of different authorities. In some countries, governments have developed 'business licence centres' that contain a centralised database of all required permits. It is important not to underestimate the need to obtain all necessary permits before starting a business venture. In many respects, permits may be regarded as the main indicator of the viability of a proposed business idea; if all necessary permits cannot be obtained, then the business is usually not feasible.

Registering for a business number and the goods and services tax (GST)

In Australia, the Australian Business Number (ABN) is a single identifier for all business dealings with the Australian Taxation Office (ATO), and for future dealings with other government departments and agencies under the *New Tax System (Australian Business Number) Act 1999*. All companies covered by the *Corporations Act* have an ABN. Other entities, including an individual, partnership or trust, are also entitled to an ABN if they meet the definition of an enterprise — any activity or series of activities undertaken in the form of a business. In general, the ATO encourages businesses to register for an ABN. Business owners can register electronically or obtain a registration application from the ATO. In addition to applying for an ABN, the form also provides the opportunity of applying for a tax file number and registering for GST.[19]

The goods and services tax (GST) is a broad-based tax of 10 per cent on most supplies of goods and services consumed in Australia. It is based on the *supply* of goods or services, including advice, information, real property and certain dealings with rights and obligations. When a business that is registered for GST makes a taxable supply, one-eleventh of the consideration received for that supply is GST. Businesses with an annual turnover of A$75 000 or more and non-profit organisations with an annual turnover of A$150 000 or more must register for GST. Those with a lower turnover are not required to register for GST, although they may do so if they wish and if they meet the definition of an enterprise.

GST (of 12.5%) is also New Zealand's main type of tax apart from income tax. In Singapore, GST was first introduced in 1994, and has increased from 4% to 5%. There is no GST in Malaysia, but a tax on sales; the normal rate is 10%. Currently, there is no value-added or sales tax in the Hong Kong SAR.

Competition (trade practices) law

All existing and proposed businesses need to be aware that most countries have laws governing what is 'acceptable' business conduct. These laws generally prohibit anti-competitive behaviour, such as deliberately misleading customers or suppliers, price-fixing, the formation of cartels, and unfair conduct against competitors. In Australia, there are several federal, state and territory statutes that protect consumers.

In Australia, the *Competition and Consumer Act 2010* (formerly the Trade Practices Act) governs this conduct. An independent statutory authority, the Australian Competition and Consumer Commission (ACCC) administers the Act. The broad objective of the Act is to allow each business to compete on its merits, making its own decisions and treating consumers fairly.[20] The Act provides ways of achieving this objective:

- It encourages competition in Australian markets by prohibiting anti-competitive conduct such as illegal price agreements and market-sharing agreements.
- It stops anti-competitive mergers that may result in the further concentration of ownership of the production of goods or the provision of services. Such mergers can reduce the ability of small businesses to shop around for commercially favourable prices and terms when buying goods and services.
- It prohibits unfair trading practices, such as misleading and deceptive conduct (for example, withholding relevant information, making false predictions, exaggerating sales); false representations (false statements made in advertising); and sharp selling practices (for example, bait advertising, which is advertising non-existent or limited quantities of goods and services, and referral selling, whereby a business will not sell its goods to a customer unless the customer gives referrals).
- It protects small business from unconscionable conduct and provides for better disclosure and dispute resolution for small businesses. The unconscionable conduct provision (s. 51AC) prohibits a stronger party dealing with a disadvantaged party in a harsh or oppressive manner. A disadvantage here includes illiteracy, age, poverty, illness, mental impairment and inequality in bargaining power.

New Zealand's main statute in the area of competition law is the Commerce Act 1986, which is very similar to Australian legislation. The Commerce Act is enforced by the Commerce Commission. In Singapore, a Consumer Protection (Fair Trading) Bill was passed in 2003. It has been the result of the government recognising the need to give consumers more protection against unscrupulous businesses. In Malaysia, the Consumer Protection Act 1999 provides greater protection for consumers. The Hong Kong SAR government has adopted a more sector-specific approach to both consumer protection and competition. China has the Anti-Monopoly Law 2007 while India grants protection with the Competition Act 2003.

Taxation

Another form of business regulation involves the government imposition of taxes that must be complied with. These can include sales taxes, goods and services taxes, employee payroll deductions and local government levies. In most countries, businesses need to:

- account for income tax
- account for business expenses that are claimed as deductions
- keep business records, and report and pay tax.

Income tax is levied on a person's or a business's taxable income, and must generally be paid to the central government. In Australia, sole traders do not need to complete a separate return for their business; they use their personal income tax return to report their business income and deductions. Partnerships must complete a partnership tax return to show the partnership's income and deductions, and to show how the profit or loss was shared among the partners. Companies must complete a company tax return to calculate the tax it must pay. A trust must also lodge an annual income tax return under its own income tax file number. All beneficiaries who receive an income from the trust must in turn declare this income in their personal income tax return.

Under income tax law, a person carrying on a business can claim deductions for costs that are necessarily incurred to produce assessable income, provided these expenses are not of a private, domestic or capital nature. Such deductions include motor vehicle expenses; expenses relating to the area occupied by the business in a personal home; travel expenses such as fares, car hire and accommodation; tools; employees' expenses; and interest on borrowed money. In addition to the business books, business owners are advised to keep evidence of transactions, such as invoices and receipts, and evidence of usage, such as motor vehicle logs for vehicle expenses and airline tickets for travel expenses.

Good business records help small business operators to manage their business and make sound business decisions. They are also useful if an owner wants to sell the business. Under tax law, a person carrying on a business must keep records covering all transactions. These records include any documents that are relevant for the purpose of working out the person's income and expenditure. Any books of accounts, records or documents relating to the preparation of the income tax return must be retained for five years. In Australia, other statutory provisions, such as corporate law, require a company to retain records for seven years after completion of the transaction to which they relate.

The best sources of advice on taxation obligations, including recordkeeping requirements, are qualified accountants or the relevant taxation authority. The main taxation authorities in the countries referred to here are listed in table 8.7. These authorities generally provide helpful guidebooks, as well as online information about taxation requirements.

TABLE 8.7 Main taxation authorities

Country	Authority
Australia	Australian Taxation Office, www.ato.gov.au
New Zealand	Inland Revenue Department, www.ird.govt.nz
Hong Kong	Inland Revenue Department, www.info.gov.hk/ird
Malaysia	Inland Revenue Board of Malaysia, www.hasil.org.my
Singapore	Inland Revenue Authority of Singapore, www.iras.gov.sg

SUMMARY

There are three basic types of legal structure — sole proprietorship, partnership and company. In Australia and New Zealand, a trust is also a legal structure under which a business may operate. Each of these has varying degrees of complexity and cost, as well as variations in the level of individual control that can be exercised by the business owner.

Intellectual property is another legal issue entrepreneurs must consider. Intellectual property is a valuable asset and it should be clearly identified. It is often the competitive edge that sets successful small businesses apart and, as world markets become increasingly crowded and competitive, a firm's intellectual property must be protected. Once the intellectual property has been identified, appropriate strategies should be put in place to safeguard it. There are five main types of intellectual property rights — patents, trademarks, designs, copyrights and trade secrets — which business owners can use to protect their intellectual property. Failure to protect such ideas, and to do so early, can put a key asset of the business at risk.

The business owner also needs to examine other, more generalised legal matters that may be relevant to the enterprise. Because there is a wide range of legal matters and their relevance depends on the nature of the business activity being undertaken, it can be difficult to cover all these in advance. Some of the more common ones are licences and permits, registering for an Australian Business Number (ABN) and the goods and services tax (GST), trade practices and taxation.

REVIEW QUESTIONS

1. What are the different legal structures a business can operate under, and how do they differ from one another?
2. What is intellectual property?
3. What is the difference between a patent, a trademark and an industrial design?
4. Why do certain categories of business require a licence or a permit to operate? Give some examples of such businesses in your own country.
5. What are the main duties of a business with regard to taxation?

DISCUSSION QUESTIONS

1. 'A partnership is a lot like a marriage.' How accurate is this statement?
2. What role do patents play in everyday life?
3. A patent registration granted by a national patent office does not necessarily protect an invention worldwide. What can be done to obtain international protection?
4. List and explain the main kinds of anti-competitive practices that a national trade practices law could prohibit.

SUGGESTED READING

Bainbridge, D., *Intellectual Property*, 7th edn, Pearson Education, Harlow, 2009.
Gamble, R., Du Plessis, J. & Neal, L., *Principles of Business Law*, Thomson Academic, Sydney, 2008.
Humphrey, N., *The Penguin Small Business Guide*, Penguin Books, Camberwell, 2008.

Derek Handley, The Hyperfactory

The mobile phone is a handy way to communicate with the world through voice, SMS, email and chat rooms. This technology, however, can be leveraged by shrewd brand builders to reach target audiences in new and exciting ways. Hyperfactory, founded in 2001 by New Zealand brothers Derek and Geoffrey Hardley, is one such company to do so.[21]

Hyperfactory takes advantage of multiple technologies to formulate and execute mobile strategies for content and mobile application publishers, global brands and agencies. In other words, The Hyperfactory powers businesses and brands through the mobile medium; brands, such as Toyota, Motorola, Vodafone and Coke, that rely on the company as indispensable to their mobile marketing strategies.[22] The company employs over 100 people and, in addition to its Auckland headquarters, has offices in Los Angeles, New York, Hong Kong, Hyderabad and Sydney.

The mobile advertising market

Marketing is usually defined as the 'process of planning and executing the conception, pricing, promotion and distribution of goods and services to satisfy individual or organisational need'.[23] This definition implies a sequence of marketing stages alongside a temporal and spatial buyer–seller separation. Such boundaries and distinctions are blurred when mobile devices extend traditional marketing's time-space paradigm.[24] No longer beholden to land-based internet connections, mobile devices realise e-commerce's potential of location independence and ubiquity. Early on, mobile advertising usually took the form of text messages. Now telecommunications firms are transmitting ads to handsets via video clips, web pages, music and cutting edge applications.

Advertising on mobile phones is still a minute business. According to Informa Telecoms & Media, in 2009 expenditure on mobile ads was US$871 million worldwide. Compare this with US$24 billion spent on internet advertising and US$450 billion spent on all advertising.[25] Some marketing gurus say it is destined to overtake not only internet advertising, but also the four traditional pillars of the business advertising: television, radio, print and billboards. Informa forecasts that annual spending will reach US$11.4 billion by 2012.

The mobile marketing applications

Derek Handley separates the mobile focus into two areas of operation: The first is an agency operation aimed at creatively developing relationships between brands and consumers, using their mobile phones as the medium to deliver an integrated strategy. The second is technology-based, and is designed to benefit businesses through planning, integration and deployment of mobile technology – irrespective of platform, protocol or device.[26]

An example of agency operation is the Fanta mobile applications launch of 'Fanta Virtual Tennis' and 'Fanta Stealth Sound System' in 2009, which was supported by point-of-sale material, print and online ads, as well as publicity.[27] The Fanta Virtual Tennis application is claimed as the world's first 3D augmented reality tennis game. Augmented reality is the process of superimposing digitally rendered images onto our real-world surroundings, giving the sense of an illusion or 'virtual' reality. In the case of Fanta Virtual Tennis, players can download and print out a gameboard, and then take their positions either side of it. The augmented 3D application recognises the board and displays it as a full size tennis court on each player's mobile phone screen. They can then use their handsets as tennis racquets to hit a virtual ball whose movement is determined by the phones' angle and position.[28]

The other application, the 'Fanta Stealth Sound System', was developed by The Hyperfactory and made available via the Fanta WAP site. It utilises high-pitched frequencies (inaudible to most people over 20) encoded as wolf-whistles, warnings and sound tags for phrases like 'cool' and 'let's get out of here'.[29]

The second operating area are of The Hyperfactory is the technology division. It is dedicated to ensuring that customers extract the greatest returns from mobile technology. An example of the combination of different products and services to achieve this goal is the BlackBerry Global Mobile Web Presence. The Hyperfactory commissioned to develop a mobile media plan and landing page, as well as a consumer targeted program that delivered messages customised according to the type of handset being used. 'The success of this campaign has led to more campaigns, and the relationship between BlackBerry and The Hyperfactory has since grown into a model of global collaboration for our companies,' says Handley.[30]

Questions

1. What are the main advantages and drawbacks of the company structure adopted by The Hyperfactory?
2. How can Derek Handley protect the intellectual property of The Hyperfactory?
3. What do you need to do to get consumers involved in mobile marketing activities such as those launched by Fanta?

ENDNOTES

1. Australian Bureau of Statistics, *Counts of Australian Businesses, Including Entries and Exits*, ABS, Canberra, 2007, p. 17.
2. Australian Taxation Office, *Tax Basics for Small Business*, Commonwealth of Australia, 2008, p. 1.
3. M. Soe, *Principles of Singapore Law*, 2nd edn, IBF, Singapore, 1992, p. 502.
4. S. Terry, *Establishing a Company in Hong Kong*, 3rd edn, Pitman, Hong Kong, 1996.
5. H. McCombie, 'Owning your responsibilities', *Company Director*, vol. 22, no. 4, May 2006, pp. 24–6.
6. J. Wasiliev, 'Family values — trusts are back on track', *Weekend Australian Financial Review*, 26–27 October 2002, pp. 29–32.
7. G. Hayes, 'Well begun, half done', *BRW*, 16–22 February 2006, p. 54.
8. J. Holyoak, *Intellectual Property Law*, Butterworth, London, 1995.
9. 'Battle of ideas', *The Economist*, 25 April 2009, p. 66.
10. P. Mollerup, *Marks of Excellence*, Phaidon Press, London, 1997.
11. 'The eagle has landed', *Inside Business Success*, November 1997.
12. IP Australia, *Registered Business Names Survey*, Commonwealth of Australia, Canberra, October 2005.
13. P.J. Groves, *Intellectual Property Rights and their Valuation*, Woodhead Publishing, London, 1997, p. 35.
14. C.S. Tay, *Copyright and the Protection of Designs*, SNP Corporation, Singapore, 1997.
15. Australian Copyright Council, www.copyright.org.au.
16. Intellectual Property Department, www.houston.com.hk/hkgipd.
17. K. Le Mesurier, 'Invention has its price', *BRW*, 16–22 June 2005, p. 86.
18. B. Barringer & R.D. Ireland, *Entrepreneurship — Successfully Launching New Ventures*, Prentice Hall, Upper Saddle River, NJ, 2006.

19. Australian Taxation Office, *Tax Basics for Small Business*, ATO, Canberra, July 2002.
20. Australian Competition and Consumer Commission, *Small Business and the Trade Practices Act*, ACCC, Canberra, February 2002.
21. Ernst & Young, 'Derek Handley, The Hyperfactory 'Upwardly Mobile'', www.ey.com, 2009.
22. 'The Hyperfactory taps former film studio executive to star in leading role', *Business Wire*, 27 May 2008.
23. American Marketing Association (AMA), 'AMA Board approves new marketing definition,' *Marketing News*, vol. 19, no. 1, 1985, p. 1.
24. R.T. Watson, F. Leyland, L.F. Pitt, P. Berthon & G.M. Zinkhan, 'u-commerce: expanding the universe of marketing', *Journal of the Academy of Marketing Science*, vol. 30, no. 4, 2002.
25. 'Mobile advertising', *The Economist*, 4 October, 2007.
26. Ernst & Young, ibid.
27. C. Harnick, 'Mobile's future is in full media integration: Mobile Ad Summit panel', *Mobile Marketer*, 23 September, www.mobilemarketer.com, 2009.
28. M.A. Khan, 'Coca-Cola makes mobile push for Fanta', *Mobile Marketer*, 17 December 2008.
29. C. Lovell, 'Fanta launches mobile application only audible to teenagers', *The Advertising Age*, 4 December, 2008.
30. 'The Hyperfactory helps brands create their permanent mobile-web destination on a global scale', The Hyperfactory, www.thehyperfactory.com.

CHAPTER 9

Financing new and growing business ventures

Learning objectives

After reading this chapter, you should be able to:

- identify and explain the various types of debt finance

- identify and explain the various types of equity finance

- list and explain alternative sources of finance

- distinguish the sources of finance according to provider, term and business life cycle

- discuss the financing options available at different stages of a business life cycle.

Due to the risks involved in entrepreneurial pursuits, the financing of new ventures is often the main obstacle facing many intending business start-ups. An idea, product or service may be great and well researched, supported by sound marketing policies and good management, but without adequate financing it is doomed to failure.

The struggle to get finance does not stop after the business is set up, and small businesses have traditionally been at a disadvantage in raising finance compared with large corporations.[1] This chapter explains the types of financing options available to entrepreneurs, and discusses the sources of such capital. It also explains the factors that financial institutions take into account when assessing applications for finance, and looks at alternative sources of finance, such as debt factoring and government-backed schemes.

A typology of financing

There are three main ways to categorise business financing, although these are not mutually exclusive: (1) we can examine financing options from the fund-provider's perspective and establish two categories — debt holders and equity holders; (2) financing options can be tackled from a time frame perspective, distinguishing between short- and long-term finance; and (3) financing needs and possibilities vary according to the different life stages of the business venture, so we can distinguish early-stage finance from expansion finance.

Debt versus equity

Debt finance is money borrowed from an outside party; equity finance is money provided by the owner(s) of a business venture. The main difference between equity and debt is that equity provides a residual ownership interest in the business, whereas debt does not.

The difference between debt and equity finance is that debt must be reimbursed on a fixed date, whereas equity is not reimbursed — unless the business goes into liquidation. Debt finance also requires the payment of interest at a fixed and predetermined rate, whereas equity providers receive a variable remuneration in the form of a dividend. However, the distinction tends to become blurred in the case of small enterprises because of the highly intertwined relationship between the owner–manager and the business.[2] It is very common for small business owner–managers to invest money that has been raised by means of a loan secured over their personal assets. As a result, the owner–manager is more likely to regard these funds as personal debt rather than equity.

The underlying factors that determine the options that the small business owner chooses for financing operations depends on the business needs, and whether the assessment criteria required by each mode of finance can be met. In all cases, it is recommended that owner–managers adopt the best **leverage** possible in their capital structures. Leverage can increase shareholders' return on their investments, and often there are tax advantages associated with borrowing. However, businesses that are highly leveraged may be at risk of bankruptcy if they are unable to pay their debt; they may also be unable to find new lenders in the future.

Leverage *The degree to which a business uses borrowed money; what the debt–equity ratio measures.*

Short-term versus long-term finance

Business and accounting literature usually considers short-term finance as debts that must be reimbursed within 12 months. Long-term finance encompasses all forms of finance where the term extends beyond 12 months.

Short-term finance usually takes the form of a bank overdraft, trade credit, credit card purchase or cash advance. These finance the day-to-day operations of the business, including wages of employees and purchases of inventory and supplies. Also, **bridging finance** (interim loans with a short fixed term) can be used to finance accounts-receivable contracts, which are relatively risk-free but delayed for one to three months.

Bridging finance *Financing extended to a firm using existing assets as collateral in order to acquire new assets; bridging finance is usually short term.*

Money for short-term operations may be secured against (1) any unencumbered physical assets of the business and then (2) additional funds from shareholders or personal guarantees from principals. On occasion, inventories can be used as temporary security for operations loans. Bridging finance is normally secured by assignment of all the receivables and personal guarantees. On the balance sheet, accounts receivable, inventory and supplies are shown in the current assets section, whereas the counterpart loan information is displayed in the current liabilities section.

Long-term finance can, on the other hand, take the form of a long-term loan or a mortgage. Such finance is arranged when the scheduled repayment of the loan and the estimated useful life of the assets purchased (such as building, land, machinery, computers, equipment and shelving) are expected to exceed 12 months. Long-term finance is normally secured (1) by the new asset(s) purchased (up to 65 per cent), then (2) by other unencumbered physical assets of the business (for the remaining 35 per cent) or, failing that, (3) by additional funds from shareholders or personal guarantees from the principals. On the balance sheet, the equipment purchased is shown in the non-current assets section, and the counterpart loan information is shown both in the current liabilities section (for the interest currently payable) and in the non-current liabilities section. The useful life of the assets is directly reflected in their depreciation schedules.

Debt lenders (creditors) make loans to businesses that show strong management ability and steady growth potential. A business plan, including a cash flow projection demonstrating the business's ability to repay the loan principal and interest over the term of the repayment schedule, is required. The lender will expect the entrepreneur to have appropriate insurance to protect the assets.

Demand for finance generally follows a 'pecking order' of (1) internal equity, (2) short-term debt, (3) long-term debt and (4) external equity. The pecking order can be readily applied to emerging and small firms because their closely held nature means that their owners prefer not to issue new equity, and there is greater uncertainty in accurately pricing equity and the supply of debt finance.[3] However, direct empirical testing of the pecking order hypothesis is very limited and, as yet, inconclusive.

Early-stage versus expansion finance

The type of funds needed is often also closely related to the stage of development of the firm. It is possible to distinguish between two main categories in relation to the business life cycle: early-stage financing and expansion financing.[4]

Early stage financing covers the following aspects of a new venture's launch and early days of trading:

- *Seed financing.* Seed money is necessary for product development, building a management team or completing a business plan. At this stage, an outline of the strategy is important, as is a research and development action plan identifying key milestones. This is the most difficult and expensive money to raise because it is needed before management can prove that the product will sell or that it can be produced and distributed at a competitive price. The entrepreneur's family, friends, relatives and personal savings are main sources of seed capital.
- *Start-up financing.* This represents the funds needed to facilitate the process of organising the business structure, facilities and relationships of a firm. At this stage, the business has completed testing of the product or service, and is now ready to commercialise it. This money costs companies less equity per dollar of funding than seed capital does, but more than expansion financing.
- *First-stage financing.* This is the money provided when firms have exhausted their initial capital and require additional funds to initiate full-scale production and marketing.

Much of the early-stage financing relies on boostrap finance — a means of financing start-up through highly creative acquisition and use of resources, without raising equity from traditional sources or borrowing money from a bank. Bootstrap finance is further described in the section outlining alternative sources of finance at the end of this chapter.

Expansion financing, on the other hand, applies to firms that have successfully survived the start-up phase and have become established in their industry. For these businesses, the focus is on growth and expansion. Accordingly, their financial needs usually fall into one of the following categories:

- *Second-stage financing.* This refers to funds provided to operating firms that are expanding and that need extra funds to increase their working capital; these firms may not yet be showing a profit.
- *Third-stage (or mezzanine) financing.* Mezzanine financing refers to investment provided to a company already producing and selling a product or service, to help the company achieve a critical objective, such as increasing inventories to achieve greater sales, that will enable it to go public. At this stage, the firm is making a profit and the new funds are usually applied to plant expansion, working capital or the development of an enhanced product. Mezzanine funds are typically lent to decrease a company's overall cost of financing by helping the company attract a significantly better price for its shares in a later public offering.
- *Initial public offering (IPO).* This is when a company first offers shares to the public and lists on the stock exchange. The track record of a business and management in seeking an IPO is critical. Historical information and several years' financial results and forecasts will need to be analysed and explained in a detailed review of the business for a potential investor.

Many investors and especially venture capitalists, when funding new business ventures, adopt a 'stage-financing approach' to reduce their risk. Funding a company in 'stages' means apportioning the committed money as the company meets pre-established goals. If the company fails to meet a goal, investors are relieved of their obligation to provide additional funds. In this way, investors can cut their losses when a company does not meet expectations. At the same time, the company gets a commitment for its full funding, which it can obtain by meeting its goals. Customarily, the company apportions shares to investors as the money is received.

As shown in figure 9.1 (below), financing options depend to a large extent on the business life cycle. For example, during the seed stage, would-be entrepreneurs need to rely on their personal funds, as well as those of family, friends and perhaps 'business angels' (BAs). Banks do not provide seed financing; they focus, rather, on established businesses with a track record and a cash flow stream. Similarly, venture capitalists (VCs) focus on the start-up and expansion stages. They usually sell their equity stakes through an exit mechanism (such as initial public offering, sale to strategic partner or management buy-out) before the business venture reaches its maturity.

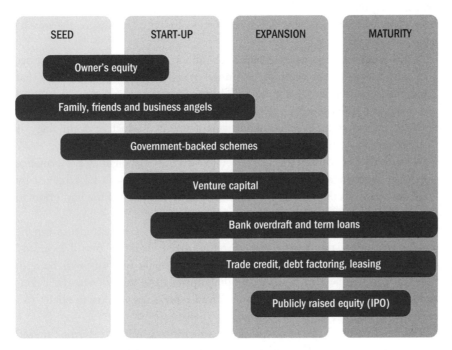

FIGURE 9.1 Financing options at different stages of the business life cycle

Financing challenges for start-ups and innovative SMEs

The entrepreneur's search for funding has never been easy. However, it has become harder in recent years with the opening of what has been called the **equity gap** — a scarcity of ready sources of outside financing in the early stage of a firm's growth.[5] The emergence of an equity gap may partly reflect cyclical or transitory influences, including the effects of poor investment decisions by VCs during the dotcom bubble and the economic downturns that may have adversely affected the prospects of smaller firms more than those of large businesses. However, there are also some intrinsic factors that may lead VCs to prefer larger or later-stage investments. These factors stem both from the supply side (the investors) and the demand side (the entrepreneurs).

Equity gap *The scarce provision of equity investments in the early stage of a firm's growth.*

The equity gap exists on the supply side because two well-trawled sources of finance no longer overlap. In their earliest stages, start-up companies characteristically rely on precarious financing, for example, the owners' savings, mortgages or cash from acquaintances. These sources might provide the first A$200 000 or so. This is not enough to bring to fruition the sort of groundbreaking ideas that can ultimately turn into a million-dollar business. So another source is needed. All this points to external equity investments as the most appropriate source of funding. A decade ago or more, A$1 million could have been raised by turning to VCs and BAs. However, the ambitiousness of VC funds have grown during their development and expansion.[6] Information asymmetries mean that VCs can face substantial costs in identifying appropriate investment opportunities. These information problems are classically greatest for smaller, younger firms and particularly innovative business seeking to expand unproven technologies, products and markets. Information difficulties present a significant obstacle to smaller-scale equity investments, given that the costs of investment does not differ proportionally with the size of the investment. These costs include:

- *Search costs*. The flow of information about small, unquoted companies seeking investment is much more limited in contrast to large companies that are quoted on public stock markets. Therefore, investors can incur significant search costs when seeking out suitable opportunities.
- *Due diligence costs*. When a management team, product or technology is unproven, it is often difficult to gauge the prospects of a business.
- *Monitoring costs*. Equity investors need to scrutinise the ongoing performance of their investment, when investing in a business. This can be achieved by taking a seat on the board, and contributing considerable time and effort to providing management support.[7]

There are problems on the demand side, too. First, entrepreneurs can be reluctant to dilute their ownership or relinquish a share of control to equity investors, and instead try to borrow or accept limits to the firm's growth. Second, being able to evaluate the available funding options and to understand the concerns and needs of investors is essential for entrepreneurs who try to obtain risk capital financing.

The financing of innovative activities poses problems not only during the seed and start-up stages. SMEs face disadvantages because they cannot exploit scale economies, and they are restricted in the types of financing they can raise for innovative projects. The process of evaluating the quality of innovative projects is quite complicated. Not only is a technical knowledge essential, owners also want to keep details of their R&D activity secret. The consequence, which can lead to credit rationing, is acute problems for many small ventures.[8]

Debt finance

Most small business owners will, at some time or another, find that their own financial resources are insufficient to meet all their needs. When this point is reached, they will need to consider accessing funds from an outside party. This requires going into debt: that is, having an obligation or outstanding liability to an outside party. The main types of debt financing available to businesses include bank overdrafts, trade credit, term loans and leasing.

Banks that provide overdrafts, term loans and mortgages are the obvious choice for many entrepreneurs. However, small businesses often fail to obtain finance for three main reasons:

- The security offered by the applicant is considered insufficient to support the bank risk.
- The term requested by the applicant to pay back the loan is considered too long from the bank's point of view.
- The business lacks a track record of performance, so the bank is unable to assess the business's ability to repay the loan.

In studies of the problems faced by bank officers dealing with loans for small businesses, research has shown that proposals submitted for businesses that are unprofitable is the variable that loan officers perceive as the most important in adversely affecting their decisions.[9] The next most important variables are the inability of the applicant to provide collateral as requested, followed by incomplete information on the loan application, the applicant's lack of knowledge of overall business management and the proposed direction of the business. Variables, such as having no account with the bank, lack of knowledge of banking facilities for small businesses and the business being managed by the owners themselves, were not important to loan officers.

Bank overdraft

An **overdraft** is a credit arrangement permitting a business to draw more funds from a bank than it has in its account. There is an upper limit on how much the business can overdraw its account. New business ventures often use a bank overdraft as a source of finance for working capital, and it often represents a large element of borrowing on the balance sheet of many small businesses.[10]

Overdraft *The amount by which withdrawals exceed deposits or the extension of credit by a lending institution to allow for such a situation.*

Overdrafts are highly flexible, so they have several advantages as a short-term funding source. Only the amount needed is drawn on and interest is paid only on the daily balance outstanding, so interest costs may be less than for a long-term standard loan. Interest payments are tax-deductible in many jurisdictions. There is also the ability to link overdrafts with bank cards or credit cards, and to use commercial bank branches and automatic teller machines to access needed funds.

However, overdrafts can have expensive administration costs, and the interest rate charged on the overdrawn sums may vary as commercial lending rates change. Moreover, owner–managers must remember that the overdrawn amount is always payable on demand, which means that the bank can recall the funds whenever it wishes.

Trade credit

Trade credit is a company's open account arrangements with its suppliers. In this situation, goods are received from the suppliers before payment is made. Suppliers are an important, but too often ignored, source of finance with no explicit cost (such as interest or dividend) to the entrepreneur who obtains such credit. Terms of trade can influence cash flow favourably by reducing the average collection period of accounts receivable at the same time as capitalising on the full duration of accounts payable periods.

Trade credit *A form of short-term debt financing whereby goods are received from the suppliers before payment is made.*

Term loan

Term loans *A loan that is repaid through regular periodic payments, usually over a period of one to ten years.*

Offered by banks and finance companies, **term loans** are a source of long-term debt. The borrower of a term loan usually contracts with the lender to repay the loan by regular periodic payments over a specified period (the term). The sum may be borrowed at a fixed interest rate, in which case the repayments will be fixed for the specified term or a variable rate is set that is subject to fluctuation. Often the loan must be secured by assets (either the business's or the owner's). A term loan is most suited to financing major long-term capital requirements, such as the purchase of manufacturing equipment or premises.

A term loan is a stable source of financing and the interest payments are often tax-deductible. The bank has no direct involvement with the running of the business and repayment costs are often fixed and predictable for the life of the loan. One problem with term loans is that associated establishment fees and other possible charges may affect the interest cost structure, making it effectively higher than the rate quoted. If the borrower defaults and has used personal assets as security for the loan, these can be seized or the lender can force the business into bankruptcy. Other disadvantages include inflexibility of conditions and variable interest rates.

When examining a loan application, loans officers will often consider the 'five Cs of credit':

- *Character* — willingness of the debtor to meet financial obligations. The integrity, trustworthiness and quality of management are assessed. The applicant's background provides useful indications about these various aspects.
- *Capacity* — the ability to meet financial obligations out of operating cash flows.
- *Contribution* — the amount of money the entrepreneur or owner–manager is putting into the project. Few lenders will advance funds if the owner is not contributing a substantial amount of money, since this would leave most of the risk in the hands of the financier, rather than the entrepreneur.
- *Collateral* — assets pledged as security. These can include real estate, bonds, shares, motor vehicles, plant and equipment.
- *Conditions* — general economic conditions related to the applicant's business (such as industry, business cycle, community and financial conditions).

Leasing

Lease *A written agreement under which a property owner allows a tenant to use the property for a specified period of time and rent.*

A **lease** gives a business access to plant or premises without paying the full cost. Leasing can be defined as an agreement whereby a lessee (the small business owner–manager) undertakes to make lease payments or rentals to the lessor, in return for which the lessor allows the lessee to use the leased property. The lessor is thus both the financier and legal owner of the property.[11]

There are two types of lease: finance leases and operating (or true) leases. The one that business operators choose depends on what they expect to do with the equipment once the lease has expired. Finance leases, also known as capital leases or conditional sales, work best for companies that intend to keep the equipment when the lease expires. The main advantage of this type of lease is that it gives the business owner the option to purchase the equipment for a nominal fee. Payments on finance leases generally represent the full value of the equipment. The lessor retains legal ownership, but all the risks and benefits are effectively transferred from the lessor to the lessee. Thus, all finance leases are required to be capitalised in the lessee's accounts and must appear in the financial statements; this requirement does not apply to operating leases. A finance lease can be a good option if the business owner does not wish to tie up large amounts of cash.

On the other hand, operating lease payments do not cover the full value of the equipment. In an operating lease, the lessor retains substantially all the risks and benefits incidental to ownership of the leased goods. At the end of the lease, the lessee can choose to walk away from the equipment, or purchase it at fair market value that, for office equipment, is usually at least 10 per cent of the original purchase price.

Leasing may be a way to gain access to costly capital equipment, such as construction and manufacturing equipment, computers, fittings and fixtures, premises and vehicles. One of the advantages of leasing is that it offers fairly minimal up-front costs. Unlike bank loans, which may require a substantial down payment, generally only two payments are required at the beginning of a lease. In addition, leasing protects against equipment obsolescence by forcing the lessor to evaluate the useful life of the equipment and to set lease terms accordingly. Finally, leasing can lessen the business tax burden. Depending on how the lease is structured, the business owner may be able to fully deduct lease payments as a business expense, rather than depreciating the value of the equipment as for a capital expenditure.

What would you do?

Anemoi Power

Your long-time friend Clem Theodore just shared with you his latest business idea: the development of a wind farm near Geraldton in Western Australia (WA). Clem is an enterprising farmer who owns a 50 ha mixed cropping and livestock property. He senses a business opportunity that may arise from the possible future introduction of a national carbon pollution reduction scheme — a system of emissions trading for greenhouse gases. The demand for green electricity will significantly increase in future years. Future governments are likely to expand the national supply of renewable energy.

Geraldton, a small town of population approximately 30 000 located in WA's Midwest, seems to be an ideal location for a wind farm. It is known for its windy nature and 'leaning trees', so named after having been buffeted by constant southerly winds. Geraldton's wind climatology is dominated by the effects of the land–sea interface. Here, summer sea breezes often reach 25 knots (46 km/h) or more near the coast.[12]

When installed on agricultural land, a windfarm has the lowest environmental impact of all energy sources. Wind farms are compatible with grazing and almost any crop that would be suitable for a site that would also support a wind farm. Upfront capital costs account for the greatest proportion of costs associated with the development of wind power. However, the operating costs are relatively low, and each additional unit of wind power costs extremely little to produce. Clem already made some enquiries with two wind turbine manufacturers, and he also contacted a wind farm operating in the region. He was told that a 2 MW wind turbine cost about A$2 million (this includes the turbine itself and the installation).

Clem owns the land where he plans to build the wind farm with ten turbines, each producing over 6000 MW per year, and he could invest A$2 million of his own money into the project. Electricity distributors would generally pay five cents per kilowatt hour and he would be eligible for another five cents per kilowatt hour subsidy. He has requested your help to develop a financing plan, and asked you if you would invest in the project, to be called Anemoi Power – after the wind gods in Greek mythology.

Questions

1. What are the potential sources of finance and resources available to Clem?
2. What additional information do you need to decide if you would personally invest in Anemoi Power?

Equity finance

The alternative to borrowing or using other people's money is to use funds belonging to the owners of the business: that is, either the original founder of the firm or other people who subsequently become part-owners of the enterprise. Sources of equity finance include owner's equity, family and friends, 'business angels', venture capital firms and the public through the initial public offering process.

Owner's equity

This type of equity is usually acquired from the owner's savings or the sale of personal assets. Using personal money means that there are no lending or interest costs payable to an outside party. Funds can be used with maximum flexibility and invested for the long term. There is no chance that an outsider can force the business to be closed for a default of payments. If the founding owner's funds are insufficient, the amount can be increased by broadening ownership of the firm to include other people who are willing to invest their money in it, or by reinvesting the profits that the business earns. However, taking in other investors as part-owners can lead to ownership dilemmas or conflicts over the distribution of profits, since such investors may expect a higher return on their investment.

Family and friends

Family members, friends, and friends of friends are the best place to start the search for capital. This is the most common avenue for financing start-ups and the most accessible for small enterprises. The attractiveness of this type of financing is obvious. First, family and friends are likely to be more flexible to forgo dividends payments until the business gains momentum. They may also be willing to invest in the business without the security of property or other collateral. Second, they are likely to be a cheaper source of funding because family and friends have an emotional attachment to the entrepreneur, and their motivation to invest is thus not purely economic.

Entrepreneurs should nevertheless be cautious with this type of financing — many cherished friendships and family relationships have been destroyed through inadequate protection and provision for personal creditor repayment related to a business failure. A common mistake is 'over-valuation', where the total valuation of the company far exceeds the substantiated and potential earnings growth value of the young enterprise.

Business angels

One of the fastest growing sources of equity finance for entrepreneurs comes from people called **business angels**.[13] 'Angel' investors are wealthy people who invest in entrepreneurial ventures, usually at an early stage. Traditionally, the type of person who becomes a business angel is retired but, as news of the concept spreads, executives and portfolio investors are now becoming angels. Like venture capital firms, many business angels provide cash to young businesses and take equity in return. However, angel investors typically invest smaller amounts of money in individual businesses than venture capitalists do, making them a suitable choice for small business owners who have exhausted the resources of family and friends but are not ready to approach venture capitalists.

Business angels *Wealthy people who invest in early-stage entrepreneurial firms and contribute their business skills.*

Start-up and first-stage finance is the most obvious benefit business angels can offer entrepreneurs, but they can also act as mentors, offering special expertise and business and professional advice. Angels often have a background in business or investment and can provide an extra pair of hands to help run the business. In some cases, they prefer to remain a silent partner. Business angels can also provide specialisation that the business may not otherwise be in a position to acquire. Therefore, the best angel for a start-up is the one who can contribute significant experience, knowledge and networking opportunities, as well as the cash needed for the business venture to grow.

Some business angels are members of angel groups, allowing them to increase their access to investment opportunities, and giving them the possibility of investing jointly with other angels to hedge their risk. These angel groups are often called **business introduction services**. Some groups provide or arrange advice services for entrepreneurs to help them become investment-ready. Business angel networks can now be found throughout the Asia–Pacific region; table 9.1 lists some of these. Both private investors and businesses register with these organisations and, after thorough interviews, the needs of businesses are matched with private investors' criteria.

Business introduction services *A service that arranges or facilitates the meeting of private investors and businesses seeking external capital.*

Venture capital

Venture capital (VC) is money provided by professionals who invest alongside owners and management in young, rapidly growing businesses with the potential to generate a high return on investment. There are several types of VC firms, but mainstream firms invest their capital through funds organised as limited partnerships in which the VC firm serves as the general partner. The most common type of VC firms are called 'private, independent VC firms', and have no affiliations with any other financial institutions. Other venture firms may be affiliates or subsidiaries of a commercial bank, investment bank or insurance company, and make investments on behalf of the parent firm's clients. A third type may be subsidiaries of industrial corporations making investments on behalf of the

Venture capital (VC) *Independently managed, dedicated pools of capital that make equity investments in high-growth businesses.*

parent itself. These latter firms are typically called 'direct investors' or 'corporate venture investors'.[14]

How does venture capital work?

Venture capitalists help businesses grow but they eventually seek to exit the investment in three to seven years. An early stage investment may take seven to ten years to mature, whereas a later-stage investment may take only three years, so the VC firm must match its investment with its desire for liquidity. The venture investment is neither a short-term nor a liquid investment and must be made carefully. In essence, venture capitalists buy a stake in an entrepreneur's idea, nurture it for a period of time and then sell their investment.[15]

When considering an investment, venture capitalists carefully screen the technical and business merits of the proposed venture. This is very important — it is estimated that, out of every hundred business plans considered by venture capitalists, only six are funded; even then, almost four of those six can be expected to fail in the medium term.[16] With these risks in mind, venture capitalists have to be highly selective in their investments, tolerant of failure and willing to adopt a long-term perspective. To help enhance the prospects of success, they work actively with the venture's management by contributing their experience and business knowledge gained from helping other businesses with similar growth challenges.

There is no standard set of rules VCs use to judge investment propositions — that is why an entrepreneur can be turned down by one VC and be accepted by another. However, the following aspects are always taken into account when evaluating an investment:

- *Team.* Investors back people. If the entrepreneur does not have a track record, there should be someone on the team who does. A team is better than a single person, especially if they have worked together with success.
- *Industry.* Most VC firms back projects in an industry they know, and where they have made money before. As a result, they often specialise in a limited number of industries. Entrepreneurs should check out the specific sectors a VC firm has targeted before approaching the firm.
- *Business model and technology.* The VC will ask for evidence that the project has a significant and defensible competitive advantage against existing and potential competitors. The entrepreneur will need a working prototype of the business's technology or product and ownership of key intellectual property rights.
- *Market opportunities.* VC firms focus on opportunities within large, rapidly growing markets and those within highly profitable niches.
- *Exit.* The VC needs to know and believe that there will be a way to sell the shareholding in the business within three to seven years. There are different exit strategies, such as initial public offering, management buy-out, and sale to another company.

How to approach a venture capitalist

Once the business plan and an executive summary have been completed, the entrepreneur can submit the proposal to the appropriate VC firms. These firms can have different investment criteria, such as:

- the amount invested in a business (for example, A$1 to A$10 million)

- the sector invested in (such as telecommunications, biotechnology and multimedia)
- the geographic focus of the fund (for example, a particular state or country)
- the particular aim of the fund (such as job creation or commercialisation of local research and development).

TABLE 9.1 Venture capital and business angel associations

Country	Venture capital and business angel associations
Australia	Australian Venture Capital Association, www.avcal.com.au Australian Association of Angel Investors, www.aaai.net.au
New Zealand	New Zealand Venture Capital Association, www.nzvca.co.nz Angel Association of New Zealand, www.angelassociation.co.nz
Hong Kong	Hong Kong Venture Capital Association, www.hkvca.com.hk
Malaysia	Malaysian Venture Capital Association, www.mvca.org.my
Singapore	Singapore Venture Capital Association, www.svca.org.sg
China	China Venture Capital Association, www.cvca.com.hk China Angels, www.chinaangels.org
India	Indian Venture Capital Association, www.indiavca.org
Asia–Pacific Region	World Business Angels Association, www.wbaa.biz Business Angel Network (South-East Asia), http://bansea.angelgroups.net

The best way to approach a VC is through a referral. As venture capital has become increasingly popular and more readily available as a source of equity funding in the last 10 years, there may be someone among the entrepreneur's network of advisers who has been through the process. Accountants and solicitors are likely to have experience and should be consulted at an early stage for guidance on who might be the appropriate backer for the deal. If the entrepreneur is not satisfied with, or able to use, personal recommendations, there are a number of directories that can help, such as the national venture capital associations in the Asia–Pacific region shown in table 9.1.

The VC firm will then evaluate the proposal and may require exclusivity for the period of the evaluation. Normally, the entrepreneur should ask for a confidentiality agreement to be signed once the investor has read the executive summary and has shown an interest in the proposal. Ideally, the VC should give a provisional response within a week or two — either a definite 'no' or a request for a meeting and further information. If the VC says no, it is useful to find out why the proposal was turned down. Once the VC firm has indicated its interest, the process can take anything between a couple of months and a year. The entrepreneur will need the VC to keep to a timetable, and must in turn comply with requests from the VC.

Publicly raised equity

Selling part ownership (shares) of an incorporated company on a public stock exchange is a way of raising finance from the general public. In this case, the

Initial public offering (IPO) *Also called flotation, going public, listing; refers to a business's initial offer of shares to the public via a stock exchange.*

business 'goes public' by making an initial offering of ordinary shares or securities to the general community. This process is called an **initial public offering (IPO)**. A large amount of money can be raised in this way, and it also serves to increase the public profile of the firm.

This method of financing has become, however, less popular over the past few years in the Asia–Pacific region. An abundance of private equity money and the improving capital market skills of private company operators mean IPOs are less attractive to expanding companies than in the past. While the popularity of public listings has been quite strong in the past, in more recent years high growth firms have become somewhat less willing to use this option.[17]

Advantages of going public

Some entrepreneurs consider that going public legitimises their efforts and confirms their success, and they plan long and hard for the opportunity to run a public company. Those who go public believe that the proceeds generated and other benefits of being a public company are worth the effort and expense required to complete a public offering. But going public is not the right decision for every business and does not ensure future success. Seeking funds from private investors or from traditional lending sources may make more sense. At times, going public may be impossible because of market conditions unrelated to a prospective candidate's strength.

Determining whether going public makes sense requires consideration of a number of factors, including timing, business history, prospects for future growth and management's personality. The advantages and disadvantages of going public should be weighed carefully before a decision is made to seek funds in public markets.[18] Some of the advantages are:

• *Capital for continued growth.* Perhaps the most obvious benefit of going public is the proceeds (cash) of the offering. This money can be used for a variety of company purposes as long as they are disclosed in the company's offering documents. Typical uses are to increase working capital, to acquire new divisions or technologies, to increase marketing efforts, to pay for research or plant modernisation or to repay debt.

• *Lower cost of capital.* Going public is often triggered by management's belief that it can raise more money and get a better price for its shares by selling to the public than to a venture capitalist or other private investor. When this is true, a public offering can raise money at lower cost and with less dilution of management's shareholdings.

• *Increased shareholder liquidity.* Going public makes it easier for company shareholders to sell their shares by creating a public market for the company's shares. Shareholders who register their shares in the company's offering hold freely tradable shares once the offering is completed. Even the shares that are not registered in the offering become more liquid.

• *Improved company image.* Going public, with all the financial disclosure and investor relations planning it requires, usually attracts the attention of the business and financial press. Free publicity, coupled with the perception that going public is a significant milestone of success, enhances a company's image.

Disadvantages of going public

The advantages of going public can be substantial but they can be outweighed by the disadvantages, depending on management's goals and the circumstances of the company. Among the disadvantages that should always be considered are:

- *Expense.* Going public is expensive. The **underwriter's** discounts alone can amount to as much as four to eight per cent of the total proceeds of the offering.[19] Other expenses include filing fees, transfer agent fee, legal fees, printing fees and accounting fees. Most of these expenses must be paid at the close of the offering.

- *Loss of confidentiality.* Going public forces a company to prepare and distribute to potential investors a complete description of the company, its history, its strengths, its weaknesses and its future plans. Detailed disclosures of financial information are required. Once information is filed, it becomes readily available to competitors, employees, customers, suppliers, union organisers and others.

- *Periodic reporting.* Going public subjects a company to a number of periodic reporting requirements with the national regulatory agency. For most companies, these and other reporting requirements, which force the company to maintain audited financial statements, increase the company's cost of doing business by imposing more stringent accounting practices, and by making additional demands on management's time.

- *Reduced control.* A public offering can reduce management's control over a company if outsiders obtain enough shares to elect a majority of the company's board of directors. Thus outside shareholders can remove members of the management team. Public companies are also more susceptible to unfriendly takeovers because their shares are easy to accumulate.

- *Shareholder pressures.* Even entrepreneurs or owner–managers who retain voting control over their companies find that going public subjects them to pressures that can affect the way they run their businesses. Many entrepreneurs find that shareholder expectations and the reporting requirements of the national regulatory agency combine to create significant pressures on a company to continually improve its performance every year.

Underwriter *An intermediary between an issuer of a security and the investing public, usually an investment bank.*

Entrepreneur profile

Peter Marshall, Tallon Marine

Although Peter Marshall discovered his entrepreneurial skills early – designing and selling jewellery to local retailers at the tender age of 12 – his Wellington secondary school somehow missed that potential. 'The headmaster said either I went or he did, and it obviously wasn't going to be him,' says Marshall. Today 52-year-old Marshall runs Tallon Marine, a marine accessories company that develops and markets a unique fixture system able to receive interchangeable boat accessories – think champagne flute holders, table lamps, rod holders and bait tables.

Launched in 2007, the Kiwi company recently signed an exclusive distribution deal with Australian marine distributor Brunswick Asia Pacific and, after beating 79 countries to a fixture and fittings category award at the 2007 IBEX (International Boat Builders Exhibition) innovation awards, is also in talks with potential distributors from the US, UK and Canada. Marshall's boat bits are starting to be big business, even though the company comprises just him, his wife Lynn, and his son-in-law. He's also anticipating 50 per cent growth over the next year and an annual turnover of more than NZ$20 million in 2011.

Marshall figures he's spent around NZ$2 million establishing Tallon Marine, if you factor in his own time, and he's also had a grant of NZ$100 000 from the New Zealand Trade and Enterprise market development fund. The company's shareholders include a few outside Kiwi investors and a number of relatives, and Marshall has a majority share under a holding company he's proudly named Wanaka Unlimited.

Marshall is still based in Wanaka [in New Zealand's South Island] – 'you have no stress and better health down south' – and was, in fact, all set to retire until the idea for Tallon Marine came along. It's probably just as well; he was getting bored. He says his early rejection at school never hurt his business career. Once he has sorted all the distribution, production and quality issues worldwide for his new venture, his big goal is to do some more fishing.

Source: Adapted from V. Bland, 'The maverick', *Unlimited*, 27 January 2008.

Alternative sources of finance

In addition to the traditional debt and equity finance already presented, there are other sources that are categorised separately because they are 'off-balance-sheet financing' or because of the specific nature and purpose of the funds that can be obtained. These alternative sources of finance are often referred to as 'boot-strapping'. **Bootstrap finance** refers to the use of methods of meeting the need for resources without relying on long-term external finance from debt holders or new owners.[20] It offers many advantages for entrepreneurs; aside from getting money from friends and family, it is probably the best way of getting a business venture operating and well positioned to seek debt financing from banks or equity finance from outside investors later. Bootstrapping relies greatly on networks, trust, cooperation and wise use of the firm's existing resources, rather than going into debt or giving away equity.[21]

Bootstrap finance
Creative financing methods of meeting the need for resources without relying on debt or equity finance.

The main sources of boostrap finance are:
- *Debt factoring*. This is a financing method where the firm sells its accounts receivable to a buyer at a discount. This method is described further in the following section.
- *Customers*. One way to use your customers to obtain financing is by having them write you a letter of credit. Another way is to obtain prepaid licences, royalties or advances from customers.
- *Real estate and equipment*. For example, entrepreneurs can simply lease a facility. This reduces start-up costs because it costs less to lease a facility than it does to buy one.
- *Government and industry partners*. Local, regional and federal government entities can provide various types of seed funding, such as grants and interest-free loans. Similarly, it is often possible to obtain seed funding from various industry partners such as enterprises, universities and industry associations.

Debt factoring and discounting

Factoring involves selling or exchanging a business's debts for cash at a discount. This is a financing system whereby an invoice is sold to a 'factor' who pays 80–90 per cent of the invoice, and assumes responsibility for the control and administration of receivables and bears the risk of non-collection. Many new and growing businesses have trouble obtaining traditional bank financing because of the length of time in business, profitability and financial strength. By factoring, they can raise cash from approved invoices in as little as 24 hours. Debt **discounting** is similar to factoring; the business sells its invoice to the financier but keeps responsibility for collecting monies owing. This is ideal if the business wants to maintain a relationship with its customers and keep track of what is happening in the industry.

Debt factoring and discounting are commonly used to meet short-term seasonal funding requirements but, in some cases, it may be an ongoing working capital facility. In situations where a bank may be unwilling to provide or extend an overdraft, debt factoring or discounting may be the most effective way to enhance the liquidity and cash flow of a firm. A key advantage is that they provide immediate cash inflow, although the firm loses collection control with debt factoring. This type of financing does not appear in the balance sheet, so it is often referred to as *off-balance-sheet financing*.

Factoring and discounting are forms of financing that do not suit all businesses. For example, they would not be suitable for retailers, contractors receiving progress payments or a business sector with a high level of trade disputes. Factoring is suitable for an SME with the following attributes:

- credit sales (not cash)
- manufacturing or wholesaling with continuous trading with established customers
- no unusual selling terms (such as consignment sales or guarantees)
- sound management and profitable trading.

Factoring *The selling of a firm's accounts receivable to a financier who assumes the credit risk and receives cash as the debtors settle their accounts.*

Discounting *The selling of a firm's accounts receivable to a financier while the firm keeps responsibility for collecting monies owing.*

Government-backed schemes

Many governments have recognised the importance of start-ups and SMEs to their national economy. As a result, they have established a variety of schemes to provide finance to new firms and fast-growing SMEs (see table 9.2). These schemes can be a valuable source of both debt and equity funding if the applicant meets the specified criteria. In general, government-backed schemes have the following criteria:

- Schemes focus on a specific stage of the firm's development. Consequently, funding can target the seed, start-up or expansion stage of a business venture.
- Schemes mostly aim to support SMEs. The size to qualify for funding can be determined in different ways: yearly sales, number of employees, assets under management or a combination of these.
- Schemes usually target specific industries. In most cases, governments tend to back firms from various high-tech sectors, such as biotechnology, biochemistry, electronics, telecommunications, software and fine mechanics. Similarly, schemes often focus on research and development (R&D) and the commercialisation of innovation.

Would-be entrepreneurs and SME owner–managers need to be aware of these features when applying to a government-backed scheme, and be prepared to go through the tedious application process.

TABLE 9.2 Government-backed schemes in selected countries

Scheme or fund	Funding	Objective	Agency/website
Australia			
Commercialisation Australia	Up to A$250 000 for proof of concept activities, and up to A$2 million for early stage commercialisation activities	To provide multi-tiered assistance to entrepreneurs, and innovative firms to take their ideas to market	Department of Innovation, Industry, Science and Research, www.innovation.gov.au
New Enterprise Initiative Scheme (NEIS)	Less than A$50 000 per year	To help unemployed people establish a business by providing income support and business advice	Department of Employment, Education and Workplace Relations, www.deewr.gov.au
New Zealand			
Seed Co-Investment Fund	Investment up to NZ$250 000 per SME alongside co-investors on a 1:1 basis	To provide seed funding for early stage businesses with strong growth potential	New Zealand Venture Investment Fund Limited, www.nzvif.com
TechNZ	Varies according to the TechNZ scheme	To support companies and people undertaking research and development projects that result in new products, processes or services	Foundation for Research Science and Technology and Technology New Zealand, www.frst.govt.nz
Hong Kong			
SME Loan Guarantee Scheme (SGS)	Up to 50% of the approved loan, subject to a maximum amount of HK$6 million	To assist SMEs secure loans when acquiring equipment and meeting their working capital needs	Administered by the Trade and Industry Department, www.smefund.tid.gov.hk. Offered through over 30 Participating Lending Institutions (PLIs)
SME Export Marketing Fund (EMF)	Grant equivalent to 50% of the total approved expenditures or HK$50 000 (whichever is less)	To help SMEs expand their businesses through active participation in export promotion activities	Trade and Industry Department, www.smefund.tid.gov.hk
Malaysia			
Bumiputera Entrepreneurs Project Fund	70% of the contract value or RM5 million, whichever is lower	To support indigenous Malay entrepreneurs who have been awarded projects by government agencies and private companies	ERF Sdn Bhd, www.erf.com.my
New Entrepreneurs Fund 2	Maximum loan: RM5 million per SME repayable over 8 years	To help stimulate the growth of indigenous Malay SMEs	Bank Negara Malaysia, www.bnm.gov.my

Scheme or fund	Funding	Objective	Agency/website
Small Entrepreneur Guarantee Scheme (SEGS)	Maximum loan amount per SME: RM50 000	To provide bank overdrafts and term loans to Malaysian-owned and controlled companies	Banka Negara Malaysia, www.bnm.gov.my Offered through the Credit Guarantee Corporation, www.iguarantee.com.my
Singapore			
Start-up Enterprise Development Scheme (SPRING SEEDS)	Investment up to S$1 million into start-ups, with differentiated value proposition alongside co-investors on a 1:1 basis	To co-finance local start-ups creating innovative products or processes	SPRING, www.spring.gov.sg
Young Entrepreneurs Scheme for Start-ups (YES)	Up to S$50 000 for youths to set-up their innovative start-up, alongside co-investors on a 4:1 basis	To provides funding support for youths to set-up their innovative start-up	SPRING, www.spring.gov.sg
Technology Enterprise Commercialisation Scheme (TECS)	Up to 100% of qualifying costs for each project, up to maximum of S$250 000 for the proof concept, and maximum S$500 000 for the proof of value	To provide early-stage funding for the commercialisation of proprietary technology ideas in start-ups	SPRING, www.spring.gov.sg
India			
Various support schemes at the central and state level	For example: loans, advances, discounting bills, term loans, export finance	To support entrepreneurs and small businesses, mainly in industry and agriculture	Public sector banks, e.g. State Bank of India, www.statebankofindia.com

SUMMARY

Obtaining finance is one of the major difficulties in establishing and running a small enterprise. There are three major issues to consider when seeking financing: (1) whether the venture should be funded through debt, equity or a combination of both; (2) whether the funding is needed on a short-term or long-term basis and (3) what point in the business life cycle the firm is at (early stage or expansion).

The first type of finance is debt, which includes short-term options, such as a bank overdraft and trade credit, as well as long-term products, such as leasing, term loans and loan capital. The second type of finance is equity in the form of owner's equity, retained profits, funding by family and friends, business angels' investments, venture capital and publicly raised equity through an initial public offering. Internal sources of finance are particularly important to small businesses. The major source of finance for many small firms, particularly at inception, is the owner/s.

In addition to the traditional debt and equity finance, entrepreneurs often rely on alternative sources of funding or bootstrapping. There are two main alternative sources: debt factoring and government-backed schemes. Debt factoring involves selling a business's debts for cash at a discount, often referred to as 'off-balance-sheet financing'. Many governments in the Asia–Pacific region have established a variety of schemes to provide finance to new firms and fast-growing SMEs. These schemes can be a valuable source of both debt and equity funding if the applicant meets the specified criteria.

REVIEW QUESTIONS

1. What are the three main ways to categorise business financing?
2. What are the specific features of debt finance? Give some examples of debt finance.
3. What is venture capital and how does it work?
4. What are the advantages and disadvantages an owner–manager should consider before seeking funds in the public market?
5. What are some alternative sources of finance for entrepreneurs?

DISCUSSION QUESTIONS

1. Why are start-ups and small firms viewed as being more risky than large enterprises?
2. Which is better — debt or equity funding? Give reasons for your answer.
3. Why does the character of a loan applicant matter to a lender, even when the loan has been guaranteed by sufficient collateral?
4. What are the similarities and differences between business angels and venture capital financiers?
5. Why might entrepreneurs and small business owner–managers face difficulties in accessing government-backed schemes?

SUGGESTED READING

Adelman, P.H. & Marks, A.M., *Entrepreneurial Finance*, 5th edn, Prentice Hall, Upper Saddle River, 2009.

Australian Bureau of Statistics, *Venture Capital and Later Stage Private Equity* Cat. no. 5678.0 Canberra, ABS, February 2009.

Gollis, C., Mooney, P. & Richardson, T., *Enterprise and Venture Capital*, 5th edn, Allen & Unwin, Sydney, 2009.

Terjesen, S. & Frederick, H., *Sources of Funding for Australian Entrepreneurs*, Howard Frederick Publishing, Brisbane, 2007.

Case study

QuickBiotech

It is late in September 2010, and Michelle Chang, a doctoral student at the National University of Singapore (NUS), is to meet her colleagues Henry Tan and Mike Hammer from the Institute of Molecular Biology again in a few days to discuss the course of action to be pursued for the establishment of QuickBiotech. Henry Tan and Mike Hammer both hold doctorates in biology and work at NUS as senior assistants. A few months before, they patented a process for the production of multi-protein complexes, which they had already put to successful use, and about which they had received favourable feedback. Now, the three colleagues want to set-up a company called QuickBiotech in order to apply the new technology to a wider field.

Background

The human body is exposed to numerous external influences (e.g. UV radiation, impact of pollutants) and internal genetic defects, which cause the proteins in our cells to malfunction. Proteins constitute the basis of all biological processes. If proteins no longer fulfil their function adequately owing to defects, this often results in life-threatening illnesses, such as cancer. This is why almost all drugs have an effect on proteins. Consequently, most research and development work for drugs and therapies need proteins, which is why both academic research institutions and the pharmaceutical companies use proteins as a basis of their research activities.

Recently, progress in fundamental research revealed the total of the proteins in a cell, which in the case of human beings amounts to more than 40 000 proteins. It became obvious that the proteins in a cell do not work individually; rather, they combine to act as protein complexes that are made up of numerous protein components. In addition, virtually all biological processes in cells are executed by such protein complexes. This has crucial consequences for research: in order to understand how proteins work, protein machines must be explored as a whole, and not only their individual protein components.

Nonetheless, academic institutes and the pharmaceutical industry have almost exclusively focused on individual, isolated proteins. The primary reason for this was that human protein machines are very difficult to produce in a pure form. Although the development of modern, recombinant methods now enables the production of individual protein components, there is still a demand for a technology that is able to provide sufficient volumes of entire protein machines, which form the basis of biological functions. This is also Michelle's, Henry's and Mike's experience in their own research at NUS. They realise that no suitable technology for the production of protein machines exists. This is why they developed their own technology: the MultiBac technology.

The technology

The MultiBac technology uses a modified, yet greatly improved version of the so-called "baculovirus gene transfer vector" to produce any combination of proteins in great volumes and of high quality. The genes of a great number of proteins, such as human ones, can be placed on this gene transfer vector. This process can be carried out in an ordinary molecular biology laboratory. The MultiBac gene transfer vector multiplies in cell cultures and constitutes no danger to human beings. Therefore, no special health and safety regulations are required to work with this system.

The gene transfer vector of the MultiBac system was developed to provide it with a unique feature, namely, that it is particularly careful in the production of the desired protein machines. For customers, this is a guarantee of the unsurpassed quality of the protein complex produced with the MultiBac technology. In comparison with conventional processes, the simplified MultiBac technology additionally saves a substantial amount of time for the production of the desired protein product: it only takes weeks rather than months. Also, the technology offers the possibility to build numerous different protein complexes from the same protein components on a modular basis and, thus, of supplying individual solutions to customers' problems.

Laboratories of renowned research institutes already use MultiBac, which NUS has made available as trial specimens. This shows that the technology works, is mature and has a selling potential. The process was patented last year by NUS, and since then it was developed in the context of employment at the university. However, the rights can be assigned to a start-up, for instance, in the form of an exclusive licence.

The next steps to launch the venture

In autumn 2010, Michelle is in the final stages of her doctoral thesis, which she wants to complete by the new year. After that, she means to work full time for the new company.

In contrast, Henry and Mike want to retain their jobs at NUS and spend less time on the company. As such, they would not be involved in the company's operative daily business but will assume an advisory function. They will receive shares in the start-up but will not be on the company payroll.

One of the key roles of Henry and Mike will be to guarantee long-term access to the latest findings in scientific research. This model, whereby some of the founders remain at university, has already proved successful in a number of other biotechnology start-ups. Research in the field of biotechnology is very costly, both in terms of time and money, so only by retaining close links with a research institution will the company ensure that it will always work with the latest technologies and, thus, remain competitive.

One of the greatest challenges currently perceived by the team is to secure funding for the new company. Although the founders are able to invest S$200 000 of their personal savings into the enterprise and, thus, realise a small-scale start-up, present plans are based on the assumption that at least S$500 000 of external capital will be needed for the first two years. These funds will primarily serve to finance Michelle's position and a small team of lab assistants in charge of producing the protein complex for the clients. The product will be sold via a network of sales agents, and other functions, such accounting and finance, will be outsourced to a professional accountant.

Questions

1. Should Michelle consider debt or equity to finance QuickBiotech? Explain your answer.
2. Would you consider any alternative sources or finance? Which one? Why?
3. What other issues need to be addressed before QuickBiotech is launched?

ENDNOTES

1. G.N. Robson, *Financing Techniques for Growing Small and Medium Sized Enterprises*, Small and Medium Enterprise Research Centre, Edith Cowan University, Perth, 1996.
2. S. Holmes, P.J. Hutchinson, D.M. Forsaith, B. Gibson & R. McMahon, *Small Enterprise Finance*, John Wiley & Sons, Brisbane 2003.
3. A. Cosh & A. Hughes, 'Size, financial structure and profitability in UK companies in the 1980s', in A. Hughes & D. Storey (eds), *Finance and the Small Firm*, Routledge, London, 1994.
4. J.S. Osteryoung, D.L. Newman & L.G. Davies, *Small Firm Finance: An Entrepreneurial Perspective*, The Dryden Press, Fort Worth, TX, 1997.
5. L. Botazzi & M. Da Rin 'Venture capital in Europe and the financing of innovative companies', *Economic Policy*, no. 34, 2002 pp. 229–69.
6. 'Business angels - Giving ideas wings', *The Economist*, 14 September, 2006.
7. '2006/250/EC: Commission Decision of 3 May 2005 on the aid scheme 'Enterprise Capital Funds', which the United Kingdom is planning to implement (notified under document number C(2005) 1144)', *Official Journal-European Union Legislation L*, vol. 49, no. 91, 2006, pp.16–32.
8. E.Müller & V. Zimmermann, 'The Importance of Equity Finance for R&D Activity – Are There Differences Between Young and Old Companies?', Discussion Papers 111, SFB/TR 15 Governance and the Efficiency of Economic Systems, Free University of Berlin, Humboldt University of Berlin, University of Bonn, University of Mannheim, University of Munich, 2006.
9. S. Harron, 'Lending to small business in Australia', *Small Enterprise Research*, vol. 4, no. 1, 1996, pp. 17–26.

10. J. English, *How to Organise and Operate a Small Business in Australia*, 6th edn, Allen & Unwin, Sydney, 1995; L. Bland, 'Invoice finance v. bank overdraft', *Secured Lender*, vol. 53, no. 1, 1997, pp. 62–4.
11. J. Petty, R. Peacock, M. Burrow, A. Keown, D. Scott & J. Martin, *Basic Financial Management*, Prentice Hall, Sydney, 1996.
12. Bureau of Meteorology, Climate of Geraldton, Australian Government, www.bom.gov.au, 2010.
13. Industry Commission, *Informal Equity Investment*, Information Paper, AGPS, Canberra, 1997.
14. C. Gollis, *Enterprise and Venture Capital*, 4th edn, Allen & Unwin, Sydney, 2002.
15. B. Zider, 'How venture capital works', *Harvard Business Review*, November–December 1998, pp. 131–9.
16. J.L. Nesheim, *High Tech Start-Up*, 2nd edn, Free Press, New York, 2000.
17. C. Roberts, 'Listing loses its appeal', *BRW*, 11–17 August 2005, p. 48.
18. J.B. Arkebauer & R. Schultz, *Going Public: Everything You Need to Know to Take Your Company Public*, 3rd edn, Dearborn Financial Publishing, New York, 1998.
19. M. Horvath, 'An insider guide to going public', *Financial Times*, Mastering Management, part 8, 20 November 2000, pp. 2–4.
20. J. Winborg & H. Landstršm, 'Financial bootstrapping in small businesses: Examining small business managers' resource acquisition behaviors', *Journal of Business Venturing*, vol. 16, no. 3, 2001, pp. 235–54.
21. H. Frederick, *Sources of Funding for New Zealand Entrepreneurs*, Ten3, Auckland, 2005, p. 4.

CHAPTER 10

Accessing business advice and assistance

Learning objectives

After reading this chapter, you should be able to:

- identify the benefits of using a professional adviser

- list the different types of adviser styles available to entrepreneurs and small business owners

- explain the three different types of advisory style

- list the issues involved in choosing an adviser

- describe the main categories of government and private sector assistance available

- explain how a business incubator works.

Business advisers can play an important role in assisting the owner–managers of new, small and growing enterprises. Successful small business managers and entrepreneurs are expected to develop a broad range of skills and competencies in many different areas. Apart from technical knowledge related to the field in which their businesses operate, entrepreneurs must learn to deal with many other issues that arise in the daily process of managing an enterprise. It is not always possible for one person to keep abreast of all these areas or to be particularly effective in all of them. For this reason, most owner–managers eventually find that they must turn to a business adviser for help.[1] A number of government and private sector assistance schemes are designed to encourage new business formation and expansion. Many of these can provide practical advice, planning services and financial support. Using these services can help a business get started or grow faster than would otherwise be the case.

This chapter provides an overview of the different types of business adviser available, the issues important in the development of an effective working relationship with them, and sources of external financial and management assistance. We explain the concept of an 'adviser' — what the term means, the different types of service that advisers offer and their varying approaches. The factors to take into account when selecting an adviser are discussed, and the range of government and private services provided to firms is explained.

The business adviser

Business adviser *Someone who works with client businesses to provide specialised skills and knowledge in one or more particular aspects of business activities.*

A **business adviser** is someone who works with client businesses to provide specialised skills and knowledge in one or more particular aspects of business activities. Such a person has developed a considerable body of knowledge and experience that can be used to help solve the problems of clients.

Many different terms are used to describe a person who works with a business in this manner. The label 'adviser' is commonly used, but there are other terms (sometimes used interchangeably): consultant, counsellor, facilitator, mentor, business coach. The difference between these is explained later in this chapter. Professional business advisers can be found in the private sector (and charge for their services), as well as in government-funded programs (many of which are free for small business owners and entrepreneurs who wish to use them).

The main benefit of an adviser is the application of particular skills and abilities to help improve the business performance of clients. Entrepreneurs and small business owners must, by virtue of the many different demands placed on them, be generalists and so, in most cases, cannot hope to acquire the same level of expertise as advisers.

In many respects, using a professional adviser is a more effective use of resources than the alternative approach of entrepreneurs trying to master the topic themselves. This is because it takes a considerable amount of time, effort and money for the owner–manager to acquire as much knowledge as the specialist adviser. Even though such services may be expensive when charged at an hourly rate, they may still be cheaper and more effective than trying to spend time mastering the topic privately.

Employing an adviser can also be more convenient, because the service can be contracted for a specific task or time period. This removes the problem of the business having to permanently dedicate one or more staff members to acquiring a particular body of knowledge. Business advisers also play an important role in bringing new ideas, information and techniques to existing businesses. Good advisers will be aware of new developments and techniques, and can suggest when these tools might be usefully employed by a business. Advisers often know from their own previous experience what works and what does not, thus allowing the entrepreneur to minimise mistakes and avoid errors.

Finally, an outside adviser can often provide an alternative point of view to that of the business owner. In this way, the merits and problems of different approaches can be discussed, debated and evaluated, and the chances of adopting a successful final solution are increased. Good advisers can provide a dispassionate, objective evaluation of business ventures — something that owners may not be able to achieve because they are too caught up in the daily management of their enterprise.

What would you do?

Off the rails?

Annabel and Andy have been working together in a commercial partnership for ten years, but in all that time they have never put their business on a professional footing. They have a small courier truck business in rural Queensland that picks up parcels, letters, bulky items and other hard-to-handle or delicate packages. Working from Andy's home and using only word-of-mouth, they have built up a loyal following because they personally hand-deliver to and pick-up from clients, and will do so on the same day, even though their vehicle occasionally breaks down.

Just recently Annabel read in the local newspaper that the well-known international courier company, Federal Express, was planning on expanding into their neighbourhood.

'This could ruin us,' she said. 'FedEx will probably be able to deliver goods much more quickly and cheaply than us. They have a better reputation, are more sophisticated and can offer more add-on services to customers. What are we going to do?'

Neither of them had any clear plans about how to deal with the possible competition.

'We could buy a new truck,' Andy suggested. 'Or perhaps we need to target a niche group of customers. We could also invest in some paid advertising.'

However, none of these options seemed enough to Annabel. 'They might help, but I'm worried we could be reacting too quickly without thinking through a long-term strategy,' she told Andy.

The results of their informal business practices have left them with a legacy. There is no accounting system, just an annual tax return; the bank account often operates in deficit; they have no formal written partnership agreement; and all of their existing contracts with clients are simply verbal agreement.

'We need to get some business advice,' said Annabel. 'But where? And how do we ensure the adviser understands our business properly?'

Questions

1. Which sort of business adviser would be most helpful in this situation? Why?
2. What written information do you think Annabel and Andy should prepare to take along to their first meeting with an adviser? Why?

The evolution of business advisory services

The level of business advice and assistance available today in the Asia–Pacific region is the result of many years of evolving responses to the needs of business operators. Although small businesses and entrepreneurs have been around for as long as commerce has existed, the provision of formal government assistance and support for small and new firms is a relatively new phenomenon. In the period after World War II, many countries adopted national policy frameworks and created formal specialised agencies to promote entrepreneurial activity and the small-firm sector. The United States, for example, created its Small Business Administration in 1953, and Japan adopted a national small-enterprise development strategy in 1947.[2] The role of these programs was to conduct research, develop policies and provide practical assistance to entrepreneurs and small-scale business ventures. This trend gathered strength and eventually resulted in similar bodies being formed throughout much of the world.

In Australia, however, government-sponsored support for small enterprises and new business ventures is a relatively recent development. It was not until the early 1970s that the federal government conducted its first review of the sector.[3] The Wiltshire Committee's report suggested that government could do much more to promote an effective small business sector; as a result, the federal government established the National Small Business Bureau in 1973.[4] This was followed in the 1980s by the creation of various small business development agencies or bureaus within each state and territory. Today, both state and federal governments provide funding to small business advisory agencies, as well as a wide variety of specific programs that offer grants, technical advice, infrastructure assistance and educational and developmental support to small firms. Many local governments also provide assistance to new and small ventures within their municipalities.

This development has been mirrored by an increased emphasis on public assistance schemes in other countries in the Asia–Pacific region. Singapore, for example, has produced a number of 'master plans' since the 1990s, each designed to map out the future development of the sector and provide tangible assistance schemes.[5] A similar approach has been used in Malaysia, which has its own economic development master plan that includes specific provision for development of the SME sector.[6] In New Zealand, both government agencies and private organisations offer an extensive range of state-run assistance and advisory centres, although the nature and duration of these has changed from time to time.

In contrast, private sector business advisers have been in existence for much longer than publicly funded agencies. Local private industry groups, such as chambers of commerce and chambers of manufacturers, were often formed during the early years of European settlement in countries such as Australia and New Zealand, whereas both formal and informal business associations have existed for many centuries in China, India and much of the Asia–Pacific region. These networks of business owners provided both formal and informal support to their members. Private sector firms such as accountancy practices, law firms and banks, have also provided advice and financial access to small and new entrepreneurial firms. Indeed, in many cases the growth of such professions has been accelerated by the existence of small firms, which usually form the bulk of their clients.

Types of professional adviser

Many different people, professions and occupations represent a source of possible beneficial advice to the business owner or entrepreneur. Some of the more important ones are discussed below.

Accountants

Accountants provide a number of useful functions. In many cases, their main role is to ensure that sound financial records are being kept; but this is only one aspect of the range of services they offer. A business accountant can also help to ensure compliance with relevant taxation laws, prepare tax returns, compile future financial projections, determine the future funding needs of the business and sources of such capital, and help the business owner make effective use of personal income. A recent study of how and why Australian SMEs use accountants for advice has shown that while they are mainly consulted for financial matters, accountants are also used as a source of business advice. Accountants are often seen as the 'most trustworthy' and reliable form of external adviser.[7] They are usually required to be registered members of a state or national professional institute, such as CPA Australia or the New Zealand Institute of Chartered Accountants (see table 10.1). They must also have completed a tertiary qualification in their field.

TABLE 10.1 Accounting institutes

Country	Institute
Australia	Institute of Chartered Accountants in Australia, www.icaa.org.au Certified Practising Accountants Australia, www.cpaaustralia.com.au National Institute of Accountants, www.nia.org.au
New Zealand	New Zealand Institute of Chartered Accountants, www.nzica.com
Hong Kong	Hong Kong Institute of Certified Public Accountants, www.hkicpa.org.hk
Malaysia	Malaysian Institute of Accountants, www.mia.org.my Malaysian Institute of Certified Public Accountants, www.micpa.com.my
Singapore	Institute of Certified Public Accountants of Singapore, www.accountants.org.sg
China	Chinese Institute of Certified Public Accountants, www.cicpa.org.cn/english
India	Institute of Chartered Accountants of India, www.icai.org
General	Confederation of Asian and Pacific Accountants, www.capa.com.my International Federation of Accountants, www.ifac.org

Lawyers

Knowledge of legal processes and consequences is important for small businesses whenever a contract has to be negotiated with an outside party, a lease is being signed, a dispute occurs over non-payment or non-performance between the business and a client, or litigation is initiated against the business. For entrepreneurs, legal advice is often needed when dealing with issues such as the registration of intellectual property and compliance with various government laws and regulations.

Lawyers should be members of their relevant professional association, hold a degree in law, and have been admitted to practise at the Bar in their state, provincial or national jurisdiction (see table 10.2). In some countries, this role is split into two different jobs — the *barrister* (who represents clients in court) and the *solicitor* (who advises clients and prepares cases for barristers).

TABLE 10.2 Law societies

Country	Pertinent body
Australia	Law Council of Australia, www.lawcouncil.asn.au
New Zealand	New Zealand Law Society, www.nz-lawsoc.org.nz
Hong Kong	Law Society of Hong Kong, www.hklawsoc.org.hk
Malaysia	Malaysian Bar Council, www.malaysianbar.org.my
Singapore	Law Society of Singapore, www.lawsoc.org.sg
China	China Law Society, www.chinalawsociety.com
India	All India Bar Association, www.allindiabar.org

Management consultants

'Consultant' is a widely used term with a number of meanings, and it is often applied indiscriminately to many different occupations. However, a properly qualified management consultant is usually taken to mean someone with extensive practical experience in a particular aspect of business. Typical management consulting roles may include human resource management advisers (consultants who advise on recruiting, employment relations, salaries and benefits, or staff terminations); trainers (who develop and implement business skills courses for clients); marketing advisers (who advise on market research, product branding, or integrated advertising and promotional campaigns); and production advisers (who examine workplace processes, quality control, error reduction, retooling, production techniques and equipment use). There is usually no mandatory requirement for a management consultant to be a member of a professional association or to have any particular level of education.

Bank managers

At first glance, it may seem that bank managers simply have a vested interest in ensuring that their clients can meet their financial obligations, such as payments on an outstanding loan, when these fall due. However, more astute managers also realise that by helping businesses to grow, they may generate more sales of banking products and services. To this end, they can represent a useful source of financial advice, money management ideas and investment options.

Financial planners

Many business owners realise that wealth generation and protection should not focus solely on the business enterprise. In many cases, it makes sound sense to diversify personal assets and income sources, so that in the event of business failure, the entrepreneur's wealth is not lost. Financial planners can help with the development of an integrated personal financial strategy, tax planning and investment advice.

Publicly funded small business agencies

Government-supported small business development agencies exist in a number of countries. In many cases, staff in these organisations provide ideas, information and advice to small business managers. Many of these people will have their own direct experience of owning or managing a small business. These agencies usually have a good working knowledge of other government programs that can help new and small firms, and so constitute an additional source of outside knowledge. An example of a publicly funded agency is provided in the Entrepreneur profile below.

Mentors

Other successful business operators can be a source of assistance to entrepreneurs. Learning from others is a highly effective way of transferring experience, building personal networks, exchanging ideas and identifying new opportunities. **Mentoring** is the process of transferring advice and ideas from one business owner to another, and is usually provided on a voluntary no-cost basis. Because it is peer-based, it often has more credibility and resonance than external advice provided by paid 'experts'. Mentors can include retired businesspeople (who often provide their advice free of charge to new start-ups) and venture capitalists who have taken an equity position in an entrepreneur's business.[8]

Mentoring *The process of transferring advice and ideas from one businessperson to another on a voluntary no-cost basis.*

Entrepreneur profile

Jack Hughes,
Darwin Region Business Enterprise Centre

Business advisory services exist to service many different communities, and the local small business agency in Australia's Northern Territory covers one of the most diverse that can be found.

With a staff of just three full-time advisers and another two part-time administrative personnel, Jack Hughes manages the Darwin Region Business Enterprise Centre (BEC). The centre services all of the Northern Territory, which encompasses Australia's most remote regions; and the population of just 215 000 people is spread out over 1.3 million km^2, most of it in remote towns situated several hundred kilometres from each other. There are only 14 000 businesses spread throughout this vast region, where distance is a significant issue in business development. In fact, the capital of the Northern Territory, Darwin, is closer to the capital cities of Indonesia, East Timor and Papua New Guinea than it is to any other Australian city.

The Darwin Region BEC opened in December 2000, and today provides counselling, mentoring and business advice to more than 1300 clients annually. There is usually no charge for these services; instead, the centre is funded by annual grants from both the Northern Territory and national governments. Another off-shoot office is located in Alice Springs, some 1500 kilometres south of Darwin.

'Only about 20% of our clients are existing businesses,' Jack says. 'Broadly, most of our queries fall into one of three categories. There are the so-called 'tyre-kickers': people thinking about starting up, but are not sure, and really just want to get more background about the pros and cons. Then there are some who have already begun, and who realise they need to know more. Finally, there are those who are about to start, who have a very clear idea of what they want to do and are looking for help to get there.'

Although Jack and his colleagues believe that encouraging and facilitating entrepreneurs is important, the centre also has a strong philosophy that ultimate responsibility rests with the client. 'We will hold their hand and guide them to a certain degree, but we make it pretty clear at the beginning that if you want to succeed in business, then you need to be proactive.'

'In small business, the founder has to be prepared to ask questions, find the necessary information, make decisions and be absolutely committed to the project. Otherwise it's not going to work. And it's important that clients fully understand this before they actually start trading.'

The personal skills of clients are also important. 'We can provide lots of advice and assistance, but ultimately it's the personal attributes that make the most contribution to a client's ability to succeed in business. Passion, persistence and sensible intelligent analysis are all skills that new entrepreneurs need to cultivate. That way, they have the capacity to make a business idea work.'

For more information about the work of the Darwin Region BEC, visit www.becnt.com.au.

Source: Based on author's interview with Jack Hughes

Personal coaches

Business coaches *A person who works with entrepreneurs, business owners or senior managers to help them deal with problems in their work and private life.*

More expensive than many other advisers, but growing in popularity, are **business coaches**. These are people who work with entrepreneurs, business owners or senior managers to help them deal with problems in their work and private life. The goal is to enhance the performance of the firm by improving the psychological environment in which a firm's key decision maker operates. A mixture of counsellor, psychologist and business adviser, the coach helps a person solve personal and work-related issues.[9]

Family and friends

In addition to professional consultants, budding entrepreneurs and existing small business operators often turn to their own range of personal contacts, such as family members and friends, for support, counselling, advice and ideas.

Other business operators

One of the most common sources of advice is other entrepreneurs. Although this may seem surprising (after all, business people may also represent a competitive threat to the firm), such people will have had many similar experiences. Like mentoring, the common background and informal transmission of acquired knowledge is often valued by small-firm owners as being more credible than that of 'the professionals'.[10]

External directors and equity investors

If an entrepreneur has raised capital from outside investors, such individuals can provide valuable ongoing feedback about business performance and management of the enterprise. Venture capitalists and 'business angels', for example, often provide such services to entrepreneurs, and may also serve as directors of the business. There has also been an increasing trend among the owner–managers of growth-oriented firms to appoint a number of outside directors to the board of their company in order to tap into their networks and gain their counsel on business problems.

How much are advisory services used?

Unfortunately, many small businesses do not fully avail themselves of the many services offered. In many cases, new and emerging firms are often unaware of what help is available, are more reluctant to ask for advice than established firms and are often sceptical of the benefits of such assistance.[11] When they do decide to seek information, it is often limited to matters like taxation and accounting; they do not access the full range of services available to help them improve the business and increase their profitability.

There is growing evidence to suggest that small business owners have a preference for particular types of service, and are more likely to use some advisers than others. Studies in Australia, New Zealand, North America and Europe show that some advisers (especially accountants, and occasionally also banks, family and friends, and fellow business owners) were clearly preferred above others, such as government agencies and professional consultants.[12] Similar results were found by Jay and Schaper, who examined the services used by the owner–managers of micro-businesses in Western Australia[13] (see table 10.3).

TABLE 10.3 Use of business advisory services by home-based businesses

Type of business adviser	Proportion of owners using adviser	Mean number of visits per year
Accountants	94%	1.56
Banks	90%	1.32
Other business operators	72%	1.16
Family or friends	68%	0.99
Lawyers	31%	0.40
Other government agency	29%	0.35
Industry association/chamber of commerce	24%	0.28
Business consultant	19%	0.22
Small business development corporation	19%	0.21
Business enterprise centre	12%	0.12
Other	9%	0.12

Source: L. Jay & M. Schaper, 'The utilisation of business advisory services by home-based businesses in Western Australia', paper presented to the 15th annual Small Enterprise Association of Australia and New Zealand (SEAANZ) conference, Adelaide, 22–24 September 2002.

As can be seen from table 10.3, there are marked differences in the types of adviser used. Accountants are the most highly used service, usually because their skills are necessary to comply with legal requirements such as tax returns and record keeping.[14] Personal contacts, local bank branches and colleagues in the same industry are also extensively used. These sources are usually free and easily accessible, and they are trusted because of the personal links the business owner has with the provider of advice. It may also reflect a limited knowledge of what services are available, or indicate a predilection, when confronted with a problem, to turn to 'those you already know'.[15] These results are not unusual. In New Zealand, a national survey of business practices also found that banks, accountants and other business operators were among the most widely used sources of assistance and that government bodies and universities were the least used. Many firms were either unaware of the services provided by government, or else perceived them to be too bureaucratic and difficult to access.[16] Likewise, SMEs in China have also been found to rely principally on private-sector business advisers, rather than government-funded programs.[17]

These studies indicate that the market for small business assistance seems to operate inefficiently. There is an over-reliance on a limited number of sources, while the services of many other advisory bodies are not extensively used. Furthermore, many business owners still report that their specific needs are not met by the advisers they do use.[18]

A separate but equally important issue to consider is the effectiveness of such advisers. Just how much difference does an adviser make to a small business owner or a budding entrepreneur? Some researchers have shown that the use of external advice can improve the survival of start-up firms or the performance of existing and growing ones.[19] However, several other authors have questioned whether advisers make any substantive difference to the actual performance of client firms, or indeed whether they can truly add value to a small firm's operations at all.[20] This issue is compounded by the difficulty of measuring an adviser's impact. Should an adviser's performance be measured quantitatively (such as in the amount of extra revenue they help their clients make), or are intangible results (such as boosting a client's confidence or helping them comply with the law) more important? Finally, is an adviser creating a successful outcome or not when he or she counsels a client to stop trading because the business is failing and likely to go further into debt if it continues?

Advisory styles

There are a number of different approaches to dealing with business problems, each of which reflects a different way of working with clients and helping to solve their problems. Although it can be difficult to accurately categorise all the ways that advisers work with clients, several researchers have developed typologies that try to explain these different perspectives.[21] Schein argues that there are three fundamentally different types (or modes) of advisory style: the expert consultant, the hired 'pair of hands' and the process facilitator.[22]

Expert consultant *A business adviser with highly developed skills in a specific area.*

Expert consultant mode

This is the classic popular idea of the **expert consultant** or business adviser. An expert is seen here as someone with a high degree of business skill in a specific area. This person is usually contracted to come into an organisation and deal with either company-wide issues or a specific problem. Just as a doctor uses acquired medical knowledge to diagnose and treat a patient's condition, the expert consultant is expected to identify what is wrong, and prescribe potential solutions for the organisation. Management consulting firms, lawyers and accountants typically fall into this category.

Although often time-efficient and effective for businesses with clearly identifiable problems, this mode has some problems. Entrepreneurs, owners and employees (the clients) may be reluctant to reveal their problems or weaknesses to the consultant. Moreover, such outside experts may often not ask the right questions and, therefore, do not uncover the full picture of what is occurring in and around the firm. They do not usually know the background of the firm and the owner/entrepreneur very well, and may prescribe solutions that are wrong because they do not take into account all the issues involved. Similarly, the client is left with no sense of ownership of the solutions proposed by the consultant. The owner or firm is told what to do and how to do it. Thus, the next problem that emerges will also have to be dealt with by another outside expert.

Hired 'pair of hands' mode

Another option is to 'buy in' advice for a limited period. The **'pair of hands' adviser** is a person whose expert services or skills are purchased for a defined length of time, often because the firm does not have the internal ('in-house') technical skills itself. An example is the use of information technology (IT) specialists who come into a company for six months to devise and set-up a software program specific to the organisation's needs. Once the assigned task is completed, the adviser leaves.

This approach does provide some longer term benefit for the small firm. It allows the business to employ staff to solve specific problems without taking on the long-term obligation of a permanent employment contract. There is also the possibility of knowledge being transferred from the adviser to in-house staff during this period. However, it still requires the entrepreneur/owner or senior staff members to be able to accurately diagnose what the problem is before making the decision to bring in a 'pair of hands'. Moreover, once the consultant departs, the firm may again find itself lacking the skills that it needs.

'Pair of hands' adviser *A specialist brought into a firm for a set period of time.*

Facilitator or process mode

A **facilitator** is a person who works alongside entrepreneurs and their staff to help them identify and solve their own problems. The facilitator does not need to be an expert in multiple fields, but rather must possess the ability to help people help themselves. The major role of the facilitator is to help business owners reflect on the processes occurring in the firm. They help business owners to become aware of their own strengths and weaknesses, to identify the problems in their business and to develop their own solutions to those problems.

This style of advice is based on a number of assumptions. Facilitators (or, as they are sometimes referred to, counsellors) argue that understanding and learning comes about only when small business clients realise for themselves what the problem is.[23] If they are simply told 'the correct answers' by an outside expert, no learning has taken place. Equally important, facilitators believe that

Facilitator *A business adviser who encourages clients to learn how to diagnose and treat their own business problems.*

true change within a business can take place only when owner–managers take responsibility for implementing changes themselves. To bring in an 'expert' or a 'hired pair of hands' who simply deals with a particular issue and then moves out of the firm is solving only a specific issue. Organisational change and development is much more enduring if entrepreneurs can be taught to recognise problems, identify their own possible solutions and make the necessary reforms themselves.

One of the strongest advocates of the facilitative approach is Ernesto Sirolli,[24] who was responsible for the establishment of the Business Enterprise Centre network (now known as BECs) in Western Australia. Sirolli has argued that only facilitation can make a real difference to entrepreneurs, since such people naturally tend to want to take responsibility for their own lives and their own business. Self-learning gives enterprising business operators the ability to continually learn and adapt to changing circumstances. In contrast, encouraging them to rely on an outside expert or 'pair of hands' simply creates a perpetual dependency situation — clients never learn to fix their own problems, and so constantly have to find someone else who can.[25]

The three different advisory styles broadly represent a continuum of approaches (see figure 10.1). At one extreme, the expert consultant is highly authoritative, making judgements and prescribing solutions; most of the decision making about the problem and how to treat it is left to the expert. At the other extreme, facilitation essentially relies on the business owner taking responsibility for dealing with the issue. The differences between the three approaches are summarised in table 10.4.

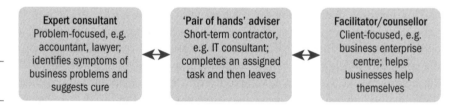

FIGURE 10.1 The three types of adviser

TABLE 10.4 Differences in advisory style

	Expert consultant	**'Pair of hands' adviser**	**Facilitator**
Level of specialist business knowledge	Highly specialised	Highly specialised	Generalist; broadly familiar with many different business fields
Problem identification	Consultant identifies	Client identifies	Client identifies
Solution implementation	Either consultant or client implements	Adviser implements	Client implements

Sourcing advisers

In addition to knowing what types of advice are available in the marketplace, entrepreneurs must also know how to access such assistance. There are a variety of different avenues that can help identify potential advisers, such as the following:

- *Professional bodies.* Organisations such as law societies and accounting institutes are often the first and most logical source to turn to for names of potential advisers. Generally, it is not difficult to obtain a list of their members in the same locality as the business. The benefit of such an approach is that it ensures the advisers are properly qualified and comply with all the relevant professional codes of conduct. However, professional bodies will usually not recommend specific individuals or firms on the list, either from fear of future liability or to avoid the impression of favouritism. The owner or entrepreneur must still make the final choice of adviser.
- *Advertisements.* Although some professional associations may limit the amount and type of self-promotion that their members may engage in, most advisers will undertake some advertising of their services. Telephone directories, professional industry journals, websites and public advertising are therefore all likely sources for names of advisers.
- *Personal recommendations.* In many cases, initial information about the relative merits of a particular adviser will be supplied by people that the entrepreneur knows personally. Friends, relatives and business colleagues will usually have their own advisers, and so may be able to provide recommendations.
- *Small business agencies.* Such bodies will often provide details of local advisers, and may be able to provide first-hand assessments of their costs and quality of service. However, to avoid claims of bias, they may be reluctant or unable to recommend specific individuals.

Choosing a professional adviser

Several commercial and personal factors should be taken into account by the owner–manager or entrepreneur when selecting an adviser (see figure 10.2).[26] Some of these issues include the following:

- *Qualifications.* Does the adviser have a recognised tertiary qualification in the professed field of expertise? Has the person undertaken any continuing education courses since graduation? Is the adviser a member of a professional body? If not, does the adviser qualify for membership? It is wise to think twice before engaging the services of anyone without such professional/peer recognition.
- *Experience and industry knowledge.* What first-hand experience does the adviser have in the entrepreneur's particular industry? Is this sufficient? If the adviser does not have relevant experience, will he or she still be able to provide an appropriate level of service? Generally, consultants who operate in the 'expert' or 'pair of hands' mode, discussed previously, will be highly technically proficient in a defined area, whereas facilitators will tend to have a much broader, generalised knowledge base.
- *Friendliness/personal rapport.* Can the owner–manager or entrepreneur relate to the adviser? Ideally, the business manager and the consultant will develop a relationship over a considerable period of time, so it is important that they are able to work well together.[27] In some situations, a client can be made to feel uneasy, awkward or uncomfortable when dealing with a particular

professional adviser. If this is the case, then it is probably better to find someone else.

- *Networking ability.* It is rare to find one adviser who has the answers to all of a client's questions. Often an array of different skills and knowledge bases is required. This is often the case during the launch of a new entrepreneurial venture, when a team of advisers, each with particular abilities, must be put together if the project is to be successfully launched. To this end, a good adviser will often have an extensive body of contacts and personal contacts who can be used as needed to help the client.[28]
- *Services provided.* What exactly will the client receive for the money? Can the adviser provide the full range of facilities and knowledge that the business owner requires? For example, an effective accountant must not be just a glorified bookkeeper. The accountant should also be able to advise on taxation law, prepare financial documents and have a good working knowledge of accounting principles.
- *Price.* How much will the adviser charge? Is this figure set at an hourly rate, or is the charge fixed, regardless of the amount of time taken? Are there likely to be any additional or hidden costs (for consumables, telephone calls and in-house visits, for example)?
- *Conflicts of interest.* Are there any situations in which the adviser may have conflicting loyalties or should not be involved in the business? Trust is an important issue for many owner–managers when selecting an adviser. For example, it would not be appropriate to engage a management consultant to develop a business plan for a particular venture if that consultant were also preparing one for a rival enterprise, as information may be transferred between the two businesses.[29]

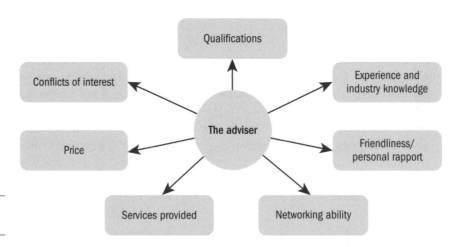

FIGURE 10.2 Adviser selection criteria

Forms of support for new and small firms

Government assistance

In recognition of the importance of entrepreneurship and small business to overall economic growth, many governments have attempted to stimulate business start-ups and growth by providing financial and informational assistance to businesses within their jurisdictions.[30] These forms of help include:

- *Business start-up assistance.* Programs include grants to start a business, training schemes for prospective business start-ups, access to low-cost or free business advisers, help in preparing a business plan, and general information provision.
- *Business development and improvement.* For existing businesses that seek to improve their performance or expand, government grants or subsidies may be provided to employ consultants to advise on different aspects of business management. These can include the areas of business planning, improved production processes, quality assurance certification, human resource management, business networking programs, the use of new information technology, and marketing campaigns. In some cases, governments may wholly subsidise these activities.
- *Infrastructure support.* Another common avenue of practical government support is the provision of key services to help a particular industry. For example, governments may meet the cost of improving road and rail links to a port to encourage the growth of industries that export by sea. Business incubators (discussed later) are another form of small-scale infrastructure assistance.
- *Tax concessions.* In some jurisdictions it is possible to claim tax reductions for costs related to business start-ups, growth and expansion. Some regional authorities in the Asia–Pacific region have also offered 'tax holidays' (where no tax needs to be paid for a set period of time) for firms that start trading in or relocate to a specific area.
- *Trade assistance.* Export credits, foreign market intelligence, trade missions and training courses have all been provided by various countries keen to enhance the level of exports undertaken by their small businesses.

Generally, government assistance is not confined to a particular department or agency. Often different forms of help are available from different government departments, so it may be necessary to make enquiries with all relevant arms of government. However, entrepreneurs and small business owners do not always have enough time or knowledge of government systems to access all these bodies. As a result, most countries now provide an agency that can act as a 'gateway' to other arms of government. Bodies such as BECs, small business development corporations, or SME first-stop shops act as integrated facilities where business-people can receive advice about their business project, suggestions for improvement, and referrals to other government schemes or departments that might be of help.

Different countries have adopted different approaches to small business and new venture development. Some regions, such as Hong Kong, have traditionally been quite minimalist in their approach. Other nations, such as Australia, have focused on information provision rather than just financial aid. One of the countries with a sophisticated national strategy for small firms is Singapore, which has developed an SME Master Plan that covers many different issues related to small enterprise formation, survival and growth.[31] Assistance to firms in Singapore includes both information and financial support.

Today, governments in many countries provide a range of both financial and advisory support services. Table 10.5 lists some specific assistance sources for new and existing small firms in different jurisdictions.

TABLE 10.5 Overview of key government agencies and services

Country	Agencies and roles
Australia	Austrade: assists with foreign investment in Australia and export-related investment in other countries, www.austrade.gov.au Business Entry Point: website providing information on numerous business support programs offered by the federal and state governments, www.business.gov.au Department of Industry, Innovation, Science and Research, www.industry.gov.au
New Zealand	Ministry of Economic Development (Manatu Ohanga), www.med.govt.nz Biz: Business Information Zone, a 'whole of government' business entry point site developed by New Zealand Trade & Enterprise department, www.biz.org.nz
Hong Kong	Trade and Industry Department, SME Information Centre, www.success.tid.gov.hk Business information portal, www.gov.hk/en/business
Malaysia	Small and Medium Enterprise Corporation Malaysia (SME Corp. Malaysia), www.smecorp.gov.my
Singapore	Standards, Productivity and Innovation for Growth (SPRING): SME first-stop office, www.spring.gov.sg Enterprise One, a business entry point service provided by SPRING, www.business.gov.sg Economic Development Board (EDB): nurtures and develops local enterprises through various financial assistance schemes, www.edb.gov.sg International Enterprise Singapore (formerly known as the Trade Development Board): helps SMEs to export their products/services through market/product development assistance schemes, www.iesingapore.gov.sg Infocomm Development Authority (IDA): encourages businesses to computerise and/or upgrade their IT operations, www.ida.gov.sg
India	Ministry of Micro, Small and Medium Enterprises, http://msme.gov.in

Private sector assistance

In addition to government sources, some private sector organisations also provide assistance to new and small firms, as do several charitable and not-for-profit associations. Sometimes the original core funding for this comes from government; at other times the organisation itself has decided that it is in its own best interests to facilitate small-firm growth or the development of new business ventures. Once again, assistance can take the form of monetary or information support. Relevant non-government groups include bodies shown in table 10.6.

TABLE 10.6 Overview of some useful non-government agencies

Country	Agencies
Australia	Australasian Institute of Enterprise Facilitators, www.aief.org.au Australian Institute of Management, www.aim.com.au Business Enterprise Centres Australia, www.becaustralia.org.au Business Innovation and Incubation Australia: national network of business incubators, www.businessincubation.com.au Council of Small Business Organisations of Australia, www.cosboa.org
New Zealand	Business Mentors/Business in the Community, www.businessmentor.org.nz Economic Development Agencies of New Zealand, www.edanz.org.nz Independent Business Foundation, www.ibf.org.nz

Country	Agencies
Hong Kong	HK Chamber of Small and Medium Business, www.hkcsmb.org.hk Small-to-Medium Enterprise Centre of the Hong Kong Trade Development Council, http://sme.tdctrade.com
Malaysia	SME Info: portal for both government and private sector information, www.smeinfo.com.my SME Resource Centre, Federation of Malaysian Manufacturers, www.fmm.org.my Malaysian Institute of Management, www.mim.org.my Malaysian International Chamber of Commerce and Industry, www.micci.com
Singapore	Association of Small and Medium Enterprises (ASME) of Singapore, www.asme.org.sg

Business incubators

An increasingly popular form of business assistance is the **business incubator**, a dedicated space provided to help businesses get established and become profitable. The typical incubator consists of one or more buildings that house offices and workspaces for business enterprises, with the incubator overseen by a centre manager experienced in working with new and growing entrepreneurial ventures. The focus is on helping businesses to successfully enter the marketplace, and then to consolidate and secure their existence. Firms can rent space on a weekly or monthly basis, but do not have to commit themselves to long-term leases. As the term *incubator* might suggest, tenants are typically expected to 'leave the nest' within two or three years of start-up, by which time it is assumed they will either be viable, and able to operate on their own, or not feasible.[32]

Business incubator *Dedicated premises provided to help firms get established and become profitable.*

The typical services offered in an incubator are:[33]

- *Convenient, reasonably priced tenancies*. Incubator rentals do not have many of the onerous conditions or long-term lease obligations found in many commercially run shopping precincts.
- *In-house business services*. These include receptionists, secretarial services, conference and meeting rooms, photocopiers, computing and internet access, and access to accounting, bookkeeping and legal professionals.
- *Business advisory services*. The manager of the centre will usually work alongside tenants to help them solve specific business problems or develop their range of generic business skills.
- *Business support*. Operating alongside other entrepreneurs gives owner–managers an immediate network of fellow businesspeople, providing mutual support, sharing ideas and knowledge and forging business collaborations.

There are three common types of business incubator. *Embedded incubators* are often part of, or share premises with, another organisation. One of the most common such alliances in Australia is with Business Enterprise Centres (BEC), which are also known in some states as 'small business centres'. The BEC manager acts as the incubator manager, providing tenants with continuous access to up-to-date business knowledge. In return, the BEC supplements its income by collecting a management fee. *Independent incubators* are 'stand-alone' facilities that operate on their own. The management of the incubator is separate from any other small business support services, and dedicated solely to dealing with incubator clients. *Specific-purpose incubators* provide support to a particular industry or trade. Common types of single-purpose incubator are technology parks and incubators dedicated to arts and crafts, biotechnology and environmentally sustainable industries.[34]

Incubators often represent a mix of public and private support. In many cases, the initial funding for the establishment of an incubator is provided by government, but ongoing management of the centre is contracted to a private sector adviser or community organisation.[35] There are currently more than 1200 business incubators operating throughout the Asia–Pacific region.[36] A list of incubator associations, by country, is provided in table 10.7.

TABLE 10.7 Business incubator associations

Country	Agencies
Australia	Business Innovation & Incubation Australia, www.businessincubation.com.au
New Zealand	Incubators New Zealand, www.incubators.org.nz
India	Indian Business Incubators' Association, www.isba.in
Asia–Pacific region	Asian Association of Business Incubation, www.aabi.info

SUMMARY

This chapter examined the importance of seeking assistance from individuals and agencies outside the business itself. Advisers can be of benefit to small and entrepreneurial firms because they bring in new ideas, provide a more effective use of resources and act as an objective source of information and analysis. Business advisory services have been in existence for a long time; however, most publicly funded services in the Asia–Pacific region have emerged only in the last 20 years.

Advice may come from a number of different sources, including accountants, lawyers, management consultants, bank managers, financial planners, small business development agencies, industry mentors, business coaches, family and friends and other business entrepreneurs. There are marked differences in the frequency with which such services are used.

There are essentially three different working styles an adviser can adopt. In the expert consultant mode, the adviser analyses, diagnoses problems and suggests change. The 'pair of hands' mode occurs when an adviser is bought in to work within the firm for a temporary period. Finally, the facilitative process mode encourages owners and entrepreneurs to take responsibility for their own situation; the adviser's main goal is to help business people learn how to help themselves.

Issues to take into account when choosing an adviser include qualifications, experience, industry knowledge, level of personal rapport, networking abilities, the range of services provided, price and the presence or absence of any conflict of interests.

Government and private sector assistance to entrepreneurs and small businesses can take many forms. This may include start-up help, business development and improvement for existing firms, provision of infrastructure, tax concessions and trade support. Business incubators represent a hybrid of public and private assistance. They provide convenient tenancies, in-house business services and advice and the opportunity to build links with kindred business operators.

REVIEW QUESTIONS

1. Briefly list and explain the function of each type of business adviser.
2. In what ways do governments provide direct assistance to new and small firms?
3. Explain the four types of service offered by a business incubator, and the three different types of incubator.
4. Where can entrepreneurs go to find the names of potential advisers for their businesses?
5. Explain the different types of business advisory styles.

DISCUSSION QUESTIONS

1. How do business advisers help a firm to improve its performance? Is there any downside in relying on advice from a business adviser?
2. Is there any particular advantage or disadvantage in seeking financial assistance or information from a private sector agency instead of a government body?
3. What are the limitations of using family and friends as your main source of business advice?

SUGGESTED READING

Carey, P., Simnett, R. & Tanewski, G., *Providing Business Advice for Small to Medium Enterprises*, Melbourne, CPA Australia, 2005.

Fombrun, C.J. & Nevins, M.D., *The Advice Business: Essential Tools and Models For Management Consulting*, Upper Saddle River, Pearson Prentice Hall, 2004.

Sirolli, E., *Ripples in the Zambezi: Passion, Predictability and Economic Development*, Institute for Science and Technology Policy, Murdoch University, Western Australia, 1995.

United Nations Economic Commission for Europe *Best Practice in Business Services* New York, United Nations, 2002.

Case study

Shepherds

Three years ago, Amelia and Rod Coppings, two New Zealanders living in Hong Kong, came up with a bright new idea for the local tourism market: helping young children, the sick and those with disabilities who were travelling on their own. After a year of thinking about the idea, talking to their friends, investing HK$150 000 of their own money in start-up costs, and attending a six-week 'business planning' course during evenings at their local polytechnic, they launched Shepherds.

Hong Kong has a large international population, including many highly-mobile, career-focused families who travel frequently into and out of the Hong Kong Special Administrative region (HKSAR). The business is targeted at meeting the special needs that such high mobility generates — namely, who will look after the travelling children if both parents are working? For a daily fee, staff from Shepherds will accompany young children travelling abroad to meet up with their parents. Shepherds staff act as surrogate parents for the trip, ensuring the child's safety and security until arrival at their destination, where they are met by their parents or legal guardian. Also, a similar service is offered now for adults with a physical illness or disability who want to undertake independent travel.

➡

Rod, 45, was previously a high-school language teacher and principal who had grown tired of the education sector. He now fills the role of office manager, bookkeeper and salesperson, while Amelia, 38, a nurse, spends much of her time on the road with the actual travelling clients. Six other employees work on a casual 'as needs' basis for the firm, assisting when Amelia cannot do all the travel herself. Although they spent the first year working from a leased office in Kowloon, for the last year they have been based at a business incubator with a free, on-site business advisory service. In the last two years, they turned over HK$750 000 and HK$780 000, but this left them with a net profit of only HK$260 000 and HK$250 000 respectively.

Rod and Amelia have been married for five years. All their assets are tied up in the business. They do not have any substantial private savings left, nor do they own any other financial assets, such as real estate.

In light of the relatively low turnover and profits, Amelia has recently suggested that they expand into other tourism areas by organising children's holidays to the outer islands around Hong Kong, nearby Taiwan or onto mainland China. She estimates that it would cost about HK$120 000 in additional marketing expenses to branch out.

Rod disagrees strongly with his wife, as he believes that they should stay focused on their original core business until it becomes more established and profitable, so they spoke to the manager of the incubator. He was enthusiastic about the proposal. 'I think expanding into other areas could work wonders for you, although I'm concerned that you haven't done any market research, developed any financial projections or put together a written business plan. And I don't know if children's tourism is the best market. What about other areas, like providing personalised tours for the numerous Australia, European and American tourists who come here each year?'

Because the business is structured as a partnership, Amelia and Rod also spoke to their accountant, Bernadette Tsui. She was more sceptical about the idea, and suggested that perhaps the most profitable option would be to close the firm and find full-time employment instead.

'You're not making much, and you probably never will. We have a shortage of skilled teachers and nurses at present, so why not take advantage of your real competitive advantage?' Bernadette said. But that certainly wasn't what Amelia wanted to hear – she still had her heart set on the children's tourism venture.

Questions

1. **List the five most important problems facing this business at present.**
2. **What information would a business adviser need in order to best help Rod and Amelia?**
3. **Which solution would you choose? Why?**

ENDNOTES

1. L.M. Dyer & C.A. Ross, 'Advising the small business client', *International Small Business Journal*, vol. 25, no. 2, 2007, pp. 130–51.
2. I. Campbell, *Perspectives on Small Business Assistance*, Law Foundation of New South Wales, Sydney, 1975.
3. Department of Trade and Industry, Commonwealth of Australia, *Report of the Committee on Small Business* (the Wiltshire Report), Government Publisher, Canberra, 1971.
4. G.G. Meredith, *Small Business Management in Australia*, 4th edn, McGraw-Hill, Sydney, 1993.

5. Singapore Standards, Productivity and Innovation for Growth (SPRING), *SME 21*, www.spring.gov.sg.
6. Government of Malaysia, Third Industrial Masterplan 2006–2020, Kuala Lumpur: Ministry of International Trade and Industry, 2006.
7. P. Carey, R. Simnett & G. Tanewski, *Providing Business Advice for Small To Medium Enterprises*, CPA Australia, Melbourne, 2005.
8. D. Leonard & W. Swap, 'Gurus in the garage', *Harvard Business Review*, vol. 78, no. 6, November–December 2000, pp. 71–82.
9. S. Sherman & A. Freas, 'The Wild West of executive coaching', *Harvard Business Review*, vol. 82, no. 11, 2004, pp. 82–90.
10. A. Leimon, F. Moscovici & G. McMahon, *Essential Business Coaching (Essential Coaching Skills and Knowledge)*, Routledge, London, 2005.
11. S. Holmes & S. Smith, 'The impact of subsidised business advice upon aspects of non-financial performance in small firms', *Small Enterprise Research*, vol. 5, no. 1, 1997, pp. 56–67.
12. P.N. Gooderham, A. Tobiassen, E. Doving & O. Nordhaug, 'Accountants as sources of business advice for small firms', *International Small Business Journal*, vol. 22, no. 5, 2004, pp. 5–22; Department of Employment, Workplace Relations and Small Business, *A Portrait of Australian Business: Results of the 1996 Business Longitudinal Survey*, Department of Employment, Workplace Relations and Small Business, Canberra, 1998; M. Battisti, *Who Does What? Business Compliance in Small Firms*, New Zealand Centre for Small & Medium Enterprise Research, Massey University, Wellington, 2009.
13. L. Jay & M. Schaper, 'The utilisation of business advisory services by home-based businesses in Western Australia', paper presented to the 15th annual Small Enterprise Association of Australia and New Zealand (SEAANZ) conference, 22–24 September 2002, Adelaide, South Australia.
14. K. Mole, 'Business advisers' impact on SMEs: An agency theory approach', *International Small Business Journal*, vol. 20, no. 2, 2002, pp. 139–62.
15. R.W. Peacock, *see* note 10.
16. S. Knuckey, H. Johnston, C. Campbell-Hunt, K. Carlew, L. Corbett & C. Massey, *Firm Foundations: A Study of New Zealand Business Practices and Performance*, Ministry of Economic Development, Wellington, 2002, pp. 192–3.
17. J. Xiao & H. Fu, 'An empirical study of usage of external business services by Chinese SMEs' *Journal of Enterprise Information Management*, vol. 22, no. 4, 2009, pp. 423–40.
18. K. Lewis, C. Massey, M. Ashby, A. Coetzer & C. Harris, 'Business assistance for SMEs: New Zealand owner-managers make their assessment', *Journal of Small Business and Enterprise Development*, vol. 14, no. 4 , pp. 551–66, 2007; N.H. Ahmad & P.S. Seet, 'Dissecting behaviours associated with business failure: A qualitative study of SME owners in Malaysia and Australia', *Asian Social Science*, vol. 5, no. 9 September 2009, pp. 98–104.
19. *See*, for example, J.J. Chrisman & W.E. McMullan, 'Outsider knowledge as a knowledge resource for new venture survival', *Journal of Small Business Management*, vol. 42, no. 3, 2004, pp. 229–44.
20. A. Gibb, 'SME policy, academic research and the growth of ignorance: Mythical concepts, myths, assumptions, rituals and confusions', *International Small Business Journal*, vol. 18, no. 3, 2002, pp. 13–35; J. Watson, J. Everett & R. Newby, 'Improving the odds of success: The effect of screening and professional advice', *Proceedings of the 45th International Council for Small Business World Conference*, 7–10 June 2000, Brisbane.
21. *See*, for example, P. Moran, *Clarifying and Enhancing the Role of Business Counsellors in Relation to Small Enterprise Development*, Durham University Business School, Durham, 1995.
22. E. Schein, *Process Consultation: Its Role in Organization Development*, 2nd edn, Addison-Wesley, Reading, Mass., 1988; E. Schein, *Process Consultation: Lessons for Managers and Consultants*, 2nd edn, Addison-Wesley, Reading, MA, 1987.

23. A.A. Gibb, 'Developing the role and capability of the small business adviser', *Leadership and Organization Development Journal*, vol. 5, no. 2, 1984, pp. 19–27.
24. E. Sirolli, *Ripples in the Zambezi: Passion, Unpredictability and Economic Development*, Institute for Science and Technology Policy, Murdoch University, Western Australia, 1995.
25. C.F. Hogan, *Understanding Facilitation*, Kogan Page, London, 2002.
26. C. Massey, 'Capturing the outcomes of enterprise agencies: A changing approach to measuring effectiveness', *Small Enterprise Research*, vol. 3, nos 1–2, 1995, pp. 57–64; Small Business Development Corporation, Western Australia, *Working with Your Business Adviser*, Small Business Development Corporation, Perth, 1997.
27. L.M. Dyer & C.A. Ross, 'Advising the small business client', *International Small Business Journal*, vol. 25, no. 2, 2007, pp. 130–51.
28. A.A. Gibb, *see* note 20.
29. G. Parkinson, 'Some advice about advisers', *Company Director*, vol. 25, no. 8, 2009, pp. 22–5; M. Schaper & C. Dunn, 'The field of service provision' in van der R. Horst, S. King-Kauanui & S. Duffy (eds) *Keystones of Entrepreneurship Knowledge*, Blackwell, Oxford, pp. 355–6, 2005.
30. T.Y. Lee & L. Low, *Local Entrepreneurship in Singapore — Private and State*, Times Academic Press, Singapore, 1990.
31. Singapore Standards, Productivity and Innovation for Growth (SPRING), *see* note 5.
32. United Nations Industrial Development Organisation, *Business Incubators*, www.unido.org, 2000.
33. P. Dowling, *Business Incubation in Australia: Best Practice Standards and an Industry Profile*, Australia and New Zealand Association of Business Incubators, Wollongong, 1997, pp. 4–5.
34. ibid., pp. 8–9.
35. Australia and New Zealand Association of Business Incubators, *Incubation Works: Case Studies of Australian Small Business Incubators and Their Impact*, ANZABI, 2004.
36. B.J. Cho & E. Son, 'The Role Dynamics of the IKED, government agencies, supporting institutes and incubation centres in Korea', *Asia–Pacific Journal of Innovation and Enterprise*, vol. 3, no. 2, 2009, pp. 57–74.

PART 3

Managing key functions

CHAPTER 11

Marketing

Learning objectives

After reading this chapter, you should be able to:

- define the concept of marketing and its importance to entrepreneurs and small business owners

- explain the five steps involved in the marketing process for new and small firms

- describe the 'seven Ps' that make up the extended marketing mix

- calculate a break-even point, contribution margin, mark-up and margin for pricing purposes

- discuss how to evaluate the effectiveness of a firm's marketing efforts.

In essence, a business exists to make a profit by identifying a market opportunity, and successfully providing goods and, increasingly, services to customers who are persuaded that they are paying the right price for the benefits that they will receive. Settling on the right price, promotional mix and distribution strategy is often easier said than done. In this chapter, we discuss marketing in the context of the entire business venture, and also in relation to the related concept of integrated marking communications. The concept of marketing and some of the different philosophies that can be adopted are examined. Then the marketing process itself is explained, followed by an examination of the 'Seven Ps' of the extended marketing mix. Special attention is paid to price setting, since many entrepreneurs have difficulty dealing with this issue. The chapter concludes with some suggestions about how to evaluate the effectiveness of a firm's marketing plan.

The concept of marketing

Marketing *The process of planning and executing the conception, pricing, promotion and distribution of ideas, goods or services to create exchanges that satisfy individual and organisational goals.*

Marketing is often considered by the entrepreneur as being the core function of the firm.[1] **Marketing** is a multistage process involving a number of different activities that must all be successfully integrated if the business venture is to succeed. Identifying a group of potential customers, understanding the reasons why they purchase, developing a strategy for communicating with those customers, and delivering a product or service to them are all part of an effective marketing plan.[2]

The research evidence suggests that there are differences in marketing approaches between large firms, small businesses and growth-oriented entrepreneurs. For example, smaller enterprises have less sophisticated marketing resources available to them, and are often driven by owner–managers focused mainly on attracting new business, rather than retaining existing clients.[3] There is also evidence suggesting that small and medium-sized enterprises do not allow the marketing function within the firm to have as much influence on strategy as their larger competitors.[4] Small firms often rely on a niche focus, identifying markets that larger competitors overlook.[5] In recent years, increased attention has been paid to the concept of 'entrepreneurial marketing'[6] — the study of how entrepreneurs undertake marketing. Compared to more established competitors, entrepreneurs involved in new, growing businesses tend to place a greater focus on creating value-adding innovations for their customers, and servicing new customer groups in dynamic and emerging markets; and they are often highly opportunistic in deciding what is the best way to reach and meet a customer's needs.[7]

An overview of the marketing process

As figure 11.1 shows, effective marketing requires entrepreneurs to carefully develop a plan through a series of considered, logical and sequential steps. It begins with a clear vision of business goals, followed by market research to better understand the likely acceptance of the product/service offering in the market and to develop priority target markets. The extended marketing mix (product, price, placement, promotion, people, process and physical evidence) must then be developed and implemented, after which the effectiveness of the marketing effort should be assessed.[8]

Goal setting

The first thing to consider in any marketing plan is how the firm wants or needs to market itself, since this will have a major impact on what strategy is adopted and whether it is successful.[9] This is often closely linked with the life cycle of the business venture, the stage in the life cycle of the product, the personal goals of the business owner and the owner's own marketing philosophy.[10]

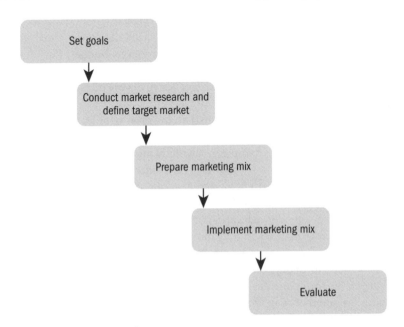

FIGURE 11.1 The marketing process

The second issue to consider is whether the product is completely new to the market. When the product that is being sold is totally original, much of the marketing effort must be devoted to alerting potential customers to the existence of the product, educating them about its features and benefits, and encouraging them to buy something new. On the other hand, if the firm intends to sell a product that is already known to consumers, then the business does not need to focus on educating buyers about what the item *is* — the firm can, instead, concentrate on explaining why people should buy from this business rather than from a competitor.

A third factor concerns the goals of the business owner. If the owner's goals are to aggressively grow and expand the business, then the marketing approach will often concentrate on issues such as achieving high levels of turnover, increasing market share, competing on price and reaching out to as many potential customers as possible. On the other hand, if lifestyle goals are the owner's priority, then it may make more sense to focus on a narrow **niche market**, where only a low level of marketing is planned to maximise return for effort required.

Niche market *A narrowly focused target market for goods and/or services.*

Understanding the market

Good market research can help identify exactly who the target market is, customers' perceptions about the product or service being offered, expenses of production, likely sales price and the factors that will induce customers to purchase or not. The right focus of the research undertaken for business planning will yield reliable and useful information to improve planning decisions.[11] The scope of the market to be researched consists of the people or firms who could benefit from the use of the new product or service, who have the means to buy it and who will be offered the opportunity to do so.[12]

A key issue here is to identify and define targeted and specific groups of customers who are *likely* to purchase, not just every customer who *could* purchase. A **target market** is the core group of customers a business intends to focus on. Successfully identifying one or more target markets allows the small firm to make the most of its limited advertising and promotions budget. This does not necessarily mean that the business will sell only to members of such a target group; it simply means that the business intends to devote its efforts to these key groups.[13]

Target market *A core group of customers that a business intends to focus its marketing efforts on.*

Markets can be segmented and targeted on the basis of at least five criteria:[14]

- *Geography.* Many small businesses make a conscious decision to sell in a particular area only. For example, a lawnmowing business in Australia may concentrate on one or two suburbs of a city, since the owner can achieve the greatest return if customers are located near one another.
- *Demographic characteristics.* Many consumers can be categorised on the basis of their age, gender, education, ethnicity, income or other features. For example, dividing markets in Singapore into Tamil-, Bahasa-, Chinese- and English-speaking groups can help entrepreneurs better develop specific strategies for each group of potential clients.
- *Psychographic features.* Lifestyle, socioeconomic status and attitudinal characteristics are another way of distinguishing consumers. University students, for example, tend to have different needs and wants (and less ready cash) than corporate executives. It rarely makes sense to try to sell to both groups using the same strategy.
- *Behavioural segmentation.* This method focuses on the ways and situations in which customers might use the product. Are they seeking particular benefits? Are they heavy or light users, loyal or past users? In addition this segmentation method includes occasion segmentation (for example, birthdays, Christmas, Fathers Day). Retailers of small bicycles, for example, can expect to sell a large proportion of their annual stock turnover in the two months leading up to Christmas.
- *Individual or business?* For many firms, their main customers are not members of the public (business-to-consumer), but rather another business or group of businesses. These are sometimes referred to as business-to-business (B2B) transactions. Secretarial services, for example, usually find that their customers are other small businesses.

When selecting segments to target, it is often a very useful strategy to diversify and have more than one client base; the business owner must carefully assess how much effort to devote to each. If all client groups generate roughly equal levels of sales and profits, then it makes sense to spread the marketing effort among all groups. However, if one group is responsible for the vast majority of profits, then efforts should focus on retaining their loyalty and custom.

Another issue to consider at this point is the difference between potential and actual customer sales. Although the number of *potential* customers in a particular target group may be large, it is rare for all these to become *actual* customers. Indeed, the number of actual customers may turn out to be only a very small proportion of the total available population. This needs to be taken into account when estimating future sales from each target group.

The marketing mix

Traditionally, marketing has been described in terms of the classic '4 Ps' of the marketing mix — product, promotion, price and placement. However, growth in the prevalence of service-based small business is increasingly moving the focus to an extended marketing mix (the 7 Ps). The 7P strategy goes beyond the 4 Ps to also consider the involvement of people, process and physical evidence in creating a marketing mix strategy.[15]

The product or service

It is logical to begin any discussion of the marketing mix with the product/service itself. What are the advantages, strengths and weaknesses of the product? How do these compare with other products already in the marketplace? One thing that many small business owners fail to appreciate is the difference between **product features** and **benefits**. The features of a product or service are a statement of what the offering is or does, whereas the benefits refer to the advantage that a consumer can receive by purchasing the good or service. Marketing a good or service on the basis of its features (what it actually is) is very different from a benefit-based approach, which promotes a good on the basis of what the customer will gain from it.[16] Table 11.1 depicts some products or services and their corresponding features and benefits to illustrate the difference. It should be clear from viewing these items that customers will not be buying because of the feature; they will buy because of the benefit derived from the product feature. Identifying and understanding the difference between a feature and a benefit of a product/service is important when designing a marketing strategy.[17]

Product feature
What a product or service is or does.

Product benefit *An advantage that a consumer can receive by purchasing a good or service.*

TABLE 11.1 Examples of product features and benefits

Product	Feature	Benefit
Fast food	Quick, mass-produced	Cheap to buy
Dog wash	Pet regularly washed by a professional	Saves time
Email	Fast, computer-based communication	Allows regular contact with friends
Dental surgery	Technically well-trained staff	Relieves tooth ache
Auto mechanic	Courtesy car available	Provides transport to work

Promotion

Integrated marketing communications (IMC) *Adopting a holistic approach to all communication methods and messages to inform, persuade and remind customers in a clear, consistent and compelling manner.*

The simple term 'promotion' is used in this chapter interchangeably with the related concept of **integrated marketing communications (IMC)**. There is a growing acceptance that businesses, big and small, should focus on a promotional strategy that communicates with customers in a coordinated manner. While the promotions outcome for small business is often aimed simply at getting a sale, it will also have an impact upon the level of awareness, trust and loyalty towards the product or service. These, often collateral, outcomes and impacts of the promotional plan are well served by an IMC approach to strategy development and implementation.[18]

The challenge is to select the right IMC promotional assortment to ensure the message delivered has impact and effect at a justifiable cost. Some of the more common tools used to achieve this are:[19]

- *Personal canvassing.* This involves personally contacting people and making them aware of what is for sale. Time-consuming and expensive, this method is best suited to firms selling high-cost items that have a limited market or to those conducting business-to-business transactions.
- *Electronic tools.* The internet is increasingly becoming the default shopping tool for many time-poor consumers, so an interesting and easy-to-find website can substantially help firms boost product sales and enquiries. Other electronic tools can also be helpful. There is a more detailed discussion of the myriad of information and communication technologies in chapter 15.
- *Print media advertising.* Newspapers, general magazines and special-interest journals are a traditional format for advertising, and are still widely used today. Advertisements can be placed in particular sections of a paper or in special-interest journals to target certain categories of reader; for example, a sports store may advertise in the sports results pages.
- *Telephone directories.* Phone listings are still an important means of customer access for many business types. Especially useful is a prominent listing in the Yellow Pages (commercial) telephone directory for businesses in most urban areas.
- *Signage.* Signs are one of the few forms of advertising that, once erected, work continuously for a business. Provided they are placed in a highly visible position in a high-traffic location, the one-off investment in a sign can result in substantial long-term exposure. Suitable positions can include above or at the front of the premises, outside one's home (if the business is home-based and such signs are permitted by the relevant authority), along major customer traffic flow areas and on the owner's and/or business's vehicles.
- *Logos and business names.* A good business name can clearly explain to a prospective customer exactly what the business does and can help it to stand out from its competitors. In contrast, names that are obscure or easily misspelt can create problems. The name can be accompanied by a simple visual graphic device (a logo) to reinforce the image.
- *Pamphlets.* Printed leaflets or flyers are a cheaper way of distributing information, usually through handouts or letterbox drops. However, most pamphlets have a low impact rate, since they are quickly discarded by readers.
- *Business cards.* Cards are a simple means of ensuring that customers, suppliers and other key stakeholders retain information about how to contact the firm.

- *Television and radio advertising.* These are broadcast (wide-ranging) media with the capacity to reach many customers at once. However, such advertisements are expensive and require professional production to maximise their impact.
- *Sponsorship.* Donating goods, money or services to a local community activity or association can also help promote the firm. Many small business owners provide sponsorship in return for having their business name prominently displayed in any related promotion of the community group or event.
- *Word of mouth.* Hardest of all to create, measure and maintain, personal recommendations are still one of the most effective ways of promoting a firm. However, referrals from other customers are usually an outcome of high levels of customer service, and can be problematic to generate intentionally.
- *Trade shows.* Industry conventions where manufacturers, suppliers and distributors come together are a good opportunity to promote a product or service. Trade shows are now common in many industries, including the mining sector, healthcare, tourism, sports retailing and manufacturing.[20]

Different promotional tools and combinations thereof will work for different types of target market and product/service offerings. However, most small firms tend to use only a few of the above channels, due to their limited financial resources and generally low levels of in-house marketing expertise.[21]

Price

Pricing is an important factor in attracting (or repelling) potential clients. Two separate but equally important issues need to be considered when developing the pricing component of the marketing mix: the pricing strategy adopted and an understanding of the mechanics governing pricing mechanisms.[22]

Pricing strategies

There are several pricing options available to small firms:
- *Going rate.* This refers to the process of establishing a price by reference to one's competitors. Adopting the same price as most other firms is a relatively straightforward, easy matter, and it is an approach used by many small-scale entrepreneurs. However, if the cost-base of the business is substantially different from the rest of the market, this pricing strategy can be problematic. For example, if a business were to spend more on manufacturing a product than its competitors charged for similar finished goods, adopting a *going rate* strategy would lead to a financial loss.
- *Cost-plus.* Commonly found in retailing (also known as mark-up pricing), this involves taking the cost price of a product and increasing it by a certain percentage to arrive at a final sales price. The amount that the product price is marked up can be set individually by the owner or can be based on standard mark-ups.
- *Maximum.* In situations where the supply of an item or service is limited, or where an oligopoly or monopoly exists, then sellers may be able to command whatever prices they believe the market can bear.
- *Perceived.* This is when the sales price of a product or service is set on the basis of what customers believe an object is worth. It is most commonly used in the marketing of luxury and rare goods, where clients may be prepared to pay

substantially more than an item's true worth because of the status and prestige that such an acquisition appears to give. Products priced in this way can have gross profit margins that are quite substantial.

- *Skimming.* When a firm introduces a new product or offering that meets with an enthusiastic market response, short-term demand may allow the business to temporarily charge an inflated price. However, in many cases, such demand often gives rise to similar product offerings from competitors, and demand eventually declines. At this point, the price will be reduced to a level that is more in keeping with a greater level of competition.

- *Discounted.* Many businesses seek to compete by offering their products at a lower price than the prevailing market norm. This is attractive to customers who are price-sensitive, and may also be used to introduce customers to a completely new product with which they are unfamiliar. However, it may also deter purchasers who believe that a lower price equals lower quality. Furthermore, it can encourage competitors to retaliate by lowering their prices even further, a process that may continue until no business is making a profit.

- *Loss.* Businesses sometimes deliberately offer a product at its cost price or even less. This may be part of a considered strategy to move old or expired stock off the shelves or to clear display space for the next season's product offerings. In some retail operations such as supermarkets, 'loss leader items' are often intentionally used to lure prospective customers into the store in the hope that they will also purchase other items that have a reasonable profit margin.

- *Price lining or price segmentation.* A common strategy for selling into multiple markets is to develop various levels of product or service as low, medium and high priced offerings. This strategy can be particularly effective when selling through multiple outlets or when selling online into different market niches.[23] For example, many businesses will offer a cheaper 'no-frills' or 'factory direct' product, identical in specification to their main product line that is only in one basic form. This strategy is often adopted by manufacturers of clothing items that are then sold under various labels but are essentially the same basic goods with different packaging and marketing effort applied.

Entrepreneur profile

Justin Miller, CEO of Sensear Pty Ltd

Sensear is a technology-based start-up that has trademarked and patented devices that simultaneously isolate and enhance speech, at the same time suppressing background noise. This allows users to safely and clearly communicate in high noise environments. The Sensear story is one where a visionary and determined entrepreneur has partnered with a talented research team to commercialise a potentially life-changing invention. The SENS™ technology provides a technically elegant and affordable hearing protection solution that promises to significantly reduce the impact of the world's most common occupational illness — noise induced hearing loss. The wearer of the device benefits from the unique feature of the SENS™ technology — the headphones or earplugs (two different forms exist, primarily for user comfort in cold and warm climates) do not need to be removed in order to communicate face to face, by two-way or by mobile phone. The secret is in the sound filtering algorithm and related microphone array technology that separates speech from damaging background noise. This transformation occurs at the same time as still permitting enough low level background noise to ensure that the wearer remains situationally aware. After several years in development, the product was launched onto the world stage in 2007, and the first shipments left the assembly line in early 2008. Since then, Sensear has attracted the attention of world-class management and private equity investors to fund and facilitate a global growth strategy. The company has offices in Melbourne, Sydney, Los Angeles, San Francisco and its headquarters in Perth, Western Australia. The distribution of the product into Europe, South America and Asia is being facilitated by the unique distribution channel that exists in the industrial safety equipment segment.

Justin describes the global distribution network for industrial safety equipment as a unique ecosystem of independent safety equipment distributors, able to professionally deliver and explain the product to a global audience. He believes that there are few product categories that offer this opportunity to enter a hi-tech product at a global level without having in place a company-owned and -supported distribution channel. In the US alone, Sensear estimates that a market exists for A\$3 billion worth of sales in the industrial safety market, predominantly in the manufacturing sector. Eventually, the potential of the technology could see the devices used in many different situations and segments from hospitality (noisy music venues), fast food (drive-through order taking), social markets for the hearing impaired (allowing those with partial hearing loss to hear clearly at noisy venues such as sporting events) and the military (communicating in the field).

Justin Miller is the quintessential entrepreneur, always looking for ways to create opportunities for promoting a product that he is justifiably passionate about. Part of the Sensear success story is the opportunistic and highly effective marketing techniques that Justin Miller espouses. Justin is a master at creating positive word of mouth at events that are likely to have a great many corporate decision-makers present. This is a product that is best demonstrated to the buyer in a noisy environment to get the full impact of the technology. Mr Miller demonstrates the technology at large air shows, by hosting 'the world's noisiest press conferences' at the end of runways and also in the pit lanes of prestigious motor racing events. In 2009 alone, the Sensear technology was presented at significant trade shows including ones in Australia (Melbourne & Avalon), USA (Las Vegas, San Diego, San Antonio and Orlando), Canada (Toronto) and Germany (Dusseldorf). Few people have the privilege to promote, support, own and champion a technology that has the potential to positively affect so many lives. Partly because of this 'social good' aspect, and also because of the passion that Justin has for the Sensear team and product, he has no plans to disengage from such an exciting opportunity. He looks forward to a time when the product is so universally known and used that 'Sensears' finds its way into the dictionary as a synonym for hearing protection.

You may like to visit the website, www.sensear.com, to learn more about the Sensear story.

Understanding the mechanics of price setting

Price setting involves more than just dealing with customers' perceptions of a product and their willingness to spend. It is also closely related to the firm's capacity to meet its own costs and to generate an acceptable return. An understanding of the principles that govern the mechanics of pricing will help astute business owners find a price that not only is acceptable in the market-place, but more importantly meets their own financial goals. It should be noted at this point that the calculations and discussions that follow do not take into account the effect of various goods and services taxes that may apply in some countries or jurisdictions.

The nature of costs

The first step in developing an understanding of the pricing process is the ability to discriminate between different types of expense. The costs involved in running any business operation can be broken down into two basic categories: fixed costs and variable costs.

Fixed costs *Expenses that remain the same, regardless of the level of activity or sales turnover a business generates.*

Fixed costs are those expenses that remain the same, regardless of the level of activity or sales turnover a business generates. Many of the day-to-day expenses of being in business (rent, administration, legal and accounting fees, insurance, electricity costs and so on) fall into this category. Such overheads are the cost of being in business. They are relatively unchanging, regardless of how many sales the business makes.

Variable costs *Expenditure items that increase or decrease as sales volume changes.*

Variable costs refer to expenditure items that increase or decrease correspondingly as sales volume moves. As more items are sold, the level of variable expenses will rise, usually in a direct relationship (so a 10 per cent increase in sales will be met with a matching 10 per cent increase in variable cost outlays). Conversely, a decline in sales is often matched by a drop in variable expenses. For a manufacturer, the main variable expense will be the raw materials used to produce a finished product; other expenses may include energy consumption and labour costs if these are directly proportionate to product output. In a retail shop, the main variable expense is the trading stock (inventory) purchased for resale to customers. In contrast, service operations are largely based on personal endeavours rather than on the sale of goods; as a consequence, such firms tend to have very few, if any, direct variable expenses.

In the rest of this chapter, the term *cost of goods sold* (COGS) is used when discussing both raw materials and trading stock. This is the major variable cost for most businesses; in fact, in many cases it is the *only* variable expense worthy of note (see table 11.2).

TABLE 11.2 Some common fixed and variable costs

Fixed costs	Variable costs
Electricity, gas and water	Cost of goods sold — raw materials, trading stock
Wages	Wages of factory staff (if a manufacturing firm)
Equipment	Wages of sales and other staff (if paid on a commission basis)
Rent of premises	
Use of professional advisers	
Insurance	

A good starting point in analysing a firm's fixed and variable costs is to examine its profit and loss statement (also called a statement of financial performance). Most items can be easily divided into one or other category, although some items will appear to be partly fixed and partly variable (for example, most firms have a fixed minimum amount of advertising that they undertake each year, although it would also be reasonable to expect this cost to directly increase if the firm wished to increase sales). In general, however, it is preferable to keep the analysis simple and to regard as variable only those items that inevitably move with the level of sales. In these situations, many firms will end up with cost of goods sold as the only variable cost.

Having completed the initial breakdown into fixed and variable costs, the business owner should next consider the role of business income. Every dollar of revenue received by a business has at least three components:

- Any price established must, first and foremost, cover the direct variable cost of producing the particular item which is sold. In other words, a certain portion of the product price or service fee must pay for the cost of the goods actually sold.
- There must also be sufficient to help defray the fixed costs (overheads) of the business.
- If anything is left over once fixed costs and variable expenses have been paid for, this represents profit for the owner. Profit is used to pay a fair return to the owner/s of the enterprise for time, effort and risk-taking in establishing and running the enterprise. Some of it must also be retained for reinvestment in the firm for future growth; and a final portion of the profit will also usually be taken away as a tax on business profits by government.

Break-even point

Each time a product is sold, it should be priced at a level that at least covers the variable expenses (cost of goods sold) and yet has enough left over to make a contribution to recovering the fixed annual costs of the enterprise. At what point have enough items been sold to fully cover all those fixed costs (and, by definition, all the variable expenses to date)? This level of sales is referred to as the **break-even point**. At break-even point, net profit is nil, but all expenses have been met.[24]

Break-even point *The level of sales where all expenses have been met, but no profit has been made.*

Break-even analysis allows the owner to calculate the point at which a business generates enough sales to meet all its costs. Beyond that level, any more items that are sold will provide a certain amount of profit. However, if sales fall below that point, then the business will run at a loss.

One conventional formula for calculating a break-even point is:

$$\text{Break-even point in units} = \frac{\text{Total fixed costs}}{\text{Unit sales price} - \text{Variable cost per unit}}$$

This equation calculates the total number of *unit sales* needed to reach the break-even point. (If the actual dollar amount is needed, this can be calculated by multiplying the total number of units by their individual selling price.) The break-even point in units can be easily calculated by using a profit and loss statement, along with a knowledge of the selling price and variable cost of the individual item.

With a little variation, the formula can also be used to calculate the level of sales needed to produce a specific level of profit:

$$\text{Number of items needed} = \frac{\text{Net profit} + \text{Total fixed costs}}{\text{Unit sales price} - \text{Variable cost per unit}}$$

EXAMPLE 1

Pure NZ Soap is a small part-time venture that buys and sells only one item – bars of soap – which it retails for NZ$2 each. The proprietor of the store buys the soap for NZ$1.20. The only variable expense is the cost of goods sold. The fixed costs are all the operating expenses (overheads). Last year, the firm sold 50 000 bars of soap, and its profit and loss statement was as follows:

Sales revenue	NZ$100 000
Less: Cost of goods sold	60 000
Gross profit	40 000
Less: Operating expenses	30 000
Net profit	$10 000

To calculate the break-even point, the following formula can be used:

$$\text{Break-even point in units} = \frac{\text{Total fixed costs}}{\text{Unit sales price} - \text{Variable cost per unit}}$$

$$= \frac{\$30\,000}{\$2.00 - \$1.20}$$

$$= 37\,500 \text{ soap bars (which is actually NZ\$75 000 worth of sales)}$$

If the owner wanted to make a net profit of NZ$20 000 this year, she could use the following formula:

$$\text{Break-even point in units} = \frac{\text{Net profit} + \text{Total fixed costs}}{\text{Unit sales price} - \text{Variable cost per unit}}$$

$$= \frac{\$20\,000 + \$30\,000}{\$2.00 - \$1.20}$$

$$= 62\,500 \text{ bars of soap (NZ\$125 000 worth of sales)}$$

Contribution margin

Calculating the break-even point using the above formula is useful but can be quite cumbersome and slow. In many cases, it would be easier if a more concise equation could be developed for such simple calculations. This is the role of the contribution margin.[25]

Contribution margin *The proportion of money left in each dollar of sales after variable costs have been met, and which is available to cover fixed costs and contribute to profits.*

The **contribution margin** represents the proportion of money left in each dollar of sales after variable costs have been met, and which is available to cover fixed costs and contribute to profits. In other words, it answers the following question: For every dollar that the business earns, how much is left over after variable costs (cost of goods sold) have been paid for? This is the amount that the owner can use to pay for fixed costs and then help generate a profit.

A contribution margin can be calculated using the formula:

$$\text{Contribution margin} = \frac{\text{Total sales} - \text{Total variable costs}}{\text{Total sales}}$$

Just like the break-even point, the information on a profit and loss statement can be used to perform this calculation. However, where the only variable cost in a business is the cost of goods sold, then the calculation of a break-even point becomes much easier, because the contribution margin will equal the gross profit margin shown on the profit and loss statement.

Once known and expressed as a percentage, the contribution margin can then be used to calculate break-even point. (Note that this figure is expressed as a dollar value, not number of items sold.)

$$\text{Break-even point in dollars} = \frac{\text{Fixed costs}}{\text{Contribution margin}}$$

It can also be used to estimate the dollar value of sales needed for a particular net profit:

$$\text{Dollar value of sales needed} = \frac{\text{Net profit} + \text{Total fixed costs}}{\text{Contribution margin}}$$

Understanding how to establish fixed and variable costs, and then using this information to calculate a contribution margin, can allow a business owner to work out whether the proposed break-even point is realistic (can the firm really make that many sales in a year at that price?) and whether a particular profit target is also achievable.

The analysis of pricing mechanisms discussed above works best with a firm that offers a single product or service. Where a number of different products at very different prices are sold, then analysis becomes somewhat more difficult.

EXAMPLE 2

Using the information provided in example 1, Pure NZ Soap's contribution margin can be calculated in the following manner:

$$\text{Contribution margin} = \frac{\text{Total sales} - \text{Total variable costs}}{\text{Total sales}}$$

$$= \frac{\$100\,000 - \$60\,000}{\$100\,000}$$

$$= 0.4$$

$$= 40\%$$

This could also have been found by referring to the profit and loss statement. Since the only variable expense is the cost of goods sold, the resulting gross profit margin is the same as the contribution margin of 40 per cent.

The contribution margin can then be used to calculate the break-even point and sales needed to make a net profit of NZ$20 000, as in the previous example, but using the simpler formula:

$$\text{Break-even point in dollars} = \frac{\text{Fixed costs}}{\text{Contribution margin}}$$

$$= \frac{\$30\,000}{0.4}$$

$$= \text{NZ}\$75\,000 \text{ worth of sales}$$

$$\text{Dollar value of sales needed} = \frac{\text{Net profit} + \text{Total fixed costs}}{\text{Contribution margin}}$$

$$= \frac{\$20\,000 + \$30\,000}{0.4}$$

$$= \text{NZ}\$125\,000 \text{ worth of sales}$$

Mark-ups and margins

Mark-up *The extent to which the price of a product is increased from its original cost of goods sold to its final selling price.*

A **mark-up** is the extent to which the price of a product is increased from its original cost of goods sold to its final selling price. It shows the percentage increase from cost price to sales price. Mark-ups are always measured in relation to the cost price, and are calculated thus:

If measuring the whole of the business:

$$\text{Mark-up} = \frac{\text{Gross profit}}{\text{Cost of goods sold}}$$

If analysing an individual product:

$$\text{Mark-up} = \frac{\text{Profit}}{\text{Cost price}}$$

The first formula can be applied if the firm's profit and loss statement is known, and the second applies when only individual product information is available.

Margin *A measure of how much of the final sales price is gross profit.*

A **margin**, on the other hand, is a measure of how much of the final sales price is gross profit. Sometimes also referred to as a gross margin, it indicates the proportion or percentage of the sales price that is gross profit (thus it is always related to the selling price):

If measuring the whole of the business:

$$\text{Margin} = \frac{\text{Gross profit}}{\text{Sales}}$$

If analysing an individual product:

$$\text{Margin} = \frac{\text{Profit}}{\text{Selling price}}$$

EXAMPLE 3

Since there is only one product on offer at Pure NZ Soap, analysis of a mark-up and margin is relatively straightforward, and can be calculated using either the profit and loss statement or the individual product information provided previously.

If measuring the whole of the business:

$$\text{Mark-up} = \frac{\text{Gross profit}}{\text{Cost of goods sold}}$$

$$= \frac{\$40\,000}{\$60\,0000}$$

$$= 0.67$$

$$= 67\%$$

If analysing an individual product:

$$\text{Mark-up} = \frac{\text{Profit}}{\text{Cost price}}$$

$$= \frac{\$0.80}{\$1.20}$$

$$= 0.67$$

$$= 67\%$$

If measuring the whole of the business:

$$\text{Margin} = \frac{\text{Gross profit}}{\text{Sales}}$$

$$= \frac{\$40\,000}{\$10\,0000}$$

$$= 0.4$$

$$= 40\%$$

If analysing an individual product:

$$\text{Margin} = \frac{\text{Profit}}{\text{Selling price}}$$

$$= \frac{\$0.80}{\$2.00}$$

$$= 0.4$$

$$= 40\%$$

Also worth noting at this point is that the final gross profit margin is *always* less than the initial mark-up, since the amount by which the product has to be increased from its original base cost of goods is always more than the resulting profit margin (see table 11.3).

TABLE 11.3 The relationship between mark-ups and margins

Mark-up on cost	... results in the following gross profit margin on sales
10.0%	9.09%
20.0%	16.67%
25.0%	20.00%
33.3%	25.00%
50.0%	33.30%
100.0%	50.00%

Source: J. English, *How to Organise and Operate a Small Business in Australia*, 7th edn, Allen & Unwin, Sydney, 1998, p. 165.

What is the relevance of mark-ups and margins? Firstly, where the only variable cost in the business is the cost of goods sold, then the gross margin will be the same as the contribution margin. This information can then be applied to calculate break-even point, or sales needed for a particular level of net profit.

Secondly, in many retail businesses, the selling price of a product is set by taking the cost price (cost of goods sold) and adding a set mark-up.

Thirdly, an understanding of mark-ups and margins can help business owners understand the significance of discounting on their final profit. In general, there is an almost exponential relationship between an increase or decrease in mark-up and the resultant effect on profitability. For example, a 10 per cent discount in sales price for Pure NZ Soap would result in its net profit reducing to nil, whereas a 10 per cent increase in sales price would double its net annual profit to NZ$20 000.

EXAMPLE 4

If Pure NZ Soap reduces the sales price of its soap by 10 per cent, then its sales revenue will also decline by 10 per cent and the resultant profit and loss statement will be:

Sales revenue	$90 000
Less: Cost of goods sold	60 000
Gross profit	30 000
Less: Operating expenses	30 000
Net profit	$nil

Note that even though the price reduction leads to decreased sales revenue, the cost of goods sold and operating expenses remain the same. Accordingly, profit is reduced to zero.

On the other hand, a 10 per cent increase in sales price from the original will produce the following result:

Sales revenue	$110 000
Less: Cost of goods sold	60 000
Gross profit	50 000
Less: Operating expenses	30 000
Net profit	$20 000

In this case, a 10 per cent price increase has led to a 100 per cent improvement in net profit compared with the original forecast.

Setting an hourly rate

For many small firms in the services sector, the above tools are of limited value, since service businesses have little, if any, cost of goods. Unlike firms that deal in tangible commodities and can evaluate their profitability and break-even point by the number of items they sell, service-based organisations often calculate their financial break-even points on a time-based process. This is especially important for self-employed business owners. Accordingly, an alternative costing method is required.

If the main or only cost of a business is the time and labour of the owner–manager, then a simple method of calculating a price is on the following basis:

$$\text{Hourly charge rate} = \frac{\text{Total funds required}}{\text{Hours available}}$$

The total funds required consist of the fixed operating costs of the business and the personal income the owner needs.

Note that the number of hours available here is not necessarily the hours a business owner is available to work, but the number of hours that can be charged out to customers — time spent working but not earning income does not count. As exercise 3 demonstrates, most people can charge out only about 1100 to 1400 hours a year.

If the resulting rate is at or below the going market rate, the business is clearly viable. However, if the hourly rate is substantially above the market rate, then the owner will need to find enough customers willing to pay at this higher rate if the business is to succeed.

EXAMPLE 5: JENNY'S HOURLY RATE

Jenny Coffey is currently working as a self-employed bookkeeper. She wants to earn a gross (before tax) personal income roughly similar to what she earned in her last paid employment (about A$75 000 per annum). It also costs her A$25 000 a year to run her business (phone calls, travel, insurance, internet costs and so on).

Jenny believes that because her business involves a lot of travel to clients' place of business, she, at best, will be able to generate about 1200 hours of chargeable work each year. Conservatively, she assumes only 1150 hours of work annually to provide some room for error.

Therefore, her rate will be:

$$= \frac{(A\$25\,000 + A\$75\,000)}{1150 \text{ hours}} = A\$86.96$$

Jenny can round up her rate to produce a final figure of A$87 per hour. This now becomes the *minimum* hourly rate that Jenny will charge for any work she does, as accepting work at below this rate will probably ensure she fails to reach her profit goal.

If you are setting an hourly rate for a business with more than one person, it is necessary to increase both the number of chargeable hours available and the net income required.

Placement

Before examining the extra components that make up the extended marketing mix, the final element in the classic 4Ps marketing mix **placement** is explored: how will the exchange of goods or services between buyers and sellers occur?[26] To ensure that this exchange occurs, the business owner must plan how to get products or services to a point where customers can purchase them. To achieve this, a placement strategy must include a distribution mechanism, as well as deal with storage and transport issues.

Placement *The exchange of goods or services between buyers and sellers.*

Distribution channels

There are a number of ways in which a business owner can sell to a consumer. One is to do so directly. This is convenient, simple and often done by many small firms. Other options involve the use of intermediaries — third parties in the distribution channel that help facilitate the sale of a product or service.[27]

Brokers can bring together the buyer (consumer) and the seller (business) to help the two parties negotiate a deal. Such an arrangement tends to be a one-off affair. However, agents (also known variously as manufacturers' agents or sales agents) act as permanent intermediaries. They market the product to consumers for a fee. Agents and brokers tend to be found in industries where there are many small product producers and retailers who lack the capacity to find one another, they still perform quite a limited service when compared to wholesalers.[28]

Wholesalers provide a more comprehensive suite of services than agents or brokers. They purchase goods from the producer, and then sell them directly to retailers. In the process, they take responsibility for storing, delivering and promoting the product. They have their own sales staff, and often provide product servicing and credit terms to purchasers. Confectionery and magazines are often sold in this way.

Retailers are the most common public face of a distribution channel. A retailer sells goods or services directly to the ultimate consumer (often the general public). They usually have a storefront, although some operate through party-plan, mail order, telephone or electronic means.

Issues to consider

The selection of a suitable distribution channel depends on a number of factors:
- *Comparative advantage.* In many cases, it makes more sense to use an intermediary than to directly sell items from the business itself. Each party has a specialised skill that they are particularly good at and which they can perform better than the other. For example, a small-scale manufacturing plant will typically not have many salespeople on its staff; its core competency is the efficient production of physical goods. Such a firm would be well advised to sell through a wholesaler or retailer and focus its own energies on remaining an effective manufacturer.
- *Industry norms.* In some business sectors, there are conventions about how items are sold. When this is the case, it is usually easier for a new firm to follow the industry trend rather than try to redesign the distribution process.
- *Pricing.* Prices have to be set so that all parties in the transactional process receive a reasonable return on their investment while making the final sales price attractive to customers. If a distribution channel contains several intermediaries, each party's ability to charge a maximum price is limited.
- *Packaging and handling of goods.* Goods must be securely packaged and stored. Damage to goods in transit (en route between the supplier and retailer) can result in lost income and customer inconvenience.
- *Payment.* Entrepreneurs need to carefully work out how payment will be made for goods that are being distributed through another firm. In some industries, an invoice is issued and payment is expected within a certain time after the goods have been delivered. In other sectors, receiving firms may be required to pay for goods in advance or at the time of their receipt. Another option is consignment, where payment is expected only if the goods in question are successfully sold to the end consumer.
- *Contractual and legal issues.* It is generally recommended that a brief written contract sets out the rights and responsibilities of all parties involved in the distribution process.

People, process and physical evidence

Planning the way that employees look and behave, as well as designing or at least acknowledging and planning for the physical interaction between employee and customer, is a vital component of a complete small business marketing strategy. All businesses should be concerned about presenting an appropriate and consistent impression and image to their clients and the general public. This is particularly the case for serviced-based firms that need to promote an essentially untouchable or intangible 'product'. Even though they might be skilled service providers, would you choose a hair salon that only swept the hair up once a day, a restaurant where the waiter had dirty finger nails, or a mechanic workshop that had several broken down cars parked in front of it? Acknowledging the importance of the extra 3 Ps of people, process and physical evidence has resulted in what is commonly referred to as the **extended marketing mix** (otherwise known as the services marketing mix).[29]

People issues related to the design of an effective marketing strategy will include discussions around employee performance standards, attitudes, motivation, behaviour, training and rewards. In general, the extended marketing mix acknowledges the key role that employees and owners play in delivering intangible services.

Determining the design of processes and the associated challenges of creating the right combination of physical evidence that portrays the right level of quality are questions of service-scape design. Creating efficient processes that maximise customer satisfaction and minimise the risk of service failure is the substantive role of operational planning. More detail on the methods of designing service delivery is the focus of a discussion on service blueprinting in chapter 12.

Extended marketing mix *The inclusion of people, process and physical evidence considerations, in addition to product, promotion, place and price to determine the marketing mix.*

What would you do?

Who are the green Chuppies?

Shuyan Wu, a talented 29-year-old interior design consultant was in the process of starting up a personalised advisory service to help residents to reduce their environmental impact. During her time as a design consultant, she observed that many young professionals were looking beyond the trappings of so-called 'Western consumerism', wanting to take positive steps to decrease their ecological footprint.

As part of developing her marketing plan she was conducting secondary research looking for the right way to segment the Beijing market into something that was manageable for her small start-up business. Some international marketing reports that she read referred to a group of Chinese consumers labelled 'Chuppies' (Chinese yuppies), or young and upwardly mobile (seeking more income and status).[30] She also knew that some international marketing experts subscribed to the concept of *Guo Qing* (pronounced gwor ching) as the 'national characteristics or circumstances' that influence the attribution of value, quality and convenience for Chinese consumers.[31] The inference was that new products and services needed to be a good 'fit' with the existing attitudes and aspirations of the typical 'Chuppy', from both an individualistic and a broader cultural perspective. However, as a resident of Soho and having worked for a number of clients near the Beijing Riviera, Shuyan sensed that some of these so-called Chuppies had quite different world views and values from the *Guo Qing* cultural norm. With this in mind, Shuyan sought a better understanding of how her target market thought and behaved. While researching the characteristics of Chinese consumers, Shuyan came across the findings of a large survey. The survey examined more than 60 000 Chinese consumers aged 16 to 40 years, living in large mainland cities and over 8 000 university students in order to develop psychographic profiles. Some key findings of the study were:

- 18% of this age group were 'experimenters', wanting the latest technology and latest gadgets
- 10% were described as 'motivated', wanting first and foremost to advance their careers
- 7% were labeled as the 'achievers', primarily because they had money (plenty of it), and aspired to have the most important of executive positions.

Some other interesting findings that would influence her segmentation strategy included the discovery that 62% of this demographic agree that men should do more housework, 58% said they had already taken measures to protect the environment and over 79% placed a high value on knowledge and learning as a means to a better life. Armed with these insights and her own knowledge, Shuyan now felt ready to begin to describe and segment her target market, which she would refer to as *green Chuppies*. She kept in mind that the intended core benefit of her service was: 'To make the customers home more environmentally friendly and energy efficient (save money and the environment) using aesthetically pleasing (looks good) and cutting edge (latest technology) design techniques'.

Questions

Using this knowledge, and your own experiences and worldviews:

1. **Describe and define the segment(s) that you think Shuyan should focus on using demographic, psychographic and behavioural segmentation methods.**
2. **Having described the segment(s), what would you suggest is the right pricing strategy for this service and why?**

Evaluation of marketing

To ensure that the marketing strategy implemented is the correct one, the entrepreneur must be satisfied that the stated goals of the original marketing process are being met. This is the purpose of marketing evaluation. One common evaluation technique is to *compare marketing expenditure with sales revenue.* In this technique, the amount of money spent on a particular marketing mechanism is compared with the level of sales or enquiries that this has generated. If an increase in marketing investment has resulted in a corresponding or greater level of sales, then the process is usually deemed a success.

Another way is to *trace the sources of sales;* in other words, how did customers find out about the business — was it via the Yellow Pages, the local newspaper, word of mouth or some other avenue? This may be as simple as asking customers at the point-of-sale they found out about the business, or it may be by more detailed means, such as a survey.

The business owner may also wish to gauge the *satisfaction of existing or previous customers.* To do this, the firm may initiate a customer feedback program using surveys, personal contacts from a member of the business, or indirect feedback from the firm's sales representatives or agents in the field.

Another evaluation tool can be *customer complaints.* These provide an interesting and valuable body of data about possible problems in the firm's marketing strategy. Continual complaints about poor delivery, for example, can indicate a problem with distribution channels.

Whatever method of evaluating marketing strategy is adopted, it must be simple to administer and capable of leading to change, if results indicate this is required.

SUMMARY

Marketing is the process of planning and executing the conception, pricing, promotion and distribution of ideas, goods or services to create exchanges that satisfy individual and organisational goals. The extended (or services) marketing mix also focuses on the role that people, processes and physical evidence play in the consumption of service-based products. There are six steps to the marketing process: goal setting, market research, target market definition, establishment of an appropriate marketing mix, implementation of the marketing mix strategy and subsequent evaluation of its performance.

Target markets of customers are either potential or actual. They can be segmented on the basis of geographical, demographic, behavioural and psychographic features. Understanding the product or service requires business owners to know the product's relative strengths and weaknesses compared with other offerings, its features and the benefits customers can derive from its use.

Marketing plans, even in small firms can benefit from a holistic or integrated approach to their planning and implementation. Hence, businesses are encouraged to plan, implement and monitor a systematic promotional campaign that ties all elements of promotion together — an integrated marketing communications perspective.

Promotional tools that can be used by small business ventures include canvassing, the internet and email, printed publications (newspapers, magazines, trade journals), telephone directories, signs, logos and business names, pamphlets, business cards, television and radio advertising, sponsorship, word-of-mouth recommendations and trade show exhibits.

Pricing strategies can include charging the going rate, cost-plus pricing, charging the maximum possible, pricing to a perceived level of value; skimming; discounting; price-lining and using loss leaders. To effectively set a price, a business owner must also understand the mechanics of price setting, including how to distinguish between fixed and variable costs, and how to calculate contribution margin, break-even point, mark-up and margin.

Placement issues cover the distribution of goods to the final customer. Matters that must be considered at this point include whether to use a direct or indirect method of distribution; the issue of comparative advantage; industry norms; the establishment of a price that gives all parties a financial interest in the sale; packaging and transport of goods; payment for sales made; and legal and contractual issues.

Planning issues involving people, processes and physical evidence arise in all businesses, but probably more so in ones that sell intangible services. Marketing decisions in this area will necessarily involve close interaction with the human resource and operational plans of the business.

The final part of the marketing process is an evaluation of the marketing effort Evaluation can be done in various ways: by comparing marketing expenditure with sales revenue generated; by tracing the sources of sales; by measuring the level of satisfaction of customers; and by analysing customer complaints.

REVIEW QUESTIONS

1. What are the 7 Ps of the extended marketing mix?
2. Outline and briefly explain the issues that determine the marketing goals set by a business owner.
3. What are the different types of pricing strategy that can be used by a firm?
4. How are a break-even point and a contribution margin calculated?
5. Explain the different types of intermediary that exist in the placement component of the marketing mix.

DISCUSSION QUESTIONS

1. Which firm is more able to market its products/services effectively: a new, small entrepreneurial venture or an established large corporation?
2. Do you think that new businesses should put more emphasis on 'price', 'place' or 'people' when developing a marketing mix strategy?
3. How does the creation of target market groups help the overall marketing process?

EXERCISES

1. *Calculating margins and mark-ups.* A retailer buys roses for A$4 per stem from the rose nursery and sells them at A$5 per stem. What are the mark-up and margin on each rose?
2. *More margins and mark-ups.* Imported small farm-prawns can be bought from Thailand for A$6.50 per kilogram; they retail at A$8 per kilogram. What are the mark-up and margin on this item?
3. *Establishing an hourly rate.* Jill is a landscape gardener planning to start-up her business in New Zealand's South Island. She wants to earn A$70 000 a year (before tax). Her total fixed costs are estimated at A$15 000, and she wants four weeks annual leave (during summer) plus another two weeks in reserve for any unforeseen problems/illness. In addition, she has identified that her industry in this location usually loses eight weeks per year to inclement weather. Because of this shortened season, she is prepared to work seven days a week when the work is available, and estimates that she will actually be completing garden installations for six hours on each of those days. She presumes there are no direct costs of goods as the owners pay for all plants and materials required for the job.
   Calculate the hourly rate required. If the going rate is $55 per hour, is her business viable?

SUGGESTED READING

Bygrave, W. & Zacharakis, A., *Entrepreneurship*, John Wiley & Sons, Hoboken, 2008.
Schindehutte, M., Morris, M.H. & Pitt, L.F., *Rethinking marketing: the entrepreneurial imperative*, Pearson Education Inc., Upper Saddle River, NJ, 2009.
Stokes, D. & Wilson, N. *Small Business Management & Entrepreneurship*, 5th edn, Thomson Learning, London, 2006.

Home Sweet Homeware

Harold Bertram, a qualified accountant was considering a return to the family business because his father's health was failing, and Harold himself was considering semi-retirement in the lovely seaside town where the store was located. The business, which had been going for nearly twenty years, sold homewares, mainly to local residents, and also made some seasonal sales to domestic tourists visiting the seaside holiday town in summer. The main direct competitors in town were a nationally known franchise giftware store and the local (four day per week, summer only) craft market.

When Harold looked closely at the recent business profits, he was concerned that the pricing of items was incorrect. He decided to look closer at the financial returns of the firm.

HOME SWEET HOMEWARE

Profit and Loss Statement
for financial year 1 July to 30 June

Sales revenue	$850 000
Less: Cost of goods sold	737 500
Gross profit	112 500
Less: Operating expenses	72 700
Net profit	$39 800

'Of the A$72 700 in expenses, A$60 200 are fixed costs and the remainder are variable costs,' his father had initially explained – pointing out that because trading conditions were difficult there had been no recent advertising outlays, in order to keep expenses low. Harold's father reminded him that at least the business was still making money when many others in town were making a loss. However, Harold thought this was still a poor return, even for a five day per week semi-retirement business. He knew the value of his own labour and decided that he needed to generate A$65 000 per annum profit to justify giving up his existing job with a large city accounting firm.

Questions

1. Calculate the break-even point of this business, using the contribution margin.
2. Harold's father said that if Harold could lift sales to A$1 million he would reach his required profit of A$65 000. Do you agree (use contribution margin again to calculate this)?
3. It seems that Harold will need to develop a marketing plan to increase sales enough to hit his A$65 000 profit target. How should he do this, bearing in mind that most forms of marketing effort will add to fixed and/or variable costs?

ENDNOTES

1. G. Hills, C. Hultman & M. Miles, 'The evolution and development of entrepreneurial marketing', *Journal of Small Business Management*, vol. 46, no. 1, 2008, pp. 99–112.
2. P. Kotler, S. Adam, S. Denize & G. Armstrong, *Principles of Marketing*, 4th edn, Pearson Education, Frenchs Forrest, 2008, p. 127; J. Summers, M. Gardiner, C.W. Lamb, J.F. Hair & C. McDaniel, *Essentials of Marketing*, Thomson, Melbourne, 2001, p. 6.
3. M. O'Dwyer, A. Gilmore & D. Carson, 'Innovative marketing in SMEs' *European Journal of Marketing*, vol. 43, no. 1, 2009, pp. 46–61.

4. M.F. Walsh & J. Lipinski, 'The role of the marketing function in small and medium sized enterprises', *Journal of Small Business and Enterprise Development*, vol. 16, no. 4, 2009, pp. 569–85.

5. K.S. Lee, G.H. Lim, S.J. Tan & H.W. Chow, 'Generic marketing strategies for small and medium-sized enterprises: A conceptual framework and examples from Asia', *Journal of Strategic Marketing*, no. 9, 2001, pp. 145–62.

6. E. Collinson & E. Shaw, 'Entrepreneurial marketing — a historical perspective on development and practice', *Management Decision*, vol. 39, no. 9, 2001, pp. 761–6; M. Schindehutte, M.H. Morris & L.F. Pitt, *Rethinking Marketing: The Entrepreneurial Imperative*, Pearson Education Inc., Upper Saddle River, NJ, 2009.

7. M.H. Morris, M. Schindehutte & R.W. LaForge, 'Entrepreneurial marketing: A construct for integrating emerging entrepreneurship and marketing perspectives', *Journal of Marketing Theory and Practice*, Fall, 2002, pp. 1–19.

8. P. Kotler, S. Adam, S. Denize & G. Armstrong, *Principles of Marketing*, pp. 17, 127.

9. D. Bangs & M. Halliday, *The Australian Market Planning Guide*, 2nd edn, Business & Professional Publishing, Sydney, 1997.

10. D. Carson & A. Gilmore, 'Marketing at the interface: Not "what" but "how"', *Journal of Marketing Theory and Practice*, vol. 8, no. 2, 2000, pp. 1–8.

11. W. Bygrave & A. Zacharakis, *Entrepreneurship*, John Wiley & Sons, Hoboken, 2008, p. 167.

12. J. Legge & K. Hindle, *Entrepreneurship: Context, Vision & Planning*, Houndmills, Palgrave Macmillan, 2004, p. 104.

13. L. Hailey, *Kickstart Marketing*, Allen & Unwin, Sydney, 2001, pp. 63–5.

14. P. Kotler et al., pp. 230–41.

15. ibid., p. 21.

16. ibid., p. 99.

17. N. Humphrey, *The Penguin Small Business Guide*, 2nd edn, Penguin Books, Camberwell Victoria, 2007, pp. 63–4.

18. P. Kotler et al., *see note* 9, p. 432.

19. M. Ali, *Practical Marketing and PR for the Small Business*, Kogan Page, London, 1998.

20. J.R. McColl-Kennedy & G.C. Kiel, *Marketing: A Strategic Approach*, Nelson Thomson, Melbourne, 2000, pp. 617–18.

21. I. Chaston & T. Mangles, *Small Business Marketing Management*, Palgrave, London, 2002; D. Carson, 'Marketing in small firms', in K. Blois (ed.), *The Oxford Textbook of Marketing*, Oxford University Press, Oxford, 2000, pp. 570–89.

22. T.S. Hatten, *Small Business: Entrepreneurship and Beyond*, Houghton Mifflin, Boston, 2006, p. 390.

23. M. Hodgetts & D.F. Kuratko, *Effective Small Business Management*, 7th edn, John Wiley & Sons, Hoboken, 2002, p. 435

24. P. Burns, *Entrepreneurship and Small Business*, Palgrave, London, 2001, p. 119.

25. J.W. English, *How to Organise and Operate a Small Business in Australia*, 7th edn, Allen & Unwin, Sydney 1998, p. 229.

26. W. Reynolds, A. Williams & W. Savage, *Your Own Business*, 3rd edn, Nelson Thomson, Melbourne, 2000, p. 287.

27. W.L. Megginson, M.J.S. Byrd & L.C. Megginson, *Small Business Management: An Entrepreneur's Guidebook*, 3rd edn, Irwin McGraw-Hill, Boston, MA, 2000, pp. 190–3.

28. P. Kotler et al., *see note* 9, pp. 416–17.

29. R. Fisk, S. Gountas, M. Hume, J. Gountas, S. Grove & J. John, *Services Marketing*, Asia-Pacific Edition, John Wiley & Sons, Milton, Qld. 2007, p. 36.

30. M. Campinella, 'UPS Survey Reveals Insights on Marketing to Chinese Consumers', *DMNews*, www.dmnews.com, 21 August 2006; P. Engardio, Chindia, *How China and India are Revolutionizing Global Business*, Mcgraw Hill New York, 2007, pp. 134–6.

31. *HBR On Doing Business in China*, Harvard Business School Press, 2004, pp. 125–7.

CHAPTER 12

Operations management

Learning objectives

After reading this chapter, you should be able to:

- define the concept of operations management and the three basic steps in the operations process

- explain the different types of physical site factors to be considered when structuring operations

- discuss production and workflow arrangements

- develop a service blueprint and describe its purpose

- discuss the issues relevant to effective inventory and supply management

- explain the ways in which an entrepreneur can evaluate, protect and improve operational performance

- describe how process systems and quality assurance work

- define the concept of risk management.

All businesses create a product of some sort, be it a tangible commodity or an intangible service. To do this, the production facilities and activities of the business must be organised in a logical way that allows the firm to operate in an efficient, effective and controlled manner.

In this chapter, the concept of operations management is defined and explained, and the three elements that constitute the operations management process are explored. Practical issues such as site selection, production, workflow and service design are examined. Special attention is given to the process and logic behind developing a service blueprint. These design and selection issues lead somewhat inevitably to a discussion related to managing and optimising inventory and evaluation of operational performance. Finally, improving operational performance is examined from quality assurance and risk assessment perspectives.

Operations as a management process

Operations management
The control of the process by which a firm makes a product.

Operations management refers to the control of the process by which a firm makes a product. The operations process consists of three elements:

- *Inputs* are the raw materials or stock from which the final product will ultimately be made.
- Processing involves the *transformation* of inputs into final products. This is a conversion phase in which staff, plant and equipment combine to change the raw materials into a product.
- The end result of the transformation process is the *output*: that is, the products made by the firm that are intended for consumption by its customers.[1]

Figure 12.1 illustrates an operations process — the production of a daily newspaper. The inputs consist of the stories filed by journalists, advertising lodged by different companies and the raw newsprint paper that is used for the published edition. The transformation process involves editing and formatting the stories, laying out pages to accommodate text and advertisements, printing the newspaper, and bundling and distributing it to the many vendors located at different shops throughout the city and its surrounding hinterland. The output is the completed newspaper that is bought by members of the public, who are usually unaware of the extraordinarily complex and detailed planning required to deliver their morning paper on time every day.

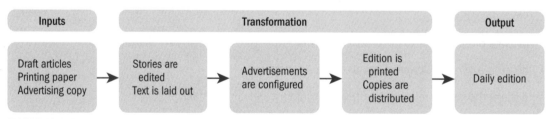

FIGURE 12.1 The operations process for a newspaper

Contemporary research into operations management has shown that effective control of these activities is an important factor in the overall success of the business venture, since it enables a firm to produce a reliable, quality product at a competitive price. Recent small business research also suggests that efficient knowledge management, human resourcing, purchasing and general management practices will further enhance overall firm productivity.[2]

Most operations management tends to focus on micro-management of particular issues, rather than on all the issues as a coherent and interlocked system.[3] However, small business managers frequently tend to overlook the importance of managing their operational workflow, and underestimate the importance of this function in achieving commercial viability for their enterprise.[4] In fact, it is via operations management that the core functions of the business venture are facilitated.[5]

To achieve successful operations management, many issues must be considered by entrepreneurs planning a new business venture such as the choice of appropriate business premises, the structuring of the production process itself, and the ongoing task of improving operations over time.[6]

These factors are discussed in more detail throughout this chapter. However, many other variables contribute to the effective management of a small firm's operations. These include the human resources of the business, the management team, pricing and distribution strategies and a coherent business plan that links operations management with other parts of the firm's activities.[7] These issues are discussed in more detail in other chapters and drawn together in the sample business plan in chapter 7.

Physical site factors

One of the first operational tasks to consider in the development of a new business venture is the physical infrastructure: that is, the site on which the firm will operate and the way in which the premises will be configured.

Premises

Firstly, the type of business premises must be determined. There are several different facilities available for new and start-up firms (see table 12.1). These give business owners a wide choice and a certain measure of flexibility when planning the business.

TABLE 12.1 Premises options for new and small firms

	Cost	Flexibility	Tenure
Home-based business	Low	High	Long term
Serviced office	Low	Low	Short term
Business incubator	Low–medium	Medium	Short–medium term
Shared premises	Low–medium	Low–medium	Medium–long term
Rented premises	Medium	Medium	Medium–long term
Purchased site	High	High	Permanent

Operating from home is an attractive option for many self-employed people and micro-sized firms in their early stages. This is especially the case for businesses operating in the services sector, where there is often little (if anything) required in the way of specialised operating equipment, storage space or street front visibility. A *home-based business* allows the business owner to keep rental costs low, if not eliminate them entirely. It also means the business can be run as a sideline or part-time venture if that is the goal. Home-based businesses are very popular — in Australia and New Zealand, about two-thirds of all small firms are based at the owner's home.[8] Many entrepreneurs with India's informal sector are also home-based workers.[9]

Serviced offices allow the firm to temporarily rent an office suite in a complex specifically established for short-term use on an as-needed basis. This arrangement allows the business owners to use rooms on a casual or ongoing basis, so they can use the more sophisticated premises when it is necessary to impress a client or when a centralised meeting location is required. Serviced offices typically provide customised telephone answering facilities and mail collection points, and can allow a small business to have an expensive office address without all the overheads usually associated with such a location.

Similarly, *business incubators* provide specialised workspace and offices for small firms. An incubator is usually a non-profit facility that provides cost-price accommodation for new businesses. The incubator itself usually consists of a collection of premises, housing many different businesses, overseen by a professional manager with experience in mentoring and advising start-up ventures. These arrangements allow new and small ventures to be located in an environment shared with other start-up firms, reducing the isolation and loneliness that can often be found when working on a new venture.[10] Lease commitments are usually run on a month-by-month basis. Incubators are discussed in more detail in chapter 10.

Sharing premises is a strategy that allows complementary businesses to reduce the overall cost of retail space, and increase returns per square metre via mutually beneficial cost sharing arrangements. Typically, a portion of the premises is sublet to a complementary and noncompeting business type that adds to the attraction power of the location. Examples of this include food outlets, such as pizza shops situated within petrol stations, beauticians occupying space within hair salons and physiotherapists occupying rooms within a medical clinic on a part-time basis.

Renting a commercial facility or industrial site is another option for new businesses. This arrangement gives starting business owners maximum choice of a location and site best suited to their needs. Entering into a lease arrangement with a property owner usually requires the tenant to be bound by a long-term lease that may run for a number of years, which can be expensive if the business venture fails and the property cannot be re-let.

Purchasing a property is another option for some business operators, but it requires a large capital outlay. Purchasing maximises the owner's ability to reconfigure the premises and gives the most freedom to operate it in the chosen manner. It also eliminates monthly rental fees and may provide a sound investment option if property prices increase. However, few starting businesses have the additional capital required for this option.

Location

Once the type of premises has been determined, the location that best suits the needs of the firm must be assessed. The choice of location can be a key strategic decision for the future success of the business, with recent research identifying the dynamic relationship between location, strategy and success.[11] In the first place, the owner must be aware of the relevant zoning, licensing and statutory requirements that limit business placements. Many local, state and federal agencies have the power to restrict the operations of different enterprises to specific geographical locations. For example, heavily polluting manufacturing plants are restricted to specified 'heavy industry' zones, and the placement of retail firms is usually limited by local governments to shopping centres and designated strip-shopping locations. There are also circumstances where historic, cultural and demographic factors have an influence upon government policy governing the types of business encouraged in a particular region (for example, Little India in Singapore).

Transport to and from the premises is also critical. The ease with which customers can get to the business will affect retail operations, which usually require high public visibility and easy access via public transport (such as buses or trains) or by private vehicle. Such positioning can drive up the price of rented premises. For manufacturing, industrial and wholesaling enterprises, an important consideration is access to reliable transport facilities that allow raw materials and goods to be moved quickly and cost-effectively. They can be based in less central (and, therefore, cheaper) localities, so long as there is ready access to road, rail, air and/or sea transport links.

Competitors also influence the location decision. For some businesses, it is an advantage to be physically separate from competitors. On the other hand, sometimes it is useful to be based near competitors when customers want a range of options before making a choice. Restaurant or coffee shop precincts are an example of this type of successful co-location of similar businesses. Similar complementary effects can arise from a manufacturer or wholesaler situated close to suppliers, thus reducing transport time and costs.

The personal preferences of the owner may be important, especially if the business is being set up with lifestyle goals as a high priority. In this case, higher profitability or reduced costs may be willingly sacrificed for reduced commuting time or proximity to a desirable residential address.

Proximity to a source of labour can also be a deciding factor for manufacturing firms or businesses with a high labour input component or that require particularly skilled or specialised workers.[12]

Globalisation of trade also plays a part in location selection decisions, such issues as shifting patterns of wealth, time zone compatibility and the international specialisation of labour and product supply are increasingly playing a part in the location decision.[13]

Internal layout

Having acquired suitable premises, the business owner must consider how the space within the given facilities will be used to maximum advantage. This is referred to as the layout or **floor plan** of the business.

Retail operations tend to take one of three basic forms: a standard grid, an open plan or a boutique (shop) layout. *Grid formats* are best suited to large numbers of independent customers who wish to guide themselves through the premises. The store is arranged in a straightforward, easily understood manner that facilitates the rapid movement of people through the premises. Typically,

Floor plan *The arrangement of operational activities within a business premises.*

there is a series of aisles with each section devoted to a common theme or related range of products.

An *open-plan arrangement* is a layout whereby products are displayed in a manner that allows customers to move easily from one area to another. Products may be displayed in any number of different ways, and need not be confined to an aisle setup.

A *boutique (shop) layout* places different groups (or types) of goods together thematically, allowing customers to browse through related products.

Manufacturing firms emphasise an internal design with a simple layout — one in which goods can be easily and quickly (hence cheaply) transferred in at one point, processed in the most efficient manner, and then removed from the premises for storage or distribution via another outlet. Four layout options exist for a small manufacturing firm, they are:

- *Fixed position.* Where the entire product is built in one location, often because of its large size. Engineering firms will sometimes adopt this strategy when fabricating large machinery components that are too big or heavy to manoeuvre.
- *Process based.* Where facilities related to similar tasks are grouped together. An important issue for manufacturers using this layout option is that much of the equipment is likely to be fixed and cannot be moved quickly from one place to another.[14]
- *Product-focused.* Where facilities are situated according to the sequence in which activities take place.
- *Cellular layout.* Where various components of the product are assembled by small product-focused work teams, and then combined for final assembly or shipping in modular form. Such systems may even have production by each cell scattered across different locations.[15]

Other types of firms have their own unique requirements. For example, wholesalers focus on arranging the maximum amount of storage space in the minimum amount of room, while still allowing easy access for removal and storage of items. Priority is given to storage volume and economies of scale when designing the floor plan for a wholesale business.

Service-based businesses face an even more variable set of requirements. They may find their workspace configurations determined by the internal structure of the business, by production requirements or, alternatively, by customer servicing needs. For example, a law firm may find that it operates best by arranging staff together in areas of activity, giving only minimal concern to customer traffic, since most clients have very little contact with the internal operations of the firm. On the other hand, a veterinary practice will need to ensure that operating rooms are located near animal accommodation for convenient access. A restaurant's priorities will be customers' easy access to seating and proximity of the kitchen to ensure food is delivered hot.

Production processes

In addition to the internal layout of the premises, there are other process issues integral to sound operations management:

- the human processes and workflows for creating the product or service must be structured in a logical, replicable and consistent manner

- the supply of raw materials and distribution of finished products need to be organised so that inputs and outputs can flow freely
- the correct operating equipment must be selected to allow the transformation process to proceed.

Workflow

In every business premises, there must be a logical system for organising the flow of production. This guides the work behaviour and activities of the people and equipment. The goal is to establish a workflow that sees inventory (inputs) move through the transformation process and emerge as completed goods or services (outputs) quickly and economically, at an acceptable standard.

One approach is to adopt *continuous production*, a system wherein the firm manufactures a fixed array of goods in a standardised format. In this process, raw materials move into the premises, are arranged and processed in a number of set steps and then emerge completed in a series of activities that is invariably the same. Factory assembly-line work has traditionally been built around such an approach, and applied to industries as varied as car manufacturing, cattle abattoirs, biscuit bakeries and timber mills.

A different strategy is to focus on a more flexible, customer-oriented system of production. When small-scale orders are required, *batch production* (sometimes called *jobbing*) is used. This involves altering the work system for each different item or small group of items produced. As a result, batch production is more labour intensive and costly per item, since different arrangements of equipment, operating systems and staff need to be ordered for each task. In addition, the operating process manager needs to put more work into ensuring that the right specifications are adhered to and clearly detailing the individual tasks.

Batching allows small firms to more efficiently deal with the special needs of a particular client. It is often used as a competitive tool against larger enterprises that have structured their entire manufacturing or production process on the basis of a production line (continuous production) strategy. Batching also tends to require more multi-skilled and highly trained employees, and provides workers with more autonomy and discretion in their work. This greater variety of work can have positive effects upon levels of employee motivation (an issue focused upon in greater detail in chapter 13). The human component of workflow design is also explored next through the process of service blueprinting.

Service blueprinting

A **service blueprint** is a variant of flow chart analysis applied originally to businesses in the services sector, but its usefulness is now recognised anywhere that customers interact with employees.[16] Creating a service blueprint is one way that intangible service acts can be visually depicted to help understand and standardise the service. The visualisation of a complex process for service-based businesses is also useful to explain the service to customers, employees and potential investors. The blueprint is also a method for identifying potential problem points in service design. Some experts advocate a highly graphic illustration resembling the storyboard of a movie, whereas others advocate a less

Service blueprint
A graphical representation of key facets of the performance of a service to convey what happens both in front of the customer and behind the scenes from a people, process and physical evidence perspective.

cluttered process flowchart approach.[17] The specific style of blueprint developed will to a large extent depend upon the intended audience.

Whichever style of blueprint is adopted, there are several key concepts inherent in all:

- *Frontstage activities* — things that occur that the customer can see, hear or feel that need to be managed to ensure a positive interaction occurs.
- *Backstage activities* — things that occur predominantly before or after the customer interaction or away from the customers' view (behind the scenes) that are integrally important for quality customer service.
- *Line of visibility* — the point beyond which the customer is unable to see any more of the service delivery process.
- *Line of interaction* — the points at which people and support systems within the service design interact.
- *Standards and scripts* — the agreed behaviours, manner and timing in which services are presented to customers.
- *Wait points* — the moments where customers will need to queue or have some idle time while their service is performed.
- *Fail points* — those 'moments of truth' where there is a risk that the service will fail leading to customer dissatisfaction.

Developing a blueprint is as much art as science. It is an iterative process that encourages an intimate yet holistic view of the actors and processes involved in the delivery of a service to a client. In an existing business, this is best done by involving all actors/stakeholders in the design of the proposed blueprint. Ideally, everyone from the courier to the counter staff, the office cleaner and the owner should be consulted.[18] Sometimes it may even be useful to involve past customers in the design effort where it is an existing business being blueprinted. Where contemplating a design for a brand new business, observing the way other organisations (quite often in different industries) serve their customers, and replicating or improving those actions, can be useful. Figure 12.2 depicts a service blueprint designed for a franchise contract cleaner during the acts of accepting and completing a domestic cleaning job. The blueprint provides the franchisee with expected timeframes and service standards at each stage, from accepting the job via SMS to completing the paperwork at the end of the day. The franchisor has identified the support people, activities and processes that it will control from behind the scenes as well as strategies for maintaining quality of service and brand reputation.

The design in figure 12.2 identifies two 'moments of truth' where a service failure is likely: at the time of booking the call and during the cleaning itself. These points would attract extra attention in accompanying documentation on how to minimise or remove the risk. In the first instance, the solution is that there are four franchisees per service area, who receive callouts on a rotation basis. A failure to complete the cleaning job to customer satisfaction at fail point two is supported with training, specialised 'signature' cleaning products and immediate customer feedback strategies. The wait point at the initial arrival of the van is a potential problem that is mitigated by providing an expected time of arrival and keeping in phone contact with the client. The risk of delay due to traffic congestion or unfamiliar destination is reduced via the use of global positioning system technologies to plan the optimum route.

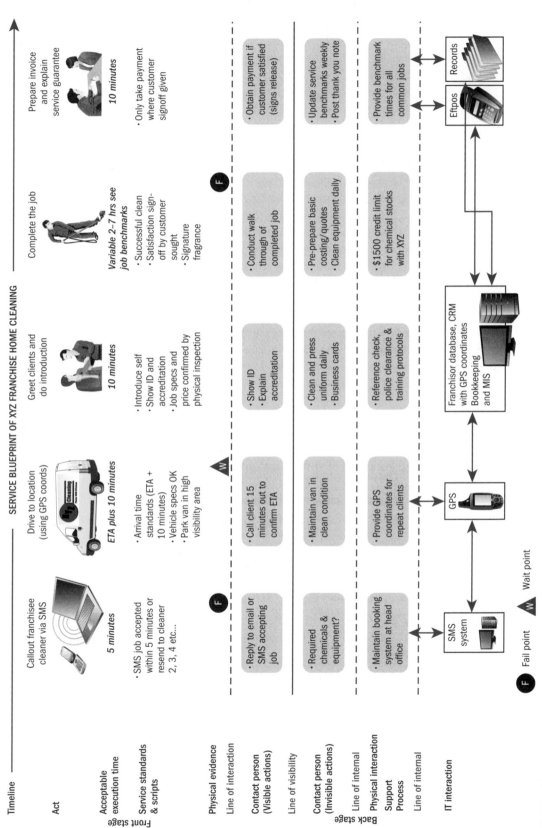

SERVICE BLUEPRINT OF XYZ FRANCHISE HOME CLEANING

Timeline →

Act	Callout franchisee cleaner via SMS	Drive to location (using GPS coords)	Greet clients and do introduction	Complete the job	Prepare invoice and explain service guarantee
Acceptable execution time	5 minutes	ETA plus 10 minutes	10 minutes	Variable 2–7 hrs see job benchmarks	10 minutes
Service standards & scripts (Front stage)	· SMS job accepted within 5 minutes or resend to cleaner 2, 3, 4 etc...	· Arrival time standards (ETA + 10 minutes) · Vehicle specs OK · Park van in high visibility area	· Introduce self · Show ID and accreditation · Job specs and price confirmed by physical inspection	· Successful clean · Satisfaction sign-off by customer sought · Signature fragrance	· Only take payment where customer signoff given

Physical evidence

Line of interaction -

Contact person (Visible actions)	(F) · Reply to email or SMS accepting job	(W) · Call client 15 minutes out to confirm ETA	· Show ID · Explain accreditation	(F) · Conduct walk through of completed job	· Obtain payment if customer satisfied (signs release)

Line of visibility -

Contact person (Invisible actions)	· Required chemicals & equipment?	· Maintain van in clean condition	· Clean and press uniform daily · Business cards	· Pre-prepare basic costing/quotes · Clean equipment daily	· Update service benchmarks weekly · Post thank you note

Line of internal (Back stage)

Physical interaction Support Process	· Maintain booking system at head office	· Provide GPS coordinates for repeat clients	· Reference check, police clearance & training protocols	· $1500 credit limit for chemical stocks with XYZ	· Provide benchmark times for all common jobs

Line of internal -

IT interaction	SMS system	GPS	Franchisor database, CRM with GPS coordinates Bookkeeping and MIS		Eftpos Records

(F) Fail point   (W) Wait point

FIGURE 12.2 Example of a service blueprint

As can be seen from this overview, service blueprints have many systems and processes occurring beneath the surface and in full view of the public, all aimed at efficiently meeting or exceeding customer expectations. The ultimate aim is to eliminate the risk of service failure and to control wait times within limits that are acceptable to the customer. All of this must be achieved at a viable cost to ensure the business remains competitive. Businesses that deliver superior, consistent and dependable service are usually in a position to charge a premium for their effort.

Inventory and supply management

Another aspect of operations management is the handling of raw materials or trading stock ('inventory'). One issue is the amount of stock that should be held by the firm. At any given time, a firm will have stock tied up in the form of finished goods, raw materials, batches of goods awaiting further processing or delivery and items being repaired. Too much stock on hand can be expensive, since a large amount of capital can be consumed in the purchase and storage of the final goods. Too little stock can mean that the firm may be unable to meet client orders as they come in.[19] To balance these conflicting demands, firms usually seek to establish an **economic order quantity (EOQ)** — that is, the amount of goods that minimises the total purchase and storage costs while still being sufficient to meet the production requirements of the business.[20]

Economic order quantity (EOQ)
The amount of goods that minimises the total purchase and storage costs while still being sufficient to meet the production requirements of the business.

There is an accepted formula for the calculation of the most efficient number of orders required per period:

$$\text{Economic Order Quantity (EOQ)} = \sqrt{\frac{2DO}{C}}$$

Where D = period demand in units, O = ordering cost per order (shipping, insurance etc) and C = the cost of carrying each unit (storage, risk of obsolescence). For example, if the cleaning franchisee depicted in the service blueprint in figure 12.2 knew that they would use 800 bottles of cleaning fluid per year, and the cost of delivering cleaning products was A$100 per order, and each bottle of fluid cost A$3 to carry, the businesses EOQ for cleaning fluid would require a quarterly order because:

$$\text{EOQ} = \sqrt{\frac{2 \times 800 \times \$100}{3}} = 230.94 \text{ units per order.}$$

This equates to 800/231 = 3.46 orders per year (round up to 4)

Just-in-time delivery
An inventory management system where materials are delivered to the firm at the time needed for production.

One approach that some firms have adopted to reduce the level of capital bound up in stock is the **just-in-time delivery** method, in which materials are delivered to the firm at the time needed for production. This can help in significantly reducing holding costs and quantities. This strategy can free up additional working capital, especially for firms that regularly deal with large quantities of physical stock. However, it requires careful attention to scheduling and ordering, both of which must be executed at the right time if the flow of inventory is to be maintained.[21] The establishment of a satisfactory supply source for inventory is important. Manufacturers and retailers are heavily dependent on the successful maintenance of an effective supply chain. Issues to consider in the selection of a supplier include cost, frequency of delivery, product range and ability to provide a satisfactory standard of materials or product. Other important aspects include intangible measures, such as the supplier's reputation in the industry, reliability, ability to deal flexibly with any changes in orders and willingness to meet any special or urgent requirements that the business may have from time to time.

In some industries, the range and number of suppliers is strictly limited, and the new business owner has little opportunity to negotiate price and the conditions under which the supplier will deliver. However, where there is a range of different supplying firms competing with one another for the small firm's trade, there is considerable room for negotiation that may lead to lower prices, bulk discounting or more flexible delivery arrangements. The growing globalisation of the supply chain means that increasingly small businesses will need to consider international sourcing of products and services. This is most evident in the manufacturing sector where what is referred to as the *China Factor* has resulted in China now employing more production workers in Chinese factories than the combined manufacturing sector workforce of the United Kingdom, Japan, Italy, USA, Canada and France.[22]

Both inventory and supply management constitute input elements into the operations process. Without an adequate input arrangement, the other parts of the operations process (transformation and outputs) will be adversely affected.

Once transformation into the final product has occurred, another supply and inventory matter arises: how will the completed products (output) be distributed to the clients of the firm? Distribution channels are discussed in chapter 11, as they form part of the firm's marketing strategy.

Entrepreneur profile

Andrew Monteiro, CEO of Journal IT

Risk assessment in the twenty-first century must include an assessment of the risks associated with finding or losing information. Most businesses would understand the need to keep their customer records and financial records secure, and probably have some form of backup system in place. However, how many SMEs take the same care with their employee and personal email records? Journal IT is a system conceived and designed by Andrew Monteiro and his team to reduce risk in a somewhat litigious society.

Andrew is a well educated and trained IT professional who was exposed to entrepreneurship from a very early age. Andrew has fond memories as a teenager of attending back yard garage sales with his father (a mechanical fitter) where they would buy items in need of minor welding/repair, and then on-sell them at the local 'swap meet' markets for a quick profit. Even at that early stage, Andrew recalls a desire to be in business for himself one day. Andrew subsequently built a diverse career in IT and developed the skills required to lead a successful team. He began his first business when still at university in 1990, selling and servicing computer hardware. He has worked as an IT engineer for a range of large and small organisations for well over a decade, as well as starting and growing his own successful information technology consultancy, Openet (openet.com.au), specialising in network design, implementation and management mainly for clients in the mining and resources sector.

The idea for Journal IT was born from a consultancy project that required the Openet team to reconstruct a chain of emails for a client; they were required to span a three year period as evidence in a court action. These emails were old data, stored on hardware and software systems that had subsequently been updated and replaced. Recreating such data can potentially be very expensive for firms. The laws of evidence in most jurisdictions do provide for the use of digital records as admissible evidence in court, but there are very few people or solutions suitable for small and medium-sized enterprises. Journal IT is an SME-focused system where businesses subscribe to have all data securely stored and indexed by a third party, allowing quick and efficient recall of old communications data. The costs start at around A$1 per mailbox per day, and reduce to 60 cents per mailbox as the size of the organisation being covered increases.

The software and systems provide clients with the assurance that every email they send or receive is being securely stored for future reference. Journal IT also provides an 'eDiscovery' search service to quickly and efficiently find email records within the system at a later date. Journal IT can also refer clients to computer forensics experts that can testify in court, as an expert witness, as to the validity of these email records. The business model offers to reduce the risks of damage to reputation, financial loss, high cost of evidence discovery, loss of business information or, at worst, compliance failure that may even lead to criminal proceedings. The service also provides a secure off-site and fully managed record storage and retrieval service with no capital expenditure required. As modern organisations become more reliant upon the internet as their primary communication tool, it seems inevitable that more SMEs will be caught without access to legally required data. Given that legal disputes are increasingly being won (and lost) on the basis of email evidence, Andrew and Journal IT have certainly identified and exploited a significant and growing gap in the IT risk management marketplace.

Source: Based on author's interview with Andrew Monteiro, Journal IT and information from journalit.com.au.

Operating equipment

For a new or intending firm, the equipment needed is also an important concern. Almost all businesses, regardless of the size or nature of the enterprise, will need an essential core of equipment. This will probably include communications equipment (telephones, facsimile, online access), a computer, a workroom, tables, chairs and filing cabinets. Beyond this, the equipment required depends on the type of business.

Retail operations usually require equipment for displaying and transporting stock. Manufacturing firms typically have the highest expenditure tied up in equipment that transforms inputs into completed outputs. Operating equipment for wholesalers includes storage apparatus and devices to move products around within warehouses. The increasing use of information technology as a business tool has generally meant that, over time, equipment needs have become more sophisticated for many businesses and, so, more expensive.

When costing a firm's equipment needs, the business owner must factor in the associated expenses of maintenance and service costs (especially for computing technology and industrial processing equipment), the expected life span of the item and the training that staff will need to operate the equipment.

Once a list of equipment has been compiled, the business owner can determine what should be purchased immediately, and what purchases can be held off until later. If finance is a problem, one option is to use a 'phased purchase' strategy where only the minimum requisite tools are obtained at the start, with other equipment being purchased as future cash inflows allow. However, this limits the ability to offer a wide product range at the time of business launch, and is rarely suitable for manufacturers, in particular. It may also be possible to purchase second-hand equipment if it is still suitable for the task required. An alternative approach is to hire or lease equipment. This has the benefit of providing immediate use of the necessary items while still minimising initial capital outlays and smoothing subsequent cash outlays.

Evaluating, improving and securing operational activities

The third challenge in operational management lies in evaluating, controlling, enhancing and securing production-related activities. The entrepreneur or owner–manager and the team of senior managers must ensure that there are sound systems in place to handle all the basic tasks, so that they can free themselves to focus on business strategy, growth and new opportunity identification. Thus there should be systems to measure and assess the level of performance, tools that can be used to improve processes and satisfactory safeguards in place to ensure that the firm is not critically damaged by unforeseen events or risks.

Assessing and controlling current operations

Different industry sectors face different types of control and evaluation problems. Retail operations, for example, need to keep control of their level of stock on hand, customer complaints and damaged or lost inventory. Service firms are more concerned with the efficient use of time per employee, since they often charge out their services on an hourly basis. Manufacturing firms need to focus on maximising usage of raw materials (inputs) and minimising rejected goods (outputs). However, all face one common issue — control of the firm's operations is an ongoing task.[23]

Effective evaluation and control in operations management often requires a number of steps such as:[24]

- *Set expected standards of performance.* Clearly communicate the production standards that the firm and its employees are expected to achieve.
- *Measure actual performance.* Understand what is being done.
- *Compare the results with the desired standards.* Identify any substantial discrepancies.
- *Make corrections.* Introduce changes as needed to bring actual performance up to standard.

In practice, the evaluation and management of current activities can be performed by addressing the following issues: (1) scheduling, (2) inspection of products and (3) measurement of firm productivity.

Scheduling mechanisms

Scheduling is setting a time frame and sequence of events required to perform a certain activity. It establishes the timelines for production and is a useful framework around which the different parts of the operation process can be organised. One of the most common scheduling tools is a timeline, which simply states what events will occur and when. Slightly more sophisticated, but visually much easier to follow, is the Gantt chart, which shows how long each part of the production process should take and tracks activities using a bar chart (see figure 12.3).[25]

Scheduling *Setting a time frame and sequence of events to perform an activity.*

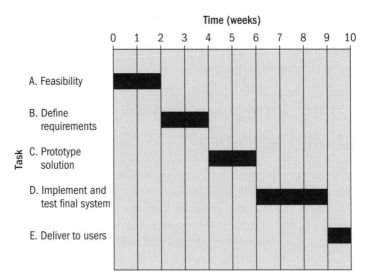

FIGURE 12.3 A Gantt chart

A variation on the Gantt chart is a PERT (performance evaluation and review technique) chart, which shows a sequential list of activities and the estimated time for the completion of each. Also known as the critical path method, it maps out the steps that culminate in the achievement of a designated outcome; however, it cannot be compiled until all events in the production process have been identified and their time requirements gauged. This encourages managers to carefully plan operating activities in advance and allows them to monitor progress.[26] Gantt charts are more useful for routine production, whereas PERT charts can be most helpful for complicated production arrangements.

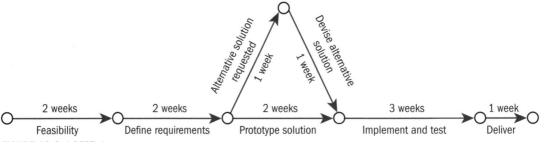

FIGURE 12.4 A PERT chart

100% inspection
When all items produced are inspected.

Acceptance (random) sampling *Inspecting random samples of product to ensure they meet the expected standard; the sample result is generalised to the entire output.*

Inspection regimes

Inspection of items being produced is another important evaluation mechanism. During the operations process, inspections may be carried out before the start of the transformation process, at key points within it, and usually also at the completion of work (the output phase). In some production systems, **100% inspection** is undertaken, with every item checked. Alternatively, **acceptance (random) sampling** may be used, especially for exceptionally large production runs. This involves taking random samples and checking that these all meet the expected standards of performance; an assumption is made that the sample results can be generalised to the entire output.

During the inspection, comparison with desired standards can be done in various ways. One approach is to use **attribute inspection**, where product acceptability is determined on the presence or absence of a key attribute. For example, the quality of a pen may be determined solely by whether it writes. Where products can reasonably be expected to display some small discrepancies that do not materially affect its utility, **variable inspection** can be used. For example, cut flowers usually vary slightly from one plant to another; as long as the variation is not significant, the flowers are deemed to fall within the desired standard.

Attribute inspection
Determining product acceptability on the presence or absence of a key attribute.

Variable inspection
Determining product acceptability by results falling within predetermined boundaries.

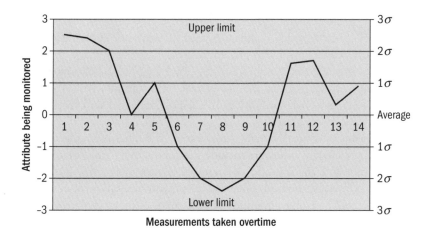

FIGURE 12.5 A variable inspection control chart

Attribute inspection charts such as the one shown in figure 12.5 can be employed as part of a quality control process to ensure that variations in key attributes fall within acceptable boundaries. In the case depicted by figure 12.5, it has been determined that variations within three standard deviations of the norm (average) would be acceptable. Such charts often form an integral part of the quality assurance processes discussed earlier.

Productivity indicators

Measuring the performance of business operations is important for maintaining effective control. If performance cannot be measured, it is much more difficult to manage. One tool to gauge the overall efficiency of operations is the **productivity ratio**. This is an indicator of the efficiency with which inputs are transformed into outputs, and can be assessed by comparing the ratio of inputs used with outputs produced.[27] The higher the ratio, the greater the efficiency of the firm. Productivity ratios can be estimated either for the whole firm, for part of it or for individuals, using the basic formula:[28]

Productivity ratio
A comparison of inputs used with outputs produced.

$$\text{Productivity} = \frac{\text{Outputs}}{\text{Inputs}}$$

For example, total productivity for a whole firm would be:[29]

$$\text{Total productivity} = \frac{\text{Value of outputs (products or services produced)}}{\text{Inputs (labour costs} + \text{capital} + \text{raw materials} + \text{other inputs)}}$$

If a firm spent A\$3 million in inputs and generated some A\$10 million in sales, its productivity ratio would be 3.33. The challenge for the managers of the business would be to ensure that this ratio did not decrease from year to year but, rather, continued to increase. Given that the cost of inputs will normally increase over time, improvement in productivity ratios is somewhat dependent upon pricing (and repricing) strategies. Firms can lose sight of how price variations of inputs and transformation costs do have an input upon productivity.

Timing of evaluation

Feedforward control
Control measures taken in advance of actual performance.

Concurrent control
Control measures performed on work in progress.

Feedback control
Control measures instituted after an event has taken place.

Control and evaluation techniques can all take place at different points in the operations process.[30] **Feedforward control** mechanisms are anticipatory evaluations or controlling measures undertaken in advance of actual performance. Gantt and PERT charts operate in this manner. A quality assurance system can also be used for feedforward control; this procedure is discussed later in the chapter.

Sometimes it is also necessary to evaluate work-in-progress. **Concurrent control** tools include methods such as the use of real-time computer-based statistical analysis, on-site personal monitoring of business activities and inspection of production work-in-progress.

Feedback control measures evaluate performance after it has taken place. Typical examples of post-event indicators include the productivity ratio, rejection rate (number of unusable goods produced), number of customer complaints or waste emissions produced by the firm. Financial documents and ratios (discussed elsewhere in this book) are other examples of such monitoring tools. These compare the financial performance of the firm (such as its annual profit or loss, and the various analytical ratios) with industry standards or with the business's own previous results. However, such tools often suffer from a significant time lag, since the documents in question may be compiled several weeks or even some months after a financial reporting period ends.

Procedural systems and quality assurance

One way to effectively organise the operating activities of any firm larger than a single-person enterprise is to compile a procedures manual. This document explains how certain activities are done, sets out the sequence of steps involved in any particular task, identifies who is responsible, and provides information to ensure the task can be done correctly.

In time, a procedures manual can act as a body of 'corporate knowledge' that exists independently of the people in the firm. Such procedures ensure uniformity, since the steps involved are clearly spelled out. If an employee leaves the firm, the manual ensures that much of the employee's practical knowledge is retained. A good operations manual can also make the business easier to sell or to franchise because the systems described are of great value and comfort to a new, inexperienced owner. There is evidence of a gap between acceptance of the value of performance measurement and actual implementation in SMEs. Although many SME owners may appreciate the value of performance measurement, they often lack knowledge on how to actually do it.[31] Therefore, it is reasonable to suggest that businesses that do bridge this gap and create a good operations manual will have developed a somewhat rare, but potentially enduring, value.

In a practical sense, a procedures manual can also form the basis of the next step in developing an effective business operation — the implementation of a quality scheme. A **quality assurance system** is a set of processes and principles designed to ensure the production of a set of consistent activities, goods or services. It is a compilation of internal rules that the business follows so that its products always conform to a predetermined standard. In this sense, 'quality' means a system that meets required standards — if the firm promises to produce goods to a certain benchmark for its customers, an effective quality system will ensure that it always does. It may not be 'quality' in the popular understanding of the word (that is, the very best type of product in its range), but it will consistently provide customers with what they have come to expect.[32] The term **total quality management (TQM)** refers to the adoption of a quality system and philosophy throughout the entire firm, not just in its operations.[33]

One common set of standards is the International Organization for Standardization (ISO) quality system series (the ISO 9000 family of standards), which provides guidelines on formalising, documenting and implementing the procedure systems by which firms supply their goods and services. Participants in an accredited quality assurance (QA) system are required to have their system audited and verified by an external assessor on a regular basis, thus ensuring that their commitment to the system is upheld. QA certification is often an important prerequisite in successfully tendering for government work or in obtaining contracts with larger firms. Moreover, some businesses also find that quality certification can be an important and useful marketing tool.[34]

The adoption of a QA system usually results in the development of a comprehensive set of detailed manuals that document almost all aspects of the firm's operations and processes. These manuals provide a clear set of guidelines for staff to follow, and help reduce the scope for errors throughout the production process. Some firms go beyond standardising QA systems to employ Six Sigma specialist consultants to help develop and implement a more structured and quantitative approach to quality management.[35] The **Six Sigma system** is founded upon statistical methods that measure deviation from an agreed standard. Such sophisticated systems are not always warranted in small business. The expenses of establishing and maintaining these systems can be substantial (especially for micro-businesses) and firms may become overly reliant on 'following the rules' rather than remaining flexible and innovative.

Quality of service and quality of product are not the same thing. It is quite plausible to purchase a good quality product yet receive bad service during the exchange. Equally it is possible to receive superior levels of service while buying an inferior product. It therefore follows that the dimensions of quality will be different for products and services. Some important quality dimensions for products and services include:[36]

- *Performance*: how well it works
- *Features*: the basics and the extras in the bundle
- *Reliability*: the likelihood that it will work every time as expected
- *Durability*: how long it will last
- *Serviceability*: how easy it is to get it fixed
- *Aesthetics*: impact on the five senses
- *Perceived quality*: the brand image (subjective)

Quality assurance system *A set of processes and principles designed to ensure the production of a set of consistent activities, goods or services.*

Total quality management (TQM) *The adoption of a quality-based philosophy throughout a firm.*

Six Sigma System *A set of quantifiable and consistently followed measures and processes designed to eliminate or at least drastically reduce errors.*

- *Tangible components*: the quality of the physical components that accompany a service, such as the people, equipment and premises
- *Responsiveness*: a preparedness to act quickly and effectively to assist customers
- *Assurance*: why the business and employee should be trusted by the client
- *Empathy*: putting oneself in the shoes of another in order to understand them better as individual customers.

The overriding principle remains that services and products are different, as are people's perceptions of what constitutes quality in both domains. The decision about what to do about maintaining a quality focus is multifaceted and often constrained by the available resources.

Risk management

It is not possible for a business owner to know for certain what will happen to the business in the future. However, it is reasonable to assume that from time to time difficulties will emerge. Many of these have the potential to create serious problems for the firm, and it is prudent to have some contingency plan for these events whenever possible.

Risk *The possibility that a situation may end with a negative outcome for the firm.*

Risk refers to the possibility that a situation may end with a negative outcome for the firm, such as a loss of sales, a loss of money or even the collapse of the business itself.[37] All entrepreneurial ventures are risky, since they involve starting a new or untried idea in a competitive marketplace where success is not guaranteed.

Risk management *The process of identifying risks in advance, assessing their likely occurrence and taking steps to reduce or eliminate them.*

Risk management is the process of identifying risks in advance, assessing their likely possibility of occurrence and then taking steps to reduce or eliminate the risk. Conducting market research into likely consumer demand for a product is a simple risk-management tool. This activity is designed to eliminate or at least reduce the risk that a product cannot be sold once it is produced. A quality assurance system is also a risk management tool, since it seeks to eliminate the possibility of faulty goods or services reaching the customer. At the macro level, the process of environment scanning, where a business owner develops a comprehensive picture of all the different external forces likely to affect the entrepreneurial venture (see chapter 6),[38] is another risk-management tool. Good risk management usually contains a **contingency plan** — a plan of how to respond should a threatened risk actually occur. Collectively, these steps are now recognised as a specific operational task and are often described as the technique of enterprise risk management.[39]

Contingency plan *How a firm will respond to a threatened risk.*

What would you do?

The cost of quali-tea!

Imagine that you purchased a small herbal tea manufacturing business last year that has now completed its fourth full year of trading. The original business was launched by the famous Tea-Tree Sisters that have now retired, leaving you with the rights to their secret recipes. The business specialises in blending what it calls the bush tea revivers, a selection of blended Australian eucalyptus and green teas, taken as a 'general restorative'. The Tea-Tree Sisters brand came to fame three years ago when a Singaporean business started importing it into Singapore under licence as an aid for concentration. This claim was never proven (or disproven) but as a result the business now exports 20% of its production volume as small batches of gift boxed tea to Singapore. The remaining 80% is sold from many popular tourism venues within Australia. Last year, your business inputs cost A$2 750 000 and generated total sales of A$3 400 000. This year, the corresponding figures have been A$3 100 000 and A$3 700 000.

Sales have been good, as people look to alternative medicine for health, and tourists seem to like the Australiana angle. The prior owners actually spent a great deal of money having the business quality certified to ISO 9001 standards to aid in marketing the product globally. You note that sales are up by A$300 000 this year compared with growth of 9% in the year prior to certification, so you think that the ISO brand may be having some sales impact.

Operationally, you are concerned that some aspects of the business are not doing too well. The error rate (defined as the number of items returned due to defective manufacture) has moved from 6.4 per 1000 in the last quarter to 7.2 during the current three-month period. Most errors seem to be complaints from local retailers about underweight packages. Although no formal records are kept, now that you think about it you seem to have had more customer complaints recently from Singapore as well. The workers tell you this has happened once before, that weights can vary because the eucalyptus leaves vary in their moisture content, particularly during summer.

Recently, one of the senior employees approached you with an innovative idea. He has been benchmarking the performance of the business against a competitor in New Zealand. He is convinced that the firm does not need to spend the A$50 000 each year that currently goes into maintaining the existing limited formal quality certification processes. He believes that there are a number of simple performance indicators at all three stages of the operations management process (inputs, transformation & outputs) that will be sufficient to keep the firm on track. Better still, these can be monitored by the staff themselves.

What should you do?

Questions

1. Give reasons why you would support maintaining the existing QA certification or moving to a self-run customised system.
2. Discuss if and why the feedback you have received so far indicates that there is a genuine production problem.

Security

Risk management at the operations level is concerned with a wide variety of threats and dangers. **Security** relates to the protection of equipment and ideas from the risks of theft, loss or unauthorised use. The protection of the physical business premises can involve the installation of movement detection alarms, patrols by contracted guards and/or the installation of suitable locks and grills. Managing security leaks or thefts by staff can be more difficult, but personal references should be thoroughly vetted before employment begins. Where intellectual property is an important asset of the firm, staff and other people granted access to the relevant idea may be required to sign a confidentiality agreement that prevents them from disclosing details to another party without authorisation. Many items of intellectual property can also be protected by trademark, patent or design registrations.

Security *The protection of equipment and ideas from the risk of theft, loss or unauthorised use.*

Insurance

Insurance

A contract to provide compensation for any damage or loss suffered by the firm if a specified act occurs.

Another element in any risk management strategy is insurance. **Insurance** is a contract to provide compensation for any damage or loss suffered by the firm if a specified act occurs. It is a safeguard against risk that provides financial compensation when an untoward event happens. The insurance contract is commonly called a policy, and the payment the firm makes to the insurer for cover is known as a premium. A common form of insurance is workers' compensation, which meets the cost of rehabilitating employees if they are injured at work.

Different forms of insurance cover different types of risks (see the box on 'Insurance products' below). However, the cost of fully insuring a business venture against *all* possible risks would be prohibitive. Where the likelihood of an event occurring is quite low, the business owner may decide that the minimal risk does not justify payment of the premium. In other situations, an insurer may be willing to provide a policy only to established businesses — new firms may not able to obtain insurance until they have an established track record that allows the insurer to confidently assess the likelihood of risk.

Insurance can be acquired by purchasing the relevant policy directly from an insurance company or through a broker who will find the most suitable policy at the best premium from a range of different insurers.

INSURANCE PRODUCTS

The following list of business product offerings provided by most Australian insurance companies indicates the many different types of insurance cover available:

- motor vehicle insurance — protects against the loss or damage of company cars
- professional indemnity — covers liability from claims arising due to breach of professional duty
- general property — protects against loss arising from flood, earthquake, fire, burglary or explosion
- business interruption — protects against costs and lost profits arising from damage to the premises by a fire or other defined event
- burglary — covers replacement of contents stolen from the business premises
- fire and other defined events — compensates for damage to buildings, contents, or customers' goods and trading stock
- money — covers funds stolen from the business site or in transit
- fraud or dishonesty — protects against loss of money or goods due to a fraudulent or dishonest act by a staff member
- machinery — compensates for breakdown of equipment
- electronic equipment — protects against physical loss, destruction or damage (including breakdown)
- negligence liability — covers claims made against the firm for damaged property or personal injury
- multiple risks — provides cover for business property against accidental damage
- personal accident and illness — provides the proprietor with funds to cover the loss of income if injured or sick

---

- tax audit — covers accountants' expenses incurred when a detailed investigation is made by the tax office.

Source: Adapted from NSW Department of State and Regional Development, 'Insurance and your industry', smallbiz.nsw.gov.au (accessed 9 May 2006).

SUMMARY

Operations management covers many different aspects of a firm. Its core focus is on ensuring maximum efficiency in the operations process, which includes the gathering of inputs, their transformation into a final product and the delivery of that output (completed product) to the firm's customers.

Physical site factors are a basic element in a firm's operational management. Several different types of business premises can be used. These include home offices, serviced offices, a business incubator site, rented premises and purchased locations. Once the appropriate site has been selected, the internal layout must be organised. Retail firms can choose between the grid, open-plan and boutique formats, whereas manufacturing premises use either a product-based or process-based layout.

Production processes deal with the issues of workflow, inventory and supply management, and operating equipment. The sequence in which work is performed is an important issue and often determines matters such as layout, staffing needs and site location. Service-based businesses require special attention to the design of processes that can be achieved via service blueprints. Inventory and supply management deal with the raw materials and trading stock held by the organisation as an integral component of the transformation process. All firms strive to reach an inventory level that approximates an economic order quantity; many firms now use a just-in-time focus to minimise the costs of holding excessive stock. A related issue is the supply of raw materials. Firms must decide which suppliers to use and the terms of supply. Business owners must also take into account the type of equipment they will need, and its cost, durability and role.

The final part of operations management is concerned with evaluating, improving and maintaining operational performance. Evaluation and control are usually performed by examining schedules, conducting inspections and measuring productivity ratios. Improvements to operational performance can be made by instituting formal procedures and by the adoption of a quality system. Risk management (protection of the existing assets of the firm) is usually done through security procedures designed to protect people, equipment and ideas, and by taking out suitable insurance policies that will provide financial compensation if a specified risk occurs.

REVIEW QUESTIONS

1. Summarise the different location options available to a new business venture. What factors should be taken into account when assessing the suitability of a particular site?
2. Explain why wait and fail points are considered 'moments of truth' in a service-based business.

3. When choosing a supplier for a new business, what issues should the owner or entrepreneur investigate?
4. Explain the meaning of the term 'quality system' and its significance to the operations of a firm.

DISCUSSION QUESTIONS

1. Describe in detail the kind of business where you think it would be important to understand EOQ.
2. In your opinion, what are the three most common risks that most businesses face? How can these be prevented or reduced?
3. Outline and briefly explain the stages of the operations evaluation and control cycle. Give an example of how this could be applied to a university course.

SUGGESTED READING

Fisk, R., Gountas, S., Hume, M., Gountas, J., Grove, S. & John, J., *Services Marketing, First Asia–Pacific Edition*, John Wiley & Sons Australia, Milton Qld., 2007.

Reid, R.D. & Sanders, N.R., *Operations Management: an integrated approach*, 3rd Edn, John Wiley & Sons, Hoboken, NJ, 2007.

Samson, D. & Singh, P.J., *Operations Management: an integrated approach*, Cambridge University Press, Port Melbourne, Vic, 2008.

Case study

James' guided computer repairs

James Chen and Abdul Aziz share a small apartment over a commercial shopfront in Subang Jaya, Malaysia, only a short walk from the post office. Abdul works part-time as an IT consultant for a local college in Subang Jaya. James has a good sales position with an international medical software design company that he got after finishing his commerce degree in neighbouring Sarawak last year, but he is keen to start his own business. While studying, his entrepreneurship and 3D design double major had him working his computer pretty hard, so it was always in need of repair/upgrades, which he performed himself, becoming a bit of a 'Mr fixit'. He believes that there are many similarly unaccredited self-taught yet technically competent people who just need to be coordinated to build a PC repair franchise network to service all areas of Kuala Lumpur.

Basically, James and Abdul plan to outsource the mobile labour component of the business using a franchise model, effectively creating a network of PC repairers on an exclusive area basis with strong marketing and operational support. James and Abdul will differentiate their service by offering to diagnose the problem via telephone before sending out the repairer, so that the right parts and a good estimate of the time available to solve the problem are supplied to the franchisee accepting the callout. This two-step strategy will allow the repairer to focus on fixing the PC effectively with an expert telephone diagnosis providing a correct fault description to the mobile repairer at least 75% of the time.

The service offer will thus have two main facets: A telephone assistance service will be operated by the franchisors (James and Abdul to begin with) where they will attempt to diagnose and correct software-related problems over the phone in a maximum of 15 minutes for a flat fee. If after 15 minutes the computer problem cannot be resolved remotely, the fee is retained as a callout fee and a local repairer is advised of the probable diagnosis and machine specifications to give them the best chance of repairing the

PC onsite. A callout is then arranged by a local franchisee network partner who has an agreed service response time, processes and standards befitting their relationship to the franchise.

Questions

1. **Create a service blueprint of the mobile service callout, focusing on the wait and fail points that may arise.**
2. **What are the key operational risks in this model?**
3. **How would you measure productivity of the franchisee and the franchisor?**

ENDNOTES

1. J. Corman & R.N. Lussier, *Small Business Management: A Planning Approach*, Irwin, Chicago, 1996, p. 217.
2. N. Ahmad & R.G. Qiu, *Journal of Intelligent Manufacturing*, 'Integrated model of operations effectiveness of small to medium-sized manufacturing enterprises' vol. 20, no. 1, 2008, pp. 79–89.
3. J.N. Pearson, J.S. Bracker & R.E. White, 'Operations management activities of small, high growth electronics firms', *Journal of Small Business Management*, vol. 28, no. 1, January 1990, pp. 20–9.
4. B.A. Saladin & R.R. Nelson, 'How small businesses view productivity and its relationship to operations management', *Journal of Small Business Management*, vol. 22, no. 1, January 1984, pp. 16–22.
5. R.S. Russell & B.W. Taylor, *Operations Management: Creating value along the supply chain*, 6th Edn, Hoboken NJ, 2009, p. 4.
6. W.L. Megginson, M.J. Byrd & L.C. Megginson, *Small Business Management: An Entrepreneur's Guidebook*, 3rd edn, Irwin McGraw-Hill, Boston, 2000, pp. 276–94.
7. J.N. Pearson et al., *see* note 3.
8. Australian Bureau of Statistics, *Characteristics of Small Business, Australia*, ABS, Canberra, 2004.
9. P.R. Todd & R.G. Javalgi, 'Internationalization of SMEs in India: Fostering entrepreneurship by leveraging information technology', *International Journal of Emerging Markets*, vol. 2, no. 2, 2007, pp. 166–80.
10. United Nations Industrial Development Organisation, *Business Incubators*, www.unido.org, 2000. (accessed 25 September 2002).
11. C.S. Galbraith, C.L. Rodriguez, & A.F. DeNoble, 'SME Competitive strategy and location behavior: an exploratory study of high technology manufacturing, *Journal of Small Business Management*, vol. 46, no. 2, 2008, pp. 183–202
12. R.D. Reid & N.R Sanders, Operations Management: An Integrated Approach, 3rd edn, John Wiley & Sons Inc., Hoboken, NJ, 2007, p. 317.
13. ibid, p. 318
14. J.W. English, *How to Organise and Operate a Small Business in Australia*, 7th edn, Allen & Unwin, Sydney, 1998, p. 275.
15. D. Samson & P.J. Singh, *Operations Management: an integrated approach*, Cambridge University Press, Port Melbourne, Vic, 2008, pp. 176–8.
16. ibid, p. 189.
17. C. Lovelock, J. Wirtz & P. Chew, *Essentials of Services Marketing*, Pearson Education, Singapore, 2009, pp. 199–223.
18. R. Fisk, S. Gountas, M. Hume, J. Gountas, S. Grove & J. John, *Services Marketing, First Asia–Pacific Edition*, John Wiley & Sons Australia, Milton Qld., 2007, p. 67.
19. T. Hill, *Small Business Production/Operations Management*, Macmillan, London, 1987, p. 140.

20. J.H. Blackstone & J.F. Cox, 'Inventory management techniques', *Journal of Small Business Management*, vol. 23, no. 2, April 1985, pp. 27–34.

21. M.L. Gulati, *Management of Production Systems*, Amexcel Publishers, New Delhi, 1999, pp. 157–64.

22. see note 5 Russell & Taylor, pp. 10–11.

23. L. Galloway, *Operations Management: The Basics*, Thomson, London, 1996.

24. W.L. Megginson et al., *see* note 4, p. 312.

25. T.S. Hatten, *Small Business: Entrepreneurship and Beyond*, Prentice Hall, Upper Saddle River, 1997.

26. J. Corman & R.N. Lussier, *see* note 1, pp. 230–1.

27. J.G. Longenecker, C.W. Moore, J.W. Petty & L.E. Palich, *Small Business Management: An Entrepreneurial Emphasis*, 13th edn, Thomson South-Western, Mason, 2006, p. 449.

28. T. Hill, *see* note 19, p. 151.

29. T.S. Hatten, *see* note 25, p. 408.

30. W.H. Newman, *Constructive Control: Design and Use of Control Systems*, Prentice Hall, Englewood Cliffs, 1975.

31. S.D. Sousa, E.M. Aspinwall & A.G. Rodrigues, 'Performance measures in English small and medium enterprises: survey results', *Benchmarking: an International Journal*, vol.13, no.1/2, 2006, pp. 120–34.

32. T. Wilde, 'A commitment to quality', in B. Whitford & R. Andrew (eds), *The Pursuit of Quality*, Beaumont Publishing, Perth, 1994, pp. 3–7.

33. D. Stringfellow, 'Challenge for Australian quality — achieving best practice', in B. Whitford & R. Andrew, ibid., pp. 8–13.

34. P.S. Wilton, *The Quality System Development Handbook*, Prentice Hall, Singapore, 1994.

35. X. Zu, L.D. Fredendall & T.J. Douglas, 'The evolving theory of quality management: the role of Six Sigma', *Journal of Operations Management*, vol. 26, no. 5, 2008, pp. 630–50.

36. D. Garvin, 'What does "Product Quality" really mean?', *Sloan Management Review*, vol. 26, no. 1, Fall 1984; A. Parasuraman, L.L. Berry & V.A. Zeithaml, 'SERVQUAL: a multiple-item scale for measuring customer perceptions of service quality', *Journal of Retailing*, vol. 64, no. 1, 1988, pp. 12–40.

37. J.G. Longenecker et al., *see* note 27, p. 464.

38. D.F. Kuratko & R.M. Hodgetts, *Entrepreneurship: A Contemporary Approach*, 5th edn, Harcourt, Fort Worth, 2001, p. 190.

39. S. Fagg, 'Has ERM earned its stripes?' *Risk Management*, April 2006, pp. 14–15.

CHAPTER 13

Human resource issues in new and small firms

Learning objectives

After reading this chapter, you should be able to:

- define and explain the concept of human resource management

- explain the importance of human resource management as a strategic business tool

- outline the major steps in acquiring, maintaining and terminating human resources

- list the main legal obligations of an employer

- explain the key differences in employment practices between large and small firms

- state how human resource management varies among countries in the Asia–Pacific region.

Apart from the single-person enterprise, all businesses will sooner or later employ other people. Additional staff increase the firm's capacity to produce goods or services, allow it to deal with an expanded client base and free up the entrepreneur/business owner to concentrate on the management and growth of the business. Some businesses employ staff at the start of operations; other small firms wait until the business has established itself. Regardless of the point at which staff are employed, there must be a consistent and logical approach to dealing with them. This involves many different issues: How will the people be recruited? On what basis will they be selected? How much should they be paid? How will the workplace be structured? What tasks will be done? What is the best way to evaluate their workplace performance? How does a manager arrange for the termination of employment at a later stage?

Many jobs in the Asia–Pacific region are in the small business sector. The Asia–Pacific Economic Cooperation forum estimates that SMEs provide more than 60 per cent of private sector jobs in the APEC region, and more than 30 per cent of all employment when workers in the government and non-profit sector are taken into account. Micro-firms account for about 30 per cent of all the private sector jobs, small-sized enterprises about 10 per cent, medium-sized firms 20 per cent, and large firms the remaining 40 per cent.[1]

This chapter gives an overview of the practical steps involved in employing people in new ventures and small firms, explains how to maximise performance from staff and briefly examines the differences in employment practices between small and large firms, and across the Asia–Pacific region.

Concept and functions of human resource management

Human resource management (HRM)
A firm's approach to managing its employees.

The term **human resource management (HRM)** can have a number of different meanings. At its simplest, HRM is simply a generic term '...denoting any approach to employment management'.[2] This covers all the aspects related to dealing with people in the workplace, and includes the tasks of recruiting, organising, paying, supervising, disciplining and monitoring them. Since no firm, not even the most sophisticated internet-based enterprise, operates without the input of its employees, HRM is a crucial function in all business entities. Indeed, staff wages and associated expenses are typically one of the largest single-cost items for most small firms,[3] so it makes sense to manage this resource as effectively as possible. Since there are many different ways a firm can structure its HRM activities, and these all directly or indirectly affect its success in other fields, a more accurate description of HRM might be:

> ...competitive advantage through the strategic deployment of a highly committed and capable workforce, using an array of cultural, structural and personnel techniques.[4]

As this definition emphasises, the most crucial aspect of successful HRM focuses on the efficient use of staff to achieve the entrepreneur's goals.

There are many different theories and perspectives on how HRM does — or should — operate within the workplace. At its simplest, however, effective HRM in all organisations revolves around three main issues (see figure 13.1):[5]

- *Acquisition.* How are employees to be found and their services secured for the use of the entrepreneurial business venture?
- *Maintenance.* How can the firm ensure the effective management of its staff once they are working within the enterprise?
- *Termination.* How are people to be let go once their services are no longer required within the firm?

These functions will be explored in further detail in the remainder of this chapter.

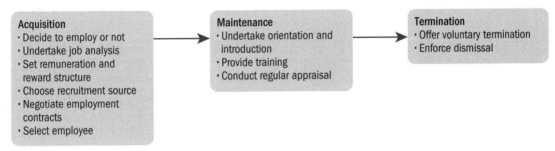

FIGURE 13.1 The three main components of human resource management

HRM as a business strategy

An essential element to bear in mind is that effective HRM involves a large element of strategic decision making by the entrepreneur or small business owner–manager. Although there are mandatory legal requirements that all firms have to adhere to, many other staff issues are determined by the business owner and senior staff. Owners, senior managers and entrepreneurs effectively have a large amount of choice in how they deal with their employees.[6]

Each strategic choice will have an impact on many other aspects of the business. For example, a participative **organisational culture** that promotes shared decision making can often make it difficult to execute decisions when market demands shift dramatically, since it will be expected that most or all employees will have a say in the final response the firm makes. In contrast, a small business run in an autocratic manner by its owner may be able to change direction quickly once the owner makes a decision, but the owner will often be shouldering a large amount of responsibility and stress because there is no delegation of command.

Organisational culture *The shared values, attitudes and behaviour of employees in a firm.*

The particular type of HRM strategy adopted can have major implications for business survival. For example, it has long been argued that particular types of organisational features are more conducive to successful entrepreneurship than others. Successful entrepreneurial firms typically contain senior managers who have a clear vision of the business, are strongly supportive of their staff and operate in a 'blame-free' culture where mistakes and risk-taking (even if unsuccessful) are seen as a necessary part of organisational and individual learning. These firms tend to encourage teamwork and the sharing of credit for success. They offer managers 'prescribed limits' within which experimentation, change and alternative approaches are encouraged. Feedback on ideas and performance is openly given.[7]

However, many large organisations have traditionally adopted strategies that are an active impediment to entrepreneurship. Formal hierarchies, a heavy emphasis on following due procedures and rules, staff specialisation in narrow areas and the division of employees into separate divisions or departments (which often leads to rivalry and mutually destructive conflict) are anathema to the concept of a flexible, adaptive organisation. However, bureaucratic structures are still essential when dealing with very large workforces or when accountability and procedural equity are important policy issues.

Whether an entrepreneurial or a traditional strategy is adopted, both benefits and costs arise. For example, the entrepreneurial structure may be quite flexible and open to innovation, but it is much more difficult to manage than an organisation with clearly defined rules and standard operating procedures. Similarly, the decision to encourage innovation and risk-taking may be laudable, but the firm must also be willing to tolerate the financial and resource costs that arise each time a mistake is made. On the other hand, a traditional structure with rigid standard procedures means that operations can be run like clockwork, but it discourages innovation and initiative. In each case, there is a trade off — between innovation and efficiency, and between flexibility and predictability. Ultimately, only the business owner can decide what constitutes an acceptable HRM trade-off of costs against benefits.

Acquisition of staff

The initial phase of the HRM model covers several activities. In the first place, the firm must make a decision to employ someone. The business owner must consider the implications this will have on the organisational structure of the firm, how the job will be structured and the methods that will be used to recruit and select an appropriate person. Issues relating to the level of remuneration (pay) and the employment contract must also be resolved.

To employ or not?

A new or existing firm becomes an employing business when the owner or entrepreneur makes the decision to recruit staff members. Before beginning the search for a new employee, the owner must make a realistic assessment of why someone is needed, and take a number of issues into account.

Growth goals

How will the employment of another person fit into the overall goals of the business? Will the new employee help achieve targets? Does the new job fit into the objectives set out in the business plan or will that document need to be revised? What staff needs are foreseen for the next few years of the business? (This issue may be extremely hard to estimate for a start-up or rapidly growing business, since future survival and organisational activities are difficult to reliably gauge in advance.)

Personal issues for the business owner

How comfortable will the owner be with the addition of another staff member? This is especially important for entrepreneurs taking on their first employee. Not all personality types are well suited to dealing with staff. Some business owners find it hard to 'let go' and effectively delegate work to another person; others may feel threatened if another person suddenly takes responsibility for part of the business. Alternatively, if an entrepreneur already has several employees, a more important recruitment issue might be whether any new staff member fits in comfortably with the existing internal culture and goals of the business that the owner–manager has created.

Marketing issues

Many human resource issues in a small enterprise are related to the overall successful marketing of the firm. If a business has built up much of its customer base on the founder's personal relationship with clients, how will a new employee taking over client relations affect that relationship? Will it be possible to guarantee the same level of customer service once the owner disengages from the marketing role? (On the other hand, recruiting new staff may have a positive outcome if the business owner is deficient in such skills.)

Operations and facilities

If a decision is made to bring in new staff members, what facilities will be required? An extra person will often mean additional expenditure on equipment and extra working space; and there will be increased administrative responsibilities and legal issues relating to employment of other people (this is discussed in more detail later in the chapter).

Financial issues

Employment of another person will have a direct impact on the financial resources of the firm. Expenditure on wages, on-costs and facilities will have an immediate impact on the cash flow of the firm and, ultimately, on the overall profitability of the enterprise. Does the firm have enough liquidity to cover the increased cash expenditure? Will the new employee ultimately generate enough revenue to cover the cost of being employed? (See the inset 'calculating employee costs and benefits').

Alternatives to employment

It is important to determine whether staff employment is, in fact, the best option for the firm. There may be alternative ways of dealing with increased demands on the firm. If the perceived employment need arises due to the need to correct a specialised problem, it may be more cost effective to bring in an expert consultant or 'pair of hands' adviser to deal with the issue (the function of these advisers is discussed in more detail in chapter 10). Alternatively, can the work arrangements of existing staff be reorganised to accommodate the demand for extra help? Could they be asked to work overtime or can the task be outsourced instead?

CALCULATING EMPLOYEE COSTS AND BENEFITS

One way of determining the cost-effectiveness of an employee is to do the following calculations. (All businesses should be able to fill in the 'Annual expenses' item, but it may not be possible to complete the 'Annual revenue' and 'Surplus/deficit' items if the job is administrative or the employee's revenue productivity is hard to measure.)

Annual expenses

Calculate the true annual cost of an additional staff member. Itemise the estimated expenditure for each of the following items (leave blank if not relevant):

Category	Cost
Yearly wage or salary	
Holiday leave loading	
Replacement of staff during their leave	
Superannuation	
Fringe benefits	
Fringe benefits tax	
Payroll tax	
Workers compensation insurance	
Other insurance premiums	
Office furniture	
Phone lines/calls	
Vehicle expenses	
Training and education	
Stationery	
Bank fees	
Administration	
Other equipment	
Total annual employee expenses	

Annual revenue

Calculate the total income the new employee is expected to generate during the year. If the firm is a retail or manufacturing operation, deduct the cost of goods sold in order to estimate the net additional income the employee will create.

Total sales income by employee	
Less: Cost of goods sold	
Net revenue produced by employee	

Surplus/deficit

Use the above two tables to complete this section. If the new employee produces a surplus, then the decision to employ is relatively straightforward.

Net revenue produced by employee	
Less: *Total annual employee expenses*	
Surplus/(deficit)	

Source: Adapted from M. Schaper, *The Australian Small Business Guide to Hiring New Staff*, Business and Professional Publishing, Sydney, 2000, pp. 19–20.

Organisational structure

Every business has a mechanism for structuring and organising the behaviour of its employees. The organisational design of a firm refers to the way in which people are allocated tasks, the way their activities are coordinated, the way information flows and decisions are made and the way units of people work together.[8] An **organisational structure chart** shows these relationships diagrammatically. Such a chart should not only cover existing employees, but also provide a map as to how any future staff will fit into the overall business.

Although there are many different ways of structuring a business, one key issue for entrepreneurial and small firms is the choice between a traditional (hierarchical) structure and an organic one. The classic hierarchical structure, which is often best exemplified by a bureaucracy, has a strict division of labour into different units, multiple layers of command and an emphasis on hierarchical information and decision making (figure 13.2).

Organisational structure chart
A diagrammatic representation of the way in which employee work relationships are structured within a business.

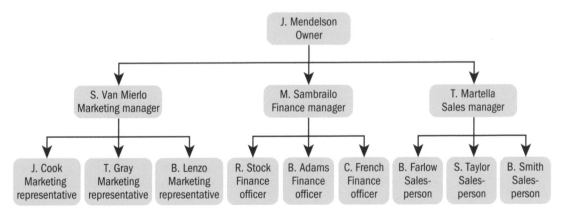

FIGURE 13.2 Simple hierarchical organisational structure

In contrast, organic structures are often found in new small firms, and they emphasise small groups sharing information, ideas and tasks; there is a flat management structure and considerable flexibility. This structure is typically associated with successful micro-firms and truly entrepreneurial large ones.

When planning the introduction of a new staff member, the organisational structure chart should be consulted to determine where the individual will fit into the business. This helps the entrepreneur determine who will be responsible for overseeing the new employee.

Job analysis

Job analysis *The process of determining the duties and skill requirements of a job, and the sort of person who might fit these demands.*

Job description *A written statement of what a job entails, how it is done and under what conditions.*

Job specification *The personal traits and experience required from a prospective employee.*

What, exactly, will the new employee be required to do, and what sort of person best fits the requirements? To answer these questions, a **job analysis** must be performed to determine the duties and skill requirements of a job and the sort of person who might fit these demands. A job analysis contains two main components: a job description and a job specification.[9]

A **job description** is a written statement of what a job entails, how it is done and under what conditions. Typical issues covered here include:
* the job title
* who to report to (name of immediate supervisor)
* work tasks and responsibilities (whether performed daily, weekly, monthly or irregularly)
* the hours of work expected.

A **job specification** details the personal traits and experience required to do the job effectively. In other words, what kind of person, with what kind of qualities, will do this job best? It includes criteria such as:
* the level of education or training a person should have
* how much previous experience (if any) is required for the job
* ability to work as part of a team (if relevant)
* communication skills
* special physical attributes (if required).

These are the elements on which job advertisements are constructed, selection criteria are devised and the suitability of applicants is assessed.

Setting selection criteria

The term *selection criteria* refers to the set of factors by which the business owner judges potential applicants for the new position, and these factors are largely based on the job analysis performed previously. Establishing a simple set of selection factors helps the owner to clarify expectations of the new employee, and to evaluate potential job applicants more accurately.

Firms seeking to develop a more entrepreneurial approach can also use selection criteria as a tool for organisational development. Rather than employees being selected simply on the basis of formal qualifications, work experience and other external indicators, prospective candidates may also be assessed on the basis of individual characteristics. This assessment can include an analysis of their risk-taking propensity, desire for autonomy, need for achievement, goal orientation and internal locus of control.

Remuneration and rewards

How much to pay is another important issue in attracting suitable candidates. While remuneration rates for many jobs are set by regulations or industrial bodies (such as the Fair Work Australia), today the majority of job pay rates are determined by market mechanisms. This means that entrepreneurs have to decide for themselves the most appropriate level of pay. Some owners have strong preconceived ideas about what an employee should be worth. In almost all countries, however, there are legal minimum levels below which pay cannot fall. Setting a pay rate too low may result in a shortage of acceptable applicants, whereas setting a pay rate too high may mean that the firm is paying more for the employee than the employee is generating for the firm.

Another issue to consider is what form the remuneration will take. One common form is a **wage** payment, in which employees are paid a base rate for working a set number of hours per week; this may be topped up by extra payments for additional work (overtime). Another form is a **salary**, which gives employees a 'total pay' package regardless of the number of hours worked; there is no provision for extra payment if additional work is required. Remuneration in some occupations, such as sales work, is often performance-based, with most of the person's income based on the number of items sold, regardless of the hours worked.

The total cost of an employee is usually much more than just the nominal rate of pay shown as wages or salary. There are numerous ancillary costs which must also be taken into account. These 'on-costs' include superannuation or pension (provident fund) contributions, insurance expenses, the provision of equipment and facilities, and fringe benefits for employees (see the inset 'How to compensate employees'). In many Asian countries, it is standard practice to provide an annual bonus to employees. On-costs may run to an extra 20–40 per cent on top of the actual wage or salary paid.

A final element to consider when structuring a compensation package is how to provide a positive incentive for creative, innovative work performance. Successful entrepreneurial firms ensure that employees receive more than just a wage or salary. They also make an effort to provide a reward system that encourages individual enterprise, reward for effort and calculated risk-taking. For example, some large corporations now remunerate in-house entrepreneurs (intrapreneurs) by offering them part-ownership (equity) in the business if their idea generates a new enterprise.

Wage *System of remuneration in which employees are paid at a set hourly rate.*

Salary *Remuneration in which employees receive a fixed 'total pay' package, regardless of the number of hours worked.*

HOW TO COMPENSATE EMPLOYEES

When negotiating an employment contract, there are many possible ways of rewarding staff. Cash and legally required benefits are simply the starting point. Some compensation packages may also include:

- additional retirement funds (over and above the minimum required by superannuation or provident fund laws)
- profit sharing
- equity involvement (employee share ownership schemes)
- flexible time schedules
- unpaid time off
- personal use of company equipment or facilities
- education expenses
- motor vehicles or transport
- recreation services (health club memberships; in-store gymnasium or massage)
- company-funded travel.

Recruitment sources

Once selection criteria and remuneration have been settled, the employee/s must be found. Many business owners are unaware of the full range of options available to them or of the issues that need to be considered when deciding on the correct recruitment medium. The most common sources of job candidates include:

- *Newspapers and websites.* Job advertisements in the print media have traditionally been one of the most common methods of recruiting applicants. It is relatively cost-effective (reaching a wide market for a fixed cost) and can sometimes be targeted at particular industries. Web-based job recruitment is the electronic version of the traditional generic newspaper advertisement. However, both tools are targeted only towards candidates who are actively looking for a new job. Other prospective employees who are already in jobs, but who could be lured away to work for the business if the right offer was made, are unlikely to be reading the situations vacant section or browsing job websites each week.

- *Unsolicited approaches.* Some interested jobseekers may have previously approached the firm seeking employment, and their applications should be kept on file for future reference. These people are obviously aware that the business exists, are keen to find a job and are interested in the work the firm performs.

- *Government employment agencies.* In some nations, government agencies provide (or fund) employment-placement organisations. They often focus on helping the unemployed or those in career transition. Such organisations can offer a cheap, relatively easy way to fill staff vacancies, but the calibre of the job applicants should be carefully assessed.

- *Competitors.* Poaching a valued employee from another business is another option. This can provide the firm with a trained, experienced person familiar with the industry and with the activities of the firm's competitors.

- *Friends and family.* The employment of family members is well documented, especially in small-scale enterprises.[10] Employing family members usually provides a common sense of purpose, a greater commitment to the long-term survival of the firm, and a sense of security that arises from working with people the owner or entrepreneur already knows and trusts. Similar considerations often apply in the recruitment of friends. However, not all family members have the necessary skills needed for particular jobs, and it can often be difficult to disentangle personal and emotional issues from workplace performance.

- *Educational and special-interest organisations.* Secondary schools, industry groups (employer associations), trade unions and universities often have a database of prospective jobseekers with specialist qualifications. This option is often valuable when a firm requires applicants to have a degree, a particular training qualification or specialist industry experience.

- *Recruitment agencies.* These consultants specialise in conducting the recruitment and selection process for client firms, and they are often engaged to 'headhunt' or seek out particular people. They use their databases of interested jobseekers, market research, personal contacts and industry sources to locate and assess potential applicants.

Once a pool of potential employees has been collated, the business owner needs to decide which seems most suitable. Jobseekers can be evaluated in a number of ways. The most common is by conducting an interview, which is usually done face-to-face. If candidates are applying from another city or country, telephone or video-conference interviews can also be held. Interview data can be supplemented by other information, such as a portfolio of previous work (useful in the creative industries), realistic job previews (where candidates spend time in the actual workplace), role-playing activities, and referees' reports.[11]

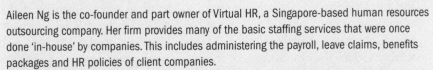

Entrepreneur profile

Aileen Ng, Virtual HR

Aileen Ng is the co-founder and part owner of Virtual HR, a Singapore-based human resources outsourcing company. Her firm provides many of the basic staffing services that were once done 'in-house' by companies. This includes administering the payroll, leave claims, benefits packages and HR policies of client companies.

As Aileen explains, 'Outsourcing to Virtual HR liberates strategy and mitigates risk. We liberate HR managers from administrative tedium to concentrate on strategic people development. We mitigate the risks that are an inevitable side effect of fast moving globalised HR and technology trends. We undertake for our clients the capital investments involved in monitoring these trends and maintaining progressive payroll and HR technology.'

Virtual HR now administers an annual payroll of S$100 million for numerous organisations spread across South-East Asia. Founded in 1996, Virtual HR's clients now include Singapore government agencies, multinational corporations and volunteer welfare organisations, mostly with a staff headcount of between 30 and 300.

When it comes to their internal HR practices, Aileen is also conscious of her company's role as an example to the Singaporean business world.

'Our staff know that working in Virtual HR means tremendous development and challenges to their professional knowledge and qualifications, and places them in the forefront of the industry. Some survive this culture, and some will fall out within three months if they do not possess the strong desire to learn.'

'We recruit mainly via staff or client referrals. We conduct multiple interviews with candidates, including using external interviewers to minimise blind spots.'

Virtual HR uses a mix of permanent and temporary staff. 'A flexible workforce allows us to engage the staff on an 'on demand' basis, and it also enables us to customise work patterns to suit our staff, such as telecommuting. These practices are not really common in Singapore, but as an HR company, we are game to test new grounds. It improves our advice to clients.'

For performance appraisals, Virtual HR uses a mix of key performance indicators (KPIs) and behavioural measures, and employees know how they are ranked against their peers. 'As in a football game or any sports, we believe you should always know your score.'

Staff are also rewarded with revenue sharing and access to a profit-sharing scheme.

'As a business operator, it is most challenging to juggle between building the business and building the people. But without financial strength, you can't reward people or develop people, no matter how strongly you believe in investing in people.'

For more information, see www.virtualHR.com.sg

Profile contributed by Geoff Baker, Murdoch University Business School.

The employment contract

An employment contract needs to be negotiated between the business owner and the employee; this document spells out pay rates, additional benefits, holiday and leave entitlements, probation periods and termination issues. In all cases, there are still minimum conditions (such as basic rates of pay, annual leave entitlements, illness and maternity leave) that must be observed, regardless of the final form the contract takes.

Employment relationships can be constructed in various ways:

- *Industrial awards.* These are prescribed minimum conditions of employment set out for particular industries by Fair Work Australia or similar regulatory entities. Employers can pay above the award, but generally may not go below these conditions. These were once common in Australia, but are increasingly being replaced by other types of employment agreement.
- *Individual written contracts.* In many cases it is possible for the employer and employee to directly negotiate most of the terms of employment, such as working hours, pay rates and fringe benefits, and then settle on a formal written contract that spells out the rights and obligations of each party and the terms on which the contract may be ended. These are sometimes referred to as workplace agreements in Australia and New Zealand, and many employment arrangements take this form of contract. In some circumstances, employee unions may negotiate the contract collectively on behalf of union members at a worksite, thus removing the need for an employer to negotiate directly with each staff member.
- *Informal contracts.* In many situations, employees work on the basis of an unwritten agreement. Pay, conditions and benefits are usually set at about the norm for a particular industry. These common law contracts are often based on the assumption by both parties that they conform to established industrial precedents. However, in the event of a dispute, it may be difficult to determine the true rights and responsibilities of both employer and employee.

Maintenance

Once a suitable employee has been found and engaged, the task of the business owner is not over. The next HRM function involves retaining people in the firm and ensuring that they work as effectively as possible. This task is sometimes more demanding than the acquisition phase.

Although it may sound like a cliché, the expression 'people are our most important asset' still holds true in many cases. Many small business owners complain that a lack of suitable staff is a key barrier to further growth, and that a lack of confidence in the ability of current employees often prevents them from letting go and allowing others to manage the firm on their behalf. This is often compounded by the entrepreneurial personality, which can find it hard to delegate work.

Orientation and induction

Once the new employee has been signed on, the business owner needs to introduce the firm's existing employees, explain current work procedures and operating processes, arrange for any necessary additional training, and perhaps also introduce the employee to customers, suppliers and other owners of the business (if any). This ensures that the new employee is fully aware of the working environment, and minimises mistakes or lost time. It is also common to have a probation period at the start of employment, during which time the employee may be dismissed for breaches of requirements or an inability to satisfactorily perform the work.

Motivation mechanisms

Motivation is the willingness of employees to exert effort to achieve business goals.[12] Motivating people to perform to the best of their ability and in ways that benefit the business organisation has always been an important issue for managers at all levels of a firm. For example, just one poorly motivated employee in a restaurant can generate many customer complaints and the loss of future customers. There is no single measure which can guarantee continued high levels of motivation, although HR theorists have put forward a number of theoretical frameworks that might help.[13]

> **Motivation** *The willingness of employees to exert effort to achieve business goals.*

In a practical sense, however, there are a number of ways a business owner can enhance motivation and performance. At a basic level, a satisfactory level of pay is necessary. As the proponents of 'equity theory' point out, employees who believe they are underpaid will cut back on their efforts or seek a new job if the gap between their remuneration and those of others is too great.[14] In many industries, performance-based pay is used as a motivating tool, via mechanisms such as piece-rate pay (payment per item produced), commission-based sales, wage incentive schemes and profit-sharing plans. Although the evidence is far from clear, such programs also appear to provide improved financial returns for firms as well.[15]

Other actions that are believed to improve employee motivation include allowing employees to work flexible hours; including them in decision-making about critical business goals; providing them with an opportunity to purchase shares (equity) in the firm; and ensuring that reward systems match individual needs. For employees with a high need for personal achievement, the opportunity for advancement or for assuming a higher level of responsibility can be an important incentive.[16] Such measures are also conducive to the development of an entrepreneurial culture within the firm.

Entrepreneur profile

Prakash Menon, NIIT

One particularly clever way of handling salaries is demonstrated by IT education expert Prakash Menon, president of NIIT (China). Menon tells of how, when he began in his position in 1988, everyone in his office left work at 5.30 pm sharp, even if critical projects were still incomplete. 'Normally, nobody in this industry leaves at 5.20 pm. The IT field is about curiosity, learning new things,' he says. 'Worldwide, you see IT people staying late in their offices.' Menon sought to address the issue by spending more time with his Chinese employees, eating with them and talking with them, in order to be closer to them.

The result? 'People still left at 5.30,' says Menon, exasperated.

Next, he tried offering more incentives, such as a family entertainment fund. This fund covered the cost of inviting all employees and their family members out once a year to thank them for their support. 'My idea was to make employees feels that the organisation was part of their life.'

Did it work? Menon sighs: 'They still left at 5.30.'

Frustrated, he asked other directors for their opinions, but no one could give him an answer. Finally, he asked a colleague directly. 'Why do you leave at 5.30 pm?' The colleague answered: 'It's very simple: if the organisation pays me this low-level salary, then I will offer this level of effort.'

That answer 'hit me like a bolt,' says Menon.

Menon revamped the payment system dramatically so that only 50% of salary for employees was fixed; the rest was variable. 'If you achieve 80% of the variable salary, then your salary is similar to the market rate. So, every employee also had the possibility of getting 20% more than the market rate.'

The scheme met with an electric reception, Menon says. 'No one went home at 5.30 from then on, and everybody's figured out how to get the 20% extra. Now the company is developing at a completely different pace.' Menon explains that he didn't actually change the compensation amount under the new scheme. 'I paid the people the same, but they felt differently. Before, they thought, 'this is a fixed salary, so why should I work harder?' It is different to India. If people in India are paid a decent salary, they immediately think they should work very hard and are loyal. They develop strong emotional ties to the company.'

Training

Another way to improve performance at work is to ensure that staff have the appropriate sets of skills to perform their tasks. Almost all industries operate in a dynamic and changing environment, and it is unlikely that employees will always come fully equipped with complete knowledge and the ability to perform their work role perfectly. Training removes or reduces shortfalls and gives the business a greater set of skills than it can productively use.

Training needs analysis *An evaluation of the skills and knowledge employees need, what they currently hold, and what gap exists.*

A **training needs analysis** is an evaluation of the skills and knowledge employees need, what they currently hold, and what (if any) gap exists between these two conditions. Such an analysis is usually made with reference to the firm's goals and its staffing (organisational) chart, and this helps the owner set out a course of future action to remedy the skills and knowledge shortfall. Ideally, such training will not only equip staff to do their current jobs more effectively, but will also allow them to further their careers within the organisation, thereby equipping the firm to better deal with future business challenges.

If managed correctly, effective training can result in direct tangible benefits for the business, including a more efficient use of staff time; reduced errors and waste within the workplace; higher sales; a greater adoption of new ideas and technologies; improved communication; enhanced customer satisfaction; and a better ability to deal with change and competition.[17] Some common training areas include:

- generic management skills
- customer service skills
- use of existing or new technology
- production processes
- business planning

- refresher courses in current business processes
- legal compliance issues
- quality systems
- environmental, health and safety issues.

Training can be undertaken in a variety of ways. Within the workplace, training can involve mentoring by other, more experienced staff; job rotation among different duties; or informal advice from work colleagues. Outside the workplace, training can be accessed via formal enrolment in a technical college or tertiary institution; participation in short-term professional development courses by accredited trainers; or development programs offered by small business agencies, private organisations and government departments.

Performance appraisal

Evaluating the performance of employees at work is also important. An employer needs to know if new recruits are achieving what they set out to do for the firm and, if not, why this is so. Some of the many appraisal mechanisms that exist include:

- *Interviews* — personal, direct evaluation of employees in a formal context.
- *Management by objectives* — providing a set of discrete goals that employees should achieve within a given time frame; employee performance is subsequently judged on capacity to meet these goals.
- *Rating scales* — questionnaires that ask supervisors to rank employees on a number of different work-related dimensions.
- *On-the-job assessment* — direct observation of employees while in their usual work environment.

There are some more subjective, informal mechanisms that are also used. These are more common in small firms, where there is limited time or inclination to undertake formal procedures, and the owner often personally knows or directly supervises the employee. These mechanisms are:

- *Stakeholder feedback* — input from immediate supervisors, the employee's workplace peers and other key people with an involvement in the firm (such as other owners of the business).
- *External feedback* — judging performance on the basis of feedback from outside parties, for example, the number and type of customer complaints or compliments about an employee.
- *Owner/entrepreneur's assessment* — informal, subjective assessment made largely on the owner/entrepreneur's personal impressions of a worker's performance to date.

It is also possible to make some evaluations about staff management on a firm-wide basis. One common indicator is the level of **staff turnover**; that is, the number of employees who leave the business. This is often the ultimate indicator of staff dissatisfaction with the working conditions in the business, and can be due to a wide combination of factors: low pay, poor in-house facilities and equipment, bad management practices or inadequate training and induction. Where a firm has a higher turnover than the industry norm, or the rate has increased over time, it is often indicative of poor employee management practices.[18]

Staff turnover *The number of employees who leave the business.*

Termination

The final component of any employment relationship occurs when the firm and employee part company.

A *voluntary termination* occurs when an employee leaves of his or her own free choice, and this situation is relatively easily handled. A staff member may be dissatisfied working in the firm or may decide to retire or pursue a new career; they may have plans to move away from the geographical area where the business is based, or else want to leave the paid workforce for a period of time.

An *enforced dismissal* is more difficult. Employees may be dismissed because the firm can no longer afford their services; there is no longer demand for the tasks they perform (they have become redundant to the business's needs); there has been a restructure of the organisation; they have a history of poor work performance; or they have broken the law or employment contract. In many small firms and entrepreneurial business ventures, where failure rates are usually much higher than in established large corporations, dismissal will also occur when the business venture itself collapses.

Termination of a worker's employment has a number of consequences for the business as a whole. Consideration must be given to the financial payouts the firm may have to make (such as payment in lieu of notice or payment of accrued leave owing) and to the effect a dismissal will have on other employees in the firm: Will it affect morale? Who will do the job of the dismissed person? In some cases, it may be necessary to ensure that a disgruntled employee does not sabotage relationships with the firm's existing suppliers or customers, or pass on valuable intellectual property to a competitor.

Sometimes there is an alternative to outright termination, such as shifting employees from full-time to part-time work (useful when there is a temporary short-term fall in demand); providing training and mentoring (to help overcome any skill deficiencies); or finding the employee work with one of the firm's strategic allies.

Given the complexities and difficulties inherent in any termination decision, voluntary or not, small business owners are strongly encouraged to seek advice from a lawyer or an employer association before dismissing an employee.

What would you do?

Engineered to succeed

You are the owner and operator of a small, specialty, mineral-processing engineering company. You have years of experience in the industry with a wide network of contacts, and a year ago decided to start your own business.

Together with just three other employees, you have rapidly built a niche role in designing and constructing mineral-processing operations in processing plants. You have won projects around the world; mostly in mineral-rich Western Australia.

With a small office, thin management structure, minimal outsourcing and careful task management, you have developed an enviable reputation in the industry for delivering projects on time and under budget.

Recently, global commodity prices have fallen, putting the mining industry into a downturn. New projects are rare and larger engineering firms are laying off excess staff. Some are even warehousing key staff – a process where the company retains the employee on a fully-paid basis, even though there are no current projects to work on. This process allows firms to retain valued, highly skilled employees who can be quickly allocated to new projects in future. Labour hire firms specialising in the mining industry are also reporting a decline in their business.

You have recently been invited to bid for a new project, of scope larger than your previous assignments. It will require an additional five staff over seven months, including two specialist engineering roles and three trade roles (such as welders and electricians). The best specialist engineers you know are either actively employed or warehoused by larger engineering firms. Winning this project will possibly see you through the downturn, and lead to potential growth for your firm during the economic recovery. However, due to the economic slump, you don't know if you can guarantee ongoing employment for these new staff beyond this contract.

The specialist engineers you know have highly sought-after skills and would prefer to have full-time permanent employment, with a guaranteed job and associated benefits. The labour hire companies say they can provide the skills you need, but when pressed for details, they are not able to provide the names of any specialists you know and trust. You are concerned that without specialist skills your firm's ability to deliver on this project, and your reputation, may be at risk.

You have just a month left to find the staff you need.

Questions
1. **What would be the most effective way to find the needed employees?**
2. **What type of employment contract would you use, and why?**

Governmental and regulatory requirements

Employers have to meet a wide range of potential legal obligations when taking on any new staff, although not all of these laws apply in every jurisdiction throughout the Asia–Pacific region.

Occupational health and safety

Employers have a general duty of care to ensure that the workplace they provide, and the conditions they expect their employees to operate in, are reasonably safe, and that all possible steps are taken to eliminate or at least minimise the risk of work-related death or injury. Most governments have specific legislation that lays down the employer's duties in this respect, and there are also agencies that police the level of workplace health and safety.[19]

Workers compensation insurance

This is insurance that is taken out to meet the cost of treating, rehabilitating or compensating any injured staff members who have been hurt in a work-related event. Premiums for this type of insurance will vary, depending on the level of risk for each industry.

Taxation

Employers must give details of their employees to taxation authorities and, in most countries, deduct tax from their wages or salaries and forward this tax to the tax office. In some cases, there may also be additional taxes or levies that firms have to deduct from employees' pay and forward to tax authorities; in Australia, such deductions include Higher Education Contribution Scheme (HECS) debts and childcare support payments.

Equal employment opportunity

In many jurisdictions, it is illegal to discriminate against job applicants on the grounds of age, sex, physical disability, ethnicity or marital status. Unless these are directly relevant to the job, such specifications must be kept out of job advertisements, selection criteria or job specification forms.

Retirement and superannuation funds

In several Asia–Pacific countries, firms are required to make payments towards their employees' retirement schemes. This is the case, for example, with the Central Provident Fund system in Singapore, the Mandatory Provident Fund in Hong Kong and the Superannuation Guarantee Levy in Australia. Firms must arrange for the required money to be forwarded to the relevant retirement or superannuation fund at predetermined intervals.

TABLE 13.1 Retirement/pension/superannuation information

Country	Authority
Australia	Superannuation Guarantee Levy, Australian Taxation Office, www.ato.gov.au
Hong Kong	Mandatory Provident Fund Schemes Authority, www.mpfahk.org
Malaysia	Employees Provident Fund, www.kwsp.gov.my
Singapore	Central Provident Fund Board, www.cpf.gov.sg
China	Ministry of Labour and Social Security, www.molss.gov.cn
India	Employees' Provident Fund Organisation, www.epfindia.com

Suitable records

To supplement other recordkeeping requirements, statutes in many countries require employers to keep adequate records of the time worked by employees, the payments made to them, leave accrued and/or used, fringe benefits, and related payments made for tax, retirement or workers compensation purposes.

Information on these employer responsibilities is usually available from professional business advisers, small business assistance agencies or accountancy practices, government departments concerned with labour or employment (see table 13.2), and the various taxation authorities (listed in chapter 8).

TABLE 13.2 Main government agencies dealing with labour or employment issues

Country	Authority
Australia	Department of Education, Employment and Workplace Relations, www.deewr.gov.au
New Zealand	Department of Labour, www.dol.govt.nz
Hong Kong	Labour Department, www.labour.gov.hk
Malaysia	Ministry of Human Resources, www.mohr.gov.my
Singapore	Ministry of Manpower, www.mom.gov.sg
China	Ministry of Human Resources and Social Security of the People's Republic of China, www.mohrss.gov.cn
India	Ministry of Labour, http://labour.nic.in or Ministry of Micro, Small and Medium Enterprises, www.laghu-udyog.com

Differences in employment practices between large and small firms

Research into HRM practices in the Asia–Pacific region has traditionally focused on large firms in the corporate sector, and there is still a shortage of comprehensive information about how owner–managers of small firms manage their staff.[20] However, the evidence to date suggests that there are a number of ways in which human resource management in small firms is different from that in large corporations and public bodies.

Firstly, HRM methods in small businesses tend to be more informal.[21] There is less reliance on standardised procedures and regulations, and more emphasis on specific judgements and solutions that attempt to deal with the issue or problem at hand.[22] For example, whereas a government department or multinational corporation might have well-established rules about how to handle leave requests or temporary recruitment of staff, in a small firm the owner or another senior manager is more likely to make a decision on the spot based on current needs and the situation. It is only as new small firms grow larger that HRM practices tend to change, become more formalised and place more emphasis on hierarchy, documentation and administrative processes.[23]

Secondly, in small businesses, managerial decision-making tends to be more closely concentrated at the top of the organisational apex (that is, in the hands of the owner), rather than diffused among different members of the firm.[24] This means that the owner or entrepreneur is more likely to be personally responsible for HRM decisions than would be the case in a large business.

Thirdly, structure and composition of the workforce are different. Several researchers have shown that small businesses tend to have a smaller proportion of union members in their workforce, more members of the owner's family working in the firm, a higher proportion of part-time workers, and staff with lower-level formal qualifications.[25] Smaller enterprises are also less likely to adopt explicit training and human resource development programs.[26]

Fourthly, there are subjective (or perceived) differences. A large problem that many small firms face is the perception among employees that a job in a new or small business is a second-rate option compared with employment in a large public corporation or government body. Although the recent history of large-scale retrenchments from corporations and government agencies has changed this view somewhat, it is still strongly held by many people. It is often assumed that career prospects are limited in small firms; that they do not have sufficient capacity to pay high wages, salaries and benefits; and, in the case of family-based businesses, that owners will always give preference to family members over talented outsiders.[27]

Finally, the training and development of staff within small firms can be less professional than in a larger private enterprise or government agency. International evidence suggests that the training provided in SMEs is more generalised, ad hoc and informal than is usually the case elsewhere.[28]

Taking these factors into account, it appears that small and new firms have more difficulty than larger organisations in attracting and retaining suitable staff, and in developing their skills to the most productive level. However, this overlooks the fact that small firms do offer some competitive advantages. They can often provide a more intimate, family-like atmosphere in which all employees know one another and people are on first-name terms. Small business owner–managers can also provide more flexibility for their staff, since the absence of formal human resource policies or strict rules allows them scope to accommodate staff needs. Also, it is often easier for employees to advance to the top of a small business than it is in a large corporation. In many situations, it is not uncommon for a valued staff member to eventually buy out the original owner or to become a part-owner. These opportunities rarely come to employees in a large corporation. In fact, recent evidence seems to support these conclusions: small firms often record lower total employee turnover rates than their larger counterparts, which appears to confirm the view that small companies are often the preferred workplace for many employees.[29]

HRM variations across the Asia–Pacific region

There are some substantial differences in HRM policies and practices among nations in the Asia–Pacific region. For example, the use of fairly comprehensive recruitment and selection procedures is common in Singapore, Malaysia, Australia and New Zealand, but less so in Hong Kong. Businesses in India and several South-East Asian countries offer substantial supplementary benefits to their employees (such as medical services, housing subsidies and 'thirteenth month' bonuses), whereas such compensation is not usually found in Australia or New Zealand.[30]

National variations can also be seen in the regulatory framework that governments in each country have established for employers. Australia and New Zealand have traditionally had a high level of union involvement in the workplace, although this has declined substantially in recent years. As a result, both countries have fairly extensive rules to protect employees. Singapore has a substantial body of employment legislation, but it focuses more on productivity and economic development than on employee protection. Malaysia has a wide variety of employment laws, but these are not as extensive as those in Australia or New Zealand. In Hong Kong, the Special Administrative Region government, like its colonial predecessors, has adopted a minimalist approach, with only limited regulation of the labour market.[31] Chinese regulations are still evolving and can often vary significantly from one province to another, especially in regards to issues such as minimum wages.[32] Indian labour laws tend to be quite complex and highly prescriptive, and it is usually quite difficult for entrepreneurs to dismiss staff.[33]

Another way that countries in the Asia–Pacific differ is in the use of family members within the firm. Although there has always been a large overlap between family-based businesses and small firms throughout the world, many of Asia's largest and most aggressive firms have continued to be family-run even as they have grown. Many Chinese-owned businesses are strongly centralised and dominated by the family patriarch. Preference in employment is often given to family members, and outsourcing, rather than recruiting new staff, is often a preferred means of entrepreneurial growth.[34] In contrast, few large entrepreneurial firms in Australia or New Zealand have remained completely in the hands of the originating family — their interests often become diluted by equity investors, and as the firm grows it is more likely to be run by a professional manager drawn from outside the family. The characteristics of Chinese-run businesses are discussed in more detail in chapter 2.

A final issue to consider is the **informal sector**. In some countries, large portions of the workforce are not regulated by the state; they operate outside the conventional framework of labour rules, regulations and compliance. India, for example, has a large level (more than half of the workforce) of informal-sector employees, who are frequently found operating in unregistered business organisations. Such employees usually do not have access to the protections provided by labour laws.[35]

Informal sector
Economic activity that is not regulated, monitored, enforced or taxed by a government.

SUMMARY

Human resource management plays a crucial role in starting a new entrepreneurial business venture and in the successful operation of existing small firms. Although there are prescribed minimum legal standards that firms must follow, there is also considerable scope for business owners to exercise their own judgement when establishing the firm's HRM activities. Successful entrepreneurial firms tend to avoid conventional hierarchical structures, and prefer more flexible working systems that place an emphasis on risk-taking, information sharing, management support and an enterprising organisational culture.

The HRM function of acquisition begins when the entrepreneur decides to employ a new staff member. Issues to take into account at this point are the growth goals of the firm, marketing and operational factors, financial implications, alternatives to employing another person and the owner's willingness to give up some responsibility and power.

Once a decision has been made to employ someone, the organisational structure chart must be reassessed, a job analysis carried out, selection criteria established, suitable compensation determined and the appropriate recruitment source chosen. When a candidate has been selected, an employment contract must be organised.

The maintenance HRM function centres around retaining and developing employees to maximise their effectiveness within the organisation. These aspects include orientation and induction, motivational mechanisms, training, and performance appraisal.

The final HRM function is that of termination. People may leave the business voluntarily or they may be dismissed, in which case there are a number of complexities that must be considered.

All governments impose a number of regulatory and legislative requirements on employing organisations. These include issues relating to occupational health and safety, workers compensation, taxation, equal employment opportunity, retirement funding and the maintenance of employment records.

There are some significant differences in employment practices between small and large firms. Small businesses tend to have more informal employment practices and may find it harder to recruit staff. To counter this, small enterprises need to emphasise that they can provide greater flexibility in their staffing arrangements and career advancement opportunities.

Differences also exist between nations in the Asia–Pacific region. Legal frameworks vary, as do the types of remuneration and benefits paid to staff. Compared with many other business models, enterprises owned by ethnic Chinese entrepreneurs tend to remain in family control and to give preference to kin, even when the enterprises grow larger.

REVIEW QUESTIONS

1. Outline the most common sources of job candidates.
2. What issues does an owner or entrepreneur need to consider before deciding whether to employ another staff member?
3. How do employment practices vary from one country to another in the Asia–Pacific region?
4. Outline and briefly explain the major legal obligations of employers.
5. List the major differences in employment practices between small and large firms.

DISCUSSION QUESTIONS

1. If you owned a small restaurant, what would be the most important orientation and induction information to give a new cook on their first day at work?
2. Which is the better approach to removing an employee: a voluntary termination or an enforced one? Why?
3. A self-employed signwriter working from a small suburban business incubator realises that he can no longer manage his workload alone, and he resolves to recruit an assistant to help him with his painting work. Such a move will mean additional equipment and outlays (estimated expense: A$20 000), and the market wage rate for such a position is about A$55 000 per annum. The signwriter also estimates that on-costs will be another 30 per cent. An assistant should help boost firm revenue by A$350 000 during his or her first year at work, with a cost of goods sold of 75 per cent. With these outlays, is employing a new person a worthwhile investment of time and money? Why?

SUGGESTED READING

Kotey, B. & Slade, P., 'Formal human resource management practices in small growing firms', *Journal of Small Business Management*, vol.43, no.1, January 2005, pp. 16–40.

Matlay, H. (ed.), 'Human Resource Aspects of Small Business and Enterprise Development', special edition of the *Journal of Small Business and Enterprise Development*, vol. 9, no. 3, 2002.

New Zealand Department of Labour *Employment Relationships: An Employers Guide*, Wellington, Department of Labour, 2009.

Schaper, M., *The Australian Small Business Guide to Hiring New Staff*, Business and Professional Publishing, Sydney, 2000.

Stone, R.J., *Managing Human Resources: An Asian Perspective*, John Wiley & Sons, Brisbane, 2009.

Case study

DotHot Fashions

DotHot Fashions is a small fashion design company, established 15 years ago by Dorothy ('Dot') Ho. Initially, Dot opened her female clothing design and retail store with only three employees: herself, her aunt Kay and her niece Kim. Both Kim and Kay contributed a small amount of the start-up capital and held a small proportion of the firm's shares. Sales were slow, and the three women were more than able to handle all of the chores. However, over the years, as the store's reputation grew and sales increased, Dot realised that she would have to hire more people. She then employed two designers, Anna and Simon, to help her with that side of the firm. This left the aunt and the niece to do the in-store retail sales and other day-to-day operational tasks.

While on a fashion tour five years ago, Dot met a young designer, Yvette Walenski, whose work she had seen previously in a show, and to which she had taken an immediate liking. Although DotHot Fashions already employed two designers, Dot felt that Yvette, with her different approach to design, would appeal to a much larger and younger clientele, and so she decided to ask her to join the company. The additional salary meant an increase in operating costs, but Yvette worked hard and enthusiastically.

During the first three years of her employment, Yvette's designs sold well and the company's sales increased dramatically. However, she was not happy about being treated as the most junior designer, especially as Dot, Anna and Simon travelled extensively and she was often left behind. Last year, Simon had a car accident and, after recovering, did not return to work. Yvette felt that the time had now come for her to be made chief designer.

However, Dot decided that both Anna and Yvette should stay in their current positions with an increase in salary, while Dot took on the extra duties. This news disappointed Yvette enormously, to the extent that she even considered looking for a new job. However, her friends pointed out that she was receiving a top salary and would soon enjoy the benefits that Anna already received.

With the extra work and increased family commitments, Dot spent the next nine months in a constant rush to meet deadlines. She vaguely noticed that Yvette was not quite herself, and that the standard of her work dropped markedly. Yvette's recent designs lacked the flair and instant marketability that had previously been her hallmark.

To overcome her tight workload, Dot concluded that it would be best to hire people to help with the in-store sales, and allow her aunt and niece to handle the non-selling activities. 'It's easier to train someone to sell than it is to teach them how to handle stock, payroll and administrative work. If I lose one of the new people and am short of a salesperson, I can always call on Aunty Kay or Kim to help out. However, if I hire a woman to take care of stock or purchasing and she leaves, the burden will fall directly on my shoulders,' she told her relatives.

Four new people have since been brought on board in the last eight weeks to do the sales tasks, and Dot has also decided to further increase the salaries of both designers, mainly to address Yvette's obvious unhappiness.

Unfortunately, things have not worked out as well as Dot had hoped. The new staff do not seem to know how to sell. Additionally, one of them has already asked for a pay rise. When Dot replied that she would have to think about it, the woman pointed out that all other retail stores in the area were paying 20 per cent more for equivalent jobs than DotHot Fashions. And, just as worrying, Yvette is not producing any new designs.

Questions

1. **Is an increase in salary likely to restore Yvette's motivation and work performance?**
2. **Evaluate Dot's performance as a human resources manager. What are her weaknesses?**
3. **Potentially, there is at least one other major human resources issue in this case that Dot appears to have overlooked. Review this case and outline what you think the undiscussed issue is.**

Case study prepared by the small-business staff, School of Accounting and Law, RMIT University.

ENDNOTES

1. APEC SME Working Group, *Profile of SMEs and SME Issues in APEC 1990–2000*, World Scientific Publishing, Singapore, p. 1.
2. J. Storey, *Human Resource Management: A Critical Text*, 3rd edn, Thomson Learning, London, 2007.
3. J.G. Longenecker, C.W. Moore, J.W. Petty & L.E. Palich, *Small Business Management: An Entrepreneurial Emphasis*, 13th edn, South-Western, Cincinnati, 2007.
4. J. Storey, *see* note 2, p. 6.
5. S.P. Robbins, P.S. Low & M.P. Mourell, *Managing Human Resources*, Prentice Hall, Sydney, 1986, pp. 9–10; A. Nankervis, R. Compton & M. Baird, *Strategic Human Resource Management*, 4th edn, Nelson Thomson, Melbourne, 2002.
6. A. Nankervis et al., *see* note 5.
7. J.B. Quinn, 'Managing innovation: Controlled chaos', *Harvard Business Review*, May–June 1985, pp. 73–84.
8. K. Bartol, D. Martin, M. Tein & G. Matthews, *Management: A Pacific Rim Focus*, 4th edn, McGraw-Hill, Sydney, 2005.
9. G. Dessler, J. Griffiths & B. Lloyd-Walker, *Human Resource Management*, 3rd edn, Prentice Hall, Melbourne, 2007, pp. 87.
10. CPA Australia, *Small Business Survey Program: Employment Issues*, CPA Australia, Melbourne, 2002, p. 4.
11. M. Schaper, *The Australian Small Business Guide to Hiring New Staff*, Business and Professional Publishing, Sydney, 2000, p. 72.
12. K. Bartol et al., *see* note 8.
13. S.P. Robbins, R. Bergman, I. Stagg & M. Coulter, *Management*, 5th edn, Prentice Hall, Sydney, 2008.
14. J.E. Dittrich & M.R. Carrell, 'Organisational equity perceptions, employee job satisfaction, and departmental absence and turnover rates', *Organisation Behavior and Human Performance*, August 1979, pp. 29–40.

15. H. Rheem, 'Performance management programs', *Harvard Business Review*, September–October 1996, pp. 8–9.
16. S.P. Robbins et al., *see* note 13.
17. D.H. Bangs, *The Personnel Planning Guide: Successful Management of Your Most Important Asset*, 3rd edn, Upstart Publishing, Dover, NH, 1986.
18. J. English, *How to Organise and Operate a Small Business in Australia*, 7th edn, Allen & Unwin, Sydney, 1998, p. 299.
19. Safework Australia, *Health and Safety*, www.safeworkaustralia.gov.au, 2009.
20. L.X. Cunningham & C. Rowley, 'Human resource management in Chinese small and medium enterprises: A review and research agenda', *Personnel Review*, vol. 36, no. 3, 2007, pp. 415–39.
21. J.M.P. De Kok, L.M. Uhlaner & A.R. Thurik, *Human Resource Management within Small and Medium-sized Firms: Facts and Explanations*, EIM Business and Policy Research, Zotermeer, The Netherlands, 2002; T. Bartram, 'Small firms, big ideas: The adoption of human resource management in Australian small firms', *Asia–Pacific Journal of Human Resources*, vol. 43, no. 1, April 2005, pp. 137–54; J. Gilbert & G. Jones, 'Managing human resources in New Zealand small businesses', *Asia–Pacific Journal of Human Resources*, vol. 38, no. 2, Summer 2000, pp. 55–69.
22. L. Sels, S. De Winne, J. Delmotte, J. Maes, D. Faems & A. Forrier, 'Linking HRM and small business performance,' *Small Business Economics*, no. 26, 2006, pp. 83–101.
23. B. Kotey & A. Sheridan, 'Changing HRM practices with firm growth', *Journal of Small Business and Enterprise Development*, vol. 11 no. 4, 2004, pp. 474–85.
24. Department of Industry, Science and Tourism, *The 1995 Business Longitudinal Survey*, AGPS, Canberra, 1997.
25. D. Lee-Ross, *HRM in Tourism and Hospitality: International Perspectives on Small to Medium-sized Enterprises*, Cassell, London, 1999, p. xvi.
26. L.X. Cunningham & C. Rowley, 'Human resource management in Chinese small and medium enterprises: A review and research agenda', *Personnel Review*, vol. 36 no. 3, 2007, pp. 415–39.
27. M. Schaper, *see* note 11.
28. US Small Business Administration, *The Small Business Economy 2008: A Report to the President*, Small Business Administration, Washington, 2009, p. 4.
29. Australian Institute of Management, *National Salary Survey*, Australian Institute of Management, Brisbane, 2005.
30. A. Nankervis & S. Chatterjee, *Understanding Asian Management: Transition and Transformation*, Vineyard Press, Perth, 2002, pp. 16–17.
31. ibid., pp. 9, 14.
32. J. Sanderson, *Doing Business in China*, Dorling Kindersley, London, 2008, pp. 50–1.
33. Organisation for Economic Co-operative and Development (OECD), *Economic Survey of India 2007*, 2007, Chapter 4, OECD: Paris.
34. G. Redding, *The Spirit of Chinese Capitalism*, de Gruyter, Berlin, 1990.
35. S. Sakthivel & P. Joddar, 'Unorganised Sector Workforce in India: Trends, Patterns and Social Security Coverage', *Economic and Political Weekly*, 27 May 2006, pp. 2107–14; M. Mehta, 'Urban Informal Sector: Concepts, Indian Evidence and Policy Implications', *Economic and Political Weekly*, vol. 20, no. 8, 23 February 1985, pp. 326–32.

CHAPTER **14**

Financial information and management

Learning objectives

After reading this chapter, you should be able to:

- define the purposes for which financial information is collected

- prepare a sales mix forecast, a cash flow statement and a profit and loss statement

- list the main types of financial documents and explain their purpose

- explain the ways in which financial information can be analysed

- list the different financial records used in most businesses.

Accurate financial information is important in the successful development of new business ventures, as well as in the management of existing firms.[1] Although profits may not be the sole consideration for starting or running a business, most entrepreneurs and business owners understandably develop a keen interest in the financial performance of their business. Financial information plays an important role in providing a more complete picture of the operations of a business and its current status, and it helps determine whether future projects are viable.

However, to properly understand and analyse such data, business owners and entrepreneurs must be familiar with the way key financial documents operate and the way they are constructed: documents such as cash flow statements, profit and loss statements (now also referred to as *statements of financial performance*) and balance sheets (also termed *statements of financial position*).

In this chapter, the different types of financial information are described and explained. The basic documents common to all businesses (new or established, small or large) are explained. In addition, since most small and new ventures are often funded by the owner, some ways of documenting and analysing personal finances are also examined. Ratios for analysing financial data are then examined. Finally, an overview is provided of financial recordkeeping systems, so that entrepreneurs and owner–managers understand how to establish and maintain accurate data sources.

The purpose of financial information

Financial data are more than just a set of books or interesting sets of figures. When carefully collected, presented and analysed, the data represent an important source of management information.

Objectivity

Financial statements are factual documents. They represent data that have been measured and quantified, so they are objective indicators of business performance. In contrast, many of the other assessment methods used to gauge operational and managerial effectiveness (such as employee performance appraisal, the nature of customer complaints or compliments, and owner's opinions) are more likely to be based on subjective criteria, such as personal assessments, 'gut feeling' and internal comparisons, and are therefore less reliable.

Financiers' expectations

If business owners want to borrow funds from a bank, or entrepreneurs need the support of venture capitalists, then they need to provide such lenders with a clear financial picture. They need to explain how the money will be used, and to convince the lender that the business can repay its debts as they fall due. Other additional financial information, such as the ability of the owner to provide security for the loan, or any other current borrowings incurred by the entrepreneur, may also be required.[2]

Statutory requirements

Governments require businesses to keep accurate financial records, both for the purposes of collecting statistical information and, more importantly, for taxation compliance. In many cases there are legal requirements, and these cannot be avoided. For example, in both Australia and New Zealand there are statutory requirements concerning the collection of the goods and services tax and its periodical remittance to the Australian Taxation Office and NZ Inland Revenue department respectively.

Viability

For any proposed new business venture, entrepreneurs need to assure investors and themselves that the idea is, in fact, financially viable. To do this, documentation must be prepared that shows the firm can generate sufficient sales, has enough cash flow and can ultimately be financially rewarding enough to make the project worthwhile. Start-up firms often use projections of financial information, along with other data such as prices, to work out their break-even point (discussed in more detail in chapter 11). Other questions are also important. Is sufficient return on investment being generated? Are all assets being used productively? What will the business investment be worth in two years' time? Is there enough profit? Only financial information can answer these questions.

Profitability

For many business owners, one of the main goals of being in business is to generate a profit. As will be shown later in this chapter, *profit* does not necessarily mean funds available as cash. Many firms have access to large amounts of money (and are therefore seen as having sufficient liquidity), yet they can still fail to generate a profit. In order to determine whether a profit has been made, appropriate returns must be collected.[3]

Goal setting

Many small business owner–managers have established other goals for themselves, apart from profitability, which they are seeking from their enterprise. These may include a satisfactory return on investment, a comfortable level of owner's drawings, or the development of a strong asset base. Financial returns can help evaluate whether such goals are realistic and are being achieved or whether the firm is failing to meet the owner's expectations.

Purchase or sale of a business

If the sale of an existing small business is being contemplated, then astute purchasers will want to carefully scrutinise the performance of the firm to date, and will require access to a comprehensive set of financial records. Vendors who wish to enhance the asking price of their firm realise that a set of accurate, verifiable documents can sometimes help improve their final selling price.

Performance appraisal

Assessing a business can take many different forms, and financial figures form an integral part of any comprehensive monitoring program. Items as diverse as the level of sales generated (sales revenue), operating costs, sales per employee and profitability from one year to the next can all help determine business performance if appropriate financial data are collected. In many cases, such data can also be compared with industry benchmarks to determine the firm's performance relative to its competitors.

Differences between small and large firms

Is entrepreneurial and small business financial analysis similar to that undertaken by corporate entities? In many respects, the answer is 'yes', in that the documents serve largely the same purposes and take similar formats in all businesses. However, there are some differences.[4]

It is much more difficult to prepare financial forecasts for entrepreneurial firms than for existing large firms, because the former are usually geared to a new business concept and are thus extremely hard to quantify accurately. An entrepreneur is usually making a 'best informed guess' when estimating financial projections for a new venture, since nothing can be guaranteed in advance of actual operations.

In addition, small business owners typically have to take personal responsibility for collating and presenting their own financial information, whereas in a large firm this duty is the responsibility of a specialised department with full-time experts, such as in-house accounting staff. Within a small firm, even when the task is handed over to someone else, such as a bookkeeper, the owner–manager must still be able to understand the documents and make decisions based on them. Not surprisingly, most research into financial management indicates that firms tend to become better organised and more sophisticated in their handling of financial information as they grow larger.[5]

Small firms are also less willing or able to make their financial data available to external parties. This can occur for a variety of reasons: in part, it is because their recordkeeping is frequently not as sophisticated as that of larger enterprises; however, another reason is that many business owners prefer not to divulge such information in case it is used by their competitors.[6]

Finally, both small business owners and entrepreneurs tend to take more personal financial risks than staff in a large business. Much of the business funding is drawn from their own finances. Many small business ventures operate under a sole proprietorship or partnership legal structure in which the owners are personally responsible for the debts of the firm. (In contrast, a company is a legal entity in itself, and debts and liabilities belong to the company, not the owners or shareholders.)

For all these reasons, financial control is very important to small-scale firms. However, because entrepreneurs and small business owner–managers have to be skilled in so many different areas of business activity (such as marketing, human resources, operations, logistics and sales), in practice many of them tend to rely on accountants for their financial information and analysis,[7] and most owner–managers have only a general understanding of financial issues.[8] For this reason, this chapter focuses on getting the basics of such documents correct, rather than on providing a detailed accounting-based method.

Regional variations in financial management

Most of the tools of financial information collection and the methods of analysing such data are reasonably generic, and can be found in basically the same format across most jurisdictions in the Asia–Pacific region. However, it is worth noting that there are some local differences that can affect the way in which financial data is utilised.

One distinguishing feature is the **financial year** period that a firm uses. This is the twelve-month period for which annual (or yearly) financial data is collected, analysed and reported upon. It is sometimes known as a reporting year, fiscal year or budget year. The financial year typically varies from one nation to another, depending on local practice and taxation laws (see table 14.1). For example, in India it typically covers the twelve months from 1 April to 31 March, whilst in Australia and New Zealand it begins on 1 July and runs until the following 30 June.[9]

It is also worth noting that many businesses in India use an alternative system to the standard numeric terms (such as 'thousand', 'million', 'billion' and so forth) used in other countries across the Asia–Pacific region. Indian firms often record their figures in lakhs, equivalent to 100 000 in Western accounting processes, and crores, equating to ten million; they also place commas at different points within numeric figures.[10]

Financial year *The twelve-month period for which annual financial data is collected, analysed and reported upon.*

TABLE 14.1 Financial reporting year periods for various Asia–Pacific nations

Country	Criteria
Australia	From 1 July to 30 June
New Zealand	From 1 July to 30 June
Hong Kong	From 1 April to 31 March
Malaysia	From 1 January to 31 December
Singapore	From 1 January to 31 December
China	From 1 January to 31 December
India	From 1 April to 31 March

Sources: L.S. Cheang, *Business Guide To Malaysia*, Butterworth-Heinemann, Singapore, 1997, p. 142; Inland Revenue Authority of Singapore, *Deciding On The Accounting Period*, 2009, www.iras.gov.sg; R. Manian, *Doing Business in India For Dummies*, Wiley, Hoboken, New Jersey, 2007, p. 158; Inland Revenue Service, Hong Kong Special Administrative Region, *Tax Information: Profits Tax*, 2009, www.ird.gov.hk.

Types of financial information

The most common financial forecasting and reporting documents used by small businesses are the sales mix forecast, cash flow statement, profit and loss statement and balance sheet. For a new business, these financial documents will be forecasts only. In addition, information about the owner's personal expenses and personal assets and liabilities may also be required. For a completed example of these for a new business (except the balance sheet), refer to the sample business plan in the appendix to chapter 7.

Sales mix forecast

Sales mix forecast
An estimate of sales of each major product or service, the revenue generated by each of these and the resulting cost of goods sold.

A **sales mix forecast** is an estimate of the likely sales of each major product or service, the revenue generated by each of these, and the resulting cost of goods sold. It is typically prepared on a month-by-month basis. This projection helps the business owner to accurately gauge the level of sales revenue that will be generated during a year of trading.

Once the business owner has decided what products will be sold and at what price, collected market research should be used to estimate how many items of each commodity will be sold each month. This will provide an estimate of total revenue for a month.

For many items, there will also be a cost of goods sold, which represents the raw materials or trading stock (also known as *inventory*) consumed in order to generate the sales. For example, retail businesses have a very large cost of goods sold (represented by the stock they buy to sell to the purchasing public), as do manufacturers. Conversely, service-based industries typically have an extremely low cost of goods sold — if any at all.

Blueprints Business Planning Pty Ltd has a relatively simple sales mix forecast (see p. 188). There are only three key sales items outlined in its business plan: business plan preparation, training courses and the books sold during the training courses. Each of these is accorded a separate entry in the sales mix, and the number of sales for each month is estimated. For example, in July it is anticipated that there will be two sales of business plans, each worth A$2000, along with the delivery of 15 hours of training courses at A$120 per hour, and three book sales, producing a total income of A$5950. The training courses also have a small cost of goods sold (representing items such as training room hire, course materials and food for participants) of A$20 per hour of training, and the cost of goods sold for books is A$30 each, all of which produces a total cost of goods sold of A$390. This format is then replicated for the other months across the trading year, providing a total estimated monthly and annual sales revenue.

Although not foolproof, this method is more concise and sophisticated than simply making up a total sales revenue figure for the year. It can also be reviewed by outside advisers or other staff to help the business owner refine and improve the original forecast figures.

A useful additional step is to determine whether any goods will be offered for sale on credit (buy now, pay later). If so, the business owner must calculate when this money will actually be collected. In the example of Blueprints

Business Planning Pty Ltd, there are no credit sales. However, it is worthwhile to look at the forecasts and determine what the impact on sales revenue would be if 10 or 20 per cent of each month's sales were made on a 30-day credit basis instead.

Cash flow statement (or forecast)

A **cash flow statement (or forecast)** shows the movement of all cash into and out of the business in a given time frame. It can be used to predict the amount of funds immediately available to a business at any given moment. Although different time frames can be used, the most common reporting period is on a month-by-month basis.

Cash flow statement (or forecast) *A document that shows the movement of all cash into and out of a business during a given time frame.*

A cash flow document shows how much money the business actually receives each month and how much it spends. In this way, it outlines the pattern of revenue generation and expenditure, and the amount of cash left to meet unforeseen emergencies, to fund expansion programs, to provide additional personal drawings to the owner or to meet any other contingencies. Note that, in this context, 'cash' does not literally mean just coins or banknotes; it refers to any easily convertible commodity, such as currency, cheques, credit card sales, bank orders, electronic funds transfers and online internet-based transactions. For a cash flow document to be accurate, it is assumed that all cash funds are deposited into the business's bank account.

A cash flow forecast is worked out in the following way:
- Estimate the sales to be made over the course of a year. The sales mix is the preferred source for estimating these data. Determine not only the level of sales to be made, but also when the revenue is likely to be received. Goods sold on credit, for example, will often not be realised as cash until one or two months after the actual transfer of goods has taken place and an invoice has been issued to the customer.
- It is then necessary to calculate any other revenue that may be added to the business bank account in each month, such as additional capital contributions, bank interest earned or loans made to the business. This is important because the cash flow forecast tries to accurately show *all* money moving in and out of the business account — not just sales revenue.
- From market research and previous experience, estimate what expenses are likely to fall due each month. Again, this must include both business and non-business expenditure that is drawn from the business's bank account. Owner's drawings for personal use, for example, should be included in this figure.
- Subtract revenue from expenses to calculate a monthly surplus or deficit.
- Note the actual bank balance the business has at the start of the trading period. This is recorded as the 'Bank balance: Start of month' amount.
- Add the first month's surplus (or deficit) to this figure to arrive at the 'Bank balance: End of month' figure.

Look again at the business plan in the appendix to chapter 7, where the entrepreneur, Jessie Jones, has decided to start a new venture, Blueprints Business Planning Pty Ltd. In the first month of trading, Blueprints Business Planning will generate A$5950 in sales and receive A$10 000 in the form of the owner's capital contribution. During the course of the month, a total of A$24 030 will be spent on various expenses, leaving a cash shortfall for the first month of A$8080. The business will begin trading in July with nothing in the bank (meaning that the entry 'Bank balance: Start of month' equals zero), and at 31 July the 'Bank balance: End of month' will be overdrawn by A$8080.

Calculating the second month's income and expenditure follows the same format, except that the opening bank balance ('start of month') is exactly the same as the closing bank balance ('end of month') of the preceding month. This is because whatever funds the business has in its account at midnight on the last day of July will be exactly the same as it has on the first day of August. In the case of Blueprints Business Planning Pty Ltd, trading will begin in August with an overdraft of A$8080. Over the course of the year, the closing bank balance will change significantly each month, and although it will be overdrawn for most of the year, the firm will end with a substantial cash surplus at the close of June.

For many businesses, cash flow management is a more important issue than profitability. This is because even though a business may turn out to be profitable over the course of a year, if it does not have enough funds in its bank account to meet its debts as and when they fall due, its survival may be at risk. For example, a temporary mid-year cash flow problem may result in the business being unable to pay its rent by the due date, leading to eviction from the premises. In this case, a profitable figure on the profit and loss statement at the end of the first trading year will be meaningless, because the business no longer has any premises from which to trade.

Central to understanding this process is the concept of the cash flow cycle, or the manner in which money moves through a typical small business. In many cases the payment for raw materials, labour and other costs will precede the actual sale of the finished product to the customer, which means there is a time lag between expenditure and revenue collection. This gap must be funded in some way, so a business must have sufficient **working capital** on hand to ensure that cash flow remains positive. If the customer does not pay immediately for the goods, but instead is invoiced for them and asked to pay at a later stage, then the gap between payment for expenses and cash collection is even greater, and this, in turn, will require a commensurately greater amount of working capital.

Cash flow can be improved in a number of ways (see the inset 'Eight ways to improve cash flow'). For example, if the owner believes that the business account will be overdrawn for a long period of time, he or she might have to provide more capital or raise a long-term loan to pay for some of the start-up costs. The owner could also seek to defer the payment of some items or spread payments over a longer period of time. What other steps could the owners of Blueprints Business Planning Pty Ltd do to reduce its substantial cash overdraft?

Finally, a cash flow document is useful for quickly evaluating performance. It shows what expenditure is being made and when; it can also help show the amount of personal drawings that the owner is taking from the business (cash flow shortages often occur because the owner takes excessive amounts of money from the business). If the projection also shows that the business is likely to end up with a negative 'Bank balance: End of month' figure, then the business will

Working capital
Funds used in operating a business on a daily basis.

either need to arrange an overdraft facility or to raise more working capital and deposit it in the account before the bank balance becomes overdrawn.

EIGHT WAYS TO IMPROVE CASH FLOW

1. Wherever possible, collect payment in cash at the time of the sale.
2. Where credit is offered, always issue invoices immediately on completion of a job or sale.
3. Offer clients incentives or discounts to pay promptly (but note that this may have an impact on eventual net profit).
4. To make payment easier, allow customers to pay by credit card or online.
5. Chase up outstanding debtors on a regular basis.
6. Smooth out expenses by leasing rather than buying capital items.
7. Pay large bills (such as insurance premiums) monthly rather than yearly.
8. Minimise expenditure by reducing owner's personal drawings from the firm.

Look at Blueprints Business Planning's cash flow forecast, in which Jesse has failed to provide any estimates of bank overdraft fees and interest charges. What would such additional expenses do to the cash flow of the firm?

Profit and loss statement

A profit is the difference between revenue earned and expenses incurred. Sometimes also known as a *statement of financial performance*, *revenue statement* or *income and expenses statement*, the **profit and loss statement** is a summary of the business's trading activities over a specific time frame (usually one year). It shows the total revenue generated by the business during the period, and sets out all the expenses associated with that period's activities. An example of a profit and loss statement is shown in figure 14.1.

Profit and loss statement *A document that shows business-related revenues and expenses and the resulting profit or loss.*

Note that because the profit and loss statement is meant to accurately account for both business revenue and the expenses associated with the creation of that revenue, and to match these for a given period of time, it differs in several respects from the cash flow document. For example, it does not include revenue generated by bank loans or owner's capital contributions (since these are not sales revenue), and it also takes into account non-cash expenditure items, such as **depreciation** (the diminution of the value of an item through use). Depreciation is not a cash expense, since the business owner does not actually write a cheque to cover the wearing down of the equipment. Nevertheless, it must be taken into account when determining total business costs for a period. Similarly, sales revenue generated during this period, but not yet collected, is still brought to account in this document. In a sole proprietorship or partnership, owner's drawings are not considered standard business expenses, but rather an advance on the profits eventually earned, and so are not included in the 'operating expenses' category. Finally, expenditure on capital items is usually not included in the profit and loss statement, since these constitute one-off or irregular purchases, rather than an ongoing cost of being in business.

Depreciation *The diminution of the value of an item through use.*

As a result, the link between the profit and loss statement and the cash flow document is not always clear-cut or obvious. In fact, it is unusual for total figures in a cash flow document to exactly equal those in the profit and loss statement.

ABC Company Pty Ltd

PROFIT AND LOSS STATEMENT

for the period 1 July 2011 to 30 June 2012

Revenues

Sales revenue	A$150 000	
Less: Cost of goods sold	50 000	
Gross profit		A$100 000
Operating and administrative expenses		
Accounting and legal fees	3 000	
Advertising and marketing	8 000	
Depreciation	5 250	
Insurance	750	
Premises rental	12 500	
Stationery	500	
Staff wages	27 350	
Phone, electricity	1 400	
Travel	1 250	
Total expenses		60 000
Net profit		40 000
Less: Tax on profit		13 000
Net profit after tax		**A$27 000**

FIGURE 14.1 Format of a profit and loss statement

Balance sheet
A document that details the assets, liabilities and net worth (owner's equity) of the business.

Owner's equity (or net worth) *The difference between the assets and liabilities of a business; the value of the business to the owner if all its assets were sold and all liabilities were paid.*

Assets *Items of worth owned by the business.*

Liabilities *Debts or financial obligations of the business.*

It can be quite difficult for an individual small business owner to take all these items and variations into account, and most entrepreneurs and small business owners are not well informed about the finer points of accounting principles. Therefore, it is usually preferable for the business owner to prepare a basic profit and loss statement that simply lays out sales revenue and expenditures in the conventional format, and to leave the accountant to make any necessary revisions.

Balance sheet

Sometimes known as a *statement of financial position*, the **balance sheet** is a snapshot of the worth of a business at a given moment in time. It shows the value of all items owned by the business, the debts it has and the resultant **owner's equity (or net worth)**. These three aspects are related to each other by means of a fundamental accounting equation, which can be found in all balance sheets:

$$Assets = Liabilities + Owner's\ Equity$$

Assets are items of worth owned by a business, and can be divided into two broad groups: those that are easily converted into cash if necessary (current assets) and those which cannot be quickly converted (non-current assets). Another key component is the **liabilities** (debts or financial obligations) of the firm, which can also be divided in a similar manner into current and non-current items. Finally, the difference between the total assets and total liabilities represents the owner's equity (or net worth). Theoretically, this is the value of the business to the owner if all its assets were sold and all liabilities were paid. Owner's equity is also frequently divided into two sections: the *owner's capital contribution* represents the funds the owner has put into the business to start or expand the venture, and the *retained profits* are the profit subsequently kept within the business to fund growth or bolster firm value.

A balance sheet is typically compiled at a particular moment in time, such as at the close of business on the last trading day in the financial year. Subsequent balance sheets can then be compiled at the end of the following financial years, thereby allowing a comparison of the growth and composition of business assets and liabilities over time.

Balance sheets are difficult to prepare for start-up ventures, since it is difficult to estimate in advance the firm's net worth at the close of the next financial year. However, they are important for existing enterprises, whose owners will be keen to know if the worth of their business has increased over the last year.

No balance sheet is included for Blueprints Business Planning in its business plan, since it is a start-up venture. However, figure 14.2 shows the standard format of a balance sheet for another hypothetical firm.

XYZ Trading Solutions Pty Ltd

BALANCE SHEET

as at 1 July 2011

Assets

Current assets:

Cash at bank	A$10 000
Accounts receivable	12 000
Work in progress	22 000
Prepaid expenses	14 000

Non-current assets:

Property	50 000
Less: Depreciation	(10 000)
Equipment	132 000
Less: Depreciation	(11 000)
Goodwill	12 000
Total assets	A$231 000

Liabilities

Current liabilities:

Overdraft	$3 000
Accounts payable	18 000
Provision for taxes	5 000

Non-currrent liabilities

Long-term loans	98 000
	$124 000

Owner's equity (net worth)

Owner's capital contribution	$70 000
Retained profits	37 000
Total owner's equity	$107 000

FIGURE 14.2 Format of a balance sheet

A word about the goods and services tax

Some nations, such as Australia, Singapore and New Zealand, operate a broad-based consumption tax that requires businesses to levy and collect a tax when selling goods or services. This is most commonly referred to as a goods and services tax (GST). Similar systems apply in the United States, Europe and the United Kingdom (where it operates as a value-added tax, or VAT). What impact do these tax systems have on a firm's financial statements?

In the first place, it affects both the sales mix and the cash flow documents. Adding a 10 per cent GST to the price of goods or services in Australia, for example, will cause the sales price to increase accordingly. The cash flow will also need to reflect the outflow of GST payments to the tax office (which may occur monthly, quarterly or annually).

However, this inflated price is not shown in the profit and loss statement — only the GST-free sales revenue is given. Why? Because the GST is not revenue earned by the firm — it is money held in trust, so to speak, for a government tax authority. For example, a firm's sales of A$1100 in goods (A$1000 + 10 per cent GST) would show only A$1000 as sales revenue and no GST expense in the profit and loss statement. But the A$100 does show up on the balance sheet as a liability if it is due and has not yet been forwarded to the tax authority. (In the business plan in the appendix to chapter 7, these figures have been excluded to help simplify the explanation of the document construction process.)

Personal expenses

Drawings *The income the business owner takes out of the business.*

Sometimes it is necessary to know the level of the business owner's personal expenditure. If the firm operates as a sole proprietorship or partnership, then money taken out of the business is referred to as the owner's **drawings**. (In a company structure, an owner–manager who works in the business is regarded as an employee of the business, and so such payments are treated as part of the overall wages and salaries bill.) Compiling this figure on a month-by-month basis makes it possible to determine whether the business can afford to pay this amount to the owner on a regular basis. The amount and type of spending made by the owner can usually be broken down into a number of different categories (such as expenditure on food, clothing, housing, medical care and recreation).

This amount is then fed into the cash flow forecast to see whether the level of drawings can be maintained by the business. If not, the business owner must either reduce the level of personal expenditure or generate additional sales revenue.

For example, our entrepreneur, Jessie Jones of Blueprints Business Planning, requires a total of A$41 320 per annum to live. This amount is shown as the 'Staff — director's wages' line item, in both the cash flow forecast and the projected profit and loss statement in the firm's business plan (in the appendix to chapter 7). Since both documents show that the firm can accommodate this expenditure and still remain both liquid and profitable, Jessie has been able to demonstrate that the business is a viable full-time income source for her.

Owner's assets and liabilities

It may be necessary for the business owner to provide information on the composition and level of per sonal worth. This is often required by financiers, who will typically lend funds to small businesses only if the funds can be secured against the owner's personal assets. Many entrepreneurs seeking to launch new ventures face similar hurdles. This **owner's assets and liabilities** document is similar to a business balance sheet, in that both documents present a statement of assets and liabilities, and the resulting difference between them (net worth).

Jessie Jones's personal assets are included in Blueprints Business Planning's business plan. They show a person with considerable assets (A$840 000) and substantial net personal worth (A$637 800). Therefore, in financial terms, it seems that Jessie would be a successful applicant for bank finance should it be required.

Owner's assets and liabilities *A document that shows the private assets, liabilities and net worth of a business owner.*

Forecasts or historical documents?

All the documents discussed can be prepared either as estimates of likely future performance, or as historical records (that is, a chronicle of what has actually happened). Tax returns, for example, are a form of historical profit and loss statement, whereas a sales revenue budget for the next year is essentially a forecast of the next year's sales mix. New business ventures are based heavily on future estimates, whereas existing firms use both historical (actual) data and trend projections when preparing forecasts. In many cases, it pays to compare the two sets of documents, since original forecasts can often be substantially different from what is finally achieved, and they need to be examined to find out where the discrepancies lie and how they can be corrected in the future.

Entrepreneur profile

Eric Rongley: In search of paying customers

Problems with cash flow — specifically, getting paid by customers and clients — can be fatal for start-ups anywhere in the world, but the toll is especially high for foreign ventures based in China. Consider the rocky start experienced by the Shanghai-based firm Bleum. US software executive Eric Rongley launched his specialised software company using his personal savings, which he then had to top up with another US$50 000 borrowed from friends.

The business was difficult to start because of a Catch-22: Bleum needed a big team of software engineers in order to attract customers — but it also needed customers in order to pay the employees. In the beginning, it was lopsided, Rongley recalls. 'I had a payroll of 30 people, but no customers.'

During the first year of operation, projects began pouring in and Bleum was busy — but still going broke. After the first 12 months of operation, the company had burned through most of the start-up funding, and little money was coming in.

Rongley says his main mistake was in not following his business instincts. After having spent two years working in China for a US-based company, he had launched Bleum knowing that the safest business plan for his high-end services was to focus on offshore clients. But just after launching, he switched tactics. 'I didn't have enough money to attract offshore clients at first,' he says. 'So I thought: I'll do local projects first, and build up the company's strength and the team while I save more money.'

But as an unknown start-up in an emerging field for the China market, Rongley found that domestic customers were quite happy to try Bleum's services, but were very slow (or even unwilling) to pay for them. 'In the first year, we focused on the local market, which promptly depleted all of my cash,' he says.

The main problem, he says, was his own lack of understanding of Chinese business culture. First, Rongley and his Chinese clients had a very different concept of a business contract. 'This is the difficult thing when doing business in China. In the West, we negotiate a deal and we struggle through the initial negotiation because we don't want to struggle after that. But in Asia, the first agreement is just one part of the ongoing process of working together – the perception is that both sides will keep negotiating as they do business.' In other words, an agreement for payment is just a guideline, which the Chinese side expects to discuss and alter as actual business begins.

Second, Rongley didn't fully understand the Chinese business mindset and the bias against young and weak startups. He thought his experience in launching operations for a US company in India would help him succeed in China. 'I figured that I knew how to adapt the business model to China. But after I launched my own business, I found I didn't understand how business is done in China,' he says, [Chinese] business people have a different set of goals when they engage a vendor. I was hitting my head on a bunch of walls. We weren't getting paid; we had customers making unreasonable requests of us; and, most importantly, the customers in China, especially five years ago, were very immature.' Because Bleum was a young company with few resources, clients felt free to break deal terms and refuse to pay. 'I found it a very vicious marketplace for us as a small, under funded company.'

Chinese clients were extremely short term in their thinking, he remembers. Stated bluntly: many clients didn't expect Bleum to survive long in business, so they didn't feel inclined to pay for its services. 'It's kind of ironic that people in the West think Asians are very long-term thinkers. Actually, I see business here as extremely short term – I'm going to burn up this vendor because there is another sucker right behind him; and after I burn him up, there will be another one right behind him.'

At the end of the first year of operation, Rongley faced a do-or-die situation: 'All our cash was gone,' he remembers. Faced with a crisis, his first decision was to stop working for local client companies. Bleum even refused job requests from domestic clients that had paid their accounts.

His second move was to rely on his relationships in international markets to find paying customers and turn the company around. 'Because of my reputation and my network in the software industry, I was able to pick up a few projects and got started from zero again,' he says. At last, contracts – and payments – began rolling in. Says Rongley: 'By the end of the second year, we weren't doing any local work. We had to tell some of our local customers 'We are done working for you.'

Today, Rongley says he was correct in taking this 'cold turkey' approach. The lesson learned: for high-end services and products that are new to China, foreign entrepreneurs face an easier time selling to international customers that are more familiar with the value of the service or product – and are more willing to pay for them.

Analysing financial data

The collection of financial information is not an end in itself. Once compiled, the figures in a profit and loss statement or balance sheet can be used to assess the performance of the business. One simple way of doing this is to compare one year's figures with another's. However, this may not always be effective, since total (absolute) amounts may vary greatly from one time to the next. In addition, simply using dollar value figures makes it difficult to compare performances between firms, since the turnover of other businesses may be higher or lower than the owner's firm.

To this end, business analysts have developed a number of useful ratios to measure performance. Ratios have the benefit of converting absolute figures into meaningful proportions, so allowing for differences in firm size or turnover. Moreover, most industries have evolved general indicator ratios that are commonly used as benchmarks by firms within that sector. These are handy 'rules of thumb' which can be used to assess the performance of one's own business against industry standards. Ratios can also be used internally, to compare the firm's performance on a particular dimension over the years.[11]

Profitability ratios

A key issue in financial management is the creation of sufficient profit. How much profit is the business making for each dollar of goods or services that it sells? The higher the profit margin, the better. Two key profitability indicators are derived from the profit and loss statement, and they analyse the profit generated in relation to the sales performance of the business:

$$\text{Gross profit margin \%} = \frac{\text{Gross profit}}{\text{Sales turnover}}$$

$$\text{Net profit margin \%} = \frac{\text{Net profit before tax}}{\text{Sales turnover}}$$

Both the gross profit and net profit margins can be compared with industry-wide benchmarks. A low gross profit margin compared with industry norms indicates a relatively high cost of goods (raw materials or trading stock) expense item, whereas a high percentage result indicates that the manager is keeping raw materials costs down. Net profit is the bottom line for most businesses — how much is available for the owner? The average net profit margin of all Australian firms is approximately nine per cent, although some industries (such as the services sector) usually produce much higher margins, and other industries, such as retail traders and hospitality firms, underperform.[12]

There are two other useful profitability ratios that assess how effectively the existing assets of the enterprise are being used to help create a profit. These are return on equity and return on assets.

$$\text{Return on equity} = \frac{\text{Net profit before tax}}{\text{Owner's equity}}$$

What sort of return is the owner receiving for the funds he or she has invested in the business? This formula estimates the return on the investment that has been made by the owner of the business to establish and fund the venture. A high return on equity is indicative of a very productive use of one's own capital contribution; a low figure is generally regarded as a poor performance.[13]

$$\text{Return on assets} = \frac{\text{Net profit before tax}}{\text{Total assets}}$$

How well is the firm using the assets (not just the owner's contribution) under its control? Again, a higher level of return is more desirable. A declining ratio usually indicates that expenses are rising faster than sales or that increases in the firm's total asset base are occurring more rapidly than any increase in its net profit.

Liquidity ratios

These indicators are essentially measures of the business's ability to survive. A common cause of failure among small firms and new business ventures is short-term cash flow problems, such as an inability to meet the demands of creditors. Liquidity ratios are designed to evaluate how well the firm's cash flow is being managed.

$$\text{Current ratio} = \frac{\text{Current assets}}{\text{Current liabilities}}$$

This ratio is drawn from the business's balance sheet, and indicates the firm's ability to repay its short-term debts.[14] A desirable result for an established firm in many industries is a figure of about 2. Firms embarking on a period of rapid growth may have a lower figure, whereas those with a long operating cycle (such as firms that take a long time to collect debts) may have a higher figure.

$$\text{Liquid ('quick') ratio} = \frac{\text{Current assets} - \text{Trading stock}}{\text{Current liabilities}}$$

A variant of the current ratio, the liquid ratio determines how quickly a firm could meet its short-term debts if payment was required in a short period of time. Because trading stock typically takes some time to be sold, it is removed from the equation. A satisfactory ratio level here for many different types of firm is about 1, although this may vary from one industry to another.

Efficiency ratios

A number of other ratios are used to monitor particular aspects of business operations.

How efficiently are the total assets of the business being used to generate sales? A high level of asset turnover indicates that the business's asset base is being well used in order to maximise sales revenue. A declining turnover rate can be a cause for concern, since it indicates some inefficiencies in the deployment of the firm's assets and possibly also in its marketing strategy.

$$\text{Asset turnover} = \frac{\text{Sales}}{\text{Total assets}}$$

An indication of the financial structure of the business, the ownership ratio measures the proportion of the business owned by the owner–manager. When the ratio drops below 50 per cent, it indicates that financiers and creditors have more involvement in the firm than is probably desirable.

$$\text{Ownership} = \frac{\text{Owner's equity}}{\text{Total assets}}$$

The debt-to-equity ratio is another way of measuring the financial structure and risk distribution in the firm. This formula measures the extent of a firm's debt burden. A high debt ratio (say, over 1) can be a cause for concern, since it indicates the business has a high risk profile caused by excess debt.[15]

$$\text{Debt-to-equity ratio} = \frac{\text{External debts}}{\text{Owner's equity}}$$

The stock turnover ratio evaluates how many times a year the business sells, or turns over, its trading stock. The higher the resulting figure, the quicker the business is 'churning' through sales. Generally a high stock turnover rate is desirable, as a relatively quick turn around between obtaining goods and reselling them helps improve the firm's cash flow and reduces the risk of potential losses from holding outdated stock.

$$\text{Stock turnover} = \frac{\text{Annual cost of goods}}{\text{Average stock on hand}}$$

Keeping records of financial information

When a business begins to operate, there needs to be a system that allows for the systematic collection, summary and preservation of the financial transactions that take place. This recordkeeping process is an essential step for the construction of historical financial documents, and is often required by law.

Such records must usually be kept for several years after the financial year in question has ended, and must be stored in either a hard format (written documentary) or electronic format accessible to statutory bodies such as taxation authorities. In many countries, records must be maintained in a particular language (such as English in Australia).

What would you do?

Rolling in money?

As a way of raising some extra cash income, you've recently gone into business with two of your fellow students, running a hot dog stall on weekends at the local community markets. These markets attract a wide range of both local residents and tourists, and you've agreed to share the workload between you. After three weeks of trading, all three of you sit down together one night to work out exactly how much your little venture has made.

'I've kept a list of our expenditure to date, and I've been putting the money we made into a drawer at my parents' place for safekeeping,' says Kelly proudly. 'I took all of our accounts that we've been keeping in this pile of papers, and looked through them. The first week, we earned A\$150 and spent A\$120. Week two, we collected A\$240 but only spent A\$80. And last weekend our revenue was A\$230 and our expenses were A\$130.'

'Great,' states Jane. 'We've got A\$100 in the bank, so it all seems okay. Why don't we split the profits three ways? That would give us A\$33 each.'

However, Kelly isn't particularly happy with this idea. 'I did put in A\$50 of my own money at the start so we could buy our first lot of sauce, buns and sausages. I need to be reimbursed before anything else. I've got the receipt to prove it, too — it's at home with my own bank statements.'

Questions

1. What problems are evident in the current financial information management procedures of this business?
2. Which financial information management tool would you introduce into this business first — a cash flow statement or a profit and loss statement? Why?

Most businesses generate a wide range of documents that need to be recorded. These can include duplicate receipts (documentary proof of money received from clients), cash till dockets, expense receipts when purchasing items from other parties, wages records, bank statements, credit card merchant transaction records, cheque books, petty cash vouchers, copies of any contracts involving financial responsibilities (such as equipment leases, rent agreements and employment contracts), vehicle log books and invoices. (Invoices are primary documents sent to clients, billing them for work performed for which payment has not yet been received; a sample is shown in figure 14.3.) In addition to manually-recorded transactions, businesses must also maintain an accurate record of all online and electronic activity.[16]

CAMDEN, MARKS & CLARKE DESIGN PTY LTD

ABN 99 555 666 777

27 Wells Lane • Melbourne • Vic 3000 Australia

Phone: (03) 4141 4242

E-mail: rob@camdenmarksclarke.com.au

Website: www.camdenmarksclarke.com.au

TAX INVOICE   **NO. 001**

Date: 10 July 2011
To: Super Corporation Pty Ltd
  PO Box Y6E
  St Kilda Vic 3182
Customer order no. 25/X14

For preparation of corporate design including logo, stationery, building plaques	$1500
Plus 10% GST	150
Total due	A$1650

Terms: 10 working days
Contact for queries: Robert Marks

FIGURE 14.3 A sample invoice for a small firm

Records must be kept of the day-to-day financial activities of a business. Some of the more common types of records are the following:[17]

- A *sales journal* is used to record the sales made by the business, either on a daily or weekly basis.
- A *purchases journal* provides information about purchases made for business-related activities. This can include the purchase of trading stock, equipment, services and any other goods.
- A *petty cash book* is a record of minor cash expenses, such as newspapers or a carton of milk, reimbursing a taxi fare for a staff member, or the occasional small unexpected expense that must be paid immediately in cash.
- An *accounts receivable ledger* is a record of outstanding debtors (people who owe the business money). This occurs when a business sells items on credit to customers, sends out an invoice and has to wait for the payment to be made. If most sales are made in this way and the money is not collected quickly enough, then a cash flow problem can emerge. An *ageing schedule* is often used to analyse how long various accounts have been outstanding, and to determine whether the number of debtors and the outstanding amounts are increasing.
- An *accounts payable ledger* shows the outstanding bills the business must still pay to its creditors. It is a list of purchases the firm has made on credit and not yet paid for.

- An *asset register* is a list of the capital equipment purchased for the business — what items were bought, when and for what price. This information is very useful for calculating depreciation expenses in the profit and loss statement (via a *depreciation schedule*). It can also help if an insurance claim has to be made for lost, stolen or damaged assets.

Generally, all these records are brought together and consolidated in a *general ledger*. However, such a ledger can sometimes be quite complex and time-consuming for a small firm to manage, especially if staff do not have experience in bookkeeping systems. For this reason, many small business advisers recommend that firms focus on maintaining effective cash books or cash journals.[18]

Cash journals are records of all the revenue collected and expenses incurred by the business each month. They record each item of revenue and expense as and when the relevant cash or cash equivalent is paid (similar to the way in which a cash flow document is prepared). The journals provide summary details of all money spent and received, whether by hard currency, cheque, electronic transaction, credit card or money order.

As figure 14.4 shows, a cash receipts journal records all cash receipts, detailing the date collected, the source of the funds, the invoice number (to cover accounts receivable as they are collected) and the amount received. Additional columns help analyse the business activity that generated the revenue (in this example, we have used a hypothetical document for Camden, Marks & Clarke Design Pty Ltd, whose main activities are consulting, corporate designing and stationery sales). A final 'sundries' column is used to account for unusual or one-off items. A similar format applies to the cash payments journal in figure 14.5, except that the columns analyse expense categories instead of revenue. As figure 14.6 shows, this information can then be used to help prepare a cash flow statement.

A more detailed and comprehensive system of recordkeeping is desirable for larger businesses or for complicated dealings in smaller businesses. It is usually more time- and cost-effective for the business owner to delegate this duty to another staff member or to outsource it to an accountant or bookkeeper. There are many computerised accounting packages available today, such as MYOB and QuickBooks, which are tailored to the needs of a business according its size, nature and number of employees. MYOB, for example, is widely used in small to medium-sized businesses in Australia.

SIMPLE STEPS TO IMPROVE RECORDKEEPING[19]

- Open a bank account in the name of the business.
- Keep all personal expenses of the business owner separate from business expenses, if possible.
- Ensure all business expenses are paid from a business account.
- Keep a 'paper trail' to help justify all expenses.
- Make sure your staff also know how your system works.
- File all documents in an organised manner.
- Get into the habit of keeping your records up-to-date, preferably on a daily basis.
- Talk to an accountant before the start of trading, to ensure the firm's recordkeeping system meets the accountant's needs as well.

FIGURE 14.4 Format of a simple cash receipts journal for Camden, Marks & Clarke Design Pty Ltd

Date	Received from	Inv. no.	Total amount	Consulting	Corporate designing	Stationery sales	Sundries	Notes
1 July	R Marks	Nil	1000.00				1000.00	Capital owner's contribution
18 July	Super Corp.	001	1650.00		1650.00			
27 July	Bronze Bros	003	3000.00		3000.00			
29 July	Sunshine Pty Ltd	002	200.00	200.00				
Total			5850.00	200.00	4650.00		1000.00	

FIGURE 14.5 Format of a simple cash payments journal for Camden, Marks & Clarke Design Pty Ltd

Date	Payment method	Paid to	Total amount	Accounting and legal	Advertising	Bank fees	Salaries	Materials	Sundries	Notes
2 July	chq. 02	Tax solutions	100.00	100.00						Advice
3 July	Online transfer	Chronicle newspaper	25.50		25.50					
3 July	Visa credit card	BP Petrol	50.00						50.00	
15 July	Chq. 03	F Smith	200.00				200.00			
18 July	Visa credit card	FE Books	38.00					38.00		Research
28 July	Direct debit	NewBank	13.50			13.50				Account fees
Total			427.00	100.00	25.50	13.50	200.00	38.00	50.00	

CAMDEN, MARKS & CLARKE DESIGN PTY LTD

CASH FLOW STATEMENT

for the period 1 July to 31 July

Revenues	
Consulting	A$200.00
Corporate designing	4650.00
Sundries	1000.00
Total revenues	$5850.00
Expenses	
Accounting and legal fees	100.00
Advertising	25.50
Bank fees	13.50
Salaries	200.00
Materials	38.00
Sundries	50.00
Total expenses	427.00
Cash surplus (deficit)	A$5423.00

FIGURE 14.6 Format of a completed cash flow statement, based on the cash journals of Camden, Marks & Clarke Design Pty Ltd

SUMMARY

Financial information management collates objective data that can be used to create and operate business enterprises efficiently. This information can be used to evaluate the business, help raise finance, meet legal recordkeeping obligations, assess the viability and profitability of a new entrepreneurial venture, help in the sale of an existing firm and help measure goal achievements and operational performance in existing firms.

Financial documents usually required in a new or small business include the sales mix forecast, cash flow forecast/statement, profit and loss statement and balance sheet. In addition, because most new and small firms typically are funded by the owners and must pay for their upkeep, two other documents are also useful: a statement of the owner's personal assets and liabilities, and an estimate of the owner's personal drawings from the business.

Common analytical ratios used to analyse the profit and loss statement and/or balance sheet include profitability ratios (gross profit, net profit, return on equity, return on assets); liquidity ratios (current, quick); and efficiency ratios (asset turnover, ownership, debt-to-equity, stock turnover).

Financial information is collected by recording information from all invoices, receipts and documentation relating to financial transactions in journals. For a very small firm, the most important of these are the cash payments and cash receipts journals, which record all revenue and expenditure. These journals are then used by an accountant to prepare other financial documents. Computerised accounting packages are available, tailored to the needs of small and medium-sized businesses.

REVIEW QUESTIONS

1. Why is it necessary to maintain accurate financial information?
2. Explain the four basic business financial documents and two personal financial documents discussed in this chapter.
3. What are the different types of ratios that can be used to analyse the financial information provided by a small firm? How are they calculated?
4. What are the different types of financial record found in most businesses?
5. How can cash journals be used to compile a cash flow document?

DISCUSSION QUESTIONS

1. What impact would a 10 per cent GST have on the financial documents in the Blueprints Business Planning Pty Ltd business plan (shown in the appendix to chapter 7)?
2. If you were an entrepreneur planning a new business venture, would you prepare the financial forecasts yourself or use an accountant? Why?
3. How can you increase the gross profit margin in a retail business?

EXERCISES

1. *The Canberra Surf Shop — start-up costs and budget*
   This exercise will give you practice in developing a cash flow document. Read through the description and then complete the cash flow statement for the Canberra Surf Shop, using the blank pro forma statement provided.
   Part 1: The first month
   In the first month of business (January), the Canberra Surf Shop is largely preoccupied with setting up. As a result, it earns only A$1000 in sales. These are cash sales and not credit — the owner, Maxine Gold, hasn't yet made arrangements to provide credit facilities. She has borrowed A$12 000 in a long-term loan from the bank. No other money is used to fund the shop's operations.

   However, there have been plenty of start-up costs. The accountant charged A$900 for advice on establishing a bookkeeping system; A$450 was spent on advertising; Eastern Power Corporation required a prepayment of A$300 for the electricity supply; the insurance broker asked for the first insurance premium payment of A$100; and a video display unit was leased for two months, with a monthly payback fee of A$200. No loan repayments are due to the bank as yet, but running the car to the coast to examine the surf tour possibilities cost A$500 in repairs and fuel. A good lease was negotiated on the shop, but two months payment (at a cost of A$400 per month) was required in advance. The new logo on the stationery looks good; it cost A$400 to design and print. However, while preparing to open, Maxine's only staff member, John, put a ladder through an uninsured A$1200 plate glass window that had to be replaced immediately. Despite this, Maxine still paid him his A$460 weekly wage (gross — it includes A$60 a week in tax, which must be remitted to the taxation authorities immediately).

   Getting started meant that the firm charged up a telephone bill of A$360. Finally, the Canberra Surf Shop spent A$6800 to purchase new clothing stock, and another A$3000 to buy some surfboards, skateboards and a windsurfer to sell.

Required:

(a) Prepare a cash flow projection for the first month of operations of the Canberra Surf Shop (using the pro forma statement provided). Make sure it also includes the owner's drawings of A$500 for all her hard work to date. What is the cash position at the end of January? Is there a surplus or shortfall and how much is it? (Assume that the first month equals four weeks exactly, and that all figures are exclusive of GST.)

Part 2: Second month of operations

Things are moving! February has been good to the shop. Maxine earned A$16 500 in sales this month (all cash — still no credit card facilities). Better still, some additional clothing stock cost only A$6850 to buy.

Of course, there were expenses. Advertising, John's wages, the phone, insurance and video leasing expenses all cost the same as last month. In addition, there was an electricity bill of A$150, bank charges of A$6 and the first instalment on the loan repayments of A$644. The business was also charged A$20 in bank interest for the overdraft caused by last month's cash shortfall.

Despite this, Maxine paid herself only A$500 again this month. This is a smart move — Maxine is looking after her cash flow!

Required:

(b) Complete the cash flow statement (using the pro forma sheet provided) for the Canberra Surf Shop's second month of operations. How is the cash flow looking now? How much cash (if any) will the owner have on hand at the start of the third month?

(c) Add the columns and thus create the company's profit and loss statement for the two-month period.

2. *Preparing some financial records for Blueprints Business Planning Pty Ltd*

Jessie Jones finds that running a full-time business alone can be more complicated than originally expected. During the course of the first month (July), she makes four sales totalling A$3000 (one for training and the others for business planning), but also spends up considerably: A$500 is paid to Aherns Ltd for office furniture on 2 July, and A$1000 is paid to OfficeWorks for stationery three days later. On 15 July, Jessie pays herself A$800, and a fortnight later another A$400. The cost of company formation (A$1200) was paid to the Australian Securities and Investments Commission on 1 July.

On the first day of the month, she managed to secure A$4500 of the original capital contribution forecast in the business plan (all from herself), and the promise of another A$1500 if she needs it. She paid A$600 to Telstra Corporation on 25 July for phone line installation.

Of her clients, the first job (worth A$900 from Newrise Computing for a business plan) is paid for as soon as it is completed on 12 July. The second job worth A$500 (for a one-day training course for Squirrel Health Shops) is paid for on 25 July. The other clients — Mercury Energy (A$1500) and Indifferent Enterprises (A$100) — have not paid by the end of July.

Canberra Surf Shop

CASH FLOW STATEMENT

For the period 1 January to 28 February

Item	January	February

All expenses are paid by cheque, and in sequential order. The business starts activities with no money in the bank.

Devise cash receipts and cash payments journals, a cash flow statement and a profit and loss statement for the firm's first month of trading. What is the total cash revenue and expenses? What is the closing bank balance in the cash flow? What profit (or loss) has the firm recorded? How do these compare with the forecasts in the original business plan?

Use the blank pro forma sheets provided to do your calculations.

Blueprints Business Planning Pty Ltd

CASH RECEIPTS JOURNAL

for the month of July

Blueprints Business Planning Pty Ltd

CASH PAYMENTS JOURNAL

for the month of July

Blueprints Business Planning Pty Ltd

FINANCIAL STATEMENTS

for the month of July

Item	Cash flow	Profit and loss

SUGGESTED READING

Bragg, S.M. & Burton, E.J. *Accounting and Finance for Your Small Business*, 2nd edition, John Wiley & Sons, New York, 2006.

Holmes, S., Hutchinson, P., Forsaith, D., Gibson, B. & McMahon, R., *Small Enterprise Finance*, John Wiley & Sons, Brisbane, 2003.

O'Berry, D., *Small Business Cash Flow: Strategies for Making Your Business a Financial Success*, John Wiley & Sons, Brisbane, 2006.

Case study

House Canvas Pty Ltd

Karen and Alex decided to set up their own business. They had studied architecture together at Melbourne University, and shared a house in the early years when they were working for different, large architectural practices.

With her flair for bold colours and contemporary fashions, Karen was the extrovert of the pair. Vivacious, well spoken and a keen networker, she was a natural marketer and promoter. On the other hand, Alex was quiet and sedate. He worked hard, made sure that all the administration was done, and got back to the drawing board only when he was satisfied that all necessary compliance and paperwork had been completed.

Initially they had planned to work in the field they had trained for, but they quickly dropped their interest in architecture when it became apparent that there were many more opportunities available in the design field. Using Karen's extensive contacts, and networking with the many art students they had met while at university, the duo found that the real demand was for interior and exterior design of new houses and commercial buildings.

Many architectural practices simply design the outside of the buildings they plan for clients; they usually do not attempt to devise a 'whole-of-building' plan that also covers the interior. Using their architectural skills, Karen and Alex were able to provide customers with innovative, exciting house designs and furniture that fitted in neatly with the architect's plans.

After a year working under a partnership structure, they realised that they couldn't do all the work themselves. They found an external investor, and the business was restructured as a private company, in which Alex and Karen held 16 000 shares each. The third owner (with the balance of the shares) was Marian Borst, who owned a building company and had interests in several other businesses related to real estate. Part of the start-up funds were used to buy a strata-titled office; they regarded this as a smart investment that would give them secure premises, and provide some of the furnishing stock necessary to equip clients' buildings.

The business has now been trading for two years as a private company, and during this time they have been able to pick up several large contracts with building developers. Work of this nature is often unpredictable. Demand is closely tied to the overall fortunes of the housing and construction industries, which in turn are based on broader economic fundamentals. Tastes for interior fashions change quickly, and clients are not always willing to pay the high prices that Karen and Alex charge.

The company operates under a relatively lean structure. The growing demand for their services means that other staff have had to be employed, although most work is outsourced to subcontractors. The only people working in the office are Karen, Alex, another architect and a design student from the local technical college who works part-time.

Recordkeeping and accounting services are provided by an external accountancy practice. The firm invoices its work, providing generous credit terms. Their work is highly valued, and they operate in a relatively exclusive, specialised market niche. Marian has indicated before that she would be willing to buy out the pair if Alex finally wanted to fulfil his long-term dream of working with the underprivileged in Africa, and if Karen decided to move on. Although the office space is shown in the books at purchase (historical) cost, it has actually appreciated in value significantly, and is now worth much more than the A$280 000 they originally paid for it – perhaps as much as A$400 000.

Business has remained brisk. The two operators are now trying to work out what next to do with their business. Should they expand and take on more staff? This may require borrowing funds. Should they take a 'steady as she goes' approach and continue as they are doing? Or should they sell out while the going is good?

Questions

1. Analyse the attached financial documents. Is the business growing or declining?

2. Are there any financial problems evident in the current figures?

3. What options do you think Karen and Alex should pursue: expansion, a continuation of current performance, or sell their interest in the firm?

(*Note*: All figures shown in the financial statements are exclusive of GST.)

HOUSE CANVAS PTY LTD

PROFIT AND LOSS STATEMENT

for the financial years 1 July to 30 June

	Year 1	Year 2
Sales revenue	A$1 000 000	A$1 150 000
Less: Sales returns and allowances	35 000	45 000
Net sales	965 000	1 105 000
Less: Cost of goods sold	505 000	630 000
Gross profit	460 000	475 000
Less: Operating expenses		
Salaries	220 000	230 000
Office expenses	95 000	80 000
Less: Financial expenses	2 500	3 000
Net profit	$142 500	$162 000

HOUSE CANVAS PTY LTD

BALANCE SHEET

for the financial years 1 July to 30 June

	Year 1	Year 2
Assets		
Current assets:		
Cash	A$60 000	A$80 000
Accounts receivable	200 000	280 000
Less: Allowance for doubtful debts	(10 000)	(14 000)
Stock	100 000	80 000
Prepaid expenses	5 000	4 000
Total current assets	355 000	430 000
Non-current assets:		
Office building	280 000	280 000

Less: Accumulated depreciation	(50 000)	(60 000)
Equipment	140 000	140 000
Less: Accumulated depreciation	(60 000)	(80 000)
Total non-current assets	310 000	280 000
Total assets	$665 000	$710 000
Liabilities		
Current liabilities		
Accounts payable	$66 000	$32 000
Taxes payable	28 000	11 000
Loan instalment	20 000	20 000
Total current liabilities	114 000	63 000
Non-current liabilities		
Bank loan	200 000	180 000
Total liabilities	$314 000	$243 000
Owners' equity		
Ordinary shares (50 000 at $2)	$100 000	$100 000
Retained profits	251 000	367 000
Total owners' equity	$351 000	$467 000

ENDNOTES

1. R.G.P. McMahon, 'Business growth and performance and the financial reporting practices of Australian manufacturing SMEs', *Journal of Small Business Management*, vol. 39, no. 2, April 2001, pp. 152–64.
2. J.C. Brau, 'How do banks price owner–manager agency costs? An examination of small business borrowing', *Journal of Small Business Management*, vol. 40, no. 4, October 2002, pp. 273–86.
3. A. Ah-Yeung, *A Guide To Keeping Business Records*, Inland Revenue Department, Hong Kong, 1995.
4. D. Davis, P. Dunn & K. Boswell, 'The importance of capturing and using financial information in small business,' *American Journal of Economics & Business Administration*, vol. 1, no. 1, 2009, pp. 27–33.
5. K. Moores & J. Mula, *Managing and Controlling Family Owned Businesses: A Life Cycle Perspective of Australian Firms*, Research Report, Bond University, Gold Coast, 1993.
6. A.N. Berger & G.F. Udell, 'The economics of small business finance: The roles of private equity and debt markets in the financial growth cycle,' *Journal of Banking and Finance*, no. 22, 1998, pp. 873–97.
7. J. Pope & H. Abdul-Jabbar, 'Small and Medium-Sized enterprises and Tax Compliance Burden in Malaysia: Issues and Challenges for Tax Administration', *Small Enterprise Research*, vol. 16, no. 1, 2008, pp. 47–60.
8. R.G.P. McMahon & S. Holmes, 'Small business financial management practices in North America: A literature review', *Journal of Small Business Management*, vol. 29, no. 2, April 1991, pp. 19–30.
9. R. Manian, *Doing Business in India For Dummies*, Wiley, Hoboken, New Jersey, 2007, p. 158.
10. For a more detailed explanation, ibid. p. 145.
11. J.W. English, *How to Organise and Operate a Small Business in Australia*, 7th edn, Allen & Unwin, Sydney, 1998.

12. C. James, 'Why it's hard to make a buck', *Australian Financial Review*, 3–4 August 2002, pp. 22–3; Australian Bureau of Statistics, *Business Operations and Industry Performance 2000–2001*, cat. no. 8142.0, ABS, Canberra, 2002, p. 8.

13. B. Brown, 'How to rate a company', *Weekend Australian*, 3–4 August 2002, p. 33.

14. ibid.

15. ibid.

16. Inland Revenue Authority of Singapore, *Basic Record-Keeping Guide for Small Businesses*, Singapore, 2008, p. 2.

17. J.W. English, *see* note 6.

18. G. Gaujers, J.A. Harper & J. Browne, *Guide to Managing a Successful Small Business in Australia*, McGraw-Hill, Sydney, 1999.

19. Inland Revenue Authority of Singapore, *Basic Record-Keeping Guide for Small Businesses*, Singapore, 2008, p. 10.

PART 4

Selected topics

CHAPTER 15 ICT as a business tool   373

CHAPTER 16 Managing growth and transition   397

CHAPTER 17 Corporate entrepreneurship   423

CHAPTER 18 Contemporary issues in small business and
             entrepreneurship   449

ICT as a business tool

Learning objectives

After reading this chapter, you should be able to:

- explain the extent and role of ICT use within SMEs

- explain the information systems concepts related to turning data into knowledge

- describe the level of ICT implementation evident in a business

- identify a broad range of ICT tools useful for SMEs

- detail a range of reasons for SMEs engaging in e-commerce

- discuss ways that businesses can attract visitors to their website.

The founder of Microsoft, Bill Gates, predicted in 1995 that the internet and technology convergence would be a great leveller for small business, allowing SMEs to compete with larger organisations.[1] By 2008, over 84 per cent of the online population in the Asia–Pacific region had made an online purchase, representing an increase in the market of 40 per cent in two years.[2] In developed economies, such as Australia, business use of broadband is approaching saturation, with over 95 per cent of SMEs having a broadband internet connection.[3] Moreover, in regions of the world where high-speed wireless broadband is widely available, the trend towards convergence of mobile devices and computing is reaching a critical mass, with information and communication technologies (ICT) tools becoming highly portable and accessible to SMEs.[4]

Technology convergence is creating a world in which data is networked to a point where information is abundant, accessible and ubiquitous. The pace of change creates somewhat daunting challenges and equally exciting opportunities for the use of ICT in SMEs. The competitive pressures of globalisation are driving new means of communication and collaboration in global networks of individuals and organisations, 24 hours a day seven days a week. A key challenge for SMEs in this dynamic environment is the application of technologies in the effective management of information and communication systems.[5]

The relationship between effective ICT systems and small business is a complex one. For instance, many small business owner–managers ask themselves how should their small firm be expected to utilise all the information around them? One way of approaching this question is to first consider what represents an 'information system' (IS) within the broader ICT concept. In smaller organisations, IS will often be a nebulous and undefined series of operations — simply a means to an end, but it can be much more than that. In the first section of this chapter, the role of information and communication systems is explained, providing a definition of ICT and related concepts. The typical path to the adoption of electronic commerce by SMEs will be described. The second section describes the different categories of information and communication systems that may serve the strategic, tactical and operational needs of SMEs. The third section will focus specifically on electronic commerce. Within this third section the various potential business uses of the internet and some related ICT will be explored.

Information and communication technologies (ICT)
Technology and related processes and networks that handle information and aid communication, encompassing radio, audio and video data, often utilising telephony or the internet to receive, store, retrieve, manipulate, share and utilise information.

Defining ICT in the SME context

The term **information and communication technologies (ICT)** as it is applied in this text for SMEs is somewhat of a catch-all phrase, incorporating the use of various information handling technologies and processes, such as computers, wireless devices, mobile phones, personal digital assistants (PDAs), global positioning system (GPS), Voice over Internet Protocol (VoIP), fixed-line telephones and, in particular, the use of the internet for e-commerce. This definition also encompasses the software applications and hardware solutions that support an e-commerce strategy. The concept also covers other less obvious hardware technologies, such as barcode scanners and many types of embedded 'chips' in other machines and appliances. Additionally, ICT includes recent developments in collaborative online networks and communities, such as wikis and weblogs (blogs).

The role and importance of ICT for SMEs

As the OECD has noted, ICT now touches on most aspects of human behaviour.[6]

Today, every business must be able to receive, process and utilise a significant amount of information. Every business collects and blends a wide variety of information, distributes it and uses it throughout the business. This information is used to provide accurate and timely outputs for internal and external consumption. Although there are many fundamentals of small business planning that are somewhat unchanging and predictable, the digital age is remodelling many facets of the business landscape, resulting in new market dynamics, wherein global competitive pressures and emergent communication technologies (at very low cost) have combined in many forms to change the rules of the game. In particular, the growth in use of the internet and related ICT has given rise to:

- rapidly falling costs of ICT
- rapidly expanding capabilities of ICT
- growing networks of users of various ICTs reaching local and global critical mass
- rising numbers of efficient online low cost marketplaces
- small firms having greater access to global markets at no higher cost than large firms.[7]

In support of the growing importance of ICT, patterns do seem to be emerging, particularly in high-tech sectors in the economy, of a greater level of 'performance spread' between the profits of firms. Essentially, the gap between the winners and losers and their use of ICT is widening, good reason for firms to ensure that they make the right ICT decisions.[8] In addition to appreciating the implications of these changes for business models and strategies, small business owner–managers must also understand the function and purpose of their ICT systems. To do this the owner should consider the key factors that are likely to influence the design and implementation of their ICT system.

The importance of data, information and knowledge

Understanding the distinction between data, information and knowledge is important for an appreciation of what constitutes an ICT system, and why ICT strategies are sometimes ineffective. **Data** are facts and figures that may or may not be useful to a user in their raw form. When this data is processed, it is converted into **information**, which is more likely to be of use in creating **knowledge** for future use. For example, recording the *data* from a sale is only useful once it becomes part of the accumulated financial (profit), marketing (sales) and operational (inventory) information system. Then, this knowledge of prior sales data patterns can be used to make decisions on pricing the product, ordering future inventory, predicting future sales and a plethora of other knowledge-based outcomes. For the small business owner, knowledge developed within the business needs to be followed by action that improves such things as profitability, productivity and sales. Accumulating knowledge without a clear use in mind is unlikely to lead to a more effective or efficient business model.

Data *Streams of raw facts and figures.*

Information *Data that has been converted into something meaningful and useful.*

Knowledge *The accumulated intellectual capital, including information created that guides actions and decisions.*

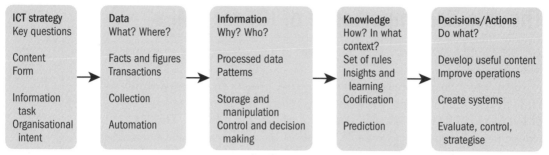

ICT strategy Key questions	Data What? Where?	Information Why? Who?	Knowledge How? In what context?	Decisions/Actions Do what?
Content Form	Facts and figures Transactions	Processed data Patterns	Set of rules Insights and learning	Develop useful content Improve operations
Information task	Collection	Storage and manipulation	Codification	Create systems
Organisational intent	Automation	Control and decision making	Prediction	Evaluate, control, strategise

FIGURE 15.1 Key features of data, information and knowledge leading to decisions and action

This model of data, information and knowledge offers a number of instructive lessons for SMEs including:[9]

- Data from multiple single transactions can build into an information flow that creates knowledge.
- Once information is organised and analysed it can lead to organisational learning that creates valuable knowledge.
- Decisions and actions derived from knowledge can be implemented within an organisation to create systems that improve productivity, and aid in the management tasks of evaluation, control and strategy.
- All data, information and knowledge should be collected and created in a planned manner that increases the likelihood of productive actions or decisions.

Knowledge processing systems have grown more important as SMEs and their advisers realise that often it is valuable knowledge that leads to competitive advantage, that 'knowledge is power'. ICT tools are often the conduit through which this power is channelled. Creating knowledge using ICT as a tool to gather and process data is as much art as it is science. It is a human activity where **tacit knowledge** is transformed into **explicit knowledge**. The ultimate value of the knowledge created is in its capacity to support decisions and actions, as well as provide timely, accurate information to various stakeholders. The value of such transformed knowledge is clearly seen in the price that potential franchisees are prepared to pay to become part of a good franchise group. Part of what the franchisee is buying is the proven concepts (tacit knowledge) that have been transformed into valuable processes and procedures (explicit knowledge) and made available for a fee.

Tacit knowledge
Knowledge that the business has developed through experience but is not easily recorded to capture its value.

Explicit knowledge
More formally recognised knowledge that has been codified and can be communicated to others.

ICT adoption by SMEs

Most studies of ICT in SMEs focus on identifying ICT adoption factors; this means that researchers have become relatively good at understanding why and when SMEs adopt ICT. However, recent meta-analyses (the study of other studies) in both the SME and e-commerce literature confirm that most research has focused on the SMEs' use of *available* ICT (well known technologies), rather than on the *supply* of new (less known) and innovative ICT.[10] The acquisition of suitable ICT can be a highly technical problem that often requires the assistance of external experts. There is a strong argument for seeking specialist advice when selecting and implementing ICT. External consultants typically accumulate more depth and breadth of knowledge on ICT implementation through economies of scale and scope. As such, they can become important mediators in the adoption of ICT.[11] However, it is often the attitude of the owner–manager towards ICT strategy and tactics that is a decisive factor in successful implementation. In small companies, owner–managers are closely involved with every aspect of the company. The company is likely to have been formed around the individual competencies of the founders; they provide the primary knowledge base of the company. It is worth reflecting on three types of attitude and management style of owner–managers that influence decisions related to ICT:[12]

- *Positive owner–managers* personally use ICT in their company and find the technology fascinating. They unreservedly acknowledge that implementing ICTs will increase their organisation's efficiency and effectiveness. Therefore, they identify opportunities for innovative use of new ICT on a continuous basis. In terms of management style, this kind of owner–manager typically develops and uses policies that encourage collaboration and a shared management style.[13]
- *Negative owner–managers* have a tendency to resist suggestions that ICT can improve business efficiency and effectiveness. They typically hesitate to invest in ICT and only implement out of necessity. Negative owner–managers often report being annoyed at having to rely on ICT solutions to remain in business and having to be dependent on external experts.
- *Uncertain/traditionalist owner–managers* are ambivalent about ICT. Such owner–managers usually express hesitation to invest in technology, and anxiety using ICT tools. They feel comfortable controlling all decisions and keeping things exactly as they always were.

Before deciding on an ICT strategy, understanding the prevailing attitudes of the owner–manager is an important first step. Failure to do so ignores the centrality of the owner's personal goals and attitudes in shaping the mission and vision of the business.

Information systems for SMEs

As a subset of business ICT, there are a range of **information systems (IS)** specifically designed to assist with decision making and routinisation of work. The decisions to be made can be at any level in an organisation, and no single system can provide all the information an organisation needs. Figure 15.2 illustrates the potential range of systems found in SMEs. Small businesses have, in general, only two hierarchical levels: *management*, which includes the owner and possibly one or two other managers, and the *operational* level, which includes all other employees. Medium-sized enterprises might have an intermediary level, comprising of supervisors and team leaders. The decision frontiers can be further divided into functional areas, such as manufacturing, marketing and sales, finance, accounting, and human resources. Typically, owner–manager decisions will have a more strategic direction whereas supervisors, team leaders and general staff will require systems that assist with short-term, tactical or day-to-day operations. There are also operational systems where rules and standard operating procedures can largely remove the need for decision making from repetitive tasks.

Information systems (IS) *An information system collects, processes, stores, analyses and disseminates information in a planned and specific manner.*

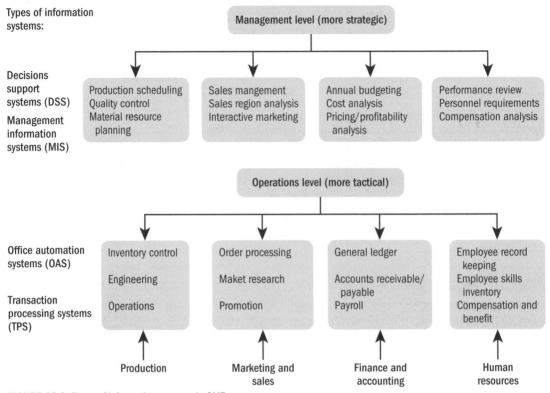

Types of information systems:

Management level (more strategic)

Decisions support systems (DSS)

Management information systems (MIS)

Production scheduling Quality control Material resource planning	Sales mangement Sales region analysis Interactive marketing	Annual budgeting Cost analysis Pricing/profitability analysis	Performance review Personnel requirements Compensation analysis

Operations level (more tactical)

Office automation systems (OAS)

Transaction processing systems (TPS)

Inventory control Engineering Operations	Order processing Maket research Promotion	General ledger Accounts receivable/ payable Payroll	Employee record keeping Employee skills inventory Compensation and benefit

| Production | Marketing and sales | Finance and accounting | Human resources |

FIGURE 15.2 Types of information systems in SMEs

Operation-level systems monitor elementary activities and transactions of the business, such as sales, receipts, cash deposits, payroll, and flow of material in a factory. The principal purpose at this level is to answer routine questions and to track the flow of transactions through the organisation. How many units have been produced today? How many sales took place today? When was a specific supplier account settled? On the other hand, management-level systems support the monitoring, controlling, decision making and planning activities. The principal question addressed by such systems is — how well are things working? Management-level systems typically provide periodic reports gathered from multiple sources, rather than real-time feedback on single operational issues. An example is a system that provides an overview of all ongoing projects at the end of each month against the sales and costs budgeted for the different projects. There are four main forms of IS that can play a significant role in many SMEs discussed in detail below.

Transaction processing systems (TPS)

Transaction processing systems (TPS)
A computerised system that processes and records the daily routine transactions necessary to conduct the business.

Transaction processing systems (TPS) collect, record and process the data that results from routine business transactions. Typical examples are systems that process sales, purchases, inventory changes, employee recordkeeping and production output. These systems are, of themselves, often relatively standardised because operational standards tend to have evolved throughout industries and markets to allow common practices to emerge.[14] Examples would include the predominant accounting packages for SMEs. These databases are important because they provide the raw data that can be processed and used by management information systems and decision support systems.[15] TPS systems are usually designed to interface with other technologies that capture data (input devices), such as bar code readers, radio devices and electronic tills. These systems are often designed around the accounting and taxation external regulatory environment in which the organisation operates.

At the operational level, tasks, resources and goals are predefined and highly structured. Therefore, most TPS contain enough structure to enforce rules and procedures for work done by clerks or operators. For example, the decision to purchase parts or raw material can be made by administrative staff according to a predefined criterion, such as a minimum inventory level.

Office automation systems (OAS)

An **office automation system (OAS)** is an application designed to increase the productivity of data workers in offices by supporting coordination and communication activities. OAS software is often standardised and mass-produced and as such, the relatively low purchase and implementation cost makes OAS a common and early stage ICT adoption choice for SMEs.

Office automation system (OAS)
A computer system that facilitates everyday information tasks in offices.

Typical OASs handle and manage documents (through text and image processing systems and presentation packages), calculating (through spreadsheets), scheduling (through enterprise collaboration systems), and communication (through telephone, fax, email and VoIP). Some important tools generally grouped within the OAS category include:

- *Text and image processing systems* that store, revise and print documents containing text or image data. These systems started with word processors but have evolved to produce professional-quality documents combining output from word processors with design, graphics, and special layout features.
- *Enterprise collaboration systems*, which are information systems that use a variety of information technologies to help employees communicate ideas, share resources and coordinate tasks. Such systems could rely on the internet or the company's intranet or extranet, and collaboration software. This software integrates electronic communication tools (e.g. email, voicemail, web publishing) and other collaborative work management tools (e.g. electronic calendar, workflow systems, document sharing) to help members of a team to collaborate.
- *Communication systems*, which fall into two broad categories: multi-user 'teleconferencing' systems and systems for facilitating individual communications. Teleconferencing is the use of electronic transmission to permit two or more people to 'meet' and discuss an idea or an issue. Typical examples of teleconferencing include audio conferencing (a single telephone call involving three or more people participating from at least two locations) and video-conferencing (a form of teleconferencing in which the participants can see the other distant participants using webcams or video equipment).

These technologies are all rapidly changing form and scope as more and more regions and businesses acquire broadband internet capabilities. For example, the increased carrying capacity of the infrastructure that supports broadband internet access has allowed organisations such as Skype® to provide global video

**Voice over
Internet Protocols
(VoIP)** *Voice
communications
using digital
internet protocols
transmitted via a
telecommunication
network.*

**Natural Language
Generation
(NLG)** *Computer-
generated voice,
capable of
synthesising spoken
words from text.*

**Interactive
Voice Response
(IVR)** *Applications
that use NLG to
automate human
service contact.*

**Management
information
system (MIS)** *A
management-level
information system
that serves planning,
controlling and
decision making by
providing summary
information.*

call systems and **Voice over Internet Protocols (VoIP)** at relatively low cost (even for free within their own network of users).

In addition, new voice and language-related applications are now maturing into SME markets using **Natural Language Generation (NLG)** technologies to communicate directly with customers. Examples of this include **Interactive Voice Response (IVR)** systems specifically designed for SMEs that want to automate service functions using the customers' spoken instructions. There are also speech-to-text conversion applications that convert the spoken word to text, offering productivity savings for firms that need to codify a great deal of spoken words (for example the legal profession). The capability of such solutions to automate service delivery functions within small firms has been identified as a significant productivity improvement opportunity for SMEs.[16]

Management information systems (MIS)

A **management information system (MIS)** provides managers with information that supports much of their day-to-day planning, controlling and decision-making needs. MIS provide a variety of reports and displays to management. Most of these systems use simple routines, such as summaries and comparisons, as opposed to sophisticated mathematical models or statistical techniques. Reports and displays generated by a MIS can be furnished either on demand or periodically, according to a predetermined schedule.

A MIS will typically extract and summarise data, allowing managers to monitor and direct the business and to provide employees with accurate feedback about easily measured aspects of their work. For example, printing out a long list of every sale that occurred during a day or a week in a chain of retail stores would be cumbersome as a way of visualising and tracking performance. However, the same data could be summarised into measures of performance, such as sales per location, per employee and per line. In this example, the transaction data remains essential, but the MIS focuses on results for management. MIS capabilities are somewhat of an extension of use of TPS and OAS, therefore many providers are now extending their products to include more MIS functionality across their product range. For example, MYOB (a well-known accounting software company) offers add-on functions (MIS) for its bookkeeping and accounting packages (TPS & OAS) that produce high level performance dashboards for small businesses at a very low cost relative to the potential benefit.[17]

Decision support systems (DSS)

**Decision support
system (DSS)** *An
interactive system
that provides support
to managers during
semi-structured and
unstructured decision
making.*

A **decision support system (DSS)** is an integrated set of computer tools that allows a decision maker to interact directly with computers to create information useful in making unanticipated, semi-structured and unstructured decisions.[18] A DSS can help small business owner–managers to generate the information they need in an interactive, simulation-based process involving, for instance, plant expansion, new products, staff recruitment and marketing. Anything that presents a strategic choice is potentially a topic for DSS.

DSS are different from transaction processing systems, which focus on processing data generated by business transactions and operations, though they extract data from the firm databases maintained by TPS. They are also different from MIS, which focus on providing managers with prespecified information (reports) that can be used to help them make more effective, structured types of decisions. Therefore, the common thread running through the wide range of DSS applications is that the situation emphasises analytical work rather than transaction processing, general office or management work, in other words, *strategic* management. ICT consultants can help a small business to build a DSS at surprisingly moderate costs because many of the hardware and software components required are mass-produced items. However, where a small business cannot justify the expense of creating a custom DSS solution, there are also 'off the shelf' tools being offered commercially.[19] This mass-distribution of basic decision support software is blurring the distinction between MIS and DSS for SMEs somewhat.

Implementing an ICT strategy

This chapter has already explored the owners' attitude to using ICT, focusing primarily on established businesses. However, new business start-ups (particularly micro-enterprises) may not have any knowledge or attitude at all related to ICT. The United Nations Asia–Pacific Development Information Program (UN-APDIP) model of ICT adoption considers businesses that start with no ICT capabilities whatsoever.[20] New micro-enterprises will typically start their ICT foray with only a simple phone and entry-level computer, and then they will develop a rudimentary PC based model using basic software and a printer. Following this, businesses then engage in the use of the internet and may gravitate to productivity-enhancing low cost software and hardware, such as VoIP and file sharing, with perhaps some fundamental level of e-commerce. Eventually some businesses will graduate to a fourth level of sophistication where ICT is used proactively to assist with marketing strategy (e-business), customer relations, resource planning and inventory management. This last step (advanced IT use) is often what separates the small business that is content (or destined) to stay small from firms with the strategic intent to grow larger.[21]

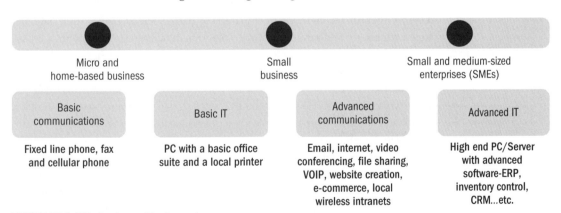

FIGURE 15.3 ICT adoption and business size

Source: Adapted from V. Kotelnikov, Small and Medium Enterprises and ICT, United Nations Development Programme – Asia–Pacific Development Information Programme (UNDP-APDI), www.apdip.net, 2007, p. 6.

Without careful control, a lack of a focus on the role of ICT implemented can result in lower productivity due to duplication and underutilisation of systems.

However, a proactive strategy to maximise the benefit of ICT investments can lead to greater growth and efficiency for SMEs.[22]

Types of ICT used by SMEs

There are a myriad of tools available to assist small business, table 15.1 lists a range of ICT that SMEs can use to boost efficiency and effectiveness.

TABLE 15.1 A selection of ICT tools for SMEs

Internet-based services	PC software	PC hardware and peripherals	Telephone, radio and satellite communications	Other
• VoIP (e.g. Skype) • Video sharing (e.g. Youtube) • Facebook, Myspace, LinkedIn. • Webmail (e.g. gmail, hotmail, yahoomail) • Web storage (e.g. Flickr) • Extranets • Mapping tools (e.g. Google Earth) • Search engines • Web logs (blogs)	• Intranets • Virtual tours • Design software • Office suites • Accounting packages • Recordkeeping • Data compression and storage • Speech to text • Email programs • Blog authoring software • Interactive voice recognition (IVR)	• Microphones • Webcams • LAN servers • DVD/CD burners • Portable hard drives • Flash memory cards • Thumb drives • Scanners • Printers • Loudspeakers • Video/LCD displays • Data projectors	• Landline phone • Wi-Fi, Bluetooth & infrared devices • Facsimile machine • Cell/mobile phone • Cordless phone • Switchboards • SMS • Global Position Systems (GPS) • UHF/VHF radios • Radio frequency identification (RFID) • Hands-free kits	• Digital recorder • Digital camera • Digital video • PDA • Public address systems • Queue management systems • Tills • Laser scanners • Radio scanners • Barcodes

Table 15.1 is divided into five categories of ICT tools. First is a representative selection of internet-based applications and services that can often be utilised at relatively low (or no) direct cost. The next two categories relate to the software and hardware configuration of the business's personal computers. The fourth category focuses on methods of transferring data, such as digital radio signals, digital telephony and satellite technologies. The final column represents a cross-section of disparate technologies, which are not 'top of mind' when first thinking of ICT, but of great importance none-the-less. In many respects the decisions made across these five categories of ICT are interrelated. Take for example the use of VoIP. This service requires a PC with certain minimum specifications, a broadband internet connection and peripheral hardware to record digital audio and video (a webcam).

There are examples where infrastructure constraints within a particular region will dictate choices other than the somewhat PC-centric view discussed above. For example, a recent study on ICT used by Australian SMEs notes that 20 per cent of rural businesses were overlooking PC based internet solutions (when compared to metropolitan SMEs) in favour of 3G mobile phone solutions.[23] This may be because of bandwidth constraints of the existing copper wire networks. Overwhelmingly, the message is that a business that wishes to take advantage of the opportunities that the internet opens up must make the 'right' yet flexible decisions in terms of technology acquisition and use.

The internet

Online activities can be classified into four layers of the internet economy, infrastructure, applications, intermediaries and e-commerce. SMEs are not generally involved with developing the infrastructure of the internet, rather they are users of this infrastructure. However, infrastructure plays a vital role in enabling the advantages of e-commerce. Each year the Economist Intelligence Unit (EIU) estimates the relative readiness of a country's consumers, businesses, governments and infrastructure to benefit from ICT. In 2008, the EIU particularly identified Voice over Internet Protocol (VoIP) as an emerging opportunity for SMEs. VoIP is predicted to significantly reduce communication costs and inefficiencies as long as the required bandwidth infrastructure is widely deployed.[24] Industry experts agree that businesses seriously considering e-commerce strategies must have access to reliable high-speed internet connections.[25] As can be seen from table 15.2, most economies in the Asia–Pacific region are either holding or improving their ranking in this regard. This bodes well for the competitiveness of the region in the digital economy of the twenty-first century.

TABLE 15.2 Two-year movement in e-readiness rankings

Country	2006	2008	Movement	Country	2006	2008	Movement
Australia	8	4	+4	Taiwan	23	19	+4
New Zealand	14	16	−2	India	53	54	−1
Hong Kong	10	2	+8	China	57	56	+1
Singapore	13	6	+5	Malaysia	37	33	−4

Source: Extracted from the 2006 and 2008 E-readiness reports of the European Intelligence Unit.[26]

Business uses of the internet

There are a number of business models that will have varying impact upon the degree and type of business strategies and ICT solutions adopted. The five business models that are typically defined in e-commerce marketing strategies are:

- *business to government (B2G)*: supplying goods or services to government
- *business to business (B2B)*: supplying goods or services to another business
- *business to consumer (B2C)*: supplying goods or services to an end consumer
- *consumer to consumer (C2C)*: users selling or trading goods with each other
- *consumer to business (C2B):* where the consumer invites business to bid to supply the goods or service they require.[27]

B2G and B2B businesses have a tendency to adopt e-commerce strategies that support logistics functions and data exchange. This is primarily because of the closer working relationships and networks that exist in these business models. Smaller organisations in the B2B and B2G arena tend to have a much more arms-length relationship with supply chain partners and clients. Because of this, smaller SMEs have less impetus to adopt sophisticated e-commerce, unless required to do so by influential network partners.[28] By definition, the customer driven models of C2C and C2B do not involve any SME-initiated transactions. Well known examples of these include eBay and Craigslist (C2C), and Google Video (C2B). Although these businesses are certainly not owned by SMEs, customer-driven marketplaces can be a fruitful revenue source for SMEs prepared to tender for their customers. The main focus of discussion past this point will relate to B2C and to a lesser extent B2B models where the vast majority of e-commerce small businesses exist.

Stages of e-commerce adoption

According to Daniel, Wilson & Myers, the path that SMEs take when adopting e-commerce can be portrayed as a number defined stages:[29]

- *Stage one* involves using a web browser to communicate via email and locate information online. This stage also includes the enterprise conducting basic banking operations online.
- *Stage two* is indicated by the creation of a home page to provide information about the company products. This home page is basically an electronic brochure. The decision to establish a viable, dedicated website is a significant step toward the full adoption of e-commerce. This is where the first significant resistance is shown by some SMEs to moving their business online. This resistance is attributed to the risk of failure, raising doubts about the value of the investment in both time and money.
- *Stage three* is reached when the business is using its own website to receive orders and payments and procure goods online. Websites that support such retailing applications generally display a high level of interactivity, flexibility and customisation. One of the major barriers to fully embracing this form of business-to-consumer e-commerce is the reluctance to change existing business practice. For example, a lot of SMEs feel comfortable with their established distribution channels and supplier arrangements. In spite of the obvious status quo, use of e-commerce by one major supplier, distributor or competitor could provide the necessary trigger for many businesses to become more active in adopting e-commerce. This stage also signals potential pricing problems in various distribution channels where e-commerce can begin to cannibalise other distribution channel sales.
- *Stage four* involves alterations to critical business processes. An example of this would be the integration of the business information system in an electronic data interchange (EDI) to exchange information and accomplish transactions. Such an application integrates the suppliers' and customers' systems to provide them (among other capabilities) with just-in-time inventory and production capability.

Why engage in e-commerce?

Probably the most often cited reason for adopting an e-commerce strategy is that it can provide an incremental increase in sales through rich, low cost marketing communications. Looking somewhat deeper than this simple yet compelling reason, there are many other benefits and advantages of engaging in e-commerce including:

- global reach
- open for business 24 hours, seven days per week, 52 weeks per year
- telecommuting opportunities for staff[30]
- enhanced customer service via interactivity
- measurable sales conversion and customer relationship management[31]

- flexibility that allows the entrepreneur to work on the business at times that are convenient
- information rich medium allows for detailed product and service education
- lower costs than brick and mortar
- support of rapid growth strategies.[32]

Given the range and scope of e-commerce tools available, it would be useful to classify the technology into several categories. Doing this may then focus the small business owner on strategic uses for technology rather than *ad hoc* adoption of solutions.

Figure 15.4 depicts seven types of internet use evident in the potential e-commerce strategies of SMEs.[33]

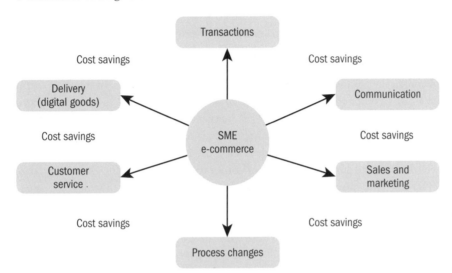

FIGURE 15.4 Types of e-commerce used in SMEs

The seven types of e-commerce solutions are:
- *Transactions.* These include such things as electronic banking, paying for supplied goods online and receiving payment from clients online.
- *Communication.* This comprises a cluster that includes using the internet as an information and research resource as well as a tool for communication within the business (intranets), and externally via email, chat forums and, more recently, through Really Simple Syndication (RSS) feeds, weblogs, social networks and VoIP. The focus of the communication could be to customers or suppliers or other stakeholders, such as shareholders, industry peers, investors and staff.
- *Sales and marketing.* This covers all advertising online as well as websites designed to provide information to customers and systems created to take orders online.
- *Changes to business process.* Such issues encompass systems to facilitate self-service by customers and suppliers as well as using the internet as a means to recruit new staff. This category also includes methods of document and design exchange with customers and suppliers.
- *Customer service.* Users might include the development of FAQs (lists of frequently asked questions), facilitating after-sales contact and providing an opportunity to accept suggestions (suggestion schemes online), as well as conducting polls and questionnaires to better understand client needs.

- *Product or service delivery.* The internet can be used as a method of delivering the product or service because the item for sale can be digitised.
- *Cost savings.* Some researchers identify reduced costs as a separate cluster where the sole purpose of the e-commerce initiative is to save money. Alternatively, it is reasonable to argue that cost savings can occur by implementing any of the other six types of e-commerce. As a consequence, figure 15.4 depicts cost saving as a benefit that is possible in any e-business strategy.

Whatever the intended business use of the internet, it is necessary to first of all make choices in regard to software selection. The volume of software applications that have and are being developed for SMEs is somewhat confronting. To give this statement perspective, in 2008 a popular web forum on the topic of e-commerce software applications for SMEs identified over 270 'top apps' (top pick applications) useful new applications designed to assist small business. This was in addition to an original list of 230 applications identified just one year prior.[34] That is, 500 useful 'top apps' applications available online at the click of a button, and of course the payment of a fee to hire or buy the application software. This could be a case of more choice without any real increase in quality. However, it is more likely reflective of the maturing of the market for SME software applications. A discussion on the many types of applications available, or upon their uses and merits is beyond the scope of this book. Suffice to say that many are low cost, well-known and supported by major corporations. In fact, some are even no cost 'freeware' (programs that are free to use), such as Open Office which is a selection of integrated applications that provide much of the functionality of the basic Microsoft Office suite at no cost to download and use. Although the old saying *you get what you pay for* may still hold true, there are such exceptions to the rule.

Building a web presence

Uniform Resource Locator (URL) *The technical name for a web address.*

The essence of most promotional strategies is to increase the awareness and likeability of a service or product (brand) and then move beyond this to elicit a sale. The online equivalent of the 'brand' name is the domain name or **Uniform Resource Locator (URL)**. Selecting a domain name for a new business is an activity that should be considered during the selection of the trading name to ensure availability. In the Asia–Pacific region, the body with responsibility for providing resource allocation and registration services is the Asia–Pacific Network Information Centre (APNIC). APNIC accredits and approves various organisations within 56 economies in Asia and Oceania to allocate domain names. A list of Asia–Pacific national trustees of domain names appears in table 15.3.[35]

TABLE 15.3 Asia–Pacific national trustees of domain names

Country	Organisation	Website
Australia	Australian Domain Name Administration	www.auda.org.au
New Zealand	Domain Name Commission	www.dnc.org.nz
Singapore	Singapore Network Information Centre	www.nic.net.sg
China	China Internet Network Information Centre	www.cnic.net.cn
Malaysia	.my Domain Registry	www.domainregistry.my
India	InRegistry	www.registry.in

These organisations typically provide substantial online advice, assistance and tutorials on selection of an appropriate URL, including a lookup facility called *Whois Search* that will provide the contact details of prior registered owners of any URL within their jurisdiction. Once ownership rights to the preferred URL are confirmed and purchased, attention can then move to website development and promotional strategy. Website design is a complex area and professionals are usually called upon to design the web presence. However, the owner should at a minimum know some of the key promotional tools, display methods and emerging technologies that could support the overall business strategy.

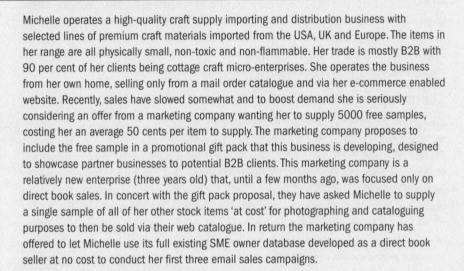

What would you do?

Michelle's Craft Supplies

Michelle operates a high-quality craft supply importing and distribution business with selected lines of premium craft materials imported from the USA, UK and Europe. The items in her range are all physically small, non-toxic and non-flammable. Her trade is mostly B2B with 90 per cent of her clients being cottage craft micro-enterprises. She operates the business from her own home, selling only from a mail order catalogue and via her e-commerce enabled website. Recently, sales have slowed somewhat and to boost demand she is seriously considering an offer from a marketing company wanting her to supply 5000 free samples, costing her an average 50 cents per item to supply. The marketing company proposes to include the free sample in a promotional gift pack that this business is developing, designed to showcase partner businesses to potential B2B clients. This marketing company is a relatively new enterprise (three years old) that, until a few months ago, was focused only on direct book sales. In concert with the gift pack proposal, they have asked Michelle to supply a single sample of all of her other stock items 'at cost' for photographing and cataloguing purposes to then be sold via their web catalogue. In return the marketing company has offered to let Michelle use its full existing SME owner database developed as a direct book seller at no cost to conduct her first three email sales campaigns.

Questions

1. Would you accept their offer?
2. What concerns do you have about these internet-based promotional ideas?

Attracting visitors to a website

Chapter 11 examined a range of promotional tools and highlighted the importance of including the website URL prominently in most other promotions. This section looks specifically at internet based methods of driving traffic to a website. Beyond having a website that has unique content that customers value, there are two main methods of generating page views via another website. Advertising space can be purchased on third party websites that prospective clients are likely to be visiting, or traffic can be attracted via high rankings on search engines and prominent listing in directories.

Advertising on third party websites

The business model of many content-rich websites involves attracting web traffic to their sites for the content, and then selling advertising space in the form of banners, sidebars, digital coupons, free gifts and advertorials. The advertiser then delivers the potential customer into the website of the advertising business. This model is quite similar to traditional forms of advertising, such as newspapers and magazines, but via a different medium. A twist on this formula is the advent of **affiliate programs** where businesses are paid on a per-click basis for providing 'click-throughs' from their web page. Caution is required when joining affiliate programs that focus on click-through, since these affiliate programs sometimes have little in the way of useful content, basically designed to trick the viewer to visit another site. Because of such unethical behaviour, most search engines have policies that exclude these valueless pyramid systems (referred to as link farms) from their rankings.[36] Other slightly different systems may also be referred to as affiliate programs that operate to *reward sales*, not click-throughs to avoid the link farm problem. Therefore, it is important when considering joining affiliate programs to consider how the search engines view the particular brand and business model of individual programs. Joining the wrong programs can now actually have a detrimental effect on rankings.

Affiliate programs *The payment of rewards for page views, site visits or sales generated from another website's referral marketing efforts.*

Search engines

Designing an effective website is not principally about aesthetics, unfortunately some extremely attractive looking websites get very few visits. Yes, a website should be aesthetically pleasing, but it is more important for most businesses to generate visits to the site in the first instance. This can either be achieved by paying for traffic from search engines and directories, or by raising the relevance of the website according to the ranking criteria of the search engines. The capability to understand and thus improve the ranking of a web page is something of a 'holy grail' among web design professionals. The skill is broadly referred to as **search engine optimisation (SEO)** and is somewhat like a forensic detective trying to deconstruct the secret code (algorithms) of the search engines. Some criteria of the search engine rankings are known, such as placing highly relevant text and code referred to as 'meta-tags'; linking to popular external websites with reciprocal arrangements; selecting specific websites to link with for relevance and keeping the content current and relevant. To understand the popularity of web pages that you may want to partner with, there are online services available that track this (for example, see Linkpopularity.com).

Search engine optimisation (SEO) *Increasing the ranking of websites on search engines via better design and implementation strategy.*

Many search engines also provide opportunities for pay-per-click advertising alongside their free listing and ranking services to create a highly visible and desirable marketplace for search terms. The search engines can then sell volumes of guaranteed 'click-throughs' using a competitive but anonymous bidding process (for example, see Google Adwords, google.adwords.com). Some search engines also invite paid inclusions that cause the listing to be raised in the rankings or to be positioned in sidebars created specifically to display paid advertisements.

Over time SEO strategies have been characterised as being Black Hat or White Hat (and many shades of grey in between). White Hat techniques are ethically focused upon improving the quality and appearance of a website, and thus making it more useful and popular with users. Black Hat techniques, on the contrary, try to trick the search engines into raising them in rankings without providing any utility to the end user. The worst of these Black Hat techniques can make the website less user friendly because the sole objective is increasing rankings, not providing useful accessible content. Search engines are continually developing policy and techniques to reduce the number of pages that are rewarded in rankings via blatant Black Hat strategies. The following Entrepreneur profile provides an example of search engine optimisation.

Entrepreneur profile

Brenda Bourne, the 'web woman' of Mole Creek

In the 1980s, when travelling around Europe with her husband Kirk, Brenda fell in love with the idea of owning and operating a hosted accommodation business. Some years later when they had sufficient capital saved up to have a chance of succeeding, the couple left their stable jobs in government and industry to start living their dream. They purchased 100 acres of verdant grazing land on the south coast of Western Australia. They then set about building their own house (themselves), complete with bed & breakfast (B&B) guest rooms. To supplement the B&B income, they also experimented with running Highland cattle, and Brenda decided to learn how to develop a website to promote the business. Being an innovative and curious self-starter, Brenda then taught herself how to optimise websites for listing with the major search engines. Brenda and Kirk also began building 'Country Cousins', a network of similar high-quality farm-based B&Bs throughout Western Australia. Understanding the power of the internet to promote the network to a global audience, Brenda set about propelling this small group of mostly semi-retired internet sceptics into a page one listing with the major search engines. Some six years later, this group of mature entrepreneurs are converts to the potential of e-commerce, with significant bookings generated from their website network. Remember that Country Cousins expressed a desire to be recognised as a farm-based B&B network. If you type in 'farms, B&B and Western Australia' into a Google search you will most likely see www.countrycousins.com.au ranked second. The success story does not stop there. In 2007, when on a short holiday in Mole Creek, Tasmania, Kirk spotted another opportunity to renovate a splendid timber homestead in a beautiful, secluded location nestled under the slopes of one of Tasmania's most famous natural attractions, the Great Western Tiers. It was an opportunity 'too good to overlook'. In no time at all they had sold their thriving business in Western Australia (at the right price) and started all over again on this new endeavour, 2600 kilometres away. However, Brenda had no intention of deserting the Country Cousins network before passing on some of her search engine optimising tips. Not surprisingly, the new Country Cousins webmaster (a bubbly retired teacher in her 70s) now also has her own property ranked 4th with Google for the same search string: farms, B&B and Western Australia – Brenda has taught them well.

   Brenda is focused on small-accommodation web design offering affordable web design for small businesses (see webwoman.com.au), and now runs this business alongside Kirk's passion – horse training. In true entrepreneurial spirit, Brenda and Kirk have formed an association of over 90 like-minded B&B owners under the banner tasmaniabedandbreakfasts. com.au. Time will tell how long it takes for this endeavour to obtain and retain number one rankings on the major search engines for travellers searching for a Tasmanian Bed and Breakfast experience!

Source: Based on author's interview with Brenda Bourne.

Other website attraction strategies

Accepting that the creation of valuable new content is probably the best way of encouraging repeat visits, there are other strategies to drive repeat traffic to a website. Common methods of developing a deeper relationship online with existing clients involve creation of valued client lists, newsletters and discount offers in much the same manner as traditional mail-order strategies. The key difference is that the cost of communication with customers online is not impacted by printing and postage expense. As a result of the very low cost of delivery, unethical individuals and organisations have engaged in excessive use of unsolicited email marketing (**spam**). Most reputable marketing and advertising professionals now abide by self-imposed codes of conduct that stipulate that the use of email as a marketing tool must be via an 'opt-in' system where respondents have given their permission to be placed on a list. However, over 36 per cent of all global spam originates somewhere in Asia, making it the worst continent for spam origination in 2008.[37] Some governments in the Asia–Pacific region have found it necessary to pass laws making it illegal to send unsolicited emails. Whether the practice is illegal or not in a particular jurisdiction, it is an ineffective and intrusive method to be avoided by ethical businesses. To avoid the accusation of originating spam, other forms of opt-in content delivery are proliferating. For example, smart businesses looking to expand their reach online are developing content that can be shared, with information sharing technologies such as RSS feeds and podcasts gaining in popularity and acceptance.

Spam *Unsolicited communications sent to a large number of recipients via any communications method, most often via email.*

Web 2.0 social networking and web logging (blogging)

A relatively recent phenomenon that is now reaching critical mass is the uptake of social networking sites such as Facebook, Myspace, Linkedin and Bebo, to name a few.[38] From an online consumer behaviour perspective, social networking and blogging sites now account for almost 10 per cent of all internet time, as such this 'word of mouth' networked medium represents a significant opportunity for SMEs to market to and communicate with new and existing customers. These web-based meeting places and information sharing platforms are being used by a growing number of entrepreneurial small business owners, in particular they are popular with micro-enterprises selling single items online as they present an opportunity to demonstrate goods and explain services previously not available to SMEs.[39] The potential for viral and guerrilla marketing tactics is also heightened in these new forums, as was explored and explained in chapter 11 (Marketing). In addition to the marketing opportunities that Web 2.0 technologies inspire, there are also opportunities for business owners to form interactive support networks over vast distances, something particularly attractive to rural businesses who have limited opportunity to network with others in their industry.

Radio and satellite dependent devices

For many businesses in sectors such as manufacturing, agriculture and transport, handheld and base VHF/UHF radio receiver/transmitters are an effective low cost method of communication over short distances that should not be overlooked in developing an ICT strategy. Where practical, the cost of handheld receiver/transmitters is often a lower cost option than using a mobile phone, and incurs no volume charge when communicating between handsets. Privacy is, of course, a consideration since these un-encoded analogue signals are easily intercepted.

Limited range **wireless networks** based around the WiFi 802.11 standard are also prominent. Although not as cheap or compact as some other wireless technologies, WiFi has been widely adopted because of its balance of speed, range and capability.[40] The prevalence of lower cost mobile phone services has also encouraged the proliferation of communication via short message service (SMS). There are now a range of applications available to utilise SMS to support communication with geographically disbursed staff and offices. In addition, **global positioning system (GPS)** technologies that exist to track and plan geographic movement of people and product are becoming widespread. Many of the VoIP service providers are also building SMS services into their products at extremely low cost. In terms of transmitting digital radio signals, the growth in the use of satellite dependent technologies also includes such things as satellite phones capable of operating in very remote locations.

This chapter began with a discussion on convergence, and it seems appropriate that the discussion concludes by considering the evolution of **personal digital assistants (PDAs)**. The PDA is in effect evolving into a mobile internet connected device that is a hybrid of personal computer, personal assistant, GPS and high-speed internet connection. Many mobile **smart phones** and small **netbooks** are now available with such a wide variety of additional applications that it is becoming difficult to differentiate between these products.

SUMMARY

This chapter has considered ICT as a broad array of information handling and communication capabilities, ranging from simple barcode scanners to fully functional e-commerce websites. Innovation in ICT has had an enormous impact on business with the OECD identifying that the personal computer, mobile phone and internet have touched nearly every economic and social norm of countries in the Asia–Pacific region. Therefore, business owners who have an attitude of only adopting ICT when forced to do so are unlikely to succeed, particularly in industries where knowledge is the primary source of value.

In such a rapidly evolving ICT landscape it is probably advisable to employ the skills of specialist consultancies for all but the most basic of ICT strategies, to ensure strategic and operational goals are met. However, it remains important for the SME owner to understand the purpose of an information system and how data is collected, stored and manipulated to create information and knowledge. From this broad understanding of IS, a numbers of specific types were examined, specifically TPS, OAS, MIS and DSS. Not all SMEs need complex ICT; some micro- and home-based businesses can thrive with the simplest of ICT systems that revolve around nothing more complicated than a mobile phone, fax machine and fixed phone line. Many small businesses only require a basic office set-up of PC and printer with internet access for communication via email, and some simple information searching and online banking facilities. However, businesses that continue to grow will need to use the more advanced capabilities of their PC and the internet. This will often include development of a website with e-commerce capabilities and communication applications that

Wireless networks *Short range radio signal that allows computers and other enabled devices to communicate without a physical connection.*

Global positioning system (GPS) *A device using satellite signals to triangulate position in longitude, latitude and altitude for navigation purposes.*

Personal digital assistants (PDAs) *A hand-held computer that can support a range of useful productivity enhancing applications.*

Smart phones *High-end telephony devices that have the functionality of a mini PC, including using a standardised operating system and wireless internet connectivity.*

Netbooks *A relatively low cost mini (under 25 cm screen) personal computer that is designed for portability, extended battery power use and internet connectivity, primarily used for consuming rather than creating or storing data.*

require broadband connection speeds. Medium-sized enterprises will sometimes need to acquire higher computing capability and specialised software to support customised processes.

Regardless of the organisation's size, there is a plethora of software tools available to assist, with more applications emerging every day. In the face of all of this technological choice, the challenge is to acquire hardware and software that achieves organisational outcomes at minimum cost and maximum efficiency. Fortunately for most businesses in the Asia–Pacific region the infrastructure that supports many of the innovations they require is of an already high standard.

The reasons and benefits of engaging in e-commerce include improvement of communication, better sales and marketing; streamlined administrative processes; improved customer services; efficient delivery of digital goods; seamless transaction processing and a range of opportunities to reduce costs. Getting onto the web is one thing; effectively advertising the business online is another matter entirely, requiring special attention be paid to developing a search engine strategy and most likely engaging in search engine optimisation.

There are other strategies for getting noticed on the internet that involve a blended use of traditional promotional mix strategies and their online equivalents. SMEs have begun using recently developed ICT tools such as social networks, pay-per-click or affiliate programs, SMS campaigns, RSS feeds and podcasts to attract and retain clients. In particular, technologies such as VoIP and WiFi are being used to reduce communication costs and increase communication capabilities. In the areas of logistics and transport, the use of GPS is also having a significant impact, particularly on operational plans.

This chapter has focused on key uses of ICT and, in particular, the adoption and use of the internet for SMEs. The opportunities for strategic and tactical advantage through the positive adoption of the right ICT have been discussed, and this has led to a focus on some specific functions and forms of ICT that show great promise. No doubt there will be a crop of amazing new tools developed and released each year to keep SMEs forever searching for the competitive edge that the right ICT strategy can provide.

REVIEW QUESTIONS

1. What is the difference between data, information and knowledge? Why is it important to make the distinction?
2. What are the four or five main types of information systems found in SMEs?
3. Give an example of each of the seven categories of e-commerce uses, shown in figure 15.4.
4. Explain why search engine optimisation is more important that visual appearance of the website.
5. Select six internet-based applications that you consider very useful to SMEs and describe their significance.

DISCUSSION QUESTIONS

1. How do you think a hairdresser might improve their business by implementing an ICT strategy?
2. Which of the five types of business model has the most potential to exploit further ICT solutions?

3. How important do you think a business owner's personal technical knowledge of ICT is for adopting e-commerce in stages one and two of the e-commerce adoption model?
4. Suggest an example of a technology that does not fit within the seven types of e-commerce discussed in relation to figure 15.4. Why does it not fit?
5. Where and how do you think communication technology convergence may benefit SMEs?

SUGGESTED READING

Napier, H.A., Rivers, O.N., Wagner, S.W. & Napier, J.B., *Creating a Winning E-business*, 2nd edition, Thomson Course Technology, Boston, 2006.

O'Brien, T., 2004, *Exploiting the Internet: A Practical Guide for Growing Enterprises*, Tri-Obi Productions, Melbourne.

Rainer (Jr), K.R., & Turban, E., *Introduction to Information Systems*, 2nd edition, John Wiley & Sons, USA, 2009.

Case study

3Floorsup

3Floorsup is a private web development company founded by Steven Quayle and Patrick O'Meara and based in Melbourne, Australia. Steven and Patrick first met via their personal networks at ages 17 and 23 years respectively. Steven began working with Patrick on various ad-hoc consultancy opportunities, and subsequently formed a partnership in 2006 to launch their business 3Floorsup. Steven has a degree in marketing and has always been self-employed. He started in business as a self-employed tennis coach and eventually turned his mind to creating a marketing consultancy. Patrick has a degree in design (multimedia systems) and has worked for some of Melbourne's leading web design companies. These partners possess a complementary array of skills and abilities that has served their fast-growing business well. The business name 3Floorsup relates to a frightening three-storey fall that Patrick survived during the formative period of their business. The fall had him relying heavily on the internet and mobile communications during the time he was recuperating. So, it seems that right from the beginning ICT was to play a significant role in their business.

In a spin-off division of the main business, 3Floorsup have developed a web-based management system for use by commercial wind farm operators to store and analyse wind turbine maintenance data called WTGservice.com. This has transformed what started as a quality focused home-based web development business into a rapidly expanding global opportunity via the world's fastest growing renewable energy source — wind power. Since developing this capability, their business has literally been swept around the world on the winds of change. The pair recognised that wind farms are high-tech capital intensive businesses that would benefit from a servicing system that manages assets, inventory, servicing schedules, reporting and quality in an integrated manner. Their software design achieves this at the same time as retaining the flexibility to allow application in varying markets and circumstances worldwide.

The fully developed product was launched in 2008, marketed under the new trading name and website WTGservice.com. At that time, it was the only commercially available 100 per cent web-based system specifically developed for wind farms. After an initial focus on the domestic market in Australia, further growth was targeted via international sales in the USA, India and China. The India-China roll-out proved a major breakthrough and was aided by a City of Melbourne innovation grant for A$25 000. The money helped 3Floorsup modify the software so that the program can be easily translated to any language, thus allowing a global sales focus.

Comparing the e-commerce strategies reflected in the websites of the two businesses, the 3Floorsup.com.au website is a stylish showcase of their web design capabilities, whereas WTGService.com is a clean uncluttered site with a greater focus on information and technical content. Neither website attempts to sell a product online. Both aim to inform and then encourage a contact call for a later personal sales approach. The virtual nature of the internet allows the two entities to portray different images and contexts while operating from the same office, now in suburban Melbourne. Steven and Patrick do not want clients to confuse the two businesses during the initial sales pitch, so they have deliberately designed for this duel web persona.

The first international contract for WTGService.com came from India, signed with a world 'top ten' wind power producer. This deal took over four months of initial analysis, coupled with rigorous and frequent communications between employees, clients and third parties related to the power producer. Steven's experiences in India were typified by stories of exponential growth and a dynamic, even chaotic environment — very exciting times. In subsequent related dealings in mainland China, the pace was a little slower and Steven was often left trying to guess whether the local partners were happy with his approach. He has learned that it takes time and a great deal of close and prolonged communication to make progress with the Chinese division of the business. These international experiences have helped 3Floorsup to focus on implementing an e-commerce and ICT strategy that is capable of delivering accurate, relevant, timely and accessible information to internal and external users worldwide.

Because the WTGService.com business model involves a great deal of technical communications and sales-related international travel, Steven identified early on that ICT could assist with reliable and rapid communication. Information discussed between employees is recorded in digital format detailing all decisions made, as well as technical and operational aspects of these decisions. Steven initiated this system, which he refers to as 'project wiki', so data can be entered by owners and employees to produce an accessible online knowledge base. A wiki is a collaborative software tool that permits participants with access rights to collectively store, search, edit and access data online. The system allows employees to retrieve data 24/7, anywhere in the world. This capability has proven especially important in dealings with India, where there is a requirement to share information with the client's rapidly expanding workforce. In addition to this, while travelling Steven often finds himself communicating with the Melbourne office via MSN (Microsoft Live Messenger) or Skype to clarify programming issues, confirm urgent requirements and make time critical decisions. Steven certainly agrees that he would not have been able to grow the business as quickly or as successfully without using a variety of ICT tools to do so.

Source: Case study prepared by Pamela Tan, Curtin Business School, Curtin University of Technology based on interviews with Managing Director, Steven Quayle.

Questions

1. As both the web design and wind turbine maintenance businesses grow, how do you think their respective information systems should evolve or devolve?
2. Do you think that 3Floorsup has a typical ICT implementation for its size, age and industry?
3. How would you describe and categorise Steven's attitude and management style as it relates to ICT adoption?

4. Do you think that WTGservice.com should aim to be a stage four e-commerce business with the application offered for purchase online and wind farm systems integrated with WTGservices.com via the internet? Explain your reasoning.
5. How would you categorise the types of e-commerce uses that are described in this case?

ENDNOTES

1. B. Gates, *The Road Ahead*, Penguin Books, New York, 1995.
2. AC Neilsen 2008a, *Trends in online shopping, a global Neilsen consumer report*, February, p. 1.
3. Australian Communications and Media Authority (ACMA), 2009, *Convergence and communications, report 2: take up and use of communications by small and medium enterprises*, Commonwealth of Australia, Canberra.
4. AC Neilsen 2008b, *Critical Mass: The Worldwide State of the Mobile Web*, p. 2.
5. The Allen Consulting Group 2001, *Built for Business: Australia's Internet Economy*, A Report by the Allen Consulting Group, Commissioned by Cisco Systems, Sydney: The Allen Consulting Group Pty Ltd.
6. OECD, *Working party on indicators for the information society; guide to measuring the information society*, unclassified report DSTI/ICCP/IIS (2005) 6/FINAL, www.oecd.org.
7. M. Schindehutte, M.H. Morris & L.F. Pitt, 2009, *Rethinking marketing: the entrepreneurial imperative*, Pearson Education, New Jersey, pp. 271–88.
8. A. McAfee, & E. Brynjolfsson, 2008 'Investing in the IT that makes a competitive difference', *Harvard Business Review*, July-August Vol. 86, Iss.7/8, p. 98–107.
9. M. Earl, 2000, Every Business is an information business, in Marchand, D.A., & Davenport, T. (eds.) *Mastering Information Management*, London: Prentice Hall, pp. 16–22.
10. C.M. Parker, & T. Castleman, 2007, 'New directions for research on SME-eBusiness: insights from an analysis of journal articles from 2003 to 2006', *Journal of Information Systems and Small Business*, vol. 1, no. 1-2, pp. 21–40.
11. P. Attewell, 1992, 'Technology diffusion and organizational learning: the case of business computing', *Organization Science*, vol. 3, no. 1, pp. 1–19.
12. E.R. Winston & D. Dologite, 2002, 'How does attitude impact IT implementation: A study of small business owners', *Journal of End User Computing*, vol. 14, No. 2, pp. 16–29.
13. P. Julien, & L. Raymond, 1994, 'Factors of new technology adaptation in the retail sector', *Entrepreneurship Theory and Practice*, Summer, pp. 79–90.
14. K.R.(Jr) Rainer & E. Turban, 2009, *Introduction to Information Systems*, 2nd edition, John Wiley & Sons, USA, p. 233.
15. J. O'Brien, 1999, *Management Information Systems*, 4th edition, New York: Irwin/McGraw-Hill, p. 56.
16. A.J. Galacher, 2006, 'Communications — the emancipation of small business', BT Technology Journal, vol. 24, no. 4, pp. 135–50.
17. MYOB, 2009, MYOB BusinessAnalyst, http://myob.com.
18. J.O. Hicks, 1993, *Management Information Systems*, 3rd edition, Minneapolis: West Publishing Company.
19. P. Seltsikas, & L.K. Brown, 2006, 'Application Service Provision (ASP) for e-business transformation by SMEs'. *International Journal of Information and Technology Management*, vol. 5, no. 4, pp. 308–20.
20. V. Kotelnikov, 2007, Small and Medium Enterprises and ICT, United Nations Development Programme — Asia-Pacific Development Information Programme (UNDP-APDI), www.apdip.net.

21. M. Levy, P. Powell, L. Worral, 2005, Strategic intent and e-business in SMEs: enablers and inhibitors, Information Resources Management Journal, vol. 18, no. 4, pp. 1–20.

22. J. Thorburn, S. Arunachala, and A. Gunasekaran, 2000, 'Tracing of information links empirically (TILE) in small and medium enterprises', *Logistics and Information Management*, Vo. 13, No. 4, pp. 248–55.

23. Australian Communications and Media Authority, 2009, Convergence and communications, report 2: Take-up and use of communications by small and medium enterprises, Commonwealth of Australia, Canberra, www.acma.gov.au.

24. *ibid.*

25. T. O'Brien, 2004, *Exploiting the Internet: a practical guide for growing enterprises*, Tri-Obi Productions, Melbourne.

26. Economist Intelligence Unit [EIU], 2008, *E-readiness rankings*, viewed 28 March, 2009, http://a330.g.akamai.net; Economist Intelligence Unit [EIU], 2008, *E-readiness rankings*, http://graphics.eiu.com.

27. H.A. Napier, O.N. Rivers, S.W. Wagner, & J.B. Napier, 2006, *Creating a winning E-business*, 2nd edition, Thomson Course Technology, Boston.

28. R. Barton, A. Thomas, 2009, Implementation of intelligent systems, enabling integration of SMEs to high-value supply chain networks. *Engineering Applications of Artificial Intelligence* doi:10.1016/j.engappai.2008.10.016.

29. E. Daniel, D. Wilson, and A. Myers, 2002, Adoption of E-commerce by SMEs in the UK — Towards a stage model, *International Small Business Journal*, vol. 20, no. 3, pp. 253–70.

30. K.R. Rainer, and E. Turban, 2009, *Introduction to Information Systems*, 2nd edition, John Wiley & Sons, USA, p. 157.

31. T. O'Brien, 2004, *Exploiting the Internet: a practical guide for growing enterprises*, Tri-Obi Productions, Melbourne.

32. T. Zimmerer, N. Scarborough, D. Wilson, 2008, *Essentials of entrepreneurship and small business management*, 5th edition, Pearson Education, Upper Saddle River, New Jersey.

33. S. Chau, 2003, 'The use of E-commerce amongst thirty-four Australian SMEs: An experiment of a strategic business tool?' *Journal of Systems and Information Technology*, vol. 7, no. 1-2, pp. 49–66.; Sensis, 2008, e-business report: the online experience of small and medium enterprises, 25 September 2008, www.about.sensis.com.au; L.T. Eriksson, J. Hultman, & L. Naldi, 2008, 'Small business e-commerce development in Sweden — an empirical survey', *Journal of Small Business and Enterprise Development*, vol. 15, no.3. pp. 555–75.

34. C. Chapman, 2008, *Online business toolbox: tools and resources for running a business online*, www.mashable.com.

35. Internet assigned Number Authority (IANA), Root Zone Database, www.iana.org.

36. Napier, Rivers, Wagner & Napier, *see* note 27.

37. Sophos, 2009, Security threat report, viewed 26 April 2009, www.sophos.com.

38. AC Neilsen, 2009, *Global faces and networked places*, March, 2009, http://blog.nielsen.com.

39. E. Alampay, 2008, 'Filipino entrepreneurs on the Internet: when social networking websites meet mobile commerce', *Science Technology & Society*, vol. 13, no. 2, pp. 211–31.

40. W. Hanson, K. Kalyanam, 2007, Internet marketing & e-commerce, Thomson South-Western, Mason, Ohio.

CHAPTER 16

Managing growth and transition

Learning objectives

After reading this chapter, you should be able to:

- explain the various dimensions of growth in a business enterprise
- discuss the four basic theories that explain how and why organisations grow
- explain the various business growth strategies
- outline the changing role of the entrepreneur as the business grows
- identify different methods of 'harvesting' a business venture.

Most small businesses have one of the following goals: to survive; to consolidate and continue to be successful; or to expand and grow. However, on closer inspection, it becomes clear that these three basic activities are often variations on the same theme, and they can be reduced to a focus on expansion and growth in one way or another. After all, growth is a dynamic process and means more than just an increase in size. It also encompasses development and change within an organisation, and it alters the way the organisation interacts with its external environment.

Once a business has grown, what happens next? Entrepreneurship is seen by many as a journey, not a destination. A common sentiment among successful entrepreneurs is that it is the challenge and exhilaration of starting up and building a venture that gives them the greatest kick. Once they have reached this goal, they may seek to enjoy the fruits of their labour through various 'harvest' strategies, such as management buy-outs, mergers and acquisitions, public offerings or outright sale.

This chapter outlines the various dimensions of growth, and presents four basic theories on how organisations change. Finally, several strategies for harvesting and maximising return from the successful business venture are detailed.

The dimensions of business growth

The growth of the venture can be seen from various perspectives, such as: (1) *financial* — growth in income, expenditure and profits; (2) *strategic* — growth in market share and competitive advantages; and (3) *organisational* — growth in organisational form, process and structure.[1]

The various dimensions of business growth must be considered in relation to one another (figure 16.1). Financial growth is a measure of the business's performance in serving the need of its markets, and thus it is a measure of the resources the market has allocated to the firm. The firm must convert those resources into assets. These assets are configured by the organisational structure. Financial growth provides the means by which a business can obtain additional resources (such as staff, equipment, information) to fuel strategic growth and to acquire additional assets. In turn, financial growth is fuelled by the performance of the strategic options taken, and by the accumulation of assets within an extended organisational structure.

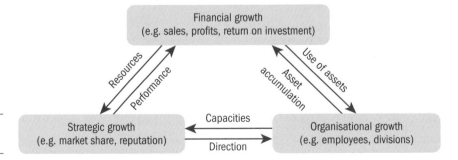

FIGURE 16.1 The dimensions of growth

Financial growth

Financial growth relates to the development of the business as a commercial entity. It is concerned with increases in sales, the investment needed to achieve those sales and the resulting profits. It is also concerned with increases in what the business owns: its assets. These different financial elements help to establish the value of the business — that is, the price a potential buyer would be willing to pay for it.

Analysis of the various financial documents of a business venture, such as its balance sheet and profit and loss statement, can give those interested (the entrepreneur, investors, fiscal authorities and other stakeholders) a general overview of the financial health of the venture. However, there is no absolute measure of performance, and the performance of the firm must be considered relative to its industry and over a period of time. This means that it is important for the firm to compare itself with industry-wide benchmarks in order to assess its own financial performance.

Growth will also bring some financial problems. Some growth will create a need for more spending. If extra stock, larger premises, new tools or additional staff are needed, money has to be found to pay for them. New loans may need to be taken out (in the case of long-term asset purchases), or additional working capital may need to be found for short-term requirements. Although some businesses will already have retained profits that can be drawn on, others may have to set up or extend their overdraft facilities. Businesses that do not have enough cash flow to service debt and to finance current expenses will find themselves in trouble; others may find that they do not have a suitable track record or security to obtain a loan, and so they stagnate from a lack of capital.

Strategic growth

Strategic growth relates to the changes that take place in the way the organisation interacts with its environment as a coherent (or strategic) whole. This is concerned mainly with the way the business develops its capabilities in order to exploit a presence in the marketplace. From a strategic perspective, businesses are able to successfully compete in the market by developing and maintaining a competitive advantage. Growth represents the business's success in drawing in resources from its environment. It is a sign that business has been effective in competing in the marketplace. However, a competitive advantage is not static. Sustaining an advantage simultaneously develops and enhances it. Growth will influence the two basic sources of competitive advantage identified by Porter: cost and differentiation.[2]

The main source of cost advantage is experience effects. As a result of the learning experience, costs tend to fall in an exponential way as output increases linearly. Cost leadership means that the customer can be offered a lower price, leading in turn to an increase in demand and thus an increase in output.

A differentiation strategy stems mainly from knowledge advantages. These arise from knowing something about the customer, the market or the product that competitors do not know, thus enabling the business to offer something of value to the customer. The customer is prepared to pay a premium for the extra value perceived. The development of a knowledge-based advantage depends on two factors: the significance of the knowledge advantage and the rate at which it will be eroded. Clearly, these two factors work against each other. The more valuable the knowledge, the more that competitors will be encouraged to get hold of it for themselves.

Organisational growth

Organisational growth relates to the changes that take place in the organisational structure, process and culture as it grows and develops. The structure of the organisation and the way that structure develops as the organisation grows are both a response to the circumstances in which the organisation finds itself, and a reaction to the opportunities with which it is presented. One well-explored approach to understanding how an organisation defines its structure is provided by contingency theory. In essence, contingency theory regards the structure of an organisation as dependent on contingencies or types of factors[3] such as organisational size, operational technology, strategy, business environment and the role of the entrepreneur.

The choice of not growing

Although market forces may press for quantitative growth, this does not necessarily coincide with the personal interests of the small business owner. The relationships between personal and organisational objectives are important to understand, because they often overlap in the small firm. Thus, for the majority of small business owner–managers, the need to maximise growth, or indeed to grow at all, is not self-evident. Growth is rarely seen as an end in itself, and will often be sacrificed in pursuit of other objectives.

The first barrier to growth relates to the choice of the owner–manager. Exploiting the growth potential of a firm requires an active commitment to growth on the part of the owner–manager. In many instances a fundamental reluctance to grow, fear of the risks of growth, or a desire to use the business simply to support an established lifestyle rather than to generate maximum capital appreciation constitute the major barriers to growth.

The second inhibitor of growth is the belief on the part of owner–managers that continued growth of the firm will lead to an erosion of their managerial and financial control over the business. The willingness to forgo growth in favour of maintaining financial self-sufficiency and managerial control inevitably sets limits on a small venture's growth.

However, there is a more fundamental reason to caution against the universal and uncritical growth ideology, and for small business owner–managers — whenever possible — to secure profitability before they go ahead with growth. Empirical evidence on the relationship between growth and performance is inconclusive. In addition, to the extent a relationship exists, it has not been determined whether this is primarily because growth leads to profits or, conversely, because profitability drives growth.[4]

Conceptualising growth and organisational change

In a review of development and change in organisations, Van de Ven and Poole identified four basic theories about how and why organisations change.[5] These are based on the notions of life cycle, teleology, evolution and dialectic. These four theories represent different sequences of change events that are driven by different conceptual motors and operate at different levels.

Life cycle

The notion of life cycle suggests that the business venture undergoes a pattern of growth and development much as a living organism does. A life cycle model depicts change in an organisation as progressing through a necessary sequence of stages. Numerous authors have proposed stages of growth or life cycle models of organisations.[6] These authors vary in the number of stages they propose and the labels they use, but the prevailing themes are clear. Often, the stages follow a pattern of start-up, growth, formalisation and so on. As it is a matter of mathematics and economics that keep rapid growth from continuing indefinitely, growth is typically a 'stage' between struggling inception and relative stability later on.

New venture development

This first stage consists of activities associated with the incubation and initial formation of the venture. At this stage, the budding entrepreneur displays a strong intention to start a business. Intention is a conscious state of mind that directs attention and, therefore, experience and action, towards a specific object (goal) or a pathway to achieve it (means).[7] This concept goes beyond that of entrepreneurial propensity: people with the intention of starting a business have not only a propensity to start, but also rational behaviour that will allow them to reach their goal. They have already, therefore, taken some steps towards this goal — developed a prototype, gathered some information, conducted initial market-research and saved some money.

Start-up

The second stage encompasses all the foundation work needed to formally launch the business venture. During the start-up stage, a business plan is drafted and presented to the potential key stakeholders in the venture — investors, suppliers and employees. The entrepreneur puts together various resources: financial, human and information. Different measures can be taken to protect any intellectual property owned by the firm, such as registering a patent, a trademark or a design. The entrepreneur must also decide on a business name and legal form of organisation.

At this stage, the founders of the venture are usually technically or entrepreneurially oriented, and they generally disdain management activities; their physical and mental energies are absorbed in making and selling the new product. Another characteristic is the frequent and informal communication among employees. Long hours of work are rewarded by modest salaries and the promise of ownership benefits. Decisions and motivation are highly sensitive to marketplace feedback; management acts as customers react.

Growth

Sustained growth is typically characterised by a strong increase in demand and sales, leading in turn to a growing number of employees. This 'go-go' phase is often accelerated by technological breakthrough, aggressive or ingenious marketing, a hungry market, sluggish competition or some combination of these. Three basic challenges[8] usually confront rapid-growth firms:

- *Instant size.* When firms double or triple in size very quickly, this in turn creates problems of disaffection, inadequate skills and inadequate systems.
- *A sense of infallibility.* By virtue of their success to date, owner–managers often view their strategies and behaviour as infallible and immune from criticism.
- *Internal turmoil.* There is a stream of new faces — people who do not know one another and who do not know the firm. The business founders find themselves burdened with unwanted management responsibilities. They long for the 'good old days' and try to act as they did in the past. Decision making suffers, internal political battles abound and people burn out.

Maturity

The firm enters the maturity or stabilisation stage just after reaching its prime, when everything comes together. During this period, the business is consistently able to meets its customers' changing needs; internal discipline and organisational culture are operating effectively; and production is run with maximum efficiency.

However, this highly desirable state of affairs can quickly be lost. The maturity stage is often characterised by increased competition, consumer indifference to the firm's products and services and a saturation of the market. Internally, staff welcome new ideas but without the excitement of the growing stages. Financial managers begin to impose controls for short-term results. The emphasis on marketing and research and development wanes. This phase is often a 'swing stage', in that it precedes the period when the firm will either innovate and move back into the growth mode or, alternatively, start to decline.

At this point, a crisis of leadership often occurs. Obviously, a strong manager is needed — one who has the necessary knowledge and skills to introduce new business techniques. But finding that manager is easier said than done. The founders often resist stepping aside, even though they are probably temperamentally unsuited to the job. Those ventures that survive the leadership crisis by installing a capable business manager usually embark on a period of sustained growth.[9]

Rebirth or decline

Several models of life cycle theory consider that decline is not inevitable for firms reaching maturity. Firms can face a 'rebirth' before they eventually decline. For example, 'continued entrepreneurship' could be the basis of the growth rate of established firms.[10] In any case, expanding the business means expanding the amount of trade it undertakes. For example, expansion from any base can be achieved by launching new products or services or by entering new markets.

If the enterprise fails to implement one of those strategies and to innovate, it will face a decline in its activities. Not making waves becomes a way of life. Outward signs of respectability, such as dress, office decoration and titles, take on enormous importance. The business institutes witch-hunts to find out *who* did something wrong rather than trying to discover *what* went wrong and how to fix it. A strong bureaucracy is typical within firms at this stage — there are systems for everything, and employees go by the book. Cost reduction takes precedence over efforts to increase revenues.

In all life cycle models, the development stage of the business determines the importance of different management tasks and leadership styles. Research has focused mainly on differences in internal organisational characteristics (such as leadership and policies, structure and strategy) across theorised stages. Table 16.1 provides a summary of these characteristics.

TABLE 16.1 Life cycle stage characteristics

Feature	New venture development	Start-up	Growth	Maturity	Rebirth or decline
Size	One or two people, part-time	Small	Medium to large	Large	Growing (rebirth) or declining
Sales growth rate	Non-existent	Inconsistent	Rapid and positive	Slow	Bounce back (rebirth) or declining
Business tasks	Evaluate opportunity; build prototype	Set up the organisation; launch product	Capacity expansion; set up operating systems	Expense control; establish management systems	Revitalisation (new products, new markets, diversification) or recrimination (decline)
Organisational structure	Embryonic	Individualistic and entrepreneurial	Directive	Delegative	Participative (rebirth) or autocratic (decline)
Control systems	Embryonic	Market results	Standards and cost centres	Reports and profits centres	Mutual goal setting (rebirth) or red tape (decline)

Teleology

Teleology is the study of design and purpose, and it argues that 'form follows function'. In teleology theory, the purpose or goal of management, such as growth, is the final cause for guiding movement of the organisation. In this perspective, the business venture sets goals, and by adapting its actions it tries to reach its goals. Therefore, a teleological model views development as a cycle of goal formulation, implementation, evaluation and modification of goals based on what was learned by the organisation. Central to this theory is the notion of purpose in organisational change and growth. Entrepreneurs can use their vision of the future to pull the organisation forward. Comparable with the life cycle theory, teleology theory focuses on a single organisation. However, teleology theory does not prescribe a sequence of events or specify in which direction an organisation must develop to reach its goals. It can only set a possible path and then rely on norms of decisions or actions.

A business venture can pursue different goals; growth can be one of them. Similarly, there are different ways to reach growth objectives. Also, growth is not necessarily a result of accomplishing the goals. Growth can have different meanings — a business can pursue growth in size (employees, sales); in profit (profit before tax, return on investment); in value (shareholder value, stakeholder value); and in quality (image, know-how, innovation).

Evolution

Evolution is a theoretical scheme that explains changes in structural forms of organisations across communities or industries. As in biological evolution, organisational change proceeds through a continuous circle of variation, selection and retention. Variations — the creation of new forms of organisation — are often seen to emerge by chance; they just happen. The selection of organisations occurs through the competition for scarce resources, and the environment selects entities that best fit the resource base of an environmental niche. Retention involves forces (including relative inertia and persistence) that perpetuate and maintain certain organisational forms.

Although one cannot predict which business venture will survive or fail, the overall population persists and evolves through time, according to the specified population dynamics. Birth rates, merge rates and mortality rates influence the characteristics of the population. This process is influenced by competition and legitimation. As a metaphor, evolution reminds entrepreneurs that they are operating in a competitive environment, that they must compete for scarce resources and that the venture must be efficient ('fit') in the tasks it undertakes. As business ventures perform reliably and accountably over time, they demonstrate their fitness and may acquire legitimacy.

Dialectic

The dialectical theory focuses on stability and change based on the collision of power between opposing entities. The dialectical theory begins with the assumption that organisations or members within organisations compete with each other for domination and control. This creates a collision between the entities. Change is the result of the appearance of opposing views (thesis and antithesis) and balance or imbalance of power between entities. Change occurs if an organisation or a stakeholder has sufficient power to confront and engage the status quo (the existing state). If this is not the case, the status quo will remain.

In organisational change and development, the dialectic illuminates conflict and conflict resolution at a number of levels; for example, between stakeholder groups such as investors and employees, and within stakeholder groups. The latter would include, for example, political manoeuvring by managerial factions within the business. Accordingly, one of the central tasks of the entrepreneur is to resolve conflicts and bring together stakeholders (whose interests may differ), so that all benefit.

Entrepreneur profile

Shi Zhengrong, Suntech

In 1963, Shi was born into a family of peasant farmers in China. However, after developing fluency in English and receiving a Bachelor's degree in Optical Science and a Master's degree in Laser Physics in Hangzhou and Shanghai respectively, he was chosen to undertake further graduate studies in Australia. He joined the University of New South Wales in Sydney, and pursued a Ph.D. in electrical engineering.

In the course of his research, Shi assisted in the development of thin-film solar cells. These were commercialised in 1995 by an Australian photovoltaic company, who appointed Shi as deputy director of research. Five years later, he received Australian citizenship and began negotiations with the Chinese government to secure US$6 million for a solar cell manufacturing plant near Shanghai.

Shi founded Suntech in 2001, and by 2005 the company was one of the word's largest photovoltaic manufacturers. It was then listed on the New York Stock Exchange, whereupon the share price rocketed.

The rise wasn't always smooth, and Shi was required to have more than technical skills to make Suntech succeed. Sharp elbows helped too. When the company showed it could be profitable early on, board members appointed by the government suddenly became interested. Shi and the government-appointed chairman clashed in late 2003 over how rapidly to expand the business, and on the amount Shi was spending on the equipment needed to do so. 'For some reason he didn't seem to trust me,' says Shi. In 2004, he went to the other board members and persuaded them to ease the chairman out. 'That's when I realised that having a controlling position in the company was critical.' So he got a capital injection from Goldman Sachs, and bought out the rest of the state-sponsored shareholders in 2005 for US$100 million.

Climate change by then had become a global issue, and governments around the world began boosting subsidies for renewable energy. Suntech's stock hit an all-time high of US$85 in late 2007. Its biggest markets for the solar panels and modules it makes are in Europe. In the following years, the rapid success of Chinese solar companies such as Suntech has spawned lots of imitators. The market became plagued by overcapacity, and at the end of 2008 Suntech fired 800 employees — the first layoffs in the company's short lifetime. However, Shi believes that the scale of enterprise that Suntech has already achieved will enable the company to withstand the industry-wide shakeout.

Source: Adapted from Ernst & Young, 'The sun shines on Dr Shi', *Entrepreneur*, 2008, pp. 21–22; B. Powell, 'China's new king of solar', *Fortune*, 11 February, 2009.

Growth strategies and growth enablers

Research has shown that fast growing companies are extremely competent at building growth perpetuating systems, which help them create sustained growth from entrepreneurial ideas. These systems incorporate three elements — visions, strategies and business models — to drive such growth, and their efficacy depends on them being clearly communicated throughout the organisation.

Growth strategies can be either internal or external. The former utilises measures within the company, such as international expansion, improving products or increasing market share, whereas the latter is focused outwards and may include forging third party relationships through licensing, strategic alliances or even acquisitions.[11]

For these 'seeds' to grow effectively, they need to be planted in an environment populated by 'growth enablers'. Growth enablers comprise elements that favour growth: an attractive growth culture, networks that serve as growth platforms and the characteristics of the company and its founder(s).

Internal growth strategies

Internal growth strategies involve efforts taken within the firm itself. The distinctive attribute of internally generated growth is that a business relies on its own resources, competencies and employees. Internally generated growth is often called 'organic' growth because it does not rely on outside intervention. Almost all companies grow organically during the early stages of their life cycle.

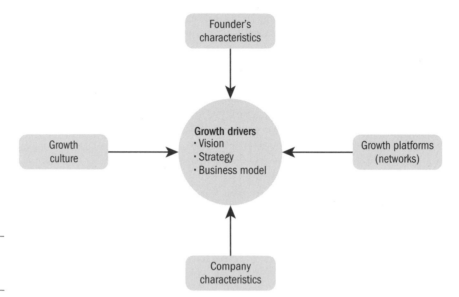

FIGURE 16.2 Growth drivers and growth enablers

Increasing market share

When they first begin, most new ventures capture only a small portion of the market they enter. A useful growth strategy, therefore, involves increasing this share through greater marketing efforts of increased production capacity and efficiency. An increase in a product's market share is typically accomplished by increasing advertising expenditures, offering sales promotions, lowering the price or increasing the size of the sales force.

Increased market penetration can also occur though increased capacity of efficiency, which permits a firm to have greater volume of product or service to sell. In a manufacturing context, an increase in product capacity can occur by expanding plant and equipment, or by outsourcing a portion of the production process to another company. For example, a firm that previously manufactured and packaged its products may outsource the packaging function to another company, and as a result free up factory space to increase production of the basic product.[12]

New product development

New product development involves designing, producing and selling new products or services as a means of increasing firm revenues and profitability. In many fast-paced industries, new product development is a competitive necessity. New products must be developed to replace existing ones and to keep ahead of competitors as the customers' expectations develop.

Whatever the nature of the product, its complexity and the resources involved in its launch, the key is to remember that a product is not a thing but rather a means to an end. The value of a product lies in the benefits it can bring to its users. The entrepreneur must apply the same market-oriented insights to the development of new products as were brought to the innovation on which the business was originally founded. Because new ventures have limited resources and competences, they should follow these guidelines to move toward the new products they seek:

- *Focus on the markets they know — the ones they are already serving.* Existing customers can provide valuable information about problems that need to be solved and how to position the product in the marketplace.
- *Develop new product or services that are related to the ones the company already offers.* Jumping off into 'left field' is not a useful option for new ventures. A much better strategy for obtaining growth is to stick with products or services that are closely linked to the ones they now produce or provide.
- *Get pricing and quality right.* New ventures cannot afford to find out the hard way that they have set the price for a product too high. Not only must new products meet customers' needs, they must also do so at a price that offers good value. Similarly, offering new products that are lower in quality than earlier ones can be a fatal mistake. Every product thus represents a balance between quality and pricing.

Improving existing products or services

Although the word 'new' is something many companies like to place on their packaging, the word 'improved' may sometimes be more appropriate. In order to attain high growth, it's not always essential to have completely new products or services; significant improvements in the existing ones may be as, or even more, effective.

Improving an item means increasing its value and price potential from the customer's perspective. There are different ways to improve a product or service, such as enhancing quality, making it larger or smaller, making it more convenient to use, improving its durability or making it more up to date.

International expansion

In its early stages, a business tends to serve a local geographic area. Many entrepreneurial businesses grow simply by expanding from original location to additional geographic sites. Ultimately, this might include expansion into the international arena through exporting, alliances or even setting up subsidiaries overseas. In fact, few businesses can achieve any real size without taking on the international option.

Several factors have facilitated the development of international trade over the past decades. For example, tariffs and trade barriers have significantly decreased at the global level as a result of successive rounds of negotiations that led to the World Trade Organization (WTO). At the regional level, Australia, New Zealand and the ten members of the Association of South-East Asian Nations (ASEAN) signed a free trade agreement in 2009. Technological developments, such as the internet, and the increasing mobility of capital and people led to further globalisation of the economy.

External growth strategies

External growth strategies rely on establishing relationships with third parties, such as licensing, strategic alliances and acquisitions. In a sense, these strategies all involve leveraging the company's resources be entering into mutually beneficial arrangement with other organisations. An emphasis on external strategies usually results in a more fast-paced, collaborative approach toward growth than the slower-paced internal strategies. There are other advantages in external strategies, including getting access to proprietary products or services, obtaining technical expertise and generating economies of scale.

There exist some disadvantages too. Cooperation with third parties can lead to a clash of corporate cultures, increased business complexity and the loss of organisational flexibility.

Strategic alliances

A strategic alliance is a partnership between two or more firms that is developed to achieve a specific goal. Various studies show that participation in alliances can boost a firm's rate of patenting, product innovation and foreign sales.[13] Technological alliances and marketing alliances are two of the most common forms of alliances.

Technological alliances feature cooperation in research and development, engineering and manufacturing. Research and development alliances often bring together entrepreneurial firms with specific technical skills and larger, more mature firms with experience in development and marketing. By pooling their complementary assets, these firms can typically produce a product and bring it to market faster and cheaper than either firm could alone. Marketing alliances, on the other hand, typically match a company that has a distribution system with a company that has a product to sell, in order to increase sales of product or service.

Licensing

Licensing is the granting of permission by one company to another company to use a specific form of its intellectual property under clearly defined conditions. Virtually any intellectual property a company owns that is protected by a patent, trademark, or copyright can be licensed to a third party. Licensing can be a very effective way of earning income, particularly for intellectual property-rich firms, such as software and biotech companies.

The terms of a license are spelled out through a licensing agreement, which is a formal contract between a licensor — the company that owns the intellectual property — and the licensee — the company purchasing the right to use it. Several types of licensing exist, but two that are increasingly important are technology licensing, and merchandise and character licensing. Technology licensing involves granting the right to use knowledge contained in a utility patent (a patent for a specific kind of product) to the purchaser. In contrast, merchandise and character licensing involves licensing a recognised trademark or brand that the licensor controls.

Acquisitions

Another way to grow externally is to acquire other businesses in their entirety and 'add' them onto the existing business venture. There are three sorts of acquisition, and these differ in the way in which the integrated firm sits in relation to the venture in the value chain.

The first type of acquisition is vertical integration. This happens when the venture acquires a firm that is either upstream or downstream in the value-production chain — that is, it acquires a business that is a customer or a supplier. The acquisition of customers is referred to as 'forward' integration and that of a supplier as 'backward' integration. The second type of acquisition occurs when the venture integrates a business that is at the same level of value production as itself — that is, a business that is, ostensibly at least, a competitor. The third type of acquisition occurs in the remaining cases when the integrated business is not a supplier, nor a customer nor a competitor. These might be referred as 'lateral' or 'unrelated' integrations.

Growth enablers

Strategies are the 'seeds' for an organisation growth and development. These seeds need suitable conditions or enablers for growth to materialise. Growth enablers include the founder's and company characteristics, an appealing and motivating growth culture, and the presence of networks as growth platforms.

Founder characteristics

Entrepreneurs at the helm of high-growth ventures seem to possess characteristics that contribute to the success of their companies. First, they are passionate about what they are doing, and know the direction they are heading. In addition, they are remain tenacious even after major setbacks. Third, these entrepreneurs have a clear growth vision for their companies, which is made very clear in vision statements and other sources.[14]

Even if entrepreneurs do want to achieve rapid growth, it may not be feasible because they lack the managerial skills needed to effectively attain this goal. In other words, they lack what is known as managerial capacity — the skill and experience necessary to take advantage of opportunities for new products or services that could help expand their business.

Company characteristics

Founders are only one of the growth enablers that are necessary to achieve company goals. Companies must also have mechanisms in place to enable even the most brilliant and passionate entrepreneurs to generate growth in sales and profits. There are three characteristics which distinguish high-growth companies from others. First, the central value that often appears in the venture's mission's statement is growth. Second, the building of relationships with external partners — suppliers, research institutions or even competitors — is more evident in high growth companies. These relationships can take various forms such a strategic alliance, joint-venture or licensing agreements. Finally, high-growth companies plan for growth. Specific goals are set and strategies for reaching them are developed.

Company culture

The entrepreneurial vibe that pervades a new business in its early days and powers its success should be sustained through the development of a healthy growth culture. In order for everyone in the company to share a dedication to growth, they should hold a sense of ownership in the vision, strategies and the day-to-day responsibilities towards their peers and other stakeholders. The placement of a charismatic leader, supported by a committed and skilled key management team and an efficient internal communication network, will foster such an atmosphere and fortify team spirit.

A good management team will be motivated, proactive and not averse to taking risks. Its people distinguish themselves through frequent promotion and their emphasis on continuous education and training. A growth-oriented company often supports such learning through programs, and will also set up incentives (for example, stock options) to motivate its employees.

Networks as growth as platforms

Growth invariably requires the development of suitable networks, which are both internal and external to the company. For example, partnerships with customers and with suppliers often enable a better understanding of the marketplace and how it changes. There is no one particular partner arrangement that facilitates growth; rather, it is the company's 'network ability' to engage with others on an equal footing.

Internal networks help too. Dynamic enterprises tend to build a network of autonomous business units that, nevertheless, share critical information and experience. Such companies predominantly have flatter hierarchies and project-focused teams that, with advanced IT support, function more openly, quickly and independently. This configuration is one that attracts like-minded entrepreneurial workers and allows them to work in closer proximity to their markets.[15]

From the entrepreneur to the manager

Managing any business venture is a tough job. Managing a rapidly growing enterprise, however, presents a particular challenge because the essential nature of the manager's job changes with growth. As the number of employees increases, and the volume and complexity of work expands, entrepreneurs must change their fundamental approach to managing. To understand this evolution, it is essential to first define the manager's job in a way that explains the pressures being added to the system, the changes that are transpiring as a result and the responses available to the manager.

Defining the manager's job

In order to frame the management task in a way that allows us to predict and understand the challenges that growth creates, we need to develop a model of the manager's job. Roberts[16] suggested a model that revolves around three key elements that are part of the manager's responsibilities:

- *Strategy and operation*. What task should the enterprise perform? The firm's activities are driven by its goals and its strategy. The strategy is the rationale for a set of operating activities, so the goal-setting and strategic-planning processes are key pieces in the management of the business. Where strategy is an idea or an objective, however, the firm's operations are that idea made real. Thus, the firm's strategy and operation are the set of tasks and activities that the firm is required to execute.
- *Organising*. How should tasks be structured and coordinated? This aspect of the manager's responsibilities includes all the choices about how to accomplish

the strategy and operating activities — how these responsibilities are assigned to organisational units; how they are broken down into specific tasks within units; how these tasks are grouped to comprise a job; how those jobs are defined according to performance standards and procedures, tied together with systems, and coordinated to achieve the desired objectives.

- *Staffing*. Who should do the work? This element includes the people who actually fill the jobs and do the work, as well as their selection, training, development and compensation.

These three sets of duties cannot be managed in isolation. There must be some fit between strategy and structure, and between implementation and the skills and capabilities of the people in the organisation.

The steps towards professional management

Many issues need to be considered when small entrepreneur-driven structures evolve into larger, professionally managed ones. For example, strategic planning in younger and smaller firms tends to be based on personal feel or intuition, or on 'firefighting' approaches. Consequently, such firms will undergo a great deal of pain and distress unless those making the decisions learn to adopt rational and systematic approaches to decision making as their organisations grow.[17] In order to make their businesses grow beyond a certain point, entrepreneurs must be prepared to move from an *entrepreneurial* management style, with centralised decision making and informal control, to a *professional* management style that involves the delegation of decision-making responsibility and the use of formal control mechanisms.

The following four steps[18] have been identified as contributing to any successful transition to professional management:

- *Recognise the need for change*. This is often extremely difficult because it is a by-product of success. Success reinforces beliefs and behaviour that are appropriate to the entrepreneurial mode but inappropriate for the needs of a larger, more complex firm. Often, a crisis will highlight the need for change. However, knowledgeable business advisers can help the entrepreneur avoid a crisis by spotting the warning signs, and indicating the need and path for change.

- *Develop human resources*. Given the change of personal role in the organisation, the entrepreneur's next step is to develop the human resources required to implement the growth model chosen. Often, people who can accept and execute responsibility are not present in the entrepreneurial organisation, because the entrepreneur's style has made it difficult for self-sufficient, independent employees to remain with the firm.

- *Delegate responsibility*. The power of professional management arises from placing decision-making responsibility close to the sources of information. Typically, this means delegating responsibility to managers who are close to customers, suppliers and other partners of the firm. The entrepreneur–CEO must be careful, however, not to give up responsibility on key policy issues that require personal perspective.

- *Develop formal controls*. The final step in the transition process is developing formal control mechanisms. Successful entrepreneurs realise that, with the onset of delegation, they can no longer control the behaviour of individuals in the organisation; the focus of control must shift from behaviour to performance.

The founder's dilemma

Many entrepreneurs strive for the success of Bill Gates or Richard Branson, each of whom have launched companies and expanded their business empires. However, Wasserman[19] indicates that successful founders-cum-CEOs are quite the rarity, and that it's the founders who surrender more equity to entice co-founders, employees and investors who are the ones more likely to build a more valuable business. Founders need to consider the trade-off between maximising their wealth or control of the company — for often greater returns necessitate bringing in a more experienced CEO to best tend to the growing company's needs.

Those founders who seek wealth over control will be more enthusiastic about ceding leadership, and will readily open their capital to external investors or depend on seasoned executives to manage and grow their business ventures. By stepping down, they'll receive a smaller piece of a bigger pie.

Conversely, should founders determine control over their empire as a measure of success, they'll be happier with a bigger piece of a smaller pie. This type of entrepreneur would be ideally suited to businesses that don't require a lot of capital investment, and where they already possess the necessary skills and contacts. In order to ensure they have developed the management skills required, they may delay the launch of the business until late in their careers.

What would you do?

Softy Fruits

Softy Fruits Sdn Bhd is a soft drink and fruit juice manufacturer located in Miri, Western Malaysia. The company was established in 1973 by Mr. Yap Beng Leong, and currently employs 85 staff. Softy Fruits sells most of its products in eastern Malaysia and nearby Brunei. The company produces two different flavours of lemonade, and three types of fruit juice (mango, pink guava and lychee). Mr. Yap is now over seventy years old and would like his youngest daughter Stacy to take over the business in the near future. Mr. Yap approached you to get some advice about his succession planning.

Stacy recently obtained her Bachelor of Commerce degree, and she has been working with her father for the past 18 months. To clearly signal that Stacy is to be his successor, Mr. Yap appointed her Deputy Managing Director immediately after she started working for Softy Fruits. Stacy is now in charge of the newly created function of business development. They both share an office so that father can teach daughter the ropes of the trade. Mr. Yap is thrilled to work with his daughter, as it gives him extra motivation to arrive at the office every morning for his usual 8 am start. He is still overseeing the daily business activities together with Mr. Lim, his trusted accountant, who has been with the company from the beginning.

Stacy has conducted a lot of research on the beverage industry. After reading a report from Euromonitor, she discovered that Malaysia has a large and increasingly sophisticated soft drinks industry. In 2009, soft drinks in Malaysia continued to post strong growth and achieved sales of 967 million litres. Stacy is also aware that as Malaysians become more health conscious, competitors are embarking on healthier alternatives that will appeal to these consumers. Some of the best performers were bottled water, fruit juice and functional drinks.

However, Stacy is not very happy with her job. She recently clashed with her father about the growth strategies she had informally suggested. 'This is going to cost a lot of money,' said Mr Yap. 'You know that we have always pursued a low cost niche strategy,' she was told. Another issue of concern was the recent appointment of Mr Lim's son, Steve, as key account manager for the restaurants in eastern Malaysia. Stacy has known Steve Lim for many years, but she has always disliked him, and considers him to be lazy and incompetent. However, Stacy's father was adamant that Steve deserved at least one chance. 'Remember that Softy Fruits is like one big family,' he said.

Questions

1. Identify the current weaknesses of Softy Fruits' leadership style and strategy.
2. What growth strategy would you recommend the company adopts in order to expand its business?

Harvesting

If building and growing a business are the first two steps in creating wealth, **harvesting** can be regarded as the third. The harvesting of a venture is one of the more significant events in the life of an entrepreneurial firm and its owner. After a total immersion in the business, a huge workload, many sacrifices and quite often burnout, many entrepreneurs want to reap a reward for the effort they have put into launching and nurturing a business venture. Entrepreneurship is often seen as a journey, not a destination, by many people who become 'serial entrepreneurs' — that is, people who build new firms and then exit them to get a maximum profit before starting yet another firm.

Harvesting *The process entrepreneurs and investors use to exit a business and realise their investment.*

This section outlines the key elements to take into consideration when planning an exit. Four exit strategies are presented: sale to a strategic partner or corporate investor, management buy-out, strategic alliance and merger and initial public offering.

Key elements to consider when planning an exit

If the entrepreneur is to take full advantage of an investment opportunity, it is essential not only to evaluate the merits of the opportunity at the outset, but also to anticipate options for exiting the business. If the entrepreneur's goal with the venture is to provide a living, then the exit strategy is of no concern. But if the goal is to create value for the owners and the other stakeholders in the business, a harvest strategy is very important. The exit is more than simply leaving the business; it is the final piece in creating the ultimate value to all participants in the venture, especially the owner, managers and employees.[20] Even if the entrepreneur does not plan to sell the business, there is still a need to prepare a succession plan in the event of retirement, illness or death of the founder. In any case, exit should be an active decision, rather than a passive, externally driven process.

As shown in figure 16.3, there are three main elements to be considered when planning an exit:

• *Strategic elements linked to the business environment*. An exit is attractive for the entrepreneur only if potential buyers are interested in the firm. The business must have a good stream of successful products that are well established in the market. In other words, the entrepreneur must be able to show that the business has a track record and that there is some potential for growth once the entrepreneur has pulled out of the business.

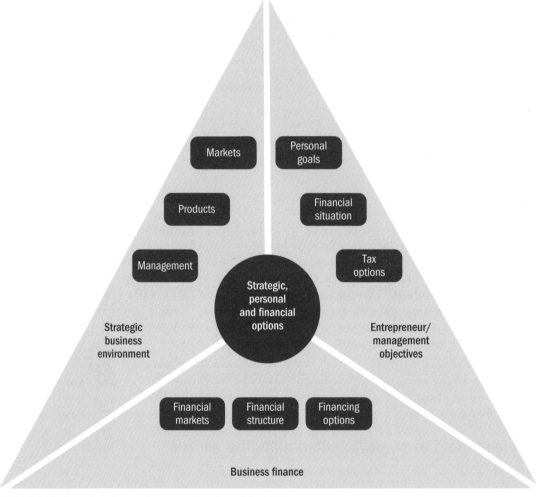

FIGURE 16.3 Balancing of strategic, personal and financial goals in a harvest strategy

- *Entrepreneur's personal aspirations.* For most entrepreneurs, the business venture is a dominant part of their lives. Thus, the decision to harvest cannot effectively be separated from the entrepreneur's personal goals and objectives. Without an understanding of what is important in life, the entrepreneur is apt to make a bad decision when it comes to harvesting a firm. The view of other stakeholders, such as outside investors and employees, also needs to be considered. Outside investors typically have expectations about their investment that include the firm either going public or being acquired by other investors.
- *Business financial situation.* The business financial situation is another key dimension to consider. For example, it might be difficult to list a business that has a high debt-to-equity ratio (leverage), in which case it may be preferable

to sell to a corporate investor who can restructure the balance sheet. Exit strategies offer different financing options for businesses in need of extra funds for pursuing growth. For example, an initial public offering is considered by many business owners as a means of raising growth capital rather than as a tool for facilitating the exit of the founders.

Whatever the final decision by the entrepreneur and others regarding the harvest strategy, opportunities to sell or go public come and go with the condition of the economy and the industry. Entrepreneurs must not only *choose* an exit strategy, but also be aware of *when* they can exit. For example, adverse financial market conditions stopped many entrepreneurs floating their businesses on the stock market during the dotcom crash and the 2008 financial crisis. Timing is important and entrepreneurs must be sensitive to the opening and closing of a window of opportunity. In shaping a harvest strategy, Timmons and Spinelli[21] suggested the following guidelines and cautions:

- *Patience.* Several years are required to launch and build most successful businesses, so patience is invaluable. A harvest strategy is more sensible if it allows for a time frame of at least three to five years and as long as seven to ten.
- *Vision.* The other side of the patience coin is not to panic as a result of unexpected events. Selling under duress is usually the worst thing to do.
- *Realistic valuation.* If impatience is the enemy of an attractive harvest, then greed is its executioner. The entrepreneur should value the business from different angles (such as book value, replacement value and discounted cash flows) to obtain a fair market value.
- *Outside advice.* It is best to find an adviser who can help craft a harvest strategy while the business is still growing, and at the same time help determine the value of the firm. Talking to an entrepreneur who has been through the experience of a merger or a sale can also give some useful pointers.

Sale to a financial or a strategic buyer

Selling the business outright is by far the most common harvest method. Sales fall into several broad categories, depending on the buyers: financial sales, strategic sales and management or employee buy-outs. Here we focus on financial and strategic sales, while management buy-outs are discussed in the next section.

A financial buyer may be a competitor in the industry or a business wishing to achieve 'vertical integration' and diversification by absorbing another business into its core business. In financial sales, buyers look mainly to a firm's stand-alone cash-generating potential as the source of value. Often, this value relates to stimulating future sales growth, reducing costs or both. Financial buyers are in business to make deals, so they may overlook some weaknesses. This has important implications for the seller, because new owners will often make changes to the firm's operations or break up the firm and sell the pieces. They often leave day-to-day operations unchanged, but they buy with a view to selling, which could disrupt the business's life a second time.

Strategic buyers, unlike financial buyers, expect the acquired business to fit in with their other holdings. Generally, these are corporate buyers seeking to effect or further a 'consolidation' strategy. In other words, strategic buyers seek to buy a number of businesses and then cobble them together to eliminate redundant and excess costs, and derive economies of scale wherever possible to decrease expenses and, similarly, increase profitability. The best match sometimes comes about if they seek out the potential seller after having determined that the business fits their plans. Consequently, strategic sales often result in the most attractive price for the seller.

Management buy-out

Management buy-out (MBO) *The purchase of a controlling interest in a business by its management in order to take over assets and operations.*

Another harvest strategy, called a **management buy-out (MBO)**, is one in which a founder can realise a gain from the business by selling to managers or existing partners in the business. The MBO usually entails high levels of debt (leverage) and, therefore, the new owner–managers must stay clearly focused on the operating performance if they are to meet debt payments and use assets effectively. If the business has both assets and good cash flow, the financing can be arranged via banks or other financial institutions. Even if assets are thin, a healthy cash flow that can service the debt to fund the purchase price may convince lenders to support an MBO.

Three factors are generally considered essential to conducting a successful MBO: (1) the ability to borrow significant sums against the business's assets; (2) the ability to retain or attract a strong management team; and (3) the potential for the participants' (including management's) investment to increase substantially in value. The ability of a business to support significant leverage depends on whether it can service the principal- and interest-payment obligations that accompany that leverage. This in turn requires a business to be capable of generating large sums of cash on a regular basis or to have substantial assets that can be sold to pay off the debt. This usually means a business with a history of operations sufficient to support the borrowing required to fund the deal.

When a management buy-out occurs, it often means that the division or business being purchased has a strong management team in place that requires few or no changes to make it complete. It is, after all, the investor's and lender's confidence in management's ability to run the business profitably and to expand its operations that make the buy-out possible. Attracting and keeping good management also means cutting them in for a significant portion of the deal. In other words, management usually acquires a healthy percentage of the business's equity. This motivates them to stay with the business and make it grow.

Strategic alliance and merger

Strategic alliance *An ongoing relationship between two businesses, which combine efforts for a specific purpose.*

Merger *The combining of two or more entities into one through a purchase acquisition or a pooling of interests.*

The entrepreneur can also use the framework of a strategic alliance to sell part of the business to a minority investor. In addition to the cash raised, there are generally wider benefits arising from this cooperation. For example, the investor can induce some economies of scale by pooling common resources or by collaborating in an allied area where the firm needs some expertise. Within a **strategic alliance**, the two allies remain legally independent, although a substantial part of their activities depends on the alliance (economic interdependence).

If the strategic alliance takes place between competitors, it can often lead to a **merger** of the two businesses later. In this case, a new legal entity is formed. The newly created enterprise will have a higher profile and an increased ability to continue growing, and may at a later stage be sold or offered to the public.

Initial public offering

In the eyes of many entrepreneurs, taking their firm public through an initial public offering (IPO) is the 'holy grail' of harvest strategies. Through the IPO, shares are offered for sale on a public stock exchange. Because the effect of this decision is to change the fundamental financial nature of the business, it must be done with a great deal of care. The merits of going public versus being acquired rest largely on the contention that IPOs provide higher valuations, and therefore better returns, than can be expected from a straight sale. Other advantages to the firm of going public are the negotiability of its securities, the potential use of future issues of its shares to acquire other businesses and an increase in the stature of the business.

However, there are disadvantages in going public. First, there is the loss of privacy as numerous reports are required by government agencies. Secondly, going public establishes the need for the board of directors to approve certain types of decisions, imposing additional restrictions on management. Thirdly, there is a significant cost associated with going public — not only is there the cost of the IPO itself, but there are also ongoing costs associated with the provision of information required by regulators.

Although IPOs are attractive for several reasons, many privately held firms will never find themselves in a position to go public. They will not qualify because they are too small or they are not in the 'right industry', or they lack the management skills to do so. Therefore, the IPO strategy is appropriate for a very limited set of firms.

SUMMARY

The growth of the venture can be approached from the financial, strategic and organisational perspectives. These three dimensions interact with one another and cannot be considered separately in the dynamics of growth. Although market forces may press for quantitative growth, this does not necessarily coincide with the personal interests of the entrepreneur. The relationship between personal and organisational objectives is important to understand, because they often overlap in the small firm.

Four basic theories can explain how and why organisations change: life cycle, teleology, evolution and dialectic. The notion of life cycle suggests that the business venture undergoes a pattern of growth and development much as a living organism does. Often, the stages follow the pattern of new venture development, start-up, growth, maturity and rebirth or decline. In teleology theory, the purpose or goal of management is the final cause for guiding movement of the organisation. In this perspective, the business venture sets goals and adapts its actions to reach its goals. The third approach, evolution, is a theoretical scheme that explains changes in structural forms of populations of organisations across communities or industries. As in biological evolution, organisational change proceeds through a continuous circle of variation, selection and retention. The fourth theory, dialectics, focuses on stability and change based on the collision of power between opposing entities.

High growth companies set specific goals and they develop strategies for reaching them. It is possible to distinguish between two main categories of growth strategies: internal and external strategies. Internal strategies for encouraging growth involves actions within companies themselves, such as efforts to increase market share, new product developments or internal expansions. Conversely, external growth strategies rely on establishing relationships with third parties through strategic alliances, licensing or acquisitions.

Managing a rapidly growing enterprise presents a particular challenge because the essential nature of the manager's job changes with growth. Fundamentally, the key responsibilities of the manager revolve around operating, organising and staffing. In order to make their businesses continue to grow beyond a certain point, entrepreneurs must be prepared to move from an entrepreneurial management style with centralised decision making and informal control towards a professional management style that involves the delegation of decision-making responsibility and the use of formal control mechanisms.

If building and growing a business are the first two steps in creating wealth, harvesting can be regarded as the third. Harvesting is the process that entrepreneurs and investors use to exit a business and realise their investment in a firm. There are four main exit strategies that entrepreneurs can use to harvest a venture: sale to strategic partner or corporate investor, management buy-out, strategic alliance and merger and initial public offering.

REVIEW QUESTIONS

1. What are the different dimensions of business growth?
2. What are the four basic theories that explain how and why organisations change?
3. What are the different strategies a venture can consider to grow its business?
4. What are the key steps for a successful transition towards professional management?
5. What are the main elements to be considered when planning an exit?

DISCUSSION QUESTIONS

1. Why are many owner–managers not interested in growing their business?
2. To what extent do the four organisational change theories (life cycle, teleology, dialectics, evolution) differ from the unit of change and mode of change perspective?
3. What are the weaknesses of the life cycle theory?
4. Why is it generally more difficult to manage growth and transition issues in family businesses?
5. 'Harvesting a business venture is as much about choosing an exit strategy as deciding when to exit.' Explain.

SUGGESTED READING

Collins, J., *Good to Great: Why Some Companies Make the Leap and Others Don't*, HarperCollins, New York, 2001.
Gunther McGrath, R. & MacMillan, I.C., MarketBusters: 40 Moves that Drive Exceptional Business Growth, Harvard Business School Press, Boston, MA, 2005.
Little, S.S., *The 7 Irrefutable Rules of Small Business Growth*, John Wiley & Sons, New York, 2005.

Case study

Les Mills International

Jill Tattersall, Chief Executive Officer at Les Mills International (LMI), world leader in the development of fitness programs, located in Auckland, recently heard that the potential distributor for the Western US region had declined the offer to represent LMI. She wondered whether LMI should set up its own agency or continue to search for another option.

Les Mills – Background

Les Mills opened his first gym in Auckland in 1968, and subsequently developed a series of standardised exercise-to-music classes that were franchised to other gyms, first in New Zealand and later Australia. After focusing on building a chain of local gyms, in 1990, he invented the BODYPUMP (a weight-lifting class) in his own living room. Today, LMI offers a series of different programs, including BODYCOMBAT (martial arts), BODYBALANCE (yoga, pilates and tai chi), BODYSTEP (high energy cardio), BODYJAM (a free flow dance format) and BODYATTACK (high intensity cardio aerobics).

Les Mills International was incorporated in 1997, funded by Phillip Mills (61%) and a group of private investors, to license Les Mills programs worldwide and to separate licensing from the health clubs business in New Zealand. Today, LMI classes are running in more than 13 000 clubs in 70 countries.

The company employs some of the world's best instructors, who trial new classes every three months, based on intensive market research to respond to consumer feedback and industry trends. When the class is judged 'perfect', it is videotaped and dispatched with a licensed music CD and written choreography notes to the 70 000 accredited Les Mills instructors around the world, who then teach to the club members.

There is also a management system to support licensed clubs, covering areas such as the recruitment of instructors, studio design and marketing. The company protects its intellectual property through trademark registration and through the vigilance of its distributors.

Purpose, vision and goal

Phillip Mills says, 'Our purpose is to inspire life-changing fitness experiences, every time, everywhere.' He adds, 'Our long-term vision is that Les Mills International will play a role in reducing obesity and its associated diseases in the Western world, and try to make people fitter, healthier and happier worldwide.' He aims to grow the numbers of gyms, offering Les Mills classes to 25 000 by 2015.

Phillip feels it is important to reach as much of the world market as possible, capitalising on his 'first mover advantage.' He therefore believes that a licensing approach for club owners was the proper way to go, using national or regional distributors to sell club owners on becoming LMI licensees, to distribute LMI programs, provide training programs and translate LMI materials into local languages. Although there was no initial cash payment to LMI for the right to become a distributor, the distributor was responsible for hiring the appropriate staff and assuming their adequate training with the help of LMI professionals. Phillip says, 'What we provide is a quality assurance method for clubs.'

The distributor would collect all licensing monthly fees from club owners and remit about 25% of this total to LMI. Normally, a distributor, starting from scratch, could expect to break-even within one and a half to three years, once 250 to 300 clubs had been signed up.

The US market

Phillip Mills believes the US market, with at least 20 000 gyms, represents half of the total world market for LMI programs, and that more than 20 per cent of the US population attend gyms. Attending gyms has become the most popular 'sport' in the US. Jill Tattersall and Phillip Mills consider the Western US region a crucial one in the US market. California is seen as the key state in this region, which also included Arizona, Nevada, Washington, Oregon, Utah and Alaska. LMI has currently 100 licensed clubs in this region but no distributor. Approaches have been made to several potential distributors. None of these turned out to be suitable for a variety of reasons, including lack of financing.

One prospective distributor looked promising however. First contacted at a Las Vegas trade show, this potential distributor seemed to meet LMI's requirements. Over the subsequent months negotiations were carried out and it appeared that an agreement might be reached. However, now, the prospective distributor for the Western US region had declined the LMI offer, ending months of speculation.

Sources: Based on author's interview with Jill Tattersall and Phillip Mills.

Questions

1. **What alternatives do you have to develop the Western US region and what decision criteria are applicable?**
2. **What factors explain the rapid growth of Les Mills International over the past years?**
3. **What current social trends may have an impact on Les Mills International?**

ENDNOTES

1. P.A. Wickham, *Strategic Entrepreneurship — A Decision Making Approach to New Venture Creation and Management*, 4th edn, Pitman Publishing, London, 2006.
2. M.E. Porter, *Competitive Strategy*, Free Press, New York, 1980.
3. A. Van de Ven & M.S. Poole, 'Explaining development and change in organisations', *Academy of Management Review*, vol. 20, no. 3, 1995, pp. 510–40.
4. P. Davidsson, L. Achtenhagen, & L. Naldi, *Research on Small Firm Growth: A Review*. European Institute of Small Business, 2005.
5. A. Van de Ven & M.S. Poole, see note 3.
6. S. Hanks, C. Watson, E. Jansen & G. Chandler, 'Tightening the life-cycle construct: A taxonomic study of growth stage configurations in high-technology organisations', *Entrepreneurship Theory and Practice*, vol. 18, no. 2, 1993, pp. 5–29.
7. B. Bird, *Entrepreneurial Behavior*, Scott Foresman and Company, Glenview, IL, 1989, p. 8.
8. D.C. Hambrick & L.M. Crozier, 'Stumblers and stars in the management of rapid growth', *Journal of Business Venturing*, no. 1, 1985, pp. 31–45.
9. L. Grenier, 'Evolution and revolution as organisations grow', *Harvard Business Review*, May–June 1998, pp. 55–67.
10. P. Davidsson, 'Continued entrepreneurship: Ability, need and opportunity as determinants for small firm growth', *Journal of Business Venturing*, vol. 6, 1991, pp. 405–29.
11. The Boston Consulting Group, '*What goliath can learn from David: the hidden role models in value creation and entrepreneurship*', April 2000.
12. B.R. Barringer & R.D. Ireland, *Entrepreneurship — Successfully Launching New Ventures*, 3rd edn, Prentice Hall, Upper Saddle River, 2010, p. 485.
13. S.A. Moskalev & D.L. Deeds, 'Joint ventures around the globe from 1990-200: forms, types, industries, countries and ownerships patterns', *Review of Financial Economics*, no. 1, 2007, pp. 29–67.

14. Byron, R. & Shane, S., *Entrepreneurship: A Process Perspective*, 2nd edn., South-western Publishing, Oklahoma City, 2007, p. 358

15. The Boston Consulting Group, ibid.

16. M.J. Roberts, 'The challenge of growth', Teaching note 9-393-106, Harvard Business School Publishing, Boston, MA, 1993.

17. E. Flamholtz & Y. Randle, *Growing Pains: Transitioning from an Entrepreneurship to a Professionally Managed Firm*, 4th edn, Jossey-Bass, San Francisco, 2007.

18. M.J. Roberts, 'Managing rapid growth', Teaching note 9-387-054, Harvard Business School Publishing, Boston, 1989.

19. N. Wassermann, 'The founder's dilemma', *Harvard Business Review*, February 2008, pp. 103–109.

20. W. Petty, 'Harvesting', in W.D. Bygrave, *The Portable MBA in Entrepreneurship*, 2nd edn, John Wiley & Sons, New York, 1997, pp. 415–43.

21. J. Timmons & S. Spinelli, *New Venture Creation: Entrepreneurship for the 21st Century*, 7th edn, Irwin, Chicago, 2007, p. 621.

CHAPTER **17**

Corporate entrepreneurship

Learning objectives

After reading this chapter, you should be able to:

- define the concept of corporate entrepreneurship and its different forms

- explain the importance of corporate entrepreneurship for established businesses

- discuss the process of new venture development

- identify the key steps in developing entrepreneurial spirit in organisations.

Most established organisations find it hard to maintain the initial entrepreneurial spirit that helped them to make it through the start-up stage. As businesses grow, they usually become more structured and more rigid. Managers from many organisations across the Asia–Pacific region have reported that although they are satisfied with their operating prowess, they are dissatisfied with their ability to implement change. 'How do the excellent innovators do it?' they ask, presuming that excellent innovators exist. 'What drives the development of new promising opportunities?' Others question how to expand an organisation beyond its core business. And most fundamental of all: 'How do we find new ideas?'

The difficulties behind these questions arise from the inherent conflict between the need for organisations to control existing operations and the need to create the kind of environment that will permit new ideas to flourish and old ones to die a timely death. Businesses have traditionally faced many difficulties in identifying opportunities and subsequently turning them into new product and successful product lines.

Faced with this challenge, large organisations have two main strategies for remaining at the forefront of innovation. The first strategy consists of buying young firms with great potential. Some giants, including General Electric and Cisco, have been remarkably successful at snapping up and integrating scores of firms. But many others worry about the prices they have to pay, and about hanging on to the talent that dreamt up the idea. The second strategy consists, therefore, of developing more ideas in-house; hence, the craze for corporate entrepreneurship — delegating power and setting up internal ideas factories.

This chapter provides a rationale and a definitional framework for corporate entrepreneurship. Successful organisations develop a disciplined, milestone-focused approach to screening and funding new ventures. The five main stages of this new venture development process are presented, and the key steps to follow in instilling an entrepreneurial spirit in organisations are discussed.

Dimensions of and rationale for corporate entrepreneurship

The management structures and processes necessary for routine operations are very different from those required for managing innovation. The pressures of corporate long-range strategic planning on the one hand and short-term financial control on the other combine to produce an environment that favours planned and stable growth based on incremental innovation. Through corporate entrepreneurship, established organisations attempt to exploit their internal resources and provide an environment that is more conducive to radical innovation. This section presents a definition of corporate entrepreneurship and its various underlying dimensions. A rationale for corporate entrepreneurship is outlined, showing that discontinuous opportunities generate disproportionate wealth.

Towards a definition of corporate entrepreneurship

Although organisation creation and innovation are generally regarded as key factors in entrepreneurship, the challenges that entrepreneurs face vary according to whether they are operating independently or as part of an existing organisation.

Thus, we need to differentiate between the settings in which entrepreneurship takes place.

Dimensions of corporate entrepreneurship

Today, there is no universally accepted definition of corporate entrepreneurship. Some authors emphasise its analogy to new business creation, and view corporate entrepreneurship as a concept limited to new venture creation within existing organisations. Others argue that the concept of corporate entrepreneurship should encompass the struggle of large firms to renew themselves by carrying out new combinations of resources that alter the relationships between them and their environment. It is possible to combine these different views and to define **corporate entrepreneurship** as the process whereby an individual or a group, in association with an existing organisation, creates a new organisation or initiates renewal or innovation within that organisation.[1]

Within the realm of existing organisations, entrepreneurship encompasses three dimensions that are not necessarily interrelated:

- **Corporate venturing** refers to corporate entrepreneurial efforts that lead to the creation of new business ventures in established organisations.[2] The new ventures — the equivalent of internal start-ups — may reside inside or outside the boundaries of the firm. *Internal corporate venturing* refers to the corporate venturing activities that result in the creation of organisational entities, such as a new division or subsidiary, within an existing firm. *External corporate venturing* refers to corporate venturing activities that result in the creation of semi-autonomous or autonomous organisational entities outside the existing firm, for example, spin-offs, joint ventures and venture capital initiatives.
- **Strategic renewal** involves the creation of new wealth through new combinations of resources within the firm. Renewal activities occur within the existing organisation and are not treated as new business by the organisation. This includes actions such as refocusing a business competitively, making major changes in marketing or distribution, redirecting product development and reshaping operations.[3]
- Innovation is also an entrepreneurial activity since it involves new combinations that may dramatically alter the bases of competition in an industry or lead to the creation of a new industry, even though it may not be immediately manifested in organisation creation or renewal. For example, innovation can lead simply to the development of new products, services or processes.

The relationship between the dimensions discussed above is presented in figure 17.1. In light of these manifestations, it is evident that corporate entrepreneurship is not confined to a particular business size or a particular stage of an organisation's life cycle, such as the start-up phase. In a competitive environment, entrepreneurship is an essential element in the long-range success of every business organisation, small or large, new or long-established.

Internal corporate venturing

Internal corporate venturing activities are located within existing organisations, but they are created in differing ways, involve different levels of innovation and differ in importance. This suggests that internal corporate ventures may vary in terms of at least three aspects that may affect their development and performance.

Corporate entrepreneurship
The process whereby an individual or a group, in association with an existing organisation, creates a new organisation or initiates renewal or innovation within that organisation.

Corporate venturing
The development of new business ventures inside or at the periphery of an organisation.

Strategic renewal
The new combinations of resources that result in significant changes to an organisation's strategy or structure.

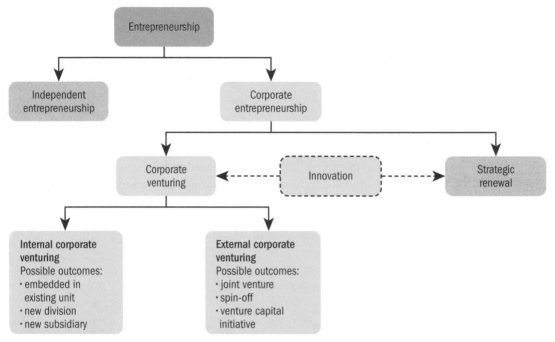

FIGURE 17.1 Hierarchy of terminology in corporate entrepreneurship

Source: Adapted from P. Sharma & J.J. Chrisman, 'Toward a reconciliation of the definitional issues in the field of corporate entrepreneurship', *Entrepreneurship Theory and Practice*, vol. 23, no. 3, 1999, p. 20.

The first aspect is structural autonomy — that is, the location of the venture within an organisation. The venture may be completely integrated into an existing division, or a separate new division may be created or a subsidiary may be set up that is isolated from the rest of the organisation and reports directly to top management. The best place to locate a venture will depend on how much managerial attention it needs, the resources required and whether it needs to be protected from criticism and opposition from other parts of the organisation.

The second aspect is the extent of innovation, or how 'new' it is in the marketplace. This aspect may range from extensions, duplications and synthesis-type innovations to those innovations that 'break the mould' (inventions). If a venture is completely new and even creates new markets, then the innovating firm will face significantly greater challenges.

The third aspect is the nature of sponsorship. What is the degree of formal authorisation for the venture? Corporate ventures may be formally sponsored by top management or they may be informal, independent initiatives of employees without formal organisational sponsorship.[4] The nature of sponsorship has some organisational implications for corporate entrepreneurship. For example, an organisational champion is very important in the case of independent entrepreneurial efforts, but it may not be as critical in the case of formally sponsored efforts.

The three aspects often interact. Consider the case of bricks-and-mortar firms pursuing e-business opportunities. In this situation firms prefer to create a separate subsidiary for several reasons: (1) it demands a clear statement of the new venture's strategy and facilitates an aggressive approach to new business development; (2) it enables greater freedom and flexibility to tailor individual venture business models to specific competitive situations; (3) it facilitates separate valuation by existing and potential investors; and (4) it makes it easier to attract and retain top talent.[5]

External corporate venturing

External corporate venturing can take several forms: **spin-offs**, joint ventures and venture capital initiatives. Both spin-offs and joint ventures lead to the creation of a new business venture outside the existing organisation. The difference between the two is that the former is entirely independent whereas the latter is semi-autonomous — the firm holds an equity stake in the new venture, and usually has a say in the management.

Spin-off *An individual or organisational unit leaving an existing firm to start as an independent new firm.*

Spin-offs have been a particularly popular form of external entrepreneurship over the last decade, giving entrepreneurial-minded employees the chance to take internally spawned projects and create independent concerns. Businesses have always spun off new firms, but what has been different over the past few years is a growing awareness on the part of the parent organisation that new products, which do not fit into their strategic plans, can sometimes be best developed and marketed by an independent firm. Organisations that are downsizing find that it is easier to maintain an equity position in a spin-off than to develop a venture from within.

Another way to capitalise on clever ideas that fall by the corporate wayside is to develop a corporate venture capital fund. Xerox, for example, set up Technology Ventures in its Palo Alto Research Center (PARC) and elsewhere; this business unit was given US$30 million to exploit ideas that 'didn't fit' within the firm. If researchers are turned down by top management at headquarters, they are free to take their ideas to Xerox Technology Ventures. However, the venture fund insists that corporate entrepreneurs stay at PARC until they perfect a proper working model of their money-making scheme. They are then moved into low-cost commercial premises, with a professional business manager to help them stay on track. In return, the founders get a 20 per cent stake in their new venture.[6]

Entrepreneur profile

Tony Fernandes, AirAsia

Tony Fernandes founded Tune Air Sdn Bhd in 2001, with a vision of making air travel more affordable for Malaysians. With this vision in mind, he approached Malaysia's then prime minister, Mahathir Mohamad, to see whether he would get official support for his plan to challenge Malaysia Airline's local monopoly. The shrewd Mr Mahathir said that he would agree, but on condition that Tony took over an existing airline: AirAsia, a struggling subsidiary of a government-owned conglomerate. AirAsia was virtually bankrupt at the time, and its fleet consisted of two ageing Boeing jets. Tony and three partners bought AirAsia for one ringgit, and took over the 40 million ringgit of debt. The project was to create a new aviation product in Malaysia by remodelling AirAsia into a low-fare, no-frills carrier. This premise was based on the success of low-fare airlines, such as US-based Southwest Airlines and Ireland's Ryanair.

Under the leadership of Mr Fernandes, the fledgling airline has become a thriving business. In its first full year of operation, AirAsia carried just over a million passengers. In 2009, it flew 22 million passengers (or 'guests', as Tony Fernandes calls them). The airline currently operates more than 110 domestic and international flights from its hubs at Kuala Lumpur International Airport (KLIA), Johor Bahru in Malaysia, Bangkok International Airport, and Soekarno-Hatta International Airport in Jakarta. What's more, AirAsia has been profitable for all but the second half of 2008.

'Tony might be the CEO of the company, but he is also the mascot of the company. Because wherever he goes, whatever he does, he represents the company,' says Mohshin Aziz, Head of Investor Relations at AirAsia. There is a cultural symmetry between what Tony Fernandes tries to present and what the company actually represents. 'He is rarely seen without his baseball cap, open-neck shirt and jeans.' adds Mr Aziz.

AirAsia has a flat hierarchy and a distinctive open culture. The headquarters of the company are located in its low-cost terminal at KLIA, and the offices have a view of the planes and runway. This constantly reminds the employees of the company's core business, and keeps them focused. If people need help, colleagues will go into the terminal and carry bags. Anyone can rise to do another's job. The airline employs pilots who started out as baggage handlers and stewards; for his part, Tony also practises what the preaches. Every month he spends a day as baggage-handler; every two months, a day as cabin crew; every three months, a day as check-in clerk.[7]

All employees are actively encouraged to make suggestions on how to improve services and processes, and resolve problems. To this effect, 'midnight sessions' (so-called because they take place after working hours) are regularly held throughout the company. During these sessions, top management will brief staff about operational issues, main concerns and the latest financial results; feedback is also sought from employees.

Source: Based on author's interview with Mohshin Aziz, Head of Investor Relations at AirAsia and 'Cheap, but not nasty', *Indian Express*, 27 Feb., www.indianexpress.com, 2009.

Rationale for corporate entrepreneurship

Existing organisations can introduce two basic types of innovation into the marketplace — incremental or radical innovations. *Incremental innovations* usually come from tweaking existing designs and listening to big customers, who usually just want steady improvements that yield higher margins. Incremental innovations use established technologies and can be implemented easily and rapidly. *Radical innovations*, on the other hand, are based on disruptive technologies and often present teething troubles that spoil the customers' bottom line. As explained below, radical innovations result from the pursuit of **discontinuous opportunities** that have the potential to generate disproportionate wealth.

Discontinuous opportunities
Innovations that move beyond existing business models to create new products and enter new markets.

Identifying and pursuing discontinuous opportunities

In the area of new business development, and especially new business incubation, discontinuous opportunities generate disproportionate wealth. For example, although discontinuous opportunities generally trigger only 14 per cent of new business launches in existing companies, they generate 38 per cent of their revenues and 61 per cent of their profits.[8]

In the Asia–Pacific region, firms have traditionally excelled in making things, growing their market share and, at best, exploiting adjacent opportunities. All this, however, is changing. Asian businesses are moving quickly away from providing a manufacturing base for the rest of the world to being providers of products and services for their indigenous markets. The cash cow of the future is creativity and innovation. Discontinuous opportunities occupy a distinct and challenging corner of the new business development arena (see figure 17.2). These opportunities are challenging because they typically entail both creating new products and entering new markets. Discontinuous business opportunities can be discovered and pursued only if existing organisations have developed adequate corporate entrepreneurship strategies.

Discontinuous opportunities assume two forms:

- *White-space opportunities* involve entering new industries, developing new technologies and marketing new products. Because they are not modifications of existing product lines, pursuit of white-space opportunities often requires knowledge and capabilities that the organisation does not currently possess.
- *Disruptive opportunities* are new technologies or business models that constitute a threat to established business lines. Because these opportunities are often related to the organisation's core business, senior management often considers existing business units to be the logical home for their stewardship. However, this tendency risks neglect of disruptive opportunities or even 'drowning' by established businesses fearing cannibalisation.[9]

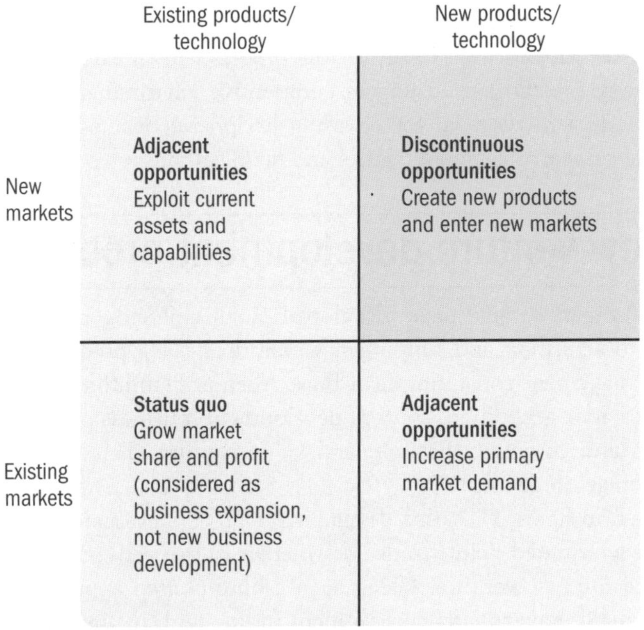

	Existing products/ technology	New products/ technology
New markets	**Adjacent opportunities** Exploit current assets and capabilities	**Discontinuous opportunities** Create new products and enter new markets
Existing markets	**Status quo** Grow market share and profit (considered as business expansion, not new business development)	**Adjacent opportunities** Increase primary market demand

FIGURE 17.2 The new business development arena

Source: Adapted from *The New Venture Division: Attributes of an Effective New Business Incubation Structure*, Corporate Executive Board, Washington, 2000, p. 4.

Reasons for corporate entrepreneurship

There are several motives for developing corporate entrepreneurship in an organisation:[10]

- *To grow and diversify the business.* Corporate ventures are often formed in an effort to create new businesses in a corporate context, and therefore represent an attempt to grow via diversification. Organisations that merely improve existing products, services and processes in order to grow their market share and their profits face stagnation sooner or later. To grow and counter the threat induced by start-ups in the marketplace, existing organisations must develop new products and enter new market segments.

- *To satisfy and retain bright and motivated staff.* In today's knowledge society, organisations employ better qualified staff to develop increasingly sophisticated products and services. As a consequence, the key to a sustained competitive advantage often resides in the organisational capabilities that a business is able to develop. In the war for talent, it is essential that organisations retain their best and brightest staff by giving them enough room to generate new ideas and allowing them to pursue promising new opportunities.

- *To exploit underused resources in new ways.* This includes both technological and human resources. Typically, a business has two choices where existing resources are underused: (1) outsource the process or (2) generate additional contributions from external clients. However, if the business wants to retain direct and in-house control of the technology or personnel, it can form an internal venture to offer the service to external clients.

- *To get rid of non-core activities.* Much has been written of the benefits of strategic focus, 'getting back to basics' and creating the 'lean organisation' — rationalisation, which prompts the organisation to divest itself of any activities that can be outsourced. However, this process can threaten the skill diversity required for an ever-changing competitive environment. New ventures can provide a mechanism for releasing peripheral business activities while retaining some management control and financial interest.

The new venture development process

Successful organisations have developed a disciplined, milestone-focused approach to screening and funding new ventures. This process, according to leading management consulting firm Booz Allen & Hamilton,[11] comprises five main stages: idea generation, concept development, business plan development, incubation and commercialisation, and value capture. This section discusses these five stages in detail.

As shown in figure 17.3, this development process evaluates each new venture at predetermined points to decide whether to proceed, refine, accelerate or discontinue the new venture. Using such a time-phased approach, an organisation gradually increases its commitment in line with the availability of more information. As the business venture moves through critical 'decision gates', its performance is measured against pre-established targets, and resource decisions are made. Meanwhile, the process itself 'learns' and becomes 'smarter' as the organisation gathers and assesses more information about the economic and competitive environment and the individual venture's operating history. This is a dynamic screening method that evolves as the venture matures, and it ensures the continuous reliability of the conception at each stage.

Idea generation

The first step of the new venture development process is idea generation. At this stage, quantity, rather than quality, matters. Innovative organisations are those that systematically generate ideas and do not let any idea slip away. Empirical evidence has shown that entrepreneurial businesses need to generate hundreds of ideas to end up with a handful of plausible programs for developing new products. Several large organisations, including 3M, Procter & Gamble, and Cisco, have therefore established 'ideas factories'. Rather than leaving it to chance, these organisations have taken the following steps to help bring out any creative potential in their employees.

Stage	Idea generation	Concept development	Business plan development	Incubation and commercialisation	Value capture
Objective	*Unleash creativity*	*Refine*	*Define*	*Free-standing organisation*	*Unleash value*
Timing	3 hours to 2 days	1 week	3 weeks to 4 months	3 months to 2 years	3 to 4 years
Elements	• Internal development • External sourcing • Idea capture • Idea screening	• Idea evaluation • Concept refinement • Idea becomes a business opportunity	• Business model development • Potential partner identification • Evaluation framework • Target market and customer value proposition validated	• Prototyping, trials • Launch planning • Resource acquisition • Business plan refinement • Technology product development • Management team	• Determination of exit strategy • Preparation for liquidity event • Communication and marketing
Output △ Major decision gates	• High potential ideas	• 2-page elaboration of each idea with recommendation △	• Business plan △	• Internal start-up △	• Value/liquidity event △
Decision	• Good idea	• Opportunity • Worth investment in resources to flesh out	• Business economics feasible • Worth investment to launch	• Readiness to launch • Readiness to wean from core	• Timing of liquidity event • Nature of liquidity event

FIGURE 17.3 New venture development process

Source: G. Neilson, J. Albrinck, J. Hornery et al., *E-Business and Beyond: Organizing for Success in New Ventures*, Booz Allen & Hamilton, New York, 2001, p. 10.

- *Allow unofficial activity*. Work conducted without direct official support is what makes it possible for an organisation to go where it never expected to. Unless an organisation makes provision for such activity, relatively few creative acts will occur. Some organisations have established policies that encourage certain employees to devote a certain percentage of their time to unofficial projects. Hewlett Packard's policy is 10 per cent, and Toshiba and 3M allow 15 per cent.
- *Encourage spontaneous discoveries*. An oft-cited example is that of Charles Goodyear, who, after almost two decades of frustration in his search for a useful form of rubber, discovered the answer to his problem — vulcanisation — when he accidentally dropped a mixture of rubber and sulphur on a hot stove. To promote 'fortunate accidents', organisations should encourage tinkering and empirical research work.
- *Create diverse stimuli*. Stimuli are the sparks for creative ideas. Idealab, for example, conducts monthly brainstorming sessions and focuses on those

ideas that generate the most passion among staff members. Siemens holds 'idea competitions' in which employees are asked to submit ideas to a cross-functional screening committee. IBM opened an online suggestions box called 'Think Place' where ideas are logged for all to see and improve upon. Organisations can influence the set of stimuli that employees are exposed to by rotating people in jobs they would not normally do.

Crowdsourcing *The act of taking tasks traditionally performed by an employee or contractor, and outsourcing them to a group (crowd) of people or community in the form of an open call.*

• **Crowdsourcing**. Some of the greatest ideas often come from amongst creative throngs of experts — consumers, engineers, students or current users. Crowdsourcing can represent an effective way to harness the wisdom of crowds. For example, Cisco Systems run an external innovation competition called the I-Prize in the fall of 2007. In the end, more than 2500 innovators from 104 countries submitted about 1200 distinct ideas.[12]

Most of the time, corporate entrepreneurship opportunities are conceived because employees have access to unique information through social ties, and because they are willing to accept ideas based on subjective criteria.[13] This starting point is important because it provides an explanation for how organisations learn to extend their knowledge in ways that are inconsistent with the dominant belief. Although other objective circumstances, such as industry structure, may determine whether new ideas emerge as market opportunities, the subjective 'opportunity structure' — how the entrepreneur views and interprets the situation — helps the introduction of new ideas.

The question is, then, 'Where does the new information come from?' Based on social network theory, it appears that weak, informal ties provide employees with information to generate ideas and to collect resources in order to engage in the most promising opportunities. Thus, it can be assumed that people who maintain relationships not necessarily associated with their formal position are more likely to be a source of entrepreneurial ideas within the business venture. This suggests that the real work in most organisations is done informally through personal contacts.[14] In the dynamic working environment, modern managers perpetually use their personal contacts when they need to meet an impossible deadline, get advice on a strategic decision or obtain support to back up their ideas.

Concept development

In the concept development phase, a promising one-sentence idea is transformed into a two-page outline of the opportunity, covering such topics as concept description, target market, value for the customer, competition, potential business models and opportunity size. Two or three people who bring the relevant knowledge and skills to the assignment, such as industry and technical expertise or organisational knowledge, flesh out the concept to determine whether it is worth putting resources into.

For an idea to get accepted at 3M, for example, it must first win the personal backing of at least one member of the main board. Only then will an interdisciplinary venture team of researchers, engineers, marketers and accountants be set up to push the idea further. This step is important because evidence suggests that the innovator who first recognises an opportunity may not be the one to champion it for resources within the organisation. Indeed, many innovators are technically minded and find it difficult to explain their ideas in business terms — this may be due to a simple lack of communication skills, but it is more likely to result from the isolation created by the individual's mind set and unique set of social relationships. Conversely, product champions are able to turn a new idea into a concrete new project in which technical and marketing development can begin to take shape.

One of the keys to success at this stage is speed. Concept development should take only weeks, yet many organisations let ideas languish for months, so by the time the idea has formed into a testable business model, the market has changed or competition has usurped the idea. Organisations need to expedite the flow of innovative ideas through this phase and establish an approval 'board' to usher to the next stage those ideas that meet the feasibility test. For example, at Royal Dutch Shell, ideas are submitted to innovations teams by email. Using a screening method devised by an external consultant, six-person 'GameChanger' teams meet weekly to assess ideas. The GameChanger teams assessed 320 proposals during their first two years of operation.

Business plan development

The new business model is designed and simulated at this stage, which can take up to four months. Management seeks to validate the uniqueness of the business model and the value proposition for its target market. A full-scale business plan is developed and new staff are brought into the venture, since those who are best able to generate ideas are not necessarily the best at translating them into workable business plans.

The need for resources during the process of testing determines which people corporate entrepreneurs will attempt to influence. During this process of validation, corporate entrepreneurs become central figures in an emergent network (for example, a venture team in the 3M case). In addition, corporate venture groups often draw on external resources, such as venture capital firms and incubators, at this stage. A successful pilot study, for instance, usually leads to more widespread acceptance of the idea's feasibility and desirability. Other forms of empirical support, such as market research or consultant studies, may also be used to lend objective credibility to a proposal and thereby gain more support.

Effective business plans reflect both a strong grasp of technology and a firm understanding of the business and market that the new venture is tackling. Moreover, they are 'reality-tested' with key constituencies, such as customers and investors. Ultimately, a document is produced that details such items as market opportunity, competitive evaluation, business model, organisational structure and financial projections.

Incubation and commercialisation

During the incubation phase, it is important that the technological feasibility of the venture is fully tested. Prototypes of the product are built and feedback from potential users is obtained. Resources must also be acquired or borrowed to establish the validity of the business model and test its value proposition. This often takes the form of seed funding, and dedicated advisers or sponsors are assigned to the emergent venture. Partnerships are established both internally and externally (with legal and technology experts, for example) to bring the new venture along. Strict discipline and management skills are needed to recruit and train staff, secure funding, complete the evaluation of the business concept, establish the organisational entity and create contracts with suppliers and potential customers.

This stage of testing may lead to at least three different types of outcome. First, the results may be positive, and the initiative becomes viewed as unequivocally successful. At the other extreme, a test of the idea can be a complete failure, thus ending the entrepreneurial process. Between these two extremes, the testing of new ideas may produce mixed results. Ideas may be seen as meritorious but requiring unacceptable levels of effort to make them practical. On the other hand, initial ideas may prove impractical at first, but the fine-tuning of the first tests may make them viable.

Commercialisation marks the point at which a business plan graduates from theory into practice. At this point, the business model gets its first dose of marketplace experience. As the concept is fully commercialised, it is rapidly tested and scaled up. The venture must prove its ability to produce multiple versions of the products, and even start multiple complementary product lines. Although the venture team needs to recognise that the business model will evolve, implementation speed is vital. Learning needs to be rapidly absorbed and incorporated. The duration of this stage is typically between three months and two years.

Value capture

Contrary to the traditional marketing approach of product innovation, which merely focuses on increasing sales or market share, the aim of corporate entrepreneurship is to create value. Several mechanisms exist for capturing value from new businesses once they have been commercialised. These include initial public offerings (IPO), selling to an external bidder, establishing joint ventures, creating separate subsidiaries or divisions and incorporating new ventures back into the parent organisation.

The strategy an organisation chooses depends on a number of factors. For example, if the parent company wants to turn its new venture into cash, it will probably choose an IPO or find a private buyer. This type of strategy is often selected when the new venture does not belong to the core activities of the parent, and if it is built on a discontinuous business model that does not fit into the current corporate culture. Alternatively, if the venture can drive growth in the business and if it encompasses a traditional business model, management would be inclined to form a new division or even to incorporate the new venture into an existing division.

Best-practice companies have a clear mechanism for unleashing the value created by new ventures. For example, Xerox takes one of three approaches: (1) if the venture is related to a Xerox core competency but does not fit neatly into an existing business unit, it may become its own separate Xerox company; (2) the venture may be assigned directly to a compatible Xerox business division; (3) the new venture may be spun off to a venture capital firm if it does not strategically fit with Xerox's existing businesses or overall portfolio.

Kerala Food

Mumbai-based Kerala Food is a manufacturer of Indian wheat pellets and food condiments. The company was established in 1965 by Pankaj Bardia, who successfully grew the business to 145 employees before retiring in 2008. His eldest son Vimal took over as owner–manager. Vimal was thrilled by his job, and he had grand plans for the company's future — although he realised that he first had to get performance on track. He had regularly been working weekends, using the time to pore over Kerala Food's books in an effort to discern why annual revenues were stuck at 37 million rupees and profits hadn't risen in four years.

Kerala Food is like as well-oiled machine, Vimal told to himself — not many bells and whistles to what we do, but we do it well. This may, in part, explain the disruption experienced when the R&D manager, Shilpa Chatterjee, developed a new line of products. Shilpa, a young recruit poached from food giant Nestlé, had recently prepared various samosas and pakoras (small, spicy fritters) recipes and suggested that Kerala Food enter the fast growing snack food segment. Many of her peers considered Shilpa a troublemaker (someone who kept pestering others to abandon their conventional way of doing things). In the last couple of months, Shilpa developed the new recipes with the help of Vivek Kumar, the marketing manager and an old friend of Vimal.

Just like Shilpa, Vivek's behaviour doesn't go down well with a lot of people when he badgers them to depart from the company's institutionalised products and processes, especially when he does it in an abrasive manner. He also finds joy in flouting the office norms; working outside the regular office hours and dressing casually, in stark contrast to the business attire adopted by his colleagues. However, his approach to work seems to suit him, as he always gets a lot done and has recently won several key accounts.

Vimal recently began to reflect upon Kerala Food's organisational culture. It seems the company's formal dress code and the polite way employees treated one another was like a throwback to the 1960s when Karala Food was first established. The company had retained much of its old ways, which emerged under the patriarchal leadership style of Pankaj Bardia. Employees were loyal and conservative both in mind and manner. Most of them would spend their entire career working for Kerala Food, and most of the new recruits were usually the sons or daughters of long time employees, or their friends. Kerala Food was like one big family and Vimal was regularly invited to family functions by his employees.[15]

Questions

1. What should Vimal Bardia do with Shilpa and Vivek? Why?
2. What would you do in order develop an entrepreneurial spirit at Kerala Food?

The key steps in developing entrepreneurial spirit

Developing an entrepreneurial spirit inside an existing organisation requires four steps, as shown in figure 17.4: (1) develop a vision and a strategy, (2) create a culture of innovation, (3) develop organisational support and (4) reward results accordingly. This process requires time and constant effort. Evidence suggests that most firms build up the attributes of corporate entrepreneurship in long-drawn-out processes over many years, not in a one-shot, single event.

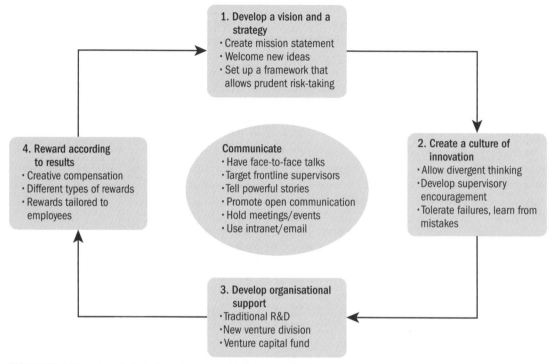

FIGURE 17.4 Four steps for fostering entrepreneurship in an organisation

Develop a vision and a strategy

The first step towards instilling an entrepreneurial spirit in an existing organisation is to develop a clearly understandable vision and a strategy. Leaders of highly innovative organisations welcome new ideas, and by their decisions, actions and communications they demonstrate that innovation propels profitability. Executives, through their words and actions, help people to overcome their fear of failure and, in the process, create a culture of intelligent risk-taking that leads to sustained innovation. These leaders do not just accept failure; they encourage it.

Welcome new ideas

Usually, the vision of the organisation is translated into a mission statement, which states the purpose of an organisation and identifies the scope of its operations in product and market terms, and reflects its values and priorities. Essentially, the mission statement defines the organisation and provides an answer to the question: 'What kind of organisation do we want to be?' It will help an organisation make consistent decisions, motivate employees, build organisational unity, integrate short-term objectives with longer term goals and enhance communication.

Leaders of highly innovative organisations emphasise developing whole new business concepts and product platforms, and systematically 'destroying one's own'. Continual innovation is their sole business. All other business concerns flow from this single overriding purpose.

Allow prudent risk-taking

IBM's Thomas Watson once said: 'The fastest way to succeed is to double your failure rate'. In recent years, more and more executives have embraced this point of view, coming to understand what innovators have always known: that failure is a prerequisite to invention. A business cannot develop a breakthrough product or process if it is not willing to encourage risk-taking and learn from subsequent mistakes.

The growing acceptance of failure is changing the way businesses approach corporate entrepreneurship. Some build exit strategies into their projects to ensure that doomed efforts do not drag on indefinitely. Some conduct a large number of market experiments, knowing that, although most of their tests will not pay off, even the failures will provide valuable insights into customer preferences. Others launch two or more projects with the goal of sending teams in different directions simultaneously. This approach creates the potential for a healthy cross-fertilisation of new ideas and techniques.

This approach to mistake making is characteristic of 'failure-tolerant leaders' — executives who help people overcome their fear of failure and, in the process, create a culture of intelligent risk-taking that leads to sustained innovation.[16] These leaders do not simply accept failure; they encourage it. They break down the bureaucratic barriers that separate them from their employees and associate with the people they lead.

Create a culture of innovation

Once the vision and the strategy have been established, organisations can work on their corporate culture. An entrepreneurial culture allows divergent thinking, develops supervisory encouragement and tolerates failure.

Allow divergent thinking

Traditional corporate control systems limit creativity through their dependence on convergent thinking. *Convergent thinking* focuses on clear problems and provides well-known solutions quickly. Order, simplicity, routine, clear responsibilities and predictability are the bases of convergent thinking. This is hardly the kind of environment in which discontinuous opportunities can be nurtured.

Conversely, *divergent thinking* focuses on broadening the context of decision making. Essentially, it requires three central skills — conversation, observation and reflection — to identify new business ideas.[17] Managing for divergent thinking means providing plenty of information to stimulate people to ask the right questions. It requires good selection and motivation of employees rather than control of people's actions; ample resources, including time, to achieve results; and genuine respect for other people's capabilities and potential.

Develop supervisory encouragement

Leaders of successful, continually innovative organisations create a sense of community across the whole organisation. In these organisations, everyone identifies with a common purpose, knows why they are working together and participates in innovation as the basic way the organisation creates and brings new value to customers. Creativity and innovation activities are not delegated to just a few people or functional areas. It is not necessary for a top manager to be the technical inventor or innovator, but to be the innovation leader calling for, recognising and acknowledging innovative results in others.

It is not enough, however, to launch change from the top and hope that communication about change will open like a parachute, blanketing everyone evenly. Entrepreneurial leaders must establish their vision by working with others, especially by finding, empowering and championing 'middle manager entrepreneurs'.[18] These are the frontline supervisors who assume the career risk of pursuing a new idea within the corporation, and who find the necessary resources, deal with problems so an idea can germinate, and bear the brunt of institutional inertia and resistance. In addition, frontline supervisors greatly influence the attitudes and behaviour of others.

Supervisory encouragement by both top managers and middle managers not only creates a vision for innovation, but sustains it, making people feel as if their work matters to the organisation or to some important group of people. Not every idea is worthy of consideration, of course, but in many organisations managers habitually show a lack of enthusiasm that damages creativity. They look for reasons *not* to use a new idea, instead of searching for reasons to explore it further. Negativity also shows in the way managers threaten or dismiss people whose ideas do not work.

Tolerate failures

Encouraging employees to innovate invariably implies tolerating failures. Successful innovators know that learning the hard way, through mistakes, is often the best way to create a business with staying power. 3M has one of the most famous cases of this — the glue that would not work because it was too weak became, eventually, the adhesive for Post-it Notes. Consequently, it is important to give employees permission to occasionally fail and to learn from failure. Furthermore, dead ends can sometimes be very enlightening. In many business situations, knowing what does not work can be as useful as knowing what does.

Creating a culture in which people feel comfortable with failure also requires abandoning the traditional approach to personal competition. The idea that achievement is maximised when people compete is not necessarily true — when the road to success requires making others fail, innovation can get left by the wayside. Competition infects co-workers with a desire to win rather than solve problems and move projects forward. In the process, employees inhibit the free flow of information that is vital to innovation. Those who feel they are competing with co-workers will want to protect information rather than share it.

Some future-minded organisations, such as Royal Dutch Shell and Monsanto, have developed work groups that emphasise collaboration. The main objective of these groups is to exchange information, not to hide it as so often happens in the heat of competition. 3M has encouraged idea sharing for decades, from the informal morning-tea brainstorming sessions years ago to today's more formal Tech Forums and in-house trade shows.

Develop organisational support

The innovation process is enhanced when the whole organisation supports it. Such support is the job of an organisation's leaders, who must put in place appropriate structures and procedures and emphasise values which make it clear that innovative efforts are a top priority. Three main structures can harness the creativity of employees and help incubate new opportunities: traditional research and development departments, new venture divisions and venture capital funds. Choosing between these structures consists basically of balancing separation and integration of new activities. This section discusses this dilemma, and then focuses on the new venture division and venture capital structures.

Should new activities be separated or integrated?

Separation is the model of choice when the new and the old differ greatly, as in the case of an internet start-up launched by an industrial company. Another reason in favour of separation is that planning and resource allocation processes designed for an established business can stifle the prospects of a new one. Established businesses have customers, organisational structures and prejudices that dispose them to stay with the familiar when deciding where to make their investments. In the fight for corporate capital, talent and commitment, new ideas often fail to attract managerial attention, particularly in their early stages; when compared with an existing business, an idea of unproven worth can seem insubstantial. A separate enterprise can also operate under its own resource allocation criteria, performance measurement systems and reward structures.

Although separation can take a business a long way towards achieving the goals of growth and performance, it has several problems, mainly because it pushes the recognition and selection tasks involved in innovation and business building to the higher levels of management. In strictly partitioned organisations, senior executives are responsible for detecting new possibilities and patterns, and for bringing new ideas into focus. Top managers, already struggling to maintain contact with existing customers, markets and employees, are faced with a growing information overload. In some cases, new ideas are suppressed too quickly; in others, top managers champion projects whose potential has not been assessed accurately. Moreover, since separation creates new organisational boundaries, it also limits the flow of information and ideas, and thereby makes it more likely that they may be lost.[19]

Thus, while ventures do need space to develop, strict separation prevents them from obtaining invaluable resources and robs their parents of the vitality they can generate. A delicate blend of separation and cooperation will help achieve both focused performance and faster growth. In other words, companies have to become 'ambidextrous' in order to develop radical innovations and protect their traditional businesses. Ambidextrous organisations separate their new, exploratory units from their traditional, exploitative ones, allowing for different processes and cultures; at the same time, they maintain tight links across units at the senior executive level. Such companies manage organisational separation through a tightly integrated senior team.[20]

New venture divisions

Many organisations engage in corporate venturing through autonomous new venture divisions (NVDs). NVDs are separate organisational units under the broader corporate umbrella, and they have the task of incubating mainly discontinuous opportunities from concept through to commercialisation and value capture. These in-house venture divisions play the role of corporate incubators, providing emergent businesses with a suite of services in an attempt to leverage the investing corporation's existing assets within the emergent business.

Figure 17.5 shows an NVD model. This NVD model combines traditional corporate business development and venture capital principles. In other words, NVDs provide business ventures with a customised level of corporate sponsorship and support, along with the flexibility and autonomy of an entrepreneurial environment.

NVDs manage corporate venturing differently from the way traditional in-house research and development (R&D) does. Venture investments are typically riskier and less subject to rigid management of internal costs than conventional corporate R&D. Protecting venture investments from such controls is one reason ideas are incubated and start-ups are housed under a separate umbrella. In addition, in NVDs' corporate venturing activities, returns are part financial and part strategic, whereas with pure venture capital, investors' expected financial returns are paramount. Clearly, corporate venturing investments should follow the best practices of venture capital firms, but the twin objectives of financial and strategic returns must be balanced in ways that do not concern venture capitalists. Several organisations have established NVDs to build new businesses, including Xerox, Nokia, Nortel and Amway.

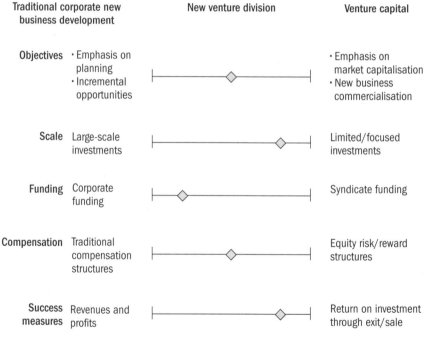

FIGURE 17.5 Characteristics of new venture divisions

Source: Based on the work of R.A. Burgelman & L.R. Sayles, *Inside Corporate Innovation: Strategy, Structure and Managerial Skills*, The Free Press, New York, 1986.

Venture capital funds

In an attempt to recreate the financial incentives that drive the traditional venture capital (VC) model and gain more direct interaction with early-stage companies, many organisations have set up venture capital funds. Fund managers are often given an interest in the fund to motivate them to produce financial returns in the same manner as a traditional venture fund. The corporate venture fund is therefore good at producing financial returns and, through its independence, is able to avoid some of the internal pressures to invest in businesses where the prospects for financial return are somewhat secondary to other corporate interests.

There are essentially two types of venture capital initiative: internal and external. Internal venture programs replicate all the characteristics of the VC model within the company itself. A venture board of managers is set up to act as an internal VC firm, and employees submit business plans to this board for funding. Internal programs are most appropriate for organisations seeking to increase the volume of ideas they generate, to capture greater value from their ideas, or to increase internal entrepreneurship. But internal programs can run into trouble if few of the required capabilities exist in-house.

External venture funds, on the other hand, involve establishing a VC fund for making investments in the wider start-up community, either directly or via established VC firms. Compared with internal programs, external programs can provide access to a wider variety of new products and technologies and generate better opportunities for technology and skill transfer. They represent a safer financial bet, allowing an organisation to both spread its investments across a more diversified portfolio and to leverage more easily the skills of professional VC firms. External programs are thus the better solution for organisations seeking to import good ideas, play catch-up in a rapidly evolving industry and hedge their bets across a broad array of new technologies.[21]

Reward according to results

Traditional reward systems in organisations are designed for people who enjoy power and status. These systems encourage safe, conservative behaviour. Promotion with broadened responsibilities and higher salaries attracts and motivates employees to become managers. These things, however, are rarely strong motivators for corporate entrepreneurs, whose main focus is achievement. This section suggests that organisations need to compensate creatively by using a mix of financial and non-financial rewards.

Creative compensation

Organisations must compensate creatively. For example, innovative organisations consistently reward creativity, but they avoid using money to 'bribe' people who come up with innovative ideas. Because monetary rewards may make people feel they are being controlled, such a tactic may not work. An organisation's leaders can support creativity by requiring information sharing and collaboration and by ensuring that political problems do not fester. Thus, it is just as important to reward the team as it is to reward the individual, depending on the situation.

Once one moves beyond the idea generation and concept development stages, compensation of the managers who run the corporate venturing function is important. Organisations often tend to stick with the 'outsourced model' (such as an external VC program), even when an internally managed fund would probably be more effective. The problem stems from a fundamental conflict. To ensure that corporations have the best people making their investment decisions, they must offer compensation in line with the market for investment managers/ venture capitalists. At the same time, the compensation of their corporate venturing managers should ideally be in line with that of their peers in other parts of the organisation. Consequently, many organisations have implemented schemes they hope will meet the expectations of corporate entrepreneurs, such as bonuses linked to the performance of companies in the investment portfolio, or equity in the start-up businesses (or in a side fund that tracks them).

Different types of reward

In the Asia–Pacific region, cash is often the favoured motivational tool, followed by travel and promotion.[22] There has been a push to introduce new types of reward over the past few years. The concept of travel-based motivation and rewards is still new, but it is beginning to take hold. Several Asian businesses are influenced by the Japanese, who have used travel as a reward for a number of years. Personal recognition is another important type of reward. At 3M the abundance of rewards and recognition — big, little, weekly or annually — such as the 'Circle of Technical Excellence', reinforces the view that people are the company's most important resource for stimulating innovation.

Companies can also adopt broader compensation schemes such as incentive share options. These are rights to purchase company securities, usually ordinary shares, which are issued to company employees and others that the company wants to hire. They are designed to attract new employees and motivate existing employees by giving them the right to purchase company shares in the future at present-day prices. If the company is successful, and its shares increase in value, employees can purchase shares in the future at a price far below the then fair market value of the shares.

Tailor rewards to employees

It is important to tailor compensation to fit the values held by employees, giving each employee the right mix of incentives and rewards (such as monetary bonuses, incentive share options, development opportunities and lifestyle perks). For example, partners and other employees in some corporate VC funds are compensated in much the same way as private VC fund partners are, sharing in the performance gains of the whole portfolio. Employees are enticed to each new individual venture with compensation similar to that of an external start-up company — that is, with equity ownership in the business.

Successful organisations clearly communicate how they will treat people and how they will differentiate individual performance and risk-taking in new ventures. This declaration may be prompted by a visionary leader's initiative, the organisation's core culture (whether performance driven or entrepreneurial) or the need to survive. Whatever the case, the declaration encourages employees to take part in a self-selection process if they are willing to innovate and to bear risks in return for the potential upside of a new venture.

Communication

Communication is essential for sharing the vision of top management, for developing an entrepreneurial culture and for stimulating creativity and innovation throughout the corporate structure. Communication should be about facts and should target frontline supervisors and other key players in the organisation. It is important to promote an open communication to nurture ideas and capabilities.

Communicate facts and target frontline supervisors

Instilling a spirit of entrepreneurship in an organisation entails changing the corporate strategy, culture and administration. The only effective way to communicate a value is to act in accordance with it and give others the incentive to do the same. For example, creating a risk-friendly environment requires demonstrating that stumbles on the innovation path are forgiven.

Members of senior management must state clearly what they plan to do and set those facts down on paper. Communication should first target frontline supervisors because they are the opinion leaders in the organisation. They greatly influence the attitudes and behaviours of others and are critical to the success of any change in corporate culture. Supervisor briefings are an effective way to gain their acceptance. These are face-to-face meetings between a senior manager working on the development of corporate entrepreneurship and a small group of frontline supervisors.[23]

Promote open communication for sharing ideas

Many things that seem to happen naturally in smaller businesses do not happen so easily in larger ones. One of these is communication within the organisation. If communication occurs only through established channels, employees who do not normally interact with one another will never interact. To promote communication, it is essential to provide opportunities (communal areas, informal gatherings) for employees to meet. The advantage lies in ensuring that every employee can understand the organisation's activities well enough to be able to tap into its resources and expertise.

Communication technologies have also made sharing ideas easier. These now extend well beyond basic email into various kinds of real-time and asynchronous electronic connections — chat rooms and news groups; conferencing systems; technologies for surveys, voting, joint document preparation and so on. Electronic communications are ideal for involving creative people who might be shunned or perceived as marginal in organisations that rely too heavily on face-to-face idea exchange.

SUMMARY

Most established organisations find it hard to maintain the initial entrepreneurial spirit that helped them survive the start-up stage. As organisations grow, they usually become more structured and more rigid. Through corporate entrepreneurship, established organisations attempt to exploit their internal resources in order to pursue opportunities that will help the business grow and diversify. Other reasons for developing corporate entrepreneurship include retaining and motivating the brightest staff, exploiting underused resources and getting rid of non-core activities. Corporate entrepreneurship can be defined as the process whereby an individual or a group, in association with an existing organisation, creates a new organisation or initiates renewal or innovation within that organisation.

Successful organisations have developed a disciplined, milestone-focused approach to screening and funding new ventures. Such an approach usually comprises five main stages: idea generation, concept development, business plan development, incubation and commercialisation, and value capture. This development process evaluates each new venture at predetermined milestones to decide whether to proceed, refine, accelerate or discontinue the venture. Using such a time-phased approach, organisations gradually increase their commitment in line with the availability of more information. As the venture moves through critical 'decision gates', its performance is measured against established targets and expectations, and resource decisions are made. To deal effectively with the implementation issues, corporate management must recognise and empower internal entrepreneurs and product champions.

Developing an entrepreneurial spirit inside an existing organisation requires four steps: (1) develop a vision and a strategy, (2) create a culture of innovation, (3) develop organisational support and (4) reward results accordingly. This process requires time and relentless effort. Evidence suggests that most firms build up the attributes of corporate entrepreneurship in long-drawn-out processes over many years, not in a one-shot, single event. This change process must be sustained by appropriate communication. In the initial phase of sharing the vision and initiating the change, communication should focus on facts and target frontline supervisors because they are the opinion leaders in the organisation. It is important to promote open communication in order to nurture ideas and capabilities.

REVIEW QUESTIONS

1. What is the rationale for developing corporate entrepreneurship in an organisation?
2. What are the dimensions of corporate entrepreneurship?
3. What is corporate venturing?
4. What are the stages of the new venture development process inside an organisation?
5. What are the key steps an organisation could follow to develop an entrepreneurial spirit?

DISCUSSION QUESTIONS

1. Why does corporate venturing usually go beyond the new product development often discussed in marketing courses?
2. How is corporate venturing different from traditional business development practices, such as takeovers, corporate R&D and venture capital financing?
3. To what extent do an organisation's social networks play a role in the discovery and pursuit of new business opportunities?
4. What are the arguments in favour of separating new venture development activities from existing operations in the organisation?
5. What is the role of the organisation's executives in developing and sustaining corporate entrepreneurship?

SUGGESTED READING

Burns, P., *Corporate Entrepreneurship: Building an Entrepreneurial Organisation*, 2nd edition, Palgrave MacMillan, Houndmills, 2008.
Jouret, G. 'Inside Cisco's search for the next big idea', *Harvard Business Review*, September 2009, pp. 43–5.
Wolcott, R.C. & Lippitz, M.J., 'The four models of corporate entrepreneurship', *MIT Sloan Management Review*, Fall 2007, vol. 49, no. 1, pp. 75–82.

Sino Automation

In August 2010, Wong Peng (Ken), Business Development Manager in the business unit 'Product' at Sino Automation was reflecting on the progress made by his team for the development of the new Spectra Flow technology. The technology was a bulk analyser that provided a reliable elemental analysis for consistent stockpile and raw mix composition. The technology could enable both the minerals industry and the building materials industry to improve profitability by gaining higher output, based on maintaining consistent quality in production processes. While Ken was happy with the technological development to date, he was unsure if the technology would be deployed. He had to submit a business plan to the head of his business unit by the end of September, and a decision would be made at the divisional level by the end of November.

The Spectra Flow technology

Sino Automation is a leading automation technology company with headquarters in Shanghai. Its core business comprises of three divisions: automation products, process automation and robotics. In 2010, the company had 53 000 employees on its payroll, and it generated US$15 billion of revenues. The process automation division where Ken was working focused on the development, manufacturing and sale of control systems and application-specific automation solutions for process industries. Such industries included chemicals and pharmaceutical, oil and gas, and minerals.

The Spectra Flow technology was developed to offer a better service to minerals industries, including open pit and underground mining, cement, and primary aluminium production. The technology was the brainchild of Dr. Mike Ormond, an American-born physicist who had been working internationally for more than 15 years for Sino Automation. Mike, who had recently turned 67, officially retired in 2008. However, he was still working on a couple of projects for Sino Automation as a freelance consultant.

Over the past decade, Mike recognised that there was a need in the minerals market for a better system of real-time analysis of the composition of raw materials being transported on a conveyor belt. The current systems were usually relying on radioactives, which are both expensive and difficult to transport because of the numerous security clearance needed.

The Spectra Flow technology utilises the full infrared spectra provided by a special lamp to analyse the target bulk material as it passes on an existing conveyor belt. It is a unique system in that it allows real-time analysis throughout the mineral manufacturing process without requiring hazardous materials like radioactive sources or X-rays. Spectra Flow technology could be safely deployed for the work environment and require no special permits for its use, and no specially certified or skilled personnel.

Corporate entrepreneurhip at Sino Automation

Sino Automation's move into corporate entrepreneurship is relatively new. In 2008, the CEO Li Kequiang realised that a major company rethink was in order to correct its growth decline, which was at odds with its improvement in returns and margins over the last five years. So, Li asked a Sino Automation senior manager to lead a small internal group to remedy this problem, and they eventually came up with the program 'Growth Initiative 2020'. This initiative's aims were to assist employees with the conceptualisation and commercialisation of new products. This was typically achieved by enrolling them in two-day 'business accelerator courses' so concepts would be generated and prioritised, followed by a four to eight week business plan development period. During this time, the employee team would consult with senior management to iron out any conceptual problems. With the aid of a facilitator, they would then present their plan to the business division for approval.

Once one business unit succeeded under this scheme, others quickly developed an interest in it. Over time, the venture teams became critical change agents.[24] Although consultants would sometimes help the process, ultimately the best advocates came from the company's veteran ranks — those who are well-known, respected and experienced in making change happen within the organisation.

The core of the Growth Initiative 2020 was staffed with ten full-time employees. Becoming part of this group became a sought-after opportunity for up-and-coming managers wanting to gain senior-level exposure and have a direct impact on the company's growth. Sino Automation's senior executives actively and openly supported the program, and they mandated its adoption by the company's different business units. To motivate employees to participate in the program, the CEO allocated US$ 100 000 of 'prize money' per year to reward the ten best projects.

The next steps

Ken, however, has been wary about the chances of Spectra Flow because the project was developed outside the Growth Initiative 2020. Mike Ormond had developed the technology on a shoe-string budget with the help a couple new, bright recruits in the business unit. The development cost amounted to a mere US$20 000, and it had taken less than six months to build a working prototype. Although Mike was a respected researcher, he lacked social competences, and the draft business plan he submitted to Ken was patchy. Also, Ken didn't want to compromise his promotion as business unit head. The promotion committee meets regularly in November each year and, to date, Ken has received positive feedback from his supervisor in the various assessments. He has consistently reached his targets over the past years and his peers describe him as a 'competent and loyal manager'.

Spectra Flow, however, presents a number of risks. Mike has just asked a handful of customers if they would be interested in the technology, but no comprehensive market research has been conducted. Although Mike and his team built a prototype, the project would have to move to the industrialisation stage, where the machine would be built in large series. Ken knows that such innovations often present teething troubles that spoil the clients' bottom line. Another Sino Automation business development manager was recently denied a promotion because the innovation he championed turned out to be a failure.

This is a fictional case.

Questions

1. What is your assessment of the Spectra Flow project development to date?
2. What course of action would you recommend to Ken?
3. Is the Market Driven Growth Initiative an adequate tool to develop corporate entrepreneurship at Sino Automation? What improvements would you recommend?

ENDNOTES

1. P. Sharma & J.J. Chrisman, 'Toward a reconciliation of the definitional issues in the field of corporate entrepreneurship', *Entrepreneurship Theory and Practice*, vol. 23, no. 3, 1999, p. 18.
2. ibid.
3. W. Guth & A. Ginsberg, 'Guest editors' introduction: Corporate entrepreneurship', *Strategic Management Journal*, no. 11, 1990, pp. 297–308.

4. S.A. Zahra, 'A conceptual model of entrepreneurship as firm behaviour: A critique and extension', *Entrepreneurship Theory and Practice*, vol. 17, no. 4, 1993, pp. 5–21.

5. J. Albrinck et al., 'Adventures in corporate venturing', *Strateg & Business*, no. 22, 2000, pp. 119–29.

6. 'Adopting orphans', *Economist*, 20 February 1999, pp. 17–18.

7. *The Economist*, 'Cheap, but not nasty', 21 March, 2009, p. 72

8. K.W. Chan & R. Mauborgne, 'Value innovation: The strategic logic of high growth', *Harvard Business Review*, January–February 1997, p. 104.

9. S.N. Joni et al., 'Innovations from the inside', *Management Review*, September 1997, p. 50.

10. J. Tidd, J. Bessant & K. Pavitt, *Managing Innovation*, John Wiley & Sons, Chichester, 1999, pp. 277–80.

11. G. Neilson, J. Albrinck, J. Hornery et al., *E-Business and Beyond: Organizing for Success in New Ventures*, Booz Allen & Hamilton, New York, 2001.

12. Cisco press release, Cisco Selects Winner of Global I-Prize Innovation Contest, 14 October, 2008.

13. S.W. Floyd & B. Wooldridge, 'Knowledge creation and social networks in corporate entrepreneurship: The renewal of organizational capability', *Entrepreneurship Theory and Practice*, vol. 23, no. 3, 1999, pp. 123–43.

14. R. Cross & L. Prusak, 'The people who make organisations go — or stop', *Harvard Business Review*, June 2002, pp. 105–12.

15. S. Wetlaufer, 'What's stifling the creativity at Coolburst?', *Harvard Business Review on Breakthrough Thinking*, Harvard Business School Press, 1999, pp.122–42.

16. R. Farson & R. Keyes, 'The failure-tolerant leader', *Harvard Business Review*, Special issue 'The innovation enterprise', August 2002, pp. 64–71.

17. R.N. Foster & S. Kaplan, *Creative Destruction*, Currency, New York, 2001.

18. J. Kao, *Entrepreneurship, Creativity and Innovation*, Prentice Hall, Englewood Cliffs, NJ, 1989, p. 397.

19. J.D. Day, P.Y. Mang, A. Richter & J. Roberts, 'The innovation organisation — why new ventures need more than a room of their own', *The McKinsey Quarterly*, no. 2, 2001, pp. 14–19.

20. C.A. O'Reilly & M.L. Tushman, 'The ambidextrous organization', *Harvard Business Review*, April 2004, pp. 74–81.

21. P. Brody & D. Ehrlich, 'Can big companies become successful venture capitalists?' *The McKinsey Quarterly*, no. 2, 1998, pp. 50–63.

22. 'Revving up Asia's workers', *Asian Business*, February 1996, pp. 41–4.

23. T.J. Larkin & S. Larkin, 'Reaching and changing frontline employees', *Harvard Business Review*, May–June 1996, pp. 95–104.

24. R.C. Wolcott and M.J. Lippitz, 'The Four Models of Corporate Entrepreneurship', *MIT Sloane Management Review*, 1 October, 2007.

CHAPTER **18**

Contemporary issues in small business and entrepreneurship

Learning objectives

After reading this chapter, you should be able to:

- define the concept of social entrepreneurship

- identify ways in which eco-efficient small firms can reduce or eliminate harmful environmental impacts

- explain the differences between male-owned and female-owned small businesses

- explain how home-based businesses differ from other small firms.

Businesses do not operate in a vacuum. Small firms are part of the broader community, and to be successful they need to have an understanding of social issues in the societies in which they operate. The hallmark of successful entrepreneurs and small business owners is their ability to identify and respond to new issues long before the impact is understood by competitors. These business owners make a conscious effort to stay ahead of new trends, and take the initiative in dealing with them by keeping in mind the likely impact of such changes when developing their own business strategies. In this chapter, we discuss and analyse some of the contemporary trends in the Asia–Pacific region that are affecting entrepreneurs and small firms, or which are likely to affect them in the near future.

Social entrepreneurship

Traditionally, entrepreneurship has been seen as occurring exclusively in the for-profit (private) sector of an economy. Most textbooks focus either on individual entrepreneurs seeking to start or grow their own businesses or on 'intrapreneurs' working within an existing large firm. However, in recent years there has been a growing awareness of the contribution of entrepreneurial behaviour within the not-for-profit sector, and as a tool of community development.

Social entrepreneur

An enterprising person who applies entrepreneurial principles and skills to the resolution of social or community problems.

Social entrepreneurs are agents of social change who apply entrepreneurial principles and skills to the resolution of community problems and for the improvement of society in general. They apply the traditional tools of an entrepreneur to produce more effective solutions to social problems, and display many of the personal attributes found among private-sector entrepreneurs. They take risks and seek innovative approaches in order to help improve the lives of individual people, groups and society, not just for personal gain.[1]

Such entrepreneurs can be found in a variety of settings. Some social entrepreneurs have been advocates of widespread change in society. These are people who have recognised that there are problems or needs that are not being met, and who have attempted to remedy this deficiency. Such social entrepreneurs typically respond by organising resources such as money and equipment, building and motivating a team of committed people to work with the entrepreneur, developing a customer base and building an awareness of the unmet need among government authorities and the broader community. In this respect, they are not dissimilar to entrepreneurs who launch new business ventures in new or emergent industries.

The other main form of social entrepreneurship is the successful application of sound business principles to not-for-profit and non-government organisations (NGOs) to produce better-managed charities, healthcare organisations, educational institutions and environmental groups. These entrepreneurial managers are people who apply existing management concepts such as business planning, financial accountability, human resource management and marketing to an organisation that traditionally has not operated on such principles. The intention of such work is to produce an NGO that is better able to meet the needs of its clients.

The rise of social entrepreneurship is due to a number of factors. The first form of social entrepreneur, the *social change entrepreneur*, has always existed; however, more researchers have become aware of such enterprising behaviour and its similarity to the conventional notion of entrepreneurship. The second type of social entrepreneur, the *entrepreneurial manager*, has been driven by an increasing emphasis in many societies on more cost-effective use of welfare and charitable funds, by increasing levels of business education among managers and by the realisation that business skills can often help produce better outcomes for a community.

Some examples of social entrepreneurs include Maria Montessori (creator of the Montessori educational teaching system in Italy), Florence Nightingale (instigator of many modern nursing techniques) and Muhammed Yunus (originator of the microfinance organisation the Grameen Bank).[2] Although social entrepreneurs share many attributes with other businesspeople, there are still some significant differences. Many social entrepreneurs lack conventional business skills or have even greater difficulty in accessing venture capital than entrepreneurs. Also, they often have to work within the different constraints imposed by not-for-profit organisations. Such entities are usually overseen by management committees. This is something the self-employed entrepreneur does not have to deal with. These committees place a strong focus on measuring performance against a 'triple bottom line' of environmental, social and financial outcomes. In contrast, private sector, conventional entrepreneurs may focus only on monetary returns. Finally, whereas private entrepreneurs usually seek to retain ownership of their intellectual property and ideas, many social entrepreneurs actively seek to share their innovations and to disseminate information to as many interested parties as possible, so as to extend community benefits (see table 18.1).

TABLE 18.1 Social entrepreneurship organisations

Organisation	Website
Ashoka Foundation	www.ashoka.org
Schwab Foundation for Social Entrepreneurship	www.schwabfound.org
Social Enterprise Australasia	www.social-e.org.au
Social Traders	www.socialtraders.com.au

Entrepreneur profile

Tim Bauer, Envirofit

American mechanical engineer, Tim Bauer, is a social entrepreneur. He is one of a new breed, sometimes called 'BOPreneurs' ('base of pyramid' entrepreneurs) committed to improving the lives of the 3 billion people globally, who earn less than US$3 a day. He is a co-founder of the not-for-profit organisation Envirofit. Its goal is to use innovative technological solutions to help address indoor and outdoor air pollution in developing countries.

In South-East Asia, Envirofit are involved in retrofitting dirty two-stroke engines with clean fuel efficient direct injection technology. The two-stroke engine is commonplace in South-East Asia, for example, in the Philippines 94 per cent of motorcycles use them; and in India,

Pakistan and Thailand usage is between 50 and 90 per cent for vehicles, such as motorcycles, motorised tricycles, tuk-tuks and auto-rickshaws. Collectively, the 100 million dirty two-stroke engines in South-East Asia contribute the equivalent of five billion cars' worth of air pollution. Tim's solution to this environmental challenge was to design, build and distribute a kit that transforms dirty two-stroke engines into direct fuel-injection mechanisms and so reduces their polluting effects.

The kit can be installed in two to four hours and has an immediate impact, in that, it both reduces pollution (i.e. cuts emissions of carbon dioxide by 76 per cent) and fuel costs for the driver. This reduction in costs is critical for many of the drivers who earn as little as a few dollars a day. To assist drivers with the initial outlay for the kit (approximately US$350), Tim has created partnerships that facilitate access to microcredit programmes for the drivers.

The organisation Envirofit was created in 2003 as a means of developing, commercialising and distributing the retrofit kit. It is based in Fort Collins, Colorado, USA. It also has ties to Colorado State University, and now has over 60 employees worldwide. As well as the retrofit kits, Envirofit also produces and distributes Clean Cookstoves that emit less toxic emissions and are more fuel efficient. In 2008, Tim was one of ten Rolex Enterprise Award winners, and Envirofit was the 2008 winner of the Green Tech category of the Popular Science 'Best of what's new' awards.

Visit the Envirofit website for more information, www.envirofit.org.

Sources: Envirofit, www.envirofit.org; Rolex Awards, 'Retrofitting for the environment', www.rolexawards.com, 2008.

Environmental issues

Environmental responsibility *The need to protect and enhance the natural environment.*

Closely related to the concept of social responsibility is that of **environmental responsibility**, which refers to the need of firms to protect and enhance the natural environment. Environmental issues are becoming increasingly important to all businesses in the twenty-first century; on the one hand, they pose risks, such as the threat of legal action and public disapproval for poor environmental performance; while on the other hand, they provide opportunities, such as a source of niche marketing, reduced waste and costs, and innovation.[3] In addition, increasing population, a declining quality of air and water, biodiversity loss and the need to minimise the use of raw materials are beginning to affect many more communities and the businesses that operate within them.

Small and medium-sized enterprises are often overlooked when the causes of and solutions to environmental problems are examined. This is despite the fact that they account for the majority of the world's business enterprises, about half of all employment and much of the total level of economic output in each country. Although no definite figures exist, it is also commonly claimed that they are responsible for about 70 per cent of global pollution.[4]

Small firms have only a minor individual impact on the environment, but when taken together they have a substantial collective influence. Moreover, it is often easier to reach key decision makers in such enterprises. This is because management and ownership of the firm are frequently synonymous; indeed, one of the defining features of a small business is that ownership is usually restricted to one or two people who are also the key decision makers in the enterprise.[5] As a result, this provides a unique opportunity for individual owner–managers to put their values into practice in the workplace, and to influence the behaviour of employees, consumers and other stakeholders.[6]

However, the involvement of small firms in measures to protect the natural environment has been one of mixed results so far. Most research in this area has indicated that there is a substantial gap between the environmental views and attitudes of small business owner–managers (which are generally positive and supportive) and the actual practices of their firms (which generally tend to lag behind). Several researchers have shown that although many small business owner–managers have a high awareness of their role in environmental remediation, and have a strong desire to actively do something, their actual performance often falls far short of what is desired.[7] Most owners do not have enough free time or access to the necessary information needed to make their firms greener.[8] This is the so-called SME problem in environmental management.[9] To date, most small-firm responses to environmental issues have focused on 'end-of-pipe' solutions: cleaning up and remedying only the most obvious environmental damage, such as pollution or waste that they directly create. Although this is useful, there is a lot more that can be done.

At a basic level, there is a series of simple and practical steps that can be taken to improve the day-to-day environmental impact of every small business; these are listed in the box that follows.

IMPROVING ENVIRONMENTAL OUTCOMES

Here are ten simple ways in which small firms can contribute to a better environment for the future and potentially reduce costs:

- re-use and recycle when possible
- only print and photocopy when necessary, and use recycled paper
- don't light empty rooms
- turn off equipment at night (e.g. photocopiers, monitors, printers)
- return used print cartridges and buy recycled ones
- return old mobile phones and batteries for recycling
- select suppliers who use less packaging
- watch out for unnecessary water and power usage
- service vehicles regularly, as this helps with fuel efficiency and lower emissions
- encourage staff to carpool and use public transport.

Source: Adapted from the Energy and environment SME toolkit, published by the Federation of Small Businesses in Scotland and the Scottish Energy Office of the Scottish Executive. www.fsb.org.uk.

Eco-efficiency

In the medium to long term, firms and entrepreneurs also need to focus on management systems that are environmentally sustainable and promote innovation

Eco-efficiency
A management strategy that focuses on the delivery of competitively priced goods and services which satisfy consumer needs while progressively reducing ecological impacts throughout the product life cycle.

and enhanced competitiveness.[10] **Eco-efficiency** is a management strategy that jointly promotes both environmental and economic performance. The World Business Council for Sustainable Development (WBCSD), which first coined the concept, has defined it as:

...the delivery of competitively priced goods and services that satisfy human needs and bring quality of life, while progressively reducing ecological impacts and resource intensity throughout the product life-cycle, to a level at least in line with the earth's estimated carrying capacity.[11]

The WBCSD identified seven components of eco-efficiency that, if acted upon properly, can contribute to business growth:

- reduce the material intensity of goods and services
- reduce the energy intensity of goods and services
- reduce toxic dispersion
- enhance material recyclability
- maximise sustainable use of renewable resources
- extend product durability
- increase the service intensity of goods and services.

'Ecopreneurship'

In recent years a growing number of business operators have realised that eco-efficiency can also provide a strong long-term competitive advantage for them. Thus, some 'ecopreneurs' have recognised that they can harness consumer concerns about the state of the environment to develop new market niches, and others have identified long-term market changes that they should adapt to.[12] Ecopreneurs display many of the characteristics of conventional entrepreneurs, including a willingness to take calculated risks, an ability to identify new and emergent business opportunities and the capacity to 'think outside the box' and use new and innovative business practices (in this case, environmentally friendly ones) to increase profitability and performance. Table 18.2 lists some sources of environmental information for entrepreneurs and small business operators.

TABLE 18.2 Sources of environmental information

Organisation	Website
APEC Sustainable Development Forum	www.apecsec.org.sg
EnviroLink Network	www.envirolink.org
Greening of Industry Network	www.greeningofindustry.org
World Business Council for Sustainable Development	www.wbcsd.org
Business Council for Sustainable Development in Malaysia	www.bcsdm.com.my
NZ Business Council for Sustainable Development	www.nzbcsd.org.nz
CSRchina.net	www.csrchina.net
TERI-BCSB India	http://bcsd.teri.res.in

Wee Sang Kiang, Eveready Manufacturing

Wee Sang Kiang is the Managing Director of Eveready Manufacturing, a firm in Singapore at the cutting edge of technology for plastic recycling. He started the business in 1978, and it is one of Singapore's largest plastic processing companies. It has two factories in Singapore, as well as an industrial and agricultural film manufacturing plant in Malaysia. The firm can process all forms, sizes and shapes of plastic waste, and recycles them into resins. The recycled resins are then either returned to the customer or sold to plastic manufacturers as raw materials. Eveready focuses on treating the plastic waste in an environmentally friendly fashion.

With a diverse range of technology and recycling equipment, the firm can process both post-industrial and post-consumer plastic waste. With advanced knowledge of plastic compounding, the firm can also modify the recycled plastic resins with additives, to enhance their physical or mechanical properties (e.g. make them flame retardant or glass fibre reinforced). Eveready commits to engaging in the R&D process with clients to help reach the desired product specifications.

Eveready's factories process up to 1000 tonnes of resin per month. In 2008, the firm developed an automated sorting system. The system uses infra-red technology to scan large amounts of plastic material from a single waste stream and sort them into three different outputs. Two tonnes of waste can be sorted in one hour with about 99 per cent accuracy. This is a huge advancement, as typically this process is labour intensive and therefore very costly. It took two years to design, develop and build the system. Wee Sang Kiang obtained support to develop the innovative system from SPRING, the Singaporean government agency responsible for promoting economic growth and productivity.

Eveready is the first firm in Singapore to develop an automated waste sorting system. The innovation has the potential to transform the process of plastic recycling in South-East Asia, and to increase the recycling rate in Singapore, in particular. There is also the potential for the technology itself to be exported to other countries to improve their plastic recycling processes.

For more information, visit the Eveready Manufacturing website, www.eveready-mfg.com.

Source: Eveready Manufacturing, www.eveready-mfg.com

Profit or principle?

Dave runs his own business selling original image-based products (e.g. calendars, posters, framed images, apparel). He has been operating successfully for the past five years, and he divides his time between New Zealand and Hong Kong. His business premises are in New Zealand and he employs ten staff. The turnover for the business has been increasing annually, and he is looking to grow the business further. His goal is to spend time in India taking photographs to start a new product range and exploring new market opportunities.

Dave has established relationships with a number of reputable retail chains in New Zealand and Hong Kong who stock his products. His preference is to pursue outlets that sell other lines produced by designers, but he established these retail chain relationships early on in the life of the business and they have helped sustain cash flow (especially during the recent economic downturn). Recently, the large retail stores Dave has relationships with have started to 'green' their supply chains. They have begun to pressure him to switch to more sustainable options with regard to product packaging, and to reduce how much packaging he uses.

Dave himself is a keen environmentalist and is very aware of his carbon footprint, both personally and in terms of his business. He has investigated environmentally-friendly packaging for his products before but rejected them because they were too costly and were not strong enough to protect his products during transport. This is important to Dave since 50 per cent of his business comes from offshore clients who purchase products through his website. As he seeks to expand the business with image ranges from other countries, this proportion of his sales is likely to increase, so packaging options are a critical choice.

Dave has explained the rationale behind his decision making to the companies concerned, and described how he engages in other socially and environmentally responsible behaviours (e.g. carbon offsetting for travel, sponsorship of a local design competition for young people and taking back packaging from his products). He feels the companies involved are more interested in making environmental claims for marketing purposes than listening to his overall environmental strategy.

Questions

1. Do you think Dave should do what the large retail stores want or should he sever those relationships? Give reasons to justify your answer.
2. How could Dave communicate to his customers the socially and environmentally responsible practices his firm engages in? Give some examples.

Gender differences

In recent years, more and more women have become involved in small businesses, mainly as the owners of their own firms. While most businesses are still run by men, almost one-fifth of all small businesses in Australia are now owned and operated by women, while another fifth are jointly run by men and women.[13] Across the Pacific region, the number of women running their own businesses has grown substantially in recent years. In New Zealand, 14% of males and 8% of females are self-employed.[14] The proportion of the self-employed population who are women has been consistently increasing — in 1991, 29% of those self-employed were women and by 2006 the percentage had increased to 36%.[15] A similar trend is evident in Singapore, where the number of women entering self-employment has exceeded that of men since the early 1980s.[16] A recent global analysis by the Organisation for Economic Cooperation and Development has indicated that the number of firms created and managed by women is expanding, and usually outstrips the creation rate among men.[17]

There are several reasons for this increase. Many women in large firms find that they are victims of the 'glass ceiling' — the invisible and informal barriers to promotion that often mean women have difficulty in career advancement within established corporations. In addition, the growth of the services economy has meant that there is a greater demand for knowledge-based and personal service industries, sectors in which women have traditionally been employed in large numbers. A further impetus is rising levels of post-secondary education, creating a growth in the number of women with the skills and qualifications needed to operate a business. The rise of the internet and the increasing acceptance of home-based and part-time business operations have also made it easier for women to start their own business at home, operate it with minimal costs and yet still focus on family and social needs.

However, the role and number of women entrepreneurs is significant in more than just a purely numerical sense. Growing numbers of female owner–managers also provide a different perspective on how to create, manage and grow new business ventures. It has often been argued that women begin new businesses with a different set of experiences, opportunities and goals than do men. For example, women and men tend to predominate in different industry sectors, and may therefore have different notions about what makes a successful enterprise, what customers' needs are, and how the firm should be managed. (This difference can also make it harder for females to successfully launch a new venture in a field dominated by men, and vice versa.) There are often greater social expectations placed on women to balance their business activities with household and family needs. This pressure is especially strong in many ethnic Chinese communities across the Asia–Pacific region.[18] Sometimes the motivation for starting a business is also different. Women, for example, often state that a prime motivation is to meet personal as well as business goals and to reject stereotypes imposed on them by others.[19] There is also evidence that the leadership and managerial styles of women are different from those of men. It has been suggested that women tend to provide a more participative, democratic and consultative style of business management, whereas men tend to be more directive and autocratic in their approach.[20]

Historically, female entrepreneurs have faced different barriers to starting a new firm. A significant barrier is that they have greater difficulty than men do in raising finance for new business ventures. This is often cited in research on women in small business, and appears to arise from a combination of factors. Although gender-based discrimination may be one cause, another possible reason is the fact that women tend to accumulate less capital than men. This condition arises because women are often paid less than men, or suffer career interruptions when they leave the workforce to start and raise a family. Other barriers include a lack of personal business networks and connections, a shortage of mentors and role models, and social typecasting, which assumes that women give a higher priority to their family responsibilities than their business activities.[21]

These perceived differences in entrepreneurial intention, opportunities and managerial approach appear to be reflected, at least to some extent, in empirical findings. Men are still more likely to own a business (or work for themselves) than women are, as can be seen in the analysis of working life in New Zealand in table 18.3.

Likewise, studies of Australian small businesses have found that female-managed firms tend to have lower sales revenue and profits than male-run businesses, suggesting that they may be more risk-averse and more focused on lifestyle considerations.[22] The great majority of businesses run by women tend to be concentrated in the services sector and at the smaller end of the size scale.

TABLE 18.3 Gender differences in work in New Zealand: Distribution of men and women by self-employment category, 2006 Census

	Men		Women		Total	
Employer	98 208	37%	44 673	30%	142 881	34%
Self-employed without employees	152 238	57%	82 713	55%	234 951	56%
Unpaid family worker	16 473	6%	23 094	15%	39 567	9%
Total self-employed	266 919	100%	150 480	100%	417 399	100%

Source: Statistics New Zealand and data from Ministry of Women's Affairs, New Zealand, *Women in enterprise: A report on women in small and medium enterprises in New Zealand*, Ministry of Women's Affairs and Ministry of Economic Development, New Zealand, Wellington, 2008, p.12.

Despite this, small businesses owned by women usually have a higher survival rate than those run by men.[23] This finding is not as surprising as it might at first seem. Firms that are small in scale, such as home-based micro-enterprises, which have low or neglible debt levels (perhaps due to an inability to borrow funds) and which are based on personal skills and services appear to have a greater ability to ride out the inevitable threats and challenges that all business must face from time to time. Table 18.4 lists some regional business organisations for women in the Asia–Pacific region.

TABLE 18.4 Some regional business organisations for women and information links

Country	Organisation and website
Australia	Business and Professional Women Australia, www.bpw.com.au
New Zealand	Her Business, www.herbusinessmagazine.com
Hong Kong	HK Association of Business and Professional Women, www.hkabpw.org
Malaysia	National Association of Women Entrepreneurs of Malaysia, www.nawem.org.my
Singapore	Business and Professional Women's Association, www.sbpwa.org.sg
China	All-China Women's Federation, womenofchina.cn
Regional	Asian Women in Business, www.awib.org

Home-based businesses

Home-based businesses (HBB) *An enterprise in which all or most of the work is performed at or from the owner–operator's private residence; also known as 'small office, home office' (SOHO).*

Home-based businesses (HBBs) represent the majority of small businesses operating in Australia, New Zealand and many other countries today, yet their role and impact are often overlooked or poorly understood. Many businesspeople and researchers are often surprised by the size and significance of this sector, which is sometimes also referred to as 'small office, home office' (SOHO).

HBBs consist of two main types of businesses. The first are businesses operated *at home*, where most of the firm's work is carried out at the operator's residence. Typical enterprises in this category include home-based accounting and professional practices. The second (and most numerous) type of home-based enterprise consists of businesses operated *from home*, where owner–operators perform most of their work out in the field or at clients' premises. In this operating model, operators simply use their residence as a base where administration, recordkeeping, raw materials and other resources are maintained. Carpenters, plumbers, bricklayers and other tradespeople typically fall into this category.

Traditionally, HBBs have been regarded as a small-scale phenomenon with limited relevance to the wider economy. In reality, however, HBBs are a major structural force in almost all economies. For example, in Australia HBBs make up more than two-thirds of all small businesses, which makes them the largest cohort of businesses in the economy. They are also the fastest growing group, increasing from 58 per cent of all small firms in 1997 to 68 per cent in 2004.[24] HBBs are equally important to the economy of New Zealand, where it is estimated that there are now over 200 000 such firms, making them the largest single group of businesses in that country.[25] Home-based businesses have been less well known in Singapore, and formal registration of a home office within government-owned residential apartments has been permitted only in recent years. By the end of 2003, there were about 7400 registered home offices in the republic. Most of these, like their Australian and New Zealand counterparts, were concentrated in the services sector, and most operated as either a sole proprietorship or partnership, and with only limited capital (typically under S$10 000).[26] Unfortunately, data about HBBs in other parts of the Asia–Pacific region are much harder to come by.

HBBs were once perceived to be highly risky enterprises with low financial returns and only marginal prospects for long-term survival, but many researchers today suggest that the opposite is often true: most HBBs endure for a relatively long period of time (typically more than five years), and are capable of generating significant economic returns for their owner–operators.[27]

A more detailed picture of the characteristics of HBBs is provided by Australian research. The typical HBB in Australia tends to display characteristics that set it apart from other small-, medium- and large-sized enterprises. There is a higher proportion of women who own such businesses, and a higher proportion holding degrees or post-secondary education qualifications. The archetypal HBB operator is usually between 30 and 50 years old, and working only part-time in the enterprise. Most operators have had no formal management training, and fund their venture entirely from their own personal finances. Almost 70 per cent have no staff, and their use of technology is much lower than in larger firms.[28]

The emergence of HBBs as a key part of the small business sector has been driven by a number of factors, all of which have served to encourage high levels of growth in this category. At the macroeconomic level, the rapid expansion in the services sector of the Australian economy has opened up numerous opportunities for businesses that can be operated from the owner's home. Unlike manufacturing, wholesaling or retailing, service-based firms rely largely on individual skills, and do not need large storage areas or a location in a retail shopping complex. Not surprisingly, therefore, most HBBs are in the services sector. At the micro-economic level, the expansion of the HBB sector has been encouraged by increasing flexibility in local government zoning and regulations, which permit the use of homes as business premises, and an increased willingness by small-scale entrepreneurs to set up enterprises that are low in capital outlay, allow more time with the family and can be operated part-time if desired.

There are several advantages in working from home. They include the ability to exercise independence and total control over the working environment, thus providing maximum flexibility and versatility in the entrepreneur's worklife. There is usually more free time available to spend with friends and family. Home-based entrepreneurs are also able to save time and money through reduced travelling costs, no rental fees for premises, and use of personal household facilities to double as work tools (such as personal computers).

Working from home, however, is not for everyone. Many small business owners do not have the requisite discipline needed to succeed under the unique conditions that a residential business imposes. These include isolation and loneliness, as the operator does not have ready access to colleagues; a weakened professional image, which can arise when customers do not believe that an HBB is a bona fide enterprise; the inability to properly manage one's time so as to prevent personal activities intruding on the working day, and vice versa; and the difficulty of increasing the size of the business. Self-motivation, the ability to effectively manage one's time, and the discipline to ignore non-work distractions are all important ingredients of the successful HBB operator.

There are also some practical administrative and legal decisions that small business owners should bear in mind before opting to work from home (see the inset 'HBBs — some questions'). They need to ensure that their financial recordkeeping is in order, so that work and personal expenses can be accurately separated and accounted for when preparing financial returns. They also have to bear in mind that local government laws may limit the size and type of firm that can be based at home, the operating hours of the business, customer parking and the extent to which signage and other advertising can be displayed outside the home. There are also personal security and insurance issues to consider. It may be risky to invite strangers into the home, and a domestic insurance policy usually does not cover losses suffered as a result of operating a business within the house.

It is important to remember the limitations imposed by a home-based business. Although a residential location may be a cost-effective place in which to start an enterprise, in the medium- to long-term it is usually suitable only for business owners who have limited growth goals, or who wish to remain self-employed. Entrepreneurs who seek to expand in the marketplace, increase their range of product and service offerings or employ staff to work with them will inevitably find that they need to either outsource such activities or move into commercial premises where greater economies of scale can be instituted.

TABLE 18.5 Home-based business organisations

Organisation	Website
Micro and Home Business Network, Australia	www.mbn.com.au
Home Business New Zealand	www.homebizbuzz.co.nz
Home based business network	www.homebasedbusiness.sbdc.com.au
Mompreneurs Asia	www.mompreneurasia.com

HBBs — SOME QUESTIONS

Premises
- Is the office secure?
- Is the office large enough?
- Is the office separate from the rest of the house, with separate entry for customers?
- If the business grows, how will expansion be accommodated within the house?
- Will there be any outside signage to help clients find their way?

Image
- Do the business stationery and website look professional?
- Is there a separate phone line to deal exclusively with work-related calls?
- Does the office within the house look suitable for entertaining clients?
- Does the outside of the house look suitably well kept?

Management
- Is there someone who can act as a back-up if the owner–operator is incapacitated?
- Does the owner have suitable time-management skills to keep work and play times separate?
- Do other members of the household know that they should not interrupt during working hours?

Finance
- How does the home office affect loan costs (mortgage repayments)?
- How will personal and work-related costs be apportioned for household expenses such as electricity, water and gas?

Legal
- Does the existing insurance policy cover HBB activities?
- Is third-party liability required for visitors to the house?
- Does the local authority allow an HBB to operate here?
- If the house is rented, will the landlord allow an HBB to be based here?

SUMMARY

There are currently a number of trends emerging in society, which entrepreneurs and small business owners need to be aware of. The concept of what constitutes 'entrepreneurship' has been expanded to embrace people working outside the private sector of the economy. It is important to understand that entrepreneurship can be successfully applied to the not-for-profit sector as a tool for community improvement, through the activities of social entrepreneurs. Emphasis is also growing on ensuring that the environmental impact of small firms (waste, pollution and so on) is reduced wherever possible. This may be difficult, since research shows that owner–managers and entrepreneurs may have good intentions but fail to produce positive outcomes; many are not paying enough attention to eco-efficiency. The role of women in entrepreneurship has become more important in recent years. The number of females running their own firms has increased substantially, and is likely to continue to do so. Home-based businesses constitute the largest segment of the small business sector, and have their own special administrative and legal problems that need to be taken into account before an entrepreneur becomes a home-based operator.

REVIEW QUESTIONS

1. What is the difference between social responsiveness and social responsibility?
2. What are the seven components that an eco-efficient firm uses in its activities?
3. How does a social entrepreneur differ from a conventional one?
4. List the ways in which women and men differ in the management of a small business.

DISCUSSION QUESTIONS

1. Are the economic needs and concerns of a small business owner always opposed to those of the broader community?
2. What steps could be taken to increase the number of social entrepreneurship initiatives in either:
   (a) a country
   (b) a district or suburb?
3. Is it valid to claim that women are more consultative owner–managers than men? Why?

SUGGESTED READING

de Bruin, A., Brush, C.G., & Welter, F., 'Special issues on female entrepreneurship', *Entrepreneurship Theory & Practice*, vol. 30, no. 5, 2006, and vol. 31, no. 3, 2007.

Hillary R., (ed.), *Small and Medium-Sized Enterprises and the Environment: Business Imperatives*, Greenleaf, Sheffield, 2000.

Nicholls, A., *Social entrepreneurship: New Models of Sustainable Social Change*, Oxford University Press, Oxford, 2006.

Sayers, J, & Monin, N. (eds), *The Global Garage: Home-Based Business in New Zealand*, Thomson Dunmore Press, Southbank, Victoria, 2005.

Case study

Sand and Sea

'Sand and Sea' is a home-based business, owned by Verity and Bob Chugurgh, who live in Auckland's North Shore, New Zealand. Verity started up the home-based business in 2005, when her two young children started school. Before Verity married she had completed a Bachelor of Fine Arts degree. She had worked in a marketing management role, and had travelled extensively throughout the Middle East, Europe and Asia. While the kids were in pre-school, Verity developed her skills as a jeweller — a craft that intrigued her at art school. She specialised in one-off 'art' pieces, and had developed a reputation as a jewellery artist, known for her beautiful, unusual designs with a natural New Zealand theme, using the materials of her local environment and a New Zealand colour palette.

With the kids off to school Verity started to earn a little money selling her high-end pieces, some of which fetched NZ$600 per necklace. For the most part, she created close copies of her award-winning designs, which she retailed at about NZ$60. She started off by selling to her friends and family, and soon word-of-mouth grew so that she was making jewellery full time, and was making a small profit. Although Verity enjoyed the autonomy of her money-making venture, and being able to do something she loved, she was getting bored with the laborious job of making each individual piece of jewellery herself. However, she did not want to directly employ someone to work for her as she did not have the workspace, and she wanted to be free from the compliance burdens of being an employer and managing others.

At the beginning of 2009 Verity's husband Bob lost his job. He had been working on contract as a software developer, but the economic downturn that began in 2008 meant that his work had completely dried up. Verity and Bob decided to build the jewellery business together, taking advantage of Bob's software development skills to more aggressively promote Verity's designs, and find a global customer base for her jewellery.

Together Bob and Verity decided to rethink the entire business. They came up with a list of workable ideas that they wished to implement. First, Verity decided to move away from producing her own jewellery to focus only on design. Because Verity's work celebrated the natural New Zealand environment – the bush, the mountains and the beach – they decided that their new venture needed to promote environmental sustainability, and be readily seen doing this. In addition, both Verity and Bob felt that for the business to be truly a shared business, they needed to take advantage of Bob's skills and provide a complementary online experience and have excellent customer service. These three issues are to be the core of their new strategy; artistic integrity, environmental sustainability and a superlative and unique online customer service experience.

Bob and Verity have decided to place five per cent of their profits into the Forest and Bird Protection Society, which they believe is a popular and suitable charity organisation that fits into their brand image. They will use a sustainable and environmentally friendly theme in their brand image. In addition, both Verity and Bob wish to retain complete control of the business by neither employing a manager nor any other staff. They have decided to source most of their feature materials locally, and to source the rest cheaply from Asia. They will also work with a small manufacturing firm in China who would assemble Verity's designs at a fraction of the cost she could do so in New Zealand. One advantage of Verity and Bob's home-based business is that it is relatively inexpensive to run. They have an office in the house, but conduct most of their face-to-face business over the internet using Skype. Although either Mike or Verity will need to occasionally travel to Asia to find suitable beads and materials, most of the natural materials can be sourced locally.

Verity will continue to enter artistic competitions and hold exhibits of her work, including contributing to such events as the Wearable Arts Awards. Bob will develop the site and provide all customer service contact, which he can do predominantly through email. Bob has ideas about providing an educational area, teaching people how to bead for themselves, a special online kids' area for designing jewellery, using recycled materials from the home and even an area where people could create their own jewellery concepts. The aim of these ideas is to drive traffic to the site and build the brand internationally.

Case study prepared by Dr Janet Sayers, Massey University.

Questions

1. Do you think this business might succeed? Why or why not?
2. What are the advantages and disadvantages of a home-based business, and what are the major challenges of growing a business like this?
3. How can Verity and Bob protect their business ideas from being 'poached' by larger businesses?

ENDNOTES

1. J.G. Dees, 'The meaning of social entrepreneurship', *Stanford Graduate School of Business*, www.gsb.stanford.edu, 1998.
2. Ashoka Foundation, 'What is a social entrepreneur?', www.ashoka.org, 2002.
3. J. Gonzalez-Benito, & O. Gonzalez-Benito, 'Environmental proactivity and business performance: An empirical analysis', *Omega*, 33, 2005, pp. 1–15.
4. R. Hillary (ed.), *Small and Medium-Sized Enterprises and the Environment: Business Imperatives*, Greenleaf, Sheffield, 2000.
5. Australian Bureau of Statistics, *Small Business in Australia 1999*, cat. no. 1321.0, ABS, Canberra, 2000.
6. D.J. Storey, *Understanding the Small Business Sector*, Routledge, London, 1994.
7. F.J. Tilley, 'The gap between the environmental attitudes and the environmental behaviour of small firms', *Business Strategy and the Environment*, no. 8, 1999, pp. 238–48.
8. M. Schaper, 'Small firms and environmental management: Predictors of green purchasing in Western Australian pharmacies', *International Small Business Journal*, vol. 20, no. 3. August 2002, pp. 235–49.
9. J.Q. Merritt, 'EM into SME won't go? Attitudes, awareness and practices in the London borough of Croydon', *Business Strategy and the Environment*, vol. 7, no. 2, May 1998, pp. 90–100.
10. Asia–Pacific Economic Co-operation Forum, *Eco-Efficiency in Small and Medium Enterprises*, APEC Secretariat, Singapore, 1998.
11. World Business Council for Sustainable Development, *Cleaner Production and Ecoefficiency: Complementary Approaches to Sustainable Development*, WBCSD, Geneva, 1997, p. 3.
12. R. Isaak, *Green Logic: Ecopreneurship, Theory and Ethics*, Greenleaf, London, 1998.
13. Australian Bureau of Statistics, *Characteristics of Small Business 2004, Australia*, cat. no. 8127.0, ABS, Canberra, 2005, p. 33; figures exclude agricultural enterprises.
14. Ministry of Economic Development, New Zealand, *SMEs in New Zealand: Structure and Dynamics*, Ministry of Economic Development, Wellington, 2009.
15. Ministry of Women's Affairs & Ministry of Economic Development, New Zealand, *Women in enterprise: A report on women in small and medium enterprises in New Zealand*, Ministry of Women's Affairs and Ministry of Economic Development, New Zealand, Wellington, 2008.
16. J. Lee, 'The motivation of women entrepreneurs in Singapore', *International Journal of Entrepreneurial Behaviour and Research*, vol. 3, no. 2, 1997, pp. 93–110.
17. Organisation for Economic Cooperation and Development, *Women Entrepreneurs in Small and Medium Enterprises*, OECD, Paris, 1997, pp. 20–3.
18. P. Chu, 'The characteristics of Chinese female entrepreneurs: Motivation and personality', *Journal of Enterprising Culture*, vol. 8, no. 1, 2000, pp. 67–84.
19. B. Roffey, A. Stanger, D. Forsaith, E. McInnes, F. Petrone, C. Symes & M. Xydias, *Women in Small Business: A Review of Research*, Department of Industry, Science and Tourism, Canberra, 1996, p. xxi.
20. S.P. Robbins, R. Bergman, I. Stagg & M. Coulter, *Management*, 2nd edn, Prentice Hall, Sydney, 2000, p. 623.
21. B. Roffey et al., *see* note 19.
22. J. Watson, 'Examining the impact on performance of demographic differences between male and female controlled SMEs', *Small Enterprise Research*, vol. 9, no. 2, 2001, pp. 55–70.
23. B. Roffey et al., *see* note 19.
24. C. Wang, E.A. Walker, J. Redmond, & J. Breen, 'Home-based businesses: Australia's hidden economic engine', *Monash Business Review*, vol. 4, no. 2, July 2008, pp. 1–13.
25. Home Business New Zealand, 'Insights into the home business community in New Zealand', www.homebizbuzz.co.nz, 2002.

26. K. Goh & T.W. Chian, 'Profile of home offices in Singapore,' *Statistics Singapore Newsletter*, March 2004, pp. 12–15.
27. A.M. Stanger, 'Home-based business marginality: A review of home-based business performance and its determinants', Paper presented to the 45th International Council for Small Business World Conference, 7–10 June 2001, Brisbane, Australia; W. Good & M. Levy, 'Home-based business: A phenomenon of growing importance', *Journal of Small Business and Entrepreneurship*, vol. 10, no. 1, 1992, pp. 34–46.
28. Australian Bureau of Statistics, *Characteristics of Small Business 2004*, *Australia*, cat. no. 8127.0, ABS, Canberra, 2005, figures exclude agricultural enterprises.

Glossary

100% inspection When all items produced are inspected   304

acceptance (random) sampling Inspecting random samples of product to ensure they meet the expected standard; the sample result is generalised to the entire output   304

affiliate programs The payment of rewards for page views, site visits or sales generated from another website's referral marketing efforts   388

arbitrage The action of taking advantage of a discrepancy in value that exists in the marketplace. Those who ferret out such discrepancies in value and realise profits by acting on them are called arbitrageurs   37

assets Items of worth owned by the business   350

attribute inspection Determining product acceptability on the presence or absence of a key attribute   305

attribute listing The identification and listing of all major characteristics of a product, object or idea   57

balance sheet A document that details the assets, liabilities and net worth (owner's equity) of the business   350

blue ocean strategy A strategy aiming to develop compelling value innovations that create uncontested market space   142

bootstrap finance Creative financing methods of meeting the need for resources without relying on debt or equity finance   234

brainstorming A conference technique by which a group tries to find a solution for a specific problem by amassing spontaneous ideas from its members   58

break-even point The level of sales where all expenses have been met, but no profit has been made   277

bridging finance Financing extended to a firm using existing assets as collateral in order to acquire new assets; bridging finance is usually short term   221

business adviser Someone who works with client businesses to provide specialised skills and knowledge in one or more particular aspects of business operations   244

business angels Wealthy people who invest in entrepreneurial firms and contribute their business skills   229

business coaches A person who works with entrepreneurs, business owners or senior managers to help them deal with problems in their work and private life   250

business dynamics Also called business churning; the extent to which firms enter an industry, grow, decline and exit an industry   14

business exit Any situation in which a business ceases to exist, through closure, liquidation, bankruptcy, sale or transfer to another owner, or merger   89

business incubator Dedicated premises provided to help firms get established and become profitable   259

business introduction services A service that arranges or facilitates the meeting of private investors and businesses seeking external capital   229

business model A conceptual tool describing the elements and relationships that outline how a company creates and markets value   146

business plan A written document that explains and analyses an existing or proposed business venture   156

business system franchise An arrangement whereby the franchisor supplies the product, and gives comprehensive guidelines on how the business is to be run   118

business-planning process A series of logical steps governing the creation, implementation and revision of a business plan   167

cash flow statement (or forecast) A document that shows the movement of all cash into and out of a business during a given time frame   347

collateral Property used as security for a loan. If the debt is not paid, the lender has the right to sell the collateral to recover the value of the loan   40

company A separate legal entity that has an existence independent of its owners and managers   199

concurrent control Control measures performed on work in progress   306

contingency plan How a firm will respond to a threatened risk   308

contribution margin The proportion of money left in each dollar of sales after variable costs have been met, and which is available to cover fixed costs and contribute to profits   278

copyright The exclusive right granted by law to a copyright holder to make and distribute copies of, or otherwise control, their literary, musical, dramatic or artistic work   209

corporate entrepreneurship The process whereby an individual or a group, in association with an existing organisation, creates a new organisation or initiates renewal or innovation within that organisation   425

corporate venturing The development of new business ventures inside or at the periphery of an organisation   425

creative destruction The process of simultaneous emergence and disappearance of technologies, products and firms in the marketplace as a result of innovation   12

creativity The production of new and useful ideas   54

crowdsourcing The act of taking tasks traditionally performed by an employee or contractor, and outsourcing them to a group (crowd) of people or community in the form of an open call   432

data Streams of raw facts and figures   375

decision support system (DSS) An interactive system that provides support to managers during semi-structured and unstructured decision making   380

depreciation The diminution of the value of an item through use   349

dialogic A system with a circular causality process   30

discontinuous opportunities Innovations that move beyond existing business models to create new products and enter new markets   428

discounting The selling of a firm's accounts receivable to a financier while the firm keeps responsibility for collecting monies owing   235

drawings The income the business owner takes out of the business   352

due diligence A process of detailed scrutiny aimed at obtaining all the information needed to comprehensively evaluate a business for purchase, and to establish whether the projected business is a worthwhile investment   116

eco-efficiency A management strategy that focuses on the delivery of competitively priced goods and services which satisfy consumer needs while progressively reducing ecological impacts throughout the product life cycle   453

economic order quantity (EOQ) The amount of goods that minimises the total purchase and storage costs while still being sufficient to meet the production requirements of the business   300

entrepreneurship The process, brought about by individuals, of identifying new opportunities and converting them into marketable products or services   5

entry costs The price of starting up or buying a business enterprise   107

environmental responsibility The need to protect and enhance the natural environment   452

environmental scanning Analysing and understanding the internal and external forces that may affect a company's products, markets or operating systems   130

equity gap The scarce provision of equity investments in the early stage of a firm's growth   223

exit costs The price involved in liquidating or closing a business enterprise   107

expert consultant A business adviser with highly developed skills in a specific area   252

explicit knowledge More formally recognised knowledge that has been codified and can be communicated to others   376

extended marketing mix The inclusion of people, process and physical evidence considerations, in addition to product, promotion, place and price to determine the marketing mix   285

facilitator A business adviser who encourages clients to learn how to diagnose and treat their own business problems   253

factoring The selling of a firm's accounts receivable to a financier who assumes the credit risk and receives cash as the debtors settle their accounts   235

feedback control Control measures instituted after an event has taken place   306

feedforward control Control measures taken in advance of actual performance   306

financial year The twelve-month period for which annual financial data is collected, analysed and reported upon   345

fixed costs Expenses that remain the same, regardless of the level of activity or sales turnover a business generates   276

floor plan The arrangement of operational activities within a business premises   295

focus group A small group of people with an interviewer trained to solicit their views about a particular issue or product   137

forced analogy Also called forced relationship; the action of making an association between two unlike things in order to obtain new insights   56

franchise An arrangement whereby the originator of a business product or operating system permits another business owner to sell the goods and/ or to use the business operating system on the originator's behalf   117

franchisee The business/person given contractual permission by the original owner of a system or product to operate a business franchise system or sell a product   117

franchisor A business or individual who owns the rights to a particular business franchise system or product   117

global positioning system (GPS) A device using satellite signals to triangulate position in longitude, latitude and altitude for navigation purposes   391

goodwill An intangible commodity; the extra value ascribed to a business, piece of intellectual property, brand name, or other business-related activity   114

harvesting The process entrepreneurs and investors use to exit a business and realise their investment   413

heuristics Simplifying strategies that can be used to make judgements quickly and efficiently. Heuristics result from cognition, i.e. the intellectual processes through which information is obtained, transformed, stored, retrieved and used   33

home-based businesses (HBB) An enterprise in which all or most of the work is performed at or from the owner–operator's private residence; also known as 'small office, home office' (SOHO)   458

human resource management (HRM) A firm's approach to managing its employees   316

ill-will Negative perceptions or attitudes towards a firm; an intangible commodity that detracts from the overall value of a business   116

in-depth personal interview An interview that encourages respondents to explain their views, and which probes responses to explore an issue in greater detail   137

Industrial Revolution The term used to describe the changes brought about by the introduction of technology and methods of mass production in the eighteenth and nineteenth centuries   4

informal sector Economic activity that is not regulated, monitored, enforced or taxed by a government   335

information and communication technologies (ICT) Technology and related processes and networks that handle information and aid communication, encompassing radio, audio and video data, often utilising telephony or the internet to receive, store, retrieve, manipulate, share and utilise information   374

information systems (IS) An information system collects, processes, stores, analyses and disseminates information in a planned and specific manner   377

information Data that has been converted into something meaningful and useful   375

initial public offering (IPO) Also called flotation, going public, listing; refers to a business's initial offer of shares to the public via a stock exchange   232

insurance A contract to provide compensation for any damage or loss suffered by the firm if a specified act occurs   310

integrated marketing communications (IMC) Adopting a holistic approach to all communication methods and messages to inform, persuade and remind customers in a clear, consistent and compelling manner   272

interactive voice response (IVR) Applications that use NLG to automate human service contact   380

job analysis The process of determining the duties and skill requirements of a job, and the sort of person who might fit these demands   322

job description A written statement of what a job entails, how it is done and under what conditions   322

job specification The personal traits and experience required from a prospective employee   322

just-in-time delivery An inventory management system where materials are delivered to the firm at the time needed for production   300

knowledge The accumulated intellectual capital, including information created that guides actions and decisions   375

lease A written agreement under which a property owner allows a tenant to use the property for a specified period of time and rent   226

leverage The degree to which a business uses borrowed money; what the debt–equity ratio measures   220

liabilities Debts or financial obligations of the business   350

locus of control The extent to which individuals believe that they can control events that affect them   38

management buy-out (MBO) The purchase of a controlling interest in a business by its management in order to take over assets and operations   416

management information system (MIS) A management-level information system that serves planning, controlling and decision making by providing summary information   380

margin A measure of how much of the final sales price is gross profit   280

market research The use of information to identify and define marketing opportunities and problems   128

marketing The process of planning and executing the conception, pricing, promotion and distribution of ideas, goods or services to create exchanges that satisfy individual and organisational goals   268

mark-up The extent to which the price of a product is increased from its original cost of goods sold to its final selling price   280

mentoring The process of transferring advice and ideas from one businessperson to another on a voluntary no-cost basis   249

merger The combining of two or more entities into one through a purchase acquisition or a pooling of interests   416

mind maps A visual method of mapping information to stimulate the generation and analysis of it   57

motivation The willingness of employees to exert effort to achieve business goals   327

natural language generation (NLG) Computer-generated voice, capable of synthesising spoken words from text   380

need for achievement A person's desire either for excellence or to succeed in competitive situations   38

netbooks A relatively low cost mini (under 25 cm screen) personal computer that is designed for portability, extended battery power use and internet connectivity, primarily used for consuming rather than creating or storing data   391

niche market A narrowly focused target market for goods and/or services   269

office automation aystem (OAS) A computer system that facilitates everyday information tasks in offices   379

operations management The control of the process by which a firm makes a product   292

opportunity A situation in which a new product, service or process can be introduced and sold at greater than its cost of production   7

opportunity cost The cost of passing up one investment in favour of another   34

organisational culture The shared values, attitudes and behaviour of employees in a firm   317

organisational structure chart A diagrammatic representation of the way in which employee work relationships are structured within a business   321

overdraft The amount by which withdrawals exceed deposits or the extension of credit by a lending institution to allow for such a situation   225

owner's assets and liabilities A document that shows the private assets, liabilities and net worth of a business owner   353

owner's equity (or net worth) The difference between the assets and liabilities of a business; the value of the business to the owner if all its assets were sold and all liabilities were paid   350

'pair of hands' adviser A specialist brought into a firm for a set period of time   253

partnership agreement A written document that covers all matters relating to the partnership   199

partnership A relationship that exists between people carrying on a business in common with a view to making a profit   198

patent A legal document giving inventors the exclusive rights to their invention for a number of years   206

personal digital assistants (PDAs) A hand-held computer that can support a range of useful productivity enhancing applications   391

placement The exchange of goods or services between buyers and sellers   283

primary data Information that is collected first-hand for a specific research problem   135

problem reversal The action of viewing a problem from an opposite angle by asking questions such as 'What if we did the opposite?' and 'What is everyone else not doing?'   56

product benefit An advantage that a consumer can receive by purchasing a good or service   271

product feature What a product or service is or does   271

product franchise A franchise to sell a particular product or service   118

productivity ratio A comparison of inputs used with outputs produced   305

profit and loss statement A document that shows business-related revenues and expenses and the resulting profit or loss   349

quality assurance system A set of processes and principles designed to ensure the production of a set of consistent activities, goods or services   307

resource Any thing or quality that is useful   144

restraint of trade clause A contractual restriction on the right of a business vendor to operate a similar business in rivalry with the new purchaser of the firm   117

risk The possibility that a situation may end with a negative outcome for the firm   308

risk management The process of identifying risks in advance, assessing their likely occurrence and taking steps to reduce or eliminate them   308

salary Remuneration in which employees receive a fixed 'total pay' package, regardless of the number of hours worked   323

sales mix forecast An estimate of sales of each major product or service, the revenue generated by each of these and the resulting cost of goods sold   346

scheduling Setting a time frame and sequence of events to perform an activity   303

search engine optimisation (SEO) Increasing the ranking of websites on search engines via better design and implementation strategy   388

secondary data Information from business research that has been done previously   132

security The protection of equipment and ideas from the risk of theft, loss or unauthorised use   309

service blueprint A service blueprint is a graphical representation of key facets of the performance of a service to convey what happens both in front of the customer and behind the scenes from a people, process and physical evidence perspective   297

Six Sigma system A set of quantifiable and consistently followed measures and processes designed to eliminate or at least drastically reduce errors   307

small business A small-scale, independent firm usually managed, funded and operated by its owners, and whose staff size, financial resources and assets are comparatively limited in scale   79

smart phones High-end telephony devices that have the functionality of a mini PC, including using a standardised operating system and wireless internet connectivity   391

social entrepreneur An enterprising person who applies entrepreneurial principles and skills to the resolution of social or community problems   450

social network The sum of relationships that a person maintains with other people as a result of social activity   45

sole proprietor or **sole trader** A person who wholly owns and operates a business   196

spam Unsolicited communications sent to a large number of recipients via any communications method, most often via email   390

spin-off An individual or organisational unit leaving an existing firm to start as an independent new firm   427

staff turnover The number of employees who leave the business   329

strategic alliance An ongoing relationship between two businesses, which combine efforts for a specific purpose   416

strategic plan A plan that sets out the long-term focus of the business, its mission and its vision, and attempts to understand the environment in which the business operates   166

strategic renewal The new combinations of resources that result in significant changes to an organisation's strategy or structure   425

strategic resources Resources which provide a sustained competitive advantage to a firm   145

survey A system for collecting information using a questionnaire   137

tacit knowledge Knowledge that the business has developed through experience but is not easily recorded to capture its value   376

target market A core group of customers that a business intends to focus its marketing efforts on   270

term loans A loan that is repaid through regular periodic payments, usually over a period of one to ten years   226

total quality management (TQM) The adoption of a quality-based philosophy throughout a firm   307

trade credit A form of short-term debt financing whereby goods are received from the suppliers before payment is made   225

trade secret Any idea, formula, pattern, device, process or information that provides a business with a competitive advantage   210

trademark A word, phrase, logo, symbol, colour, sound or smell used by a business to identify a product and distinguish it from those of its competitors   208

training needs analysis An evaluation of the skills and knowledge employees need, what they currently hold, and what gap exists   328

transaction processing systems (TPS) A computerised system that processes and records the daily routine transactions necessary to conduct the business   378

trust An obligation imposed on trustees to deal with the trust property (over which they have control) for the benefit of the beneficiaries   201

trust deed A written document that evidences the creation of the trust. It sets out the terms and conditions on which the trust assets are held by the trustees, and outlines the rights of the beneficiaries   201

underwriter An intermediary between an issuer of a security and the investing public, usually an investment bank   233

uniform resource locator (URL) The technical name for a web address   386

variable costs Expenditure items that increase or decrease as sales volume changes   276

variable inspection Determining product acceptability by results falling within predetermined boundaries   305

venture capital (VC) Independently managed, dedicated pools of capital that focus equity investments in high-growth businesses   229

voice over internet protocols (VoIP) Voice communications using digital Internet protocols transmitted via a telecommunication network   380

wage System of remuneration in which employees are paid at a set hourly rate   323

wireless networks Short range radio signal that allows computers and other enabled devices to communicate without a physical connection   391

working capital Funds used in operating a business on a daily basis   348

Index